THE HIDDEN DYNAMICS OF CHINESE REVOLUTION

THE HIDDEN DYNAMICS OF CHINESE REVOLUTION

Writings and Speeches of **Leon Trotsky on China** (1925–1940)

With
Introduction by
Rajesh Tyagi

AAKAR

THE HIDDEN DYNAMICS OF CHINESE REVOLUTION
Writings and Speeches of
Leon Trotsky on China
(1925–1940)

First Published, 2009

ISBN 978-81-89833-52-7 (Pb)

Published by
AAKAR BOOKS
28 E Pocket IV, Mayur Vihar Phase I, Delhi-110 091
Phone : 011-2279 5505 Telefax : 011-2279 5641
aakarbooks@gmail.com; www.aakarbooks.com

Printed at
Arpit Printographers
E-mail : arpitprinto@yahoo.com

Dedicated to
the Chinese workers, who sacrificed their lives
in Shanghai and Canton for the cause of
the Proletarian Revolution in China

Acknowledgements

I express my gratitude to all my friends who had contributed in one way or the other in bringing out this book of historic importance. Special mention has to be made of Shri K.K. Saxena of Aakar Books who had been instrumental in publication of this book and Ms. Ritu Singh who has taken great pains in thorough checking of the draft of the book.

Contents

Preface

The last decade of the 20th century had been witness to the crumbling down of decaying Stalinist regimes, in the USSR and countries of Eastern Europe i.e. Germany, Hungary, Poland, Bulgaria, Yugoslavia, Czechoslovakia and so on. The historic mission of the Capitalism for a world conquest, cut halfway by the mighty tide of the October Socialist Revolution of 1917, thus completed itself, towards the end of the 20th century.

Amazingly, Leon Trotsky, the co-mentor with Lenin, of the Russian Revolution and the Third International (Comintern), had long ago predicted this end of the destiny of Stalinism. In no ambiguous terms Trotsky claimed that Soviet Russia under Stalin would either degenerate or fall. Rather, he said, it would first degenerate and then fall. Soviet Russia had since completely degenerated into a bureaucratic state during the lifetime of Stalin himself, continued to decay further after him and ultimately fell to its destiny as predicted by Trotsky. Its satellite formations in Europe, which had followed its trajectory, shared the same fate with it. The Chinese regime of 1949, the Asian model of Stalinism, has joined the voyage of world capitalism, with its bureaucratic apparatus and red flag.

The prediction of Trotsky, coming true, has renewed the interest of more young generations, especially in backward countries, in the works and writings of Leon Trotsky.

The miserable explanations, offered by the epigones of Leninism—Stalinists and Maoists, for collapse of the bureaucratic models of 'actually existing socialism', which they had proudly nurtured and defended for decades altogether, find no takers now.

Two generations now separate ours from Trotsky. These three generations, their students and youth, have been mis-educated by the epigones, on the basis of their false analysis of the meaning of Russian and Chinese revolutions, turning them away from the struggle to arm the working class and through it the vast peasantry, with a proletarian perspective.

The distortion and falsification of the history of the Chinese Revolution at the hands of epigones, has virtually extricated its living soul—the unprecedented heroic role played in it by the young and inexperienced working class, despite the pernicious influence exercised over it by its opportunist leadership. There has been a well orchestrated attempt to present the history of the Chinese Revolution, causing all references to the heroic battles fought by the Proletariat in Chinese cities against its enemies, disappear in thin air.

Stalinists and Maoists, both, have maliciously suppressed the real essence and nature of the dispute which Trotsky had raised against the Stalinist degeneration of the Comintern, and instead continued to curse 'Trotskyism' and its 'original sin'—the proposition of 'permanent revolution'—and shell them with pure slanders, invented by them. As a reader of this book would himself see, the vicious propaganda against Trotskyism, conducted by its enemies, in the last more than three-fourth of a century presents but a warped version of this debate of extraordinary importance then going on within the world communist movement, between its two main trends, one led by Trotsky, the other by Stalin.

The struggle of Trotsky against the attitude of Comintern on the strategy of the Chinese Revolution of 1925–27, is the crucial part of his overall struggle against its degeneration at the hands of the Stalinist school, and for re-orientation of the world communist movement. Writings of Trotsky on China (1925–1940), included in this book, present a step-by-step account of the political struggle between the two camps inside the Third International—The Stalinists in control of Comintern on one side, and the left oppositionists, led by Trotsky, on the other. They show as to how Stalinist bureaucracy turned the Chinese Revolution, with very bright prospects of success, into a big game of loser's win. The Menshevik quest of Stalinists for a revolutionary bourgeois in China, led them in the first phase of the Chinese Revolution to capitulate and throw the Chinese proletariat bound hand and foot before the Chinese bourgeois, instead of seizing power by fighting against it. When this 'revolutionary ally' betrayed and butchered the proletariat, as foreseen by Trotsky, then in the second phase, the same Stalinist bureaucracy forced the proletariat to stage untimely uprisings and thereby commit suicide. Destruction of the proletariat, inflicted by the Stalinist bureaucracy, however, raised this bureaucracy higher and higher among the desperate masses.

Destruction of Stalinist states in the Soviet Union and East Europe, one after the other, and growing over of China to a bureaucratic-capitalist state, around the last decade of the past century, has led to integration of the world under complete domination of Imperialism, though at a time when the gigantic productive forces unleashed by it, are already in head-on collision with its production relations, above all with the nation state. The decline of Stalinism, eventually coincides with crisis of world capitalism itself, generating a vacuum to be filled by the revolutionary intervention of world proletariat.

The immense importance of Trotsky's writings on China lies in their focus upon the nature and the course of development of the revolutionary process in the peripheral and backward regions of the world as an integral part of the world socialist revolution. These writings expose the futility of the Stalinist programme of building of 'Socialism in one country', showing that the productive forces necessary for building socialism cannot be reconciled within a single country. Opposing the Menshevik policy of Stalinists, in assigning a revolutionary role to the bourgeois in backward countries, Trotsky argued that unlike the European revolutions of the previous century, the revolutions in backward countries would not be carried by or in conjunction with the bourgeois, but exactly in opposition to it. The proletariat, leading the poor peasantry behind it, would consummate the bourgeois tasks through its dictatorship, while crossing over to resolution of Socialist tasks. Trotsky conceived the question of revolutionary power as dictatorship of the Proletariat, supported by peasantry. He ridiculed the old formula of a 'two class dictatorship' and its further dilution by Stalinists and Maoists in the 'bloc of four classes', including the bourgeois as well.

The Internationalist perspective of Trotsky, elaborated upon in the theory of permanent revolution, stood in direct opposition to the reactionary nationalist perspective of the Stalinist bureaucracy. His writings on China contain a splendid account of his struggle against the reactionary perception of Stalinism.

The writings of Trotsky on China encompass three historic phases of the Chinese Revolution. In the first phase, Trotsky struggles against the forcing of Chinese proletariat into an illegitimate alliance with Chinese bourgeois—the KMT-CCP alliance. During this phase, the young Chinese proletariat and its party CCP, is continuously forced by Stalinist Comintern to subjugate itself to the political will, programme, principles and discipline of bourgeois-nationalist KMT, first with its right wing under Chiang Kai Shek and then with its left wing under Wang Ching Wei. The first phase ends with butchering of the proletariat first by Chiang and then Wang. The second phase starts with the struggle of Left Opposition against coercing of Chinese proletariat, already dispersed and weakened, to untimely uprisings, by the Stalinists, in order to cover up their past misdeeds. This second phase ends with failed workers' uprisings, where even the remnants of workers revolution stand completely destroyed. Then starts the third phase, with bureaucracy, the only surviving pillar of hope, spreading its wings to take advantage of the defeat and dispersal of the working class, substituting itself for the working class, reorganising the Chinese CP into an apparatus subordinate to itself, finally staking its own claim to power. Trotsky fights it till the end of his life. With physical elimination of Trotsky in July 1940, following the elimination of the entire old guard of Bolshevik leaders, those close associates of Lenin, at the hands of the murder machine of Stalin, ends this third phase of his works.

It is more important today than ever, to understand the revolutionary principles in defence of which both Lenin and Trotsky kept fighting for their entire life. It is the writings of Trotsky which explain coherently how an entire era of proletarian revolutions was destroyed by the Stalinist bureaucracy, after the death of Lenin, which then itself perished under its own weight.

Introduction to the book contains a brief account of the eventful history of China, which though unusual for an introduction to a book of this sort—a compilation of writings—was felt desirable that a brief narration of factual matrix out of which arose the political discourse, around the questions of utmost relevance and importance of our epoch, should be given for reference. Similarly, the conflicts of perspective during three Russian Revolutions, also find mention in short. The appeal of Chen Tu Shiu is added to the book as appendix, for its importance in throwing light on the conflicts inside the CCP during the crucial period.

We hope that this publication of Trotsky's writings, speeches and letters would succeed in presenting the more objective, real but hidden side of the Chinese Revolution, to its readers.

Introduction

The works of Leon Trotsky, on China and the Chinese Revolution, starting from 1925 till his elimination in 1940, unfold before us the true nature and meaning of the grandiose conflict, which took place in the Third International (Comintern) on the question of its attitude towards the Chinese Revolution, between its two opposite currents—Trotskyism and Stalinism.

Trotsky's writings on the Chinese Revolution are of immense significance for Marxists all over the world, particularly in backward countries, for a whole series of reasons: because the dispute on the attitude of Comintern towards the Chinese Revolution, is a vital part of Trotsky's struggle against Stalinist degeneration of world revolution; because these writings contain extensive elaboration of the theory and perspective of 'Permanent Revolution'; because an understanding of the character and nature of the defeats, suffered by the Chinese proletariat in 1925–27, is crucial for understanding the subsequent evolution of CCP, Mao's adaptation to the defeat of working class, and finally the character of the regime that emerged in China in 1949.

In the literature, poured in bulk in the backward countries of the world, through the official channels of the Soviet Union and China, one would seek in vain a discussion on the disputes which came up before Comintern on the question of Chinese Revolution. While suppressing the true essence of this historic debate, only slanders against Trotsky and his theory of 'permanent revolution', were spread consciously. It is thus all the more necessary for Marxists in the backward world to comprehend the works of Leon Trotsky, to equip themselves with a more objective understanding towards the real meaning of the struggle waged by Trotsky against his adversaries, in an attempt to save the International communist movement, from the destruction that could be averted.

I

One can hardly understand the true essence of the struggle of Trotsky against Stalinism, without tracing back to the origin and development of these two currents, embedded in the soil of three Russian revolutions—1905, February 1917 and October 1917.

Russia confronted the prospects of a social revolution at the turn of the 20th century, when world capitalism had entered onto the stage of Imperialism, thereby undermining the strength of the nation state and subjugating the national bourgeois into its agency. The West had accomplished its national bourgeois revolutions long ago, and had since become unaccustomed to revolutions, while the East was yet to experience one. The prediction of Marx that these bourgeois revolutions would be a direct prelude to the Socialist revolution in Europe, could not materialise for the betrayal of reformist leadership, which intentionally held back the proletariat from taking power in Europe. It was around this time that the countries of the backward world, with belated historic development, were dragged into the whirlpool of world capitalism, one after the other, and as a consequence, a new class—the class of Proletarians appeared in backward countries. On the eve of the First World War, this process gained extraordinary momentum.

China, after Russia, entered onto the world capitalism at a very belated stage in history. For this belated entry, the bourgeois of these backward countries found itself in a situation of social as well as political paralysis, in the clutches of Imperialism. The national bourgeois, which had made revolutions in 19th century Europe, lost all its vigour by the turn of 20th century, having become a tutelage, an agency of Imperialism. Expansion of Capitalism to these countries, however, generated new contradictions and aggravated the old ones in them. The decisive factor was the appearance of modern Proletariat—the industrial working class—in the countries of backward Orient, whose thick concentration in cities, flared up the entire political scenario.

Marx originally thought that France would begin the social revolution, Germany continue it and England would finish it. Socialist Europe was thus to lead the world on the path of social revolution. No country of the backward world, including Russia, found any mention in this road-map. As we know, history did not follow this trajectory. The focus of revolution had shifted to the backward world, at least for the time being, where social contradictions immediately started to translate themselves in a real revolution. As all the problems of revolution were posed afresh, after half a century of German revolution and 35 years since the French, the old thesis were not of much use for seeking answers to them.

II

The proletariat of one of the most backward countries of the world—Russia, was called upon by the force of circumstances, to fire the first shot of social revolution. The fundamental task, posed before the revolutionaries, was the determination of essence and character of the revolution itself and the role and relationship of various classes in it. Different political trends in Russia, not only had serious disagreements among them on this issue, but approached it from different positions.

Initially, Marxism could grow at a very slow pace and with great difficulty in struggle against the peasant-socialism in Russia, called 'Narodism'. In ten years since 1885, when the 'Emancipation of Labor Group', the first Marxist organization was established by G.V. Plekhanov, only ten small study circles could grow in Russia. Narodism dominated the political thought of its times in Russia and had a great influence over the youth in Russia. Early proponents of Narodism, like Herzen and Chernishevsky, had a wide audience among the youth. Narodniks thought that Russia had its own peculiarities in contrast to the West and capitalism was not going to take root in Russia. For them, the peasantry and not the working class, was the real driving force behind the impending revolution in Russia, and the 'peasant commune' was the prototype of a new society. Russian Marxists, who identified themselves and claimed under the banner of social-democracy in those times, refuted the thesis of Narodism, showing that capitalism had already become a fact in Russia and that the impending revolution in Russia was bourgeois-democratic, arising out of the contradictions between the developing forces of capitalism and the ossified absolutism. However, as the real revolutionary struggle sharpened, the daydream of 'peasant socialism' nurtured by Narodniks, took no time to evaporate. After a hard and long-drawn struggle, Narodism got down from the stage of history, clearing the way for Marxist theory and practice, around the end of the 19th century.

The social-democracy, though it succeeded in refuting the thesis of Narodism, while establishing that Capitalism was a truth of Russian life and the character of the ongoing revolution was bourgeois democratic and not peasant socialist, yet the term 'bourgeois-democratic' was an abstract formulation, and an admission of general nature to it, could not have answered the concrete question: which class would lead the revolution against autocracy and would take the power.

III

In their response to this concrete question, even Social Democrats were seriously divided in their perspective. These currents of thought had almost crystallized them in definite political tendencies by the beginning of 1904.

The character of the Russian Revolution was Bourgeois-Democratic; from this simple formulation, Menshevik ideologues, like Plekhanov, Martinov, Axelrod and Zasulich, Martov derived that it was the turn of the liberal bourgeois to lead the revolution and establish its rule. They assumed that the resulting capitalist development, would provide conditions for the proletariat to acquire political maturity, and an expansion of the basis of class struggle. Hence, the stage for socialist revolution would be set only after a period of peaceful development of capitalism. They saw the role of the proletariat in the revolution as an ally of the bourgeois, that too with a caution that the proletariat, through its revolutionary actions, should not scare the liberal bourgeois. Mensheviks, in fact, reduced the role of the workers to a 'democratic left wing of the bourgeois', and virtually replaced constitutional-reformism for the revolution. In doing this, the Mensheviks drew a crude analogy with the bourgeois revolutions of the 19th century in the West, where bourgeois could take power as leader of the national-democratic revolutions and not only arrest the revolution after addressing the bourgeois democratic tasks, in which only it was interested, but turn the power in its hands against the revolution. The proletariat was thus to complete the second stage revolution—the Socialist revolution—in these countries of the West. Mensheviks ignored that in the countries of the East, with belated historical development, the revolution was to take a different course as the bourgeois in these countries was totally incapable of assuming the leadership of the revolution or to advance the revolutionary cause, even an inch further. Born in the age of general and complete decline of the world capitalism as a whole, the bourgeois in these countries is paralytic. It is instead the Proletariat who as leader of the entire nation, would establish its hegemony upon the revolution and after its victory would convert it to its dictatorship.

Proceeding from the same premises of bourgeois-revolution, Lenin, however, took a big stride forward. Lenin propounded that the proletariat, and not the bourgeois, was the leader of the revolution, who in alliance with the peasantry, would establish a 'democratic dictatorship', and would clear the ground for a capitalistic growth in Russia. He thought that this democratic revolution in Russia would give spark to the European proletariat, who in turn and after taking power in the West, would aid the Russian proletariat to take power and build socialism. This proposition of Lenin—'democratic dictatorship of proletariat and peasantry'—bore an intentional algebraic character, leaving the question of alignment of forces in this dictatorship, open for the future. However, the formulation admitted many possibilities, including the majority and domination of peasantry in the 'democratic dictatorship' and also existence of an independent peasant party in the dual sense, i.e. independent from both the bourgeois and the proletariat at the same time. Lenin imagined that this 'democratic dictatorship of proletariat and peasantry' would clear the ground in Russia, for full and free growth of capitalism, on a European module instead of the Asiatic one. In his famous work 'two tactics of social democracy in a democratic revolution', Lenin elaborated upon this viewpoint:

> *"Marxists are absolutely convinced of the bourgeois character of the Russian Revolution. What does that mean? It means that the democratic reforms in the political system and the social and economic reforms that have become a necessity for Russia, do not in themselves imply the undermining of Capitalism, the undermining of bourgeois rule; on the contrary, they will for the first time, really clear the ground for a wide and rapid, European and not Asiatic development of Capitalism; they will for the first time, make it possible for the Bourgeois to rule as a class."*

Lenin's idea was thus for a 'bourgeois democratic republic, but without bourgeois', that is, for a petty bourgeois republic.

Both these currents of the Marxist school, though seriously differing with each other on the question of who would lead the revolution, were trapped between economic materialism on the one hand and nationalist perspective on the other. Both conceived the nature and prospects of revolution in Russia, corresponding to different historical stages determined by the given level of economic development and the growth of productive forces in Russia alone, in isolation from the rest of the world. Both assessed the strength and role of the proletariat, within the confines of Russia and arrived at the common misunderstanding that the proletariat in Russia was not strong enough to take the power in its hands. According to the Mensheviks, the power would be taken by the bourgeois first, before the proletariat could muster enough maturity and strength to take it alone, while the Bolsheviks thought that it would have to be shared with the peasantry till a democratic revolution is accomplished.

Neither of the two had thought that the proletariat could take power in Russia, as the leader of the democratic revolution, even before it takes power in the West!

Proceeding from the very premise of bourgeois revolution,

Leon Trotsky, only 25 at the time, approached the issue in a fundamentally different manner. Estimating the character and prospects of the revolution in Russia and the role and relationship of classes in it from the proletarian internationalist perspective, Trotsky advanced the hypothesis, with possibility of the proletariat taking power in Russia, as leader of the democratic revolution, even before the proletariat could take power in the West. Trotsky observed :

> *"It is possible for the workers to come to power in an economically backward country, sooner than in an advanced country"*. Further, he said : *"Bourgeois nature of the revolution cannot be cited to blur the fact that the chief actor in the revolution is the proletariat, who is impelled towards the power by the course the revolution"*. Again, he said : *"In the revolution at the beginning of the twentieth century, the direct objective tasks of which are also bourgeois, there emerges as a near prospect, the inevitable, or at least the probable, political domination of the proletariat"*.

Trotsky clarified that though the immediate tasks before the revolution in Russia were of a bourgeois character as against the forces of medievalism, but simultaneously the revolution would have a socialist edge as the main actor in it was the proletariat and not the bourgeois, unlike the bourgeois revolutions in the West. Precisely because of this, Trotsky said, no Chinese wall can be drawn between the democratic and socialist tasks of the revolution in Russia, and the democratic revolution would serve only as a 'prelude' to socialist revolution. He commented: *"As soon as the Proletariat takes power, the division of programme into a maximum and minimum, loses all its significance"*. Trotsky opposed the theory of 'revolution in stages'—first democratic, then socialist, the false and artificial compartmentalization of the course of history in two stages, which both factions of Russian social-democracy, the Mensheviks and Bolsheviks, adhered to at that time. This 'two stage theory' justified the nomenclature of social-democracy, i.e. socialism in words, democracy in action. Trotsky argued that the revolutionary process in the backward countries, where the leader of the revolution is the proletariat, would take an entirely different course. The fact that the proletariat and not the bourgeois was the leader of the revolution in backward countries like Russia, distinguished it from the bourgeois revolutions of the 19th century in the West. Trotsky pointed out that in the backward countries like Russia, the bourgeois is too weak to take power as the leader of the nation, against the forces of local medievalism and foreign capitalism. It can take power only in alliance with them and thereby as an agent of counter-revolution, against the proletariat and peasantry.

Trotsky observed that the proletariat can take power in Russia as agent of agrarian revolution, with the aid of Russian peasantry, and can retain it in its hands. He warned that any other permutation would put the power in the hands of the bourgeois. Trotsky thought that though the proletariat can start the revolution in a single country, through seizure of power, the revolution can be accomplished only on a world scale, with the aid of proletariat of the world. Thus, Trotsky clearly said that the fate of the Russian Revolution cannot be decided in Russia alone but would be decided on the world arena, as the same was inseparably bound with the destiny of the world proletariat.

In refutation of the objection by the Social Democrats that Russia was not ripe for a Socialist Revolution, Trotsky claimed that it is not Russia, but the world economy as a whole, which was ripe for socialism. It is a different thing, if the dictatorship of the proletariat leads to socialism or not or at what tempo or through what stages, would depend upon the fate of European and world capitalism.

Trotsky disagreed with Lenin's formulation—'democratic dictatorship of proletariat and peasantry', which, according to him was unrealizable in practice. Trotsky argued that two classes together cannot constitute a 'dictatorship'. According to Trotsky, either the proletariat would take the power, or it would fall in the hands of the bourgeois. Although the peasantry would play a decisive role in the power struggle, its role would remain only of a lever to power, which would catapult either of the two classes to power. In any case, neither the peasantry can play a role independent of both the classes—the proletariat and the bourgeois—nor can it take power for itself as a class. In history, the peasantry has always supported a person or class against the other, but has never come to power itself. Underlining the algebraic nature of Lenin's formulation—

'democratic dictatorship of two classes'—Trotsky pointed out that the formulation, because of its algebraic character, neither specified the correlation of class forces, nor the mechanics of this dictatorship. Trotsky said that the formulation of Lenin pointed out only broad contours of the future power, leaving the question of its exact structure and composition, open to multiple interpretations. One of the probable interpretations Trotsky allowed was 'Dictatorship of the Proletariat, followed by the peasantry'. Trotsky underlined that never during the whole history of capitalism had there existed a dictatorship of two classes, nor there can be.

Lenin and Trotsky stood close to each other on all issues of vital importance in the revolutionary discourse. Differences between Lenin and Trotsky, were of a purely ideological nature and secondary in their importance. Lenin and Trotsky both looked at the Proletarian revolution in the developed West, specially in Germany, as the only guarantee for the Russian Revolution to stay in place.

IV

Thus three main currents of Social Democracy, with different strategic hypotheses for the characterization of the revolution and the role of various classes therein, held sway on the political arena of Russia, when the uprising of 1905 approached them, for a first actual test on the ground of a real revolution and its verification through class struggle. Although the powerful uprising melted the autocratic power to a great extent, it fell short of an overturn, as the proletariat neither aspired nor was prepared to consolidate the power in its hands. The bourgeois as a class and the petty-bourgeois peasantry could not have carried out the revolutionary overturn. However, the uprising of 1905 threw immense light upon the mechanics of impending revolution in Russia, showing the inability and weakness of the bourgeois to carry out the revolution and the strength and potential of the proletariat, though insufficiently mature and prepared by then, could not decisiviely verify the different hypotheses of revolution.

Then came February 1917. With the abdication of the Tsar, dual power came into existence. On the one hand a formal government, the Provisional government, was formed with Prince Lvov at the head of it, dominated by the SRs who were the biggest party in the Duma. Later, the Mensheviks also joined it. On the other hand stood the Soviets of workers and soldiers, which were organs of real power. Worker Soviets were all powerful and the provisional government was powerless against them. It had to appeal to the Soviets, whenever it was put under threat of overthrow, e.g. the Kornilov affair. Very soon, the crisis of this government called for change of guard and Kerensky became head of it. Though power rested in the hands of armed workers who were supported by the peasantry, the unfortunate part was that the Bolsheviks were in a minority in the Soviets and the leadership of the Soviets was in the hands of Mensheviks, who actively assisted the bourgeois government by holding back the workers and voluntarily surrendered the power to it. Lenin remarked that the power could fall in to the hands of the bourgeois only because of the surrender by the Menshevik leadership before it. The bourgeois thus came to power relying not upon its own strength, but the betrayal of revolution by the Mensheviks.

Unable to appreciate the character of this government, even the majority of the Bolshevik leaders came out in open support of this Government. Kamenev, Muranov and above all Stalin, who had returned from Siberia, took over the editing of *Pravda* and openly declared support for the bourgeois government. Lenin wrote 'letters from Afar' opposing this bogus policy. Out of the five letters only the first one was published, that too after editing. The situation changed only when Lenin returned to Russia on April 3, 1917, from exile in Switzerland. He vehemently opposed the Bolshevik leaders for the support they rendered to the Provisional Government. Lenin presented his famous 'April thesis' to a Bolshevik Conference on the 4th of April, 1917, in which he abandoned the old formulation of a 'two class dictatorship' and called for overthrow of the Provisional government. Lenin proposed the slogan 'All Power to the Soviets', asking for seizure of factories by workers and the lands by peasants. The thesis met with instant opposition from prominent Bolshevik leaders, who accused Lenin of having gone over to the positions of Trotsky. These Bolshevik leaders still confided in the old formula of a 'democratic revolution' and looked upon the February revolution as a democratic revolution in Russia. These Bolshevik leaders, opposing Lenin, were confident that the provisional government was the embodiment of a 'democratic dictatorship of proletariat and peasantry' and it deserved support of all revolutionary forces. The proletariat in their view was not mature enough to take power. Lenin stood in staunch opposition to it, arguing in favour of a proletarian uprising, and was instantly accused of 'Trotskyism'. It was virtually true. The February Revolution had endorsed the prognosis of Trotsky that either the workers or the bourgeois would take the power, rejecting all other hypothesis, and the genius in Lenin was the first to recognize it in his April thesis. *Pravda*, the official organ of the Bolshevik Party, published the thesis of Lenin only after three days, with a note that the ideas were the personal opinion of Lenin and that the thesis was unacceptable to Bolshevik leaders. It was very hard for Lenin to win a vote in support of his thesis. The result of the new position of the Party was the victory of the Great October Proletarian Revolution. It goes without saying that the October Revolution was carried out under the leadership of Lenin fully supported by Trotsky, against the wishes of majority of the Bolshevik leaders, who thought that a proletarian upsurge in Russia was premature.

After presentation of the 'April Thesis', there remained no difference between the approach of Lenin and Trotsky and they virtually merged into a single and inseparable revolutionary current. Lenin abandoned the hypothesis of a 'democratic dictatorship of two classes' and Trotsky abandoned his soft position towards Menshevism, after it exposed itself as tutelage of the bourgeois. All historic significance of the differences of opinion between Lenin and Trotsky, which already were of secondary importance, came to an end with the April Thesis and they remained only of archival importance.

One cannot be mistaken in seeing that both Lenin and Trotsky, the co-mentors of the Russian Revolution, stood very close to each other in their perspective. Due to this proximity of views, they always remained together at all critical junctures of history. They agreed with each other in all material aspects of revolutionary thought and strategy, as opposed to the Mensheviks or even many of the Bolshevik leaders, who took positions hostile to Lenin. Both Lenin and Trotsky shared a common viewpoint on all issues of vital importance, i.e. the political impotence and reactionary character of the bourgeois in backward countries, the leading role of Proletariat in the revolution, alliance of proletariat with poor peasantry, etc. The fact is that the perspective of Trotsky cannot be separated from that of Lenin. Leninism and Trotskyism, constituted together the revolutionary stream in Russian Marxist Movement as against Menshevism, which demanded surrender of revolutionary posts to Bourgeois. Trotsky always claimed himself to be a disciple of Lenin. It was the struggle launched by Lenin upon the internal and external enemies of the Proletarian Revolution, which Trotsky continued after the untimely demise of Lenin and till his own extermination at the hands of enemies of the revolution.

As this book would reveal, 'Trotskyism' was the invention of Russian bureaucracy, which itself had become the chief instrument of counter-revolution, immediately after the demise of Lenin in 1924. The bureaucracy segregated the views and positions of Trotsky from the live context of political struggle and posed them against Leninism. In fact, in the garb of fighting 'Trotskyism', the soul of Leninism was covertly targeted by the bureaucracy, which ultimately succeeded in destroying the gains of the October Revolution.

Anyway, the Provisional government in Russia continued to expose itself as a pure and simple bourgeois government, closely integrated with local reaction on the one hand and foreign imperialism on the other. It did not even attempt a single step to resolve any of the bourgeois-democratic tasks—the land reforms, the national issue, end to the war, etc. Civil liberties, however, were won by the masses with the force of arms.

Then occurred the incident of July 4. A peaceful demonstration of workers and soldiers was fired upon in Petrograd, under the orders of the Provisional government. Dual power ended at once and an open dictatorship of the bourgeois was established. The slogan of 'all power to Soviets' had to be withdrawn. The provisional Government—the coalition of SRs and Mensheviks, thus unfolded itself as a dictatorship of the bourgeois, instead of the 'democratic dictatorship of workers and peasants'. The provisional government remained a bourgeois government from start to end.

The Mensheviks and SRs both exhausted themselves in rendering support to the bourgeois government. A section of the peasantry under left SRs joined the Bolsheviks against right SRs. The Bolshevik party led the Proletariat to overturn the bourgeois government and established a proletarian dictatorship in Russia, cutting short the consolidation of bourgeois power, well in time.

The very short course of revolution from February to October, completely and decisively refuted the formulations— 'revolution in two stages' and the 'two class dictatorship' and endorsed the prognosis of Lenin and Trotsky. The great success of the October Revolution put its co-leaders Lenin and Trotsky, at the head of the revolution.

The bourgeois democratic tasks, which the bourgeois government did not even address, were resolved within no time by the Proletarian State. The October Proletarian Revolution was the tangible embodiment of the 'permanent revolution' where the proletariat, while solving the democratic tasks, took to the socialist ones, without interruption in the course. This was exactly what Trotsky had been arguing!

Experience revealed what theory was unable to foresee! commented Trotsky.

The thunder of the Russian Revolution immediately created a tide of revolutionary wave in Europe and elsewhere on the globe. The maturing proletarian revolutions in the West got a big shot in the arm. The 18 months between the first and second congress of Comintern (March 1919–July 1920) were eventful. A strike wave swept across entire Europe. Successful uprisings were staged in Hungary and Austria. Sections of Comintern were organized in many countries. The armies of Denikin and Kolchak were defeated by the Red Army in civil war in Russia.

Though a situation of high tide of revolution was created all over the globe, with the proletariat in the West ready to follow the Russian path, leading to brighter prospects for the dream of a World Proletarian Revolution coming true, yet the betrayal by the reformist leadership of the West reversed the course of victory and pushed it within no time to a low ebb. This betrayal led to one defeat after another for the proletariat. In Italy, a fully ripe revolution was thrown out of gear by autumn of 1920 by treachery of socialist leaders; while in Germany the adventurous coup in March 1921 resulted in failure.

Immediately upon its advent, the new proletarian Soviet power in Russia was also coerced into the tangles of civil war and foreign aggression on all sides. This colossal engagement on two fronts—domestic and foreign—exhausted the resources of Russia—both human and material—to a great extent. The only hope was the maturing and impending revolutions in Europe, especially Germany. This hope also shattered very soon with defeat of attempts at revolutions in European countries (1919–1924) due to betrayal by the reformist leadership of Second International. These defeats, specially the debacle of Germany, created an overall situation of low ebb in the world socialist movement, pushing down the world proletariat to demoralization and dimming of the revolutionary fervent born out of the Great October Proletarian revolution in Russia. As no support could come from proletariat of the West and consequently the Russian Proletariat was completely isolated, left to face its own destiny. The Soviet Union, which had barely come out of the civil war and imperialist aggression, was now relegated to complete isolation, surrounded from all sides only by its enemies. The best of its revolutionary fighters had already perished in civil war and foreign aggression in Russia. Same was the situation in the countries of Europe where the unsuccessful workers uprisings, due to betrayal by reformist leadership, had resulted in a bloody backlash at the hands of a counter-revolution which followed, taking its toll upon best of the elements of first line in the revolution, the flowers of revolutionary movement. Proletarian leaders like Rosa Luxemburg and Karl Leibknekth were murdered by the enemy.

Lenin and Trotsky both were, however, convinced that the depression in world revolutionary movement was only a temporary phenomenon, arising out of the betrayal by the reformist leaders of the Second International, and was reversible in the near future. They vowed to reverse it, through revolutionary consolidation of world proletariat under the leadership of Comintern, the world party of the proletariat.

Then came the untimely demise of Lenin in 1924. This was the biggest casualty for the world proletariat. In the background of general defeat and demoralization of the working class, a wave of hopelessness gripped the Soviet Union. Scared by the defeats of working class and the bloody reaction that followed, a section of the second line leadership, which was now in command, started to lose faith in the great revolutionary agenda of 'wiping out the capitalism from the face of the earth, through a world socialist revolution' as set out by the Third International (Comintern) in its founding document. This section of leadership in Soviet Union, developed serious doubts about the concept of world socialist revolution and started to dissociate itself from this great battle-cry of world proletariat. Thus, overcoming the initial revolutionary fervent of the working class, generated by the tide of revolution around 1917, specially by the success of proletarian overturn in Russia and which found its expression in the ideas of Lenin and Trotsky; the reaction, now set—in to hold the ground inside Soviet Union, in the background of later defeats of proletariat in different countries. In the face of setbacks to initial attempts at uprisings, the then leadership prepared itself to surrender the avowed positions of striving for a world revolution, taking to confiding inside the Soviet Union. From a strategic offensive against the world capitalism thus began the degeneration to a strategic defensive. There started a reactionary current—from Proletarian Internationalism to Russian Nationalism.

This reactionary nationalist tendency, then discovered its logical embodiment in the emerging bureaucracy, headed by Joseph Stalin, which had already gripped the ranks of second line leadership. The bureaucracy in its turn, discovered the ideology in the 'Great Russian chauvinism' of the Tsarist era, and systematically evolved a whole nationalist perspective. The 'Georgian Affair', which took place in Lenin's lifetime and which immediately attracted the ire of Lenin, was a clear sign of revival of 'White Russian Chauvinism' and the bureaucratic tendencies throwing their stranglehold upon the Soviet Union. Lenin was bitter against the bureaucracy and vowed to fight it. In his 'Last Testament', Lenin suggested removal of Stalin from the top offices in Soviet Union. But this struggle was cut short by his untimely demise. After Lenin, the bureaucracy openly distanced itself from the idea of world revolution and turned to take all strings of the life in the Soviet Union in its hands, by usurping the power inside the Soviet Union for itself, i.e. in exclusion of the working class. In the person of Stalin, it found its leadership. Trotsky wrote that before Stalin could find bureaucracy, the bureaucracy found him. Like all reactionaries of the world, the Stalinist bureaucracy, then stepped out to embrace everything that was rotten and outmode in the past and present. It revived the relics of the past to refute the living present. Everything which was discarded since then by the revolutionary experience of three revolutions, was thus taken out from the dustbin of history. It started with beating the retreat from the perspective of world socialist revolution on the pretension of building socialism within the confines of one country—the Soviet Union. 'Socialism in one Country' became the orientation of world proletarian movement. The programme of world socialist revolution, for accomplishment of which the Third International (Comintern) was formed, was thus completely discarded. Instead of extending the revolution further over the globe, the bureaucracy set out to enjoy the fruits of the victorious revolution of Russian Proletariat.

Trotsky warned that the forces of socialism can only be reconciled on a world scale and not within the confines of one country, as Stalinists thought. But Stalin, the architect of this project, persisted in his daydreams of building Socialism in one country, that too in a backward country like Russia. Gigantic resources were to be generated to touch even the level of capitalist countries of the west, what to say of building socialism. The only path to execute the cynical project of Stalin, was thus to hard press the working people of the Soviet Union to the extreme, in order to generate the immense resources required for it. This execution was not possible through the power based on Workers Soviets. Thus a coercive apparatus was required over and above the proletariat. Stalinists then carved out such power in the form of a bureaucratic apparatus. A bureaucratic crust first emerged to develop into a whole apparatus. The bureaucratic tendencies which had emerged during lifetime of Lenin as a shadow of pre-revolutionary Russia upon the Proletarian State and against which Lenin had vowed to fight in his last days, now found an opportunity to consolidate themselves in a tangible apparatus of bureaucracy.

Even after putting the working people to extreme hardship, the reactionary, sectarian-nationalist programme of building socialism in Soviet Russia, in isolation from rest of the world, started to suffer its destiny—debacle after debacle—and very soon turned into a hollow fantasy of conservative nationalism, that is the Stalinism. Resistance came from working people against their extreme exploitation, their deprivation from affairs of state and the failures of Stalinist project of building socialism in one country. A need arose thus for more and more repression to put down the resistance of working people, which further strengthened the bureaucracy as the sole apparatus capable for such repression upon working people. Through the colossal machinery of violence, in the form of armed forces of State, now at its disposal, the bureaucracy now had a free hand to get rid of everything what was live and revolutionary in the Soviet Union.

Taking benefit of its official position and power in Soviet Union, the Stalinist bureaucracy captured Comintern, the world party of proletariat and then started to divert all resources and forces at the disposal of world proletariat to strengthen its position inside Soviet Russia, instead of utilising the resources of the Soviet Union for expansion of revolution to other parts of the world. Through Comintern, the Stalinist bureaucracy, took control of the Communist parties of the world and gradually converted them to its agencies, executing its bureaucratic commands. It transformed the Communist parties into bureaucratic apparatuses, directly subordinate to Kremlin, in the name of communist discipline.

V

The young and inexperienced Chinese Proletariat and its party, were the first to become casualty under the axe of this bureaucracy. After Russia, it was the turn for the Chinese proletariat to deal with the complicated questions arising out of the revolution in a backward agrarian country, with historically belated development. Although the very rich experience of the Russian Revolution was available to Chinese revolutionaries, instead of utilizing it, they permitted themselves to be misled by the false preaching of Comintern, thereby depriving themselves of the fruits of this experience.

Its leadership, working under direct command of Stalinist Comintern, was instrumental in eliminating the proletariat from political scene in China, despite the heroic fight waged by proletariat against its enemies. The Chinese proletariat was subjected, against its will, to the capitulationist and servile Menshevik policy of trailing behind the bourgeois nationalists in KMT instead of conducting a class war against it. After this collaborationist policy was beaten, first by the right KMT under Chiang Kai Shek and then by the left KMT under Wang Jing Wei, the bureaucracy found its position weakened inside the Comintern and Soviet Union. The path Comintern dictated to them, instead, led to tragic end of a mature revolutionary situation in China. In order to wash off its face the stains of shameful defeats of its policy, one after the other, it forced the demoralised and wounded Chinese proletariat to enter into misadventures of extreme nature and commit suicide thereby. This opportunist policy, full of zigzags, alternating between capitulation and misadventure, in no time resulted in abortion of an apparently mature revolutionary situation in China during 1925–27, leading to the brutal slaughter of the flowers of the working class at the hands of its class enemies. The defeats followed by destruction, pushed the Chinese working class into the dungeons of history for decades to come.

The bureaucracy prepared the defeats and defeats facilitated bureaucracy in occupying the positions vacated by the working class. Defeat of the working class virtually unfolded itself as conquest for the bureaucracy, which advanced its own claim to power and captured it in 1949, using the banner of the proletariat.

This catastrophic reversal of the proletarian revolution maturing in China in 1927, and consequent annihilation of revolutionary proletariat, demonstrated, however, as to how disastrous can be the consequences when the Menshevik policy is applied to a revolutionary situation.

The writings of Leon Trotsky on China, from 1925 till his elimination by Stalin in 1940, present a splendid account of his unrelenting struggle against Menshevism, as exported to China by the Stalinist Comintern.

VI

China, at the end of 19th century, having very little connections with the outside world, was reeling, as before, under a completely decayed and outmode dynasty of Manchu Emperors, who ruled through a bureaucratic network of civil servants, interested only in maintaining status quo, resisting any effort for development or change in China. Saturated by the peasantry, China was living almost in its cocoon, isolated from the rest of the world. Its restricted foreign trade with Europe was highly imbalanced against itself, helping only to exhaust its finances, while China was forced to borrow from foreign powers to purchase even the basic necessities, like iron and steel. The opium war imposed upon China by Britain in 19th century, drained all its silver reserves and forced it further to borrow for future trade against its will, from the western powers. In 1894, Japan made an attempt to usurp part of Chinese territory, but was thwarted by its rivals—Britain, France and Russia. Japan though got a sea-port and 35 million pounds as indemnity from China, for which China had to borrow 48 million pounds. Every time, it was peasantry which continued to be burdened by the foreign loans. The already abominable conditions of Chinese peasantry hardly permitted it to bear anymore the ever increasing burden.

At the turn of the 20th century, the oriental despotism of Manchu rule, decaying for long in China, had fallen almost in tatters, virtually collapsed. China faced chaos and division of its territory under the barbaric domination of landlords in rural areas, who engaged in intense exploitation of the peasantry with no form of redress. The foreign capitalists, taking advantage of this chaos and division in China, had snatched "concessions" at gun point from Manchu emperors, to establish their own industry in big cities and sea-ports of China, with policing rights of their own. The Manchu Dynasty, breathing its last, capitulating both before foreign powers and local warlords, had already abandoned the people to face their destiny, i.e. to be exploited as cheap labour while continuing to pay taxes for repayment of foreign loans, through their sweat and blood. This ruthless exploitation continued to be answered by the unrelenting peasantry, through sporadic local peasant uprisings, which succeeded in creating breathing space for the peasantry, but failed in uprooting the regime of exploitation, through consolidation of power on a national scale. Thus, though totally decayed, Manchu Empire continued in China, with cities under the domination of different foreign powers, and the vast rural territories under control of warlords.

VII

More than a decade thus passed in this chaos, during which time numerous secret societies, bourgeois and petty-bourgeois, were formed in China to fight against Manchu Rule and foreign domination, but without any success. The abortive attempt by Sun Yat Sen in 1885 to carry out an uprising had failed.

In 1900, the Boxer uprising, carried out by the peasantry, resulted in imposition of protocols upon China by the European powers, compelling China to introduce thorough reforms on western patterns, abandoning its old Confucian structures. The army was modernized. Western curriculum was introduced in education as well as in the Civil services. Education for women was permitted in China and Chinese students started to go abroad for western studies. With this, new modes of thought, Marxism included, started to enter into China.

This was the time when Capitalism on a world scale as a whole had already embarked upon the stage of Imperialism and the Bourgeois as a class had lost its revolutionary energy, to bring about a social revolution against the inertia of medieval societies. Early bourgeois, the local manufacturers and traders, were born at this time of overall decline of capitalism. The proletariat was yet a non-entity in China, and was yet to born as a social class.

Completely strangled by dynastic stagnation and intervention of foreign capitalists, the Chinese bourgeois, however, was forced to act. Taking advantage of the tensions among foreign imperialist powers on the eve of the World War-I, and with a ready to act force of rebellious peasantry at its disposal, the Chinese bourgeois was set to take the power in its hands. It took to the banner of Nationalism, to mobilize the nation, especially the peasantry behind it, with an agenda for unification of China as a modern nation into a democratic republic of western style, by overthrowing the Manchu Dynasty and foreign domination, both. In 1905, various anti-Manchu movements joined hands to form a secret Society 'Tong Meng Hui', with Sun Yat Sen as its leader.

In the backdrop of growing unrest, Manchus had to retreat to introduce political reforms. In 1909, Provincial Assemblies were established by Manchus and in 1910 a National Consultative Assembly was established, to assist the Imperial Court, but it frequently remained at odds with the Government.

However, the reforms could not save the rotten regime for long. The Manchu Dynasty was ultimately overthrown by a powerful peasant uprising carefully prepared under the leadership of liberal-democratic bourgeois, under the banner of nationalist Tung Meng Hui. In total, ten attempts were made around this time, in different provinces but the actual revolution began with the uprising at Szechwan province in southwest China. The uprising started with a narrow motivation of Capitalists against nationalisation of Railways, only to become a mass uprising against the Manchu dynasty as a whole. On August 24, 1911, students took to the streets. The army tried to arrest leaders of the movement, leading to open conflicts between protestors and the army; 32 were killed on the spot. People took to arms and fought with the army. Coming out of its narrow ambit, the movement had by now taken the form of a mass political movement, demanding an end to the Manchu rule and establishment of a parliamentary republic. On October 10, 1911, armed rebellion started at Wuchang city, capital of Hubei province, among discontented and modernised army units, who declared their support to nationalists. Wuchang was seized with little resistance, following which many other provinces also declared their cessation from the Manchu

Empire. By the end of November, about two-third of provinces had ceased from the Empire. In December 1911, a delegation from Central and Northern regions, resolved to constitute a republic and elected Sun Yat Sen, its provisional president. On January 1, 1912 the formal declaration of republic was made. However, the Manchu Empire still survived with its seat in Beijing, with Hunan and Hupeh provinces still remaining inside it.

Desperate for their survival, Manchus had to appoint Yuan Shi Kai as Governor-General of these two provinces. Taking advantage of the situation, Yuan bargained with Manchus to concentrate maximum power in his hands. He forced the Manchus to summon the National Assembly, and got himself elected as Prime Minister. With the support of fifty generals of the Imperial Army, which was now the last resort for Manchus, Yuan then succeeded in securing abdication of the Manchu Emperors.

Seeing that the fall of the Manchu dynasty was imminent, Yuan then brokered a deal with the Nationalists, to accept him as President of the republic in place of Sun Yat Sen, putting them under threat of a civil war in case of refusal. The weak Chinese bourgeois relented, without resistance.

Pursuant to the dual deal, the Emperor abdicated on 12th February and Sun Yat Sen on 13th February. Yuan thus succeeded in concentrating all power in his hands, by putting both the Nationalists and Emperors under threat of a civil war between them. On 5th April the Chinese Republic was recognised officially by the United States. The Ministry he formed was full of cronies, while nationalists were almost excluded.

In February 1912, five secret societies, bourgeois and petty bourgeois, prominent among them the 'Tung Meng Hui' came together to form the Kuomintang (KMT), a nationalist party, to establish a bourgeois republic with western style democracy. Then, peasantry was called to throw its forces behind KMT. In the elections to the National Assembly, held in December 1912, KMT won majority seats. KMT planned to control Yuan through the Parliament and elected Government. Yuan tried to bribe KMT leader Sung Chaio Jen, failing which he got him assassinated on March 20, 1913, when he was to leave for Peking to take leadership of new Parliament and threatened the Parliament with troops. Parliament impeached Yuan. In July, provinces tried to secede from the Republic, but Yuan brought them in line.

Yuan forced Parliament to elect him president in October 1913. The Parliament then adopted a Constitution with a cabinet system of Government, instead of presidential system, putting Yuan under the elected Government. A bourgeois Parliament, which tried to control Yuan, itself had become casualty to the corruption of its own members, who were bent upon filling their own coffers, above anything else. By force of arms, Yuan dissolved the Parliament forever. The bourgeois Parliament had denigrated itself so much in the eyes of people, for the corruption and misdeeds of its leaders, that its dissolution by Yuan met with no resistance from the people. The bourgeois republic, failing to mobilise the support of people behind it, thus could not survive and virtually shattered under its own weight.

Yuan Shi Kai, himself having no faith in principles of bourgeois democracy or republic of western style, rather contempt against it and with a totalitarian mindset, staged a coup to restore the Empire and become Emperor of China. KMT was banned and its leader Sun Yat Sen flew to Japan, where he remained in hibernation for about five years. Till 1916, Yuan remained the virtual dictator of China. However, not satisfied with this, he attempted yet another coup to regain the dynastic rule with himself as Emperor, which failed. Though Yuan made the Parliament vote in favour of establishment of Monarchy and got himself appointed Emperor by the provincial delegates in December, he failed to correctly estimate the anti-monarchic sentiments of the people. Uprisings and secessions started. Under pressure of his aides, Yuan had to give up the dreams of the Empire by March 1916, but it was too late by then. Taking advantage of the chaos which followed, the militarists under Yuan set up themselves against him and succeeded in usurping different territories all over Northern China. Humiliated and deserted, Yuan was forced to abandon his dreams of settling an Empire. Yuan died from an ailment in 1916.

After failure of the bourgeois in carrying out a successful revolution, to assume and retain power in its hands, China once again became fragmented with the warlords usurping Northern China, while only South China remained under domination of Bourgeois Nationalist Government having its seat at Wuhan, leaving cities under control of foreign powers. Triple power thus existed in China—South, dominated by KMT, North by different warlords, and its cities under direct control of foreign powers.

The intervention of Yuan, pursuant to weakness and corruption of bourgeois nationalist leadership, had aborted the bourgeois revolution midway. Thus, neither a republic nor a Monarchy could settle in China. The dream of the Chinese bourgeois, to have a democratic republic on the pattern of western capitalism, stood shattered even before the complete destruction of the Empire. What now survived was the bare desire to unify the country, minus the dreams of a democratic republic. This was possible with military methods, and the Chinese bourgeois was left with the only option to tread this path.

The Chinese bourgeois utterly failed to accomplish its historic mission either of unifying China or liberating it from the shackles of medievalism and colonialism. Already on the path of decay, the Chinese bourgeois, like the bourgeois in all other backward countries, could not have delivered anything more than that. It was at this time that a bourgeois resolution on the other side of the globe, i.e. in Spain, also suffered the same fate-miscarriage in the offing. This demonstrated that the bourgeois as a class has lost all its revolutionary energy worldwide and is unable to carry out bourgeois-deomcratic revolutions either in Asia (China) or in Europe (Spain). The responsibility accomplishing the bourgeois democratic tasks in China, which the bourgeois could not do, thus essentially fell on the shoulders of the very young Chinese proletariat.

VIII

In the backdrop of this scenario approached World War I. China was forced to enter into it, against its will, on the orders of the Allies, which was an apparent manouevre of the Allies to seize the 'concessions' given by China to Germany, for themselves. At the end of the War, the Allies, who succeeded in getting these concessions from 'great powers', tried to alienate them from Japan, through the Versailles Treaty, which created a furore in China. Huge protests of students erupted against the Versailles Treaty, forcing the Government to refuse to sign the treaty. The demonstration which started on 4th May 1919, with 5,000 students, gathering at Tiananmen Square in Peking, spread to 16 provinces, involving 1,00,000 people, and went down in history of China as '4th May Movement'. Chen Tu Shiu, its leader, a professor in Peking University, became the hero of the masses. This was the awakening and entry of a new generation of China onto the political stage, which turned towards the Proletariat to take the destiny of China, still in the stranglehold of the forces of old society, in its hands.

The 4th May Movement brought forward a leadership of a different type, inspired by the Great October Proletarian Revolution in Russia, which consolidated itself into a small group of intellectuals by 1920 and formally organised itself under the banner of the Chinese Communist Party (CCP) in 1921. The CCP had about 50 members and a Central Committee of 3, with Chen-Tu-Shiu its Secretary. Journals, including *The Communist* were published and mass organisations, like the Socialist Youth League were formed. Small political groups were formed in Shanghai, Wuhan, Changsha, Canton and Tsinan. A group was also formed in Paris. A Committee of Workers' Movement was organised in Shanghai. Mass organisations among workers, youth and women were working in 1920 itself. In its activities, the CCP cooperated with nationalists as well as anarchist elements.

During the making of the CCP was organised the 'Shanghai Mechanical Workers' Union'—the first organisation of industrial proletariat, directly under the Communist influence. In January 1921, the Committee of Workers' Movement was organised in Shanghai. At the same time, Hongkong-Chinese Seamen's Union was also organised which launched a nationwide, first really militant strike action, twelve months later in 1922. Around June 1921 a full fledged Labour Secretariat was established in Shanghai with its branches in other industrial cities of Wuhan, Tsinan, Peking, Canton and Changsha.

In October 1921, a big strike was organised against British American Tobacco Company. In January1922, Chinese Seamen's Union, with 10,000 workers struck in Hongkong. Other workers in Hongkong and Canton supported the strike. Nationalists also supported the strike. By February 1922, one lakh workers had got involved, virtually paralysing the entire Hongkong. This strike forced the British to withdraw their offensive against the right to Unionise and to accept a substantial increase in wages. In May 1922 was called the first Congress of the National General Labour Union (NGLU), which came to represent one-fifth of the total workers in China. It raised the slogan of an 8-hour working day, mutual aid and overthrow of the Imperialists and Warlords.

The 7th February 1923 was the climax of the strike wave. The Govt. in Peking crushed the strike organised by the Hankow Railroad Workers, by use of force. A gathering of 10,000 strikers was fired upon, killing more than 40 on the spot, injuring above 300 and dismissing thousands from their jobs.

As one can see, by mid-1922 there was a developed working class movement in China, though only about 120 Communists were in touch with the national organisation of the CCP existing in 16 provinces, having a formal structure in only 10. Serious attempts were also made to organise among the peasantry. By 1923, the CCP successfully led about 1,50,000 workers in about one hundred small and big strikes. The CCP as well as the working class, thus became a real force in China.

IX

The Chinese bourgeois, however, failing to achieve its mission of establishment of a western style democracy in China on its own, turned towards the United States in hope of aid to crush the warlords. But, like other Imperialist powers, the United States was interested in China only as a 'market' and had vested interests against its unification and development as a modern country. Though intensely repulsive against Communism, Sun Yat Sen, having no alternative, had to turn to the Soviet Union for help. Lenin not only promised the requisite aid to KMT in the form of weapons, machines, advice, training, etc. but also pledged to return the territories of China conquered by the Tsars.

The Comintern under Lenin supported KMT nationalists, as at that time it was the only platform in opposition to the Imperialists and Warlords and no independent proletarian current existed in China. However, with the formation of the CCP subsequently, the political divide between the working class and bourgeois was sealed organisationally. Both hostile classes of the modern world now existed in China face to face with each other.

X

Towards the end of the second decade of the 20th century, China was still developing at snail's pace with a primitive economy and stagnated politics at its helm, frequently hit by famines small and big and it was only its highly centralised system of distribution that could save its population from perishing during those famines. Few cities with a population of over 50,000 could develop in China, habited by 6% of its people, 4% habiting small towns and over 90% still living in vast rural China. Production and distribution was highly organized. While villages contributed mainly through agriculture produce and handicraft goods, towns contributed mainly through manufacture. Industry in China, having concentration in big cities and sea ports, was developed mainly by foreign capitalists. The tariff laws imposed on China prevented building of its own industrial base.

Foreign intervention had disturbed the centuries-old static, self-reliant and balanced economy of China by introducing cheap manufactured goods and by disrupting the central organization of economy. Primitive and by then isolated economy of China faced total degradation with Imperialist advent. The foreign intervention, had resulted in growth of industry only for a little, while China as a whole remained a backward peasant country, reeling under the double yoke of domestic feudalism and foreign imperialism.

Yet this intervention made a great contribution by default, independent of the will of its perpetrators, by producing the real liberator of a stagnated Chinese Society—the Proletariat.

The Proletariat was numerous, hardly half per cent of the total population, mainly concentrated in Shanghai, Canton, Hankow and around Wuhan. Shanghai alone had 20% of the total proletariat with 3,00,000 workers, Canton 2,00,000, Hankow 2,00,000 and 1,00,000 in and around Wuhan. Around half of the Proletariat was employed in foreign industry. However, the strength of the proletariat cannot be measured by its numbers, as the same lies in its social position having core installations of modern capitalism in its hands—factories, railways, transport, communication, etc. and its vital role in backward countries as the sole and natural leader of subjugated nation, especially its peasantry. Above all, the strength of the proletariat lies in its existence as an international class, hostile to the world bourgeois.

XI

But, by the time the working class could consolidate to assert itself in China, independent of the nationalist bourgeois, through its class organizations (CCP and Labor Unions) and class actions (strikes), the leadership of the Comintern as well as that of Soviet Russia had fallen, unfortunately, to the hands of bureaucracy headed by Stalin. This bureaucracy, emerging out of the second line leadership of the Russian Revolution and riding to power in Russia in the background of defeat and debacles to the world proletarian revolution (1919–1924), was interested primarily in consolidating its own positions inside the Soviet Union, especially in tis opportunist strife against the Left opposition led by Trotsky, and was taking the Comintern for a ride in the power game, with interests of World Proletarian Revolution put on the backburner.

The Comintern under Stalin-Bukharin, openly advocated that the Proletariat, instead of contending for the leadership in the Chinese Revolution, has rather to perform the 'coolie service' in it, of which, according to them, the national bourgeois was the leader. This 'tutelage' policy, becoming the official line of Stalinist Comintern, though belied again and again by the experience of three revolutions in Russia and further ratified by the course of events in China itself, was cynically imposed upon the CCP, forcing it to trail behind the bourgeois-landlord KMT, against its will.

The ongoing revolution of China was bourgeois in nature—from this, the Stalinists derived the wrong conclusion, drawing an analogy with Mensheviks in Russia, which view was fully discarded by three Russian Revolutions, that the bourgeois was the natural leader of the Chinese Revolution and the proletariat had a role only subservient to it. This led the Stalinists to the 'two stage' Menshevik theory of revolution—first democratic and then socialist. The old Bolshevik formula of a 'democratic dictatorship of proletariat and peasantry', instead of the dictatorship of the proletariat, which already stood discarded by the course of Russian Revolution and abandoned by Lenin himself in his April thesis, was also recalled to service in Chinese Revolution by the Stalinist Comintern; re-dressing and stretching the same even further, to appear under a new slogan—'bloc of four classes'; wherein the bourgeois was also attributed a revolu-tionary role. KMT for them was the real embodiment of this popular front, a living 'bloc of four classes'—National bour-geois, Petty bourgeois, peasantry and in the last—Proletariat.

From the small numeric existence of the proletariat inside China, epigones of Leninism made a wrong estimation of the actual historic role and strength of the Chinese proletariat and thus mis-oriented themselves on the question of mechanics of class forces in Chinese Revolution. The official line of Comintern under Stalin, basing itself upon the essentially conservative nationalist perspective, assumed the Chinese working class as incapable of providing leadership to a democratic revolution in China and developing it to a proletarian overturn. They pinned their false hopes on Chinese bourgeois under Kuomintang and advocated "tailism" as the only practical policy for the proletariat. The policy of Comintern at that time can be no better reflected than in the words of Borodin, the then agent of Comintern in China, who told the Chinese Communists that at that stage they essentially have to do the 'coolie work' for the bourgeois. The bogus formula of 'Stagism'—the two stage theory of revolution, an innovation of Menshevism and now advocated by Stalinists, artificially confining the integrated course of history into separate compartments—the bourgeois democratic and the proletarian socialist—one trailing behind another, only in their assumptions, was an offshoot of this reactionary nationalist perspective. The other side of this coin was the equally fictitious slogan invested by Stalin himself: 'Socialism in one country', which he advanced to betray the great proletarian cause of world revolution.

The political inability of the Stalinists to approach the question of Chinese revolution from a proletarian internationalist perspective and estimate the strength of the Chinese proletariat as an integral part of world proletarian army, led them straight to political bankruptcy, by artificially belittling the role of proletariat in their falsely assumed democratic stage of Revolution. The nationalist perspective led the Stalinists to advocate 'tailism' for the proletariat, as they assumed that the Chinese proletariat was too weak to take the power in China. This was the estimation of epigones of Leninism at a time when, after exhaustion of the bourgeois democracy, which had crumbled in no time under its own weight, the stage in history was already set in China for the proletariat to establish its hegemony over the revolution and take the power in its hands. Instead, the Stalinists imposed the policy of total servility to the bourgeois, upon the proletariat, prescribing it as a panacea for democratic stage of revolution. When this outmode and retrogressive policy backfired, an attempt was made to cover it through putchism, using the proletariat as cannon fodder for the misadventures of bureaucracy, resulting in complete destruction of the young Chinese proletariat. The policy proved to be abortive not only for the impending revolution in China, but for the World Proletarian Revolution.

In its second congress in 1922, the CCP for the first time resolved to form a United Front with the KMT, while maintaining its independence. When the Comintern, which had supported KMT till now, proposed the United front between KMT and CCP, the leader of KMT, Sun-Yat-Sen outright rejected the proposal, saying that he saw no role for communism in China. However, unable to afford to lose material support from the Comintern and Soviet Russia, Sun permitted entry to communists in KMT, on the condition of submission to the discipline of KMT by the communists. Maring, the Comintern representative in China at that time, agreed to the proposal of KMT. In August 1922, a meeting of leading communists, with Chen-Tu-Shiu at its head, considered and rejected this directive of the Comintern.

But the Comintern did not concede to the politically correct position of CCP. Stalinist bureaucracy inside the Comintern used their official position to put pressure upon the leadership of CCP to bend before Nationalists and enter KMT in their individual capacity. Stalinists, instead of recognising the KMT as a bourgeois party, termed it a "bloc of four classes"—national bourgeois, petty bourgeois, workers and peasants, which was rather further dilution of the formula of "Dictatorship of two classes—Proletariat and peasantry". The formula had already been discarded by the Russian revolutions. But the unwilling CCP was forced to enter the KMT, against its will and adhere to its discipline, abandoning all its independent positions and actions in practice. Though the Chinese communists succeeded in having a reservation in retaining membership of CCP simultaneously, was hardly of any consequence in practice.

Trotsky marks this subjugation of the CCP to the bourgeois discipline of KMT, saying that the CCP was neither permitted to publish its political paper, nor to criticize the bourgeois-Confucian principles of Sun Yat Sen.

XII

On 4.9.1922, with concurrence of the Comintern, Sun Yat Sen proposed to reorganise the KMT and raise an armed force to defeat warlordism. In this reorganisation in January 1923, it was ensured by the bourgeois-nationalists that the Communists get completely excluded from the military organisation of KMT. However, this invited no objection from the Comintern, which continued to support KMT as before. Chiang Kai Shek was sent to Soviet Russia to learn military organization and collect arms.

The Third congress of the CCP, taking place in June 1923, debated the issue of Communists remaining inside the KMT, with the majority proposing a come-out of it. Maring, the then agent of Comintern in China, dictated the maintenance of a statusquo.

CCP at that time was leading militant struggles of working class and virtually needed an independent class policy, in place of servitude in shackles inside a bourgeois party. As the working class struggles were being fought under the banner of the bourgeois KMT, the proletarian current remained dimmed as overshadowed by the bourgeois leadership of KMT. Trotsky opposed this policy of Tailism, being advocated by the Stalinist bureaucracy, and supported independence of action for the CCP. Stalinists instead forced the party to remain as a fraction inside the KMT.

In 1924, Whampoa Military Academy was established to train the armed forces of KMT, where Communists were permitted only in the political wing and barred from military organs. The Chinese communists, about 1000 members of CCP by that time, united themselves with the left wing of Nationalists against the rights. In 1924, there was a great urge from the leaders of CCP itself to abandon the KMT and take to the independent road, but, under pressure from the Comintern, the United front had to be preserved under the banner of KMT.

In 1925, Sun Yat Sen died and thereafter it escalated tensions inside the Nationalist KMT between its right wing under Chiang Kai Shek, the Commander of National Army and its left wing under Wang Ching Wei, the Chairman of National Government. By this time, the CCP, relaxing its membership norms and becoming a mass proletarian party, had augmented itself to about 10,000. A fresh wave of powerful strikes swept Chinese cities, which put workers face to face with the bourgeois. Tensions between KMT and CCP thus sharpened more and more, every passing day.

The start of 1925 was eventful and impregnated by revolutionary opportunities and prospects for the Chinese proletariat. February saw big strikes by workers taking place against Japanese Textile Mills. The National Railroad Union again emerged after its ruthless suppression, to hold its second congress. Leaders of Chinese Seamen's Union joined the CCP. As many as 166 Workers' Unions came to the platform of National General Labor Union (NGLU), representing five lakh workers in different cities in China and held a congress. As the working class organization grew, it moved towards the left, more and more.

During this period were formed peasant associations under the lead of CCP. These peasant associations, by 1927 had claimed about 90 lakh membership in 16 provinces. This was a ready reserve for the CCP, for accomplishing a real revolution under the leadership of the proletariat, with peasantry following.

On 30th May 1925, thousands of workers gathered on Nanking Road, in response to the call for a demonstration given by the Central Committee of CCP against the killing of a striker on May 15, 1925, by armed guards in Shanghai Cotton Mills. The demonstration was fired upon by International Settlement Police under a British Officer, where twelve workers were killed and scores of others were either wounded or arrested. The proletariat responded to it by organizing a bigger demonstration, culminating in a general strike on the next day. Then was organised the Shanghai General Labor Union (SGLU). Strike spread to other regions. In Hong Kong and Canton was total strike and blockade of ports. There was total disruption of normal life. On 23rd June, a general strike was called by NGLU and a huge demonstration was taken out in Shanghai, which was again drowned in blood by British and French troops stationed there, firing and killing 80 people on the spot. The strike intensified, making it a big showdown between the working class and the Imperialists. Hong Kong was boycotted and evacuated by workers, bringing it to a virtual halt. Sailors threw their support behind the strike. This strike, the longest in Chinese history, lasted 16 months, with no ship moving in or out from Hong Kong ports for more than a year. This movement, known as '30th May Movement' in Chinese history, brought the working class to centre-stage of political events.

XIII

Around a proletarian axis, a powerful centripetal force was already in motion by 1925, with a following not only among the peasantry but in urban petty bourgeois too. This was the intensity of the actions of working class, which according to epigones, was not ready to take the leadership of revolution into its hands! Workers already possessed sufficient power to close down all the Imperialist Enterprises in cities, at once. It was the Workers' Movement only which could have gravitated the petty bourgeois and even bourgeois layers of population, to the left and could have pressed them into real action against the Imperialists and Warlords. The CCP by now was deeply rooted in the masses. The time had come for the proletariat to move to overthrow the Foreign and Chinese bourgeois, along with warlords, and take the power in its hands.

The proletariat and CCP were ready for this, but Stalinists were not. CCP was held back by the Comintern. Preparing for revolution first of all required a departure from the bourgeois leadership of KMT, which Comintern resented tooth and nail. Trotsky consistently advocated for immediate and unconditional departure, but Stalinists prevailed. Trotsky argued against any United Front of Workers with the bourgeois. At the second congress of KMT, both Chiang and Wang, leaders of right and left KMT, advocated for preservation of the United Front, as the same resulted in servitude of Communists to the Bourgeois-Nationalists. Trotsky called for organization of Soviets of Workers and peasants, which Stalin opposed, saying that there was no revolutionary situation in China and that KMT itself would act in place of the Soviets.

XIII

On 20th March 1926, Chiang Kai-shek staged a coup in Shanghai declaring martial law, on the pretext of an abduction attempt allegedly made upon him at Zhingshan warship. A total of 50 CCP members along with Soviet advisors to KMT, were put under arrest on the charge of plotting against the KMT. This was the gift from the bourgeois to the Comintern. Even the Comintern did not wake up. Instead of calling upon the CCP to leave KMT, it still argued for preservation of a united front with the bourgeois. Chiang released communists and Soviet advisors but imposed strict restrictions upon CCP. Chiang barred CCP from criticising the principles of Sun Yat Sen, it forbade Nationalists from joining CCP without prior permission, asked for a membership list of CCP and rejected communists from all leading posts in the KMT and Government. Still, Borodin and Stalin asked Communists to bow down to KMT. All degrading conditions imposed by Chiang were accepted by the Comintern, without shame. Circumstances were pressing for ending the United Front with Chiang, and preparing for an insurrection, but the Stalinists did not change their line. All attempts to leave KMT or even take it over in alliance with the left KMT were opposed by Stalin and the Comintern under him. The CCP was subdued inside the KMT by manoeuvre of Chiang and treachery of Stalin.

The CCP at this moment resolved to raise its own armed forces and demanded from Comintern that 5,000 rifles out of those supplied to KMT be given to it to arm the peasants of Kwangtung province who followed CCP, but the Comintern refused, saying that the armed peasants cannot participate in Northern Expedition against warlords, rather they would invite the suspicion of KMT and make the peasants oppose KMT. The Stalinist Comintern openly commanded the CCP to follow the leadership of KMT and surrender to its discipline. The great opportunity was thus lost at will. Chen Tu Shiu wrote later that "By this time the party was already not the party of the proletariat, having become completely the extreme left wing of the bourgeois and beginning to fall into the deep pit of opportunism". During all this time, Stalin continued to label Chiang as great revolutionary. As Chen wrote later, "without fighting against Stalin, one could not have fought with Chiang".

In July 1926 started the Northern Expedition of KMT, in agreement with the Comintern, with the purported aim to unify China by defeating the Warlords through military means. Taking advantage, the CCP stepped up agitations alongside the route of Army, preparing the peasantry to seize lands of the landlords and organize armed uprisings. The Comintern prevented these uprisings, virtually aborting the social revolution itself, especially in rural China and thereby leaving the civil war through military expedition, under the command of KMT, as the only option. The CCP was forced by Comintern to hold back the peasantry from taking lands of KMT officers and small landlords. This punctured the entire purpose of the peasant uprisings. While Stalin was advising restraint to Communists, Chiang rejected all demands of peasants, except for a cut of 25% in land revenue.

The same was the situation in the cities, where the entire economy was destabilised by the proletariat through militant strikes, violent demonstrations and armed picketing. But as soon as the KMT came in control of the cities, strikes were banned and pickets disarmed. The CCP itself was forced by the Comintern to help end the strikes. The calling off of the Hong Kong Canton strike in October 1926 by the CCP is a glaring example of it. In fact, while remaining inside KMT, the character of the CCP had undergone a sea change, and it had become a bureaucratic machine on the patterns of bourgeois KMT itself, blindly executing the commands taken from the Comintern. It was more or less a national agency of Stalinist Comintern, in China.

In January 1927, KMT armies under Wang Ching Wei captured the city of Wuhan with the help of the CCP, and declared it the new seat of Nationalist Government.

Stalin continued to call for use of the 'revolutionary potential' of the 'revolutionary' nationalist government, terming Chiang Kai Shek as a great revolutionary leader, while himself exchanging pleasantries and portraits with him. Even on the basic question of land distribution, Stalin argued against breaking off the agreement with KMT, assuring that the KMT's agrarian policy itself would foster an agrarian revolution. Trotsky vehemently protested against it, convinced that the colonial bourgeois could not advance the revolution under its leadership. Trotsky had warned that the Northern Expedition under the leadership of bourgeois KMT would soon turn into an expedition against the proletariat. But Stalinists, blinding themselves by illusions on the role of Chinese bourgeois, failed to see through the real agenda. Leaders of the CCP knew that the advice of Stalin was worthless, but they were forced to continue with the United Front. History, though, was forwarding a clear option—either social revolution or a united front. Trotsky called for immediate abandonment of KMT, while at the same time preparing the proletariat through its consolidation in the Soviets to seize power. But Stalinists were determined not to listen. Stalin opposed the idea of organization of the Soviets on the ground that there was no revolutionary situation in China and that KMT itself was a substitute for the Soviets.

At the end of February 1927, Chiang's troops were approaching Shanghai in the Northern Expedition. According to bogus and self-abortive plan of Stalin, which permitted the proletariat to be used as cannon fodder, the CCP was asked to take control of Shanghai first and then to hand it over to KMT as it approached the city. When Chiang's forces were 25 miles from the city, the CCP-led SGLU began a series of strikes and protests against the warlords and imperialists who controlled the city. Street fighting erupted, culminating in bloody repression of the proletariat. Chiang calmly watched the butchering of the proletariat, deliberately holding his forces back, instead of coming to its aid.

After the mayhem of the proletariat, the strike was called off on February 24, 1927.

Again, on March 21, 1927, the forces of KMT moved towards Shanghai and SGLU was again made to call for insurrection. Responding to the call of the CCP, over 5,00,000 workers rose in unison, demonstrating extraordinary heroism, stormed the police stations, drove the warlords out and virtually seized the city of Shanghai. The blue flag of KMT was trampled underfoot by the workers. Worried at the Shanghai insurrection, nationalists started repression upon communists in other cities, while Chiang stopped the campaign against the warlords, deciding to break with communists. The Comintern, however directed CCP to bury the weapons, stop the hostilities, applaud KMT in Shanghai, and hand over the power peacefully to it. Following the command, the Shanghai proletariat was then called upon by CCP to give rather a triumphant welcome to Chiang. With workers applauding the KMT, the CCP and workers' organizations were effectively paralysed.

However, Chiang Kai Shek had something else on his mind. He arrived in Shanghai on 26th March. On April 2, 1927 he secretly organized Central Monitoring Committee in Shanghai, hired criminal gangs and organized rightist groups to attack the CCP. While Chiang was preparing himself for this violent showdown, the Comintern was busy in preaching for preservation of the United Front. Before the sunrise of April 12, the gangs attacked the districts under control of workers—Zhabei, Nanshi, and Pudong—wounding and killing the workers. Chiang Kai Shek passed an emergency decree, declaring the workers' militias illegal and the 26th Army under him disarmed the workers, wounding more than 300. When workers and students protested against it, the Army opened fire, killing more than 100 and wounding hundreds. Chiang banned CCP and all its organizations; 5,000 went missing, more than a thousand were taken prisoner and more than 300 were executed on the spot. Communists in Canton, Xiamen, Fuzhou, Ningbo, Nanking, Hangzhou and Changsha, were arrested and killed. On April 28, even the communists taking refuge in the Soviet Embassy in Beijing, were the killed. Chiang's troops, along with other reactionary secret societies, roamed the streets of Shanghai, executing workers on the spot. Workers, who had applauded Chiang only few days back, were not in a position to fight back the armed assault, so demonstrations were ineffective. No preparations were made to arm the working class, even though Chinese communists were alarmed by Chiang's refusal to support the workers' uprising. Days before the Shanghai massacre, the Comintern and Chiang were exchanging fraternal pleasantries. On 6th April, Stalin had expressed confidence in KMT and Chiang, saying that they cannot do otherwise except to carry out assault against imperialism. Chiang had deliberately kept his armies away from fighting the imperialists and warlords in Shanghai, hoping to negotiate with them after the workers were crushed. When workers won the battle, Chiang led his army against them into Shanghai. Chiang declared a new Government in Nanking, in opposition to the Nationalist government in Wuhan.

XV

The Northern Expedition, as Trotsky had predicted much in advance, culminated in the an expedition of the bourgeois against the proletariat. Trotsky still called for reversal of policy, demanding a war against bourgeois-nationalist KMT.

Still, the fantasy of Stalinists about the United Front was far from over.

Stalin first kept silent on the Shanghai coup, and then started to shift the blame elsewhere. Stalinists started to accuse in meetings the workers for committing 'excesses' and provoking Chiang Kai Shek thereby.

On April 27, 1927, the Comintern held a meeting of its Executive Committee on China. M.N. Roy reported from China that the coup has strengthened the bonds between left KMT and CCP. Thus, the United Front was to continue now under the banner of KMT as a 'bloc of four classes', with the only change that the right KMT now under Chiang Kai-shek was to be replaced with left KMT under Wang Ching Wei and the government in Wuhan led by him. This was exactly the line adopted at the 5th congress of the CCP. Now Wang, instead of Chiang, was the great revolutionary leader, and communists must submit to its discipline and domination as before Chiang, while Wang and Chiang both remaining inside the same party-KMT. The policy of Stalin thus remained unaltered. Trotsky severely criticised Roy's report and demanded immediate withdrawal from KMT, which went unheard. Chen Tu Shiu also sent a report supporting withdrawal from KMT. But Bukharin, the then Chairman of the Comintern, criticised the recommendation for withdrawal, advocating for continuance of work inside KMT, this time under Wang Ching Wei. The CCP was now commanded to join the left wing of KMT under Wang Ching Wei and submit to its discipline. The CCP was made to enter into the coalition Government under left KMT, with its seat at Wuhan in South China, with two Communist Ministers—Peng Shu Tse and Tang Ping Shan, inducted therein as ministers for labour and agriculture, the classical ministries for hostages.

This was the same Wang who had refused to move against Chiang at the time of Shanghai coup. Trotsky argued against relying upon the left-KMT, and called for organisation of Workers' Soviets as the chief organ of proletarian power, ahead of the uprisings themselves. But Stalin declared, "the revolutionary KMT in Wuhan by a determined fight against militarism and imperialism will in fact be converted into an organ of the revolutionary dictatorship of the proletariat and peasantry". Similar things had been said about Chiang just two months before. Instead of Chiang, now Wang was being named as leader of the revolution. In any case, CCP was to tail itself behind the bourgeois KMT. After the right wing, now it was the turn for its left. Rules to be applied were same. No agrarian revolution, no anti-KMT agitation, no excesses, no provocation. CCP Ministers were used to hold back the workers and peasants from revolution itself, instead of pulling the government to the left. Minister of labour was used to abort the strikes, while the Minister of Agriculture was made to order firing upon the peasants seizing the lands of landlords. Revolution was once again paralysed. The idea of organizing Soviets, advanced by Trotsky, was mocked at by the Stalinists saying that Soviets can be organised only at the eve of uprising, and according to them, there was no such revolutionary situation in China.

On the eve of revolution in China, however everytime caught the Stalinists unawares, and the Chinese proletariat without the necessary drill.

Stalinists continued in their slumber till Wang Ching Wei also carried out a similar anti-communist coup in Changsha in Hunan province on May 21, 1927, before abandoning Wuhan, and the irreparable damage was inflicted, once again, this time by left KMT.

On May 25, 1927, Trotsky again warned that Chiang and Wang are the sides of the same bourgeois coin, both are natural friends being agency of Chinese bourgeois and that both are avowed enemies of working class. Trotsky now officially dissociated himself from the policy of Stalin in the meeting of the Comintern (Second Speech on Chinese question). Trotsky repeatedly warned against violent repression at the hands of Wang. But the same fell on deaf ears of Stalinist bureaucracy.

On July 15, 1927, Wang carried out a bloodbath of communists, and brutally crushed the labour movement in Wuhan. The armies of Wang butchered a whole peasant army led by CCP around Wuhan, arrested CCP leaders and expelled all communists from KMT. This was the gift to Stalin from left KMT, which Stalin was terming as the organ of revolutionary democratic dictatorship. The proletariat was badly wounded and was bleeding profusely.

XVI

Instead of accepting defeat and instead of changing the orientation and strategy, Stalin boasted before the 15th Congress of the Russian Communist Party in December 1927 that the Chinese Revolution was not defeated but had moved to a higher plane. Trotsky said that the revolution stood completely crushed, both CCP and the labour organisations were destroyed and that a period of counter revolution had set in. On the contrary, Stalin now said that the time was now ripe for leaving KMT (after communists were already expelled from KMT!) and the time had come to organise uprisings of workers. Trotsky opposed this putschist policy, vehemently. Trotsky said that at the time when revolution was already crushed, the uprisings were merely a misadventure of extreme nature and a bureaucratic fantasy, aimed at concealing the disastrous consequences of the capitulationist line of Stalin, hitherto applied, behind the smokescreen of false revolutionism.

Trotsky warned that the Chinese working class, already defeated and crushed, would not be able to afford this bureaucratic luxury. He called for patience, saying that necessary preparations should be made for armed uprisings, keeping the uprising themselves in abeyance for the time being. Trotsky suggested arming and organisation of the workers on a mass scale through the Soviets, as a condition precedent for successful uprising.

The voice of left opposition once again went unheard. The Stalinists were in extraordinary haste to cover up their criminal past of collaboration with KMT which had led to total annihilation of revolution in China by then, with some miraculous victory. Stalinists were not in a mood to spare any time for making preparations. The Chinese proletariat was thus forced into the gamble of armed insurrection, against all odds. As history showed, the consequences were disastrous.

The uprisings were doomed to fail and they did, but only after taking a very big toll upon the working class. In the coming four months, from August to December, during which the puschist policy was applied, the armed revolutionaries and advanced workers who were still alive were completely eliminated, as the mass of workers remained passive due to its demoralisation in earlier debacles. First in the Nanchung Uprising, then in the Hunan-Hupeh harvest uprising, then in the Haifing Soviet Movement and finally in the Canton insurrection in December 1927, one defeat followed the other, inflicting immeasurable damage. Six thousand revolutionaries were butchered by the KMT in Canton alone. The surviving potential of the CCP, after the Shanghai massacre, to go underground and re-organize the workers and peasants was now completely destroyed. The revolution which had suffered a crushing defeat in April 1927 due to capitulationist and tailist policy of Stalin, was now killed completely through putchism and misadventures. The CCP, acting directly under the commands of the Comintern, was virtually forced to commit suicide, as Chen Tu Shiu, its leader, conceded thereafter in his "Open Appeal".

As the events themselves revealed, not only were the uprisings called at the most inopportune moment, when the morale of the proletariat, already mauled and wounded, was at its lowest ebb, but also no serious preparations were undertaken to ensure the success of the uprisings. Above all, no Soviets were elected among the proletariat to consolidate the power and to become the organ of revolution. In Canton, a Soviet was conjured out of thin air, to be appointed from above at the eve of the uprising, instead of electing it among the workers and permitting it time to earn legitimacy among the proletariat. Consequently, it failed to play any role in the uprising. It was clear that the leadership had not undertaken the preparations seriously, rather, it had played at the insurrection.

XVII

However, despite the opportunism of its leadership, the Chinese proletariat showed unprecedented heroism during the Canton uprising. With the battle-cry against its class enemies, 'Down with Kuomintang', it trampled underfoot the emblem and flags of bourgeois nationalists. Imperialists and warlords were driven out of Canton by the proletariat. Canton remained in the hands of the Proletariat for four days, before the latter was butchered by the armies of Chiang with the weapons supplied by the Comintern.

In fact, the revolution did not fail, but was aborted at the hands of Stalinist bureaucracy. The crushing failures of 1927 still could have been used as a lesson, though at a very high price, to dissociate from the policy of class collaboration, but the Stalinists still did not care. Instead of a reviewing of their servile and capitulationist policy in its entirety, the Stalinists triggered the dirty blame game against those who questioned their policy.

After destroying the CCP, Wang Ching Wei fled to Europe, abandoning Wuhan to be taken over by Chiang. In June 1928, the warlord capital Beijing was also captured by Chiang's army. Another massacre of communists and workers was then carried out in Tsinan.

XVIII

In 1928, Trotsky was expelled from the Russian Communist Party and then from the Comintern, and was ultimately exiled from Russia. In 1929, Chinese Communist Party was also purged of all supporters of left opposition. Putting the whole blame of the mess of 1927 on Chen Tu Shiu, for a crime for which he was in no way responsible, the Comintern expelled him in 1929 from the CCP, the party which he had founded.

Trotsky rightly claimed that Stalin was truly the gravedigger of the second Chinese Revolution. From beginning to end, the Comintern under Stalin, remained saturated with illusions about the political character and position of the colonial bourgeois. Its wrong assumption of weakness of the proletariat as a class, pushed it into the arms of Chinese bourgeois under the slogan 'bloc of four classes'. It recognized the KMT, under bourgeois domination, as an embodiment of the 'bloc of four classes' and thus the only body for carrying out the 'National Democratic Revolution'.

After missing the shots, the CCP misled and confused the working class and peasantry and finally pushed them to the knell of death. Having subordinated the Chinese working class to the bourgeois, it put brakes on revolution, supported reactionary generals of bourgeois KMT, now the right KMT and then the left, prevented the appearance of Soviets, and liquidated those that appeared. Chen Tu Shiu, its leader at that time, later admitted, "I decisively recognise that the objective conditions were second in importance as the cause of the failure of the last Chinese revolution. The main cause was the error of opportunism, the error of our policy in dealing with Kuomintang".

XIX

The story of the aborted proletarian revolution in China on the one hand is the story of unprecedented heroism displayed by the young proletariat which took upon itself the task of carrying out a revolutionary transformation of China, against all odds, but failed due to bankruptcy of its nationalist bureaucratic leadership, while on the other, it is also a narrative of the misdeeds of its leadership which forced the young proletariat to accept servility and then to commit suicide. Taking advantage of their stranglehold over the Comintern, Stalinists gained the upper hand in China, unfortunately, in the absence of a revolutionary opposition. They ordered the Chinese proletariat to march to the valley of death and then usurped its place at the head of peasant wars to steal the march to power through the bureaucratic overturn of 1949.

After crushing the Canton Uprising in December 1927, the proletariat had gone into shades of history, disabled for the time being to march at the head of the revolution in China and provide it leadership. A period of short lull thus set in. But the Chinese peasantry, crushed under the double yoke of medievalism and Imperialism, by then itself was in dire need of a real revolution. On its own, the peasantry could not have set a revolution in motion at the national level, it could only have brought about sporadic uprisings, which it was already doing. These uprisings, however, needed to be consolidated on a national level into a real revolutionary upheaval. The proletariat, the natural executor and leader of this process, due to its decimation after its crushing defeat in Canton, was not in a position to perform this historic task. Deprived of the natural leadership of the proletariat, the peasantry needed another force to consolidate its actions on the national level. The bureaucracy, which had organised itself under the banner of the CCP by then, succeeded in winning over the confidence of the rebellious peasantry, through deception, by posing itself to be the legitimate heir of the Chinese proletariat, whose heroic actions in Chinese cities in the recent past, were fresh in the memory of the peasant mass. The bureaucracy also succeeded in claiming credit for the Great October Revolution in Russia. Using this camouflage, the bureaucracy first established its hegemony over the peasant wars already going on for a long time in remote rural areas, aligned them under its command, raising an Army, and thus rode to power in 1949.

Though the working class was crushed in the cities, yet the heroic battles it had fought against its enemies, irrespective of the blunders of its leadership, were sufficient and bound to shake up the peasantry from its slumber. The proletarian tide of the past continued to spread in waves in the peripheral remote peasant regions of the country. The heroic actions of the city proletariat continued for a long time to find their belated echo in the form of sporadic peasant uprisings, against the power of local and foreign oppressors, in the vast and underdeveloped territories of China.

After the 1927 devastation which had completely uprooted the Chinese CP as a political party, the surviving cadres escaped to rural regions of China to save their lives. Those who had fled the cities in the wake of the counter-revolution, carried with them the stories of heroic action of the city proletariat and spread it into the peasantry.

XX

The retreat of CCP from the cities to the rural areas, leaving the cities under control and domination of the KMT and the city proletariat at the mercy of the bourgeois, led to a virtual divorce between the Chinese CP and the proletariat. Instead of fighting for reversal of defeats suffered by it because of incorrect orientation of its leadership, the CCP adapted itself to those defeats, abandoned all the work among the city proletariat, leaving it to suffer its own destiny and beat a retreat into rural regions. It then placed itself directly at the head of rural petty bourgeois peasantry, instead of taking its leadership through the proletariat.

Work in cities, as well the urban proletariat, were consciously abandoned, leaving the cities and their proletariat without leadership and under the terrorist dictatorship of KMT. Under the new strategy, the rural peasantry was declared to be the revolutionary class capable on its own of accomplishing the democratic revolution in China, without leadership of the urban proletariat as a class. Small peasant bands were then organised into varied formations of peasant armies, which continued engagement in partisan warfare.

After complete destruction of the old CCP at the hands of Stalinists, the party started to be reorganised under direct command of the Stalinist Comintern, exclusively from the peasantry—the rural petty bourgeois, instead of the proletariat. It continued to swell its ranks from among the peasant cadres, distancing more and more from its earlier proletarian base and composition. The more it associated itself with the peasantry, the more it dissociated itself from the working class. Through the purges designed in the aftermath of the tragic failure of revolution, the Comintern consciously harnessed the CCP into a bureaucratic machine, with a self-serving motive. Within no time the CCP emerged again as a full fledged bureaucratic apparatus, with the making of a peasant party in its slogans, appearance and composition. To be able to place itself at the head of the rebellious Chinese peasantry, the bureaucracy needed to claim to its credit the heroic legacy of City Proletariat, which was though destroyed as a political force by the bureaucracy itself. Thus, it took to the red banner and the name of Chinese CP, and thereby deceiving the peasantry to follow its lead, succeeded in placing itself directly at the head of peasant armies. This CCP was now totally different from the original CCP, and was more a bureaucratic machine subservient to the Stalinist Comintern, rather than a political party.

The bureaucracy easily succeeded in its cunning manoeuvre, as the city proletariat—the actual and legitimate claimant of this leadership of agrarian revolution—was completely crushed by December 1927, and was thus unable to consolidate itself to provide leadership to the widespread peasant unrest. Thus, the time was most conducive for the Stalinist bureaucracy to push down the proletariat from the political stage. It could take advantage of the situation by consolidating itself into an apparatus like a machine in place of it, in the name of the CCP, under the red banner of Marxism which could claim great moral authority and prestige being the banner of victorious proletariat in Russian Revolution and the banner of recent militant struggle of Chinese proletariat itself.

The new CCP was reorganised and swelled in size during the period of a general decline of revolution, victory of the counter-revolution and complete destruction of the Chinese proletariat. Trotsky wrote in 'The Chinese Question after the Sixth Congress' on October 4, 1928, that "after losing its proletarian nucleus, the CCP did not remain in conformity with its historic destiny". What survived was the banner of the old CCP, under which the bureaucracy organised itself in the name of the CCP, which completely abandoned both the cities and proletariat. At the time of its coming into power in 1949, the party had a total membership of 3.5 million, of which not even one per cent was proletarian. The new CCP adapted itself to the defeat of the proletariat, by abandoning it.

In what way was the contradiction between the class composition of the CCP, recruited mainly from the petty bourgeois peasantry on the one hand and its Red banner—the banner of Revolutionary proletariat—on the other hand, resolved by the bureaucracy? It was resolved by its imposing itself as a bureaucratic supra-class organisation in the name of the CCP, holding balance among the four classes and thereby depriving both the proletariat and the peasantry, of any actual role, power or authority, inside the Chinese CP. This, by logical corollary, meant that the role of the CCP was now to maintain the equilibrium among the different social classes, a political status quo by holding back the proletariat and the peasantry from advancing against the combined force of the bourgeois and landlords, i.e. the KMT. This apparently bourgeois policy was executed by the CCP under the class collaborationist slogan—'bloc of four classes', in which even the balance continued to be held by bourgeois leaders like Chiang and Wang, with the CCP doing its cherished 'coolie service' in it.

For historic reasons also, the bureaucracy did not find it difficult to have its foothold over the peasant wars in China. The Chinese society as a whole, customarily, had a slavish adherence to the bureaucratic rule, as the dynastic empire in China, for centuries together, had ruled through a network of civil servants. The bureaucracy, thus, had at its service, both a long-standing tradition and a settled taste for it in the Chinese society, which had become accustomed to following a tailor-made structure of command. The proletariat, which was bound to rebel against the bureaucratic rule, was pacified by its untimely uprooting, by the disastrous policy of the Comintern alternating between capitulation and misadventures.

The Chinese proletariat, badly destroyed at the hands of the Stalinist Comintern in 1927, continued to be pushed back by the Chinese bureaucracy through manoeuvres, and was prevented from consolidating itself in opposition to the bureaucracy. In the absence of the proletariat, which was the only legitimate claimant for the leadership of the Chinese nation, the bureaucracy seized the opportunity for itself. While deliberately keeping the working class at bay, first, the bureaucracy with red banner in its hands, got itself at the head of the peasant war, established its domination over it, and then got itself catapulted to power in 1949, using the peasant war as a lever to capture power.

XXI

Those who could escape from the cities of Shanghai and Canton, after the defeat of the insurrection in 1927, took shelter in Hunan, Shanwei and Kiangsi, where the peasant movement was started and armed bands were organized in larger formations, to establish a guerilla army with temporary base. Till 1931-34, Kiangsi Soviet existed as the seat of the CCP, with an area more than 30,000 sq. km under its control.

The KMT then launched five encirclement campaigns, one after the other, against these bases prepared by the CCP amongst peasant regions. The first four were fought by the peasantry, but the fifth, inflicted very heavy casualties, and was ready to annihilate all forces of the CCP and Kinagsi Soviet. All attempts to break off the cordon to escape failed after taking a heavy toll. Top leaders and big formations were annihilated while attempting to escape. Escape became possible only as the secret military plan (the iron bucket plan) prepared by Chiang was leaked to the CCP, by one KMT high official, Mo Xiong, who was sympathetic to the revolutionary cause. Disguising himself as a beggar enroute to the CCP headquarters inside the KMT ring, he delivered the secret plan to the CCP. The CCP then planned to abandon the base region and retreat in a long march to escape the annihilation. The long march started on October 16, 1934, after a force of 1,30,000-strong carried out a surprise attack on KMT lines at Yudu, broke it successfully and marched out of the KMT ring. The escape took the KMT forces by surprise, who arrived at the region after 16 days of the escape, with full preparations for total annihilation of the CCP.

It was not a single long march but in fact several formations that had marched through separate routes from south to north and west. This long march concluded in October 1935, with different formations arriving in Yenan in Shaanxi, at different times. Of the 86,000 who proceeded on the march, only about 7,000 could survive, including the new recruits during the march. Nine-tenth of the forces perished in one year. In Yenan, fresh recruits again reinforced the armies, which now organized themselves as regular formations of red armies.

Though as a peasant war, this civil war in China fought between 1930–1937 had a progressive character on the side of the peasantry, being a war fought against the bourgeois-landlords, but as a peasant war only, that too under the command of Stalinist bureaucracy, instead of the proletariat, it was devoid of any revolutionary perspective and was doomed to fail as a revolutionary war capable of triggering a social revolution in China. However, the bureaucracy itself was not interested in triggering a social revolution in China.

XXII

Then came the Japanese invasion of China in which the CCP once again found an opportunity to extend its friendly embrace to the nationalists. The Second United front was struck between KMT and CCP to fight the foreign invasion, again with domination of KMT and Chiang as its leader. In relation to the war, the policy of bureaucracy was again saturated with collaborationism. The bureaucracy presented the invasion as a national event confronting all the social classes in China in the same way, devoid of its class refraction. This was to further reinforce its policy of collaboration with the Chinese bourgeois, this time in the name of a national war against Japan. The CCP forced the peasantry to stop agrarian movement against the landlords, including seizure of lands inside rural China. Trotsky vehemently opposed it, saying that the war against foreign invasion in no way diminishes the class contradictions in China, but flares them up to their zenith. He advocated deepening of the class struggle, instead of its abandonment. In his work, 'The Chinese Revolution and the Thesis of Comrade Stalin', Trotsky wrote: "Imperialist yoke is being supposed to serve as justification for the policy of bloc of four classes. To proceed from an abstract conception of National oppression, without its class refraction in China, would be false". He warned that the proletariat is the only consistent fighter against national oppression, while all sections of bourgeois, are connected to Imperialism through so many strings and thus would dwindle in struggle. The very first assault of Japan on nationalist Capital Nanking in December 1937, endorsed this prognosis of Trotsky. This assault which went down in history as the 'rape of Nanking', succeeded with little resistance of two days only, after the bourgeois nationalist armies of KMT flew from Nanking, leaving the people open to brutalities of Fascist invaders. The assault counted more than one lakh men murdered and one lakh women raped. Japan took control of China and the CCP stopped all class struggle.

The Japanese occupation continued in China till the end of World War-II, resulting in the eventual defeat of the Axis forces and surrender of Japan, after the atomic bombing of Hiroshima and Nagasaki. Russian forces entered Manchuria, the most industrialized part of Chinese territory, ousted the Japanese, seized their weaponry and took control. Another important consequence of World War-II, was the extreme weakening of the KMT because of its exhaustion in continuous engagement with Japanese armies. An added advantage was the exposure of the corruption and misdeeds of KMT officers, including its collaboration with Japanese Imperialists, before the Chinese people, during more than a decade. All this made it convenient for the CCP to take power in its hands, with the help of the Soviet Union. The arms seized from the Japanese in Manchuria, were given by the Soviet Union to the Red Army under the CCP, to fight the KMT, though it was apparently clear that the motivating factor behind this aid was simply the national interest of Russian bureaucracy, which could have hardly afforded presence of the power of the KMT, friendly to the US and thus potentially hostile to it, alongside its extensive southern borders. On its side, the United States saw no prospects at that time in continuing with the very costly aid to armies of KMT as the Soviet bureaucracy itself was ready to do everything to doubly assure the bourgeois countries, that it stands no more for the perspective of world revolution. Dissolution of the Comintern in 1943 by Stalin, itself was the best proof of the intentions. Abandoned by the US, KMT had to leave China to cross over to Taiwan, where it found its new seat. Thus, the CCP came to power in China in 1949, with Mao-Tse-Tung as its Premier.

XXIII

When Mao-Tse-Tung himself proclaimed the foundation of Peoples' Republic of China on October 1, 1949, at Tiananmen Square, he made no mention of the dictatorship of the proletariat. Rather, he conceived the overturn as an achievement of the 'Chinese People', instead of the world proletariat. Following the bogus concepts of 'stagism' and 'multi-class democratic dictatorship', power was assumed in the name of 'bloc of four classes', which included the Chinese bourgeois. In this coalition, the proletariat however was to remain a mute spectator, and the bureaucracy to be the master of all, being the balance holder among the conflicting interests of different social classes.

The bureaucracy had come to power in China in 1949, not as an agency of world socialist revolution but as a balance-holder among the antagonistic interests of various national classes in China. While getting power in the name of 'bloc of four classes', it deliberately shut its eyes towards the antagonistic class position of different classes.

The regime of this bureaucracy, established in 1949 in China, after the peasant armies led by Mao-Tse-Tung overthrew the US-backed Nationalist government of Chiang, represented a power, bourgeois in nature, basing itself primarily upon the fictitious 'bloc of four classes', instead of the proletariat. This Bonapartist regime, deceptively painted in red, consciously preserved various forms of capitalism instead of destroying them, and ultimately grew over to a full-fledged agency of world capitalist order. It fought with Chiang's KMT and defeated it, not because of its class hostility to it, but as the national interests of Soviet bureaucracy so demanded, which was in control of the CCP. The Russian bureaucracy could not have afforded to tolerate the presence of a US-backed regime next door to it. Both the regimes—Soviet as well as Chinese—had adopted a purely nationalist outlook, in opposition to proletarian international-ism. The relationship between Russia and China, itself, was determined by purely nationalist considerations, like their relations to other countries of the world. Their friendships, as well as conflicts with each other and the rest of the world were inspired and depended only upon these narrow national considerations. Mao-Nixon friendship, at the height of the mayhem by the US in Vietnam, is a burning example of it. Neither of the two even dreamed about the world proletarian revolution, rather, they engaged themselves only in the defence of their national regimes and a war for supremacy.

And how did this regime deal with the proletariat after the power fell into its hands in 1949? The bureaucracy, from the very inception, did not permit the proletariat or even the peasantry to carry forward the revolution. A blanket ban was imposed on workers' strikes, not only in the nationalized enterprises but in private too. It blatantly denied any improvement in wage structure, rather demanded from workers surplus labour for added working hours, on the pretext of raising 'national productivity'. By a decree, it forbade the efforts of the workers to seize the industrial and commercial lands of landlords. In ultimate land distribution, it was the same previous landowners, who, as if by way of fiction, got back the best lands for their use. Relying upon the apparatus of the party and the Red Army, the Maoist bureaucracy blocked all initiative of the working people, asking them to become mute spectators of its deeds. When it failed to persuade, it used force for compliance. It crushed the resistance, from wherever it came. When the proletariat, when resisted the policy, it was fired upon and whole massacres were carried out.

Changes which were carried out after the 1949 overturn were strictly confined to the bourgeois framework, having no proletarian edge at all. Only big bourgeois enterprises were nationalized, consciously sparing the middle and small. In the countryside, the peasant movement was thwarted from taking more lands. This confirmed the prediction of Trotsky that the third Chinese revolution would either come as a proletarian revolution or no revolution at all. The coming into power of the bureaucracy in China in 1949, virtually proved abortive of the impending social revolution. The regime of bureaucracy did never attempt to overstep the bourgeois framework, to take to proletarian path.

XXIV

But, the ball of history could not have rested on the top head of the social pyramid for long. The emancipation of productive forces during more than two decades of civil war and fight against foreign aggression in China, in the background of the immense advance of world capitalism, in the aftermath of World War II, unleashed a rapid growth of Capitalism, through the changed relations of production. This naturally swelled the ranks of the middle classes and provoked wild petty bourgeois aspirations inside them. As the petty-bourgeois continued to grow, its upper layers developed a strong aspiration for Capitalist road and apathy for proletarian path. Chinese bureaucracy became the agency to serve the interests of this new bourgeois class in China.

Strong resistance came from lower rungs of the society, especially from the proletarian layers, which smelled the bourgeois nature of the new regime and still more strong bourgeois currents hidden inside the party and the

Government. The party itself, due to its petty bourgeois composition, started to dwindle and was torn apart by a developed political crisis. The leaders of various factions inside the CCP, however, used this antagonism among social classes and the general unrest among the mass, to settle their factional accounts with each other. The factional struggle inside the party, which did not reflect or correspond to the antagonism among the social classes of its time, dominated the party, while the party continued to alienate itself from the working people and developed more and more into an apparatus based on command structure.

Adhering to the model of Stalinist Russia, being built under the masterplan of 'Socialism in One Country', the 1949 regime in China, imbued with the same nationalist conservative perspective, instead of focusing upon destruction of World Capitalism, took to building of Socialism in China, a backward country dominated by the peasantry. Very soon it became clear that the far backward productive forces in China even as compared to Russia, what to say of the advanced Capitalist West, would not permit the making of Socialism in China by itself, unless the revolution is spread to the advanced Capitalist countries of the West. But the Maoist regime, instead of realising its mistake and making a sharp turn towards the perspective of World Proletarian Revolution, persisted in the bogus Stalinist project of building Socialism in one country, in isolation to the World Proletarian Revolution.

In its zeal to achieve the farcical target of building of Socialism in China, which according to it could not be achieved through ordinary economic and political measures, it made the Chinese proletariat and peasantry the scapegoat for its cynical projects. First it resorted to blind cooperatisation, which failed in no time. Then was launched the purely bureaucratic project—The Great Leap Forward, in 1958, setting the target before itself to surpass the industrial tempo of the US and Britain by 1972. As was destined beforehand, the Great Leap Forward proved to be a real Great Leap backward. The move badly failed. The economy was shattered and China lost what it could achieve even after the 1949 overturn. The failure of the Great Leap, an apparent misadventure of Maoist bureaucracy, was a virtual jolt not only to the Maoists but to China as a whole. But, instead of making a review of its strategic positions, the bureaucracy still persisted in its reactionary venture. It now started the peoples' communes, which could gather no moss and were dismantled in no time.

XXV

The failure of the bureaucracy in touching upon even the lowest levels of world Capitalism of its times, leave aside Socialism, resulted in its general degradation in the eyes both of its friends and foes. Factional conflicts inside the party were accelerated further. Maoism was degrading itself by virtue of its failures whenever an application of the same was made. The Sino-Soviet conflict arose after Khrushchev, the heir to Stalin, tried to wash off his hands on the failures of Chinese bureaucracy. Mao in turn started to criticise Khrushchev as a revisionist.

In its zeal to find a way out of the situation, where the party bureaucracy, unfolding itself by that time as agency of Capitalism, stood totally degraded in the eyes of working people, who eventually showed a rebellious mood against bureaucratic degradation, a new manoeuvre was started in the name of 'Great Proletarian Cultural Revolution'. Instead of changing its perspective, even now, to that of the World Proletarian Revolution, as the left oppositionists had advanced against Stalin, the Chinese Stalinists devoted themselves this time to start what they termed a 'Great Proletarian Cultural Revolution' in China, a country dominated overwhelmingly by the illiterate peasantry. To execute this cultural revolution, schools, colleges and universities were closed down for more than four years, thereby depriving the populace now even of literacy. Libraries were burnt down and literature destroyed. This obviously was an absurdity and stupidity at its extreme.

This venture also utterly failed. After 'Great Leap', it was the 'Great Cultural Revolution' which had completely failed. Both the attempts of the bureaucracy to deviate the loaded train of Capitalism from its tracks, met with no success at all. But they succeeded in yet other motive. During this entire period, purges continued to take place where the Chinese Stalinists taking advantage of the unconscious mass unrest, used the same against the left oppositionists and against each other, as well.

The meltdown, however, continued and the flames of mass upheavals were doused by bureaucratic froth of 'actually existing socialism', starting a march to capitalism under the banner of Socialism. With the passage of time, both the Red flag and the Red Armies vanished into thin air, clearing the way for unbridled Capitalism, which holds sway in China today.

When the mass of the people in China demanded freedom from the stranglehold of bureaucratic regime, by now fully integrated with world Capitalism, they met with violent repression at the hands of the Chinese bureaucracy, then under Deng Xiao Ping. Tiananmen was the reply of Chinese bureaucracy to the people, the same Tiananmen which witnessed the start of 4th May movement in 1919. It goes without saying that Deng Xiaoping and the capitalist roaders like him, who made it to top positions in the party and the Government headed by it, did not come as a bolt from the blue, but were nurtured inside the shell of the party itself, which held the red Banner in its hands only to deceive the toiling masses. Deng Xiaoping was the true inheritor of Mao regime.

XXVI

Pursuing its collaborationist policy, Stalin dissolved the Comintern in June 1943, to appease and reassure the capitalist leaders of the world of his collaborationist intentions. The world party of revolution—the third international—formed by Lenin and Trotsky, with the avowed objective 'to wipe out Capitalism from the face of the earth' was thus annihilated by the epigones of Leninism.

Trotsky, who was expelled from CPSU, was banished from the Soviet Union in 1928 and then expelled from the Comintern in 1929, continued his fight from within and then without the Comintern. One by one, the entire old guard of the Russian revolution, all the leaders around Lenin, were eliminated by the Stalinist bureaucracy, after it succeeded in strengthening its positions against the left-opposition. Trotsky still continued to fight for the correct line, but after Hitler rose to power in Germany, Trotsky and the left oppositionists found their struggle inside the Comintern to be insufficient and formed the

Fourth International with the objective to fight fascism, Imperialism and Stalinism.

The destiny of Trotskyism remained inseparably bound throughout with the tides and ebbs of the world proletarian revolution. It staged an upsurge with tides of December 1905, February 1917 and October 1917; it relegated to the background, only with low ebbs in the proletarian revolutions around the 1920s. Contrary to it, Stalinism, the reactionary tendency, leaned towards the right reaction. It rose to power on the back of the defeat of working class and it declined with the crisis of world capitalism. It had emerged and had taken ground, in the backdrop of the defeats suffered by the world proletariat around the 1920s, while its destruction started and continued with the crisis of world imperialism, spiraling since 1991. Stalinism had come to existence as product of an adaptation between the bureaucracy and reactionary nationalism, and in opposition to the idea of proletarian internationalism. Both bureaucracy and nationalist perspective had simultaneously emerged in the Soviet Union, complementary to each other, as a result of demoralization of the world proletariat after the temporary debacles of the 1920s, which could have been reversed very soon, if a consistent Internationalist policy had been adopted.

Trotsky's critique of the Comintern and CCP, from 1925 till 1940, presents a beautiful and eye-opening account of the true nature and role of the Comintern under Stalin. It passes like a golden thread through the unfortunate story of Chinese Revolution where the young Chinese proletariat, which performed heroic action in Chinese cities, was butchered at the hands of its enemies, because of the bogus policies of Comintern—alternating between capitulation and putschism. The writings of Trotsky show how the Stalinist bureaucracy, taking advantage of destruction of proletariat at its own hands, placed itself at the head of peasant wars and rode to power in 1949. More precisely, the Stalinist bureaucracy not only took advantage of the defeats and destructions of the Chinese Proletariat, but remained instrumental in sowing these defeats and ultimate destruction. The theory of permanent revolution, as against the reactionary formula of the 'two-stage theory', thus received but a negative confirmation in what can be termed as a monstrous revolutionary catastrophe—the abortion of Chinese revolution.

After their complete decay into anti-people regimes of dictatorship of bureaucracy, the Stalinist States crumbled approximately without any resistance. The 1990s became the beginning of the end of these bureaucratic regimes and within no time Stalinism shattered to vacate the stage of history.

In 1940, Trotsky was murdered in Mexico, where he was living in exile, by Mercader, a member of Stalin's death squads. Needless to say, after the demise of Trotsky, the leaders of the Fourth International could not pursue a consistent revolutionary policy to consolidate the revolutionary forces of the world. But the immortal legacy of Trotsky lives on to inspire the next generations of Marxists and workers for carrying out the historic task, left behind by this Marxist genius. The new age—the age of proletarian Internationalism—would rehabilitate Trotsky as the pioneer revolutionary thinker of our epoch.

1

The 'Moscow Spirit'

To the Memory of the Murdered Workers and Students of Shanghai

June 6, 1925

The Times, the leading newspaper of the English bourgeoisie, writes that the movement of the Chinese masses reveals a 'Moscow Spirit'. Well, for once we are prepared to agree with the conservative denunciators. The English press in China and in the British Isles brands the striking workers and students as Bolshevists. Well, we are prepared to a certain extent to support even this terrible revelation. The fact is the Chinese workers object to being shot down by the Japanese police, so they have declared a protest strike and are proclaiming their indignation in the streets. Is it not evident that here the 'Moscow Spirit' prevails? The Chinese students, filled with sympathy for the workers in their struggle, have joined in the strike against the exercise of violence by foreigners. It is evident, as far as the students are concerned, that we have to deal with the Bolshevists.

We of Moscow are prepared to accept all these accusations and revelations. We should like however to add that the best agents for spreading the 'Moscow Spirit' in the East are the capitalist politicians and journalists. To the question of the ignorant coolie: "What is a Bolshevist?" the English bourgeois press replies: "A Bolshevist is a Chinese worker who does not wish to be shot by Japanese and English police; a Bolshevist is a Chinese student who stretches out a brotherly hand to the Chinese worker who is streaming with blood; a Bolshevist is a

Chinese peasant who resents the fact that foreigners, whose arguments are deeds of violence, behave on his land as though they were lord and master." The reactionary press of both hemispheres gives this excellent description of Bolshevism.

Is it possible to carry on in the East a better, more convincing, more stirring propaganda? And to what purpose, may we ask, do we need in the East or, for that matter, in the West either, secret agents with Moscow gold in one pocket and with poison and dynamite in the other? Would any trained agents be capable of doing a thousandth part of the educational work which *The Times* and its companions carry on gratuitously—this must be acknowledged—throughout the world? If a so-called Moscow agent were to tell the oppressed Chinese that the policy of Moscow is a policy of the liberation of the oppressed classes and subjugated nations, the Chinese would very likely not believe him—has he not often been deceived by foreigners! But when Moscow's worst enemy, in the form of the English Conservative newspapers, tells him the same about Moscow, he will believe it implicitly.

When the half-naked and half-starved Chinese worker who is oppressed and degraded begins to become conscious of his dignity as a human being, he is told: Moscow agents have egged you on! If he allies himself with other workers to defend his elementary human rights, he is told: this is the "Moscow Spirit". If in the streets of his own town, he tries to defend his right to existence and development, he hears cries of: This is Bolshevism!

Thus the course of revolutionary education advances step by step under the direction of the foreign police and of the journalists, whose attitude of mind is similar to that of the police. And in order to imprint the political lessons deeply on his memory, the English police, after having shot down dozens and hundreds of Chinese workers and students, drags him into the cellars of the English prisons in Shanghai. Thus a shortcut to political knowledge is accomplished. From now onwards every Chinese will know that the "Moscow Spirit" is the spirit of revolutionary solidarity which unites the oppressed in the fight against the oppressors; and that on the other hand, the atmosphere which pervades the cellars of the English prisons of Shanghai incorporates the spirit of "British freedom".

We would have concluded at this point, for, is there much to add to this eloquent and convincing propaganda of the capitalist press on behalf of Moscow? But it occurs to us that liberal Labour politicians of the MacDonald type are eagerly listening to our conversation with the Conservatives. "You see," they say, pointing didactically at the chief editor of the *Times*, "We have always said that our Conservatives work for Bolshevism." And this also is true. The Conservatives, or rather the reactionaries—all capitalist parties are now reactionary—represent an enormous historical force which is supported by capital and gives expression to its chief interests. MacDonald is right in that there would be no Bolshevism, either in the East or in the West, if the forces of capital did not exist. As long, however, as the force and the yoke of capital does exist, the 'Moscow Spirit' will make its way throughout the world.

For the 'adjustment' of events in Shanghai, and in order to counteract the influence of 'Moscow', the liberals and Mensheviks suggest the idea of an international conference on the Chinese question, but they are shutting their eyes to the fact that at this conference the decision would lie in the hands of the same gentlemen at whose command workers and students are shot down in Shanghai.

Possibly MacDonald has a programme ready for this conference. If not, we can submit our own to him. It is very simple. The Chinese house belongs to the Chinese. No one has a right to enter this house without knocking at the door. The owner has the right to admit none but friends and to refuse entrance to those whom he considers his enemies. This is the beginning of our programme. You will certainly reject it, because to your nostrils it seems to be thoroughly saturated with the explosive 'Moscow Spirit'. But just for this reason it will penetrate into the consciousness of the oppressed Chinese and of every honest English worker. This programme contains in itself the most powerful innate force. This is the banner under which the workers and students of Shanghai are dying. The blood which has been shed in the streets of Shanghai will infect the masses with the 'Moscow Spirit'. This spirit penetrates everywhere and is invincible. It will overcome the whole world by liberating it.

2

Problems of our Policy with Respect to China and Japan

March 25, 1926

In the case of China we must take into consideration factors which fall into three categories: (a) China's internal forces; (b) the militarist organizations which, while expressing China's internal forces in one or another form, are to a great extent dependent upon foreign governments; (c) foreign imperialist forces on the one hand, and the forces of the USSR and the proletarian revolutionary movement on the other.

All of the difficulty in finding an orientation flows from the interrelation of factors in these three categories from which everything derives its internal logic and tempo of development. Of course, in the development of a newly awakened country with a population of 400 million, domestic factors are, in the last analysis, decisive. We must base our fundamental orientation on the development of these internal forces, i.e., chiefly on drawing the peasantry into the revolution and ensuring that proletarian organizations are in the leadership. Our decisive advantage is that we have the opportunity to conduct in China a policy of great historic scope.

While doing this it goes without saying that we cannot ignore the struggle of the militarist groups with all its episodic ups and downs, but we must not allow these episodes to draw us away from our fundamental political line.

I. The International Orientation of the Chinese Revolution and the USSR

1. There is no information which would make us think that there will be a pause, however temporary, in the development of the internal forces of the Chinese revolution. On the contrary, we have every reason to believe that in the period ahead the movement of the broad popular masses—of workers and peasants—will be developed and consolidated. We, for our part, must do everything possible to give this movement its maximum scope. But the international situation has become far more difficult in light of Europe's well recognized stabilization, the Locarno Pact, and particularly given the way the imperialists have posed the China problem in its full scope. Under these circumstances. China's leading revolutionary forces, and even more, the Soviet government must do everything possible to impede the formation of a united imperialist front against China. At the present moment, Japan could become extremely dangerous to the Chinese Revolution in view of both its geographic position and its vital economic and military interests in Manchuria. The Chinese revolutionary movement has approached that stage when the question of its relations with Japan takes on the greatest importance. It is necessary to try to gain a respite, and this means in fact to 'postpone' the question of the political fate of Manchuria, i.e., to actually be reconciled to the fact that southern Manchuria will remain in Japanese hands in the period ahead.
2. This political orientation, which in no case means, of course, a cessation of the general political struggle against Japanese imperialism, must be submitted in its entirety for the approval of the Chinese Communist Party and the Kuomintang. It is necessary however to consider in advance how difficult it will be for the revolutionary elements and broad public opinion in China to accept this orientation in view of the intense hostility toward Japan. Nevertheless, this orientation is

dictated by the internal needs of the Chinese revolution which, until there is a new revolutionary wave in Europe and Asia, will not be able to withstand a combined onslaught from the imperialists. The interests of the Chinese revolution fully coincide in this case, as in others, with the interests of the Soviet Union, which needs an extended respite just as much as the Chinese revolutionary movement needs to gain time.

3. From what has been said it is clear that the orientation toward intensifying the contradictions between the imperialist powers in the Far East and above all, the orientation toward coming to a certain understanding with Japan must be carefully prepared with respect to the general attitude of China's revolutionary forces so that this policy will not be incorrectly interpreted by ill-informed elements as a sacrifice of China's interests, for purposes of a settlement in Soviet–Japanese political relations.
4. To properly orient Chinese public opinion it is particularly important to recognize the need to strengthen revolutionary and anti-imperialist influence on the Chinese press, not only by creating new organs but by influencing those already in existence.
5. In the event that Manchurian autonomy is established, which is what Japan is trying to bring about, we should get Chang Tso-lin to give up his campaign into the South and generally to stop meddling in the internal affairs of the rest of China. Under no circumstances, of course, can we take the initiative or even indirect responsibility in this matter, but a clear understanding of the implication of Manchurian autonomy under the present conditions in itself dictates the necessary line of conduct for the leading circles of the Chinese revolutionary movement on the one hand, and for us on the other.
6. In view of the general political plan outlined above, it is now more important for us than ever before to eliminate all unnecessary, incidental, and secondary issues that disturb Chinese public opinion. There is absolutely no

doubt that in the actions of the various departmental representatives there were inadmissible great-power mannerisms compromising the Soviet administration and creating an impression of Soviet imperialism. It is necessary to impress upon the corresponding agencies and persons the vital importance for us of such a policy and of even such an external form of the policy in relation to China so that any trace of suspicion of great-power intentions will be eliminated. This line—based on the closest attention to China's rights, emphasizing its sovereignty, etc.—must be carried out on every level. In every individual instance of a violation of this policy, no matter how slight, the culprits should be punished and this fact brought to the attention of Chinese public opinion.

7. We must in various ways openly declare: Our policy is based fully on sympathy with the struggle of the Chinese popular masses for a single independent government and for democracy. We reject, however, the idea of any kind of military intervention whatever on our part. The Chinese problem can and must be solved by the Chinese people themselves. Until the realization of a unified China, the Soviet government endeavours to establish and maintain loyal relations with all of the governments existing in China, central as well as provincial.
8. In Manchuria our diplomatic work must be wholly and completely transferred from Harbin to Mukden.
9. We should negotiate with Chang Tso-lin on the following basis: It is clear to us that under the existing circumstances the Manchurian government must maintain good, stable relations with us. We will not encroach upon these relations. But at the same time, it is to the Manchurian government's advantage to have stable and peaceful relations with us, thereby guaranteeing itself a certain independence in relation to Tokyo. During the negotiations we must point out to Chang Tso-lin that certain Japanese circles are ready to have him replaced with another buffer general, but that

we see no reason for him to be placed with another person while normal relations exist.

10. Working out a strictly businesslike administrative structure for the CER [Chinese Eastern Railroad] is the basic element in negotiations with Manchuria, i.e., an explicit procedure for settling (on an equal footing) all contested or disputed questions; in the event of any complications turning the question over to Mukden. Simultaneously our railway administrator, the consul in Harbin, and the consul general in Mukden will be instructed that any attempt by the railway authorities to solve problems unilaterally, over the head of the Chinese authorities or—even worse—by means of ultimatums to the latter must be punished without mercy.
11. Following an agreement with Chang Tso-lin and the corresponding recognition of this agreement in Peking, an effort should be made to have a Chinese–Japanese–Soviet railway conference called with the aim of all three powers working out a joint economic and construction plan for the railroad in Manchuria, and an economic agreement concerning Manchuria based on full respect for mutual interests and rights.
12. While strictly keeping the actual apparatus of the CER in the hands of the Soviet government—which in the next period is the only way to protect the railroad from imperialist seizure—it is necessary to immediately adopt broad measures of a cultural-political nature aimed at the Sinification of the railroad. (a) The administration should be bilingual; station signs and instructions posted in the stations and in the cars, etc., should be bilingual. (b) Chinese schools for railroad workers should be established combining technical and political training. (c) At appropriate points along the railroad, cultural-educational institutions should be established for the Chinese workers and the Chinese settlements adjacent to the railroad.
13. It is necessary (for Comrade Serebryakov) to check whether turning the railroad directly over to the People's

Commissariat of Communications could be interpreted by the Chinese as a step toward our unilateral seizure of the railroad. All details of changing the railroad's administrative structure must be carefully thought through and worked out with the appropriate Chinese authorities.

14. We must take advantage of the present moment, while our activity on the railroad is totally unencumbered, to conduct a purge of the CER over a month-long period in accordance with the Politburo's decision . . . transferring the elements of the administration and the workers who are of little use or who have compromised themselves to the railroads of the Soviet Union and replacing them in Manchuria with workers from the central railroads who are thoroughly reliable and politically educated.
15. On the other hand, it is necessary right now to carefully compile (and subsequently examine) all cases of tyranny and violence on the part of Chinese militarists, police, and Russian White Guard elements against Russian workers and employees of the CER, and also all cases of conflict between Russians and Chinese on national-social grounds. It is also necessary to devise the course and means for defending the personal and national dignity of Russian workers so that conflicts on this basis, rather than kindling chauvinist sentiments on both sides, on the contrary, will have a political and educational significance. It is necessary to set up special conciliation commissions or courts of honour attached to the trade unions, with both sides participating on an equal basis, under the actual guidance of serious communists who understand the full importance and acuteness of the national question. The means for protecting the railroad employees from the tyranny of local Chinese authorities must be worked out in an appropriate agreement (with Mukden and Peking) and furnished with all of the necessary organizational guarantees. In this regard it is necessary to issue instructions and proclamations in

Russian and Chinese and distribute them along the railroad line, posting them in the stations and similar premises as well as in the cars.

16. The staff of the consulate general in Harbin should be reorganized to conform with the policies described above.
17. One of the points of the agreement with Chang Tso-lin (and later on with Japan) should protect People's Revolutionary Mongolia from Chang Tso-lin's encroachments.
18. Instead of immediately starting joint negotiations with Japan, we should concentrate on actually improving relations by carrying out all of the measures outlined above, and by influencing Japanese public opinion accordingly; and the People's Commissariat of Foreign Affairs shall be instructed to work out systematic measures in keeping with this approach. Without deciding beforehand the form of a possible tripartite agreement (USSR, Japan, China) the ground should be prepared politically and diplomatically in such a way that it will be impossible for the Chinese to interpret any concessions China may find itself temporarily forced to make to Japan as a division of spheres of influence with our participation. Chinese public opinion, especially in left-wing circles, should be made well aware that the only Chinese concessions to Japanese imperialism that we are prepared to tolerate are those necessary for the popular revolutionary movement in China itself in order to defend itself against a united imperialist offensive. With this perspective the possible joint negotiations should have as their aim, at the cost of some concessions, driving a wedge between Japan and Britain
19. In case it turns out that the people's armies have to surrender ground to Wu P'eifu for a long period, it may prove expedient to try to reach an agreement with the latter in order to weaken his dependence on Britain while at the same time carrying out an ongoing struggle against Britain, the main and implacable foe of Chinese independence.

20. With regard to the people's armies it is necessary to conduct comprehensive political, educational, and organizational work (in the Kuomintang and Communist Party) in order to convert them into an effective stronghold of the popular revolutionary movement, independent of personal influence.
21. Canton: During a period of slow development of the revolutionary movement in China, Canton has to be considered as not just a temporary revolutionary beachhead, but also an enormous country with a population of 37 million. It needs a correct and stable economic and political administration. The Canton government should concentrate all its efforts on strengthening the republic internally by means of agrarian, financial, administrative, and political reforms; by drawing the broad popular masses into the political life of the South Chinese Republic, and by strengthening the latter's internal defensive capacity.

    The Canton government should in the present period emphatically reject any idea of an aggressive military campaign and, in general, any activity that would push the imperialists onto the path of military intervention.

    Note: Inquire of Comrade Rakovsky whether there is some chance for the Canton government to arrange either officially or unofficially some kind of modus vivendi with France, and if it would not be expedient to send a representative of the Canton government to Paris with the aim of sounding out the French government along this line.
22. In view of the fact that in a whole number of resolutions that have been adopted there are components that urge the leadership of the Kuomintang to assume a cautious and yielding stance on questions raised and meticulously outlined here, in order to avoid any kind of political deviation whatever from the general line, it is necessary to thoroughly explain that such concessions as are made necessary by circumstances must in no way

reduce the revolutionary scope of the movement or curtail the broadest agitation either in China or beyond its borders for purposes of assisting the revolutionary movements of the neighbouring oppressed colonial countries, etc., etc.

23. In view of the fact that the Chinese reactionaries, at the instigation of the imperialists, have demanded that Comrade Karakhan be recalled, we must recognize the necessity for organizing a very energetic political campaign in China (and as much as possible in other countries, above all in Britain and Japan) against this outrageous demand, explaining the meaning and content of the liberation policy Comrade Karakhan has been pursuing as a representative of the Soviet Union.

II. Railroad Problems in Manchuria

1. It would be advisable to postpone the Manchurian railroad conference until attitudes toward the CER have improved.
2. On railroad construction the CER should make preliminary arrangements with Mukden, keeping in mind that the USSR cannot proceed independently with railroad construction in Manchuria.
3. For the purpose of expanding CER railroad construction, expenditures on CER improvements should be cut back so that all available resources can be diverted toward construction.
4. The plan advanced by the People's Commissariat of Communications for CER construction should be adopted.
5. For the construction of the individual spur tracks it would be advisable to form joint-stock companies that can attract local Chinese capital, with the Chinese taking the initiative wherever possible.
6. The CER should not restrict its tasks to laying spur tracks, but should also project the construction of paved roads for automobile transport and the development of shipping.

7. The CER should try with every means available to prevent the Japanese from constructing railroad lines to its north and also toward Hailun and to prevent linking up railroad lines such as the Kirin line with the CER.
8. In order to exert pressure on Japan we should spread information that we are constructing railroads from China across eastern Mongolia.
9. Our aim should be to begin work as soon as possible on a railroad running from Verkhneudinsk to Urga and Kalgan, and from Khabarovsk to Sovetskaya Gavan.
10. The People's Commissariat of Communications should be instructed to ascertain what kind of disagreements between the CER and the Southern Manchurian Railroads on the questions of tariffs, rebates, or cost reductions on poor-quality goods, and freight distribution should be brought up at the conference of the governments.
11. We should reply in the following manner to Dobuchi in connection with Comrade Serebryakov's trip: that the problems facing us will be ascertained on the spot since Serebryakov will personally visit Tokyo. After that our side will make concrete proposals aimed at settling disputed questions and eliminating friction on the basis of principles of mutual respect for the interests of all three parties concerned.

III. On Japanese Immigration

When resolving the question of Japanese immigration to the Soviet Far East we must take into account the intense interest the Japanese public is showing in this matter. However, in view of the danger of Japanese colonization in the Far East, every step we take will have to be cautious and gradual. It is premature at this time to fix the number of Japanese immigrants who are to be allowed into the USSR, but, in any case, Japanese immigration should not be large. It should be strictly regulated and should result in the breaking up of Japanese-controlled resources by means of a special agency set up for that purpose. The Japanese colonists should be settled in a checkerboard fashion, being alternated with a reinforcement of colonization from central Russia. The land that is parceled out should be acceptable to the Japanese peasants and should be suited to the peculiarities of Japanese agriculture. There are areas of land suitable for the Japanese colonists in the vicinity of Khabarovsk and further south, but not in the Siberian interior. We must not allow Korean immigration into these regions under the pretense that it is Japanese. The question of Korean immigration must be examined separately. The Koreans can be granted land that is considerably farther into the depths of Siberia.

3

First Letter to Radek

August 30, 1926

Dear Karl Berngardovich:

1. I'm writing to you on the question of the Chinese Communist Party in the Kuomintang. This question deserves attention and elaboration. I agree entirely with what you wrote in this regard. But it must be made concrete for the uninitiated readers, and that is essentially everyone. It is extremely important to organize the basic factual data on the development of the Kuomintang and the Communist Party (the areas where they have spread; the growth of the strike movement, the Kuomintang, the Communist Party, and the trade unions; the conflicts within the Kuomintang; etc.).

   It is very important, in my opinion, to compare the situation in China with the situation in India. Why is it that the Indian Communist Party is not joining a national-revolutionary organization? How are things going in this regard in the Dutch Indies?

   The fact of the matter is that the existence of national and even colonial oppression does not at all necessitate the entry of the Communist Party into a national-revolutionary party. The question depends above all on the differentiation of class forces and how this is bound up with foreign oppression. Politically the question presents itself thus: is the Communist Party destined for an extended period of time to play the role of a propaganda circle recruiting isolated co-thinkers (inside a revolutionary democratic party), or can the Communist Party in the coming period assume the leadership of the workers' movement? In China there is no doubt that the conditions are of the second order. But this must be demonstrated, perhaps if only in a very general way, but with an accompanying selection of the essential factual material. Do not forget that at the party conference Bukharin will give a report on questions of international policy, and the question of the Kuomintang will also undoubtedly come up there.

2. How are "questions and answers" going?
3. Did you write the letter?
4. On the agenda of the party conference is the question of trade unions. As far as I know, you have been following Trud and the trade union press. It is very important to expand this work and systematize it in view of the exceptional importance of the question.

I am writing a little, receiving guests, being photographed with comrades at the SPA, and shooting quail, which I hope you are doing too.

4

The Chinese Communist Party and the Kuomintang

September 27, 1926

Facts and documents from the political life of China in the recent period provide an absolutely indisputable answer to the problem of further relations between the Communist Party and the Kuomintang. The revolutionary struggle in China has, since 1925, entered a new phase, which is characterized above all by the active intervention of broad layers of the proletariat, by strikes and the formation of trade unions. The peasants are unquestionably being drawn into motion to an increasing degree. At the same time, the commercial bourgeoisie, and the elements of the intelligentsia linked with it, are breaking off to the right, assuming a hostile attitude toward strikes, communists, and the USSR.

It is quite clear that in the light of these fundamental facts the question of revising relations between the Communist Party and the Kuomintang must necessarily be raised. The attempt to avoid such a revision by claiming that national-colonial oppression in China requires the permanent entry of the Communist Party in the Kuomintang cannot stand up under criticism. At one time, the Western European opportunists used to demand that we Russian Social Democrats should work in the same organization not only with the Social Revolutionaries but also with the "Liberationists" on the grounds that we were all engaged in the struggle against tsarism. On the other hand, with regard to British India or the Dutch Indies, the very question of the Communist Party entering the national-revolutionary organizations does not arise. As far as China is concerned, the solution to the problem of relations between the Communist Party and the Kuomintang differs at different periods of the revolutionary movement. The main criterion for us is not the constant fact of national oppression but the changing course of the class struggle, both within Chinese society and along the line of encounter between the classes and parties of China and imperialism.

The leftward movement of the masses of Chinese workers is as certain a fact as the rightward movement of the Chinese bourgeoisie. Insofar as the Kuomintang has been based on the political and organizational union of the workers and the bourgeoisie, it must now be torn apart by the centrifugal tendencies of the class struggle. There are no magic political formulas or clever tactical devices to counter these trends, nor can there be.

The participation of the CCP in the Kuomintang was perfectly correct in the period when the CCP was a propaganda society which was only preparing itself for future independent political activity but which, at the same time, sought to take part in the ongoing national liberation struggle. The last two years have seen the rise of a mighty strike wave among the Chinese workers.

The CCP report estimates that the trade unions during this period have drawn in some 1.2 million workers. Exaggeration in such matters is of course inevitable. Moreover, we know how unstable new union organizations are in situations of constant ebb and flow. But the fact of the Chinese proletariat's mighty awakening, its desire for struggle and for independent class organization, is absolutely undeniable.

This very fact confronts the CCP with the task of graduating from the preparatory class it now finds itself in to a higher grade. Its immediate political task must now be to fight for direct independent leadership of the awakened working class—not of course in order to remove the working class from the framework of the national-revolutionary struggle, but to assure it the role of not only the most resolute fighter, but also of political leader with hegemony in the struggle of the Chinese masses.

Those who favour the CCP's remaining in the Kuomintang —argue that "the predominant role of the petty bourgeoisie in the composition of the Kuomintang makes it possible for us to work within the party for a prolonged period on the basis of our own politics". This argument is fundamentally unsound. The petty bourgeoisie, by itself, however numerous it may be, cannot decide the main line of revolutionary policy. The differentiation of the political struggle along class lines, the sharp divergence between the proletariat and the bourgeoisie, implies a struggle between them for influence over the petty bourgeoisie, and it implies the vacillation of the petty bourgeoisie between the merchants, on the one hand, and the workers and communists, on the other. To think that the petty bourgeoisie can be won over by clever manoeuvres or good advice within the Kuomintang is hopeless utopianism. The Communist Party will be more able to exert direct and indirect influence upon the petty bourgeoisie of town and country the stronger the party is itself, that is, the more it has won over the Chinese working class. But that is possible only on the basis of an independent class party and class policy.

We have taken the above-quoted argument in favour of the CCP's remaining in the Kuomintang from the July 14, 1926, resolution of the CCP Central Committee plenum. This resolution, along with other documents of the plenum, testifies to the extremely contradictory policies of the CCP and to the dangers flowing from that. The documents of the July plenum of the CCP Central Committee testify at every step to the "intensified process, during the past year, by which each of the two poles—bourgeoisie and proletariat—has defined its own separate position" (quoted from the same resolution).

The resolutions, documents, and reports record, first, the growth of the Kuomintang right wing, then the rightward movement of the Kuomintang centre, and after that, the vacillations and splits in the Kuomintang left. And all of this has followed the pattern of, stepped-up attacks on the communists. For their part, the communists have been retreating steadily, from one position to the next, within the Kuomintang. Their concessions, as we shall see, are both of an organizational nature and of the kind involving matters of principle. They have agreed to limit the number of communists on leading bodies of the Kuomintang to no more than one-third. They have even agreed to accept a resolution declaring the teachings of Sun Yat-sen inviolable. But, as ever, each new concession only brings renewed pressure against the communists on the part of the Kuomintang forces. All of these processes, as we have said, are absolutely inevitable, given the class differentiation. Nevertheless, the Central Committee plenum rejected the views of those Chinese communists who proposed withdrawal from the Kuomintang. The resolution states:

> A completely incorrect point of view, which distorts the prospects for development of the liberation struggle in China, is held by those comrades who think that the Communist Party—if it were to break organizationally with the Kuomintang, that is, if it were to dissolve the alliance with the urban commercial and professional bourgeoisie, the revolutionary intelligentsia, and partly, the government—could now, by itself, lead the proletariat and behind it the other oppressed masses to carry out the bourgeois-democratic revolution.

This line of argument seems to us, however, completely untenable. Whether the CCP will prove capable in the future, as an independent and decisive force, of leading the proletariat and peasantry to liberate and unify the country, no one can now predict. The further course of the revolutionary struggle in China depends on the play of far too many internal and international forces. Of course, the Communist Party's struggle for influence over the proletariat and for the hegemony of that class in the national-revolutionary movement may not lead to victory in the next years. But that is no argument at all against an independent class policy, which is inconceivable without an independent class organization. It is fundamentally wrong to suggest that withdrawal from the Kuomintang means the breakup of the alliance with the petty bourgeoisie. The essential point is that the vague and formless alliance of the proletariat with the petty-bourgeois, merchant, and other elements, which is reflected in the Kuomintang, is now no longer even possible. The class differentiation has passed over into the realm of politics. From now on the alliance between the proletariat and the petty bourgeoisie can be based only on strictly defined and clearly stated agreements.

The drawing of organizational lines, which inevitably flows from the class differentiation, does not rule out but, on the contrary, presupposes—under existing conditions a political bloc with the Kuomintang as a whole or with particular elements of it, throughout the republic or in particular provinces, depending on the circumstances. But first of all, the CCP must ensure its own complete organizational independence and clarity of political programme and tactics in the struggle for influence over the awakened proletarian masses. Only with this kind of approach can one speak seriously of drawing the broad masses of the Chinese peasantry into the struggle.

The direction of the CCP's thinking can best be made clear by quoting the most striking passages from the CCP declaration issued by the July Central Committee plenum (July 12, 1926):

The urgent demand of the Chinese people is for the alleviation of all these sufferings. This is not Bolshevism. Perhaps one could say that it is Bolshevism for the sake of saving our people, but it is not Bolshevism for the sake of communism.

Further on, this manifesto states:

They [the bourgeoisie] do not understand that the minimal expression of the class struggle that has occurred in the organization of the workers and in the strikes does not at all reduce the fighting capacity of the anti-imperialist and antimilitarist forces. Moreover, they do not understand that the welfare of the Chinese bourgeoisie depends on the success of the war waged in conjunction with the proletariat against the imperialists and militarists, and not at all upon the continuation of the class struggle by the proletariat.

The path of struggle is to "call for a nationwide conference". This should be done by the Kuomintang "as the party whose mission it is to carry out the national revolution". To the objection that the militarists would make it impossible to convene a national assembly truly representative of the people, the manifesto replies with generalities about control being exercised by the parties and unity of all classes. In Point 23 of the platform a demand is inserted, and only in twelfth place, for freedom to form coalitions, freedom of assembly, etc. The concluding section of the declaration states:

They [the militarists] say that our platform is revolutionary. That may be. However, it corresponds to the most urgent and vital demands and needs of all layers of the people. And a united fighting front of all classes of the population should be based on a common platform. Those who take part in this struggle should firmly defend these demands. They should fight for the common interests, not egoistically defend the interests of their own class.

The entire declaration is permeated from beginning to end with the desire to convince the bourgeoisie and not to win the proletariat. This kind of position establishes the premises for inevitable retreats before the right, center, and pseudo left leaders of the Kuomintang. The politics expressed in this declaration in fact have nothing to do with Marxism. This is Sun Yat-senism, slightly touched up with Marxist terminology.

Under these conditions it can no longer come as a surprise that the communists found it possible to accept the following policy statement of the Kuomintang Central Committee, adopted on Chiang Kai-shek's motion:

The Kuomintang must see to it that every member of another party entering the Kuomintang [i.e., the Communist Party-L.T.] understands that Sun Yat-senism, founded by Sun Yat-sen, is the basic principle of the Kuomintang and that there must not be any doubts or criticism expressed in regard to Sun Yat-sen or Sun Yat-senism.

It is quite obvious that when matters are presented this way, the whole reason for the CCP's existence disappears.

Sun Yat-senism as an idealist, petty-bourgeois doctrine of national solidarity was able to play a relatively progressive role in the period when the communists could get along in the same organization with the students and progressive merchants on the basis of a vague and informal alliance. The present class differentiation within Chinese society and within the Kuomintang is not only an irreversible but also a profoundly progressive fact.

Moreover, it means that Sun Yat-senism has become altogether a thing of the past. It would be suicidal for the CCP to refrain from criticizing this doctrine which, as events unfold, is sure to bind the Chinese Revolution hand and foot and ever more tightly. The imposition of this kind of obligation results from enforced organizational cohabitation within the bounds of a single political organization in which the communists voluntarily accept the position of a systematically discriminated-against minority.

The way out of this profoundly contradictory and absolutely unacceptable situation cannot be found along the lines pursued by the last plenum of the CCP. The way out does not lie in trying to "take the place of" the left wing in the Kuomintang, or in gently and unobtrusively trying to educate and nudge them along, nor in trying to "help create a left-Kuomintang periphery out of the organizations of the petty bourgeoisie". All these recipes and even the way they are formulated are cruelly reminiscent of the old Menshevik cuisine. The way out is to draw the line organizationally as the necessary prerequisite for an independent policy, keeping one's eyes, not on the left Kuomintang, but above all, on the awakened workers. Only under this condition can a bloc with the Kuomintang or with any of its elements be anything more than a castle of sand. The sooner the policy of the CCP is turned around, the better for the Chinese Revolution.

Two Conclusions

1. In the foregoing we have criticized the recent decisions of the CCP Central Committee. On the basis of past experience we can expect attempts to depict our criticism as an expression of hostility toward the fraternal Chinese party.

   One or another sentence may be torn out of context with the aim of showing that to us, the CCP is a "brake" on the revolutionary movement. There is no need to comment on the harm done by such low-grade "criticism". But facts are stronger than fabrications and insinuations. Properly evaluated and foreseen in time, the facts can still prove convincing even if the insinuations are disseminated in huge editions. Our criticism of the central leadership of the CCP is dictated by the desire to help the proletarian revolutionists of China to avoid mistakes that have long since been tested out in the experience of other countries. The responsibility for the CCP Central Committee's mistakes lies first of all with the leading group of our own party. The policy of remaining in the Kuomintang in spite of the whole trend of developments was dictated from Moscow, as the highest precept of Leninism. The Chinese communists had no alternative but to accept the political conclusions flowing from this organizational precept.

2. Politics is expressed through organization. That is why opportunism in organizational matters is entirely possible, as Lenin taught us. Such opportunism can be expressed in various ways, depending on the circumstances. One form of organization—opportunism is tailendism, i.e., the desire to hold on to organizational forms and relations that have become outdated and therefore turn into their opposites. We have seen organizational tailendism in the recent period in two cases: (a) on the question of the Anglo-Russian Committee; 10 and (b) on the question of the relations between the CCP and the Kuomintang. In both cases, the tailendism consisted in clinging to an organizational form that had already been stood on its head by the course of the class struggle. In both cases the outdated organizational form has helped right-wing elements and bound the left hand and foot. We must learn from these two examples.

[Postscript dated September 30, 1926]

From Comintern leaders in China we have heard a voice of warning-though phrased, to be sure, in a very cautious way—

on the question of relations between the CCP and Kuomintang. Thus, the report on CCP tactics toward the Kuomintang which was received after the May plenum of the Kuomintang Central Committee states:

In carrying out these decisions, i.e. the decisions defining our organizational ties with the Kuomintang, we should stretch them somewhat, that is, remain formally within the Kuomintang, but in practice, make a division of labor that would, as much as possible, give them the form of collaboration between two parties, i.e., make a gradual transition from the form of collaboration based on inner unity to that of contacts and consultations between allies.

Thus, from China the proposal has come that we, without formally negating the directives, should violate them in fact and turn the relations between the CCP and Kuomintang in the direction of an alliance between two independent parties. This proposal, which was called for by the whole course of events, met with no sympathy, however, and as a result we have had the decisions of the July plenum of the CCP Central Committee, decisions that are obviously mistaken, profoundly contradictory, and tending in a dangerous direction.

5

Second Letter to Radek

March 4, 1927

Dear Friend:

It seems to me that your way of formulating the problems with respect to the Chinese Communist Party is inadequate, and owing to what it leaves out, must inevitably lead, upon its subsequent application, to mistaken conclusions, i.e., for all intents and purposes to support for the status quo with some left-wing criticism.

You write that the treacherous bourgeois politics of the Kuomintang have "not yet created a mass movement against the Kuomintang and have not fostered an understanding of the need for a special class party of the proletariat and the poorest peasantry". Undoubtedly, the supporters of the present situation will try to latch onto these words. This was precisely the reason Stalin revived the "theory of stages", explaining that "it is impossible to skip over a stage", etc. Since the masses have not become conscious of the need, therefore . . . and so on. Our reasoning is just the opposite: in order to make it easier for the masses to understand how treacherous Kuomintang policy is, what is needed is an absolutely independent party, even if small, criticizing, explaining, exposing, and so forth; and by so doing, paving the way for the "new stage".

It is as if the present situation in China had been specifically created so that the masses would not understand the need for an independent party. Indeed, with the full authority of the International and the Russian Revolution we are telling China's working class vanguard that they already have an independent party—the Communist Party; that by force of the peculiar conditions in China this Communist Party must become a part of the Kuomintang at the present stage of the revolution; that Lenin's precepts demand this, and so on. Then the Kuomintang tells the communists: "Since Lenin's precepts demand that you join the Kuomintang, I, the Kuomintang, demand that you renounce Lenin's precepts and recognize the precepts of Sun Yat-sen".

To pose in the abstract the question of a painless transition from Sun Yat-sen to Lenin by presenting Leninism as the logical extension of Sun Yat-senism (although this method can in certain instances be used pedagogically with respect to the young revolutionary dilettantes of China) has, of course, proven to be untenable on the great historical scale. The class struggle has torn up the little artificial bridge we had constructed between Sun Yat-sen and Lenin. The Chinese proletariat must go through the process of directly and openly overcoming Sun Yat-sen, through an open struggle against Sun Yat-senism. If Marx demanded this even with respect to Lassalle, can it really be that we must not pose such a task with respect to Sun Yat-sen? Any moves to obscure, delay, or camouflage on this fundamental question will be not only dangerous but utterly disastrous for the Chinese proletariat.

When should the communists have withdrawn from the Kuomintang? My memory of the history of the Chinese revolution in recent years is not concrete enough, and I do not have the materials at hand; therefore, I will not venture to say whether it was necessary to pose this question point-blank as early as 1923, 1924, or 1925. In that period the preparatory arrangement expressed in your letter, evidently counting on a transitional state of a year or two, would have, perhaps, been admissible. But we are dreadfully late. We have turned the Chinese Communist Party into a variety of Menshevism, and worse yet, not into the best variety; i.e., not into the Menshevism of 1905, when it temporarily united with Bolshevism, but into the Menshevism of 1917, when it joined hands with the right SR movement and supported the Cadets. In giving our blessing to or merely tolerating this situation, we hamper the development of the class consciousness of the Chinese workers, only to afterward cite the insufficient development of their consciousness as the reason for dragging out still further the present state of things. With such a policy we are caught in a vicious circle.

If it were to turn out that the Chinese communists do not want to withdraw from the Kuomintang even in the present conditions of an unfolding class struggle, this would mean not that withdrawal is unnecessary, but that what we have there is a Martynovist party. I am afraid that to a large degree this is precisely how things stand.

Our task would then be reduced to extracting the genuinely revolutionary elements from the Martynovist party and beginning the work of building a Bolshevik party, outside not only the Kuomintang, but also outside the present "Communist" Party of China. I say this hypothetically because I do not know the actual relationship of forces inside the Communist Party; in fact, I doubt that it could have developed much at all yet in view of the absence of a clear and precise formulation of the problem by any side whatever. If we want to try to save the Chinese Communist Party from ultimately degenerating into Menshevism, we do not have the right to put aside one day longer the demand for withdrawal from the Kuomintang.

You propose that we restrict ourselves to the call for the Communist Party to emerge from underground. But this misses the point. To emerge from underground work means to breach Kuomintang legality. How would it be done? On the spur of the moment? Without warning? Without an attempt to come to an understanding with the Kuomintang on new terms? Without making an agreement with the left wing? But this would be the worst kind of breach; one that would be depicted as treachery. We are not starting out in China with a blank slate. All aspects of the problem of the relationship between the communists and the Kuomintang have been discussed in China. The problem brought about conflicts, was resolved, and resulted in a specific structuring. To ignore what has gone on before is impermissible. The problem must be posed in terms of revising the party constitution. The communists should directly and openly propose that the organizational structure be revised, by mutual agreement, to provide for the full independence of both parties In the absence of such a clear and precise formulation, the tactic of "emerging from underground" will be incomprehensible to the communists themselves; but the fact of the matter is that they must understand what the tactic will lead to and have a perspective for the future. Of course, withdrawal from the Kuomintang is a painful process. A neglected illness always requires more drastic treatment. It is wrong to be afraid that we will "alienate the petty bourgeoisie". There will be an endless number of zigzags and waverings on the part of the petty bourgeoisie. It is very likely that our withdrawal from the Kuomintang will at first give rise to just such a zigzag. But the petty bourgeoisie can be won over only by a concrete policy, not by maintaining disguises, making diplomatic manoeuvres, etc. In order to develop a policy that has the potential for winning over the petty bourgeoisie, it is necessary to have the instrument for this policy, i.e., an independent party.

That is why I have come to the following conclusions:

1. We must recognize that for the Communist Party to remain in the Kuomintang any longer threatens to have dire consequences for the proletariat and for the revolution; and above all, it threatens the Chinese Communist Party itself with a total degeneration into Menshevism.
2. We must recognize that if there is to be a leadership for the Chinese proletariat, a systematic struggle to gain influence in the trade unions, and finally, a leadership in the struggle of the proletariat to influence the peasant masses, there must be a totally independent, i.e., truly Communist (Bolshevik) Party.
3. The question of the forms and methods of coordination of the activities of the Communist Party and the Kuomintang must be fully and completely subordinated to the demand for the independence of the party.
4. All the genuinely revolutionary elements of the Chinese Communist Party must advance the programme for

action indicated above, demanding that its Central Committee raise before the Kuomintang and the working masses—in its full scope and unequivocally—the question of revising organizational relationships. Simultaneously, communists must everywhere "emerge from underground", i.e., actually begin to work as an independent party.

5. A congress of the Chinese Communist Party must be prepared under the call for the organizational independence of the Chinese Communist Party and the complete independence of its class politics and on the basis of a merciless struggle of its Bolshevik elements against the Menshevik elements within the party itself.

6

A Brief Note

March 22, 1927

I confess that at the present time the situation in China arouses in me far greater concern than does any other problem. I have just received a telegram to the effect that Shanghai has been occupied by Nationalist troops. The wider the territory under Nationalist rule and the more the Kuomintang takes on the character of a governing party, the more it becomes bourgeois. In this regard, the inclusion of Shanghai in the territory of the Nationalist government has an out-and-out decisive character.

At the same time, we read Kalinin's and Rudzutak's speeches, in which they expound and repeat the idea that the Nationalist government is the government of all the classes of the Chinese people (those are their words!). Thus, it seems that in China a government can exist that transcends class lines. Marxism has been completely forgotten. Forgotten too have been Lenin's theses on democracy (the First Congress of the Comintern). When you read such things in *Pravda,* at first you do not believe your eyes, you reread it and reread it again. . . But then, on this question Kalinin and Rudzutak are expressing in full the policy of the Chinese Communist Party, i.e., to put it more accurately, the Comintern's present policy on the Chinese question. The greater the successes of the national revolution in China, the greater are the dangers that await us with the present policy. (There will be some wise soul who will conclude from these words that I am against reaping the Chinese "harvest"—in other words, against the victory of the national revolution in China.)

The present policy is incorrect, even if we approach the matter from a "purely national" point of view, "abstracted" from the international revolution. There can be no doubt that the Nationalist government in China, upon seizing huge territories and finding itself face to face with gigantic and extremely difficult problems, upon experiencing the need for foreign capital and clashing daily with the workers, will make a sharp turn to the right, toward America to a certain extent and Britain. At this moment the working class finds itself without leadership, for it is quite impossible to consider as an independent leadership of the working class the "communist" appendage of the Kuomintang, which puts into the workers' heads the idea that the Nationalist government is a government of all classes. We find ourselves in the position of a hen who has hatched a duckling.

Evidently those who are in charge of this policy conceive of the following course of development: first we will carry things to a complete victory for the Nationalist troops, i.e., the unification of China; then we will begin to remove the Communist Party from the Kuomintang. The concept is Menshevik through and through. First we complete the bourgeois revolution, and then, . . . etc. With this concept, we are turning ourselves into not a class force of history, but some sort of classless inspectorate above the historical process as a whole. And, of course, we will fall flat on our faces at the very first turn. This turn will in all likelihood be the occupation of Shanghai.

The communists cannot, of course, relinquish support for the Nationalist army and the Nationalist government, nor, it appears, can they refuse to become part of the Nationalist government. But the question of the complete organizational independence of the Communist Party, i.e., of its withdrawal from the Kuomintang, must not be put off one day longer. We have lost far too much time as it is. The communists can form a united government with the Kuomintang on the condition of the total separation of the parties forming the political bloc. So it was with us and the left SRs." Vladimir Ilyich demanded that the Hungarian communists follow the same course and reproached them for having entered into an amalgamation of parties—that act having been, incidentally, one of the reasons the Hungarian revolution was crushed so quickly.

Is it permissible to continue any longer the flirtation with Sun Yat-senism, which is turning into the ideological shackles of the Chinese proletariat and tomorrow will become (is already becoming today) the main instrument of the Chinese bourgeois reaction! I believe that this sort of flirtation is criminal. But in order to cut the umbilical cord of Sun Yat-senism, there must be someone to cut it. An independent Communist Party is needed. Revolutionary selection within the Communist Party itself, i.e., its Bolshevization not in word but in deed, will undoubtedly occur around this question.

References to national oppression as a justification for a Menshevik policy are absolutely untenable. First of all one must remember that the whole Second International (Jaurès, Vandervelde, and the others) in demanding the unity of the Bolsheviks not only with the Mensheviks but also with the SRs was taking as its starting point the oppression of tsarism. As if a struggle against tsarism or against national oppression is not the class struggle! In Georgia, Finland, Latvia, etc., the yoke of tsarism took the form of the most savage national oppression, more complete than Britain's or even Japan's oppression of China. However, from this it did not follow that the Georgians, Finns, or Latvians should not build an independent party.

It seems to me that we must again, in one way or another, present this question to the Politburo. Of course, there is the danger that instead of a serious discussion of this problem in the Central Committee, there will be factional slander. But can we be silent when nothing less than the head of the Chinese proletariat is at stake?

7

Letter to Alsky

March 29, 1927

Dear Comrade Alsky,

Thank you for sending me the book. I read it today, all to my interest and benefit. I think you are absolutely right when you object to naming the Southern Nationalist government "workers' and peasants'." Defining it in such a way is, of course, a serious mistake as should be especially obvious now after the occupation of Shanghai with the powerful class contradictions this entails.

But this is precisely why I believe that you have made an error, expressed with particular clarity on page 141, where you say that in China, "two camps that are bitterly hostile to one another" have come into being: in one are the imperialists and militarists and certain layers of the Chinese bourgeoisie; and in the other are "the workers, artisans, petty bourgeoisie, students, intelligentsia, and certain groups from the middle bourgeoisie with a nationalist orientation." In fact, there are three camps in China—the reactionaries, the liberal bourgeoisie, and the proletariat—fighting for hegemony over the lower strata of the petty bourgeoisie and peasantry. It is true that before 1926 this division was less obvious than it is now, but even then it was a fact. But your book was published in 1927, and it was of the utmost importance to specifically describe this situation. If not, your review of Mif's book, and your evaluation in a number of places, and especially on page 141, would—in my opinion—provide the basis for grossly incorrect and dangerous conclusions. The Kuomintang in its present form creates the illusion that two camps exist, furthering the national-revolutionary disguise of the bourgeoisie, and consequently, making its betrayal easier. The Communist Party's entry into the Kuomintang, on the other hand, makes an independent proletarian policy impossible. It would be the purest charlatanism and betrayal of Marxism—you, of course, would agree—to point to the revolutionary heroism of the proletariat and the successes of the Canton forces as proof that in the sphere of proletarian politics everything is going favourably. That the workers and the revolutionary soldiers won back Shanghai is magnificent. But the question still remains: Who did they win it back for? If one thinks that "two bitterly hostile camps exist in China, it is clear that Shanghai has passed from the hands of one camp into the hands of the other. But if one bears in mind that there are three camps in China, then the question posed above takes on its full meaning.

The problem of a struggle for a workers' and peasants' government should in no case be identified with the problem of noncapitalist roads" of development for China. The latter can only be posed provisionally and only within the perspective of the development of world revolution. Only an ignoramus of the socialist-reactionary variety could think that present-day China, with its current technological and economic foundations, can through its own efforts jump over the capitalist phase. A conception of this type would be the worst caricature of the theory of socialism in one country, and carrying this conception to the absurd would render the Comintern a service, clearing its activity of such rubbish once and for all thereafter. If, thus, the problem of the Chinese revolution growing over into a socialist revolution is right now merely a long-term option wholly dependent upon the development of the world proletarian revolution, the problem of the struggle for a workers' and peasants' government has the most immediate importance for the course of the Chinese revolution as well as for the education in revolution of the proletariat and its party.

We know how complex and contradictory the course of the revolution is, especially in such a huge and—to an overwhelming extent—backward country like China. The revolution can still pass through a series of ebbs and flows. What we must safeguard in the course of the revolution is above all the independent party of the proletariat that is constantly evaluating the revolution from the point of view of three camps, and is capable of fighting for hegemony in the third camp and, by so doing, in the entire revolution.

I must say, I totally fail to comprehend why the call for soviets is not being raised in China. It is precisely through soviets that the crystallization of the class forces can keep pace with the new stage of the revolution instead of conforming to the organizational-political traditions of a bygone day, of the kind being offered by the present-day Kuomintang. How the Kuomintang will reorganize itself after the Communist Party withdraws from it—this particular question is of secondary importance to us. The indispensable condition is an independent proletarian party. The form for its closest collaboration with the rural and urban petty bourgeoisie is the soviets as organs of the struggle for power or as organs of power.

Large sections of the Chinese National Revolutionary Army are still green, and bourgeois landowners' sons wield great influence within the ranks of the commanding staff. Because of this, the future of the revolution is in danger. Once more, I do not see any other way to oppose this danger than soldiers' deputies joining workers' deputies, and so on.

It goes without saying, the means for selecting the deputies would have to be very carefully adapted to suit the conditions and particular features of a city, a village of a given area, the army, etc., so as not to give an accidental advantage to the reactionary elements or bring disorganization to the revolutionary forces, and so on. But I repeat: I see no other means for testing and organizing the revolutionary movement and the revolutionary power that grows out of it than a system of soviets. Why is nothing said about it? Explain it to me, please! This is what I can in no way understand.

Instead of clearly and concisely posing the question of the struggle for a workers' and peasants' (and artisans' and soldiers') soviet of deputies they are devoting themselves to the artificial and, therefore, reactionary perpetuation of an organization of the past—the Kuomintang-forcing the Communist Party to submit to the discipline of a bourgeois organization, at the same time consoling the party with talk about "non-capitalist roads" of development.

In his speech, Comrade Radek stated that the present-day Kuomintang must be preserved "as a transmission belt". When people move away from Marxism, they invariably substitute all sorts of meaningless images for a class understanding. A transmission belt is an excellent device. One only needs to know what it is transmitting from and what it is transmitting toward. While driving the Communist Party away from a strictly defined organizational position and subjecting it to the ideological discipline of Sun Yat-senism, the Kuomintang will necessarily and inevitably transfer power to the most influential, weighty, and organized elements of the "united" national camp, i.e., bluntly speaking, to the liberal bourgeoisie. Thus, the Kuomintang under the present conditions is a "transmission belt" for delivering the revolutionary popular masses into the hands of the bourgeoisie, for politically subjugating them to it. Any other interpretation is stupidity or charlatanism.

Members of the Kuomintang (those with brains) not only demand that communists unconditionally observe "revolutionary discipline" but when doing this they refer to the experience of the October Revolution with its dictatorship of one party. We, for our part, are supporting such a way of formulating the question insofar as we are compelling the Chinese Communist Party—against its will-to be part of a united Kuomintang and to submit to its discipline. In so doing we are leaving out of our reckoning the "petty detail" that what is taking place in China is not a socialist overturn but a bourgeois-national revolution, the "completion" of which means not the dictatorship of one party but a guarantee of the maximum democracy; so, from our point of view it means above all total freedom for the party of the proletariat. Now, when the wave is rising, there is nothing easier than to warm up our singing voices on "non-capitalist roads of development". But with the first big revolutionary lull, or especially a full-fledged ebb, it can become immediately obvious that China lacks the fundamental instrument for revolutionary struggle and revolutionary successes—an independent Communist Party acquiring experience and understanding the situation.

[Postscript, March 29, 1927]

PS: In your book it says that the Hong Kong-Canton Strike Committee represented the "Chinese version of the soviet of workers' deputies". This is absolutely true if "Chinese version" is understood not in the sense of some sort of decisive national peculiarity, but in the sense of the character of a stage of development of the soviet system: it was a soviet of deputies of the type that existed in the summer of 1905 in Ivanovo Voznesensk. Why can't this system be developed further? What is standing in its way? I maintain that it is the fact that the Communist Party has been bound hand and foot. If it is called upon to openly struggle for influence over the workers and through the workers over the peasantry under the banner of Marxism, and not Sun Yat-senism, and in direct struggle against the reactionary application of Sun Yat-senism, simultaneously collaborating with all revolutionary elements, groups, and layers of the petty bourgeoisie in the city and in the countryside; then it is impossible to devise a better form for such a struggle and for such collaboration than soviets.

PPS: I would not attach such great importance to your words about "two camps" if in the beginning of your book there were not a dedication to the Kuomintang and the Communist Party. I believe such a dedication is a serious mistake. The Kuomintang and the Communist Party are parties representing two opposing classes. It is not possible for one and the same book to be simultaneously dedicated to both. It is permissible to be in an alliance with the Kuomintang, but such an ally must be as carefully watched as an enemy. However, to be sentimental about such an ally is impermissible.

8

To the Politburo of the AUCP (B) Central Committee

March 31, 1927

Dear Comrades:

It is only through the papers that I am able at present to follow the events in China. What instructions you have given I do not know. But one cannot help noticing that nowhere in our press, in dealing with the development of the Chinese revolution (primarily its military aspect), has the question of soviets been raised. But it seems to me that at the present stage this question takes on absolutely decisive significance.

1. The Chinese revolution has taken over such major proletarian centers as Shanghai and Hankow, not to mention other less important places. Everything seems to point to the fact that the first thing that should be done in these proletarian centers is to organize soviets of workers' deputies.
2. Revolutionary collaboration between the proletariat and the urban and rural poor is a matter of life and death for the further progress of the Chinese revolution. Regardless of how one views the question of the further relations between the CCP and the Kuomintang, one thing is clear: day-to-day political, administrative and practical collaboration between the hundreds of thousands of workers and the millions of semiproletarian and petty-bourgeois elements in town and countryside cannot be achieved solely through the

essentially elitist organization of the Kuomintang, with its roughly 300,000 party members. This kind of actual, genuine, day-to-day collaboration among the masses of the people awakened by the revolution can only be brought about in reality through the creation of soviets of workers', artisans' and peasants' deputies

3. The national army, whose political education has only begun, will inevitably become swollen out of proportion as it is joined by new, provincial forces, completely green and raw as far as politics is concerned. The officer cadre, as far as one can tell from the available materials, is characterized by bourgeois and landlord origins and by sympathies tending to favor those same classes. Apprehensions regarding a Chinese variant of Bonapartism are apparently rather strong among revolutionary circles in China, nor can one say by any means that these fears are unfounded. Under existing conditions it would seem there is no more effective measure for countering such dangers than the establishment of soldiers' sections of soviets, beginning with the garrisons in the major proletarian centers.
4. It goes without saying that the formation of soviets must be done very carefully, in accordance with all the class relations, local conditions, and other special features and factors, so as not to give any accidental advantage to reactionary elements in one place or another, not to cause disturbances among the troops, etc. Nevertheless, everything points to the fact that this task of truly consolidating the conquered territories by forming soviets of the working and exploited masses of the Chinese population cannot be postponed any longer.
5. Only in this way can there, and will there, be a radical agrarian transformation-by "reformist" means where circumstances permit, and by "revolutionary" means where there are landlords with military detachments supporting them.
6. Today, many are being persuaded to desert or betray, especially if they are generals. The creation of rank-

and-file soviets would help to radically alter this pattern. Without ruthless reprisals against the militarists, the heads of outlaw bands, the innumerable "generals" and bandits, it will be impossible, in a China that has suffered years of civil war, to establish a stable democratic system. But stern measures of reprisal are unthinkable without the creation of a firm base of support for them among the lower ranks of society. Such a base can only be found in soviets of workers', soldiers', and poor people's deputies.

7. Needless to say, such soviets should and will become agencies in the struggle for power or actual organs of power on the local level.
8. All social layers and groups which in fact cooperate with and support the revolution in particular situations, at particular times, in particular localities, would elect their deputies to the soviets. This cooperation and support would be shown, on the one hand, by the attitude of such layers toward the workers, their strikes, etc., and on the other, by their attitude toward the national army. The lines of political cooperation as well as of political demarcation would follow the course of the class struggle, and not the artificial organizational schemes of the Kuomintang (such as the formula of one-third for the communists and two-thirds for merchants and intellectuals, etc.).
9. I will not raise the question of the relations between the CCP and the Kuomintang here. But I do think that a system of soviets would also help to place this question in its proper framework in a very short time. A system of soviets in China would not be, at least not in the coming period, an instrument of proletarian dictatorship, but one of revolutionary national liberation and democratic unification of the country. The soviets in this period would not be under the dictatorship of one party but under the direction of a bloc of parties with inevitable internal struggle between them, inevitable shifts, etc. The Kuomintang's attempt, using

the model of the Russian experience, to set up a one-party dictatorship, i.e., of the Kuomintang, with the Communist Party totally subordinated to it, is in essence counter-revolutionary and will inevitably produce fascist tendencies. The dictatorship of the proletariat in the Soviet Union, under conditions of capitalist encirclement, was possible only in the form of the dictatorship of the Communist Party. But in China, what is occurring is a national-democratic revolution, not a socialist one. A national democratic revolution is supposed to assure the proletariat full freedom for the class struggle and, consequently, full independence for the Communist Party as the leader of that struggle. The revolution cannot succeed without prolonged, close, and even more deepgoing collaboration between the proletariat and the plebeian masses of the towns and villages. This can be realized through the soviets in the form of blocs between parties, through the influence of worker delegates on non-party deputies, etc.

9

Class Relations in the Chinese Revolution

April 3, 1927

Issue 11 of the *Communist International* (March 18, 1927) printed as an editorial an article on the Fifth Congress of the Chinese CP and the Kuomintang which is in every way an exceptional mockery of the basic elements of Marxist theory and Bolshevik politics. This article cannot be characterized otherwise than as the worst expression of right Menshevism on questions of revolution.

As its starting point the article takes the proposition that "the problem of problems of the Chinese revolution at the present moment is the position of the Kuomintang, the further development of the Kuomintang as a party at the head of the South China state" (p. 4). Thus the problem of problems is not the awakening and the unification of millions of workers under the leadership of trade unions and the Communist Party, nor the drawing of poor peasants and artisans into the mainstream of the movement, nor the deepening of the struggle of the CP to win over the proletariat, nor the struggle of the proletariat for influence over the many-millioned masses of the disinherited —no, "the problem of problems" (!) is the position of the Kuomintang, i.e., a party organization which embraces, according to official figures, some 300,000 members—students, intellectuals, liberal merchants in general, and in part peasants and workers.

"For a political party," declares the article, "300,000 members is quite a considerable number." A paltry parliamentary appraisal! If these 300,000 had emanated from the experience of past class struggles, and the experience of leading proletarian strikes and peasant movements, then, naturally, even a smaller number of members could successfully assume the leadership of the revolution on its new and broader mass stage. But these 300,000 represent in their majority the result of individual recruitment among the tops. We have here the unification of national-liberals or Cadets with right SRs, with an admixture of young communists who are compelled in the period of their political training to submit to the discipline and even the ideology of a bourgeois-nationalist organization.

"The development of the Kuomintang," continues the article, "reveals alarming [!] symptoms from the standpoint of the interests of the Chinese revolution" (p. 4). And what is the nature of these "alarming" symptoms? Apparently it is this, that the power is in the hands of the Kuomintang center, and "the center has in the recent period gravitated in most instances definitely to the right." It should be noted that all political definitions in this article are of a formal, parliamentary, and ceremonial character, emptied of all class content. What is the meaning of this gravitation-to the right? What kind of Kuomintang "center" is this? It consists of the tops of the petty-bourgeois intelligentsia, middle-ranking functionaries, and so on. Like all petty bourgeois, this center is incapable of carrying out an independent policy, especially in the period when millions of workers and peasants have entered the arena. This petty-bourgeois center can produce an ally for the proletariat only on the condition that the proletariat carries out an independent policy. But there cannot even be talk of such a policy in China in the absence of an independent class party there.

Communists do not simply "join" the Kuomintang but they submit to its discipline and even obligate themselves not to criticize Sun Yat-senism. Under these conditions, the petty-bourgeois intellectual center can only trail behind the nationalist-liberal bourgeoisie, which is bound up by imperceptible gradations with the compradorian, i.e., overtly imperialist bourgeoisie; and, in proportion as the struggle of the masses sharpens, go over openly to its side. Thus the Kuomintang is a party apparatus adapted for the political subjection of the mass movement through the medium of a top intellectual center to an out-and-out right, i.e., manifestly bourgeois leadership, which under these conditions unfailingly subjects the Nationalist government to itself, and will continue to do so. The article cites the fact that "lefts" predominate in conferences, congresses, and the Executive Committee of the Kuomintang, but that this solacing circumstance is "not reflected in the composition and politics of the Nationalist government". How astonishing! But, after all, the left petty bourgeoisie exists only to display its radicalism in articles, and at conferences and banquets, while handing the power over to the middle and big bourgeoisie.

Thus the "alarming" symptoms in the Kuomintang consist in this, that the Kuomintang does not personify the pure idea of a national liberation revolution, which the author of the article sucked out of his thumb, but rather reflects the class mechanics of the Chinese Revolution. The author finds "alarming" the fact that the history of the Chinese people is unfolding in the form of a class struggle, proving thereby no exception to the history of all mankind. The article further informs us that the "Kuomintang and the Nationalist government are seriously concerned [a remarkable expression!] about the growth of the labor movement." What does this mean? It only means that the intellectual petty bourgeoisie has become scared by fear of the bourgeoisie before the awakening of the working masses. In proportion as the revolution extends and deepens its base, radicalizes its methods, sharpens its slogans, groups and layers of proprietors and intellectual burghers bound up with them will inevitably split from it at the top.

One part of the national government is joined with blood-ties to the bourgeoisie, and another part, fearful of breaking with it, becomes "concerned" about the growth of the labor movement, and seeks to harness the latter. By this delicate expression, "concerned," as previously by the words "alarming symptoms," the article refers to the sharpening of class relations, and to the attempts of the nationalist-liberal bourgeoisie, by using the Kuomintang as a tool and by issuing orders through it to the Nationalist government, to place a halter on the proletariat. When and where have we ever appraised class relations as is done by the lead article in the Communist International? Whence come these ideas? What is their source?

What methods are proposed in the article to overcome these "alarming symptoms"? On these questions the article polemicizes against the June (1926) plenum of the Central Committee of the Chinese CP, which adopted the position that it was necessary for the CP as an independent organization to conclude a bloc with the Kuomintang. The article rejects this idea. It also rejects the proposal to organize a left faction in the Kuomintang as an ally of the CP. No, the task—it teaches—consists in "assuring a firm left orientation to the whole Kuomintang". The question is solved easily. What is needed at the new stage of development, at a time when the workers are engaging in strikes against the capitalists, when the peasants are seeking, against the opposition of the Nationalist government, to drive out the landlords—what is needed at this new stage is to assure "a firm left orientation" to the Kuomintang, which represents the unification of a section of the bourgeoisie suffering from the strikes, a section of the landed intelligentsia suffering from the agrarian movement, the urban petty-bourgeois intellectuals who are fearful of "repelling" the bourgeoisie to the side of reaction, and finally the Communist Party which is bound hand and foot. It is this Kuomintang which must acquire "a firm left orientation".

Nobody knows what class line this "firm left orientation" must express. And how is it to be attained? Very simply: It is necessary "to saturate it [the Kuomintang] with revolutionary worker and peasant elements" (p. 6). Saturate the Kuomintang with workers and peasants? But the whole trouble is that workers and peasants, unacquainted with the pure idea of national revolution, are trying to utilize the revolution in order to "saturate" themselves a little before they saturate the

Kuomintang with themselves. To this end they are engaging in strikes and agrarian uprisings. But these unpleasant manifestations of class mechanics hinder the Kuomintang from acquiring "a firm left orientation". To call a striking worker to join the Kuomintang is to run up against his objection: Why should I join a party that crushes strikes through the government appointed by it? The resourceful author of the article would probably reply to him: By joining a common party with the bourgeoisie, you will be able to push it to the left, you will eliminate "alarming symptoms" and dispel the clouds of its "concern". In answer to this, the Shanghai striker will say that workers can exert pressure on their government and even achieve a change in government not through individual pressure on the bourgeoisie within the framework of a common party, but through an independent class party. Incidentally, it may well be that the Shanghai striker, who has already given evidence of advanced maturity, would not even continue to discuss any further, but shrug his shoulders, and give up his interlocutor as hopeless.

The article goes on to quote one of the leading communists who stated at the December 1926 party conference that the Kuomintang was dead and decomposing and that the communists have no reason for hanging on to a stinking corpse. In this connection the article says: "This comrade obviously (!!) had in mind the fact that recently the Nationalist government and especially government organs in the provinces have come out on a number of occasions against the development of the revolutionary struggle of the working class and peasantry"(p. 7).

The penetration of the author of this article is truly astounding. When a Chinese communist says that the bourgeois-nationalist tops are dead so far as the revolution is concerned, he "obviously" has in mind the fact that the Nationalist government has been shooting strikers on a small scale. "Obviously"! Of course, "alarming symptoms" are in evidence, but "this danger may be averted, if we do not look upon the Kuomintang as a stinking corpse" (p. 7). The whole thing depends, it seems, on how one looks upon the

Kuomintang. Classes and their parties depend on how we view them. The Kuomintang is not a corpse, it is only ailing. What of? Of a lack of blood of revolutionary workers and peasants. It is necessary for the Communist Party to "assist in the influx of this blood," etc. In short, what is needed is to perform the very-popular-of-late operation of blood transfusion, not on an individual but on a class scale. But, after all, the gist of the matter is that the bourgeoisie has begun to transfuse blood in its own way, by shooting, or helping to shoot, or winking its eyes at shootings of strikers and revolutionary peasants. In short, while fulfilling this splendid prescription we run up against one and the same difficulty, which is, the class struggle.

The gist of the entire article is in its desire to have the Chinese revolution make a detour around the class struggle, by taking an economic, rational, and expedient road. In a word by using the method of the Mensheviks, and at that, in the periods of their greatest backsliding. And this article appears in the theoretical organ of the Communist International which was founded on an irreconcilable break with the Second International!

The article upbraids the Chinese communists for not participating in the Nationalist government and its local organs. They would be able there to push the government to the left from within, guard it against false actions toward the masses, etc., etc. The entire experience of the past, and above all the experience of the Russian revolution, has been scrapped. The authority of the leadership of the revolution is handed completely over to the Kuomintang, the responsibility for violence over the workers must be assumed by the communists. Bound hand and foot within the Kuomintang, the communists are powerless to offer the many-millioned masses an independent line in the field of foreign and domestic politics. But the workers are justified in charging the communists, especially if they participate in the Nationalist government, with complicity in all anti-proletarian and anti-people actions of the nationalist bourgeoisie. The entire experience of our revolution has been scrapped.

If the communists, despite the mass labor movement,

despite the powerful growth of the trade unions and the revolutionary agrarian movement in the villages, are obliged as hitherto to constitute a subordinate section of a bourgeois party, and enter as an impotent appendage into a national government formed by this bourgeois party, then it must be flatly stated that the time has not yet come for the formation of the Communist Party of China. For it is far better not to build a Communist Party at all than to compromise it in the epoch of revolution, i.e., precisely at the time when the ties between the party and the working masses are sealed with blood, and when great traditions are created which exert their influence for decades.

Developing a scintillating program in the spirit of right Menshevism in its period of decline, the article refurbishes it in the modest modern spirit by consoling China with the fact that she possesses objective pre-conditions for "skipping over the capitalist stage of development". Not a word is said in this connection to the effect that the anti-capitalist perspective of China's development is unconditionally and directly dependent upon the general course of the world proletarian revolution. Only the proletariat of the most advanced capitalist countries—with the organized assistance of the Chinese proletariat—will be able to take in tow the 400 million atomized, pauperized, backward peasant economy, and through a series of intermediate stages lead it to socialism, on the basis of a worldwide exchange of commodities, and direct technical and organizational assistance from the outside. To believe that without the victory of the proletariat in the most advanced capitalist countries, and prior to this victory, China is capable with her own forces of "skipping over the capitalist stage of development" is to trample underfoot the ABCs of Marxism. This does not concern our author. He simply promises China a non-capitalist path—obviously in recompense for injuries she has borne, and also for the dependent character of the proletarian movement, and especially the degraded, disfranchised position of the Chinese CP. How can and must the question of the capitalist and socialist paths of China's development be posed in reality?

Above all it must be made clear to the vanguard of the Chinese proletariat that China has no prerequisites whatever economically for an independent transition to socialism; that the revolution now unfolding under the leadership of the Kuomintang is a bourgeois-national revolution, that it can have as its consequence, even in the event of complete victory, only the further development of productive forces on the basis of capitalism. But it is necessary to develop no less forcefully before the Chinese proletariat the converse side of the question as well: The belated bourgeois-national revolution is unfolding in China in conditions of the imperialist decay of capitalism. As Russian experience has already shown—in contrast, say, to the English—politics does not at all develop in parity with economics. China's further development must be taken in an international perspective. Despite the backwardness of the Chinese economy, and in part precisely due to this backwardness, the Chinese revolution is wholly capable of bringing to political power an alliance of workers and peasants, under the leadership of the proletariat. This regime will be China's political link with the world revolution.

In the course of the transitional period, the Chinese revolution will have a genuinely democratic, worker-and-peasant character. In its economic life, commodity–capitalist relations will inevitably predominate. The political regime will be primarily directed to secure the masses as great a share as possible in the fruits of the development of the productive forces and, at the same time, in the political and cultural utilization of the resources of the state. The further development of this perspective—the possibility of the democratic revolution growing over into the socialist revolution—depends completely and exclusively on the course of the world revolution, and on the economic and political successes of the Soviet Union, as an integral part of this world revolution. If the Chinese Revolution were to triumph under its present bourgeois-nationalist leadership, it would very quickly go to the right, demonstrate its good intentions to the capitalist countries, soon gain recognition on their part, offer them concessions on new bases, obtain loans, in a word, enter into the system of capitalist states as a less degraded, less colonial, but still profoundly dependent entity. Furthermore, the Chinese republic would hold in relation to the Soviet Union in the best variant the same position as the present Turkish republic.

A different path of development can be opened up only if the proletariat plays the leading role in the national democratic revolution. But the first and most elementary precondition for this is the complete independence of the Communist Party, and an open struggle waged by it, with banners unfurled, for the leadership of the working class and the hegemony in the revolution. Failing this, all talk of noncapitalist paths of development serves only to cover up right Menshevist politics by left SR phraseology of the [Russian] pre-revolutionary period —the most revolting of all conceivable combinations. A program of assisting in the "influx of workers' and peasants' blood into the Kuomintang" (what an infamous phraseology!) gives nothing and means nothing. There also happen to be different kinds of workers' and peasants' blood. The blood which is being shed by workers of China is not blood shed for class-conscious tasks. Workers who enter the Kuomintang will become followers of the Kuomintang, i.e., the proletarian raw material will be recast in the petty-bourgeois Sun Yat-senist mould. To prevent this from taking place, the workers must receive their education in a Communist Party. And for this, the Communist Party must be completely free from any outward restrictions to leading the workers in their struggle and opposing Leninism to Sun Yat-senism.

However, it may be the author of the article envisions, in the ancient and truly Martynovist style, the following perspective: first, the national bourgeoisie completes the national-bourgeois revolution through the medium of the Kuomintang which is, with the assistance of Chinese Mensheviks, infused with workers' and peasants' blood. And following this so-to-speak Menshevik stage of the national revolution will come the turn of the Bolshevik stage: the Communist Party withdraws from the Kuomintang, the proletariat breaks with the bourgeoisie, wins the peasantry away from it and leads the country to a "democratic dictatorship of workers and peasants". It is very likely that the author is guided by a conception which is a result of his failure to digest the two stratifications in the 1905 period—the Menshevik and the Bolshevik. But such a perspective must be declared pedantic nonsense.

It is impossible to achieve the national democratic revolution twice: first in the bourgeois and then in the proletarian spirit. To be sure, if we were to hinder the proletarian vanguard from breaking with the bourgeoisie in time and utilizing the revolutionary situation to prove to the masses in the nonrecurring events of the supreme struggle its energetic and unwavering loyalty to the cause of the toilers; if we were to accomplish this end by further enslaving the CP to the Kuomintang, then the time would sooner or later come when the proletarian vanguard would break belatedly with the bourgeoisie, in all likelihood not under the banner of communism, and would perhaps renounce politics altogether. The past of the European labor movement would provide the revolutionary proletarians of China with a corresponding ideology in the shape of syndicalism, anarchism, etc. Under these conditions, the Chinese nationalist-democratic state would very easily arrive at methods of fascism or semi-fascism.

We have observed this in the case of Poland. Was it so very long ago that Pilsudski was one of the leaders of the petty-bourgeois revolutionary organization, the Polish Socialist Party? Was it so very long ago that he sat in the Peter and Paul Fortress? His entire past gave him influence and authority among petty-bourgeois circles and in the army; and he used this authority for a fascist coup directed wholly against the proletariat. Will anyone wish to deny that in the staff of the Kuomintang its own Pilsudskis will be found? They will. Candidates can already be designated. If the Polish Pilsudski required three decades to complete his evolution, then the Chinese Pilsudski will require an interval far more brief to accomplish his transition from the national revolution to national fascism. We are living in the imperialist epoch when the tempo of development is extremely accelerated, when convulsions follow upon convulsions, and each country learns from the experience of another. To pursue the policy of a dependent Communist

Party supplying workers to the Kuomintang is to prepare the conditions for the most successful and triumphant establishment of a fascist dictatorship in China at that not very distant moment when the proletariat, despite everything, will be forced to recoil from the Kuomintang.

Menshevism, even in the period of its revolutionary "flowering", sought to be not the class party of the proletariat which rises to all-national and then world tasks (Bolshevism) but a supervisor of national development, in which capacity the party of the proletariat was assigned in advance a subordinate place (to collaborate, to push, to effect blood transfusion, and so on). But aspiring to such pseudo-Marxist supervision of history has always proved in action to be pedantic idiocy. The Mensheviks completely revealed this as far back as 1905; Kautsky did likewise somewhat later but no less decisively.

A national revolution in the sense of a struggle against national dependency is achieved through the mechanics of classes. Chinese militarists represent a class organization. The compradorian bourgeoisie represents the most "mature" detachment of the Chinese bourgeoisie which does not want a Chinese February lest it arrive at a Chinese October or even a semi-October. The section of the Chinese bourgeoisie which still participates in the Kuomintang, constituting there an internal brake and an auxiliary detachment of the compradorian bourgeoisie and of the foreign imperialists, will on the morrow seek to lean upon the bombardment of Nanking in order to exert pressure on the revolutionary rank and file and above all to put a harness on the proletariat. They will succeed in doing so unless the proletariat is able to counteract them from day to day by a well-directed class resistance. This is impossible so long as the Communist Party remains subordinate to the Kuomintang, which is headed by the auxiliary detachment of the compradorian bourgeoisie and foreign imperialists. It is indeed embarrassing to have to explain this in the year 1927 and doubly embarrassing to have to direct these ideas against the lead article in the organ of the Comintern!

As the Chinese revolution extends geographically it at the

same time deepens socially. Shanghai and Hankow—the two most important industrial centers which together embrace about three-quarters of a million workers—are in the hands of the Nationalist government.' Nanking was subjected to a bombardment by the imperialists. The struggle immediately passed into a higher stage. Having captured Hankow and Shanghai, the revolution has thereby drawn into itself the most developed class contradictions in China. It will no longer be possible to orient the policies on the handicraft petty trade peasant of the South. It is necessary to orient either on the proletariat or the bourgeoisie.

The proletariat must orient itself on the many million rank and file in the struggle against the bourgeoisie. We have this on the one hand. And on the other, the imperialists show by their Nanking butchery that they are in no jesting mood. Are they hoping in this way to terrorize Chinese workers or to bring the agrarian movement to a halt? Hardly. In any case, this is not their immediate aim. They desire above all to compel the bourgeois tops of the nationalist movement to understand that the time has come for them to break with the rank and file if they do not wish to have the guns of world imperialism trained upon them. The bombardment of Nanking is propaganda for the ideas of compradorism, i.e., the salutary nature of ties with world capitalism which is mighty, united, and armed, which can provide not only profits but also armed aid against one's own workers and peasants.

It is frivolous to assert that the bombardment of Nanking will fuse the whole Chinese nation as one man, etc. Such declamation suits middle-class democrats. The revolution has risen to a new level and a more profound differentiation within the nationalist camp. Its splitting into a revolutionary and a reformist-compradorian wing flows with iron necessity from the situation as a whole. The British guns, after the initial wave of "universal" indignation, will only speed this process. Hereafter, to drive workers and peasants into the political camp of the bourgeoisie and to keep the Communist Party as a hostage within the ranks of the Kuomintang is objectively tantamount to conducting a policy of betrayal.

Should the representatives of the CP participate in the Nationalist government? Into a government that would correspond to the new phase of the revolution, into a revolutionary workers' and peasants government, they must unquestionably enter into the present Nationalist government, under no conditions. But before raising the question of communist representation in a revolutionary power, it is necessary to consider the question of the Communist Party itself. After the capture of Shanghai by the revolution, former political relations have already become absolutely intolerable. It is necessary to approve as unconditionally correct the resolution of the June plenum of the CC of the Chinese CP, which demands that the party withdraw from the Kuomintang and conclude a bloc with that organization through its left wing.

To deny the need for organizing a left faction within the Kuomintang and to recommend instead that the Kuomintang as a whole be made to acquire a left orientation, as is done by the leading article in the *Communist International*, is merely to occupy oneself with babbling. How can a political organization be given a left orientation if not by gathering within it the partisans of this orientation and setting them up against their opponents? The Kuomintang will, of course, object to this. It is quite possible that they will begin citing the resolution of our Tenth Party Congress against factions. We have already witnessed a masquerade of this kind on the question of the dictatorship of a single party. The arch-right-wingers in the Kuomintang insist upon its unconditional necessity, citing the AUCP as an example in point. Similarly they will insist that a single party effecting the revolutionary dictatorship cannot tolerate factions in its midst. But this only signifies that the right wing of the nationalist camp, which assumed power through the Kuomintang, seeks in this way to prohibit the independent party of the working class and to deprive the radical elements of the petty bourgeoisie of any possibility of obtaining within the party a real influence on its leadership. The author of the article which we analyzed above goes all the way in all these questions to meet the bourgeois wing of the Kuomintang.

We must clearly understand that the Chinese bourgeoisie

is still trying to cover itself with the authority of the Russian revolution and that, in particular, it is plagiarizing from the forms of the future dictatorship of the Chinese proletariat in order to strengthen its own dictatorship against the proletariat. That is why it is of utmost importance today not to permit any muddling in the determination of the stage through which the Chinese Revolution is passing. It is a question not of the socialist but of a bourgeois-democratic revolution. And within the latter, it is a question of the struggle between two methods—bourgeois-conciliationist as against worker-peasant. It is possible today only to speculate as to the manner and conditions in which the national democratic revolution can rise to the socialist revolution, whether it will occur with or without an interruption and whether this interruption will be long or brief. The further march of events will bring the necessary clarification. But to smear over the question of the bourgeois character of the present revolution with general considerations of a noncapitalist development is to befuddle the Communist Party and to disarm the proletariat. Let us hope we shall not live to see the International Central Control Commission calling the Chinese communists to account for an attempt to build a left faction in the Kuomintang.

From the standpoint of the class interests of the proletariat—and we take them as our criterion—the task of the bourgeois revolution is to secure the maximum of freedom for the workers in their struggle against the bourgeoisie. From this standpoint the philosophy of the leaders of the Kuomintang in regard to a single centralized party that permits neither any other parties nor any factions within itself is a philosophy hostile to the proletariat, a counterrevolutionary philosophy which lays down the ideological foundations for Chinese fascism in the future. It is absurd to say that the withdrawal of the Chinese CP from the Kuomintang signifies a break of collaboration. It is the termination not of collaboration but of servitude. Political collaboration presupposes equality between the sides and an agreement between them. Such is not the case in China. The proletariat does not enter into an agreement with the petty bourgeoisie but rather submits to its leadership under a veiled form, with an organizational seal set upon this submission. In its present form the Kuomintang is the embodiment of an "unequal treaty" between the bourgeoisie and the proletariat. If the Chinese Revolution as a whole demands the abrogation of unequal treaties with the imperialist powers, then the Chinese proletariat must liquidate the unequal treaty with its own bourgeoisie. It is necessary to summon the Chinese workers to the creation of soviets. The proletariat of Hong Kong during the general strike created an organization very close in structure and functions to the elementary type of workers' soviets. With this experience as a basis, it is necessary to go further. The Shanghai proletariat already possesses the priceless experience of struggle and is fully capable of creating soviets of workers' deputies which will set an example for all China and thereby become the center of attraction for all genuinely revolutionary organizations.

10

On the Slogan of Soviets in China

April 16, 1927

Dear Comrades,

Yesterday, during the discussion on the Chinese question, one of Comrade Stalin's main retorts to Comrade Zinoviev's criticisms and mine of the basic errors in our policy on the problems of the Chinese revolution was to repeat the words: "Why didn't Zinoviev say ..?" "Why didn't Trotsky write ..?" I will not undertake here to go back to what we have said and written on this question. Undoubtedly, if our suggestions and advice had been treated with less prejudice and hostility and given more serious consideration at the time, we could have avoided the most important errors.

I will not dwell on the fact that of late fundamental questions are being resolved in closed sessions of the Politburo to which members of the Central Committee are not admitted. The object of this letter is not to recall what has happened in the past, but to pose the basic problem of the present and future: the Question of soviets in China. Comrade Stalin has now opposed the call for the Chinese workers and oppressed masses in general to set up soviets. However, this question has decisive importance for the further development of the Chinese Revolution. Without soviets the entire Chinese Revolution is going to serve the upper stratum of the Chinese bourgeoisie and through it the imperialists.

The plenum did not address itself to this fundamental question. However, the question is becoming extremely acute. It cannot be postponed any longer because the entire fate of the Chinese Revolution is bound up with the question of the formation of soviets. That is why I am raising this question here.

This is Comrade Stalin's reasoning: "Soviets are the essential organs of the struggle for power; to call for soviets means in fact to usher in the proletarian dictatorship, the Chinese October." But why did we have soviets in 1905? "We were struggling against tsarism," answers Stalin. "There is no struggle against tsarism in China. Since we are not heading directly for an October, we should not call for the formation of soviets."

This entire logic represents such a flagrant distortion of the meaning of our entire revolutionary experience, illuminated theoretically by Lenin, that I could never have believed a serious and responsible revolutionary would say such things if I had not heard them with my own ears.

Let us try to briefly analyze the problem.

1. Against the tsar it was permissible to form soviets while not yet conducting a struggle for the proletarian dictatorship. Why, then, is it impermissible, by means of soviets, to wage a struggle against the bloc of Chinese militarists, compradors, landlords, and foreign imperialists without posing as the immediate task the establishment of a proletarian dictatorship? Why?

   If one thinks, as Stalin did (and still does?), that the unification of China must be achieved by the bourgeois Kuomintang leadership which, through the Kuomintang, has made the Communist Party subordinate to itself, deprived the CP of its elementary independence (even its press!), and ruled captured territories by means of a reactionary bureaucracy—if this represents the national revolution, then, of course, there can be no place for soviets. If one recognizes, however, that the bourgeois Kuomintang leadership, not just the right wing but the left centrists, too, are incapable of carrying the democratic nationalist revolution to its conclusion or even halfway, and that it will without fail reach an agreement with the imperialists—if this is understood, then it was necessary in good time and now it is even more necessary to prepare to replace that leadership. A replacement does not mean the pure and simple replacement of Chiang Kai-shek with Wang Ching-wei: that would turn out to be the same old brew, with some more slops added. The problem will not be solved by changing the faces. A change means preparing a revolutionary government that relies not on the verbal, but on the real and practical support of the workers, petty bourgeoisie, peasants, and the masses of soldiers in the army. This can be achieved only by providing the masses with the kind of organization that meets the needs of the revolutionary conditions and of the awakening masses with their yearning for independence, a change in their living conditions, etc. This organization is the soviet.

2. Stalin imagines that first the bourgeoisie, with the support of the masses who are not organized for revolution (organized, they would not have begun to support it), must carry to completion the struggle against imperialism, and then we will begin preparations for soviets. This idea is false to the core! The whole question is how the struggle against imperialism and Chinese reaction will be waged and who will play the leading role in this struggle. It is possible to proceed toward the democratic worker–peasant dictatorship only on the basis of the unfolding struggle against imperialism which will be long and drawn out; only on the basis of a struggle against the national-liberal bourgeoisie for influence over the workers and peasants; only on the basis of a mass organization of workers and peasants not just against imperialism but also against the Chinese bourgeoisie. The only form this organization can take is soviets.
3. "Soviets must not be organized in the army's rear," says Stalin. This is the generals' point of view but not ours. The generals also think that trade unions should not be organized in the army's rear. We know, however, that both soviets and trade unions in the rear are an excellent aid to the revolutionary army. "But, don't you see,

soviets are organs for insurrection," replies Stalin. "That means you intend to organize an insurrection at the army's rear and seize power." This is a false and caricatured formulation of the problem! It is true that soviets are organs of the struggle for power. But they are not at all born as such; they develop in this direction. But only through the experience of struggle can they mature for the role of organs for the dictatorship (in this case, the democratic dictatorship). If we seriously intend to strive for a democratic workers' and peasants' dictatorship, the soviets will have to have the necessary time to develop and intervene in the unfolding events–those involving the military included–so that they, the soviets, can become firmly established, gain experience, and subsequently make a bid for power.

"But, you see, the [KMT] center will not permit soviets." We have nothing in common with this point of view. What the center permits or does not permit will depend on the relationship of forces. This relationship must be shifted to the advantage of the proletariat. While the awakened but unorganized masses follow the lead of the political organization of the Kuomintang upper echelon, they necessarily give the big bourgeoisie and the generals a powerful advantage over the proletariat. To argue that China has not yet reached its October and for this reason to keep the masses in a state of disarray actually means to weaken the proletariat by our own efforts while strengthening the bourgeoisie and its center, and then to plead that this center will not permit soviets at the army's rear.

4. But why can't the workers simply join the Kuomintang? Really, isn't it an adequate organization? To pose the question thus, one has to forget completely everything we have done and learned. The Kuomintang is a party organization tightly controlled by the topmost layer, despite the popularity of its banner. Is it really conceivable that hundreds of thousands, even millions of workers and peasants will join a party organization during the revolution? Where and when has this

happened? In fact, the importance of a soviet is that there, on the spot, it draws in those sections of the masses who have in no way become mature enough for the party and will not be for a number of years. To declare that the Kuomintang is a substitute for soviets is to engage in intolerable sophistry. The Kuomintang has 300,000 members. At present these 300,000 (if the number is not exaggerated) are dispersed. Only now is there talk about the need for Kuomintang elections, i.e., elections to fill the leadership organs by polling party members; but it goes without saying that there is no talk of the election of Kuomintang members by the millions of the masses. The fact is that to have to resort to such sophisms as equating the Kuomintang with soviets shows that soviets are knocking at the door and that they cannot be driven off by doctrinaire schemas about whether it is October or not October.

5. But wouldn't the formation of soviets lead to "a premature insurrection"? Premature insurrections erupt more easily and frequently in cases where the masses lack an authoritative organization that embodies their revolutionary will. That is to say, the absence of soviets in the major revolutionary centers will lead to chaotic, premature, and pointless outbreaks as a result of the unorganized state of the class struggle and the absence of correct political leadership. This has always been the case. Every revolutionary experience testifies to it.
6. What will soviets do? The first and most urgent thing they will do is provide an organization for the workers and help them in organizing their fraternization with the soldiers. The first order of business for the soviet of workers' deputies of a given industrial city or region should be to draw into its ranks soldiers' deputies, representatives from the garrisons. This is the surest way–or, to be precise, the only way–to effect a serious guarantee against Bonapartist 20 and fascist attempts by the Kuomintang higher-ups and any other riffraff. Failure to organize soviets of workers' and soldiers'

deputies will mean turning the soldier into cannon fodder for Chiang Kai-shek and setting the stage for a bloody massacre of the workers like the one that occurred in Shanghai.

7. In the cities, this must (obviously not be restricted to workers only. It is necessary that the petty artisans, small shopkeepers, and the city's oppressed lower strata in general be drawn into the soviets. This will facilitate the workers' revolutionary envelopment of the army. If this is not done, however, the fate of Shanghai, and with it the revolution, will depend on some vile Bonapartist.
8. This should by no means be limited to the cities. The network of soviets should be extended as soon as possible from the major industrial centers to the countryside, relying on the existing peasant unions, broadening their framework, expanding their program, and linking them up with the workers and soldiers.
9. What will the soviets do? They will struggle against the local reactionary bureaucracies, learning and teaching the masses to understand the connection between the local authorities and those who rule the country. They will struggle against those same bureaucracies, against the militarist gangs, against the landlords, etc., in the rural areas. They thus become organs of the agrarian revolution that cannot be postponed until China is unified ("until there is a constituent assembly").
10. Commissars are powerless figures under the reactionary generals, often outright lackeys who are appointed by these very generals. The only way a commissar can have any weight in the present epoch is by relying on strong local mass organs, and not simply on a political party—especially one like the Kuomintang, which has no serious organizational structure or one like the Communist Party, which is bound hand and foot and deprived of even an independent newspaper. The formation of workers', peasants', and soldiers' soviets prepares the ground for a really revolutionary democratization of the National Revolutionary Army which otherwise will

inevitably become the tool of a homegrown Chinese Bonapartism.

11. Through the soviets a real and genuine—not doctrinaire and artificial-regroupment of forces will take place. All of the classes, layers, and strata that are involved in or that will become involved in the real, present struggle against native and foreign reactionaries will enter the soviets. The goading by the various Kuomintang "leaders", the conniving, the counterposing of one person to another, and combinations of these things—all of this backstage chicanery, inadequacy, and impotence, now fully exposed, will be replaced by the other, far more serious, real revolutionary class selection. The alignment of forces will proceed as follows: for or against the soviets, i.e., for preparing the transition of the revolution to a higher stage, or for a deal between the Chinese bourgeoisie and imperialism. If the question is not posed this way, all prospects for a democratic worker–peasant dictatorship, etc.—not to mention noncapitalist paths of development—will remain merely talk to console us while the masses of Chinese people remain the cannon fodder of a revolution led by corrupt nationalist liberals.
12. Whoever opposes the formation of soviets must say: All power to the Kuomintang. But the Kuomintang tells the communists, "place yourself under my command", prohibits them from criticizing Sun Yat-Senism, and does not even let them have a newspaper, pointing out that in Russia, too, there is a one-party dictatorship. But, in Russia the one-party dictatorship is the expression of the proletarian dictatorship and the socialist revolution, whereas the Kuomintang is a bourgeois party in a bourgeois revolution. Without soviets a dictatorship in the existing concrete situation means disarming the workers, gagging the communists, a state of disorganization among the masses, and Chiang Kai-shek-type coups.
13. Does this mean war with the Kuomintang? Nonsense! Nonsense! Nonsense! The problem here is organizing collaboration with the Kuomintang on a far broader and deeper basis—on the basis of millions of workers,

soldiers, peasants, and other deputies' soviets. Of course, this collaboration presupposes the full and unconditional freedom for the Communist Party to criticize the Kuomintang, and this freedom to criticize presupposes the freedom of the communist press and communist organization.

14. Unless there is a total political split in the Kuomintang, unless it is purged of all Chiang Kai-shekist elements in general, there can be no joint revolutionary work with it. The differentiation, cleansing, and tempering within the Kuomintang will proceed more easily and most assuredly on the question of soviets than on any other. We will work hand in hand with the section of the old Kuomintang that will support the soviets and participate in them, i.e., that will get into real contact with the real masses. Of course, while working hand in hand with a revolutionary Kuomintang, we will keep a very vigilant eye on this ally and openly criticize its indecisiveness, retreats, and errors, not to mention possible treachery. In this way, on the basis of the closest collaboration with the Kuomintang, we will strive to further broaden the Communist Party's influence on the soviets and through the soviets.
15. But wouldn't soviets mean dual power for an indefinite period? 21 On one side would be the national-revolutionary government (if, when thoroughly reorganized, it holds its own and experiences an upturn), and on the other side, the soviets. Yes, this means dual power or elements of dual power. "But we were against dual power." We were against a dual-power regime insofar as we were striving to seize power ourselves as the proletarian party. We were for dual power i.e., a system of soviets, while there was a Provisional Government insofar as soviets restricted any bourgeois pretensions to dictatorship. Dual power during the February Revolution was progressive insofar as it contained new revolutionary possibilities. But this progressiveness was only temporary. The way out of the contradiction was the proletarian dictatorship. Dual

power lasted only eight months in our case. In China this transitional regime under certain conditions could last considerably longer, and vary in different parts of the country. To call for and begin organizing soviets means in fact to begin introducing in China elements of dual power. This is both necessary and healthy. This alone will open up further prospects of a revolutionary democratic dictatorship of the proletariat and peasantry. Without this, all talk about this dictatorship is simply chatter which the Chinese popular masses know nothing about.

16. I will not examine here the very important question of future possibilities and paths for the development of the future worker–peasant dictatorship into the proletarian dictatorship and an immediate socialist revolution since it is not now on the agenda. That there is such a perspective and that it has every chance of becoming a reality—given a favorable tempo of development of the proletarian revolution in the West—is, for every Marxist, indisputable. This can and should be discussed. But this perspective need not turn into a philosophic compensation for the present situation when the armed bourgeois traitors have the upper hand. The basic and vital task now is to prepare for the next stage, the only one from which subsequent prospects and possibilities can emerge.
17. That the Chinese revolution at this stage is national-democratic, i.e., bourgeois, is elementary to us all. Our politics, however, do not flow simply from the revolution having a bourgeois label but from the actual development of class relations within this revolution. Comrade Martynov proceeds very clearly and explicitly from the old Menshevik conception that since the revolution is bourgeois but anti-imperialist, the section of the Chinese bourgeoisie whose interest is to overthrow imperialism cannot step aside from this revolution. Chiang Kai-shek answered Martynov on this score by making a deal with the imperialists and crushing the Shanghai proletariat. This is precisely where Comrade Stalin goes astray.

11

The Friendly Exchange of Portraits Between Stalin and Chiang Kai-shek

April 18, 1927

To the Eastern Secretariat of the ECCI:

Returned from leave of absence, I found the photograph of Chiang Kai-shek sent me through the Eastern Department of the ECCI and the request promptly to send him my autographed picture. Had I received such a request through the Foreign Office, then, regardless of my attitude toward this request, I would find the fact itself explainable. But it is absolutely incomprehensible to me why the Eastern Department of the ECCI—the international organization of the communist vanguard of the proletariat occupies itself with such a thoroughly compromising matter as the spreading of portraits of Chiang Kai-shek. And this, moreover, as a result of a malicious irony of fate, on the eve of the coup d'etat carried out by him. I do not doubt that this job, unseemly for the ECCI, was done by some employee of the Eastern Department not empowered to do it, without the knowledge of the leading persons and especially of the Presidium of the ECCI, as a consequence of which I deem it necessary to bring this distasteful affair to your attention. The picture of Chiang Kai-shek I am herewith returning.

With communist greetings,

L. Trotsky

Copy: To the Presidium of the ECCI and the Political Bureau of the Central Committee.

12

The Chinese Revolution and the Theses of Comrade Stalin

May 7, 1927

The theses of Comrade Stalin entitled *Problems of the Chinese Revolution*[1] were published in *Pravda* on April 21, 1927, a few days after the close of the plenary session of the Central Committee [2], to which these theses were never presented and at which they were never discussed (although all the members of the plenum were still in Moscow).

Moreover, the theses of comrade Stalin are erroneous to such a point, they turn the matter upside down to such a degree, they are so permeated with the spirit of *chvostism*, they are so inclined to perpetuate the mistakes already made, that to remain silent about them would be a positive crime.

The Lessons of the Chinese Events Must Be Drawn

1. The prohibition of an open discussion of the theoretical and tactical problems of the Chinese Revolution has been motivated of late by the fact that such a discussion would delight the enemies of the USSR. Naturally it would be quite impermissible to make public facts that could be seized upon by enemies, who, incidentally, do not shrink from the direct invention of "facts" and "documents". But there is no need at all for such a discussion. It is only a question of determining the driving forces of the Chinese revolution and of estimating the basic line of its political direction. In other words, it is a question of discussing *the same questions to which the theses of*

comrade Stalin are devoted. If these theses can be published, then why cannot a criticism of them be published?

It is an unheard-of mistake to contend that a discussion of the problems of the Chinese Revolution can injure our state interests. If this were so, then not only the Communist Party of the Soviet Union but every other party of the Communist International, including the Chinese, would have to abstain from any discussion. But the interests of the Chinese Revolution, as well as the interests of the education of all the Communist parties in the world, demand an open, energetic, exhaustive discussion of all the problems of the Chinese Revolution, especially those in dispute. It is not true that the interests of the Communist International conflict with the state interests of the USSR. The renunciation of discussion of the mistakes is not dictated by the interests of a workers' state, but by a false "apparatus-like" bureaucratic attitude towards the Chinese revolution as well as towards the interests of the USSR.

2. The April defeat of the Chinese Revolution is not only a defeat for the opportunist line but also a defeat for the bureaucratic methods of the leadership, through which the Party is confronted with every decision as an accomplished fact: the decision, it is explained, does not justify criticism until facts demonstrate its annulment, whereupon it is just as automatically, that is, behind the back of the Party, replaced by a decision which is frequently more erroneous, like the present theses of Stalin. Such a method, which, in and by itself, is incompatible with the development of a revolutionary party, becomes an especially heavy obstacle to young parties that can and should learn independently from the experiences of defeats and mistakes.

The theses of comrade Stalin are published. At least within the limits of these theses, the questions of the Chinese Revolution can and must be discussed openly and from every angle.

The Yoke of Imperialism and the Class Struggle

3. The peculiarity of the Chinese Revolution—in comparison, for example, with our revolution of 1905—lies

above all in the semi-colonial position in China. A policy that disregarded the powerful pressure of imperialism on the internal life of China would be radically false. But a policy that proceeded from an abstract conception of national oppression without its class refraction and reflection would be no less false. The main source of the mistakes in the theses of comrade Stalin, as in the whole leading line in general, is the false conception of the role of imperialism and its influence on the class relationships of China.

The imperialist yoke is supposed to serve as a justification for the policy of the "bloc of four classes". The yoke of imperialism leads allegedly to the fact that "all" (!) the classes of China look upon the Canton government as the "national government of the whole of China in the same way" (!). (Speech of comrade Kalinin, *Izvestia,* March 6) This is essentially the position of the right Guomindang man, Dai Tshi Tao, who pretends that the laws of the class struggle do not exist for China —because of imperialist pressure.

China is an oppressed semi-colonial country. The development of the productive forces of China, which is proceeding in capitalist forms, demands the shaking off of the imperialist yoke. The war of China for its national independence is a progressive war, because it flows from the necessities of the economic and cultural development of China itself, as well as because it facilitates the development of the revolution of the British proletariat and that of the whole world proletariat.

But this by no means signifies that the imperialist yoke is a mechanical one, subjugating "all" the classes of China in the "same" way. The powerful role of foreign capital in the life of China has caused very strong sections of the Chinese bourgeoisie, the bureaucracy and the military to join their destiny with that of imperialism. Without this tie, the enormous role of the so-called "militarists" in the life of modern China would be inconceivable.

It would further be profound *naiveté* to believe that an abyss lies between the so-called comprador bourgeoisie, that is, the economic and political agency of foreign capital in China, and the so-called "national" bourgeoisie. No, these two sections stand incomparably closer to each other than the bourgeoisie and the masses of workers and peasants. The bourgeoisie participated in the national war as an internal brake, looking upon the worker and peasant masses with growing hostility, and becoming ever readier to conclude a compromise with imperialism.

Installed within the Guomindang and its leadership, the national bourgeoisie has been essentially an instrument of the compradors and imperialism. It can remain in the camp of the national war only because of the weakness of the worker and peasant masses, the lack of development of the class struggle, the lack of independence of the Chinese Communist Party and the docility of the Guomindang in the hands of the bourgeoisie.

It is a gross mistake to think that imperialism mechanically welds together all the classes of China from without. That is the position of the Chinese Kadet, Dai Tshi Tao, but in no wise ours. The revolutionary struggle against imperialism does not weaken, but rather strengthens the political differentiation of the classes. Imperialism is a highly powerful force in the internal relationships of China. The main source of this force is not the warships in the waters of the Yangtze Kiang—they are only auxiliaries—but the economic and political bond between foreign capital and the native bourgeoisie. The struggle against imperialism, precisely because of its economic and military power, demands a powerful exertion of forces from the very depths of the Chinese people. To really arouse the workers and peasants against imperialism is possible only by connecting their basic and most profound life interests with the cause of the country's liberation. A workers' strike—small or large—an agrarian rebellion, an uprising of the oppressed sections in city and country against the usurer, against the bureaucracy, against the local military satraps, all that arouses the multitudes, that welds them together, that educates, steels, is a real step forward on the road to the revolutionary and social liberation of the Chinese people. Without that, the military successes and failures of the right, semi-right or semi-left generals will remain foam on the surface of the ocean. But everything that brings the oppressed and exploited masses of the toilers to their feet inevitably pushes the national bourgeoisie into an open bloc with the imperialists. The class struggle between the bourgeoisie and the masses of workers and peasants is not weakened, but, on the contrary, is sharpened by imperialist oppression, to the point of bloody civil war at every serious conflict. The Chinese bourgeoisie always has a solid rearguard behind it in imperialism, which will always help it with money, goods and shells against the workers and peasants.

Only wretched philistines and sycophants, who hope in their hearts to obtain freedom for China as an imperialist bounty for the good behaviour of the masses, can believe that the national liberation of China can be achieved by moderating the class struggle, by curbing strikes and agrarian uprisings, by abandoning the arming of the masses, etc. When comrade Martynov proposes that strikes and the struggle on the land be replaced by a solution of the questions through the medium of governmental arbitration, then he differs in no way from Dai Tshi Tao, the philosophical inspirer of Chiang Kai-shek's policy.

Democratic or Socialist Revolution?

4. The senseless contention is attributed to the Opposition that China now stands on the eve of a socialist dictatorship of the proletariat. There is nothing original in this "criticism". On the eve of 1905 and later on, the Mensheviks frequently declared that Lenin's tactic would be correct if Russia were directly on the eve of the socialist revolution. Lenin, however, explained to them that his tactic was the only road to the radical victory of the democratic revolution which, under favourable conditions, would begin to grow over into a socialist revolution.

The question of the "non-capitalist" path of development of China was posed in a conditional form by Lenin, for whom, as for us, it was and is ABC wisdom that the Chinese revolution, left to its own forces, that is, *without the direct support of the victorious proletariat of the USSR and the working class of all advanced countries*, could end only with the conquest of the broadest possibilities for the capitalist development of the country, with more favourable conditions for the labour movement.

5. No less basically false is the contention that the question as to whether the Chinese proletariat needs an independent party; whether this party needs a bloc with the Guomindang or must subordinate itself to it; whether soviets are necessary, etc., must be solved in accordance with how we conceive the course and the tempo of the *further* stages of the Chinese Revolution. It is quite possible that China will have to pass through a relatively prolonged stage of parliamentarism, beginning with a Constituent Assembly. This demand is inscribed on the banner of the Communist Party. If the bourgeois democratic revolution does not grow into a socialist revolution in the near future, then in all probability the workers' and peasants' soviets will pass from the scene for a definite stage and give way to a bourgeois régime, which, depending on the progress of the world revolution, will in turn give way, at a new historical stage, to the dictatorship of the proletariat.

6. But first of all, the inevitability of the capitalist path has by no means been proved; and secondly—this argument is now incomparably more timely for us—the bourgeois tasks can be solved in various ways. The slogan of the Constituent Assembly becomes an empty abstraction, often simple charlatanry, if one does not add who will convoke it and with what program. Chiang Kai-shek can raise the slogan of a Constituent Assembly against us even tomorrow, just as he has now raised his "workers' and peasants' program" against us. We want a Constituent Assembly convoked not by Chiang Kai-shek but by the executive committee of the workers' and peasants' soviets. That is the only serious and sure road.

7. Basically untenable is the endeavour of comrade Bukharin to justify the opportunist and compromising line by referring to the allegedly predominant role of the "remnants of feudalism" in Chinese economy. Even if comrade Bukharin's estimation of Chinese economy rested on an economic analysis and not on scholastic definitions, the "remnants of feudalism" would still be unable to justify the policy which so manifestly facilitated the April *coup d'état*.

The Chinese Revolution has a national bourgeois character principally because the development of the productive forces of Chinese capitalism collides with its governmental customs dependence upon the countries of imperialism. The obstruction of the development of Chinese industry and the throttling of the internal market involve the conservation and rebirth of the most backward forms of production in agriculture, of the most parasitic forms of exploitation, of the most barbaric forms of oppression and violence, the growth of surplus population, as well as the persistence and aggravation of pauperism and all sorts of slavery. No matter how great the specific weight of the typically "feudal" elements in Chinese economy may be, they can be swept away only in a revolutionary way, and consequently not in alliance with the bourgeoisie but in direct struggle against it. The more complicated and tortuous is the interlacing of feudal and capitalist relations, the less the agrarian question can be solved by legislation from above, the more indispensable is the revolutionary initiative of the peasant masses in close union with the workers and the poor population of the cities, the falser is the policy that clings convulsively to the alliance with the bourgeoisie and the large landowner and subordinates its work among the masses to this alliance. The policy of the "bloc of four classes" not only prepared the bloc of the bourgeoisie with imperialism, but also meant the preservation of all the survivals of barbarism in administration and in economy.

To invoke the bourgeois character of the Chinese Revolution, in particular against the soviets, is simply to renounce the experiences of our bourgeois revolutions of 1905 and February 1917. In these revolutions, the immediate and essential objective was the abolition of the autocratic and feudal régime. This aim did not exclude, but demanded the arming of the workers and the formation of soviets. Here is how Lenin treated the subject after the February revolution:

> "For an effective struggle against the tsarist monarchy, for a real assurance of liberty not only in words, not in elegant promises of the rhetoricians of liberalism, the workers must *not* support the new government, but the government must 'support' the workers. For the only *guarantee* of freedom and of the final destruction of tsarism is *the arming of the proletariat*, the consolidation, the

extension, the development of the role, the significance, and the power of the workers' and soldiers' soviets. Everything else is phrases and lies of the politicians in the liberal and radical camps who are deceiving themselves. Support the arming of the workers or at least do not obstruct this process, and freedom in Russia will be invincible, the monarchy irretrievable, the republic assured. Otherwise the people will be deceived. Promises are cheap. They cost nothing. All the bourgeois politicians in *all* the bourgeois revolutions have 'fed' the people with promises and stupefied the workers. Our revolution is a bourgeois revolution, *therefore* the workers must support the bourgeoisie; that is what the worthless politicians from the camp of the liquidators say. Our revolution is a bourgeois revolution, say we, the Marxists; *therefore* the workers must open the eyes of the people to the deception of the bourgeois politicians, must teach it to put no trust in words, to rely upon *its own* forces, *its own* organization, *its own* unity, *its own* arms."[2]

The Chinese revolutionist who casts the over-cunning resolutions and comments on the bloc of four classes out of his head, will firmly grasp the sense of these simple words of Lenin, will be sure not to go astray and will attain the goal.

The School of Martynov in the Chinese Question

8. The official leadership of the Chinese Revolution has been oriented all this time on a "general national united front" or on the "bloc of four classes" (cf. the report of Bukharin; the leader in the *Communist International,* no.11; the unpublished speech by Stalin to the Moscow functionaries on April 5, 1927; the article by Martynov in *Pravda* on April 10; the leader in *Pravda* of March 16; the speech by comrade Kalinin in *Izvestia* of March 6, 1927; the speech by comrade Rudzutak in *Pravda* of March 9, 1927; etc., etc.). Matters had gone so far on this track, that on the eve of Chiang Kai-shek's *coup d'état, Pravda,* in order to expose the Opposition, proclaimed that revolutionary China was not being ruled by a bourgeois government but by a "government of the bloc of four classes".

The philosophy of Martynov, which has the sorry courage to carry all the mistakes of Stalin and Bukharin in the questions of Chinese policy to their logical conclusion, does not meet a trace of objection. Yet it is tantamount to trampling under foot the fundamental principles of Marxism. It reproduces the crudest features of Russian and international Menshevism, applied to the conditions of the Chinese Revolution. Not for nothing does the present leader of the Mensheviks, Dan, write in the last number of *Sotsialisticheski Vestnik*:

> "'In principle' the Bolsheviks were also for retaining the 'united front' in the Chinese revolution up to the completion of the task of national liberation. On April 10, Martynov, in *Pravda*, most effectively and despite the obligatory abuse of the Social Democrats, in a quite 'Menshevik manner' showed the 'Left' Oppositionist Radek the correctness of the *official* position which insists on the necessity of retaining the 'bloc of four classes', on not hastening to overthrow the coalition government in which the workers sit side by side with the big bourgeoisie, not to impose 'socialist tasks' upon it prematurely."[3]

Everyone who knows the history of the struggle of Bolshevism against Menshevism, particularly in the question of relations to the liberal bourgeoisie, must acknowledge that Dan's approval of the "rational principles" of the Martynov school is not accidental, but follows with perfect legitimacy. It is only unnatural that this school should raise its voice with impunity in the ranks of the Comintern.

The old Menshevik tactic of 1905 to 1917, which was crushed under foot by the march of events, is now transferred to China by the Martynov school, much the same as capitalist trade dumps its most inferior merchandise, which finds no market in the mother country, into the colonies. The merchandise has not even been renovated. The arguments are the same, letter for letter, as they were twenty years ago. Only, where formerly the word *autocracy* stood, the word *imperialism* has been substituted for it in the text. Naturally, British imperialism is different from autocracy. But the Menshevik reference to it does not differ in the slightest from its reference to autocracy. The struggle against foreign imperialism is as much a class struggle as the struggle against autocracy. That it cannot be exorcized by the idea of the national united front, is far too eloquently proved by the bloody April events, a direct consequence of the policy of the bloc of four classes.

What the "Line" Looked Like in Practice

9. On the past period, which terminated with the April *coup d'état*, the theses of comrade Stalin announce:

> "The line adopted was the only correct line."

What did it look like in practice? An eloquent reply is supplied by Tang Pingshan, the Communist minister of agriculture, in his report at the Seventh Plenum of the ECCI in December 1926.

> "Since the establishment of the national government in Canton last July, which is nominally a government of the left wing, *the power has actually been in the hands of the right wing* ... The movement of the workers and peasants cannot develop to its full breadth as a result of various obstacles. After the March putsch a *military dictatorship of the centre* [that is, Chiang Kai-shek] was established, while the political power remained as before in the hands of the right wing. The whole political power, which should properly [!] have belonged to the left wing, is finally lost."

So: the left "should have" had the power, but finally lost it; the state power belonged to the right, the military authority, which is incomparably more powerful, arid was entirely in the hands of the "centre" of Chiang Kai-shek, which became the centre of the conspiracy. Under such conditions, it is not difficult to understand why "the movement of the workers and peasants" could not develop as it should have.

Tang Pingshan gives an even more precise characterization of what the "only correct line" looked like in reality:

> "... *We sacrificed the interests of the workers and peasants in practice* ... After lengthy negotiations with us, the government did not as much as promulgate a trade-union law ... The government did not accept the demands of the peasantry, which we presented to it in the name of various social organizations. When conflicts arose between the large landowners and the poor peasants, the government always took the side of the former."

How could all this happen? Tang Pingshan cautiously names two reasons:

(a) *"The left leaders are not capable of consolidating and extending their influence by means of political power"*;

(b) *The right wing "won the possibility to act, partly* as a result of our wrong tactic".

10. Such are the political relations that received the pompous title of the "bloc of four classes". Such "blocs" abound in the revolutionary as well as the parliamentary history of bourgeois countries: the big bourgeoisie leads the petty-bourgeois democrats, the phrase-mongers of the national united front, behind it, and the latter, in turn, confuse the workers and drag them along behind the bourgeoisie. When the proletarian "tail", despite the efforts of the petty-bourgeois phrase-mongers, begins to stir too violently, the bourgeoisie orders its generals to stamp on it. Then the opportunists observe with an air of profundity that the bourgeoisie has "betrayed" the national cause.

11. But did not the Chinese bourgeoisie "nevertheless" fight against imperialism? This argument too is an empty commonplace. The compromisers of every country, in similar cases, have always assured the workers that the liberal bourgeoisie is fighting against reaction. The Chinese bourgeoisie utilized the petty-bourgeois democracy only in order to conclude an alliance with imperialism against the workers. The Northern expedition only served to strengthen the bourgeoisie and weaken the workers. A tactic that prepared such a result is a false tactic. "We sacrificed the interests of the workers and peasants in practice," says Tang Pingshan. What for? To support the bloc of four classes. And the results? A colossal success of the bourgeois counter-revolution, the consolidation of shattered imperialism, the weakening of the USSR. Such a policy is criminal. Unless it is mercilessly condemned, we cannot take a step forward.

The Theses Justify a Line for which there is no Justification

12. The theses endeavour even now to justify the policy which united the party of the proletariat with the big bourgeoisie within the framework of one organization, the Guomindang, where the whole leadership was in the hands of the bourgeoisie. The theses declare: "This was the line ... for the utilization of the rights, their connections and experiences,

in so far as they submitted [!] to the discipline of the Guomindang." Now we know very well how the bourgeoisie submitted to "discipline" and how the proletariat utilized the rights, that is, the big and middle bourgeoisie, their "connections" (with the imperialists) and their "experiences" (in strangling and shooting the workers). The story of this "utilization" is written in the book of the Chinese Revolution with letters of blood. But this does not prevent the theses from saying: "The subsequent events fully confirmed the correctness of this line." Further than this no one can go!

From an enormous counter-revolutionary *coup d'état*, the theses of Stalin draw the positively miserable conclusion that the policy of "isolating the right" within the united Guomindang must be "replaced" by a policy of "determined struggle" against the right. All this after the right-wing "comrades" have begun to speak in the language of machine-guns.

13. The theses refer, to be sure, to a "previous prediction" on the inevitability of the bourgeoisie's withdrawal from the revolution. But are such prophecies by themselves sufficient for a Bolshevik policy? The prediction that the bourgeoisie will quit is an empty commonplace unless definite political conclusions are drawn from it. In the already quoted article, which approves the semi-official line of Martynov, Dan writes: "In a movement that embraces such antagonistic classes, *the united front cannot of course last forever*."[4]

So Dan also acknowledges the "inevitability of the bourgeoisie's withdrawal". In practice, however, the policy of Menshevism in the revolution consists of retaining the united front at any cost, as long as possible, at the price of adapting its own policy to the policy of the bourgeoisie, at the price of cutting down the slogans and the activity of the masses, and even, as in China, at the price of the organizational subordination of the workers' party to the political apparatus of the bourgeoisie. The Bolshevik way, however, consists of an unconditional political and organizational demarcation from the bourgeoisie, of a relentless exposure of the bourgeoisie from the very first steps of the revolution, of a destruction of all petty-bourgeois illusions about the united front with the bourgeoisie, of tireless struggle with the bourgeoisie for the leadership of the masses, of the merciless expulsion from the Communist Party of all those elements who sow vain hopes in the bourgeoisie or idealize them.

Two Paths and the Mistakes of the Past

14. The theses of comrade Stalin, to be sure, seek to oppose to each other the two paths of development of the Chinese revolution: one under the leadership of the bourgeoisie, with its suppression of the proletariat and an inevitable alliance with foreign imperialism; the other under the leadership of the proletariat against the bourgeoisie.

But in order that this second prospect of the bourgeois-democratic revolution should not remain an empty phrase, it must be said openly and plainly that the whole leadership of the Chinese Revolution up to now has been in irreconcilable contradiction to it. The Opposition has been and is subjected to a rabid criticism precisely because, from the very beginning, it brought to the fore the Leninist manner of putting the question, that is, the path of the struggle of the proletariat against the bourgeoisie for the leadership of the oppressed masses of city and country within the framework and on the foundation of the national-democratic revolution.

15. From the theses of Stalin it follows that the proletariat can separate itself from the bourgeoisie only after the latter has tossed it aside, disarmed it, beheaded it and crushed it under foot. But this is precisely the way the abortive revolution of 1848 developed, where the proletariat had no banner of its own, but followed at the heels of the petty-bourgeois democracy, which in turn trotted behind the liberal bourgeoisie and led the workers under the sabre of Cavaignac. Great though the real peculiarities of the Chinese situation may be, the fundamentals that characterized the development of the 1848 revolution have been repeated in the Chinese Revolution with such deadly precision as though neither the lessons of 1848, 1871, 1905 and 1917 nor those of the Communist Party of the Soviet Union and the Comintern had ever existed.

That Chiang Kai-shek played the role of a republican-liberal

Cavaignac has already become a commonplace. The theses of Stalin, following the Opposition, recognize this analogy. But the analogy must be supplemented. Cavaignac would have been impossible without the Ledru-Rollins, the Louis Blancs and the other phrasemongers of the all-inclusive national front. And who played these roles in China? Not only Wang Jingwei, but also the leaders of the Chinese Communist Party, above all their inspirers of the ECCI. Unless this is stated openly, explained and deeply impressed, the philosophy of the two paths of development will only serve to screen opportunism *à la* Louis Blanc and Martynov, that is, to prepare a repetition of the April tragedy at a new stage of the Chinese Revolution.

The Position of the Chinese Communist Party

16. In order to have the right to speak about the struggle for the Bolshevik path of the democratic revolution, one must possess the principal instrument of proletarian policy; *an independent proletarian party* which fights under its own banner and never permits its policy and organization to be dissolved in the policy and organization of other classes. Without assuring the complete theoretical, political and organizational independence of the Communist Party, all talk about "two paths" is a mockery of Bolshevism. The Chinese Communist Party, in this whole period, has not been *in alliance* with the revolutionary petty-bourgeois section of the Guomindang, but *in subordination* to the whole Guomindang, led in reality by the bourgeoisie which had the army and the power in its hands. The Communist Party submitted to the political discipline of Chiang Kai-shek. The Communist Party signed the obligation not to criticize Sun-Yat-Sen-ism, a petty-bourgeois theory which is directed not only against imperialism, but also against the class struggle. The Communist Party did not have its own press, that is, it lacked the principal weapon of an independent party. Under such conditions, to speak of the struggle of the proletariat for hegemony means to deceive oneself and others.

17. By what is the submissive, indistinct, and politically unworthy position of the Communist Party in Chiang Kai-shek's Guomindang to be explained? By the insistence upon

the unity of the national front under the actual leadership of the bourgeoisie which allegedly "could not" withdraw from the revolution (the school of Martynov), that is, the rejection in practice of the second, Bolshevik path of which the theses of Stalin speak as an afterthought, solely for camouflage purposes.

To justify such a policy by the necessity for an alliance of the workers and peasants, is to reduce this alliance itself to a phrase, to a screen for the commanding role of the bourgeoisie. The dependence of the Communist Party, an inevitable result of the "bloc of the four classes", was the main obstacle in the path of the workers' and peasants' movement, and therefore also of the real alliance between the proletariat and the peasantry, without which the victory of the Chinese Revolution cannot even be thought of.

18. What should the Communist Party do in the future?

In the theses, there is only a single sentence on this, but one capable of sowing the greatest confusion and causing irreparable harm. "... While fighting in the ranks of the revolutionary Guomindang," say Stalin's theses, "the Communist Party must *preserve its independence* more than ever before." Preserve? But to this day the Communist Party has had no such independence. Precisely its lack of independence is the source of all the evils and all the mistakes. In this fundamental question, the theses, instead of making an end once and for all to the practice of yesterday, propose to retain it "more than ever before". But this means that they want to retain the ideological, political and organizational dependence of the proletarian party upon a petty-bourgeois party, which is inevitably converted into an instrument of the big bourgeoisie.

In order to justify a false policy, one is forced to call dependence independence, and to demand the preservation of what ought to be buried for all time.

19. Chinese Bolshevism can rise only under a merciless self-criticism by the best elements of the Communist Party. To support them in this is our direct duty. The attempt to cover up the mistakes of the past by artificially curbing a discussion of them, will cause enormous harm, primarily to the Chinese Communist Party. If we do not help it to purge itself, in the

shortest period, from Menshevism and the Mensheviks, it will enter a prolonged crisis, with splits, desertions, and an embittered struggle of various groups. What is more, the heavy defeats of opportunism may clear a road to anarcho-syndicalist influences.

If, in spite of a workers' mass movement, in spite of the powerful rise of the trade unions, in spite of the revolutionary agrarian movement on the land, the Communist Party should remain as before an integral appendage to a bourgeois party, and what is more, should it enter the national government created by this bourgeois party, it would be better to say frankly: the time has not yet come for a Communist party in China. It is better not to constitute any Communist party at all than to discredit it so cruelly at the time of a revolution, that is, just at the time when the Party is being joined to the working masses with bonds of blood and when great traditions are being created that are destined to live for decades.

Who was Mistaken on the Tempo?

20. In Stalin's theses there is of course a whole section devoted to the "mistakes of the Opposition". Instead of hitting out at the right, that is, at the mistakes of Stalin himself, the theses are intent upon striking at the left, thereby deepening the mistakes, piling up confusion, making the way out more difficult, and driving the line of the leadership down into the swamp of compromise.

21. The main accusation: the Opposition "does not understand that the revolution in China cannot develop at a rapid tempo". For some reason or other, the theses drag in here the tempo of the October Revolution. If the question of tempo is raised, it must not be measured with the external yardstick of the October Revolution, but with the internal class relationships of the Chinese Revolution itself. The Chinese bourgeoisie, as is known, paid no attention to the precepts about a slow tempo. In April 1927, it considered it quite opportune to throw off the mask of the united front which had served it so well, in order to open an attack upon the revolution with all its strength. The Communist Party, the proletariat, as well as the Left Guomindang people, showed themselves completely

unprepared for this blow. Why? Because the leadership counted upon a slower tempo, because it remained hopelessly behindhand, because it was infected with *chvostism*.

On April 23, that is, after the *coup d'état* by Chiang Kai-shek, the Central Committee of the Guomindang, together with the "left" Wuhan government, published a manifesto, which said:

> "*It only remains for us to regret* [!] *that we did not act when there was still time*. For that we apologize [!] sincerely."[5]

In these doleful and whining avowals lies, against the will of their authors, a pitiless refutation of the Stalinist philosophy on the "tempo" of the Chinese Revolution.

22. We continued to maintain the bloc with the bourgeoisie at a time when the working masses were driving towards independent struggle. We attempted to utilize the experiences of the "rights" and became playthings in their hands. We carried on an ostrich policy in the press, by suppressing and concealing from our own party the first *coup d'état* by Chiang Kai-shek in March 1926, the shootings of workers and peasants, and in general all the facts that marked the counter-revolutionary character of the Guomindang leadership. We neglected to look after the independence of our own party. We founded no newspaper for it. "We sacrificed the interests of the workers and peasants in practice" (Tang Pingshan). We did not take a single serious step to win over the soldiers. We allowed the Chiang Kai-shek band to establish a "military dictatorship of the centre", that is, a dictatorship of the bourgeois counter-revolution. On the very eve of the *coup d'état* we blew the trumpets for Chiang Kai-shek. We declared that he had "submitted to discipline", and that we had succeeded "by a skilful tactical manoeuvre in forestalling an abrupt turn to the right that threatened the Chinese revolution."[6] We remained behind the events all along the line. At every step we lost in tempo to the benefit of the bourgeoisie. In this way we prepared the most favourable conditions for the bourgeois counter-revolution. The Left Guomindang at least offers us its "sincere apology". The theses of Stalin, on the contrary, draw from this whole chain of truly unparalleled chvostist mistakes the

remarkable conclusion that the Opposition demands. a too rapid tempo.

23. Ever more frequently one hears accusations at our party meetings against the "ultra-left" Shanghaiers and in general against the Chinese workers for having provoked Chiang Kai-shek by their "excesses". No one cites any examples; and what would they prove, anyway? Not a single real people's revolution, drawing millions into its vortex, proceeds without so-called "excesses". A policy which seeks to prescribe for the masses just awakening a line of march that will not disturb the bourgeois "order" is a policy of incurable philistines. It will always break its head against the logic of civil war when, while pronouncing belated curses upon the Cavaignacs and Kornilovs, it denounces at the same time the alleged "excesses" of the left.

The "mistake" of the Chinese workers lies in the fact that the critical moment of the revolution found them unprepared, unorganized and unarmed. But that is not their mistake, it is their misfortune. The responsibility for it falls entirely upon a bad leadership, which let every interval pass.

Does a New Revolutionary Centre Already Exist or Must One First be Created?

24. On the present state of the Chinese revolution, the theses proclaim: "Chiang Kai-shek's *coup d'état* means that there will now be two camps, two governments, two armies, two centres in the South: a revolutionary centre in Wuhan and a counter-revolutionary centre in Nanking." What an inexact, superficial, vulgar characterization! It is not simply a question of two halves of the Guomindang but of a new grouping of class forces. To believe that the Wuhan government is already a finished centre, which will simply continue the revolution from the point where it was brought to a stop and beaten to the ground by Chiang Kai-shek, is to regard the counter-revolutionary *coup d'état* in April as a personal "desertion", an "episode"; in a word, it is to understand nothing.

The workers were not simply crushed. They were crushed by those who led them. Can one believe that the masses will now follow the Left Guomindang with the same confidence that they accorded the whole Guomindang yesterday? From now on the struggle must be conducted not only against the former militarists allied with imperialism, but also against the "national" bourgeoisie which, as a result of our radically incorrect policy, has captured the military apparatus and considerable sections of the army.

For the struggle on a new, higher stage of the revolution, the deceived masses must above all be inspired with confidence in themselves, and the not yet awakened masses must be aroused. For this, it must first of all be demonstrated that not a trace has been left of that disgraceful policy which "sacrificed the interests of the workers and peasants" (cf. Tang Pingshan) in order to support the bloc of the four classes. Anyone who will lean in the direction of this policy must be mercilessly driven out of the Chinese Communist Party.

The miserably superficial and bureaucratic idea must be thrown aside that now, after the sanguinary experiences, millions of workers and peasants can be set in motion and led if only the "banner" of the Guomindang is waved around in the air a little. (We will surrender the blue banner of the Guomindang to nobody! cries Bukharin.)

No, the masses need a revolutionary program and a fighting organization which grows out of their own ranks and contains within itself the guarantee of contact with the masses and of loyalty to them. The Wuhan authorities are not enough for this: workers', peasants' and soldiers' soviets are needed for this, soviets of the toilers.

Soviets and the Arming of the Workers and Peasants

25. After rejecting the vital and indispensable slogan of soviets, the theses of comrade Stalin declare somewhat unexpectedly that the principal "antidote [?] to the counter-revolution is the arming of the workers and peasants". The arming of the workers is undoubtedly a necessary thing. We will have no differences at all on this point. But how are we to explain why it was considered correct up to now to arm the workers to a "minimum" extent for the welfare of the

revolution? that the representatives of the Comintern actually *opposed* the arming of the workers? (cf. the letter of the four comrades to the delegation of the CPSU in the Comintern); that in spite of the full possibility of arming themselves the workers found themselves unarmed at the moment of the *coup d'état*? All this is to be explained by the desire not to break with Chiang Kai-shek, not to offend Chiang Kai-shek, not to push him to the right. The marvelous "antidote" was lacking precisely on the day when it was most needed. Today the workers are not arming themselves in Wuhan either—so as "not to drive away" Wang Jingwei.

26. The arming of the workers and peasants is an excellent thing. But one must be logical. In Southern China there are already armed peasants; they are the so-called National armies. Yet, far from being an "antidote to the counter-revolution", they have been its tool. Why? Because the political leadership, instead of embracing the masses of the army through soldiers' soviets has contented itself with a purely external copy of our political departments and commissars, which, without an independent revolutionary party and without soldiers' soviets, have been transformed into an empty camouflage for bourgeois militarism.

27. The theses of Stalin reject the slogan of soviets with the argument that it would be a "slogan of struggle against the government of the revolutionary Guomindang". But in that case, what is the meaning of the words: "The principal antidote to the counter-revolution is the arming of the workers and peasants"? Against whom will the workers and peasants arm themselves? Will it not be against the governmental authority of the revolutionary Guomindang?

The slogan of arming the workers and peasants, if it is not a phrase, a subterfuge, a masquerade, but a call to action, is not less sharp in character than the slogan of workers' and peasants' soviets. Is it likely that the armed masses will tolerate at their side or over them the governmental authority of a bureaucracy alien and hostile to them? The real arming of the workers and peasants under present circumstances inevitably involves the formation of soviets.

28. Further: Who will arm the masses? Who will direct the armed men?

So long as the national armies marched forward and the Northern armies yielded ground, the arming of the workers could proceed with relative ease. The timely organization of workers', peasants' and soldiers' soviets would have meant a real "antidote" to the counter-revolution. Unfortunately, the mistakes of the past are irreparable. The whole situation has now taken a sharp turn for the worse. The few weapons seized spontaneously by the workers (are not these the "excesses" that are spoken of?) have been torn from them. The advance to the North has been suspended. Under these conditions the arming of the workers and peasants is a labourious and difficult task. To declare that the time for the soviets has not yet arrived and at the same time to launch the slogan for arming the workers and peasants, is to sow confusion. Only the soviets, at a further development of the revolution, can become the organs capable of really conducting the arming of the workers and of directing these armed masses.

Why is it Impossible to Form Soviets?

29. To this, the theses reply: "In the first place soviets cannot be created at any convenient moment, they are created only in the period of a special rise of the revolutionary wave." If these words have any sense at all, it is this: We let pass the favourable moment when we did not call upon the masses to create soviets at the beginning of the last period of powerful revolutionary rise. Once again: the mistakes of the past are irreparable. If we are of the opinion that the Chinese Revolution has been crushed for a long time, then the slogan of soviets will naturally find no echo in the masses. But all the more unfounded then is the slogan of the arming of the workers and peasants. We do not believe, however, that the consequences of the false policy pursued are so heavy and profound. There are many facts that speak for the possibility and the likelihood of a new revolutionary rise in the near future. Among other things, it is indicated by the fact that Chiang Kai-shek is forced to flirt with the masses, to promise the workers the eight-hour day, and all

sorts of relief to the peasants, etc. In the event of a further extension of the agrarian movement and a turning of the petty-bourgeois masses of the city against Chiang Kai-shek as an open agent of imperialism, more favourable conditions can arise in the near future under which the now battered proletarian vanguard will reassemble the ranks of the toilers for a new offensive. Whether this will take place a month sooner or later is of no concern; in any case we must prepare for it now with our own program and our own organizations. In other words: *the slogan of soviets will henceforth accompany the whole further course of the Chinese revolution and reflect its destinies.*

30. "In the second place," say the theses, "soviets are not formed for chattering; they are created primarily as organs of struggle against the existing state power, and for the conquest of power." That soviets are not created for chattering is perhaps the only correct point in the theses. But a revolutionist does not propose the arming of the workers and peasants for chattering either. Whoever says here: at the present stage only chatter can be the result of soviets, but on the contrary, something serious will come out of the arming of the workers and peasants, is either making fun of himself or of others.

31. A third argument: since there is now a series of Left Guomindang organizations in Wuhan, which in their solemn manifesto of April 23 apologized for having overslept the *coup d'état* of Chiang Kai-shek, the theses draw the conclusion: the creation of soviets would mean an insurrection against the Left Guomindang, "for there is no other governmental authority in this region at present than that of the revolutionary Guomindang".

These words fairly reek with the apparatus-like, bureaucratic conception of revolutionary authority. The government is not regarded as the expression and consolidation of the developing struggle of the classes, but as the self-sufficient expression of the will of the Guomindang. The classes come and go but the continuity of the Guomindang goes on for ever. But it is not enough to call Wuhan the centre of the revolution for it really to be that. The provincial Guomindang of Chiang Kai-shek had an old, reactionary, mercenary bureaucracy at its disposal. What has the Left Guomindang? For the time being, nothing or almost nothing. The slogan of soviets is a call for the creation of real organs of the new state power right through the transitional régime of a dual government.

32. And what will be the attitude of the soviets to the "government of the revolutionary Guomindang", allegedly the "only" governmental authority "in this region"? A truly classic question! The attitude of the soviets to the revolutionary Guomindang will correspond to the attitude of the revolutionary Guomindang to the soviets. In other words: to the extent that the soviets arise, arm themselves, consolidate themselves, they will tolerate over them only such a government as bases itself upon the armed workers and peasants. What makes the soviet system valuable is the fact that, especially in directly revolutionary epochs, it furnishes the best means of guaranteeing agreement between the central and local government authorities.

33. Comrade Stalin, as far back as 1925, called the Guomindang a "workers' and peasants' party" (!?).[7] This definition has nothing in common with Marxism. But it is clear that with this incorrect formulation comrade Stalin wanted to express the idea that the basis of the Guomindang is an anti-bourgeois alliance of the workers and peasants. This was absolutely false for the period in which it was said: the workers and peasants, it is true, did follow the Guomindang, but they were led by the bourgeoisie and we know where it led them. Such a party is called bourgeois, and not workers' and peasants'. After the "withdrawal" of the bourgeoisie (that is, after it massacred the unarmed and unprepared proletariat), the revolution, according to Stalin, passes over to a new stage, in which it is to be led by the Left Guomindang, that is, by one, at least so we are to assume, that will finally realize the Stalinist idea of the "workers' and peasants' party". The question arises: why then will the creation of workers' and peasants' soviets mean a war against the authority of the workers' and peasants' Guomindang?

34. Another argument: To call for the creation of soviets "means to hand the enemies of the Chinese people a new

weapon to combat the revolution, to manufacture new legends and to pretend that there is no national revolution in China, but an artificial transplanting of Moscow sovietization".

This stupefying argument means that if we develop, extend and deepen the revolutionary movement of the masses, the enemies of the Chinese people will redouble their efforts to calumniate it. This argument has no other sense. Therefore it has no sense at all.

Perhaps the theses have not in mind the enemies of the Chinese people, but the fear of the popular masses themselves of a Moscow sovietization? But on what is such a consideration based? It is well known that all the varieties of the "national" bourgeoisie, right, centre and left, zealously smear themselves with a protective Muscovite colouration in all their political work: they create commissars, political army posts, political departments, plenums of the central committee, control commissions, etc. The Chinese bourgeoisie is not at all afraid of transplanting Muscovite forms, which it carefully debases to serve its own class aims. But why do they apply them? Not out of love for Moscow, but rather because they are popular with the masses of the people. The Chinese peasant knows that the soviets gave the land to the Russian peasant, and whoever does not know this ought to learn it. The Chinese workers know that the soviets guaranteed the liberty of the Russian proletariat. The experience of the counter-revolution of Chiang Kai-shek must have made the advanced workers understand that without an independent organization embracing the whole proletariat and assuring its collaboration with the oppressed masses in the city and on the land, the revolution cannot triumph. The creation of soviets follows for the Chinese masses from their own experience, and is far from being an "artificially transplanted sovietization" for them. A policy that is afraid to call things by their right name is a false policy. One must be guided by the revolutionary masses and by the objective needs of the revolution, but not by what the enemy will say.

35. It is said: The Hankow government is nevertheless a fact. Feng Yuxiang is a fact, Tang Shengzhi is a fact, and they have armed forces at their disposal; neither the Wuhan

government nor Feng Yuxiang, nor Tang Shengzhi wants soviets. To create soviets would mean to break with these allies. Although this argument is not openly formulated in the theses, it is nevertheless decisive for many comrades. We have already heard from Stalin on the Hankow government: the "revolutionary centre", the "only governmental authority". At the same time an advertising campaign is launched for Feng Yuxiang in our party meetings: "a former worker", "a faithful revolutionist", "a reliable man", etc. All this is a repetition of the past mistakes under circumstances in which these mistakes can become even more disastrous. The Hankow government and the army command can be against the soviets only because they will have nothing to do with a radical agrarian program, with a real break with the large landowners and the bourgeoisie, because they secretly cherish the thought of a compromise with the right. But then it becomes all the more important to form soviets. This is the only way to push the revolutionary elements of Hankow to the left and force the counter-revolutionists to retire.

36. But even if the soviets do not carry on a war with the "only" government of Hankow, will they not still bring with them the elements of dual power? Without a doubt. Whoever is really for the course towards a workers' and peasants' government, not only in words but in deeds, must understand that this course leads through a certain period of dual power. How long this period will last, what concrete forms it will assume, will depend upon how the "only" government in Hankow conducts itself, upon the independence and initiative of the Communist Party, upon how rapidly the soviets develop, etc. It will be our task, in any case, to strengthen the element of the workers and peasants in the dual power and by that provide the genuine workers' and peasants' soviet government with a fully developed democratic program.

37. But dozens of foreign warships are anchored in the Yangtze river which can sweep away Shanghai, Hankow, etc. Is it not insanity to form soviets under such conditions? This argument too is, of course, not formulated in Stalin's theses, but it is paraded around everywhere in Party meetings

(Martynov, Yaroslavsky and others). The school of Martynov would like to kill the idea of the soviets with fear of the British naval artillery. This artifice is not a new one. In 1917, the Social Revolutionists and the Mensheviks sought to frighten us by declaring that the seizure of power by the soviets would mean the occupation of Kronstadt and Petrograd by the Allies. We answered: only the deepening of the revolution can save it. Foreign imperialism will only reconcile itself to such a "revolution" as strengthens its own positions in China at the price of a few concessions to the Chinese bourgeoisie. Every real people's revolution that undermines the colonial foundation of imperialism will inevitably meet with the latter's furious resistance. We did try to stop halfway, but this "only correct line" protected Nanking from the cannon of imperialism as little as it did the Chinese workers from the machine-guns of Chiang Kai-shek. Only the transition of the Chinese revolution to the phase of real mass action, only the formation of workers', peasants' and soldiers' soviets, only the deepening of the social program of the revolution, are capable, as our own experiences prove, of bringing confusion into the ranks of the foreign armed forces by arousing their sympathy for the soviets and thus really protecting the revolution from blows from without.

What do the Theses of Stalin Propose in Place of Soviets?

38. The creation of "revolutionary peasant committees, workers' trade unions, and other mass organizations as preparatory elements for the soviets of the future". What should be the course of these organizations? We do not find a single word on this in the theses. The phrase that these are "preparatory elements for the soviets of the future" is only a phrase and nothing more. What will these organizations do now? They will have to conduct strikes, boycotts, break the backbone of the bureaucratic apparatus, annihilate the counter-revolutionary military bands, drive out the large landowners, disarm the detachments of the usurers and the rich peasants, arm the workers and peasants, in a word, solve all the problems of the democratic and agrarian revolution that are on the order

of the day, and in this way raise themselves to the position of local organs of power. But then they will be soviets, only of a kind that are badly suited to their tasks. The theses therefore propose, if these proposals are to be taken seriously at all, to create substitutes for soviets, instead of soviets themselves.

39. During all the preceding mass movements, the trade unions were compelled to fulfil functions closely approaching the functions of soviets (Hong Kong, Shanghai, and elsewhere). But these were precisely the functions for which the trade unions were entirely insufficient. They embrace a too small number of workers. They do not at all embrace the petty-bourgeois masses in the city that incline towards the proletariat. But such tasks as the carrying through of strikes with the least possible losses to the poorer population of the city, the distribution of provisions, participation in tax policy, participation in the formation of armed forces, to say nothing of carrying through the agrarian revolution in the provinces, can be accomplished with the necessary sweep only when the directing organization embraces not only all the sections of the proletariat, but connects them intimately in the course of its activities with the poor population in the city and country. One would at least think that the military *coup d'état* of Chiang Kai-shek had finally hammered into the mind of every revolutionist the fact that trade unions separated from the army are one thing, and united workers' and soldiers' soviets, on the other hand, are quite another thing. Revolutionary trade unions and peasants' committees can arouse the hatred of the enemy no less than soviets. But they are far less capable than soviets of warding off its blows.

If we are to speak seriously of the alliance of the proletariat with the oppressed masses in the city and country—not of an "alliance" between the leaders, a semi-adulterated alliance through dubious representatives, but of a real fighting alliance built and steeled in the struggles of the masses against the enemy —then such an alliance can have no other organizational form than that of soviets. This can be denied only by those who rely more upon compromising leaders than upon the revolutionary masses below.

Should we Break with the Left Guomindang?

From the foregoing remarks may be seen how ill-founded are the whispers about a break of the Communist Party with the Guomindang. "This is tantamount," say the theses, "to deserting the field of struggle and leaving our allies in the Guomindang in the lurch to the delight of the enemies of the revolution." These pathetic lines are quite out of place. It is not a question of a break but of preparing a bloc, not on the basis of subordination but on the basis of a genuine equality of rights. A revolutionary Guomindang has yet to be formed. We are in favour of the Communists working inside the Guomindang and patiently drawing the workers and peasants over to their side. The Communist Party can gain a petty-bourgeois ally, not by prostrating itself before the Guomindang at every one of its vacillations, but only if it appeals to the workers openly and directly, in its own name, under its own banner, organizes them around it and shows the Guomindang by example and by deed what a party of the masses is, by supporting every forward step of the Guomindang, by relentlessly unmasking every vacillation, every step backward, and by creating a real revolutionary foundation for a bloc with the Guomindang in the form of workers', peasants' and soldiers' soviets.

40. It is absurd to assert that the Opposition stands for the "political isolation" of the Communist Party. This assertion contains just as much truth as the one that the Opposition stood for withdrawing from the British trade unions. Both accusations have only served to mask the bloc with the right Guomindang and with the traitorous General Council. The Opposition is energetically in favour of strengthening and developing the bloc with the revolutionary elements of the Guomindang, for a compact fighting alliance of the workers with the poor population of the city and country, for the course towards the revolutionary dictatorship of the workers, peasants and the urban petty-bourgeoisie.

For this it is necessary:

a. to recognize as disastrous such forms of the bloc in which the Communist Party sacrifices the interests of the workers and peasants to the utopian aim of holding the bourgeoisie in the camp of the national revolution;

b. to reject categorically such forms of the bloc in which the Communist Party hauls down its banner and sacrifices the growth of its own influence and its own authority in the interest of its allies;
c. to approve a bloc with clearly formulated common tasks, but not to base it upon misunderstanding, diplomatic manoeuvres, sycophancy and hypocrisy;
d. to lay down the conditions and limits of the bloc with thorough precision and let them be known to all;
e. for the Communist Party to retain full freedom of criticism, and to watch over its allies with no less vigilance than over an enemy, without forgetting for a moment that an ally who bases himself upon other classes or depends upon other classes is only a temporary confederate who can be transformed by the force of circumstances into an opponent and an enemy;
f. to set the connection with the petty-bourgeois masses higher than a connection with their party leaders;
g. finally, to rely only upon ourselves, upon our own organization, arms and power.

Only by observing these conditions will a really revolutionary bloc of the Communist Party with the Guomindang become possible, not a bloc of the leaders, which vacillates and is subject to contingencies, but a bloc based upon all the oppressed masses of the city and country under the political hegemony of the proletarian vanguard.

The Problems of the Chinese Revolution and the Anglo-Russian Committee

41. In the direction of the Chinese Revolution we are confronted not by tactical errors, but by a radically false line. This follows clearly from everything that has been presented above. It becomes still clearer when the policy in China is compared with our policy towards the Anglo-Russian Committee. In the latter case the inconsistency of the

opportunistic line did not express itself so tragically as in China, but no less completely and convincingly.

42. In England, as in China, the line was directed towards a rapproachement with the "solid" leaders, based on personal relations, on diplomatic combinations, while renouncing in practice the deepening of the abyss between the revolutionary or leftward-developing masses and the traitorous leaders. We ran after Chiang Kai-shek and thereby drove the Chinese Communists to accept the dictatorial conditions put by Chiang Kai-shek to the Communist Party. In so far as the representatives of the All-Russian Central Council of Trade Unions ran after Purcell, Hicks, Citrine and Company and adopted in principle the position of neutrality in the trade-union movement, they recognized the General Council as the only representative of the British proletariat and obligated themselves not to interfere in the affairs of the British labour movement.

43. The decisions of the Berlin Conference of the Anglo-Russian Committee mean our renunciation of support in the future to strikers against the will of avowed strikebreakers. They are tantamount to a condemnation and a flat betrayal of the trade-union minority, all of whose activity is directed against the traitors whom we have recognized as the sole representatives of the English working class. Finally, the solemn proclamation of "non-interference" signifies our capitulation in principle to the national narrowness of the labour movement in its most backward and most conservative form.

44. Chiang Kai-shek accuses us of interfering in the internal affairs of China just as Citrine accuses us of interfering in the internal affairs of the trade unions. Both accusations are only transcriptions of the accusation of world imperialism against a workers' state which dares to interest itself in the fate of the oppressed masses of the whole world. In this case as in others, Chiang Kai-shek, like Citrine, under different conditions and at different posts, remain the agents of imperialism despite temporary conflicts with it. If we chase after collaboration with such "leaders", we are forced ever more to restrict, to limit and to emasculate our methods of revolutionary mobilization.

45. Through our false policy we not only helped the General Council to maintain its tottering positions after the strike

betrayal, but, what is more, we furnished it with all the necessary weapons for putting impudent demands to us which we meekly accepted. Under the tinkling of phrases about "hegemony", we acted in the Chinese Revolution and the British labour movement as if we were morally vanquished, and by that we prepared our material defeat. An opportunist deviation is always accompanied by a loss of faith in one's own line.

46. The businessmen of the General Council, having received a guarantee of non-interference from the All-Russian Central Council of Trade Unions, are undoubtedly persuading Chamberlain that their method of struggle against Bolshevik propaganda is far more effective than ultimatums and threats. Chamberlain, however, prefers the combined method and combines the diplomacy of the General Council with the violence of British imperialism.

47. If it is alleged against the Opposition that Baldwin or Chamberlain "also" wants the dissolution of the Anglo-Russian Committee, then one understands nothing at all of the political mechanics of the bourgeoisie. Baldwin justly feared and still fears the harmful influence of the Soviet trade unions upon the leftward-developing labour movement of Britain. The British bourgeoisie set its pressure upon the General Council against the pressure of the All-Russian Central Council of Trade Unions upon the traitorous leaders of the trade unions, and on this field the bourgeoisie triumphed all along the line. The General Council refused to accept money from the Soviet trade unions and to confer with them on the question of aid for the mine workers. In exercising its pressure upon the General Council, the British bourgeoisie, through it, exerted pressure upon the All-Russian Central Council of Trade Unions and at the Berlin Conference obtained from the latter's representatives an unprecedented capitulation on the fundamental questions of the class struggle. An Anglo-Russian Committee *of this kind* only serves the British bourgeoisie (cf. the declaration of *The Times*). This will not hinder it from continuing its pressure in the future upon the General Council, and demanding of it a break with the All-Russian Central Council of Trade Unions, for by such a policy of pressure and blackmail the British bourgeoisie wins

everything we lose by our senseless and unprincipled conduct.

48. The insinuations that Chiang Kai-shek is "in solidarity" with the Opposition, because he wants to drive the Communists out of the Guomindang, have the same value. A remark by Chiang Kai-shek is being circulated in which he is supposed to have said to another general that he agrees with the Opposition in the CPSU on this point. In the text of the document from which this "quotation" was picked out, the words of Chiang Kai-shek are not adduced as an expression of his views, but as a manifestation of his readiness and aptitude to deceit, to falsehood, and even to disguise himself for a few days as a "Left Communist" in order to be better able to stab us in the back. Still more, the document in question is one long indictment against the line and the work of the Comintern's representatives in China. Instead of picking quotations out of the document and giving them a sense contrary to that contained in the text, it would be better to make the document itself known to the Comintern. Leave aside, however, the misuse of alleged "quotations" and there remains the "coincidence" that Chiang Kai-shek has always been against a bloc with the Communists, while we are against a bloc with Chiang Kai-shek. The school of Martynov draws from this the conclusion that the policy of the Opposition "generally" serves the reaction. This accusation is not new either. The whole development of Bolshevism in Russia proceeded under the accompaniment of Menshevik accusations that the Bolsheviks were playing the game of the reaction, that they were aiding the monarchy against the Kadets, the Kadets against the SRs and Mensheviks, and so on without end. Renaudel accuses the French Communists of rendering aid to Poincaré when they attack the bloc of the radicals and the Socialists. The German Social Democrats have more than once pretended that our refusal to enter the League of Nations plays the game of the extreme imperialists, etc., etc.

The fact that the big bourgeoisie, represented by Chiang Kai-shek, needs to break with the proletariat, and the revolutionary proletariat on the other hand needs to break with bourgeoisie, is not an evidence of their solidarity, but of the irreconcilable class antagonism between them. The hopeless compromisers stand between the bourgeoisie and the proletariat and accuse both the "extreme" wings of disrupting the national front and rendering assistance to the reaction. To accuse the Opposition of playing the game of Chamberlain, Thomas or Chiang Kai-shek is to show a narrow-minded opportunism, and at the same time to recognize involuntarily the proletarian and revolutionary character of our political line.

49. The Berlin Conference of the Anglo-Russian Committee which coincided with the beginning of British intervention in China, did not even dare to allude to the question of effective measures to take against the hangman's work of British imperialism in the Far East. Could a more striking proof be found that the Anglo-Russian Committee is incapable of moving as much as a finger towards really preventing war? But it is not simply useless. It has brought immeasurable harm to the revolutionary movement, like every illusion and hypocrisy. By referring to its collaboration with the All-Russian Central Council of Trade Unions in the "struggle for peace", the General Council is able to soothe and lull the consciousness of the British proletariat, stirred by the danger of war. The All-Russian Central Council of Trade Unions now appears before the British working class and the working class of the whole world as a sort of guarantor for the international policy of the traitors of the General Council. The criticism directed by the revolutionary elements in Britain against the General Council thereby becomes weakened and blunted. Thanks to Purcell, Hicks and Company, the MacDonalds and Thomases get the possibility of keeping the working masses in a stupor up to the threshold of war itself, in order to call upon them then for the defence of the democratic fatherland. When comrade Tomsky, in his last interview (*Pravda,* May 8), criticized the Thomases, Havelock Wilsons and the other hirelings of the Stock Exchange, he did not mention by a single word the subversive, disintegrating, lulling, and therefore much more pernicious work of Purcell, Hicks and Company. These "allies" are not mentioned by name in the interview as though they do not even exist. Then why a bloc with them? But they do exist.

Without them Thomas does not exist politically. Without Thomas there exists no Baldwin, that is, the capitalist régime in England. Contrary to our best intentions, our support of the bloc with Purcell is actually support of the whole British régime and the facilitation of its work in China. After all that has happened, this is clear to every revolutionist who has gone through the school of Lenin. In a like manner, our collaboration with Chiang Kai-shek blunted the class vigilance of the Chinese proletariat, and thereby facilitated the April *coup d'état.*

The Theory of Stages and the Theory of Socialism in One Country

50. The *chvostist* theory of "stages" or "steps" repeatedly proclaimed by Stalin in recent times, has served as the motivation in principle for the opportunist tactic. If the complete organizational and political independence of the Chinese Communist Party is demanded, it means that steps are being skipped over. If soviet organizations are demanded for drawing the worker and peasant masses into the civil war, it means that "stages" are being skipped over. If the dissolution of the political bloc with the traitors of the General Council, who are now carrying on the basest work, is demanded, it means that stages are being skipped over. The conservative bourgeois-national Guomindang government, the military command of Chiang Kai-shek, the General Council—in a word, any one of the institutions created by the pressure of the possessing and ruling classes, and constituting a barrier for the revolutionary class movement, becomes, according to this theory, a great historical stage, to which one's policy must be adapted until "the masses themselves" pass through it. Once we set out on this road, our policy must be inevitably transformed from a revolutionary factor into a conservative one. The course of the Chinese revolution and the fate of the Anglo-Russian Committee are an imminent warning in this regard.

51. Such facts as the defeat of the great strikes of the British proletariat last year, as the Chinese Revolution this year, cannot go by without consequences for the international labour movement, just as the defeat of the German proletariat in the

autumn of 1923 did not pass without leaving its traces. An unavoidable temporary weakening of the revolutionary positions is in itself a great evil. It can become irreparable for a long time if the orientation is wrong, if the strategic line is false. Precisely now, in the period of a temporary revolutionary ebb, the struggle against all manifestations of opportunism and national limitedness and for the line of revolutionary internationalism is more necessary than ever.

By recognizing the principle of non-interference, our delegation, regardless of its intentions, promotes the most conservative, most defeatist tendencies in the working class. There is nothing perplexing in the fact that the most backward and weariest sections of the workers of the USSR consider interference in the British strike struggle or the Chinese revolution a mistake. Ever more frequently they argue: "Are we not taught that we can build up socialism in our country, even without the victory of the revolution in other countries, if only there no intervention? Then we must carry on such a policy as does not provoke intervention. Our interference in British and Chinese affairs is a mistake, because without yielding positive results it drives the world bourgeoisie on to the road of military intervention and thus threatens the construction of socialism in our country."

There is no doubt and there can be none that now, after the new defeats of the international revolutionary movement, the theory of socialism in one country will serve, independent of the will of its creators, to justify, to motivate and to sanctify all the tendencies directed towards restricting the revolutionary objectives, towards quenching the ardour of the struggle, towards a national and conservative narrowness.

The slightest digression towards the side of "non-interference", whether covered or not with the theory of socialism in one country, only increases the imperialist danger instead of diminishing it.

It is perfectly clear and incontestable with regard to the Chinese Revolution that only a deeper mass impulsion, a more radical social program, the slogan of the workers' and peasants' soviets, can seriously shield the revolution from a military attack from without. Only a revolution on whose banner the toilers and oppressed write plainly their own demands is capable of gripping the feelings not only of the international proletariat but also of the soldiers of capital. We know this well enough from our own experiences. We saw and proved it in the years of the civil war at Archangel, Odessa and elsewhere. The compromising and traitorous leadership did not protect Nanking from destruction. It facilitated the penetration of the enemy ships into the Yangtze. A revolutionary leadership, with a powerful social movement, can make the waters of the Yangtze too hot for the ships of Lloyd George, Chamberlain and MacDonald. In any case, this is the only way and the only hope of defence.

The extension of the soviet front is simultaneously the best defence of the USSR. Under the present circumstances, the talk that our international position has become worse, or can in any way become worse, as a result of some kind of "left" mistake, sounds absurd. If our position has grown worse, it is a result of the defeat of the Chinese Revolution, a historical and international event, regardless of whether or not we interfere in it. Were we not to interfere in the intervention of imperialism, we would only facilitate its work—against China, and against ourselves as well. But there is a difference between interference and interference. The falsest and most dangerous interference consists of the endeavour to halt the development of the revolution half-way. The struggle for peace occupies the centre of our international policy. But even the most extreme representative of the Martynov school would never dare to contend that our policy of peace can be in contradiction to the development of the Chinese Revolution, or inversely, that its development can be in contradiction to our policy of peace. The one supplements the other. The best way to defend the USSR is to vanquish the Chiang Kai-shek counter-revolution and to raise the movement to a higher stage. Whoever rejects soviets for China under such conditions, disarms the Chinese Revolution. Whoever proclaims the principle of non-interference in the relations of the European proletariat weakens its revolutionary vanguard. Both weaken the position of the USSR, the principal fortress of the international proletariat.

Thus we see how one mistake is heaped upon the others and together produce a line which digresses ever more from the line of Bolshevism. Critical voices and warnings are regarded as obstructions. The shifting of the official line towards the right is supplemented by blows at the left. To continue on this path would involve the greatest dangers for the soviet state as well as for the Comintern. Were we to conceal these dangers from the international proletarian vanguard, we would be betraying the banner of Communism.

* * *

We do not doubt for a moment that the mistakes can be repaired, the deviations overcome, and the line rectified without violent crises and convulsions. The language of facts is all too eloquent, the lessons of experience all too plain. It is only necessary that our party, of the Soviet Union as well as of the International, obtains the full possibility to weigh the facts and draw the proper conclusions from them. We firmly believe that they will draw these conclusions in the spirit of revolutionary unity.

THE SPEECH OF COMRADE CHEN DUXIU ON THE TASKS OF THE CHINESE COMMUNIST PARTY

Epilogue May 17, 1927

52. What purpose does Marxism serve in politics? To understand that which is and to foresee that which will be. Foresight must be the foundation of action. We already know what has happened to the predictions of comrade Stalin: one week before the *coup d'état* of Chiang Kai-shek, he defended him and blew the trumpet for him by calling for the utilization of the right wing, its experiences, its connections (speech to the Moscow functionaries on April 5). In the theses analysed by us, Stalin gives another example of foresight which has also been tested by life. The central question of our criticism of Stalin's theses was formulated by us above as follows: "Does there already exist a new centre of the revolution or must one first be created?" Stalin contended that after the *coup d'état* of Chiang Kai-shek there were *"two governments, two armies, two centres: the revolutionary centre in Wuhan and the counter-*

revolutionary centre in Nanking". Stalin contended that no soviets can be built because that would signify an uprising against the Wuhan centre, against the "*only government*" in Southern China. We called this characterization of the situation "false, superficial, vulgar". We called this so-called Wuhan government the "*leaders of Wuhan*" and showed that in Southern China, after the abrupt veering of the civil war to another class line, there is no government as yet, that one must be first created.

In *Pravda* of May 15 the speech of comrade Chen Duxiu at the convention of the Chinese Communist Party (April 29) is reprinted.

Neither Stalin nor we had this speech when Stalin wrote his theses and we wrote a criticism of them. Chen Duxiu characterizes the situation not on the basis of a general analysis of the circumstances but on the basis of his direct observations. Now, what does Chen Duxiu say of the new revolutionary movement? He declares plainly that "it would be a mistake" to consider the Wuhan government an organ of the revolutionary democratic dictatorship: "It is *not yet a government of the worker and peasant masses but solely a bloc of leaders*". But is this not word for word what we said against Stalin?

Stalin wrote: "There is now no other governmental power than the government of the revolutionary Guomindang." We answered him on that: "These words fairly reek with the apparatus-like and bureaucratic conception of revolutionary authority. The classes come and go but the continuity of the Guomindang government goes on forever [allegedly]. But it is not enough to call Wuhan the centre of the revolution for it really to be that" (cf. above). Instead of making it clear to the Chinese revolutionists, to the Communists primarily, that the Wuhan government will break its head against a wall if it imagines that it is itself already the only government in China; instead of turning relentlessly against the decorative hypocrisy of the petty-bourgeois revolutionists who have already destroyed so many revolutions; instead of shouting right into the ear of the uncertain, faltering, vacillating centre of Wuhan: "Do not be misled by outward appearances, do not be dazzled by the glitter of our own titles and manifestos, begin to perform the hard daily work, set masses in motion, build up workers', soldiers' and peasants' soviets, build up a revolutionary governmental power"—instead of all this, Stalin hurls himself against the slogan of the soviets and supports the worst, the most provincial and bureaucratic prejudices and superstitious views of those ill-fated revolutionists who fear people's soviets, and instead have faith in the sacred ink-blots on the notepaper of the Guomindang.

53. Comrade Chen Duxiu characterizes the situation on the basis of his own observations with exactly the same words with which we characterized the situation on the basis of theoretical consideration. No revolutionary government but only a bloc of leaders. But this does not at all mean that comrade Chen Duxiu himself draws correct conclusions from the circumstances correctly characterized by him. Since he is bound hand and foot by false directives, Chen Duxiu draws conclusions which radically contradict his own analysis. He says: "We have before us the task of beginning to build up a genuinely revolutionary and democratic government *as soon as the situation in the sphere of the national government has changed and the threat of foreign intervention and the offensive of the militarists have disappeared.*"

Here we must say directly and openly: put the question this way and you adopt the surest and shortest road to ruin. The creation of a genuinely revolutionary government basing itself on the popular masses is relegated to the moment when the dangers have disappeared. But the central danger consists precisely of the fact that instead of a revolutionary government in Southern China, there is for the time being only a bloc of leaders. Through this principal evil, all the other dangers are increased tenfold, including also the military danger. If we are to be guarded to the highest possible degree against the foreign and our "own" militarist bands, we must become strong, consolidate ourselves, organize, and arm ourselves. There are no other roads. We should not stick our heads in the sand. No artifice will help us here. The enthusiasm of the masses must be aroused, their readiness to fight and to die for their own cause. But for this the masses must be gripped as deeply as possible, politically and organizationally. Without losing even an hour, they must be given a revolutionary program of action and the organizational form of the soviets. There are no other roads. Postpone the creation of a revolutionary government until somebody has eliminated the danger of war in some way or other, and you take the surest and shortest road to ruin.

54. With regard to the agrarian movement, comrade Chen Duxiu admits honestly that the agrarian program of the Party (reduction of rent payments) is completely insufficient. The peasant movement, he says, "is being transformed into the struggle for land. The peasantry arises spontaneously and wants to settle the land question itself." Further on, comrade Chen Duxiu declares openly: "*We followed a too pacific policy*. Now it is necessary to confiscate the large estates". If the content of these words is developed in a Marxian manner, it constitutes the harshest condemnation of the whole past line of the Communist Party of China, and the Comintern as well, in the agrarian question of the Chinese revolution. Instead of anticipating the course of the agrarian movement, of establishing the slogans in time and throwing them among the peasant masses through the workers, the revolutionary soldiers and the advanced peasants, the Chinese Communist Party remained a vast distance behind the spontaneous agrarian movement. Can there be a more monstrous form of *chvostism*? "*We followed a too pacific policy*." But what does a pacific policy of a revolutionary party mean in the period of a spontaneous agrarian revolution? It signifies the most grievous historical mistake that a party of the proletariat can possibly commit. A pacific policy (the reduction of rent payments), while the peasant is already fighting spontaneously for land, is not a policy of Menshevik compromise but of liberal compromise. Only a philistine corrupted by alleged statecraft can fail to understand this, but never a revolutionist.

55. But from his correct, and therefore deadly, characterization of the relations of the party to the agrarian movement, comrade Chen Duxiu draws not only false, but positively disastrous conclusions. "It is now necessary," he says, "to confiscate the large estates, but at the same time to make

concessions to the small landowners who must be reckoned with." In principle, such a way of posing the question cannot be assailed. It must be clearly determined who and in what part of China is to be considered a small landowner, how and to what limits he must be reckoned with. But Chen Duxiu says further:

> "Nevertheless, it is necessary to await *the further development of the military actions* even for the confiscation of the large estates. The only correct decision at the present moment is the principle of deepening the revolution *only after its extension*."

This road is the surest, the most positive, the shortest road to ruin. The peasant has already risen to seize the property of the large landowners. Our party, in monstrous contradiction to its program, to its name, pursues a pacific-liberal agrarian policy. Chen Duxiu himself declares that it is "now [?] necessary to confiscate the large estates", but he immediately recalls that we "must not fall into left extremism" (Chen Duxiu's own words) and he adds that we must "await the further development of the military actions" for the confiscation of the property of the large landowners, that the revolution must first be extended and only later deepened.

But this is simply a blind repetition of the old, well-known and outworn formula of national-liberal deception of the masses: First the victory, then the reform. First we will "extend" the country—for whom: for the large landowner?—and then, after the victory, we will concern ourselves very tranquilly with the "deepening". To this, every intelligent and half-way sensible peasant will answer comrade Chen Duxiu: "If the Wuhan government today, when it finds itself encircled by foes and needs our peasant support for life and death—if this government does not dare now to give us the land of the large landowners or does not want to do it, then after it has extricated itself from its encirclement, after it has vanquished the enemy with our help, it will give us just as much land as Chiang Kai-shek gave the workers of Shanghai." It must be said quite clearly: The agrarian formula of comrade Chen Duxiu, who is bound hand and foot by the false leadership of the representatives of the Comintern, is objectively nothing else than the formula of the severance of the Chinese Communist Party from the real agrarian movement which is now proceeding in China and which is producing a new wave of the Chinese Revolution.

To strengthen this wave and to deepen it we need peasants' soviets with the unfurled banner of the agrarian revolution, not after the victory but immediately, in order to guarantee the victory.

If we do not want to permit the peasant wave to come to naught and be splattered into froth, the peasants' soviets must be united through workers' soviets in the cities and the industrial centres, and to the workers' soviets must be added the soviets of the poor population from the urban trade and handwork districts.

If we do not want to permit the bourgeoisie to drive a wedge between the revolutionary masses and the army, then soldiers' soviets must be fitted into the revolutionary chain.

As quickly as possible, as boldly as possible, as energetically as possible, the revolution must be deepened, not after the victory but immediately, or else there will be no victory.

The deepening of the agrarian revolution, the immediate seizure of the land by the peasants, will weaken Chiang Kai-shek on the spot, bring confusion into the ranks of his soldiers, and set the peasant hinterland in motion. There is no other road to victory and there can be none.

Have we really carried through three revolutions within two decades only to forget the ABC of the first of them? Whoever carries on a *pacific* policy during the agrarian revolution, is lost. Whoever postpones matters, vacillates, temporizes, loses time, is lost. The formula of Chen Duxiu is the surest road to the destruction of the revolution.

Slanderers will be found who will say that our words are dictated by a hatred of the Chinese Communist Party and its leaders. Was it not once said that our position on the Anglo-Russian Committee signified a hostile attitude towards the British Communist Party? The events confirmed the fact that it was we who acted as loyal revolutionists towards the British Communists, and not as bureaucratic sycophants. Events will confirm the fact—they confirm it every day—that our criticism of the Chinese Communists was dictated by a more serious, more Marxist, revolutionary attitude towards the Chinese revolution than was the attitude of the bureaucratic sycophants who approve of everything after the fact, provided that they do not have to foresee for the future.

The fact that the speech of comrade Chen Duxiu is reprinted in *Pravda* without a single word of commentary, that no article revealing the ruinous course of this speech is devoted to it—this fact by itself must fill every revolutionist with the greatest misgivings, for it is the central organ of Lenin's party that is involved!

Let not the pacifiers and flatterers tell us about "the unavoidable mistakes of a young Communist Party". It is not a question of isolated mistakes. It is a question of the false basic line, the consummate expression of which is the theses of comrade Stalin.

The Necessary Final Accord

In the May 9 number of *Sotsialisticheski Vestnik,* it says in the article devoted to the theses of comrade Stalin:

> "If we strip the envelope of words that is obligatory for the theses of a Communist leader, then very little can be said against the essence of the 'line' traced there. As much as possible to remain in the Guomindang, and to cling to its left wing and to the Wuhan government to the last possible moment: 'to avoid a decisive struggle under unfavourable conditions'; not to issue the slogan 'all power to the soviets' so as not 'to give new weapons into the hands of the enemies of the Chinese people for the struggle against the revolution, for creating new legends that it is not a national revolution that is taking place in China, but an artificial transplanting of Moscow sovietization'—what can actually be more sensible for the Bolsheviks now, after the 'united front' has obviously been irremediably destroyed, and so much porcelain has been smashed under the 'most unfavourable conditions'?"[8]

Thus, after *Sotsialisticheski Vestnik,* in its April 23rd number, acknowledged that Martynov analysed the tasks of the Chinese revolution in *Pravda* "very impressively" and "entirely in the

Menshevik manner", the leading article in the central organ of the Mensheviks declares in its latest number that "very little can be said against the essence of the 'line' traced" in the theses of comrade Stalin. This harmony of political lines hardly requires special elucidation.

But still more: The same article in *Sotsialisticheski Vestnik* speaks further on in a mocking tone – we quote literally!—of *"the line of Radek which, covered with extreme 'left' slogans, (withdrawal from Guomindang, 'propaganda of the soviet system' etc.), simply desires in reality to give up the game and to step aside."*[9] The line of Radek is characterized here with the words of the leading articles and the feuilletons of *Pravda*. After all, it cannot be otherwise: Radek cannot say anything openly in the press about his line, for otherwise the Party would learn that Radek's line is being confirmed by the whole course of events. The editors of *Sotsialisticheski Vestnik* not only describe "the line of Radek" with the words of *Pravda* but also evaluate them in full accord with the articles of *Pravda*: The line of the Opposition, according to Dan, gives the possibility, "covered with extreme 'left' slogans", in reality "to give up the game and to step aside". We have already read in the articles of *Pravda* that "a mass for the dead must be read" for the Chinese Revolution, that the Chinese Communists must "retire within themselves", that they must renounce "great deeds and great plans", and that all this is the "sermon of the liquidation of the Chinese Revolution"—if the line of the Opposition is adopted. This was said literally, for example, in the leading article in *Pravda* of May 16, 1927. As we see, it is word for word the same thing that Dan says, or more correctly, Dan says of the Opposition word for word what *Pravda* has said in a series of its articles. Dan approves the theses of Stalin and derides the "liquidator" Radek, who covers his liquidation with extremely left phrases. Everything is clear now: The liquidationism of Radek is the same liquidationism which is evaluated as such by the renowned revolutionist Dan. That is the lesson that the leading articles in *Sotsialisticheski Vestnik* presents to those who are still capable of learning anything.

It is surely portentous that the quoted number of *Sotsialisticheski Vestnik* should arrive in Moscow on the eve of the opening of the session of the Executive Committee of the Communist International, which must consider the problem of the Chinese Revolution in its full scope.

NOTES

1. The theses of Comrade Stalin are published in the name of the Central Committee. This does not change the fact that the theses were not examined by the plenum of the Central Committee. The Political Committee charged three members, Comrades Stalin, Bukharin and Molotov, to look over the theses of Comrade Stalin and, in case of agreement, to publish them in the name of the Central Committee. Naturally, it is not a question of the formal side of the matter, which nobody raises. But it is quite clear that such a "simplified" method of deciding questions of world importance, after the mistakes made and the heavy defeats, in no way serves the interests of the party and of the Chinese Revolution. – *L.T.*
2. First Letter from Afar, *Lenin,* Vol.XIV, part 1, pp.10-11; *Pravda,* March 21, 1917.
3. No. 8, April 23, 1927, p. 4.
4. *Sotsialisticheski Vestnik,* April 23, 1927, p. 3.
5. *Pravda,* April 23, 1927.
6. Raskolnikov's foreword to the pamphlet by Tang Pingshan.
7. *Problems of Leninism,* p. 264.
8. *Sotsialisticheski Vestnik,* no.9 [151] p. 1.
9. *Sotsialisticheski Vestnik,* no.9, [151] p. 2.

13

The Communist Party and the Kuomintang

May 10, 1927

I think the new situation calls for a review of the relationship between the Communist Party and the Kuomintang. Why should we remain in the left Kuomintang?

1. On this point the following argument is often repeated: "Since the workers and peasants support the left Kuomintang, we should remain in it, in order to win them over to the Communist Party." This argument scarcely holds up. Far more workers support the Social Democracy and Amsterdam International than the Kuomintang. The same argument could also fully apply to the Anglo-Russian Committee.

   As a general rule, when we want to break workers away from some organization and win them over, we do not join the organization; we leave it.
2. Another argument is. "Now, while they are smashing both us and the left Kuomintang, withdrawal is out of the question." I think it is much more dangerous for the organization to be combined when they are dealing us blows than it is when we are the ones dealing the blows. Bela Kun's experience in Hungary is eloquent testimony to this. Under such difficult conditions, the meaning of revolutionary firmness is clearer than ever. By remaining in the same organization with the Wang Ching-weis, we are sharing the responsibility for their waverings and

betrayals. There must be unity in striking the enemy—but a separation of political responsibility.

3. From the first argument it follows that we should remain in the left Kuomintang until we have drawn all of the workers and peasants away from it. But if this is the case, we will never leave the Kuomintang. First, because China's national democracy will have behind it not only peasants but workers as well for a good while yet. And second, by remaining in the Kuomintang we do not confront the workers with the necessity of choosing between it and the Communist Party.

   As for the peasants, they could continue to look to the Kuomintang as our peasants looked to the Social Revolutionaries, right up to the proletarian dictatorship. From precisely this flows the necessity of a bloc.

   The second argument states that we should remain in the Kuomintang until our retreat is over (i.e., until our destruction). But if our retreat were to shift to an attack, then they would say: it is impermissible to disrupt the offensive by withdrawing from the Kuomintang.

4. The analogy of the British Communist Party's entry into the Labour Party falls apart under its own weight. The British Labour Party is proletarian in composition and political differentiation is proceeding slowly by comparison. The Kuomintang is a "party" of different classes, and political differentiation among them is proceeding with extreme rapidity because of the revolution. The Chinese Communist Party has lagged behind this differentiation the whole time.

5. After the Chiang Kai-shek coup the question becomes even more crucial. As it turns out, the most vile proposals against the Communist Party and the working class at the Kuomintang's last plenum were made by Wang Ching-wei. That was on the eve of the coup .36 All available information indicates that the Hankow government at this moment continues to pursue the same line, yet the Communist Party remains the left

opposition in the Kuomintang. Moscow can talk about "remaining in the Kuomintang with full [?] political and organizational [?!] independence." But what does this mean in practice? In Hankow, surely, all of these questions are being posed at the point of a sword. The Central Committee of the Chinese Communist Party will be totally unable to comprehend what we are in fact proposing. And in moments as critical as this nothing is worse than confusion.

6. This kind of argument was also advanced: It is necessary to leave the Kuomintang, but the Communist Party must be allowed a certain time to prepare. It is easier to accept this kind of formulation. But then the Chinese Communist Party must be told openly about it. Obviously, the preparation must include the perspective that withdrawal from the Kuomintang will give way to a bloc with it and collaboration on all policy—however, with a separation of political responsibility. Unfortunately this purely practical way of posing the question has been withdrawn and replaced with the arguments of a general nature, examined briefly above.
7. Meanwhile, there can be no doubt that the Communist Party's remaining in the left Kuomintang will in the future mean the subordination of its policy to its organizational dependence, and—considering how young and inexperienced it is—this will inevitably lead it to repeat all the mistakes of the past period.

* * *

In Comrade Radek's letter of March 3, the need to remain for a time within the Kuomintang was argued as follows: "All the activity of the Kuomintang, or more precisely, its right wing and military units—directed as they are against the interests of the masses and in defense of the interests of the landlords and capitalists, as well as the Blanquist policies of the Kuomintang Central Committee—have still not produced among the masses any opposition to the Kuomintang nor led to an understanding of the need for a separate class party of the proletariat and the poorest peasantry."

At the time, I objected to this argument on the basis of which the organization of an independent workers' party is put off until the masses understand the need for such a party. But right now I will leave aside the question of principle on this matter. The meaning of the words we have quoted from Comrade Radek is clear: It is necessary to wait for actions on the part of the right wing and units of the army so that the masses understand the need for their own party. Were the "April actions" not sufficient for this? It would seem that they were.

However, new difficulties now crop up: The "April actions" which, according to the March 3 letter, should have served as the signal for an independent Communist Party, are now being proclaimed the main obstacle to this independence. We are creating an organizational trap for ourselves—one we will not be able to escape from by continually finding new political arguments.

I understand very well that on this aspect of the question our differences are not differences in principle, but how the question is interpreted organizationally under the present conditions in China has enormous significance. The very same Chinese communists who were the left appendage under Chiang Kai-shek will in a year or two become in turn the left appendage under Wang Ching-wei.

[Postscript, June 9, 1927]

The above lines were written about a month ago. Everything that has transpired since then confirms the need for clarity on the fundamental question of independence for the Chinese Communist Party. To depict the Kuomintang as a formless organization committed to no one is to distort the very meaning of the question. No matter how formless the Kuomintang is at its periphery, its central apparatus has the revolutionary dictatorship firmly in hand. The Canton Kuomintang has imitated the AUCP in this respect. The Hankow Kuomintang imitates the one in Canton (or Nanking). For the Central Committee of the Communist Party in Hankow the proposal that it enter the Kuomintang while retaining full political and organizational independence is no more than an unsolvable riddle. We know that even the present Central Committee of the present Chinese Communist Party declared itself last year in favor of a bloc from without rather than a bloc from within, that is, in favor of withdrawing from the Kuomintang. But now the Chinese Central Committee is no doubt repeatedly being told: "Look, even the Opposition in the AUCP is against withdrawing from the Kuomintang." In China this argument is undoubtedly being used, and will continue to be used, just as widely as we use the argument that the Opposition is for withdrawing from the Kuomintang.

T'an P'ing-shan's speech at the time he became minister37 shows all too clearly that for this Communist Party to remain in the Kuomintang-not "in general" but under the given concrete conditions of time and place-permits its leaders to declare they will implement the program of the Kuomintang and not that of their own party, and what is even worse, permits the party to put up with such leaders, thereby blurring the lines defining the party. This has to be stopped at all costs. A real differentiation of Bolsheviks from Mensheviks within the Communist Party itself is bound to occur over this question.

What is necessary at the present time? It is necessary to formulate the reasons we have remained in the Kuomintang up to the present. At the same time—and this is most important of all—it is necessary to formulate with just as much clarity and accuracy the reasons we must now leave the Kuomintang. The reasons for leaving it multiply by the day-one need only look at the dispatches "not for publication".

To postpone dealing with this question can only worsen the situation.

L. Trotsky

Enclosed:

1. Comrade Radek's letter of March 3,1927.
2. Comrade Trotsky's reply of March 4, 1927.
3. Comrade Trotsky's memorandum of March 22, 1927.
4. Comrade Trotsky's letter of March 29,1927.

14

The Sure Road

May 12, 1927 Moscow

The Shanghai correspondent of the *Daily Express* reports:

> "The peasants of Henan province are occupying the land and executing the big landlords who resist most stubbornly. Everywhere, control is in the hands of the Communists. Workers' soviets are formed locally which take over administrative authority."[1]

We do not know to what extent the telegram is correct in depicting the situation with such bold strokes. We have no other reports save the telegram. What is the real extent of the movement? Is it not deliberately exaggerated in order to influence the power of imagination of Messrs. MacDonald, Thomas, Purcell and Hicks with the intention of making them more pliant to the policy of Chamberlain? We do not know. But in this case, it has no decisive significance.

The peasants are seizing the land and exterminating the most counter-revolutionary big landlords. Workers' soviets are formed locally which take over administrative authority. That is what a correspondent of a reactionary paper communicates. The editorial board of *Pravda* considers this report sufficiently important to incorporate it in the contents table of the most important daily events in the world. We too are of the opinion that this is correct. But it would naturally be premature to contend that the Chinese Revolution, after the April *coup d'état* of the bourgeois counter-revolution, has already entered a new and higher stage. After a great defeat, it frequently happens that a part of the attacking masses, which was never submitted to any direct blows, passes over to the next stage of the movement and for a while outstrips the leading detachments which suffered with especial severity in the defeat. Were we to have before us such a phenomenon, the soviets of Henan would soon disappear, temporarily washed away by the general revolutionary ebb-tide.

But there is not the slightest reason to contend that we have before us only sharp rearguard encounters of a revolution which is ebbing for a long period. In spite of the fact that the April defeat was no separate "episode", but a very significant stage in the development of the counter-revolution; in spite of the agonizing blood drawn from the vanguard detachments of the working class, there is not the least reason to contend that the Chinese Revolution has been beaten back for years.

The agrarian movement, since it is more scattered, is less subject to the direct operations of the hangmen of the counter-revolution. There is the possibility that the further growth of the agrarian movement will give the proletariat the opportunity to rise again in the relatively near future and to pass over once more to the attack. Naturally, exact predictions on this point are impossible, especially from afar. The Chinese Communist Party will have to follow attentively the actual course of events and the class groupings in order to catch the moment of a new wave of attack.

The possibility of a new attack, however, will depend not only on the evolution of the agrarian movement but also upon the side towards which the broad, petty-bourgeois masses of the towns develop in the next period. The *coup d'état* of Chiang Kai-shek does not signify only the consolidation of the power of the Chinese bourgeoisie (perhaps less so), but also the re-establishment and the consolidation of the positions of foreign capital in China with all the consequences that flow from them. From this follows the probability, perhaps even the inevitability—and this in the fairly near future—of a turn of the petty-bourgeois masses against Chiang Kai-shek. The petty-bourgeoisie, which is subjected to great sufferings not only by foreign capital but also by the alliance of the national Chinese bourgeoisie with foreign capital, must, after some vacillations, turn against the bourgeois counter-revolution. It is precisely in this that lies one of the most important manifestations of the class mechanics of the national democratic revolution.

Finally, the young Chinese proletariat, by all the conditions of its existence, is so accustomed to privation and sacrifice, has so well "learned", together with the whole of the oppressed Chinese people, to look death in the eye, that we may expect from the Chinese workers, once they are properly aroused by the revolution, highly exceptional self-abnegation in struggle.

All this gives us the full right to count upon the new wave of the Chinese Revolution being separated from the wave which ended with the April defeat of the proletariat, not by long years but by short months. Naturally, nobody can establish the intervals for this either. But we would be incompetent revolutionists if we were not to steer our course upon a new rise, if we were not to work out any program of action for it, any political road or any organizational forms.

The April defeat was no "episode", it was a heavy class defeat; we will not take up here an analysis of the reasons for it. We want to speak in this article of tomorrow and not of yesterday. The heaviness of the April defeat lies not only in the fact that the proletarian centres were struck a sanguinary blow. The heaviness of the defeat lies in the fact that the workers were crushed by those who until then had stood at their head. Such a violent turn must produce not only physical disorganization but also political confusion in the ranks of the proletariat. This confusion, which is more dangerous to the revolution than the defeat itself, can be overcome only by a clear, precise, revolutionary line for tomorrow.

In this sense, the telegram of the Shanghai correspondent of the reactionary British newspaper has especial significance. In it is shown what road the revolution in China can tread should it succeed in the next period in reaching a higher level.

We have said above that the peasants' liquidation of the big landlords of Henan, like the creation of workers' soviets, may be the sharp conclusion of the last wave or the commencement of a new one, since the matter is considered from afar. This contrast of two waves can lose its significance if the interval between them is long, namely, a few weeks or even a few months. However the matter may be (and here only advice can be given, especially from a distance), the symptomatic significance of the Henan events is thoroughly clear and incontestable, regardless of their extent and sweep. The peasants and the workers of Henan are showing the road which their movement can tread, now that the heavy chains of their bloc with the bourgeoisie and the big landlords have been smashed. It would be contemptible and philistine to believe that the agrarian problem and the workers' problem in this revolution, gigantic in its tasks and in the masses it has drawn in its train, can be solved by decree from above and by arbitration committees. The worker himself wants to break the backbone of the reactionary bourgeoisie and to teach the manufacturers to respect the proletarian, his person and his rights. The peasant himself wants to sever the ties of his dependence upon the big landlords who exhaust him with their usurious practices and enslave him. Imperialism, which violently hampers the economic development of China by its customs, its financial and its military policy, condemns the worker to beggary and the peasant to the cruelest enslavement. The struggle against the big landlords, the struggle against the usurer, the struggle against the capitalists for better working conditions, is thus raised by itself to the struggle for the national independence of China, for the liberation of its productive forces from the bonds and chains of foreign imperialism. There is the principal and the mightiest foe. It is mighty not only because of its warships, but also directly by its inseparable connections with the heads of the banks, the usurers, the bureaucrats and the militarists, with the Chinese bourgeoisie, and by the more indirect but no less intimate ties with the big commercial and industrial bourgeoisie.

All these facts demonstrate that the pressure of imperialism is in no sense an external, mechanical pressure which welds all the classes together. No, it is a very deep-lying factor of internal action which accentuates the class struggle. The Chinese commercial and industrial bourgeoisie carries behind it the supplementary force of foreign capital and foreign bayonets in every one of its serious collisions with the proletariat. The masters of this capital and these bayonets play the role of more experienced and more adroit operators, who included the blood of the Chinese workers in their accounts just as they do with raw rubber and opium. If one wants to drive out foreign imperialism, if one wants to conquer the enemy, then his "peaceful", "normal" hangman's and robber's work in China must be rendered impossible. This cannot be attained, naturally, on the road of compromise of the bourgeoisie with foreign imperialism. Such a compromise may increase the share of the Chinese bourgeoisie in the product of the labour of the Chinese workers and peasants by a few per cent. But it will signify the deeper penetration of foreign imperialism into the economic and political life of China, the deeper enslavement of the Chinese worker and peasant. Victory over foreign imperialism can only be won by means of the toilers of town and country driving it out of China. For this, the masses must really rise, millions strong. They cannot rise under the bare slogan of national liberation, but only in direct struggle against the big landlords, the military satraps, the usurers, the capitalist brigands. In this struggle, the masses are already rising, steeling themselves, arming themselves. There is no other road of revolutionary training. The big bourgeois leadership of the Guomindang (the gang of Chiang Kai-shek) has opposed this road with all means. At first, only from within, by means of decrees and prohibitions, but when the "discipline" of the Guomindang did not suffice, with the aid of machine guns. The petty-bourgeois leadership of the Guomindang hesitates out of fear of a too stormy development of the mass movement. By their whole past, the petty-bourgeois radicals are more accustomed to looking to the top, to seeking combinations of all sorts of "national" groups, than to looking down below, to the real struggle of millions of workers. But if vacillations and irresolution are dangerous in all things, then in the revolution they are disastrous. The workers and peasants of Henan are showing the way out of the vacillations, and by that, the road to save the revolution.

It is not necessary to explain that only this road, that is, the deeper mass sweep, the greater social radicalism of the program, the unfurled banner of workers' and peasants' soviets, can seriously preserve the revolution from military defeats from without. We know this from our own experience. Only a revolution on whose banner the toilers and the exploited plainly inscribe their won demands is capable of winning the living sympathy of the soldiers of capitalism. We experienced and tested this out in the waters of Archangel, Odessa and other places. The leadership of compromise and treason did not preserve Nanking from destruction, and gave the enemy ships access to the Yangtze. A revolutionary leadership, given a mighty social sweep of the movement, can succeed in making the waters of the Yangtze too hot for the ships of Lloyd George, Chamberlain and MacDonald. In any case, it is only along this road that the revolution can seek and find its defence.

We have repeatedly said above that the agrarian movement and the formation of soviets can signify the conclusion of yesterday and the beginning of tomorrow. But this does not depend upon objective conditions alone. Under present conditions, the subjective factor has an enormous, perhaps a decisive significance: a correct formulation of the tasks, a firm and clear leadership. If a movement like the one that has begun in Henan is left to its own resources, it will inevitably be crushed. The confidence of the insurrectionary masses will be increased tenfold as soon as it feels a firm leadership and greater cohesion with it. A clear-headed leadership, generalizing matters in the political field and connecting them up organizationally, is alone capable of preserving the movement to a greater or lesser degree from incautious or premature side-leaps and from so-called "excesses", without which, however, as the experience of history teaches, no really revolutionary movement of the millions can reach its goal.

The task consists of giving the agrarian movement and the workers' soviets a clear program of practical action, an internal cohesion and a broad political goal. Only on this basis can a really revolutionary collaboration of the proletariat and the petty-bourgeoisie be constituted and developed, a genuine alliance of struggle of the Communist Party with the Left

Guomindang. The cadres of the latter can in general only constitute and steel themselves if they do it in most intimate contact with the revolutionary struggles of the peasants and the poor population of the city. The agrarian movement, led by peasants' and workers' soviets, will confront the Left Guomindang people with the necessity of finally choosing between the Chiang Kai-shek camp of the bourgeoisie and the camp of the workers and peasants. To put the fundamental class questions openly, that is the only way under present conditions to put an end to the vacillation of the petty-bourgeois radicals and to compel them to tread the only road which leads to victory. This can be done by our Chinese party with the support of the whole Communist International.

NOTE

1. *Pravda*, May 11, 1927.

15

A Protest to the Central Control Commission

May 17, 1927

Politburo, Presidium of the Central Control Commission:

1. The Politburo decided on May 12 not to publish my articles. It seems this concerns two articles, one, "The Chinese Revolution and the Theses of Comrade Stalin", which I sent to *Bolshevik*, and the other, "The Sure Road," which I sent to *Pravda*. I was not summoned to be present for the Politburo discussion of this question, although such would be required for even a pretense of fairness.
2. The reason given for not carrying the articles was that they criticize the Central Committee and are in the nature of a discussion. In other words, a rule is being established whereby all party members and the entire party press can only echo the Central Committee, whatever it says, whatever it does, no matter what the circumstances.
3. I consider the line of the Central Committee on the Chinese question to be fundamentally wrong. It was precisely this erroneous line that ensured the success of the April coup of the Chinese counter-revolution. Confuting the widely circulated lies and slander that the Opposition "is trying to profit from the difficulties", Zinoviev et al. offered to discuss the question of the future line for China and all of the most important questions of our policy in a closed plenum. This in itself

indicated our intention to study and decide these questions on their merits, in a formal manner, without stenographic records-consequently without seeking to "exploit" anything. The Politburo, together with the Presidium of the Central Control Commission, refuses to convene such a plenum. Thus the attempt to correct a line that is false to the core and disastrous in its effects, by means of a serious discussion in the Central Committee, has failed through the fault of the Politburo, automatically backed up as always by the Presidium of the Central Control Commission.

4. Then, Comrade Stalin's theses suddenly appear, representing a reinforcement and deepening of the most erroneous aspects of a thoroughly erroneous policy. And finally, to top it all off, the Politburo, having refused to discuss the Chinese question with us at a closed plenum (of course, it was discussed—without us—at "private" meetings) sanctioned Stalin's theses, and afterward refuses to allow anybody to pose in the press the question of why Chiang Kai-shek triumphed so easily, why the Chinese proletariat proved to be so unprepared, why our party has gotten so horribly entangled in the web of Martynovism, why Stalin's theses are pushing the Chinese Communist Party and the entire International into the swamp of opportunism, and why the *Sotsialistichesky Vestnik* so emphatically approved Martynov's article earlier, and Stalin's theses now (May 9, 1927).
5. Are the Chinese Revolution and the Comintern's entire political line really such small items that they can be swept under the rug? Can this really further the process of education in the Chinese Communist Party? Is this really the way for foreign sections of the Comintern to be developed? Can our party really survive following this course? Is such a bureaucratic Utopia really conceivable?
6. The resolution of the Politburo states that we want to force the party into a discussion. If by discussion what

is meant is the roar of the apparatus, the shouts and whistling of the claques that have been organized in advance, the packing of cells with goons trained to use violence against the Opposition, the overwhelming of workers' cells with threats and cries about a split—then, of course, we do not want such "discussion". But it is this very type of discussion our party life is brimming with. We want the party to discuss the question of the Chinese Revolution, beginning as a minimum with the party's theoretical and central organs.

7. Yes, we want a discussion on the question of the fate of the Chinese Revolution and consequently of our own fate. Why was such a discussion considered normal under Lenin throughout our party's entire history? Can anyone really believe that the theses Stalin, Molotov, and Bukharin pronounce at any given moment are the last word in historical development for the party? Yes, we want a discussion of these questions in order to demonstrate and make clear to the party that these theses are false to the core, and that carrying them out threatens to break the neck of the Chinese Revolution.
8. The Central Committee does not want a discussion. Yet what this discussion would entail is criticism of the Central Committee itself. It can be said as a general rule that the more erroneous any Central Committee line proves to be, and the more strikingly and harshly it is refuted by events, the less taste there will be for a discussion. I don't think there were ever any mistakes in the history of our party that compare with those made by Stalin and Bukharin on the Chinese question or on the question of the Anglo-Russian Committee. But the point is not what happened yesterday. Every one of us has been ready, and is ready now, to give it all up as a bad job. But these mistakes, promulgated by decree, are being extended into the future with their magnitude increased tenfold. This is what I am talking about. It is understandable that the Politburo "does not want" a discussion. But does the Politburo really have the right

to forbid a discussion of the issue, when involved are fundamental errors of the Politburo itself on questions of world-historic importance?

9. The Politburo does not want a discussion. Why? Ostensibly so as "not to upset" the party. However, the Politburo opened up an artificial discussion, contrived by the leadership, about the allegedly antiparty statement of Comrade Zinoviev at an alleged nonparty meeting. The party was not told anything about what Comrade Zinoviev said (as for me, I subscribe to every word he said). Comrade Zinoviev's speech has not been published. The affair is presented as though it was a nonparty meeting, whereas in fact the entire meeting had the character of a party meeting, even though a certain number of people who are not in the party may have been present. The "discussion" against Comrade Zinoviev proceeds at full tilt. The Central Control Commission is quiet. It is not stepping in. But when the "discussion" has made its way along the line, the Central Control Commission will also pronounce a "verdict".
10. Now, during the discussion of the Chinese question, open meetings of the party cells have been specially set up all over the country so as not to allow anyone to speak out on the mistakes of the revolutionary leadership and in order to have a chance to hold anyone who makes criticisms accountable for speaking against the party at a nonparty meeting. This is the system. It is a system organized by the leadership, a system organized for the purpose of stifling thought within the party. Actually, one could get the idea that there is no real need for members of the Bolshevik party to exchange opinions on the question of the Chinese Revolution, especially now that it has become clear that the Politburo, instead of learning from its errors, is imposing these errors on the party by decree. Compelled to make a choice in a situation like this, every honest party member should say: "It will be immeasurably more dangerous if I

conceal my criticism of the party than if, against my will, a few people who aren't in the party hear my criticism."

11. We want a party discussion of the conditions and causes of the Chinese catastrophe. In order to hinder this, the Central Committee converts Comrade Zinoviev's supremely calm and supremely moderate statement into a party "catastrophe". Despite the critical situation, the difficulties, the dangers, etc., the leadership whips up the party, shakes it up, terrorizes it, and deliberately shouts in the party's ear the lie that Comrade Zinoviev is mobilizing nonparty elements against it. By means of a one-sided, fierce, envenomed discussion on grounds that have been artificially blown up, they want to prevent the party from calmly discussing the basic issues of the Chinese Revolution. Amidst the noise, fuss, and clamor of a one-sided apparatus discussion, our articles are forbidden publication. Why are they forbidden? Because Stalin cannot answer them. Because the pathetic, empty, hurriedly stuck-together sentences of his theses that so satisfied Dan fly to pieces at a puff of criticism.
12. Discussion of the most basic issues is forbidden by referring to the difficulties of the situation, the dangers from without, and the approaching threat of war. As for these undeniable dangers, the Opposition stands out if only because it foresaw them earlier and assessed them in greater depth. The dangers are present, and moreover gigantic. But the fact is that every one of these dangers will become a hundred times more dangerous as a result of the mistakes of the leadership. The main source of the dangers lies in the defeat of the Chinese Revolution, so swiftly brought about through the absence of the necessary class base. We prevented this base from being created at the proper time by our false policy. At the present stage this is a blow to the revolution and our international position. If we go further along the path of Stalin's theses, the position of the Chinese Revolution—and that means ours as well—will further deteriorate (see Ch'en Tu-hsiu's speech 39). Then they

can point to a position that has deteriorated doubly and they can doubly forbid all criticism. The more in error the leadership is, the less possible will it be—given the present course—to criticize it.

13. They will turn the whole question inside out. In favorable conditions it is still possible to make headway even with an incorrect line. But a serious situation demands a correct line, all the more imperatively the more serious it is. If the line is incorrect and if a leadership's persistence in following the incorrect line threatens the workers' state and the international revolution with new defeats and jolts, only a pathetic bureaucrat who has lost any feeling of personal responsibility or a base careerist—of whom, by the way, there are more than a few around—can keep silent about the mistakes, once having seen them and recognized them. Stifling a principled political discussion of the disputed issues with the noise, clamor, and hooting of the artificially contrived "discussion" directed against Comrade Zinoviev means terrorizing the rank-and-file party members, depriving them of any feeling of personal responsibility, raising the apparatchik even higher above them, and allowing the careerist to thrive like a fish in water.
14. I am calling things by their proper names because innuendo can help nothing in a situation like this. It is possible to mechanistically suppress anything for a short period of time: doubts, questions, and outraged protests. But Lenin called such methods rude and disloyal. They are rude and disloyal, not because they have an unpleasant form, but because they are inherently incompatible with the nature of the party. The Chinese Revolution cannot be stuck in a bottle and sealed up. Nobody will succeed in doing this. The move to crush the Opposition that is being secretly prepared can be successful only superficially and mechanistically. The line we defend has been tested in the fire of the greatest events in world history, confirmed by the entire

> experience of Bolshevism, and reaffirmed, even though negatively, by the tragic experience of the Chinese Revolution and the Anglo-Russian Committee. This line cannot be suppressed. However, it is entirely possible to do irreparable damage to the party and the Comintern.

This is what I want to state clearly and unequivocally to the Central Committee and the Central Control Commission.

16

A Letter to the Secretariat of the Central Committee

May 18, 1927

1. My request of May 11 of this year that the Secretariat of the Central Committee indicate where and when I would be able to familiarize myself with the Politburo's decision on the Chinese question after what has transpired over the past two months has remained unanswered.
2. My request of May 11 of this year that Comrade Bukharin's draft theses on the Chinese question be made known in time for the amendments to be introduced has remained unanswered.
3. In view of the fact that Comrade Bukharin's theses basically repeat all the mistakes of Comrade Stalin's theses, I am forwarding to the Executive Committee of the Comintern my theses on the basic questions of the Chinese Revolution in connection with criticism of Comrade Stalin's theses.

17

It is Time to Understand, Time to Reconsider, and Time to Make a Change

May 27, 1927

Every day and, one might say, every hour brings news from China demonstrating the complete erroneousness of the line adopted by the plenum and the equally complete correctness of our predictions and proposals. This information is being concealed from the press. After the national bourgeoisie, exploiting the Kuomintang and our policy in the Kuomintang, smashed the workers, the so-called left Kuomintang—to whom the Communist Party was now subordinating itself—made an appeal in which it was proclaimed that "the peasants, workers, owners of businesses, and merchants-are all allies in the national revolution. . . . The Kuomintang is placing before itself the task of freeing from oppression not only the workers and peasants, but also the industrialists and merchants." (See the TASS dispatch—concealed from the press—dated May 25 from Hankow: Bulletin not for publication, no.117.)

This is precisely why the left Kuomintang is demanding that the workers observe "revolutionary discipline"—with respect to the industrialists and merchants. The left Kuomintang prohibits trade unions from arresting a counterrevolutionary, just as it prohibits peasants from seizing the landlords' land. By misleading us, the Chinese Communist Party is helping the Kuomintang in these efforts. Step by step, events are demolishing a policy based on illusions, conciliation, disregard for the class struggle, and the bloc of four classes, which was invented by Martynov and approved by Dan. This policy is erroneous, and it is ruinous. In light of the new facts and the recent dispatches, the plenum would do well to bury Bukharin's resolution, replacing it with a resolution of a few lines:

> In the first place, peasants and workers should place no faith in the leaders of the left Kuomintang but they should instead build their soviets jointly with the soldiers. In the second place, the soviets should arm the workers and the advanced peasants. In the third place, the Communist Party must assure its complete independence, create a daily press, and assume the leadership in creating the soviets. Fourth, the land must be immediately taken away from the landlords. Fifth, the reactionary bureaucracy must be immediately dismissed. Sixth, perfidious generals and other counter-revolutionists must be summarily dealt with. And finally, the general course must be toward the establishment of a revolutionary dictatorship through the soviets of workers' and peasants' deputies.

18

Hankow and Moscow

May 28, 1927 Moscow

What is happening in Hankow now? We can only judge from the telegraphic fragments which Tass does not give to the press.

The Left Guomindang continues to chew the cud of the theory of solidarity of the workers, peasants and the bourgeoisie in the "national revolution" and recommends to the workers and peasants to observe discipline—towards the bourgeoisie.

The Central Committee of the Communist Party (or the Executive Committee of the Guomindang?) calls upon the trade unions to mind "their own affairs" and to leave to the authorities of the Guomindang the struggle against the counter-revolution.

The leader of the Communist Party, Chen Duxiu, adjures the peasants *to wait* for land until the external foe is conquered.

From Moscow comes the warning not to create soviets "prematurely".

In the meantime, imperialism exerts pressure upon Chiang Kai-shek, and Chiang Kai-shek, through the bourgeoisie of Hankow, upon the Left Guomindang.

The Left Guomindang demands discipline and patience from the workers and the peasants.

This is the general picture. Its meaning is completely clear.

What is the Moscow leadership doing these days? We know nothing about it. But we need not doubt that under the influence of the recent extremely disquieting telegrams from Hankow, Moscow is sending advice there with approximately the following content: "As much of the agrarian revolution as possible"; "as many of the masses as possible in the

Guomindang", and so forth. The Communist ministers transmit these counsels to the government and to the Central Executive Committee of the Guomindang.

In this manner, the work of the Communist Party is divided into two parts: aloud, it implores the workers and peasants *to wait*; but in an undertone it whisperingly adjures the bourgeois government *to make haste*. But the revolution is a revolution precisely because the masses do not want to wait. The bourgeois "radicals" are afraid to make haste precisely because they are bourgeois radicals. And the Communist Party, instead of bringing the masses to their feet, instead of occupying the land, and building soviets, loses time with sterile counsels to both sides, in accordance with the sacrosanct prescription of Martynov on the bloc of four classes and on the replacement of the revolution by an arbitration committee.

The collapse of this policy is absolutely inevitable. Unless we correct it sharply, instantly and resolutely, the collapse will take place in the immediate future. Then a lot of papers, with Moscow's advice on them, will be brandished before our eyes: "As much of the agrarian revolution as possible, as many of the masses as possible in the Guomindang." But then we will repeat just what we say today: Such counsels are humbug. The whole revolution cannot be made dependent upon whether or not the pusillanimous bourgeois leadership of the Guomindang accepts our well-meaning advice. It cannot accept it. The agrarian revolution cannot be accomplished with the consent of Wang Jingwei, but in spite of Wang Jingwei and in struggle against him.

That is why the first task is to free our hands, to withdraw the Communist ministers from the national government, to call upon the masses to occupy the land immediately and to build up soviets.

But for this we need a really independent Communist Party, which does not implore the leaders, but resolutely leads the masses. There is no other road and there can be none.

19

First Speech on the Chinese Question

May 1927 Moscow

Comrades! In the question under discussion you have been given the theses of comrade Zinoviev which have remained unknown to the Russian party up till now. Zinoviev was not permitted to come here, although he has the full right—politically as well as formally—to do so. I am defending here the theses of comrade Zinoviev as common to us both. The first rule for the political education of a mass party is: It must know not only what is adopted by the Central Committee but also what it rejects, for only in this way does the line of the leadership become clear and comprehensible to the Party masses. And that is how things have always been with us until now. The refusal to show the Party Comrade Zinoviev's and my own reveals the intellectual weakness, the lack of certainty in their own position, the fear that the theses of the Opposition will appear more correct to the public opinion of the Party than the theses of the majority. There can be no other motives for the concealment of our theses.

My attempt to publish a criticism of Stalin's theses in the theoretical organ of the Party was unsuccessful. The Central Committee, against whose line in this question my theses are directed, prohibited their publication, as well as the publication of other articles by Zinoviev and me.

Yesterday a decision of the Editorial Committee, signed by comrade Kurella, was distributed here. It relates to information on our proceedings. What is meant by this is not quite clear to me. In any case, the Executive Committee is meeting in a strange atmosphere of silence by the press. Only one article in *Pravda* has been devoted to the Plenum and this article contains a phrase of unheard-of impudence: "He would be a criminal who would think of shaking the unity of the ranks of the Comintern", etc., etc. Everyone understands what is meant by this. Even before the drafts of the resolutions have been published, *Pravda* brands as a criminal whoever argues against the future resolutions. One can imagine how *Pravda* will inform the Party tomorrow about what is taking place here. Meanwhile, here in Moscow every expression of opinion, oral or written, in favour of the Opposition on the basic problems of the Chinese Revolution is treated as a crime against the Party. The completely false theses of comrade Stalin have been declared de facto inviolable. Still more, in the very days of the proceedings of the Executive, those comrades who, in the discussions in their Party cells, protested against the baiting of comrade Zinoviev, are simply expelled from the Party or are at least threatened with expulsion. It is in this atmosphere, comrades, that you are acting and deciding. I propose that the Executive decide that every party, the Communist Party of the Soviet Union included, shall publish completely exact and objective reports on our deliberations, supplemented by all the theses and documents distributed here. The problems of the Chinese Revolution cannot be stuck into a bottle and sealed up.

Comrades, the greatest of all dangers is the ever-sharpening Party régime. Every mistake of the leadership is made "good", so to speak, through measures against the Opposition. The day the telegram on Chiang Kai-shek's *coup d'état* was made known in Moscow, we said to each other: The Opposition will have to pay dearly for this—especially as demands for payment on their part have not been lacking recently.

The opportunity is always found to frame up a new "case" of Zinoviev, Kamenev, Trotsky, Piatakov, Smilga, etc., so as to distract the attention of the Party from the most burning questions; expulsions of the Opposition, despite the approach of the Party congress—or rather just because of it—constantly increase. The same methods in every section of the Party: in every factory, in every district, in every city. In this situation there frequently emerge, of necessity, those elements who are always ready to accept in advance everything from above, because nothing is difficult for them. They lull themselves into the hope that after Trotsky or Zinoviev have been overcome, everything will be in order. On the contrary: the régime has its own inner logic. The list has only been opened, not closed. Along this road there are only difficulties and further convulsions.

This régime weighs heavily on the International. Nobody trusts himself to speak a word of criticism openly, on the false pretence of not wanting to harm the Soviet Union. But that is exactly how the greatest harm is done. Our internal policy needs revolutionary international criticism, for the wrong tendencies in foreign policy are only an extension of the incorrect tendencies in our internal policy.

I now turn to the draft resolution of comrade Bukharin. First, a question which directly touches the point on the agenda already acted upon. Listen, comrades:

> "The Communist International is of the opinion that parties, and in general all organizations that call themselves workers' parties and workers' organizations, which do not conduct the *most decisive struggle* against intervention in China, which *lull the vigilance of the working class* and propagate a *passive attitude* on this question, objectively (sometimes also subjectively) help the imperialists ... in the preparation of war against the Soviet Union and in the preparation of new world wars in general."

These ring like honest words. But they become honest only when they are applied also to the Anglo-Russian Committee. For does it "conduct the most decisive struggle against intervention in China"? No! Does it not lull the vigilance of the working class? It does. Does it not propagate a passive attitude on this question! Without a doubt. Does it not thereby objectively (in its British half also subjectively) help the imperialists of Britain in their work of preparing the war? Obviously and without a doubt.

Compare this with what was declaimed here yesterday by Kuusinen on the Anglo-Russian Committee, in the language of Kuusinenized Purcellism. Whence this duplicity? The philosophy of customs certificates is far more appropriate in the customs office of a border state than on the tribune of the Comintern. This false and unworthy philosophy must be swept away with a broom.

Let us listen further to Bukharin's resolution:

> "The ECCI declares that the development of events [in the Chinese revolution, the estimate of its driving forces made at the last Enlarged Plenum of the CI] has confirmed the prognosis. The ECCI declares especially that the course of events has fully confirmed the prognosis of the Enlarged Plenum on the inevitable departure of the bourgeoisie from the national revolutionary united front and its going over to the side of the counter-revolution."

The workers of Shanghai and Hankow will certainly be surprised when they read that the April events developed in complete harmony with the historical line of March which comrade Bukharin had previously outlined for the Chinese revolution. Could one ever imagine a more malicious caricature and more ridiculous pedantry? The vanguard of the Chinese proletariat was smashed by that same "national" bourgeoisie which occupied the leading role in the joint party of the Guomindang, subordinating the Communist Party, on all decisive questions, to the organizational discipline of the joint party. After the counter-revolutionary coup, which struck the Chinese workers and the huge majority of the working class of the world like a bolt from the blue, the resolution says: It all took place in accordance with the best rules of the Bukharinist prognosis. This really sounds like a bad joke.

What is to be understood here by a prognosis, what does this so-called prognosis signify under the given conditions? Nothing but an empty phrase on the fact that the bourgeoisie, at a given stage of the bourgeois revolution, must separate itself from the oppressed masses of the people. That this commonplace is pathetically called a "prognosis", is a disgrace to Marxism. This banality does not separate Bolshevism from Menshevism for an instant. Ask Kautsky, Otto Bauer or Dan, and their answer will be: the bloc of the proletariat with the bourgeoisie cannot last for ever. Dan scribbled that in his rag only a short time ago.

But the kernel of the question is the following: To say that the bourgeoisie must separate itself from the national revolution is one thing. But to say that the bourgeoisie must take hold of the leadership of the revolution and the leadership of the proletariat, deceive the working class and then disarm it, smash it, and bleed it to death, is something quite different. The whole philosophy of Bukharin, in his resolution, is founded on the identity of these two prognoses. But this means that one does not want to make any fundamental contrast between the Bolshevik and Menshevik perspectives.

Let us listen to what Lenin said on this question:

> "The bourgeois politicians have fed and deceived the people with promises in *every* bourgeois revolution. Our revolution is a bourgeois revolution—*therefore* the workers must support the bourgeoisie. This is what the good-for-nothing politicians of the liquidator camp say. Our revolution is a bourgeois revolution, is what we Marxists say, and *therefore* the workers must open the eyes of the people to the deceit of the bourgeois politicians, teach them not to believe them, but to rely on their *own* forces, on their *own* solidarity, on their own *arms*." (March 1917)

Foreseeing the inevitable departure of the bourgeoisie, Bolshevik policy in the bourgeois revolution is directed towards creating an independent organization of the proletariat as soon as possible, impregnating it as deeply as possible with mistrust of the bourgeoisie, uniting the masses as soon and as broadly as possible and arming them, aiding the revolutionary uprising of the peasant masses in every way. The Menshevik policy in foreseeing the so-called departure of the bourgeoisie is directed towards postponing this moment as long as possible; while the independence of policy and organization of the proletariat is sacrificed to this aim, the workers are instilled with confidence in the progressive role of the bourgeoisie, and the necessity of political self-restraint is preached. In order to maintain the alliance with Purcell, the great strike-breaker, he must be appeased by declaiming about cordial relations and political agreement. In order to maintain the so-called bloc with the Chinese bourgeoisie, they must always be whitewashed anew, thereby facilitating the deluding of the masses by the bourgeois politicians.

Yes, the moment of the departure of the bourgeoisie can thereby be postponed. But this postponement is utilized by the bourgeoisie against the proletariat: It seizes hold of the leadership thanks to its great social advantages, it arms its loyal troops, it prevents the arming of the proletariat, political as well as military, and after it has acquired the upper hand it organizes a counter-revolutionary massacre at the first serious collision.

It is not the same thing, comrades, whether the bourgeoisie is tossed to one side or it tosses the proletarian vanguard to one side. These are the two roads of the revolution. On what road did the revolution travel up to the coup? The classic road of all previous bourgeois revolutions, of which Lenin said:

> The bourgeois politicians have fed and deceived the people with promises in *every* bourgeois revolution.

Did the false position of the leadership obstruct or facilitate this road of the Chinese bourgeoisie? It facilitated it to a great extent.

To prevent the departure of the bourgeoisie from becoming the destruction of the proletariat, the miserable theory of the bloc of four classes should have been denounced from the very beginning as genuine theoretical and political treason to the Chinese revolution. Was this done? No, just the contrary.

I have not time enough to present a historical description of the development of the revolution and of our differences, which Bukharin had full opportunity to do—extensively and falsely. I am prepared to undertake this retrospective treatment in the theoretical organ of the Party or of the International. Unfortunately, Bukharin touches on this question only where we have no opportunity to answer him properly, that is, with facts and quotations.

The following will suffice for today:

1. On March 16, one short month before the coup by Chiang Kai-shek, an editorial in *Pravda* indicted the Opposition for believing that the bourgeoisie stands at the head of the Guomindang and the national government and is preparing

treason. Instead of making this truth clear to the Chinese workers, *Pravda* denied it indignantly. It contended that Chiang Kai-shek submitted to the discipline of the Guomindang, as if the conflicting classes, especially in the feverish tempo of the revolution, could submit to common political discipline. Incidentally: if the Opposition never had anything to say against the official line, as was said here by Smilga in his ponderous manner, then why are the speeches and articles by Bukharin for the last year filled with accusations against the Opposition on the most burning questions of the Chinese Revolution?

If I have time, I will read here a letter by Radek: it is a repetition of his letter of last July. This letter was written last September and takes up the most burning questions of the Chinese Revolution.

2. Only on April 5, that is, only a week before the *coup d'état* by Chiang Kai-shek, Stalin rejected Radek's opinion at a meeting of Moscow functionaries and declared again that Chiang Kai-shek was submitting to discipline, that the admonitions were baseless, that we would use the Chinese bourgeoisie and then toss it away like a squeezed-out lemon. The whole speech of Stalin meant the soothing, the allaying of the uneasiness, the lulling to sleep of our party and the Chinese party. Thousands of comrades listened to this speech. This was on April 5. Truly, the prognosis is not so remarkable as Bukharin may claim. The stenogram of this speech by Stalin was never made public, because a few days later the squeezed-out lemon seized power with his army. As a member of the CC, I had the right to get the stenogram of this speech. But my efforts and attempts were in vain. Attempt it now, comrades, perhaps you will have better luck. I doubt it. This concealed stenogram of Stalin alone, without any other document, suffices to reveal the erroneousness of the official line, and to demonstrate how out of place it is to maintain that the events in Shanghai and Canton "confirmed" the very line that Stalin defended in Moscow a week before.

3. The CC received a report on March 17 from China, from three comrades who were sent there by the CC. This highly important document gives an actual description of what the

line of the CI really looked like. Borodin acted, in the words of the document, sometimes as a right, at other times as a Left Guomindang man, but never as a Communist. The representatives of the CI also acted in the same spirit, by transforming it a little into the *Guomintern*; they hindered the independent policy of the proletariat, its independent organization and especially its armament; to reduce this to a minimum they considered their sacred duty. Heaven forbid, with arms in hand the proletariat would frighten the great spirit of the national revolution, hovering over all the classes. Demand this document! Read it! Study it, so that you will not have to vote blindly.

I could name dozens of other articles, speeches and documents of this type over a period of about one and a half to two years. I am prepared to do it in writing at any moment, with complete accuracy and a statement of date and page. But what has been said is already enough to prove how basically false is the assertion that the events confirmed the "prognosis" of that time.

Read further in the resolution:

> The ECCI is of the opinion that the tactic of a bloc with the national bourgeoisie in the period of the revolution already passed was fully correct.

Still more. Bukharin contends even today that the renowned formula of Martynov that the national government is the government of the bloc of four classes, suffers from only one trifling defect, that Martynov did not emphasize that the bourgeoisie stands at the head of the bloc. A quite insignificant trifle! Unfortunately, Martynov's masterpiece shows many other defects. For Martynov contends quite openly and clearly in his *Pravda* article that this national Chiang Kai-shek government was no (no!) bourgeois government, but (but!) the four-class-bloc government. Thus is it written for him in the holy scriptures.

What does this mean, anyway—bloc of four classes? Have you encountered this expression in Marxist writing before? If the bourgeoisie leads the oppressed masses of the people under the bourgeois banner, and takes hold of the state power through its leadership, then this is no bloc but the political exploitation of the oppressed masses by the bourgeoisie. But the national revolution is progressive, you reply. To be sure. Capitalist development in backward countries is also progressive. But its progressive character is not conditioned by the economic *co-operation* of the classes, but by the economic *exploitation* of the proletariat and the peasantry by the bourgeoisie. Whoever does not speak of the class struggle but of class co-operation in order to characterize capitalist progress, is not a Marxist but a prophet of peace dreams. Whoever speaks of the bloc of four classes so as to emphasize the progressive character of the political exploitation of the proletariat and peasantry by the bourgeoisie, has nothing to do with Marxism, for herein really lies the political function of the opportunists, of the "conciliators", of the heralds of peace dreams.

The question of the Guomindang has the closest connection with this. What Bukharin makes out of it is real political trickery. The Guomindang is so "special", something unprecedented, something that can only be characterized by the blue flag and blue smoke—in a word: whoever does not understand this highly complicated "special thing"— and it cannot be understood for, according to Bukharin, it is just too "special"—understands nothing about the Chinese Revolution. What Bukharin himself understands about it, however, is not to be understood at all from Bukharin's words. The Guomindang is a *party*, and in time of revolution, it can be understood only as a party. In the recent period, this party has not embodied the "bloc of four classes", but the leading role of the bourgeoisie over the masses of the people, the proletariat and the Communist Party included. The word "bloc" should not be misused, especially not in the this case where it is done only for the good of the bourgeoisie. Taken politically, a bloc is the expression of an alliance of sides "with equal rights", who come to an understanding on a certain joint action. Only, this was not the case in China, and still is not to this day. The Communist Party was a subordinated part of a party at whose head stood the national-liberal bourgeoisie. Last May, the Communist Party bound itself not to criticize even the teachings of Sun Yat Sen, that is, the petty-bourgeois doctrine which is aimed not only against imperialism but also against the proletarian class struggle.

This "special" Guomindang has assimilated the lesson of the *exclusiveness* of the party which exercises the dictatorship and draws from this the conclusion as regards the Communists: "Hold your tongue!", for in Russia—they say—there is also only one party at the head of the revolution.

With us the dictatorship of the party (quite falsely disputed theoretically by Stalin) is the expression of the socialist dictatorship of the proletariat. In China we have the bourgeois revolution, and the dictatorship of the Guomindang is directed not only against the imperialists and the militarists but also against the proletarian class struggle. In that way, the bourgeoisie, supported by the petty bourgeoisie and the radicals, curbs the class struggle of the proletariat and the uprisings of the peasantry, strengthens itself at the cost of the masses of the people and the revolution. We stood for this, we made it easier for them to go on with it, we want to sanction it now also by talking nonsense about the "special nature" of the Guomindang without showing the proletariat the vicious class manoeuvres that have been and are concealed behind this "special nature".

The dictatorship of a party is a part of the socialist revolution. In the bourgeois revolution, the proletariat must absolutely insure the independence of its own party—at any price, cost what it may. The Communist Party of China has been a shackled party in the past period. It did not have so much as its own newspaper. Imagine what this means in general and especially in a revolution! Why has it not had, and has not yet to this day, its own daily paper? Because the Guomindang does not want it. Can we tolerate anything like this? This means disarming the proletariat politically. Then withdrawal from the Guomindang—cries Bukharin. —Why? Do you want to say thereby that the Communist Party cannot exist within the "revolutionary" Guomindang as a party? I can accept remaining within a really revolutionary Guomindang only under conditions of complete political and organizational freedom of action for the Communist Party, with a guaranteed common bias for action by the Guomindang together with the Communist Party.

The political conditions for this have been enumerated in the thesis of Zinoviev as well as in my own (no. 39) more precisely in points a, b, c, d, e, f, g, and h. These are the conditions for remaining in the Left Guomindang. If comrade Bukharin is for remaining unconditionally—under all circumstances and at any price—then we do not go along with him.

(Remmele: Where is that in the resolution?)

The maintenance of a bloc or the organizational form of a bloc at any price leads to the necessity of throwing oneself at the feet of one's partner. The Berlin session of the Anglo-Russian Committee teaches us that.

The Communist Party must create its own completely independent daily press, at any price. Thereby it will for the first time really begin to live and act as a political party.

Let us read further:

> The ECCI considers radically false the liquidatory [Look, look!] view that the crisis of the Chinese revolution is a long-term defeat.

On this point, we have expressed ourselves in our theses with complete clarity. That the defeat is great I consider self-evident. To seek to minimize it only means to stand in the way of the education of the Chinese party.

No one is today in a position to prophesy exactly if the defeat will last, or for how long. At any rate, in our theses we proceed from the possibility of the speedy overcoming of the defeat by the proletariat. But the preliminary condition for this is a correct policy on our part. The policy represented by comrade Chen Duxiu, the leader of the party, in his speech at the latest convention of the Communist Party of China (published recently in *Pravda*) is basically false on the two most important questions: that of the revolutionary government, and that of the agrarian revolution. If we do not correct with the greatest energy the policy of the Chinese and our own party on these two decisive questions, the defeat will become deeper and weigh heavily on the Chinese working people for a long time. What is most essential concerning this has been said in my thesis, in the postscript to the speech of comrade Chen Duxiu. I must limit myself greatly, and I point to the theses and other documents. I have promised to read also the letter from Radek to the Central Committee. Unfortunately I cannot here refute wholly frivolous and absurd assertions about the "surrender" of the Chinese Eastern Railway, etc. Bukharin, like myself, has no documents on this, because the question was considered quite cursorily at one session of the Politburo.

(Bukharin: It is shameless to deny this.)

If I am given three minutes for it, I will immediately refute the shamefaced Bukharin, for what he says is a lie. The only thing I proposed at that time—after the words of comrade Rudzutak, who said this railway becomes an instrument of imperialism now and then (for which Bukharin attacked Rudzutak)—was a declaration from our side in which we repeat, in an open and solemn manner, that which we had already said once in the Peking decisions: The moment the Chinese people has created its own democratic unified government, we will freely and gladly hand over the railway to them on the most favourable conditions. The Politburo said: No, at this time such a declaration will be interpreted as a sign of weakness, we will make this declaration a month from now. Although not in agreement with this, I raised no protest against it. It was a fleeting discussion which was only later transformed in a wretched manner, in an untruthful way, then, turned into a rounded-off formula, launched in the Party organization, in the Party cells, with warped insinuations in the press—in a word, dealt with just as has become the custom and practice with us in recent times.

Chairman: Comrade Trotsky, I call your attention to the fact that you have only eight more minutes to speak. The Presidium granted you forty-five minutes and after that I must let the Plenum decide.

Remmele: Besides that, I must request the Plenum to reject certain imputations and expressions; to speak of a shameless Bukharin is the lowest I have yet heard.

Trotsky: If I am reproached for shamelessness and I speak of the shamefaced, protest is made—against me. I speak of the shamefaced Remmele who accuses me of shamelessness. It is you who speak of shamelessness, I always speak only of shamefacedness.

Chairman: I strongly request you to abstain from such expressions. Do not think that you can behave here just as you please.

Trotsky: I bow before the objectivity of the chairman, and withdraw every suspicion of "shamefacedness".

I cannot read the whole of Radek's letter; perhaps I will do it when I speak a second time. The letter from Radek, which was sent to the CC in full agreement with myself and Zinoviev, and which raised the most burning questions of the Chinese Revolution which we are discussing here today, was not answered by the Politburo of the Party. I must therefore now speak only on the general political consequences created by the very heavy defeat of the Chinese Revolution.

Comrade Bukharin has already made the attempt to refer to the fact that Chamberlain broke off diplomatic relations. We were—I have already observed—in a very difficult situation, where we were surrounded by enemies, and Bukharin and other comrades participated then in a great party discussion to find the correct way out of the difficult situation. A revolutionary party can renounce its right to analyse the situation and draw the necessary conclusions for its policy just as little in a difficult situation as in a favourable one. For I repeat again, if a false policy can be harmless in a favourable situation it can become fatal in a difficult situation.

Are the differences of opinion great? Very great, very significant, very important! It cannot be denied that they have become deeper in the course of the last year. No one would have believed in the possibility of the Berlin decisions of the Anglo-Russian Committee a year ago, no-one in the possibility that the philosophy of the bloc of four classes would be flaunted in *Pravda,* that Stalin would present his squeezed-out lemon on the eve of Chiang Kai-shek's *coup d'état,* just as Kuusinen yesterday presented his customs certificate. Why did this quick development become possible? Because the incorrect line was checked by the two greatest events of the last year, the great strikes in Britain and the Chinese Revolution.

Comrades have come forward—and we shall certainly hear such voices again—who said: since the contradictions have become sharpened, the road leads necessarily to two parties. I deny this. We live in a period where contradictions do not ossify, because great events teach us better. There is a great and dangerous push towards the right in the line of the CI. But we have enough confidence in the force of the Bolshevik idea and the power of great events to reject decisively and determinedly every prophecy of split.

The theses of comrade Bukharin are false. And, moreover, in the most dangerous manner. They suppress the most important points of the question. They contain the danger that we shall not only fail to make up for lost time but that we shall lose still more time.

1. Instead of continually sounding alarms about wanting to withdraw from the Guomindang (which is not proposed at all) the political independence of the Communist Party must be put above all other considerations, even that of remaining in the Guomindang. A separate daily press, relentless criticism also against the Left Guomindang.

2. The postponement of the agrarian revolution until the territory is secured militarily—the idea of Chen Tu Shiu—must be condemned formally, for this program endangers the life of the revolution.

3. The postponement of the reorganization of the government until the military victory—a second idea of Chen Tu Shiu—must also be characterized as endangering the life of the revolution. The bloc of Hankow leaders is not yet a revolutionary government. To create and spread any illusions on this score means to condemn the revolution to death. Only the workers', peasants', petty-bourgeois and soldiers' soviets can serve as the basis for a revolutionary government.

Naturally, the Hankow government will have to adapt itself to the soviets in some way or other, or else—disappear.

4. The alliance between the Communist Party and a really revolutionary Guomindang must not only be maintained but must be extended and deepened on the basis of mass soviets.

Whoever speaks of arming the workers without permitting the workers to build soviets is not serious about arming them.

If the revolution develops further—and we are fully confident that it will—the impulse of the workers to build soviets will grow ever stronger. We must prepare, strengthen and extend this movement, but not hamper and apply brakes to it as the resolution proposes.

The Chinese Revolution cannot be advanced if the worst right deviations are abetted, and smuggled Menshevik goods are allowed to be circulated under the customs seal of Bolshevism—comrade Kuusinen did this for a whole hour yesterday—while on the other hand the really revolutionary warnings of the left are mechanically smothered.

Bukharin's resolution is false and dangerous. It directs the attack towards the left. The Communist Party of China, which can and must become a really Bolshevik Party in the fire of the revolution, cannot accept this resolution. Our party and the entire Comintern cannot declare this resolution their own. The world historical problem must be openly and honestly discussed by the whole International. The discussion, may it be ever so sharp politically, should not be conducted in the tone of envenomed, personal baiting and slander. All the documents, the speeches, the theses, the articles must be made available to the membership of the International.

The Chinese Revolution cannot be stuffed into a bottle and sealed from above with a signet.

20

Second Speech on the Chinese Question

May 1927 Moscow

We are all of the opinion that the Chinese Revolution lives and will continue to live. That is why the main question is not whether the Opposition issued a warning and when, and where (I assert that it did warn and take it upon myself to prove it); the question is not whether Trotsky or Maslow wanted to surrender the Chinese Eastern Railway; the question is rather what is to be done from now on to pull the revolution out of the morass into which it was led by false policy and to set it on the correct road. I want, in a few words, to go to the heart of the question and show the irreconcilable divergence between our position and Stalin's.

Stalin has again declared himself here against workers' and peasants' soviets with the argument that the Guomindang and the Wuhan government are sufficient means and instruments for the agrarian revolution. Thereby Stalin assumes, and wants the International to assume the responsibility for the policy of the Guomindang and the Wuhan government, as he repeatedly assumed the responsibility for the policy of the former "national government" of Chiang Kai-shek (particularly in his speech of April 5, the stenogram of which has, of course, been kept hidden from the International).

We have nothing in common with this policy. We do not want to assume even a shadow of responsibility for the policy of the Wuhan government and the leadership of the

Guomindang, and we urgently advise the Comintern to reject this responsibility. We say directly to the Chinese peasants: The leaders of the Left Guomindang of the type of Wang Jingwei and Co. will inevitably betray you if you follow the Wuhan heads instead of forming your own independent soviets. The agrarian revolution is a serious thing. Politicians of the Wang Jingwei type, under difficult conditions, will unite ten times with Chiang Kai-shek against the workers and peasants. Under such conditions, two Communists in a bourgeois government become impotent hostages, if not a direct mask for the preparation of a new blow against the working masses. We say to the workers of China: The peasants will not carry out the agrarian revolution to the end if they let themselves be led by petty-bourgeois radicals instead of by you, the revolutionary proletarians. Therefore, build up your workers' soviets, ally them with the peasant soviets, arm yourselves through the soviets, draw soldiers' representatives into the soviets, shoot the generals who do not recognize the soviets, shoot the bureaucrats and bourgeois liberals who will organize uprisings against the soviets. Only through peasants' and soldiers' soviets will you win over the majority of Chiang Kai-shek's soldiers to your side. You, the advanced Chinese proletarians, would be traitors to your class and to your historic mission, were you to believe that an organization of leaders, petty-bourgeois and compromising in spirit, which has no more than 250,000 members (see the report of Tang Pingshan), is capable of taking the place of workers', peasants', and soldiers' soviets embracing millions upon millions. *The Chinese bourgeois-democratic revolution will go forward and be victorious either in the soviet form or not at all.*

We will say to the Chinese Communists: The program of comrade Chen Duxiu, namely, to postpone the "reorganization" of the Hankow régime and the confiscation of the large landowners' land until the war danger is eliminated, is the surest and swiftest road to ruin. The war is a class danger. It can only be ended by crushing the great landowners, by annihilating the agents of imperialism and of Chiang Kai-shek and by the building of soviets. Precisely in that lies the agrarian revolution, the people's revolution, the workers' and peasants' revolution, i.e., the genuine national revolution (in the Leninist, but not in the Martinovist sense of the term).

Now on the internal questions of the Communist Party of the Soviet Union.

At critical moments like the present, the principal rule of revolutionary policy consists of thinking out a question to the very end and expressing one's opinion completely, with entire clarity, without any hypocrisy, without reservations. It is a question of the Opposition in the CPSU and of what is going to happen in connection with the international difficulties and the prospect of war.

It would be manifestly absurd to believe that the Opposition can simply renounce its views. Such questions are decided by the test of events. An examination of the last half year since the Seventh Plenum has, in our opinion, shown and proved that the line of the Opposition stood the test of the greatest events of the Chinese Revolution and made it possible to foresee and foretell correctly every stage in the question of the Anglo-Russian Committee, that is, in essence, the question of Amsterdam, and consequently also of the Second International.

Is common work possible? I have enumerated our diplomats to you, and I named only the most important ones. I could name hundreds and thousands of Opposition party workers in various posts at home. Will anyone dare to say that such Oppositionists, for example, as the People's Commissar for Postal and Telegraphic Communications, Ivan Nikitich Smirnov, or the head of the Workers' and Peasants' Inspection for the Army and Navy, Muralov, or the People's Commissar for the interior, Byeloborodov, fulfil their duties worse than others? But the whole trick of the Party apparatus consists of removing the Oppositionists from their work, beginning with the skilled workers in the factories. They are persecuted, shifted around, driven out, regardless of the quality of their work, solely and exclusively because of their Opposition viewpoint, which they defend with party methods. As the Party Congress approaches, they are trying to send a member of the Central Committee, comrade Smilga, one of the oldest Bolsheviks, one of the heroes of the October Revolution and the civil war, one of our outstanding economists, to the Far East, to Khabarovsk, for planning work, that is, simply to isolate him politically. In the same manner, they are trying to get rid of comrade Safarov, who has more than twenty years of uninterrupted Party work behind him, by proposing to him to leave as soon as possible, be it for Turkey, or Tierra del Fuego, or the planet Mars, or anywhere else, so long as he disappears. They are trying at all costs to ship one of the oldest Party members, Kuklin, a proletarian to the core, a former member of the Central Committee (he was removed from it for supporting the Opposition) to Britain, where he would be practically like a fish out of water. All of them are stainless revolutionists, fighters of the October Revolution and the civil war. The number of examples could be multiplied endlessly. This method is ruinous. It disorganizes the Party. Common practical work is entirely possible. This has been demonstrated by all our experience. The guarantee for such common work in the interest of our workers' state depends entirely upon the Central Committee which is, it is true, pursuing an exactly contrary course.

I repeat: conscientious common work is possible, despite the deepening of the differences during the last year. On international questions this has appeared clearly, because tremendous events have taken place there. But now developments are entering a new phase in internal questions. Not only war, but also war danger itself puts all questions harshly before us. Every class necessarily examines the fundamental questions of policy when faced with war. The kulak, the functionary, and the NEP-man raise their heads and ask: What kind of war will this be, what will we get out of it, with what methods will it be conducted? On the other hand, the town worker, the land worker and the poor peasant will also examine more sharply, in face of the war danger, the achievements of the revolution, the advantages and disadvantages of the soviet régime, and will ask: In which direction will the relationship of forces be changed by the war? Will it increase the role of the men on top or the masses below? Will it straighten out the proletarian class line of the Party or will it accelerate the shift towards the high-ups under the pretext of a "national war" (in the Stalinist interpretation)?

The bourgeois elements among us have grown very strong; the struggle of the two tendencies has its roots in the classes. Since there is only one party in our country, the struggle goes on inside our party.

With the greatest light-mindedness, or more correctly, with the most criminal light-mindedness, they have spoken here of shattering the Opposition, of splitting off the Opposition, and the speakers were those whose whole past gives them the least right to do so. But I shall not dwell on them. Such people are washed ashore by one wave and washed away by another.

Ustryalov, the shrewdest enemy of Bolshevism, has for some time demanded the expulsion of the Opposition and a split with it. Ustryalov is the representative of the new bourgeoisie which grows out of the NEP, and of the most virile section of the old bourgeoisie which wants to support itself upon the new. Ustryalov does not want to "skip over any stages". Ustryalov openly supports the policy of Stalin and only demands of Stalin greater determination in liquidating the Opposition. Ponder over these facts.

On the other hand, when MacDonald appeals against intervention, he demands that the sensible "practical politicians" should not be prevented from putting an end to "the propagandists of the Third International"—these are literally MacDonald's words—, that is, that Stalin should not be disturbed in his work of smashing the Opposition. Chamberlain, with his brigand's methods, wants to hasten the same process. The various methods are directed towards one aim: to smash the proletarian line, to destroy the international connections of the Soviet Union, to force the Russian proletariat to renounce its intervention in the affairs of the international proletariat. Can it be doubted that MacDonald will raise no objection to your refusal to permit comrade Zinoviev to attend the sessions of the Comintern? MacDonald will boast of his own farsightedness if you should carry out the policy of destroying and splitting off the opposition. MacDonald will say: The practical politicians are breaking with the propagandists of the Third International.

The attempt to depict the Opposition as a group of leaders is a gross deception. The Opposition is an expression of the class struggle. The organizational weakness of the Opposition by no means corresponds to its specific weight in the Party and the working class. The strength of the present Party régime lies, among other things, in the fact that it changes the relation of forces in the Party by artificial means. The present heavy bureaucratic régime in the Party reflects the pressure of other classes upon the proletariat. Yesterday, eighty old Party members, tested Bolsheviks, sent a declaration to the Central Committee in which they fully support the standpoint which we are developing here. They are all comrades who have behind them ten, fifteen, twenty and more years of uninterrupted work in the Bolshevik Party. To speak of any kind of "Trotskyism" in the face of all these facts, is to falsify the question in a ridiculous and wretched manner. The revisionists label the revolutionary content of Marxism with the word Blanquism, the more easily to enable them to fight against Marxism. The comrades who are turning away from the Bolshevik line label the revolutionary content of Leninism "Trotskyism", the more easily to enable them to fight against Leninism. We have had a classic example of this in the speech of comrade Kuusinen, out of whose mouth spoke a provincial German Social Democrat.

During the most recent period of Party development, the blows have been directed only against the left. The basic reason for this is the defeats of the proletariat in the international field and the strengthening of the right course flowing from them. The whole history of the working-class movement proves that great defeats result in a temporary triumph of the opportunist line. After the defeat of the great strikes in Britain and of the Chinese Revolution, they want to deliver a new blow to the Opposition, that is, to the left, revolutionary line in the Communist Party of the Soviet Union and the Communist International. There is no doubt that the most principled, most consummate speech was delivered here by the new leader of the new course, Martynov, the mountebank of the bloc of four classes. What does this signify? A still greater strengthening of the shift to the right. It means the threat that the tendencies of

Ustryalov will triumph. The Ustryalovs do not want to skip over any stages or phases, that is why the Ustryalovs are now openly for Stalin. But they do not, of course, think of remaining with him. For them, he is only a stage. For them, it is a question of destroying the left barrier in the CPSU, of weakening the proletarian line, of transforming the soviet system into an instrument of the petty bourgeoisie, so as to proceed from there on the direct road towards the restoration of capitalism, most probably in the Bonapartist form.

The war danger puts all questions harshly. Stalin's line is the line of indecision, of vacillation between left and right tendencies with actual support for the right course. The growth of the war danger will force Stalin to choose. He has made an effort here to show that the choice has already been made. After the massacre of the Chinese workers by the bourgeoisie, after the capitulation of the Political Bureau to Purcell, after the speech of Chen Duxiu in *Pravda*, Stalin sees the enemy only on the left and directs his fire against them. Dozens of old and tested Bolshevik Party comrades, chiefly from Moscow and Leningrad, warn the Party in their collective letter of the threatening internal dangers. We do not doubt that thousands of Party fighters will join with them, fighters who do not fear threats or provocations, and who, despite all mechanical barriers, will understand how to penetrate to the public opinion of the Party, and to redress the revolutionary line of Bolshevism through the Party and by Party methods.

Fraternizing with Purcell and baiting Zinoviev, eulogizing and painting up the bourgeois leaders of the Guomindang and baiting the Left Opposition in the CPSU and in other parties—one goes closely together with the other. This is a definite course. Against this course we will fight to the end. Stalin said the Opposition stands in one front with Chamberlain, with Mussolini and Zhang Zuolin. To that I answer: Nothing has facilitated the work of Chamberlain so much as the false policy of Stalin, particularly in China. The revolution cannot be made by halves. The London blow is the pay-off for the Martinovist course in China. On this path, only defeats can be accumulated.

Stalin obviously wants to make the attempt to present the Opposition as something like a defence corps for Chamberlain.

This is wholly in the spirit of his methods. Yesterday Michael Romanov, today Chamberlain. But here he will miscalculate even more than he did with his hopes in Chiang Kai-shek and Purcell. Chamberlain must be seriously fought against, and the working class in the country and throughout the world must be brought to its feet and united. The masses can be brought to their feet, united and strengthened only through a correct class line. While we fight for a correct revolutionary line against the line of Stalin, we are preparing the best conditions for the struggle against Chamberlain. It is not we who are helping Chamberlain; it is the false policy.

Not a single honest proletarian will believe the insane infamy about the united front between Chamberlain and Trotsky. But the reactionary section of the petty bourgeoisie, the rising kulakdom of the Black Hundreds, can believe this, or pretend to believe this, so as to carry through to the end the suppression of the revolutionary proletarian line and its representatives. If you give the devil of chauvinism a finger, you perish. With his poisoned accusations, Stalin is extending this finger. We say this here and we will say it openly before the international proletariat.

21

Is it not Time to Understand?

May 28, 1927 Moscow

Today's *Bulletin of Tass*[1], Number 118, not for the press, contains a few telegrams of exclusively political importance. These telegrams are not kept concealed from public opinion because they may cause harm to the soviet state or the Chinese Revolution, but because they prove the faultiness of the official course and the correctness of the line of the Opposition. We cite only the two especially striking telegrams:

> *Shanghai, May 24. TASS—The central political council in Nanking has decided to make Feng Yuxiang a member of the council.*

That Chiang Kai-shek has made Feng Yuxiang a member of the council (for the time being, perhaps, without the consent of the "cautious" Feng Yuxiang) is now known to the whole world. But it must remain a secret from the Soviet workers. Why? Because Feng Yuxiang has until recently been presented to us at home as a genuine "worker" or "peasant", as a reliable revolutionist, and so forth, that is, all the mistakes that were previously made with Chiang Kai-shek, were again made with Feng Yuxiang. Now, for the last few week, all telegrams concerning the more than dubious conduct of Feng Yuxiang have been concealed. Why? To what end? Obviously, because some are waiting with the secret hope: perhaps he will not betray us after all! And if he does betray us, they will say: this completely verifies our prediction on the abandonment of the national revolution by the bourgeoisie. But now? Instead of warning the Chinese workers and the Party, instead of stirring the masses of workers, peasants and soldiers to adopt really revolutionary measures against the treason of the generals, we keep quiet, we conceal the telegrams in our pockets. That will not help. The class logic of the revolutionary struggle cannot be concealed in one's pocket.

The second telegram:

> The Situation in Hankow
>
> Hankow, May 23. TASS—The Central Committee of the Communist Party has proposed to the 'Hupeh League for Strengthening the Revolutionary Front' to set in order the relations between the workers and the petty-bourgeoisie. The Central Committee emphasized the necessity of increasing discipline among the workers and of obedience to the decrees of the National Government and declared that the trade unions have not the right to arrest anyone, and must always apply to the authorities when they consider the arrest of this or that person necessary.

This telegram is even more important than the first. For every serious revolutionist, it illuminates the whole situation and shows the absolute faultiness of the official line, the downright disastrousness of this line, and the absolute correctness of the line of the Opposition.

Just think: the trade unions in the territory of the Hankow government are arresting the enemies of the revolution. This means that the trade unions, by the whole logic of the situation, are forced to assume the tasks of revolutionary soviets. Now what does the Central Committee of the Communist Party do? It recommends to the trade unions to refrain from non-legal actions, to submit to the "decrees" of the Wuhan authorities, and in case of emergency, when a counter-revolutionist, a traitor, or conspirator has to be arrested or shot, to apply respectfully to the authorities who, in all probability, are related or allied to the conspirator. Is this not a mockery of the revolution, of its needs and of its most elementary tasks? Instead of arousing the masses to settle with the enemy right on the spot, the Wuhan government forbids it. Still more, it forbids it not in its own name, but through the medium of the Communist Party. The Central Committee of the Communist Party, in this case, plays the role of a political clerk to cowardly bourgeois radicals and pseudo-radicals, who tremble before the revolutionary masses and believe together with Martynov that the revolution can be carried out through arbitration commissions but not through the liquidation of the enemy by the masses. Isn't this monstrous? Isn't this a mockery of the revolution?

It is noteworthy, besides, that the "Hupeh League for the Strengthening of the Revolutionary Front" is given a special commission, namely, to set in order "the relations between the workers and the petty-bourgeoisie". These relations cannot be set in order by a special League and not by special instructions, but only by a correct policy. The soviets of workers and of semi-proletarian city poor must be the broad organs of such a daily revolutionary policy. If the trade unions are forced to assume the functions of soviets, they will in certain cases almost inevitably leave out of consideration or injure the legitimate interests of the city petty-bourgeois. Thus, the absence of soviets also hits the petty-bourgeoisie and undermines its alliance with the proletariat.

Such is the situation in reality. The trade unions, driven forward by the masses, seek to correct the errors of the Chinese and Moscow leadership, and are proceeding to the immediate liquidation of the enemy. The Central Committee of the Communist Party, however, which ought to be the inspirer and leader of this summary liquidation, holds back the workers, and calls upon them to increase their "discipline" (towards the bourgeoisie), and to bow mutely before the connivance of the Hankow Kerenskys and Tseretelis with the agents of imperialism, of the bourgeoisie and of Chiang Kai-shek.

There is the Martinovist policy for you, not in words but in deeds!

A whole series of telegrams, especially from Tokyo, speaks of the "crumbling" of the Hankow government, of its impending downfall, and so forth. Of course such telegrams must be taken with the greatest caution. These are telegrams from an enemy, who awaits the downfall of the revolution, hopes for it, is on the watch for it, and thinks up all kinds of things and lies. But the two above-mentioned telegrams, like many others of a similar kind which arrive almost every day, compel us to recognize the fact that *the position of the Hankow government can become hopeless.* If it prevents the workers and peasants from putting an end to the counter-revolutionists, it will collapse. By its false policy, the Central Committee of the Communist Party is accelerating its collapse. Should the Hankow government crash under the assault of the workers', peasants' and soldiers' soviets, we will surely not regret it. And it will collapse because it opposes the creation of soviets. If the Hankow government is supported in this ruinous policy, if the Chinese workers and peasants are restrained from immediately eliminating the enemy, and from building soviets, then *the Chinese Communist Party is helping the Hankow government to collapse in the shortest time,* and to die an inglorious death, not at the hands of the worker and peasant masses, but at the hands of bourgeois reaction. What is more, with such a policy the Hankow government, before it "collapses", will most probably unite with Chiang Kai-shek—against the workers and peasants. Is it not really time to understand this?

NOTE

1. TASS, the Soviet Telegraphic Agency, was the official Soviet news agency.

22

Why have we not called for Withdrawal from the Kuomintang until Now?

June 23, 1927

The reasons we have not called for withdrawal from the Kuomintang until now (a serious blunder) can be correctly formulated in only one way that will account for both past and present. That is approximately as follows:

We have proceeded from the fact that the Communist Party has spent too much time in the Kuomintang, and that our party and the Comintern have been overly occupied with this question, but that openly calling for immediate withdrawal from the Kuomintang would even further sharpen the contradictions within our own party. We formulated the kind of conditions for the Chinese Communist Party's remaining in the Kuomintang, which—in practice, if not on paper—essentially excluded the possibility that the Chinese Communist Party would remain within the Kuomintang organization for a long period. We tried in this way to devise a transitional formula that could become a bridge our Central Committee could use to retreat from its erroneous course to a correct one. We posed the question pedagogically and not politically. As always in such cases, this turned out to be a mistake. While we were busy trying to enlighten a mistaken leadership, we were sacrificing political clarity with respect to the ranks. Because of this, the very way in which the question was raised was distorted. The Central Committee did not use our bridge, crying that the

Opposition was in fact in favor of withdrawal from the Kuomintang. We were compelled to "justify" ourselves and argue that we were not in favor of withdrawal. This clear contradiction between the pedagogical and the political was reflected in the very first lines of the Declaration of the Eighty-three.

Our basic approach on this question was correct, since we all held to the course for withdrawal from the Kuomintang. Our mistake was in pedagogically watering down, softening, and blunting our position on the basic question. It has yielded nothing but minuses for us: vagueness of position, defensive protestation, and lagging behind the events. We are putting an end to this error by openly calling for immediate withdrawal from the Kuomintang!

23

For a Special Session of the Presidium of the ECCI

July 1927

To the Presidium of the Executive Committee of the Communist International:

The recent news from China shows that placing our stakes on the Wuhan government as the "organizing center of the revolution" was a devastating mistake. Within the territory of the Wuhan government the counter-revolution organized with ease at the same time that the workers' movement was suppressed. The situation is extremely serious for both the Chinese Revolution and the USSR because a defeat for the Chinese Revolution increases the danger of war tenfold.

In view of this, we consider it especially necessary to immediately convene the Presidium of the ECCI along with members and alternates of the EC who are in Moscow to discuss the situation and correct the mistaken line that is being carried out by the Comintern in China and that was approved by the last plenum of the ECCI.

Vujovic
Zinoviev
Trotsky

24

What about China?

August 1, 1927

Let us take the entire tactical, or rather strategic line in China as a whole. The Kuomintang is the party of the liberal bourgeoisie in the period of revolution—the liberal bourgeoisie that draws behind it, deceives, and betrays the workers and peasants.

The Communist Party, in accordance with your directives, remains throughout all the betrayals within the Kuomintang and submits to its bourgeois discipline.

The Kuomintang as a whole enters into the Comintern and does not submit to its discipline, but merely utilizes the name and the authority of the Comintern to dupe the Chinese workers and peasants.

The Kuomintang serves as a shield for the landlord-generals who hold in their grip the soldier-peasants.

Moscow—at the end of last October-demands that the agrarian revolution be kept from developing so as not to scare away the landlords in command of the armies. The armies become mutual insurance societies for the landlords, large and small alike.

The landlords do not raise any objection to their military expeditions being called national revolutionary, so long as the power and the land remain in their hands. The proletariat, which composes a young revolutionary force in no way inferior to our own proletariat in 1905, is driven under the command of the Kuomintang.

Moscow offers counsel to the Chinese liberals: "Issue a law for the organization of a minimum of workers' detachments."

This, in March 1927! Why the counsel to the tops—Arm yourselves to the minimum? And why not a slogan to the rank and file—Arm yourselves to the maximum? Why the minimum and not the maximum? In order not to "scare away" the bourgeoisie, so as not to "provoke" a civil war. But the civil war came inevitably, and proved far more cruel, catching the workers unarmed and drowning them in blood.

Moscow came out against the building of soviets in the "army's rear—as if the revolution is the rump of an army!—in order not to disorganize the rear of the very same generals who two days later crushed the workers and peasants in their rear.

Did we reinforce the bourgeoisie and the landlords by compelling the communists to submit to the Kuomintang and by covering the Kuomintang with the authority of the Comintern? Yes, we did.

Did we weaken the peasantry by retarding the development of the agrarian revolution and of the soviets? Yes, we did.

Did we weaken the workers with the slogan of "minimum arming"—nay, not the slogan but the polite counsel to the bourgeois tops: "minimum arming," and "no need for soviets"? Yes, we did. Is it to be wondered at that we suffered a defeat, having done everything that could have made victory difficult?

Voroshilov gave the most correct, conscientious, and candid explanation for this entire policy. "The peasant revolution," he said, "might have interfered with the Northern Expedition of the generals." You put a brake on the revolution for the sake of a military expedition. That is exactly how Chiang Kai-shek viewed the matter. The development of the revolution might, you see, make an expedition difficult for a "nationalist" general. But, after all, the revolution itself is indeed an actual and a real expedition of the oppressed against the oppressors. To help the expedition of the generals, you put a brake on the revolution and disorganized it. Thereby the expedition of the generals was turned into a spearhead not only against the workers and the peasants but also-precisely because of that against the national revolution.

Had we duly secured the complete independence of the Communist Party, assisted it to arm itself with its press and with correct tactics; had we given it the slogans "Maximum arming of the workers!" "Extend the peasant war in the villages!" the Communist Party would have grown, not from day to day, but from hour to hour, and its cadres would have been tempered in the fires of revolutionary struggle. The slogan of soviets should have been raised from the very first days of the mass movement. Everywhere, wherever the slightest possibility existed, steps for the actual realization of soviets should have been taken. Soldiers should have been drawn into the soviets. The agrarian revolution would have disorganized the pseudo-revolutionary armies but it would have likewise transmitted the infection to the counter-revolutionary armies of the enemy. Only on this foundation could it have been possible to forge gradually a real revolutionary, i.e., workers' and peasants' army.

Comrades! We have heard here a speech made not by Voroshilov, the people's commissar for the army and navy, but by Voroshilov, a member of the Political Bureau. This speech, I say, is in itself a catastrophe. It is equivalent to a lost battle.

(Shouts from the Opposition benches: "Correct!")

Trotsky: Last May, during the plenum of the ECCI, when after finally assigning Chiang Kai-shek to the camp of reaction, you put your stakes on Wang Ching-wei, and then on T'ang Sheng-chih, I wrote a letter to the ECCI. It was on May 27. "This policy is erroneous, and it is ruinous." What did I propose? Here is literally what I wrote. On May 27, I wrote:

The plenum would do well to bury Bukharin's resolution, replacing it with a resolution of a few lines:

In the first place, peasants and workers should place no faith in the leaders of the left Kuomintang but they should instead build their soviets jointly with the soldiers. In the second place, the soviets should arm the workers and the advanced peasants. In the third place, the Communist Party must assure its complete independence, create a daily press, and assume the leadership in creating the soviets. Fourth, the land must be immediately taken away from the landlords. Fifth, the reactionary bureaucracy must be immediately dismissed. Sixth, perfidious generals and other counter-revolutionists must be summarily dealt with. And finally, the general course must be toward the establishment of a revolutionary dictatorship through the soviets of workers' and peasants' deputies. ["It is Time to Understand, Time to Reconsider, and Time to Make a Change."]

Now, compare this with: "There is no need for a civil war in the villages"; "Do not alarm the fellow travelers"; "Do not irritate the generals"; "Minimum arming of the workers"; and so on. This is Bolshevism! While our position is called in the Political Bureau Menshevism. Having turned yourselves inside out, you have firmly resolved to call white, black. But your misfortune is that international Menshevism—from Berlin to New York approves of the Chinese policy of Stalin-Bukharin, and being fully cognizant of the issues, solidarizes with your political line on the Chinese question.

Please try to understand that in question here is not the individual betrayals of the Chinese members of the Kuomintang, or of the right and left Chinese army commanders, or British trade unionists, and Chinese or British communists. When one rides in the train, it is the earth that appears to be in motion. The whole trouble lies in the fact that you placed hopes on those who were not to be relied upon; you underestimated the revolutionary training of the masses, the principal requirement for which is inoculating the masses with mistrust toward reformists, vague "left" centrists, and all vacillators in general. The fullest measure of this mistrust is the supreme virtue of Bolshevism. Young parties have still to acquire and assimilate this quality. Yet you have acted and are acting in a diametrically opposite fashion. You inoculate young parties with the hopes that the liberal bourgeoisie and the liberal labor politicians from the trade unions will move to the left. You hinder the education of the British and Chinese Bolsheviks. That is the source whence come these "betrayals" that each time catch you unaware.

Excerpted from 'The War Danger—the Defense Policy and the opposition,' in "The Stalin School of Falsification".

25

New Opportunities for the Chinese Revolution, New Tasks and New Mistakes

September 1927

Stalin and Bukharin's main concern at the present time is to claim that on the question of China the Opposition was always in complete solidarity with the Politburo majority until only recently. All the sections of the Comintern have been ordered to sermonize on this theme. This unexpected turn only serves to show how deepgoing the bankruptcy of the Stalin group is. Just yesterday they were still arguing that the Opposition, unlike Stalin-Bukharin, had a Social Democratic, semi-Menshevik position on all questions. And now they are boasting that Stalin and Bukharin have acted and spoken exactly as the Opposition has, in every respect. But since yesterday's writings have not yet been burned, their pitiful attempt to hide their mistakes can be exposed without difficulty.

The July 1926 plenum adopted the following resolution:

The plenum of the Central Committee, in approving the action of the Politburo and of the delegation of the All-Union Communist Party on the Chinese question, finds the proposals of the Opposition (Zinoviev-Trotsky) patently opportunistic and in part openly capitulationist on the following points: recalling Comrade Karakhan, relinquishing control over the Chinese Eastern Railroad, and withdrawing from the Kuomintang. The Central Committee holds that such a position would make sense only in the event of a total liquidation of the national revolutionary movement in China. . .

And so forth.

If the "China" policy of the Opposition even before July 1926 was "opportunistic and in part openly capitulationist", how can it now be said that the policy on the Chinese question was carried out with unanimous consent? It is hardly worth pausing on the questions of Karakhan's recall or the alleged relinquishing of the Chinese Eastern Railroad. The crux of the matter is our attitude toward the Kuomintang. The resolution accused the Opposition of favoring withdrawal from the Kuomintang. The Opposition stated that it was prepared to form a bloc with the Kuomintang and establish a workable understanding with its rank and file, on the condition of full and genuine independence for the Communist Party since in general such independence is the first lesson in the ABCs of Bolshevism. A struggle along this line has been going on since 1925. This struggle was recorded in numerous resolutions, reports, and articles written by the majority, where the Opposition's point of view is termed capitulationist precisely on the basis of the fact that the Opposition insisted on the independence of the Communist Party as the prerequisite for all revolutionary politics.

The Opposition exposed the incorrect policy with respect to Chiang Kai-shek. If not everyone knows of the relevant statements in the Politburo or in the Central Committee, Radek's speech at the Hall of Columns on April 5 is widely known. The most complete expression of opportunistic blindness was Stalin's speech at this same meeting, the record of which has been hidden from the party to this day. It would be sufficient to print the verbatim records of these two speeches—Radek's and Stalin's to eliminate the possibility of any further allegations to the effect that the Opposition never opposed Stalin's pro-Chiang Kai-shek line.

After Chiang Kai-shek's coup, in May 1927, the Opposition introduced the following proposal in the plenum of the Executive Committee of the Comintern:

The plenum would do well to bury Bukharin's resolution, replacing it with a resolution of a few lines:

In the first place, peasants and workers should place no faith in the leaders of the left Kuomintang but they should instead build their soviets jointly with the soldiers. In the second place, the Soviets should arm the workers and the advanced peasants. In the third place, the Communist Party must assure its complete independence, create a daily press, and assume the leadership in creating the soviets. Fourth, the land must be immediately taken away from the landlords. Fifth, the reactionary bureaucracy must be immediately dismissed. Sixth, perfidious generals and other counter-revolutionists must be summarily dealt with. And finally, the general course must be toward the establishment of a revolutionary dictatorship through the soviets of workers' and peasants' deputies. ["It is Time to Understand, Time to Reconsider, and Time to Make a Change.")

This proposal was only a brief summary of a whole series of documents previously submitted to the Politburo by the Opposition. Much time had been lost. However, if the Executive Committee of the Comintern had adopted the proposal of the Opposition in May 1927, 50 that it could have been put into practice, we would not have had this second, Wuhan chapter, which is even more disgraceful than the first, Chiang Kai-shek chapter. And we would be immeasurably stronger today.

Finally, now—in September 1927—we are introducing our current proposals, which correspond to the new stage in the development of the Chinese events.

1. It is necessary to again pose the problems of the Chinese revolution point-blank. An overall orientation is again needed because the official leadership while attempting to make some outward display of initiative in action (Bukharin's remarks at the last joint session of the Politburo and the Presidium of the Central Control Commission concerning Ho Lung and Yeh T'ing's detachments) is in fact floundering without rudder or sail. With such a policy, new defeats are inevitable. These defeats will compromise the Chinese Communist Party and the Comintern directly, i.e. not through the buffer of the Kuomintang, as has been the case until now.
2. What does the movement of new, and, to all

appearances, truly revolutionary detachments of Ho Lung and Yeh T'ing signify? Is it the brief epilogue common enough after great historic defeats, with the appearance on the scene of the extreme left wing—which didn't know how or was not able to act when it should have and is therefore doomed to defeat? Or is it the spontaneous beginning of a great new chapter in the Chinese revolution? This question is key in determining our "strategic" orientation and the tactical measures that flow from it.

3. If this question is to be defined more precisely in terms of the relations between the classes, then it must be formulated roughly as follows: After the bourgeoisie and the conciliationist petty-bourgeois higher-ups have gone over completely to the camp of the counter-revolution—having taken advantage of the workers' and peasants' movement, Moscow's backing, and the authority of Bolshevism and the Comintern, and having reduced all of this to an instrument for the political exploitation and deception of the workers and peasants—can we expect that in the antibourgeois, anti-conciliationist camp there will be enough political and organizational forces that will prove capable of inspiring the masses, who have been betrayed and, for the most part, beaten and bled white, with confidence in themselves and their own leadership? For this is the only way that a new upsurge of the Chinese revolution can be assured.
4. It is impossible to give an unqualified answer to this question, especially from the sidelines and from afar. However, it is doubtful that anyone, even in China itself-in this immense, far-flung country—can say yet whether China is fated to go through a more or less prolonged period of revolutionary decline before the movement is revived on a new, more advanced class base; or whether we can expect that, given the presence of huge masses of people living in horrifying conditions, given their exceptional readiness for self-sacrifice, given the presence of a young proletariat scattered widely

throughout the country, given the people's experiences in civil war, and given the presence of the USSR and possible help from it, a new wave of uprisings can lead directly to a victorious struggle of the proletariat and the peasant masses for power. This last, of course, provided there is the correct leadership. Neither of these possibilities is excluded. Which will prevail depends not only on the so-called objective conditions, which, moreover, do not lend themselves to any kind of complete a priori calculation, but also on our own policies—their correctness, their energetic implementation, and so on.

5. About two months ago *Pravda*, to everyone's surprise (including, apparently, its own), advanced the slogan of soviets for China. Until then Stalin had explained that soviets are appropriate only during the transitional period where the bourgeois revolution passes over into the socialist revolution. This explanation stood in glaring contradiction to the entire experience of our three revolutions, all our party's traditions, and Lenin's theoretical teachings on revolutions in the East. Nonetheless, Stalin's new teachings became the official teachings of the party, i.e., of its apparatus. (It should be noted that the new "discoveries" and "teachings," at odds with one another and, above all, with the facts, wash off the party ranks like water-soluble paints. This does not mean that they are harmless: when water-soluble paints run together, they turn everything to a dingy gray color.)
6. Advancing the slogan for soviets in July, i.e., after the revolution has suffered serious defeats—obviously ought to mean that the Chinese Revolution had directly entered the period of transition into a socialist revolution. But the question remains: why was this slogan, advanced in a single editorial only, afterward so thoroughly forgotten? And why does *Pravda* say nothing about it now, when the movement of revolutionary detachments is having notable successes

with the assistance of the working class and peasant masses? Or does the slogan for soviets, which served at a certain point as camouflage (for Stalin and Bukharin), prove unsuitable for the new offensive of the revolution?

7. As is apparent from several commentaries in *Pravda*, the official leadership is exercising restraint and caution with respect to the new revolutionary movement that is linked to the detachments of Ho Lung and Yeh T'ing, i.e., in essence it is not running the risk of openly assuming the same responsibility for an authentic revolutionary movement of workers and peasants as it did for the armies of Chiang Kai-shek, Feng Yu-hsiang, and Wang Ching-wei.
8. It is not at all a matter of "guaranteeing" success. It is a matter of politically identifying the development of the revolution in the next period with the fate of this movement and of arming this movement with the correct perspective and the correct demands, without which victory is unthinkable. A movement of numerically small and, it goes without saying, poorly armed revolutionary armies can be successful only with the active intervention in events by the workers and the rural poor peasants—in particular only if workers' and peasants' soviets are established as the organs of power. Meanwhile, *Pravda* has again concealed this slogan. Why? Apparently because it fears that the movement will be more or less rapidly crushed. Of course, such a defeat is always possible; but in the absence of the correct slogans it is inevitable. To abstain "for the time being" from advancing fundamental, vitally necessary slogans for fear of defeat means, for fear of defeat, to in fact pave the way for it.
9. To identify the revolution with Chiang Kai-shek's armies was not only supremely "ill-considered", but also the greatest of historical mistakes and the gravest of crimes. To assume responsibility for Wuhan as the center of the agrarian revolution was the second "ill-considered" act, no less serious than the first, and the second crime, no

less grave. Once burned, twice shy. "Wait-and-see" type caution with respect to the independent workers' and peasants' movement, a reluctance for the time being to arm it with the necessary slogans, i.e., to say openly to the Chinese workers and peasants for the whole world to hear: "This movement is yours"—such "caution" threatens to become the third successive error of "ill-consideration" and the worst of them all.

10. What is involved here is not whether or not we are sympathetic toward the military revolutionary movement that has begun, and not even of organizational and material aid to it. There is no need at all to waste words on that score. Bragging about aid to revolutionary armies, or for example, to the British coal miners is what an overblown functionary would do, but not a revolutionary. Every bit of aid that comes from the sidelines is necessary, but it is not decisive. The relations among the Communist Party, the revolutionary troops, the workers, and the poor peasants is what is decisive. And these relations are determined to a great extent by politics as a system of slogans and actions. You can give any kind of material aid you want to a rebelling army, but if the question of power is not posed point- blank, if the slogan for soviets is not raised, and if a complete program of economic measures linked to the establishment of soviet power is not put forward, then outside material aid to the armies will not produce the desired results, just as our aid to the British coal miners did not produce the desired results when it was accompanied by our political bloc with the General Council. In the last analysis it is not material aid that is decisive, but the correct political line.
11. Right now, on the road, I'm reading in the Ukrainian organ Visty [News] of September 13 a dispatch from Shanghai about the fact that, in the face of the approach of Ho Lung's and Yeh T'ing's revolutionary troops to Swatow, the Kuomintang authorities and garrisons abandoned the city. The editor entitled the dispatch

"Kuomintang Flees from Swatow". For many months now we have been living with the charge of "underestimating" first the Kuomintang as a whole, then the left Kuomintang, which Stalin had authorized as the revolutionary center. Bukharin vowed that he would never give up the blue flag of the Kuomintang, but meanwhile it turns out that the Kuomintang powers "flee" from Swatow with the blue flag in their hands-since (as the British so aptly say in such cases) one cannot simultaneously "run with the foxes and hunt with the hounds". Combining the red and the blue—a bloc of four classes-did not originate with Martynov. Bukharin vowed to hold onto the blue flag for a bloc of three classes. But now there turns out to be a civil war between the blue and the red flags. And one would have to be a hopeless idiot not to understand that only this civil war— against the landlords, the bourgeoisie, and the conciliators—can produce a genuine bloc of the workers and the poor, rural and urban. Those who up to now have isolated the Communist Party from the workers and the rural poor in China are precisely the ones who, in chasing after the blue flag of the Kuomintang, compromised the red flag of the proletariat.

12. But from the circumstance that a state of civil war has broken out between the revolutionary troops and the Kuomintang flows the fact that the revolutionary movement can win only under the leadership of the Communist Party and only in the form of soviets of workers', soldiers', and peasants' deputies. This presupposes a readiness on the part of the Communist Party to take on the leadership of a movement of this kind. And that in turn calls for a complete program in the period of struggle for power and the conquest of power, and after the establishment of the new regime.
13. The previous policy was deadly for the training of the Communist Party. Perhaps the most serious consequence of the wrong line of the previous period was not so much the material defeats and sacrifices as

the loss of historical conditions unique for training revolutionary cadre, tempering the proletarian vanguard, and strengthening within it a sense of independence and confidence in its strength and in its leadership. Now, on the threshold of a new stage of the revolution, the Communist Party is immeasurably weaker than it should and could be. But one must accept the facts as they are as the result of a whole combination of factors, including the criminally erroneous line of the leadership. Only the Communist Party can now assume the leadership of the revolutionary movement. The blue flag of the Kuomintang can now be had not by way of new blocs, but through civil war—that is by tearing it like a trophy from the hands of the vanquished enemy. Therefore, we must put an end to shameful, reactionary fictions: We must openly announce a break of the Communist Party with the Kuomintang, openly declare the Kuomintang an instrument of bourgeois reaction, and expel it in disgrace from the ranks of the Comintern. To fail to do so means to condemn the new movement to vacillations, confusion, and defeat.

14. This does not necessarily mean that the Communist Party will be the only revolutionary political organization in the next period. On the basis of the peasant unions and the Red Spears, in direct struggle against the Kuomintang powers and military forces, a political organization can be formed alongside the Communist Party but more or less independent of it, relying on the support of a section of the rural poor. It is fruitless to try to guess how this will occur—at least from here, where the nature of the movement's organization and cadre are not well enough visible. But one thing is obvious: the Communist Party must clearly realize that the revolution can be victorious only through it and only under its leadership, and that the peasant organizations can fight successfully only side by side with it, only under its slogans, and only under its direct political and organizational influence. But this is possible only with a

clear and precise formulation of all the political and economic tasks of the revolution by the Communist Party itself.

15. In order to justify collaboration with the bourgeoisie in the revolution (i.e., the Menshevik policy), Stalin and Bukharin have advanced two factors in turn. First it was foreign imperialism, which supposedly brings the classes of China together. It soon became obvious, however, that the bourgeoisie, in alliance with foreign imperialism, was smashing the workers and peasants. Then they advanced the second factor, Chinese feudalism, which they say impels the more "Left-Wing" section of the very same bourgeoisie and the real revolutionary ally, the loyal Wang Ching-wei, to struggle along with the workers and peasants against feudalism. But as it turned out, the bourgeoisie did not put forward a single political group that would agree to participate in revolutionary struggle against Bukharin's feudalism. And it is not accidental. In China there are no noble lords standing in opposition to the bourgeoisie. The landholder as a general rule is the urban bourgeois. The small landholder—the kulak, the gentry—is closely linked with the usurer and the urban bourgeois. Unless one is playing with words, there is no feudalism in China. In the Chinese village there are serf–owner relations which are crowned, however, not by feudal, but by bourgeois property forms and a bourgeois sociopolitical order. This type of serf-owner relationship, which is a result of agrarian over-population, given the overall lag in capitalist development, can be found—of course in much more "mild" forms—in several Balkan countries, which have known neither feudalism nor the noble estate since their emancipation from the Turkish yoke. Of course, in China poverty and bondage take inhumane forms such as were hardly to be encountered even in the age of feudalism. Nonetheless, the attempt to create feudalism in China, still more its prevalence, relies not on facts, but on the naked desire to justify

collaboration with the bourgeoisie. The facts have avenged themselves. In China there has been found no such bourgeoisie or section of the bourgeoisie that would agree to carry on a revolutionary struggle against feudalism, i.e., against itself. That is why, upon the approach of revolutionary troops to Swatow, the Kuomintang takes to its heels, carrying the blue flag under its arm and the Comintern membership card in its pocket.

16. The struggle for an agrarian revolution is a struggle against the bourgeoisie, which means against the Kuomintang. Not one section of the bourgeoisie has supported or is supporting this struggle. In the countryside, the chief enemy, due to their numerical strength, will be the gentry, the kulak, the small landed proprietor. In China, a refusal to expropriate the small exploiters, the kulaks, would mean renunciation of the agrarian revolution. The agrarian revolution in China—not according to Bukharin but in reality—is an antibourgeois revolution. Because of this—and only because of this—Martynov and Bukharin's schemes failed. But this also means that the proletariat will complete the agrarian revolution, taking behind it the poor masses of the Chinese countryside, i.e., 80, 90, or more per cent of the peasantry—in direct and unmitigated struggle against the bourgeois, the landowner, and the kulak, and against their political arm, the Kuomintang.

17. The way the question of revolutionary power is posed is determined in the same way.

    The experience with Chiang Kai-shek signified the failure of the idea of a bloc with the entire "bourgeois nation" in a struggle against imperialism and feudalism.

    The experience with Wang Ching-wei signified the failure of the bloc of "the revolutionary democracy" in the spirit of Kerensky and Tseretelli.

    Right now the business at hand for the proletariat is to win over to "revolutionary democracy" the poor lower classes of the city and countryside and lead them forward for the conquest of power, of the land, of national independence, and better living conditions for the toiling masses In other words, the business at hand is the dictatorship of the proletariat.

18. The call for a democratic dictatorship of the proletariat and peasantry, if it had been advanced, let us say, at the beginning of the Northern Expedition, in connection with the call for soviets and the arming of the workers and peasants, would have played a tremendous role in the development of the Chinese Revolution, would have completely assured a different course for it. It would have isolated the bourgeoisie and thereby the conciliationists, and it would have led to the posing of the question of the dictatorship of the proletariat under conditions infinitely more favorable than in the past. But we cannot reverse the course of history. The bourgeoisie retreated from the revolution on its own initiative—under circumstances chosen by it and most favorable to it. Exactly the same is true of the conciliationists. Because we were afraid to isolate them at the right time, they successfully isolated us. It always happens that way—and at that, not only in Shanghai, but also in Edinburgh, as is shown by the last congress of trade unions.

    But in any case, the retreat from the revolution by the bourgeoisie—the big bourgeoisie and the middle and upper petty bourgeoisie in the city and the countryside, and the intelligentsia as well—is an accomplished fact. Under these conditions, the call for a democratic dictatorship of the proletariat and peasantry—given a new revolutionary upsurge—will prove to be vague and amorphous. And any vague and amorphous slogan in a revolution becomes dangerous for the revolutionary party and the oppressed masses

    There can be virtually no doubt that Stalin will come forward tomorrow under the banner of the democratic dictatorship of the proletariat and the peasantry after giving it a conciliationist character. It would be incorrect to think that Stalin and Bukharin have understood their mistakes The course of events in China is pushing them to the left, but they are bracing themselves and pulling to the right. In the future, too, they will strive to blunt the tasks and conceal the "isolation" of the proletariat by means of a bloc with the last two honorable figures in the Kuomintang the wife and the protégé' of Sun Yat-sen. 67 Blocs of this type, organized from the top, already nothing more than a masquerade, will, however, call for very real sacrifices on the part of the proletarian party in the sense of a retreat from decisive slogans and methods of struggle. Sun Yat-sen can manage the Chinese revolution a little more cheaply than Chiang Kai-shek and Wang Ching-wei.

19. If the revolutionary movement expands, the subsequent success of Ho Lung and Yeh T'ing's troops will inevitably push a section of the left conciliationists in the direction of a "bloc" with the revolutionary forces in order to co-opt the movement and neutralize it. The conciliators will be able to move toward this goal under the very slogan of a democratic dictatorship of the proletariat and the peasantry so as to once again even more surely and at a higher level, subordinate the proletariat to themselves, narrow the scope of the movement, and prepare a new disaster, the third one in a row.

    The Leninist slogan for a democratic dictatorship of the proletariat and the peasantry that was not applied at the right time cannot be mechanically carried over into the third stage that is taking shape on the basis of a new relationship of forces. We must clearly understand that after the experience with the Kuomintang in general and with the left Kuomintang in particular, a historically overdue slogan will become a weapon of the forces working against the revolution. And for us it is no longer a question of the democratic dictatorship of the proletariat and the peasantry, but of the dictatorship of the proletariat supported by the inexhaustible masses of urban and rural poor—a dictatorship that poses for itself the objective of solving the most urgent and vital problems of the country and its working masses and in the process inevitably passes over to the path of making socialist inroads on property relations.

20. The task of the Communist Party is first and foremost the creation of a revolutionary army. A Red army of regulars must be constructed on the basis of the movement of the workers and peasants that is actually unfolding. The principle of operating with mercenary soldiers must be replaced by the principle of a systematic class levy. The organs for this levy should be trade unions and peasant unions under the leadership of the soviets and the Communist Party. It is necessary to skillfully and persistently include partisan detachments of peasants (the Red Spears, etc.) in the regular ranks. The question of the composition of the command must be correctly resolved on the basis of all the experiences of the Russian as well as the Chinese revolutions. The exploiter and the counterrevolutionary elements should be mercilessly driven out of the army.
21. The task of feeding the armies and the cities poses the problem of the food policy. Resolving this problem under conditions of civil war and blockade is inconceivable without measures of iron discipline regarding food, without the seizure of the food supplies of the big landholders, kulaks, the speculators, and without rationing in one form or another.
22. Civil war at the present stage is inconceivable in China without the dispossession of the kulaks.
23. The same tasks that the Opposition has formulated more than once, in particular at the May plenum of the Executive Committee of the Comintern, remain the most important part of the practical program for the soviets and revolutionary armies.

    The land must be immediately confiscated from the landlords—big and small—as the armies advance and as local uprisings are successful. The reactionary bureaucracy must be immediately rooted out. Traitors, counter-revolutionaries, and agents of Chiang Kai-shek and Wang Ching-wei must be dealt with on the spot.

24. Problems of industry and transport will rise point-blank before the revolutionary government. In one of his countless speeches on China, Bukharin whiningly complained about the sabotage of the bourgeoisie, who export capital and are leaving no circulating media and thus create great difficulties that the Opposition does not want to concern itself with. Bukharin has proposed no means for overcoming these difficulties. A general reference to the difficulties as an excuse for one's flabbiness is a common trick of opportunism.

    It is patently obvious that under conditions of civil war, the bourgeoisie can be prevented from sabotaging the economy, above all industry and transport, not by admonishment, but by the measures of the dictatorship through organized proletarian control of industry in those instances where it is feasible and through workers taking enterprises into their own hands in every case where it is otherwise impossible to secure a continuity of production. The same applies with respect to rail and water transportation. In short, the overall plan should be to transfer the most important enterprises, i.e., the industries and transportation facilities ripest for it, into the hands of the soviet state. The necessary steps and preparatory organizational measures to be adopted must be worked out in accordance with the entire situation depending on the overall course of development of the revolution, the strength of the enemy's resistance, etc.

    It goes without saying, all this applies first and foremost to foreign concessions.

25. There will be philistines who will cry out about our utopianism, ultra-leftism, etc. They will moan about China's backwardness, the small numerical size of the proletariat, etc.

    To this we answer first of all that we do not intend to build socialism in a single country in China either. The Chinese Revolution is not an independent, isolated phenomenon that must find solutions to all the problems posed by the revolution within the borders of China. The Chinese Revolution is one link of that chain of which the following are among the other links: the Soviet Union, the forthcoming imperialist wars, impending proletarian uprisings, etc.—in other words, the chain of wars and revolutions that constitute today's imperialist epoch. It is precisely the epoch of imperialism that has led to such a sharpening of class relations in China and made the solution of the most important tasks of the revolution impossible, not only under the leadership of the bourgeoisie, but also through the democratic dictatorship of the petty bourgeoisie and the proletariat; and by so doing the task of establishing the dictatorship of the proletariat supported by the rural and urban poor has been put on the agenda. The dictatorship of the proletariat means making socialist inroads in property relations and a transition to production under state control, i.e., passing over to the rail of the socialist revolution.

26. But are the forces of the Chinese proletariat sufficient to get the support of the hundreds of millions of Chinese poor, seize power, set up an army and state apparatus, withstand blockade and sabotage, safeguard the country's most important economic operations, etc.? In essence, this question is tantamount to another question: Does the Chinese Revolution in fact have a chance for further development and victory, since roads and methods other than those designated above do not exist?

Naturally, nobody will say for certain that the Chinese proletariat will succeed in coming to power in the near future. Only the actual struggle will be able to tell whether or not that is true. Only correct leadership can provide a victory. The revolutionary "limit", as they say, i.e., that quantity that restricts all the others, at the present time is not in the least the Chinese proletariat, but the Chinese Communist Party, which incorrect theory, an incorrect line, and incorrect leadership have

> weakened to the worst degree. By its numbers, its productive role, and the way it is distributed in the country as a whole, the Chinese proletariat represents a tremendous force and can become the leading and ruling force in the country provided there is a rapid growth and tempering of the Chinese Communist Party. Can it make up for lost and wasted time? It can. If there is a revolutionary upsurge, the party can quickly rise to the level of events. But for this to happen, it must have a clear perspective before it—not halfway measures, reluctance, or playacting with Mme. Sun Yat-sen. The task of the dictatorship of the proletariat in a country of poor peasants should be presented clearly and distinctly, and in its full scope.

Without this, support to the troops of Ho Lung and Yeh T'ing would be the purest adventurism, which could have as its only result a new crushing defeat for the movement, a new monstrous bloodletting, and a new strengthening of the forces of reaction. The Chinese Revolution at its new stage will win as a dictatorship of the proletariat, or it will not win at all.

26

Speech to the Presidium of the ECCI

September 27, 1927

1. You accuse me of violating discipline. I have no doubt that your verdict is already prepared. Today there is not one organization that discusses and decides; they only carry out orders. Even the Presidium of the Communist International is no exception.
2. What do you call factional work? Anything that is not authorized by the AUCP Secretariat. But the Secretariat tramples the rules underfoot, shatters the very foundations of party discipline, and imposes a ban on what is the inalienable right and primary duty of every party member.
3. Here is a vivid and burning example. Today's papers report that the revolutionary army has occupied Swatow. It is already several weeks that the armies of Ho Lung and Yeh T'ing have been advancing. *Pravda* calls these armies revolutionary armies. Here, at any rate, it is much closer to the truth than in regard to the armies of Chiang Kai-shek, Feng Yu-hsiang, or T'ang Sheng- chih. But I ask you: What prospects does the movement of the revolutionary army that captured Swatow raise before the Chinese Revolution? What are the slogans of the movement? What is its program? What should be its organizational forms? What has become of the slogan of Chinese soviets, which *Pravda* suddenly advanced for

a single day in July? On this point we hear not one word in the press if we exclude the fundamentally wrong article by Comrade Lozovsky.

Why is the press of the AUCP silent? Why does the Comintern press hold its tongue? After all, the resolution of the last ECCI plenum, approved following the report by Comrade Bukharin, remains in force to this day. That resolution is totally wrong. It helped the Wuhan government complete what Chiang Kai-shek had not yet accomplished.

The opportunist theses and resolutions of Stalin and Bukharin, which have twice led the Chinese Revolution to the most severe defeats, are printed without any prohibition. Marxist criticism and Marxist formulations of the problems are placed under a ban. Anyone who circulates our theses is accused of violating discipline and expelled from the party. But we say that every honest party member is duty bound to demand the publication of all the documents on the Chinese question and is duty bound to circulate our criticism of the opportunist line of Stalin-Bukharin, and to do so with all the forces and resources possible. The question of the fate of the Chinese Revolution stands immeasurably higher than the bureaucratic orders and bans of the CC Secretariat, which are presented as measures of revolutionary proletarian discipline.

4. I have said that the organs of the Comintern have remained silent in regard to the third stage of the Chinese Revolution, which could mark the beginning of a new rise, but which could also—with incorrect policies—prepare the way for a third defeat that would be the most severe and the most devastating, that would enfeeble the revolution for a number of years to come.

While the entire press remains silent and the Comintern says nothing, a new opportunist combination is all the while being quietly prepared, entirely in the spirit of the Chinese policy of Stalin-Bukharin. In Moscow a new and ever-so-modern Kuomintang is in formation, centering around the widow of Sun Yat-sen and a comrade-in-arms of Chiang Kai-shek, Eugene Ch'en. The first stage was Chiang Kai-shek; the second stage, Wang Ching- wei; the third stage is Eugene Ch'en and Company. The first two stages ended with the workers and peasants being crushed and shot down. The third stage will lead to the same thing. Instead of assuring the full independence of the Chinese Communist Party, raising its self-esteem, broadening its outlook, confront-ing it with the tasks of a dictatorship of the soviets that would unite the proletariat and the many millions of poor peasants in China—instead of that, Stalin-Bukharin are preparing a new inspectorate to be placed over the Chinese Communist Party, a new petty-bourgeois compromiser form of supervision over it, that is, new shackles to bind the proletarian vanguard hand and foot. We say to you: This will end in a third catastrophe. And do you really think we are going to keep quiet?

5. Since 1925 we have been carrying on a struggle for the independence of the Chinese Communist Party, for its emancipation from the discipline of Chiang Kai-shek. This crucial, fundamental slogan of Bolshevism was called Trotskyism. In China, the agents of the Comintern used the term "Trotskyist" for those genuine proletarian revolutionists who upheld the fundamental precondition of Bolshevik politics: the independence of the proletarian party. Against them, the Comintern agents supported Ch'en Tu-hsiu, who translated the politics of Martynov into Chinese.

   What is the Opposition guilty of? Only that it paid too much attention to the prohibitions of the Stalinist Secretariat, which have been fatal to the revolution, and that it did not immediately and publicly place before the entire Comintern, with full firmness and determination, the call for the complete independence of the Chinese Communist Party.

6. In May of this year, during the ECCI plenum, we

proposed a briefly worded motion in opposition to the thoroughly opportunist resolution of Bukharin. Our motion was as follows: The plenum would do well to bury Bukharin's resolution, replacing it with a resolution of a few lines:

In the first place, peasants and workers should place no faith in the leaders of the left Kuomintang but they should instead build their soviets jointly with the soldiers. In the second place, the soviets should arm the workers and the advanced peasants. In the third place, the Communist Party must assure its complete independence, create a daily press, and assume the leadership in creating the soviets. Fourth, the land must be immediately taken away from the landlords. Fifth, the reactionary bureaucracy must be immediately dismissed. Sixth, perfidious generals and other counter-revolutionists must be summarily dealt with. And finally, the general course must be toward the establishment of a revolutionary dictatorship through the soviets of workers' and peasants' deputies. ["It is Time to Understand, Time to Reconsider, and Time to Make a Change."]

These lines are the voice of genuine Bolshevism, temporarily stifled by the bureaucratic apparatus in service to opportunist policies. And do you really think we will fail to make these lines known to the Chinese and world proletariat? Whoever thinks that is no revolutionist.

7. To this day the China resolution of the last ECCI plenum has not been withdrawn. To this day the position of Stalin, who at first called for confidence in Chiang Kai-shek and then proclaimed the Wuhan government the leading center of the agrarian revolution, has not been condemned.

   Isn't Comrade Treint correct when he says that the Stalin-Bukharin policy given the organized silence of the entire Comintern—led the vanguard of the international proletariat astray? Didn't l'Humanite send a telegram greeting the butcher Chiang Kai-shek as the hero of the Shanghai Commune? Isn't a policy that loses sight of the deep abyss between the proletarian Communard and the general Galliffet—isn't this a criminal policy that must not only be condemned but branded criminal?

8. Even worse, the Kuomintang, to this day, remains a member of the Comintern. Which Kuomintang? The Kuomintang of Chiang Kai-shek or that of Wang Ching-wei? But now they have united. Thus the united Kuomintang of Chiang Kai-shek and Wang Ching-wei still belongs to the Comintern. You are in a hurry to expel Vujovic and myself. But you have forgotten to expel the comrades-in-arms Chiang Kai-shek and Wang Ching-wei. Perhaps you will agree to place this question on the agenda today as well.
9. The fight for the independence of the Communist Party, the fight of the proletariat for the peasantry and against the bourgeoisie, the fight for soviets of workers', peasants', and soldiers' deputies is called by the opportunists Trotskyism. Why? In order the more surely to fight against Leninism. Trotskyism is an epithet the bankrupt hide behind when they have nothing to say. The silence of the Comintern in regard to the new stage of the Chinese Revolution, unfolding before our eyes, is evidence of unparalleled confusion. The right road and destination must be pointed out clearly. We cannot be silent. We will not be silent, because we are revolutionists and not bureaucrats.

27

The Canton Uprising*

December 1927

1,2,3,...

4. Control in the party, and therefore in the country too, is in the hands of the Stalin faction, which has all the features of centrism, a centrism which is, moreover, in the period of decline and not of upsurge. That means short zigzags to the left, longer zigzags to the right. One can have no doubt that the last move to the left (the jubilee manifesto) produces the necessity of placating the right wing and its real supports in the country—not with words, but with deeds.
5. The zigzags to the left are not only expressed in hastily prepared jubilee manifestoes. The Canton rising is unquestionably an adventurist zigzag by the Comintern to the left, after the disastrous consequences of the Menshevik policy in China have made themselves fully apparent. The Canton episode is a worse and more pernicious repetition of the Estonian putsch of 1924, after the revolutionary situation in Germany of 1923 had been missed. Menshevism plus bureaucratic adventurism have dealt a double blow to the Chinese Revolution; we need not doubt that the revenge for Canton will be a new and longer zigzag to the right in the field of international politics, especially Chinese.

---

* Excerpted from the article *"On the New Stage"*.

28

The Classic Mistakes of Opportunism*

January 1928

The outcome and the lessons of the Chinese Revolution, a revolution that constitutes one of the greatest events in world history, have been kept in obscurity, barred from discussion, and have not been assimilated by the public opinion of the proletarian vanguard. In reality the Central Committee of the Russian Communist Party has prohibited discussion of the questions related to the Chinese Revolution. But without studying the mistakes that were committed—the classic mistakes of opportunism—it is impossible to imagine the future revolutionary preparation of the proletarian parties of Europe and Asia.

Aside from the question of knowing who was directly responsible for the leadership of the December events in Canton, these events furnish a striking example of putschism during the ebb of the revolutionary wave. In a revolutionary period, a deviation towards putschism is often the result of defeats whose direct cause is to be found in an opportunist leadership. The Communist International cannot take a single new step forward without first drawing the lessons of the experience of the Canton uprising, in correlation with the course of the Chinese Revolution as a whole. This is one of the main tasks of the Sixth World Congress. The repressive measures taken against the left wing will not only fail to correct the mistakes already made, but even more serious, they will teach nothing to anyone.

---

* Excerpted from the article *"Appeal of the Deportees"*.

29

On the Canton Insurrection

Three Letters to Preobrazhensky

(March–April 1928)

First Letter, March 2, 1928

Pravda prints in several installments an extensive article entitled, *The Significance and Lessons of the Canton Insurrection*. This article is truly remarkable for the invaluable, substantiated, and firsthand information it contains as well as for its lucid exposition of contradictions and confusion of a principled nature.

It begins with an evaluation of the social nature of the revolution itself. As we all know, it is a bourgeois-democratic, a workers' and peasants' revolution. Yesterday it was supposed to unfold under the banner of the Kuomintang—today it unfolds against the Kuomintang.

But according to the author's appraisal, the character of the revolution, and even the entire official policy, remains bourgeois-democratic. We turn next to the chapter that deals with the policy of the soviet power. Here we find stated that "in the interests of the workers, the Canton Soviet issued decrees establishing workers' control of production, effecting this control through factory committees [and] ... nationalization of large-scale industry, transport, and banks".

It goes on to enumerate the following measures: "the confiscation of all the apartments of the big bourgeoisie for the use of the toilers ..."

Thus the workers were in power in Canton, through their soviets. Actually the entire power was in the hands of the

Communist Party, i.e., the party of the proletariat. The program included not only the confiscation of whatever feudal estates still exist in China, not only the workers' control of production, but also the nationalization of large-scale industry, banks, and transport, as well as the confiscation of bourgeois apartments, and all their property for the use of the toilers. The question arises: If such are the methods of a bourgeois revolution, then what would the socialist revolution look like in China? What other class would do the overthrowing and by what sort of different measures? We observe that given a real development of the revolution, the formula of a bourgeois-democratic, a workers' and peasants' revolution applied to China in the present period, in the given stage of its development, proved to be a hollow fiction, a bagatelle. Those who insisted upon this formula prior to the Canton insurrection, and above all those who insist on it now, after this insurrection, are repeating (under different conditions) the principled mistake committed by Zinoviev, Kamenev, Rykov, and the rest in the year 1917.

An objection may be raised that the problem of the agrarian revolution in China has not been solved as yet! True. But neither was it solved in our own country prior to the establishment of the dictatorship of the proletariat. In our country it was not the bourgeois-democratic but the proletarian socialist revolution that achieved the agrarian revolution which, moreover, was far more deep-going than the one that is possible in China, in view of the historical conditions of the Chinese system of land ownership. It may be said that China has not matured for the socialist revolution as yet. But that would be an abstract and a lifeless manner of posing the question. Was Russia, then, if taken by itself, ripe for socialism? Russia was ripe for the dictatorship of the proletariat as the only method of solving all national problems; but so far as socialist development is concerned, the latter, proceeding from the economic and cultural conditions of a country, is indissolubly bound up with the entire future development of the world revolution. This applies in whole and in part to China as well. If eight or ten months ago this was a forecast (rather belated, at that), then today it is an irrefutable deduction from the experience of the Canton uprising. It would be erroneous to argue that the Canton uprising was an adventure by and large, and that the actual class relations were reflected in it in a distorted form.

In the first place the author of the above-mentioned article does not at all consider the Canton insurrection as an adventure, but as an entirely lawful stage in the development of the Chinese Revolution. The general official point of view is to combine the appraisal of the revolution as bourgeois-democratic with an approval of the program of action of the Canton government. But even from the standpoint of appraising the Canton insurrection as a putsch, one could not arrive at the conclusion that the formula of the bourgeois-democratic revolution is viable. The insurrection was obviously untimely. It was. But the class forces and the programs that inevitably flow from them were disclosed by the insurrection in all their lawfulness. The best proof of this is that it was possible and necessary to foresee in advance the relation of forces that was laid bare by the Canton insurrection. And this was foreseen.

This question is most closely bound up with the paramount question of the Kuomintang. Incidentally, the author of the article relates, with assumed satisfaction, that one of the fighting slogans of the Canton overturn was the cry "Down with the Kuomintang!" The banners and insignia of the Kuomintang were torn down and trampled underfoot. But only recently, even after the "betrayal" of Chiang Kai-shek, and after the "betrayal" of Wang Ching-wei, we heard solemn vows that "We will not surrender the banner of the Kuomintang!" Oh, these sorry revolutionists!

The workers of Canton outlawed the Kuomintang, proclaiming all its tendencies illegal. What does this imply? It implies that for the solution of the fundamental national tasks, not only the big but also the petty-bourgeoisie could not put forward such a force as would enable the party of the proletariat to solve jointly with it the tasks of the "bourgeois-democratic revolution". But 'we' are overlooking the many-millioned peasantry and the agrarian revolution ... A pitiable objection. For the key to the entire situation lies precisely in the fact that the task of conquering the peasant movement falls upon the proletariat, i.e., directly upon the Communist Party; and this task cannot be solved in reality differently than it was solved by the Canton workers, i.e., in the shape of the dictatorship of the proletariat whose methods from the very outset grow over inevitably into socialist methods. Conversely, the general fate of these methods, as well as of the dictatorship as a whole, is decided in the last analysis by the course of world development, which naturally does not exclude but on the contrary presupposes a correct policy on the part of the proletarian dictatorship, that consists of strengthening and developing the alliance between the workers and peasants, and of an all-sided adaptation to national conditions, on the one hand, and to the course of world development, on the other. To play with the formula of the bourgeois-democratic revolution, after the experience of the Canton insurrection, is to march against the Chinese October, for without a correct general political orientation, revolutionary uprisings cannot be victorious, no matter how heroic and self-sacrificing they may be.

To be sure, the Chinese Revolution has "passed into a new and higher phase"—but this is correct not in the sense that it will begin surging upward tomorrow or the next day, but in the sense that it has revealed the hollowness of the slogan of the bourgeois-democratic revolution. Engels said that a party that misses a favorable situation and suffers a defeat as a result, turns into a nonentity. This applies to the Chinese party as well. The defeat of the Chinese Revolution is not a bit smaller than the defeat in Germany in 1923. Of course, we must understand the reference to "nonentity" in a sensible way. Many things bespeak the fact that the next period in China will be a period of revolutionary reflux, a slow process of assimilating the lessons of the cruelest defeats, and consequently, the weakening of the direct influence of the Communist Party. Thence flows the necessity for the latter to draw profound conclusions in all questions of principles and tactics. And this is impossible without an open and all-sided discussion of all the fatal mistakes perpetrated hitherto.

Of course this activity must not turn into the activity of self-isolation. It is necessary to keep a firm hand on the pulse of the working class in order not to commit a mistake in estimating the tempo, and not only to identify a new mounting wave, but also to prepare for it in time.

Second Letter [Undated]

Your letter was also twenty-two days in transit. It is difficult to discuss vital questions under such conditions, and in my opinion the Chinese question belongs among the most vital ones, because the struggle is still unfolding in China, the partisan armies are in the field, and an armed insurrection has been placed on the agenda, as you no doubt know from the resolution of the last plenum of the ECCI [Executive Committee of the Communist International].

To begin, I want to reply to a minor but aggravating point. You say that I needlessly polemicize against you under the pseudonym of Zinoviev. In this you are entirely mistaken. I believe, incidentally, that the misunderstanding arose as a result of the irregular mail delivery. I wrote about the Canton affair at a time when I was apprised of the famous letter of the two musketeers; in addition to this, reports came from Moscow that they had been supplied with secretaries in order to expose "Trotskyism". I felt certain that Zinoviev would publish several of my letters on the Chinese question in which I set out to prove that in no case would there be such a special epoch in the Chinese revolution as an epoch of the democratic dictatorship of the proletariat and peasantry, because incomparably fewer preconditions exist there than in our own country, and as experience, and not theory, has already shown us, the democratic dictatorship of the proletariat and peasantry as such failed to materialize in our own country. Thus, my entire letter was written with a view to the past and future "exposures" on the part of Zinoviev.

In referring to the charge of ignoring the peasantry, I did not for a moment forget certain of our disputes on China—but I had no reason whatever to put in your lips this banal charge against me; for you, I trust, recognize that it is possible, without in the least ignoring the "peasantry", to arrive at a conclusion that the only road for solving the peasant question lies through the dictatorship of the proletariat. So that you, my dear E.A.—please do not take offense at a hunter's simile—assume gratuitously the role of a startled hare who concludes that the rifle is being aimed at him when the pursuit follows a totally different track.

I came to the opinion that there would not be any democratic dictatorship of the proletariat and peasantry in China from the time the Wuhan government was first formed. I based myself precisely upon the analysis of the most fundamental social facts, and not upon the manner in which they were refracted politically, which, as is well known, often assumes peculiar forms, since, in this sphere, factors of a secondary order enter in, including national tradition. I became convinced that the basic social facts have already cleared the road for themselves through all the peculiarities of political superstructures, when the Wuhan shipwreck destroyed utterly the legend of the left Kuomintang, allegedly embracing nine-tenths of the entire Kuomintang. In 1924–25, it was almost an accepted commonplace that the Kuomintang was a workers' and peasants party. This party "unexpectedly" proved to be bourgeois capitalist. Then another version was created, that the latter was only a "summit", but that the genuine Kuomintang, nine-tenths of the Kuomintang, was a revolutionary peasant party. Once again, it turned out "unexpectedly" that the left Kuomintang, in whole and in part, proceeded to smash the peasant movement which, as is well known, has great traditions in China and its own traditional organizational forms that became widespread during these years. That is why, when you write in the spirit of absolute abstraction that "it is impossible to say today whether the Chinese petty-bourgeoisie will be able to create any sort of parties analogous to our SRs, or whether such parties will be created by the right-wing communists who split off, etc." I reply to this argument from "the theory of improbabilities" as follows:

In the first place, even were the SRs to be created, there would not at all follow from this any dictatorship of the proletariat and peasantry, precisely as none followed in our own country, despite immeasurably more favorable conditions;

secondly, instead of guessing whether the petty-bourgeoisie is capable in the future—i.e., with the further aggravation of class relations—of playing a greater or lesser independent role (suppose a piece of wood suddenly fires a bullet?), one should rather ask why did the petty-bourgeoisie prove incapable of playing such a role in the recent past? When it had at its disposal the most favorable conditions the Communist Party was driven into the Kuomintang, the latter was declared a workers' and peasants' party, it was supported by the entire authority of the Communist International and the USSR, the peasant movement was far-flung and sought for leadership, the intelligentsia was widely mobilized since 1919, etc., etc.

You write that China still faces the "colossal problem of the agrarian bourgeois-democratic revolution". To Lenin, this was the root of the question. Lenin pointed out that the peasantry, even as an estate, is capable of playing a revolutionary role in the struggle against the estate of the landed nobility, and the bureaucracy indissolubly linked up with the latter, crowned by the tsarist autocracy. In the subsequent stage, says Lenin, the kulaks will break with the workers, and together with them a considerable section of the middle peasants, but this will take place during the transition to the proletarian revolution, as an integral part of the international revolution. But how do matters stand in China? China has no landed nobility; no peasant estate, fused by community of interests against the landlords. The agrarian revolution in China is aimed against the urban and rural bourgeoisie. Radek has stressed this often—even Bukharin has half-understood this now. In this lies the gist of the matter!

You write that "the social content of the first stage of the future third Chinese revolution cannot be characterized as a socialist overturn". But we run the risk here of falling into Bukharinistic scholasticism, and of occupying ourselves with splitting hairs over terminology instead of with a living characterization of the dialectic process. What was the content of our revolution from October 1917 to July 1918? We left the mills and factories in the hands of the capitalists, confining ourselves to workers' control; we expropriated the landed estates and put through the petty-bourgeois SR program of the socialization of land; and to crown it all, during this period, we had a co-participant in power in the form of the Left SRs. One could say with complete justification that "the social content of the first stage of the October Revolution cannot be characterized as a socialist overturn". I believe it was Yakovlev and several other Red professors who spilled a great deal of sophistry over this. Lenin said that we completed the bourgeois revolution en route. But the Chinese Revolution (the "third") will have to begin the drive against the kulak at its very first stages; it will have to expropriate the concessions of foreign capitalists, for, without this, there cannot be any unification of China in the sense of a genuine state sovereignty in economics and politics. In other words, the very first stage of the third Chinese Revolution will be less bourgeois in content than the first stage of the October Revolution.

On the other hand, the Canton events (as earlier Chinese events, etc.) demonstrated that the "national" bourgeoisie, too, having behind it Hong Kong, foreign advisers, and foreign cruisers, assumes such a position in relation to the slightest independent movement of workers and peasants as renders workers' control of production even less likely than was the case among us. In all probability we shall have to expropriate mills and factories, of any size, at the very first moments of the "third Chinese revolution".

To be sure, you propose simply to set aside the evidence of the Canton uprising. You say "since" the Canton insurrection was an adventure—i.e., not an undertaking that grew out of a mass movement—therefore "how can such an undertaking create a new situation ...?" Now, you yourself know that it is entirely impermissible thus to simplify the question. I would be the last person to argue against the fact that there were elements of adventurism in the Canton uprising. But to picture the Canton events as some sort of hocus-pocus from which no conclusions flow is an oversimplified attempt at evading the analysis of the actual content of the Canton experience. Wherein did adventurism lie? In the fact that the leadership, striving to cover up its past sins, monstrously forced the course of events, and caused a miscarriage. The mass movement existed, but it was inadequate and immature. It is wrong to think that presumably a miscarriage can teach us nothing about the maternal organism and the process of gestation. The enormous and theoretically decisive significance of the Canton events for the fundamental questions of the Chinese Revolution lies precisely in the fact that we have here—"thanks to" the adventure (yes! of course!)—what happens so rarely in history and politics: virtually a laboratory experiment on a gigantic scale. We paid very dearly for it, but that is all the less reason to wave its lessons aside.

The conditions for the experiment were almost "chemically pure". All the previously adopted resolutions had set down, sealed, and canonized, just like two times two equals four, that the revolution is bourgeois-agrarian, that only those "who leap over stages" could babble about the dictatorship of the proletariat based upon an alliance with the peasant poor, who compose 80 per cent of the Chinese peasantry, etc., etc. The last convention of the Communist Party of China met under this banner. A special representative of the Comintern, Comrade N., was present. We were told that the new CEC of the Chinese CP was above all suspicion. During this time, the campaign against so-called Trotskyism attained the wildest tempo, in China as well. Yet, on the very threshold of the Canton events, the CEC of the Chinese CP adopted, in the words of *Pravda*, a resolution declaring that the Chinese revolution had assumed a "permanent" character. Moreover, the representative of the Comintern, Comrade N., held the same position.

Under the "permanent" character of the revolution we must here understand the following: face to face with the supremely responsible practical task (though it was posed prematurely) the Chinese communists and even the representative of the Comintern, after taking into account the entire past experience and, as it were, all the political assets, drew the conclusion that only the workers led by the communists could lead the peasants against the landowners (the urban and rural bourgeoisie); and that only the dictatorship of the proletariat based on an alliance with the hundreds of millions of peasant poor could ensue from such a victorious struggle.

Just as during the Paris Commune, which also had in it

elements of a laboratory experiment (for the uprising took place there in a single city isolated from the rest of the country), the Proudhonists and Blanquists had to resort to steps directly contrary to their own doctrines, and thus (according to Marx) revealed all the more clearly the actual logic of class relations—so in Canton, too, the leaders, who were stuffed to the ears with prejudices against the bogie of the "permanent revolution", once they set to work, proved guilty of committing this original permanent sin from their very first steps. What happened, then, to the antitoxin of Martynovism that had been injected in bovine and asinine doses? Oh no! If this were only an adventure, i.e., a sort of hocus-pocus, showing nothing and proving nothing, then this adventure would have assumed the image and likeness of its creators. But no! This adventure came in contact with the earth, it was fed by the juices of real (though immature) mass movements and relations; and it was on this account that the said "adventure" seized its own creators by the scruff, impolitely picked them up, shook them in the air, and then deposited them on their heads, tapping their skulls, for firmness' sake, against the Chinese pavements ... As the latest resolutions and the latest article on this subject testify, these said "creators" are still standing on their heads, "permanently" dancing with their feet in the air.

It is ludicrous and impermissible to say that it is "inopportune" to draw conclusions from living events which every worker-revolutionist must think through to the end. At the time of the Ho Lung-Yeh T'ing uprising I wanted to pose openly the question that, in view of the consummation of the Kuomintang cycle of development, only the vanguard of the proletariat could aspire to power. This would presuppose a new standpoint for it, a new self-appraisal on its part—after a reevaluation of the objective situation—and this very thing would have excluded such an adventuristic approach to the situation as "We'll bide our time in a little corner, the peasant will come to our assistance by starting things, and somebody will somehow seize power and do something." At that time, certain comrades said to me, "It is inopportune to raise these questions now in connection with Ho Lung who apparently has been crushed already." I did not at all tend to overestimate Ho Lung's uprising; I did consider, nevertheless, that it was the last signal in favor of the necessity to review the orientation in the Chinese Revolution. Had these questions been opportunely posed at that time, then, perhaps, the ideological authors of the Canton adventure might have been compelled to think things over, and the Chinese party might not have been so ruthlessly destroyed; and if not, then in the light of our prognosis and our warning, the Canton events would have entered as a weighty lesson into the consciousness of hundreds and thousands, as for example, did Radek's warning about Chiang Kai-shek, on the eve of the Shanghai coup d'etat. No, the propitious time has passed. I do not know when the Chinese Revolution will revive. But we must utilize whatever time remains at our disposal entirely for preparation and, moreover, on the basis of the fresh course of events.

You write that it is necessary to study the history of China, its economic life, statistical data, etc. Nobody can object to this (unless this is intended as an argument to postpone the question to doomsday). In my own justification, however, I must say that since my arrival in Alma Ata I have occupied myself only with China (India, Polynesia, etc., for comparative study). Of course more gaps remain than completely covered places, but I must say nevertheless that in all the new (for myself) books I am reading, I find even today nothing new in principle. But the chief point still remains—the confirmation of our prognoses by experience—first in relation to the Kuomintang as a whole, then in relation to the "left" Kuomintang and the Wuhan government, and finally, in relation to the "deposit" on the third revolution, in the shape of the Canton uprising.

That is why I consider that there cannot be any postponement.

Two final questions:

You ask: Was Lenin right when during the war he defended against Bukharin the idea that Russia was still facing a bourgeois revolution? Yes, he was right. The Bukharin formulation was schematic and scholastic, i.e., it represented the self-same caricature of the permanent revolution that

Bukharin tries to ascribe to me now. But there is also another side to this same question: Was Lenin right when against Stalin, Rykov, Zinoviev, Kamenev, Frunze, Kalinin, Tomsky, etc., etc. (let alone all the Lyadovs), he advanced his April Theses? Was he right when against Zinoviev, Kamenev, Rykov, Milyutin, etc., etc., he defended the seizure of power by the proletariat? You know better than I that had Lenin failed to reach Petrograd in April 1917, there would have been no October Revolution. Up to February 1917, the slogan of the dictatorship of the proletariat and peasantry was historically progressive; after the February overturn the same slogan—of Stalin, Kamenev, and the rest—became a reactionary slogan.

From April to May 1927, I supported the slogan of the democratic dictatorship of the proletariat and peasantry for China (more correctly, I concurred with this slogan) inasmuch as the social forces had not as yet passed their political verdict, although the situation in China was immeasurably less propitious for this slogan than in Russia. After this verdict was passed by a colossal historical action (the experience of Wuhan) the slogan of democratic dictatorship became a reactionary force and will lead inevitably either to opportunism or adventurism.

You further argue that for the October leap we had the February running start. That is correct. If, even at the beginning of the Northern Expedition, we had begun to build soviets in the "emancipated" regions (and the masses were striving for that), we would have obtained the necessary running start, would have disintegrated the armies of the enemies, obtained our own army, and we would have assumed power—if not in the whole of China at once, then in a very considerable section of it. At present, of course, the revolution is on the decline. The babbling of the light-minded scribblers about the fact that the revolution is on the verge of a new upswing, inasmuch as, in China, if you please, countless executions are taking place and a cruel commercial and industrial crisis is raging—this is criminal idiocy. After three of the greatest defeats, the crisis does not arouse but on the contrary oppresses the proletariat, while the executions are destroying the politically weakened party.

We have entered the period of reflux. What will provide the impulse for a new mounting wave? Or to put it differently: What conditions will provide the necessary running start for the proletarian vanguard at the head of the worker and peasant masses? This I do not know. The future will show whether only internal processes will suffice or an impulse from without will be necessary. I am willing to allow that the first stage of the movement may repeat in an abridged and altered form the stages of the revolution that we have already passed (for example, some new parody of the "all-national front" against Chang Tso-lin); but this first phase will perhaps suffice only in order to enable the Communist Party to advance and proclaim to the popular masses its "April Theses", i.e., its program and strategy of the conquest of power by the proletariat. If, however, we enter into the new upswing, which will unfold with an incomparably more rapid tempo than in the past, with a schema of a "democratic dictatorship" that is already outworn today, then one could stake his head beforehand that in China very many Lyadovs will be found, but hardly a Lenin in order to effect (against all the Lyadovs) the tactical rearming of the party on the day after the revolutionary spurt.

Third Letter [Undated]

Dear E.A.:

Received your airmail letter yesterday. Thus, all the letters have arrived. The last letter took sixteen days in transit, i.e., six days less than ordinary mail. Two days ago I sent you a detailed answer to your objections on the Chinese revolution. But on awakening this morning I recalled that I had failed (apparently) to reply to the argument you deem most important, as I understand it. You write:

> Your basic error lies in the fact that you determine the character of a revolution on the basis of who makes it, which class, i.e., by the effective subject, while you seem to assign secondary importance to the objective social content of the process.

Then you go on to adduce as examples the November revolution in Germany, the 1789 revolution in France, and the future Chinese revolution.

This argument is in essence only a "sociological" generalization (to use Johnsonian terminology) of all your other concrete economic and historical views. But I want also to reply to your views in their generalized sociological formulation, for in so doing the "fundamental error" (on your part and not mine) stands out most clearly.

How to characterize a revolution? By the class which achieves it or by the social content lodged in it? There is a theoretical trap lodged in counterposing the former to the latter in such a general form. The Jacobin period of the French revolution was of course the period of petty-bourgeois dictatorship, in addition to which, the petty-bourgeoisie—in complete harmony with its "sociological nature"—cleared the way for the big bourgeoisie. The November revolution in Germany was the beginning of the proletarian revolution but it was checked at its very first steps by the petty-bourgeois leadership, and succeeded only in achieving a few things unfulfilled by the bourgeois revolution. What are we to call the November revolution—bourgeois or proletarian? Both the former and the latter would be incorrect. The place of the October Revolution will be determined when we both give the mechanics of this revolution and determine its results. There will be no contradiction in this case between the mechanics (understanding under it, of course, not only the motive force but also the leadership) and the results—both the former and the latter are "sociologically" indeterminate in character. I take the liberty to put the question to you: What would you call the Hungarian revolution of 1919? You will say: proletarian. Why? Didn't the "social content" of the Hungarian revolution prove to be capitalist! You will reply: This is the social content of the counterrevolution. Correct. Apply this now to China. The "social content" under the dictatorship of the proletariat (based on an alliance with the peasantry) can remain during a certain period of time not socialist as yet, but the road to bourgeois development from the dictatorship of the proletariat can lead only through counterrevolution. For this reason, so far as the social content is concerned, it is necessary to say: "We shall wait and see."

The gist of the matter lies precisely in the fact that although the political mechanics of the revolution depend in the last analysis upon an economic base (not only national but international) they cannot, however, be deduced with abstract logic from this economic base. In the first place, the base itself is very contradictory and its "maturity" does not allow of bald statistical determination; secondly, the economic base as well as the political situation must be approached not in the national but in the international framework, taking into account the dialectic action and reaction between the national and the international; thirdly, the class struggle and its political expression, unfolding on the economic foundations, also have their own imperious logic of development, which cannot be leaped over. When Lenin said in April 1917 that only the dictatorship of the proletariat could save Russia from disintegration and doom, Sukhanov (the most consistent opponent) refuted him with two fundamental arguments: (*i*) the social content of the bourgeois revolution has not yet been achieved; (*ii*) Russia had not yet matured economically for a socialist revolution. And what was Lenin's answer? Whether or not Russia has matured is something that "we shall wait and see"; this cannot be determined statistically; this will be determined by the trend of events and, moreover, only on an international scale. But, said Lenin, independently of how this social content will be determined in the end, at the present moment, today, there is no other road to the salvation of the country—from famine, war, and enslavement—except through the seizure of power by the proletariat.

That is precisely what we must say now in relation to China. First of all, it is incorrect to allege that the agrarian revolution composes the basic content of the present historical struggle. In what must this agrarian revolution consist? The universal partition of the land? But there have been several such universal partitions in Chinese history. And then the development always returned to "its proper orbit". The agrarian revolution is the destruction of the Chinese landlords and Chinese functionaries. But the national unification of China and its economic sovereignty imply its emancipation from world imperialism, for which China remains the most important safety valve against the collapse of European and, tomorrow, of American capitalism. The agrarian overturn in China without national unification and tariff autonomy (in essence: monopoly of foreign trade) would not open any way out or any perspectives for China. This is what predetermines the gigantic sweep and the monstrous sharpness of the struggle facing China today, after the experience already undergone by all the participants.

What then should a Chinese communist say to himself under these conditions? Can he really proceed to reason as follows: The social content of the Chinese Revolution can only be bourgeois (as proved by such and such charts). Therefore we must not pose ourselves the task of the dictatorship of the proletariat; the social content prescribes, in the most extreme case, a coalition dictatorship of the proletariat and peasantry. But for a coalition (in question here, of course, is a political coalition, and not a "sociological" alliance of classes) a partner is needed. Moscow taught me that the Kuomintang is such a partner. However, no left Kuomintang materialized. What to do? Obviously, there only remains for me, a Chinese communist, to console myself with the idea that "it is impossible to say today whether the Chinese petty-bourgeoisie will be able to create any sort of parties" ...or whether it will not. Suppose it suddenly does?

A Chinese communist who reasons along such a prescription would cut the throat of the Chinese Revolution.

Least of all, of course, is it a question here of summoning the Communist Party of China to an immediate insurrection for the seizure of power. The tempo depends entirely upon the circumstances. The task lies in seeing to it that the Communist Party is permeated through and through with the conviction that the third Chinese Revolution can come to a triumphant conclusion only with the dictatorship of the proletariat under the leadership of the Communist Party. Moreover, it is necessary to understand this leadership not "in a general" sense, but in the sense of the direct wielding of complete revolutionary power. And so far as the tempo with which we shall have to build socialism in China is concerned, about this "we shall wait and see".

30

Summary and Perspectives of the Chinese Revolution*

Its Lessons for the Countries of the Orient and for the Whole of the Comintern

June 1928

Leon Trotsky wrote the two documents that comprise *The Third International after Lenin* in 1928, while involuntarily exiled in Alma Ata. The documents were meant to be used for discussion at the Sixth World Congress of the Communist International. Trotsky's work—a sharp criticism against the opposing program supporting "socialism in one country"—was never distributed to or discussed by the main body at the Congress. The parts of it made available to a committee, but then recalled, were smuggled out of the country by James Cannon, a delegate and founding member of the Communist Party in the United States.

CHAPTER III
(PART 1)

Bolshevism and Menshevism and the Left wing of the German and international social democracy took definite shape on the analysis of the experiences, mistakes, and tendencies of the 1905 revolution. An analysis of the experiences of the Chinese Revolution is today of no less importance for the international proletariat.

---

* Excerpted from *The Third International after Lenin: The Draft Program of the Communist International: A Criticism of Fundamentals*, 1928.

This analysis, however, has not even begun—it is prohibited. The official literature is engaged in hastily selecting facts to suit the resolutions of the ECCI, the hollowness of which has been completely revealed. The draft program dulls the sharpest points of the Chinese problem whenever possible, but it sets the seal of approval upon the essential points of the fatal line followed by the ECCI in the Chinese question. The analysis of the great historical process is replaced by a literary defense of bankrupt schemas.

1. On the Nature of The Colonial Bourgeoisie

The draft program states: "Temporary agreements [with the national bourgeoisie of colonial countries] are admissible only in so far as the bourgeoisie does not obstruct the revolutionary organization of the workers and peasants and wages a genuine struggle against imperialism."

This formula, although it is deliberately tacked on as an incidental proposition, is one of the central postulates of the draft, for the countries of the Orient, at any rate. The main proposition deals, naturally, with the "emancipation [of the workers and peasants] from the influence of the national bourgeoisie". But we judge not from the standpoint of grammar but politically and, moreover, on the basis of experience, and therefore we say: the main proposition is only an incidental one here, while the incidental proposition contains what is most essential. The formula, taken as a whole, is a classic Menshevik noose for the proletariat of the Orient.

What "temporary agreements" are meant here? In politics, as in nature, all things are "temporary". Perhaps we are discussing here purely practical agreements *from one occasion to the next*? It goes without saying that we cannot renounce in advance such rigidly delimited and rigidly practical agreements as serve each time a quite definite aim. For example, such cases as involve agreements with the student youth of the Kuomintang for the organization of an anti-imperialist demonstration, or of obtaining assistance from the Chinese merchants for strikers in a foreign concession, etc. Such cases are not at all excluded in the future, even in China. But in that case why are *general* political conditions adduced here, namely, "... in so far as the bourgeoisie does not obstruct the revolutionary organization of the workers and peasants and wages a genuine [!] struggle against imperialism"? The sole "condition" for every agreement with the bourgeoisie, for each separate, practical, and expedient agreement adapted to each given case, consists in not allowing either the organizations or the banners to become mixed directly or indirectly for a single day or a single hour; it consists in distinguishing between the Red and the Blue, and in not believing for an instant in the capacity or readiness of the bourgeoisie either to lead a *genuine* struggle against imperialism or *not to obstruct* the workers and peasants. For practical and expedient agreements we have absolutely no use for such a condition as the one cited above. On the contrary, it could only cause us harm, running counter to the general line of our struggle against capitalism, which is not suspended even during the brief period of an "agreement". As was said long ago, purely practical agreements, such as do not bind us in the least and do not oblige us to anything politically, can be concluded with the devil himself, if that is advantageous at a given moment. But it would be absurd in such a case to demand that the devil should *generally* become converted to Christianity, and that he use his horns not against workers and peasants but exclusively for pious deeds. In presenting such conditions we act in reality as the devil's advocates, and beg him to let us become his godfathers.

By its absurd conditions, which serve to paint the bourgeoisie in bright colors in advance, the draft program states clearly and definitely (despite the diplomatic and incidental character of its thesis) that involved here are precisely long-term political blocs and not agreements for specific occasions concluded for practical reasons and rigidly confined to practical aims. But in such a case, what is meant by demands that the bourgeoisie wage a "genuine" struggle and that it "not obstruct" the workers? Do we present these conditions to the bourgeoisie itself, and demand a public promise from it? It will make you any promises you want! It will even send its delegates to Moscow, enter the Peasants' International, adhere as a "sympathizing" party to the Comintern, peek into the Red International of Labor Unions. In short, it will promise anything that will give it the opportunity (with our assistance) to dupe the workers and peasants, more efficiently, more easily, and more completely to throw sand in their eyes—until the first opportunity, such as was offered in Shanghai.

But perhaps it is not a question here of political obligations exacted from the bourgeoisie which, we repeat, it will immediately agree to in order thus to transform us into its guarantors before the working masses? Perhaps it is a question here of an "objective" and "scientific" evaluation of a given national bourgeoisie, an expert *a priori* "sociological" prognosis, as it were, of its capacity to wage a struggle and not to obstruct? Sad to say, as the most recent and freshest experience testifies, such an *a priori* prognosis makes fools out of experts as a rule. And it would not be so bad, if only they alone were involved ...

There cannot be the slightest doubt on the matter: the text deals precisely with long-term political blocs. It would be entirely superfluous to include in a program the question of occasional practical agreements. For this purpose, a matter-of-fact tactical resolution *On Our Current Tasks* would suffice. Involved here is a question of justifying and setting a programmatic seal of approval upon yesterday's orientation toward the Kuomintang, which doomed the second Chinese Revolution to destruction, and which is capable of destroying revolutions in the future.

According to the idea advanced by Bukharin, the real author of the draft, all stakes are placed precisely upon the general evaluation of the colonial bourgeoisie, whose capacity to struggle and not to obstruct must be proved not by its own oaths but in a rigorous "sociological" manner, that is by a thousand and one scholastic schemes adapted to opportunist purposes.

To bring this out more clearly let us refer back to the Bukharin evaluation of the colonial bourgeoisie. After citing the "anti-imperialist content" of colonial revolutions, and quoting Lenin (without any justification whatever), Bukharin proclaims:

> The liberal bourgeoisie in China played an objectively revolutionary role over a period of a number of years, and not

> months. Then it exhausted itself. This was not all a political 'twenty-four hour' holiday of the type of the Russian liberal revolution of 1905.

Everything here is wrong from the beginning to end.

Lenin really taught us to differentiate rigidly between an oppressed and oppressor bourgeois nation. From this follow conclusions of exceptional importance. For instance, our attitude toward a war between an imperialist and a colonial country. For a pacifist, such a war is a war like any other. For a communist, a war of a colonial nation against an imperialist nation is a bourgeois revolutionary war. Lenin thus *raised* the national liberation movements, the colonial insurrections, and wars of the oppressed nations, to the level of the bourgeois democratic revolutions, in particular, to that of the Russian revolution of 1905. But Lenin did not at all place the wars for national liberation *above* bourgeois democratic revolutions as is now done by Bukharin, after his 180 degree turn. Lenin insisted on a distinction between an oppressed bourgeois nation and a bourgeois oppressor nation. But Lenin nowhere raised and never could raise the question as if the bourgeoisie of a colonial or a semi-colonial country in an epoch of struggle for national liberation must be more progressive and more revolutionary than the bourgeoisie of a non-colonial country in the epoch of the democratic revolution. This does not flow from anything in theory; there is no confirmation of it in history. For example, pitiful as Russian liberalism was, and hybrid as was its Left half, the petty bourgeois democrats, the Social Revolutionists and Mensheviks, it would nevertheless hardly be possible to say that Chinese liberalism and Chinese bourgeois democracy rose to a higher level or were more revolutionary than their Russian prototypes.

To present matters as if there must inevitably flow from the fact of colonial oppression the revolutionary character of a national bourgeoisie is to reproduce inside out the fundamental error of Menshevism, which held that the revolutionary nature of the Russian bourgeoisie must flow from the oppression of feudalism and the autocracy.

The question of the nature and the policy of the bourgeoisie is settled by the entire internal class structure of a nation waging the revolutionary struggle; by the historical epoch in which that struggle develops; by the degree of economic, political, and military dependence of the national bourgeoisie upon world imperialism as a whole or a particular section of it; finally, and this is most important, by the degree of class activity of the native proletariat, and by the state of its connections with the international revolutionary movement.

A democratic or national liberation movement may offer the bourgeoisie an opportunity to deepen and broaden its possibilities for exploitation. Independent intervention of the proletariat on the revolutionary arena threatens to deprive the bourgeoisie of the possibility to exploit altogether.

Let us observe some facts more closely.

The present inspirers of the Comintern have untiringly repeated that Chiang Kai-shek waged a war "against imperialism" whilst Kerensky marched hand in hand with the imperialists. Ergo: whereas a ruthless struggle had to be waged against Kerensky, it was necessary to support Chiang Kai-shek.

The ties between Kerenskyism and imperialism were indisputable. One can go even still further back and point out that the Russian bourgeoisie "dethroned" Nicholas II with the blessings of British and French imperialism. Not only did Miliukov-Kerensky support the war waged by Lloyd George-Poincaré, but Lloyd George and Poincaré also supported Miliukov's and Kerensky's revolution first against the Czar, and later against the workers and peasants. This is absolutely beyond dispute.

But how did matters stand in this respect in China? The "February" revolution in China took place in 1911. That revolution was a great and progressive event, although it was accomplished with the direct participation of the imperialists. Sun Yat-sen, in his memoirs, relates how his organization relied in all its work on the "support" of the imperialist states—either Japan, France, or America. If Kerensky in 1917 continued to take part in the imperialist war, then the Chinese bourgeoisie, the one that is so "national," so "revolutionary", etc., supported

Wilson's intervention in the war with the hope that the Entente would help to emancipate China. In 1918 Sun Yat-sen addressed to the governments of the Entente his plans for the economic development and political emancipation of China. There is no foundation whatever for the assertion that the Chinese bourgeoisie, in its struggle against the Manchu Dynasty, displayed any higher revolutionary qualities than the Russian bourgeoisie in the struggle against Czarism; or that there is a principled difference between Chiang Kai-shek's and Kerensky's attitude toward imperialism.

But, says the ECCI, Chiang Kai-shek nevertheless did wage war against imperialism. To present the situation in this manner is to put too crude a face upon reality. Chiang Kai-shek waged war against certain Chinese militarists, the agents of *one* of the imperialist powers. This is not at all the same as to wage a war against imperialism. Even Tang Ping-shan understood this. In his report to the Seventh Plenum of the ECCI (at the end of 1926) Tang Ping-shan characterized the policy of the Kuomintang; center headed by Chiang Kai-shek as follows:

> In the sphere of international policy it occupies a passive position in the full meaning of that word ... It is inclined to fight only against British imperialism; so far as the Japanese imperialists are concerned, however, it is ready under certain conditions to make a compromise with them.[1]

The attitude of the Kuomintang toward imperialism was from the very outset not revolutionary but entirely opportunist. It endeavored to smash and isolate the agents of certain imperialist powers so as to make a deal with the self-same or other imperialist powers on terms more favorable for the Chinese bourgeoisie. That is all. But the gist of the matter lies in the fact that the entire formulation of the question is erroneous.

One must measure not the attitude of every given national bourgeoisie to imperialism "in general", but its attitude to the immediate revolutionary historical tasks of its own nation. The Russian bourgeoisie was the bourgeoisie of an imperialist oppressor state; the Chinese bourgeoisie, a bourgeoisie of an oppressed colonial country. The overthrow of feudal Czarism was a progressive task in old Russia. The overthrow of the imperialist yoke is a progressive historical task in China. However, the conduct of the Chinese bourgeoisie in relation to imperialism, the proletariat, and the peasantry, was not more revolutionary than the attitude of the Russian bourgeoisie towards Czarism and the revolutionary classes in Russia, but, if anything, viler and more reactionary. That is the only way to pose the question.

The Chinese bourgeoisie is sufficiently realistic and acquainted intimately enough with the nature of world imperialism to understand that a really serious struggle against the latter requires such an upheaval of the revolutionary masses as would primarily become a menace to the bourgeoisie itself. If the struggle against the Manchu Dynasty was a task of smaller historical proportions than the overthrow of Czarism, then the struggle against world imperialism is a task on a much larger scale; and if we taught the workers of Russia from the very beginning not to believe in the readiness of liberalism and the ability of petty bourgeois democracy to overthrow Czarism and to destroy feudalism, we should no less energetically have imbued the Chinese workers from the outset with the same spirit of distrust. The new and absolutely false theory promulgated by Stalin-Bukharin about the "immanent" revolutionary spirit of the colonial bourgeoisie is, in substance, a translation of Menshevism into the language of Chinese politics. It serves only to convert the oppressed position of China into an internal political premium for the Chinese bourgeoisie, and it throws an additional weight on the scale of the bourgeoisie against the scale of the trebly oppressed Chinese proletariat.

But, we are told by Stalin and Bukharin, the authors of the draft program, Chiang Kai-shek's northern expedition roused a powerful movement among the worker and peasant masses. This is incontestable. But did not the fact that Guchkov and Shulgin brought with them to Petrograd the abdication of Nicholas II play a revolutionary role? Did it not arouse the most downtrodden, exhausted, and timid strata of the populace? Did not the fact that Kerensky, who but yesterday was a Trudovik, became the President of the Ministers' Council and the Commander-in-Chief, rouse the masses of soldiers? Did it not bring them to meetings? Did it not rouse the village to its feet against the landlord? The question could be posed even more widely. Did not the entire activities of capitalism rouse the masses, did it not rescue them, to use the expression of the *Communist Manifesto*, from the idiocy of rural life? Did it not impel the proletarian battalions to the struggle? But does our historical evaluation of the objective role of capitalism as a whole or of certain actions of the bourgeoisie in particular, become a substitute for our active class revolutionary attitude toward capitalism or toward the actions of the bourgeoisie? Opportunist policies have always been based on this kind of non-dialectical, conservative, tailendist "objectivism". Marxism on the contrary invariably taught that the revolutionary consequences of one or another act of the bourgeoisie, to which it is compelled by its position, will be fuller, more decisive, less doubtful, and firmer, the more independent the proletarian vanguard will be in relation to the bourgeoisie, the less it will be inclined to place its fingers between the jaws of the bourgeoisie, to see it in bright colors, to over-estimate its revolutionary spirit or its readiness for a "united front" and for a struggle against imperialism.

The Stalinist and Bukharinist appraisal of the colonial bourgeoisie cannot stand criticism, either theoretical, historical, or political. Yet this is precisely the appraisal, as we have seen, that the draft program seeks to canonize.

* * *

One unexposed and un-condemned error always leads to another, or prepares the ground for it.

If yesterday the Chinese bourgeoisie was enrolled in the united revolutionary front, then today it is proclaimed to have "definitely gone over to the counter-revolutionary camp". It is not difficult to expose how unfounded are these transfers and enrollments which have been effected in a purely administrative manner without any serious Marxian analysis whatever.

It is absolutely self-evident that the bourgeoisie in joining the camp of the revolution does so not accidentally, not because it is light-minded, but under the pressure of its own class interests. For fear of the masses the bourgeoisie subsequently deserts the revolution or openly displays its concealed hatred of the revolution. But the bourgeoisie can go over "*definitely* to the counter-revolutionary camp", that is, free itself from the necessity of "supporting" the revolution again, or at least of flirting with it, only in the event that its fundamental class aspirations are satisfied either by revolutionary means or in another way (for instance, the Bismarckian way). Let us recall the history of the period of 1848–1871. Let us recall that the Russian bourgeoisie was able to turn its back so bluntly upon the revolution of 1905 only because the revolution gave it the State Duma, that is, it received the means whereby it could bring direct pressure to bear on the bureaucracy and make deals with it. Nevertheless, when the war of 1914–1917 revealed the inability of the "modernized" regime to secure the basic interests of the bourgeoisie, the latter again turned towards the revolution, and made its turn more sharply than in 1905.

Can anyone maintain that the revolution of 1925–1927 in China has at least partly satisfied the basic interests of Chinese capitalism? No. China is today just as far removed from real national unity and from tariff autonomy as it was prior to 1925. Yet, the creation of a unified domestic market and its protection from cheaper foreign goods is a life-and-death question for the Chinese bourgeoisie, a question second in importance only to that of maintaining the basis of its class domination over the proletariat and the peasant poor. But, for the Japanese and the British bourgeoisie the maintenance of the colonial status of China is likewise a question of no less importance than economic autonomy is for the Chinese bourgeoisie. That is why there will still be not a few Leftward zigzags in the policy of the Chinese bourgeoisie. There will be no lack of temptations in the future for the amateurs of the "national united front". To tell the Chinese communists today that their alliance with the bourgeoisie from 1924 to the end of 1927 was correct but that it is worthless now because the bourgeoisie has definitely gone over to the counter-revolutionary camp, is to disarm the Chinese communists once again in face of the coming objective changes in the situation and the inevitable Leftward zigzags of the Chinese bourgeoisie. The war now being conducted by Chiang Kai-shek against the North already overthrows completely the mechanical scheme of the authors of the draft program.

* * *

But the principled error of the official formulation of the question will doubtless appear more glaringly, more convincingly, and more incontrovertibly if we recall the fact which is still fresh in our minds, and which is of no little importance, namely, that Czarist Russia was a combination of oppressor and oppressed nations, that is of Great Russians and "foreigners", many of whom were in a completely colonial or semi-colonial status. Lenin not only demanded that the greatest attention be paid to the national problem of the peoples in Czarist Russia but also proclaimed (against Bukharin and others) that it was the elementary duty of the proletariat of the dominant nation to support the struggle of the oppressed nations for their self-determination, up to and including separation. But did the party conclude from this that the bourgeoisie of the nationalities oppressed by Czarism (the Poles, Ukrainians, Tartars, Jews, Armenians, and others) were more progressive, more radical, and more revolutionary than the Russian bourgeoisie? Historical experience bears out the fact that the Polish bourgeoisie-notwithstanding the fact that it suffered both from the yoke of the autocracy and from national oppression—was more reactionary than the Russian bourgeoisie and, in the State Dumas, always gravitated not towards the Cadets but towards the Octobrists. The same is true of the Tartar bourgeoisie. The fact that the Jews had absolutely no rights whatever did not prevent the Jewish bourgeoisie from being even more cowardly, more reactionary, and more vile than the Russian bourgeoisie. Or perhaps the Estonian bourgeoisie, the Lettish, the Georgian, or the Armenian bourgeoisie were more revolutionary than the Great Russian bourgeoisie? How could anyone forget such historical lessons!

Or should we perhaps recognize today, after the event, that Bolshevism was wrong when—in contradistinction to the Bund, the Dashnaks, the PPSers, the Georgian and other Mensheviks—it called upon the workers of all the oppressed nationalities, of all the colonial peoples in Czarist Russia, at the very dawn of the bourgeois democratic revolution, to dissociate themselves and form their own autonomous class organizations, to break ruthlessly all organizational ties not only with the liberal bourgeois, but also with the revolutionary petty bourgeois parties, to win over the working class in the struggle against these parties, and through the workers fight against these parties for influence over the peasantry? Did we not commit here a "Trotskyist" mistake? Did we not skip over, in relation to these oppressed, and in many cases very backward nations, the phase of development corresponding to the Kuomintang?

As a matter of fact how easily one could construct a theory that the PPS, Dashnak-Tsutiun, the Bund, etc., were "peculiar" forms of the necessary collaboration of the various classes in the struggle against the autocracy and against national oppression! How can such historical lessons be forgotten?

For a Marxist it was clear even prior to the Chinese events of the last three years—and today it should be clear even to the blind—that foreign imperialism, as a direct factor in the internal life of China, renders the Chinese Miliukovs and Chinese Kerenskys in the final analysis even more vile than their Russian prototypes. It is not for nothing that the very first manifesto issued by our party proclaimed that the further East we go, the lower and viler becomes the bourgeoisie, the greater are the tasks that fall upon the proletariat. This historical "law" fully applies to China as well.

> Our revolution is a bourgeois revolution, the workers must support the bourgeoisie—say the worthless politicians from the camp of the liquidators. Our revolution is a bourgeois revolution, say we who are Marxists. The workers must open the eyes of the people to the fraud of the bourgeois politicians, teach them not to place trust in promises and to rely on *their* OWN forces, on *their* OWN organization, on *their* OWN unity, and on *their* OWN weapons alone.[2]

This Leninist thesis is compulsory for the Orient as a whole. It must by all means find a place in the program of the Comintern.

2. The Stages of the Chinese Revolution

The first stage of the Guomindang was the period of domination by the national bourgeoisie, under the apologetic banner of the "bloc of four classes". The second period, after the Chiang Kai-shek *coup d'état*, was an experiment in parallel and "independent" domination by Chinese Kerenskyism. While the Russian Populists, together with the Mensheviks, openly gave their short-lived "dictatorship" the form of dual power, the Chinese "revolutionary democracy" did not reach even that stage. And inasmuch as history in general does not work to order, there is nothing left for us but to understand *that there is not and that there will not be* any other "democratic" dictatorship than the one exercised by the Guomindang since 1925. This remains true regardless of whether the semi-unification of China accomplished by the Guomindang is maintained in the coming period or whether the country is again dismembered. But precisely when the class dialectics of the revolution, having spent all its other resources, put on the order of the day the *dictatorship of the proletariat,* with the numberless millions of oppressed and downtrodden of town and country on its side, the ECCI advanced the slogan of the *democratic* dictatorship (that is, bourgeois democracy) of the workers and peasants. The reply to this formula was the Canton insurrection which, lifted the curtain over a new stage, or, more correctly, over with all its prematurity, with all the adventurism of its leaders, the coming, the *third* Chinese revolution. This must be emphasized.

Trying to insure themselves against the sins of the past, the leaders criminally forced the trend of events at the end of last year and brought about the Canton miscarriage. However, even a miscarriage can teach us a good deal concerning the organism of the mother and the process of birth. The tremendous theoretical and even decisive significance of the Canton events for the fundamental problems of the Chinese revolution is due precisely to the fact that we have here what happens so rarely in history and in politics: *a laboratory experiment on a gigantic scale*. We paid for it dearly, but that makes it all the more imperative for us to digest the lessons.

One of the fighting slogans of the Canton insurrection, as *Pravda* (no.31) relates, was the watchword: "Down with the Guomindang!" The Guomindang banners and signs were torn and trampled upon. But it was already after the "betrayal" of Chiang Kai-shek and that of Wang Jingwei (not a betrayal of his class, but of our illusions) that the ECCI pompously declared: "We will not give up the Guomindang banner." The workers of Canton prohibited the Guomindang, *proclaiming all its tendencies illegal*. This means that to solve the basic national tasks, not only the big bourgeoisie but also the small bourgeoisie failed to advance a political power, a party, a faction, in conjunction with which the proletarian party might be able to solve the tasks of the bourgeois democratic revolution. The key to the position lies in the fact that the *problem of winning the movement of the poor peasants already fell entirely on the shoulders of the proletariat*, and the Communist Party directly; the approach to a real solution of the bourgeois-democratic tasks of the revolution necessitated the concentration of all the power in the hands of the proletariat.

As to the short-lived Canton Soviet government, *Pravda* reports:

> In the interests of the workers, the decrees of the Canton Soviet proclaimed workers' control of production through factory Committees, the nationalization of big industry, transportation and the banks.

Then, measures are mentioned such as the "confiscation of all dwellings of the big bourgeoisie for the benefit of the labourers ..."

Thus, it was the Canton workers who were in power and what is more, the government was actually in the hands of the Communist Party. The program of the new government included not only the confiscation of the feudal lands, in so far as such exist in Guangdong at all, and workers' control of production, but also the nationalization of big industry, the banks and transportation and even the confiscation of the dwellings of the bourgeoisie and all their property for the benefit of the workers. The question arises: If these are the methods of a bourgeois revolution what will the proletarian revolution in China look like?

Notwithstanding the fact that the instructions of the ECCI said nothing about the proletarian dictatorship and socialist measures; notwithstanding the fact that Canton, when compared with Shanghai, Hankow and other industrial centres of the country, has more of a petty-bourgeois character, the revolutionary upheaval effected *against the Guomindang* led automatically to the proletarian dictatorship which, at its very first steps, found itself compelled by the entire situation to take more radical measures than those with which the October Revolution began. And this fact, in spite of its paradoxical appearance, is quite a normal outcome of the social relations of China as well as of the whole development of the revolution.

Large and middle-scale landownership (as it exists in China) is most closely intertwined with urban, including foreign capitalism. There is no landowning caste in China in opposition to the bourgeoisie. The most widespread, generally-hated exploiter in the village is the usurious wealthy peasant, the agent of urban banking capital. The agrarian revolution has therefore just as much of an anti-bourgeois as it has of an anti-feudal character in China. The first stage of our October Revolution, in which the wealthy peasant marched hand in hand with the middle and poor peasant, and frequently at their head, against the landlord, will not, or will hardly at all, take place in China. The agrarian revolution there will be from the very beginning, and also later on, an uprising not only against the few landlords and bureaucrats, but also against the wealthy peasants and usurers. Whereas in Russia the poor peasant committees acted only in the second stage of the October Revolution, towards the middle of 1918, in China they will appear on the scene, in one form or another, as soon as the agrarian movement revives. The breaking-up of the rich peasants will be the first and not the second step in the Chinese October.

The agrarian revolution, however, does not constitute the only basis of the present historical struggle in China. The most radical agrarian revolution, the general division of land (the Communist Party will naturally support it to the very end), will not by itself be a way out of the economic blind alley. It is now essential for China to have national unity and economic sovereignty, that is, customs autonomy, or more correctly, a monopoly of foreign trade; this means: *emancipation from world imperialism*, for which China remains the most important source not only of enrichment but also of existence, constituting a safety valve against internal explosions of capitalism, today in Europe and tomorrow in America.

This is what determines in advance the gigantic scope and monstrous sharpness of the struggle through which the masses of China must pass, the more so now, when the depth of the stream of the struggle has already been measured and felt by all or its participants.

The enormous role of foreign capitalism in Chinese industry, its habit of relying directly on its own "national" bayonets in order to defend its rapacity, makes the program of workers' control in China even less realizable than it was in Russia. The direct expropriation of the foreign capitalist enterprises, and later also the Chinese capitalist enterprises, will most likely be made imperative by the struggle, on the very morrow of the victorious insurrection.

The same objective social and historical causes which determined the "October" outcome of the Russian Revolution rise before us in China in a still more accentuated form. The bourgeois and the proletarian poles of the Chinese nation are opposed to each other even more intransigently, if this is possible, than they were in Russia, inasmuch as, on the one hand, the Chinese bourgeoisie is directly bound up with foreign imperialism and its military machine and, on the other hand, the Chinese proletariat has from the very beginning established relations with the Comintern and the Soviet Union. Numerically, the Chinese peasantry constitutes an even more overwhelming mass than the Russian peasants; but, crushed in the vice of world contradictions upon the solution of which in one way or another its fate depends, the Chinese peasantry is even less capable than the Russian of playing a leading role.

This is now no longer a theoretical forecast; it is a fact tested through and through and from all sides.

These fundamental and incontrovertible social and political prerequisites of the third Chinese Revolution show not only that the formula of a democratic dictatorship has *hopelessly outlived its usefulness*, but also that the third Chinese Revolution, in spite of the extreme backwardness of China or more correctly, because of this great backwardness, as compared with Russia, will not have a "democratic" period, be it even for six months, as was the case in the October Revolution (November 1917 to July 1918); it will be compelled from the very beginning to effect the most decisive shake-up and abolition of bourgeois property in town and country.

True, this prospect does not harmonize with the pedantic and schematic conception concerning the relationships between economics and politics. But the responsibility for this harmony which disturbs the newly adopted prejudices to which the October Revolution already dealt a serious blow, does not devolve upon "Trotskyism" but upon *the law of uneven development*. In the given case, it is exactly in place.

It would be pedantry to contend that the Chinese Communist Party, had it pursued a Bolshevik policy in the revolution of 1925–27, would *certainly* have come to power. But it is pitiful philistinism to contend that this possibility was entirely out of the question. The mass movement of workers and peasants was absolutely sufficient for it, as was also the collapse of the ruling classes. The national bourgeoisie sent its Chiang Kai-sheks and Wang Jingweis to Moscow; through its Hu Hanmins it knocked on the door of the Comintern, precisely because it felt itself hopelessly weak in the face of the revolutionary masses; it realized its weakness and sought to insure itself in advance. Neither the workers nor the peasants would have followed the national bourgeoisie if we ourselves had not drawn them behind it with a lasso. Had the Comintern pursued a more or less correct policy, the outcome of the struggle of the Communist Party for the masses would have been determined in advance: the Chinese proletariat would have supported the Communists, while the peasants' war would have supported the revolutionary proletariat.

If, at the beginning of the northern campaign, we had begun to organize soviets in the "liberated" districts (and the masses were instinctively fighting for that) we would have rallied to our side the agrarian uprisings, we would have built *our own* army; we would have undermined the opposing armies and—notwithstanding the youthfulness of the Communist Party of China—it would have been able, with a judicious Comintern guidance, to mature in these years of stress and to come to power, if not in the whole of China at once, then at least in a considerable part of it. And above all, we would have had a *party*.

But precisely in the sphere of leadership something absolutely monstrous occurred, a veritable historical catastrophe: the authority of the Soviet Union, of the Bolshevik Party and of the Comintern went entirely to the support, first of Chiang Kai-shek, against an independent policy of the Communist Party, and then to the support of Wang Jingwei, as the leader of the agrarian revolution. After having trampled underfoot the very basis of Lenin's policy and paralysed the young Chinese Communist Party, the ECCI determined in advance the victory of Chinese Kerenskyism over Bolshevism, of the Chinese Milyukovs over the Kerenskys, and of Japanese and British imperialism over the Chinese Milyukovs.

In this and in this alone lies the meaning of what happened in China in the course of 1925–27.

(PART 2)

3. Democratic Dictatorship or a Dictatorship of the Proletariat?

But how did the last Plenum of the ECCI evaluate the experiences of the Chinese Revolution, including the experience of the Canton insurrection? What further perspectives did it outline? The resolution of the February (1928) Plenum, which is the key to the corresponding sections of the draft program on this subject, says concerning the Chinese Revolution:

> It is incorrect to characterize it as a 'permanent' revolution [the position of the representative of the ECCI]. The tendency to skip [?] over the bourgeois-democratic stage of the revolution while simultaneously [?] appraising the revolution as a 'permanent'

> revolution is a mistake analogous to that committed by Trotsky in 1905 [?].

The ideological life of the Comintern since Lenin's departure from its leadership, that is, since 1923, consisted primarily in a struggle against so-called "Trotskyism" and particularly against the "permanent revolution". How is it, then, that in the fundamental question of the Chinese Revolution not only the Central Committee of the Communist Party of China, but also the official delegate of the Comintern, i.e., a leader who was sent with special instructions, happen to commit the very same "mistake" for which hundreds of men are now exiled to Siberia, and put in prison? The struggle around the Chinese question has been raging for some two and a half years. When the Opposition declared that the old Central Committee of the Communist Party of China (Chen Tu-hsiu), under the influence of the false directives from the Comintern, conducted an opportunist policy, this evaluation was declared to be "slander". The leadership of the Communist Party of China was pronounced irreproachable. The celebrated Tang Ping-shan declared amid the general approval of the Seventh Plenum of the ECCI that

> At the very first manifestations of Trotskyism, the Communist Party of China and the Young Communist League immediately adopted a unanimous resolution against Trotskyism.[3]

But when, not withstanding; these "achievements", events unfolded their tragic logic which led to the first and then to the second and even more frightful debacle of the revolution, the leadership of the Communist Party of China, formerly flawless, was re-baptized as Menshevik and deposed in the space of twenty-four hours. At the same time a decree was promulgated that the new leadership fully reflected the line of the Comintern. But no sooner did a new and a serious test arise than it was discovered that the new Central Committee of the Communist Party of China was guilty (as we have already seen, not in words, but in actions) of swerving to the position of the so-called "permanent revolution". The delegate of the Comintern took the very same path. This astonishing and truly incomprehensible fact can be explained only by the yawning "scissors" between the instructions of the ECCI and the real dynamics of the revolution.

We shall not dwell here upon the myth of the "permanent revolution" of 1905 which was placed in circulation in 1928 in order to sow confusion and bewilderment. We shall confine ourselves to an examination of how this myth broke down on the question of the Chinese revolution.

The first paragraph of the February resolution, from which the above-quoted passage was taken, gives the following motives for its negative attitude toward the so-called "permanent revolution":

> The current period of the Chinese revolution is a period of a bourgeois-democratic revolution which has not been completed either from the economic standpoint (the agrarian revolution and the abolition of feudal relations), or from the standpoint of the national struggle against imperialism (the unification of China and the establishment of national independence), or from the standpoint of the class nature of the state (the dictatorship of the proletariat and the peasantry) ...

This presentation of motives is an unbroken chain of mistakes and contradictions.

The ECCI taught that the Chinese Revolution must secure for China the opportunity to develop along the road to socialism. This goal could be achieved only if the revolution did not halt merely at the solution of the bourgeois-democratic tasks but continued to unfold, passing from one stage to the next, i.e., continued to develop uninterruptedly (*or permanently*) and thus lead China toward a socialist development. This is precisely what Marx understood by the term "permanent revolution". How then can we, on the one hand, speak of a non-capitalist path of development for China and, on the other, deny the permanent character of the revolution in general?

But—insists the resolution of the ECCI—the revolution has not been completed, either from the standpoint of the agrarian revolution or from the standpoint of the national struggle against imperialism. Hence it draws the conclusion about the bourgeois-democratic character of the "present period of the

Chinese revolution". As a matter of fact the "present period" is a period of counter-revolution. The ECCI doubtlessly intends to say that the new resurgence of the Chinese revolution, or *the third Chinese Revolution,* will bear a bourgeois-democratic character because the second Chinese Revolution of 1925–1927 solved neither the agrarian question nor the national question. However, even thus amended, this reasoning is based upon a total failure to understand the experiences and lessons of both the Chinese and the Russian revolutions.

The February 1917 revolution in Russia left unsolved all the internal and international problems which had led to the revolution—serfdom in the villages, the old bureaucracy, the war, and economic debacle. Taking this as a starting point, not only the SRs and the Mensheviks, but also a considerable section of the leadership of our own party tried to prove to Lenin that the "present period of the revolution is a period of the bourgeois-democratic revolution". In this, its basic consideration, the resolution of the ECCI merely copies the objections which the opportunists raised against the struggle for the dictatorship of the proletariat waged by Lenin in 1917.

Furthermore, it appears that the bourgeois-democratic revolution remains unaccomplished not only from the economic and national standpoint, but also from the "standpoint of the class nature of the state (the dictatorship of the proletariat and the peasantry)". This can mean only one thing: that the Chinese proletariat is forbidden to struggle for the conquest of power so long as no "genuine" democratic government stands at the helm in China. Unfortunately, no instructions are forthcoming as to where we can get it.

The confusion is further increased by the fact that the slogan of Soviets was rejected for China in the course of these two years on the ground that the creation of Soviets is permissible presumably only during the transition to the proletarian revolution (Stalin's "theory"). But when the Soviet revolution broke out in Canton and when its participants drew the conclusion that this was precisely the transition to the proletarian revolution, they were accused of "Trotskyism". Is the party to be educated by such methods? Is this the way to assist it in the solution of supreme tasks?

To save a hopeless position, the resolution of the ECCI (without any connection whatever with the entire trend of its thought) rushes in post-haste to its last argument taken from imperialism. It appears that "the tendency to skip over the bourgeois-democratic stage is all the more [!] harmful because such a formulation of the question eliminates [?] the most important national peculiarity of the Chinese revolution, which is a semi-colonial revolution".

The only meaning that these senseless words can have is that the imperialist yoke will be overthrown by some sort of non-proletarian dictatorship. But this means that the "most important national peculiarity" has been dragged in at the last moment in order to paint the Chinese national bourgeoisie or the Chinese petty-bourgeois "democracy" in bright colors. This argument can have no other meaning. But this only "meaning" has been adequately examined by us in our chapter, "On the nature of the Colonial Bourgeoisie". There is no need to return to this subject.

China is still confronted with a vast, bitter, bloody, and prolonged struggle for such elementary things as the liquidation of the most "Asiatic" forms of slavery, national emancipation, and unification of the country. But as the course of events has shown, it is precisely this that makes impossible in the future any petty-bourgeois leadership or even semi-leadership in the revolution. The unification and emancipation of China today is an international task, no less so than the existence of the USSR. This task can be solved only by means of a desperate struggle on the part of the downtrodden, hungry, and persecuted masses under the direct leadership of the proletarian vanguard's struggle not only against world imperialism, but also against its economic and political agency in China, against the bourgeoisie, including the "national" bourgeoisie and all its democratic flunkeys. And this is nothing else than the road toward the dictatorship of the proletariat.

Beginning with April, 1917, Lenin explained to his opponents, who accused him of having adopted the position of the "permanent revolution", that the dictatorship of the proletariat and the peasantry was realized partially in the epoch of dual power. He explained later that this dictatorship met with its further extension during the first period of Soviet power from November 1917 until July 1918, when the entire peasantry, together with the workers, effected the agrarian revolution while the working class did not as yet proceed with the confiscation of the mills and factories, but experimented with workers' control. So far as the "class nature of the state" was concerned, the democratic-SR-Menshevik "dictatorship" gave all that it could give—the miscarriage of dual power. As to the agrarian overturn, the revolution gave birth to a perfectly healthy and strong baby, but it was the proletarian dictatorship that functioned as the midwife. In other words, what the theoretical formula of the dictatorship of the proletariat and the peasantry had combined, was dissociated in the course of the actual class struggle. The hollow shell of semi-power was provisionally entrusted to Kerensky-Tseretelli, while the real kernel of the agrarian-democratic revolution fell to the share of the victorious working class. This dialectical dissociation of the democratic dictatorship, the leaders of the ECCI failed to understand. They drove themselves into a political blind alley by condemning mechanically any "skipping over the bourgeois-democratic stage" and by endeavoring to guide the historical process in accordance with circular letters. *If we are to understand by the bourgeois-democratic stage, the accomplishment of the agrarian revolution by means of a "democratic dictatorship", then it was the October Revolution itself that audaciously "skipped" over the bourgeois-democratic stage.* Should it not be condemned for it?

Why is it then that the historically inevitable course of events which was the highest expression of Bolshevism in Russia must prove to be "Trotskyism" in China? No doubt owing to the very same logic which declares to be suitable for China the theory of the Martynovs, a theory fought by Bolshevism for two decades in Russia.

But is it at all permissible to draw here an analogy with Russia? Our answer is that the slogan of a democratic dictatorship of the proletariat and the peasantry was constructed by the leaders of the ECCI exclusively and entirely in accordance with the method of analogy, but a formal and literary analogy and not a materialist and historical analogy. An analogy between China and Russia is entirely admissible if we find the proper approach to it, and Lenin made excellent use of such an analogy. Moreover he did so not *after* but before the events, as if he had foreseen the future blunders of the epigones. Hundreds of times Lenin had to defend the October Revolution of the proletariat that had the audacity to conquer power *notwithstanding the fact* that the bourgeois-democratic tasks had not been solved. Precisely *because of that, and precisely in order to do that,* replied Lenin. Addressing himself to the pedants, who in their arguments against the conquest of power referred to the economic immaturity of Russia for socialism, which was "incontestable" for him[4], Lenin wrote on January 16, 1923:

> It does not even occur to them, for instance, that Russia, standing on the border between civilized countries and countries which were for the first time definitely drawn by this war into the vortex of civilization, all Eastern countries and non-European countries'that Russia therefore could and should have manifested certain peculiarities which fall, of course, along the general lines of world development but which make its revolution different from all preceding revolutions of the Western European countries and which introduce certain partial innovations in approaching the countries of the Orient.[5]

The "peculiarity" which brings Russia *closer* to the countries of the Orient was seen by Lenin precisely in the fact that the young proletariat, at an early stage, had to grasp the broom and sweep feudal barbarism and all sorts of rubbish from its path toward socialism.

If, consequently, we are to take as our starting point the Leninist analogy between China and Russia, then we must say: from the standpoint of the *"political nature of the State"*, all that could have been obtained through the democratic dictatorship in China has been put to the test, first in Sun Yat-sen's Canton, then on the road from Canton to Shanghai, which culminated in the Shanghai *coup d'etat*, and then in Wuhan where the Left Kuomintang appeared in its chemically pure form, i.e., according to the directives of the ECCI, as the organizer of the agrarian revolution, but in reality as its hangman. But the social *content* of the bourgeois-democratic revolution will fill the initial period of the coming dictatorship of the Chinese proletariat and the peasant poor. To advance now the slogan of a democratic dictatorship of the proletariat and the peasantry after the role not only of the Chinese bourgeoisie, but also of Chinese "democracy" has been put to a thorough test, after it has become absolutely incontestable that "democracy" will play even a greater hangman's role in the coming battles than in the past. To advance this slogan now is simply to create the means of covering up the new varieties of Kuomintangism and to prepare a noose for the proletariat.

Let us recall for the sake of completeness what Lenin tersely said about those Bolsheviks who insisted upon counterposing to the SR-Menshevik experience the slogan of a "genuine" democratic dictatorship:

"Whoever now talks only about the 'revolutionary-democratic dictatorship of the proletariat and peasantry' has lost touch with life, has, in virtue of this circumstance, *gone over*, in practice, to the petty bourgeoisie against the proletarian *class* struggle; and he ought to be relegated to the museum of 'Bolshevik' pre-revolutionary antiquities (or, as one might call it, the museum of 'old Bolsheviks').[6]

These words ring as if they were actually spoken today. Of course it is not at all a question of calling the Communist Party of China to an immediate insurrection for the seizure of power. The pace depends entirely upon the circumstances. The consequences of defeat cannot be removed merely by revising the tactic. The revolution is now subsiding. The half-concealing resolution of the ECCI, the bombast about imminent revolutionary onslaughts, while countless people are being executed and a terrific commercial and industrial crisis rages in China, are criminal light-mindedness and nothing else. After three major defeats an economic crisis does not rouse but, on the contrary, depresses the proletariat which, us it is, has already been bled white, while the executions only destroy the politically weakened party. We are entering in China into a period of reflux, and consequently into a period in which the party deepens its theoretical roots, educates itself critically, creates and strengthens firm organizational links in all spheres of the working class movement, organizes rural nuclei, leads and unites partial, at first defensive and later offensive, battles of the workers and the peasant poor.

What will turn the tide in the mass movement? What circumstances will give the necessary revolutionary impulsion to the proletarian vanguard at the head of the many-millioned masses? This cannot be predicted. The future will show whether internal processes alone will be sufficient or an added impulsion will have to come from without.

There are sufficient grounds for assuming that the smashing of the Chinese Revolution, directly due to the false leadership, will permit the Chinese and foreign bourgeoisie to overcome to a lesser or greater degree the frightful economic crisis now raging in the country. Naturally, this will be done on the backs and bones of the workers and peasants. This phase of "stabilization" will once again group and fuse together the workers, restore their class self-confidence in order subsequently to bring them into still sharper conflict with the enemy, but on a higher historical stage. It will be possible to speak seriously about the perspective of an agrarian revolution only on the condition that there will be a new mounting wave of the proletarian movement on the offensive.

It is not excluded that the first stage of the coming third revolution may reproduce in a very abridged and modified form the stages which have already been passed, presenting, for instance, some new parody of the "national united front". But this first stage will be sufficient only to give the communist party a chance to put forward and announce its "April" thesis, that is, its program and tactics of the seizure of power, before the popular masses.

But what does the draft program say on this?

> The transition to the proletarian dictatorship is possible here [in China] only after a series of preparatory stages [?] only as a result of a whole period of the growing over [??] of the bourgeois-democratic revolution into the socialist revolution.

In other words, all the "stages" that have already been gone through are not to be taken into account. The draft program still sees ahead what has already been left behind. This is precisely what is meant by a tail-endist formulation. It opens wide the gates for new experiments in the spirit of the Kuomintang course. Thus the concealment of the old mistakes inevitably prepares the road for new errors.

If we enter the new upsurge, which will develop at an incomparably more rapid tempo than the last one, with a blueprint of "democratic dictatorship" that has already outlived its usefulness, there can be no doubt that the third Chinese revolution, like the second, will be led to its doom.

4. Adventurism as the Product of Opportunism

The second paragraph of the same resolution of the February plenum of the ECCI says:

> The first wave of the broad revolutionary movement of workers and peasants which in the main proceeded under the slogans, and to a considerable extent *under the leadership of the communist party,* is over. It ended in several centers of the revolutionary movement with *heaviest defeats* for the workers and peasants, the physical extermination of the communists and revolutionary cadres of the labor and peasant movement in general.

When the "wave" was surging high, the ECCI said that the whole movement was entirely under the blue banner and leadership of the Kuomintang which even took the place of Soviets. It is precisely on that ground that the communist party was subordinated to the Kuomintang. But that is exactly why the revolutionary movement ended with "heaviest defeats". Now when these defeats have been recognized, an attempt is being made to erase the Kuomintang from the past as if it had never existed, as if the ECCI had not declared the blue banner its own.

There have been no defeats either in Shanghai or in Wuhan in the past; there were merely transitions of the revolution "into a higher phase"—that is what we have been taught. Now the sum total of these transitions is suddenly declared to be "heaviest defeats for the workers and peasants". However, in order to mask to some extent this unprecedented political bankruptcy of forecasts and evaluations, the concluding paragraph of the resolution declares:

> The ECCI makes it the duty of all sections of the CI to fight against the social democratic and Trotskyist slanders to the effect that the Chinese revolution has been liquidated [?].

In the first paragraph of the resolution we were told that "Trotskyism" was the idea of the *permanent* Chinese Revolution, that is, a revolution which is precisely at this time growing over from the bourgeois to the socialist phase; from the last paragraph we learn that according to the "Trotskyists", "the Chinese revolution has been liquidated". How can a *"liquidated"* revolution be a *permanent* revolution? Here we have Bukharin in all his glory.

Only complete and reckless irresponsibility permits of such contradictions which corrode all revolutionary thought at its roots.

If we are to understand by "liquidation" of the revolution the fact that the labor and peasant offensive has been beaten back and drowned in blood, that the masses are in a state of retreat and decline, that before another onslaught there must be, apart from many other circumstances, a molecular process at work among the masses which requires a certain period of time, the duration of which cannot be determined beforehand; if "liquidation" is to be understood in this way, it does not in any manner differ from the "heaviest defeats" which the ECCI has finally been compelled to recognize. Or are we to understand liquidation literally, as the actual elimination of the Chinese Revolution, that is, of the very possibility and inevitability of its rebirth on a new plane? One can speak of such a perspective seriously and so as not to create confusion only in two cases— if China were doomed to dismemberment and complete extirpation, an assumption for which there is no basis whatever, or if the Chinese bourgeoisie would prove capable of solving the basic problems of Chinese life in its own non-revolutionary way. Is it not this last variant which the theoreticians of the "bloc of four classes", who directly drove the communist party under the yoke of the bourgeoisie, seek to ascribe to us now?

History repeats itself. The blind men who did not understand the scope of the defeat of 1923, for a year and a half accused us of "liquidationism" towards the German revolution. But even this lesson, which cost the International so dearly, taught them nothing. At present they use their old rubber stamps, only this time substituting China for Germany. To be sure, their need to find "liquidators" is more acute today than it was four years ago, for this time it is much too obviously apparent that if anybody did "liquidate" the second Chinese Revolution it was the authors of the "Kuomintang" course.

The strength of Marxism lies in its ability to foretell. In this sense the Opposition can point to an absolute confirmation in experience of its prognosis. At first concerning the Kuomintang as a whole, then concerning the "Left" Kuomintang and the Wuhan government, and, finally, concerning the "deposit" on the third revolution, that is the Canton insurrection. What further confirmation could there be of one's theoretical correctness?

The very same opportunist line, which through the policy of capitulation to the bourgeoisie has already brought heaviest defeats to the revolution during its first two stages, "grew over" in the third stage into a policy of adventurous raids on the bourgeoisie and thus made the defeat final.

Had the leadership not hurried yesterday to leap over the defeats which it had itself brought about, it would first of all have explained to the Communist Party of China that victory is not gained in one sweep, that on the road to the armed insurrection there still remains a period of intense, incessant, and savage struggle for political influence on the workers and peasants.

On September 27, 1927, we said to the Presidium of the ECCI:

> Today's papers report that the revolutionary army has occupied Swatow. It is already several weeks that the armies of Ho Lung and Yeh Ting have been advancing. *Pravda* calls these armies revolutionary armies ... But I ask you: what prospects does the movement of the revolutionary army which captured Swatow raise before the Chinese revolution? What are the slogans of the

> movement? What is its program? What should, be its organizational forms? What has become of the slogan of Chinese Soviets, which *Pravda* suddenly advanced for a single day in July?

Without first counterposing the communist party to the Kuomintang as a whole, without the party's agitation among the masses for Soviets and a Soviet government, without an independent mobilization of the masses under the slogans of the agrarian revolution and of national emancipation, without the creation, broadening, and strengthening of the local Soviets of workers', soldiers', and peasants' deputies, the insurrection of Ho Lung and Yeh Ting, even apart from their opportunist policy, could not fail to be only an isolated adventure, a pseudo-Communist Makhno feat; it could not fail to crash against its own isolation. And it has crashed.

The Canton insurrection was a broader and deeper repetition of the Ho Lung-Yeh Ting adventure, only with infinitely more tragic consequences.

The February resolution of the ECCI combats putschistic moods in the Communist Party of China, that is, tendencies toward armed uprisings. It does not say, however, that these tendencies are a reaction to the entire opportunist policy of 1925–1927, and an inevitable consequence of the purely military command issued from above to "change the step", without an evaluation of all that had been done, without an open revaluation of the basis of the tactic, and without a clear perspective. Ho Lung's campaign and the Canton insurrection were—and under the circumstances could not fail to be—breeders of putschism.

A real antidote to putschism as well as to opportunism can be only a clear understanding of the truth that the leadership of the armed insurrection of the workers and poor peasants, the seizure of power, and the institution of a revolutionary dictatorship fall henceforth entirely upon the shoulders of the Communist Party of China. If the latter is permeated thoroughly with the understanding of this perspective, it will be as little inclined to improvise military raids on towns or armed insurrections in traps as to chase humbly after the enemy's banner.

The resolution of the ECCI condemns itself to utter impotence by the fact alone that in arguing most abstractly concerning the inadmissibility of leaping over stages and the harmfulness of putschism, it entirely ignores the class content of the Canton insurrection and the short-lived Soviet regime which it brought into existence. We Oppositionists hold that this insurrection was an adventure of the leaders in an effort to save their "prestige". But it is clear to us that even an adventure develops according to laws which are determined by the structure of the social milieu. That is why we look to the Canton insurrection for the features of the future phase of the Chinese revolution. These features fully correspond with our theoretical analysis made prior to the Canton uprising. But how much more imperative it is for the ECCI, which holds that the Canton uprising was a correct and normal link in the chain of struggle, to give a clear class characterization of the Canton insurrection. However, there is not a word about this in the resolution of the ECCI, although the Plenum met immediately after the Canton events. Is this not the most convincing proof that the present leadership of the Comintern, because it stubbornly pursues a false policy, is compelled to occupy itself with the fictitious errors of 1905 and other years without daring to approach the Canton insurrection of 1927, the meaning of which completely upsets the blueprint for revolutions in the East which is set down in the draft program?

5. Soviets and Revolution

In the February resolution of the ECCI the representatives of the Comintern, "Comrade N. and others", are made responsible for the "absence of an *elected* Soviet in Canton as an organ of insurrection". Behind this charge in reality lies an astounding admission.

In the report of *Pravda* (No. 31), written on the basis of first-hand documents, it was stated that a Soviet government had been established in Canton. But not a word was mentioned to indicate that the Canton Soviet was *not* an elected organ, i.e., that it was not a *Soviet*—for how can there be a Soviet which was not elected? We learn this from the resolution. Let us reflect for a moment on the significance of this fact. The ECCI tells us now that a Soviet is necessary to effect an armed insurrection, but by no means prior to that time. But lo and behold! When the date for the insurrection is set, there is no Soviet. To create an elected Soviet is not an easy matter. It is necessary that the masses know from experience what a Soviet is, that they understand its form, that they have learned something in the past to accustom them to an elected Soviet organization. There was not even a sign of this in China, for the slogan of Soviets was declared to be a Trotskyist slogan precisely in the period when it should have become the nerve center of the entire movement. When, however, helter-skelter, a date was set for an insurrection so as to skip over their own defeats, they simultaneously had to *appoint* a Soviet as well. If this error is not laid bare to the core, the slogan of Soviets can be transformed into a strangling noose of the revolution.

Lenin in his time explained to the Mensheviks that the fundamental historical task of the Soviets is to organize, or help organize, the conquest of power so that on the day after the victory they become the organ of that power. The epigones and not the disciples, draw from this the conclusion that Soviets can be organized only when the 12th hour of the insurrection has struck. Lenin's broad generalization they transform *post factum* into a little recipe which does not serve the interests of the revolution but imperils it.

Before the Bolshevik Soviets in October 1917 captured power, the SR and Menshevik Soviets had existed for nine months. Twelve years before, the first revolutionary Soviets existed in Petersburg, Moscow, and scores of other cities. Before the Soviet of 1905 was extended to embrace the mills and factories of the capital, there was created in Moscow, during the strike, a Soviet of printers' deputies. Several months before this, in May 1905, a mass strike in Ivanovo-Voznesiensk set up a leading organ which already contained all the essential features of a Soviet of workers' deputies. Between the first experiment of setting up a Soviet of workers' deputies and the gigantic experiment of setting up a Soviet government, more than twelve years rolled by. Of course, such a period is not at all required for all other countries, including China. But to think that the Chinese workers are capable of building Soviets on the basis of the little recipe that has been substituted for Lenin's broad generalization is to substitute impotent and importunate pedantry for the dialectic of revolutionary action. Soviets must be set up not on the eve of the insurrection, not under the slogan of immediate seizure of power; for if the matter has reached the point of the seizure of power, if the masses are prepared for an armed insurrection *without a Soviet*, it means that there have been other organizational forms and methods which made possible the performance of the preparatory work to insure the success of the uprising. Then the question of Soviets becomes of secondary importance and is reduced to a question of organizational technique or merely to a question of denomination. The task of the Soviets is not merely to issue the call for the insurrection or to carry it out, but to *lead the masses toward the insurrection through the necessary stages*. At first the Soviet rallies the masses not to the slogan of armed insurrection, but to partial slogans, so that only later, step by step, the masses are brought towards the slogan of insurrection without scattering them on the road and without allowing the vanguard to become isolated from the class. The Soviet appears most often and primarily in connection with strike struggles which have the perspectives of revolutionary development, but are in the given moment limited merely to economic demands. The masses must sense and understand while in action that the Soviet is *their* organization, that it marshals the forces for a struggle, for resistance, for self-defense, and for an offensive. They can sense and understand this not from an action of a single day nor in general from any single act, but from the experience of several weeks, months, and perhaps years, with or without interruptions. That is why only an epigonic and bureaucratic leadership can restrain the awakening and rising masses from creating Soviets in conditions when the country is passing through an epoch of revolutionary upheavals and when the working class and the poor peasants have before them the prospect of capturing power, even though this is a perspective of one of the subsequent stages and even if this perspective can be envisaged in the given phase only by a small minority. Such was always our conception of the Soviets. We evaluated the Soviets as that broad and flexible organizational form which is accessible to the masses who have just awakened at the very first stages of their revolutionary upsurge; and which is capable of uniting the working class in its entirety, independent of the size of that section which, in the given phase, has already matured to the point of understanding the task of the seizure of power.

Is any documentary evidence really necessary? Here, for instance, is what Lenin wrote about the Soviets in the epoch of the first revolution:

> The Social Democratic Labor Party of Russia [the name of the party at that time] has never refused to utilize at moments of greater or smaller revolutionary upsurge certain non-party organizations of the type of Soviets of Workers' Deputies in order to strengthen the influence of the social democrats on the working class and to consolidate the social democratic labor movement.[7]

One could cite voluminous literary and historic evidence of this type. But one would imagine that the question is sufficiently clear without them.

In contradistinction to this the epigones have converted the Soviets into an organizational parade uniform with which the party simply dresses up the proletariat on the eve of the capture of power. But this is precisely the time when we find that the Soviets cannot be improvised in 24 hours, by order, for the direct purpose of an armed insurrection. Such experiments must inevitably assume a fictitious character and the absence of the most necessary conditions for the capture of power is masked by the external ritual of a Soviet system. That is what happened in Canton where the Soviet was simply appointed to observe the ritual. That is where the epigone formulation of the question leads.

* * *

During the polemics on the Chinese events the Opposition was accused of the following alleged flagrant contradiction: whereas from 1926 on the Opposition advanced the slogan of Soviets for China, its representatives spoke against the slogan of Soviets for Germany in the Autumn of 1923. On no other point perhaps has scholastic political thought expressed itself so glaringly as in this accusation. Yes, we demanded for China a *timely* start for the creation of Soviets as independent organizations of workers and peasants, *when the wave of revolutionary upsurge was mounting.*

The chief significance of the Soviets was to be that of *opposing the workers and peasants to the Kuomintang bourgeoisie* and its Left Kuomintang agency. The slogan of Soviets in China meant above all the break with the suicidal and infamous "bloc of four classes" and the withdrawal of the communist party from the Kuomintang. The center of gravity consequently lay not in bare organizational forms, but in the class line.

In the Autumn of 1923 in Germany it was a question of organizational form only. As a result of the extreme passivity, backwardness, and tardiness of the leadership of the Comintern and the Communist Party of Germany, the moment for a timely call for the organization of Soviets was missed. The factory committees, due to pressure from below and of their own accord, had occupied in the labor movement of Germany by the Autumn of 1923 the place which would no doubt have been much more successfully occupied by Soviets had there been a correct and daring policy on the part of the communist party. The acuteness of the situation had in the meantime reached its sharpest point. To lose any more time would have meant definitely to miss the revolutionary situation. The insurrection was finally placed on the order of the day, with very little time left. To advance the slogan of Soviets under such conditions would have been the greatest pedantic stupidity conceivable. The Soviet is not a talisman with omnipotent powers of salvation. In a situation such as had then developed, the hurried creation of Soviets would only have duplicated the factory committees. It would have become necessary to deprive the latter of their revolutionary functions and to transfer them to the newly-created and still utterly un-authoritative Soviets. And when was this to be done? Under conditions in which each day counted. This would have meant to substitute for revolutionary action a most pernicious game in organizational gew-gaws.

It is incontestable that the organizational form of a Soviet can be of enormous importance; but only at a time when it furnishes a timely reflection of the correct political line. And conversely, it can acquire a no less negative meaning if it is converted into a fiction, a fetish, a bagatelle. The German Soviets created at the very last moment in the Autumn of 1923 would have added nothing politically; they would only have caused organizational confusion. What happened in Canton was even worse yet. The Soviet which was created in a hurry to observe the ritual was only a masquerade for the adventurist putsch. That is why we discovered, after it was all over, that the Canton Soviet resembled an ancient Chinese dragon simply drawn on paper. The policy of pulling rotten strings and paper dragons is not our policy. We were against improvising Soviets by telegraph in Germany in September 1923. We were for the creation of Soviets in China in 1926. We were against the masquerade Soviet in Canton in 1927. There are no contradictions here. We have here instead the profound unity of the conception of the dynamics of the revolutionary movement and its organizational forms.

The question of the role and significance of the Soviets which had been distorted and confused and obscured by the theory and practice of recent years, has not been illuminated in the least in the draft program.

(PART 3)

6. The Question of the Character of the Coming Chinese Revolution

The slogan of the dictatorship of the proletariat, which leads behind it the peasant poor, is inseparably bound up with the question of the socialist character of the coming, third revolution in China. And inasmuch as not only history repeats itself but also the mistakes which people counterpose to its requirements, we can already hear the objection that China has not yet matured for a socialist revolution. But this is an abstract and lifeless formulation of the question. For has Russia, taken by itself, matured for socialism? According to Lenin – NO! It has matured for the dictatorship of the proletariat as the only method for solving unpostponable national tasks. But the destiny of the dictatorship as a whole is determined in the last analysis by the trend of *world* development, which, of course, does not exclude but rather presupposes a correct policy on the part of the proletarian dictatorship, the consolidation and development of the workers' and peasants' alliance, an all-sided adaptation to national conditions on the one hand, and to the trend of world development on the other. This fully holds true for China as well.

In the same article entitled *On Our Revolution* (January 16, 1923), in which Lenin establishes that the peculiarity of Russia proceeds along the lines of the peculiar development of the Eastern countries, he brands as "infinitely hackneyed" the argument of European social democracy to the effect "that we have not matured for socialism, that we lack, as some of these 'erudite' gentlemen say, the objective economic prerequisites for Socialism". But Lenin ridicules the "erudite" gentlemen not because he himself recognized the *existence* of the economic prerequisites for Socialism in Russia but because he holds that the rejection of the seizure of power does not at all follow, as pedants and philistines think, from the absence of these prerequisites necessary for an independent construction of socialism. In this article of his, Lenin for the hundred and first time, or, rather, for the thousand and first time replies to the sophisms of the heroes of the Second International: "This *incontrovertible* considerations [the immaturity of Russia for Socialism] ... is not decisive for the evaluation of our revolution."[8] That is what the authors of the draft program refuse and are unable to understand. In itself the thesis of the economic and cultural immaturity of China as well as Russia (China, of course, more so than Russia) is incontrovertible. But hence it does not at all follow that the proletariat has to renounce the conquest of power, when this conquest is dictated by the entire historical context and the revolutionary situation in the country.

The concrete, historical, political, and actual question is reducible not to whether China has economically matured for "its own" socialism, but whether China has ripened politically for the proletarian dictatorship. These two questions are not at all identical. They might be regarded as identical were it not for the law of uneven development. This is where this law is in place and fully applies to the inter-relationship between economics and politics. Then China has matured for the dictatorship of the proletariat? Only the experience of the struggle can provide a categorical answer to this question. By the same token, only the struggle can settle the question as to when and under what conditions the real unification, emancipation, and regeneration of China will take place. Anyone who says that China has not matured for the dictatorship of the proletariat declares thereby that the third Chinese Revolution is postponed for many years to come.

Of course, matters would be quite hopeless if feudal survivals did really *dominate* in Chinese economic life, as the resolutions of the ECCI asserted. But fortunately, *survivals* in general cannot dominate. The draft program on this point, too, does not rectify the errors committed, but reaffirms them in a roundabout and nebulous fashion. The draft speaks of the "predominance of medieval feudal relations both in the economics of the country and in the political superstructure ..." This is false to the core. What does *predominance* mean? Is it a question of the number of people involved? Or the dominant and leading role in the economics of the country? The extraordinarily rapid growth of home industry on the basis of the all-embracing role of mercantile and bank capital; the complete dependence of the most important agrarian districts on the market; the enormous and ever-growing role of foreign trade; the all-sided subordination of the Chinese village to the city—all these bespeak the unconditional predominance, the direct domination of capitalist relations in China. The social relations of serfdom and semi-serfdom are undeniably very strong. They stem in part from the days of feudalism; and in part they constitute a new formation, that is, the regeneration of the past on the basis of the retarded development of the productive forces, the surplus agrarian population, the activities of merchants' and usurers' capital, etc. However, it is capitalist relations that dominated and not "feudal" (more correctly, serf and, generally, pre-capitalist) relations. Only thanks to this dominant role of capitalist relations can we speak seriously of the prospects of proletarian hegemony in the national revolution. Otherwise, there is no making the ends meet.

> The strength of the proletariat in any capitalist country is infinitely greater than the proportion of the proletariat in the total population. This is due to the fact that the proletariat is in economic command of the central points and nerve centers of the entire capitalist system of economy, and also because the proletariat expresses economically and politically the *real* interests of the vast majority of the toilers under capitalism.
>
> "For this reason the proletariat, even if it constitutes the minority of the population (or in cases where the conscious and truly revolutionary vanguard of the proletariat comprises the minority of the population), is capable both of overthrowing the bourgeoisie and of attracting subsequently to its side many allies from among the masses of semi-proletarians and petty bourgeois, who will never come out beforehand for the domination of the proletariat, who will not understand the conditions and tasks of this domination, but who will convince themselves solely from their subsequent experiences of the inevitability, justice, and legitimacy of the proletarian dictatorship.[9]

The role of the Chinese proletariat in production is already very great. In the next few years it will only increase still further. Its political role, as events have shown, could have been gigantic. But the whole line of the leadership was directed entirely against permitting the proletariat to conquer the leading role.

The draft program says that successful socialist construction is possible in China "only on the condition that it is directly supported by countries under the proletarian dictatorship". Thus, here, in relation to China, the same principle is recognized which the party has always recognized in regard to Russia. But if China lacks sufficient inner forces for an *independent* construction of socialist society, then according to the theory of Stalin-Bukharin, the Chinese proletariat should not seize power at any stage of the revolution. Or it may be that the existence of the USSR settles the question in just the opposite sense. Then it follows that our technology is sufficient to build a socialist society not only in the USSR but also in China, i.e., in the two economically most backward countries with a combined population of six hundred million. Or perhaps the *inevitable* dictatorship of the proletariat in China is "inadmissible" because that dictatorship will be included in the chain of the world-wide socialist revolution, thus becoming not only its link, but its driving force? But this is precisely Lenin's basic formulation of the October Revolution, the "peculiarity" of which follows precisely along the lines of development of the Eastern countries. We see thus how the revisionist theory of socialism in one country, evolved in 1925 in order to wage a struggle against Trotskyism, distorts and confuses matters each time a new major revolutionary problem is approached.

The draft program goes still further along this same road. It counterposes China and India to "Russia before 1917" and Poland ("etc.") as countries with "a certain minimum of industry sufficient for the triumphant construction of socialism," or (as is more definitely and therefore more erroneously stated elsewhere) as countries possessing the "necessary and sufficient material prerequisites ... for the complete construction of socialism." This, as we already know, is a mere play upon Lenin's expression "necessary and sufficient" prerequisites; a fraudulent and an impermissible jugglery because Lenin definitely enumerates the *political and organizational prerequisites*, including the *technical, cultural, and international* prerequisites. But the chief point that remains is: how can one determine a priori the "minimum of industry" sufficient for the complete building of socialism once it is a question of an uninterrupted world struggle between two economic systems, two social orders, and a struggle, moreover, in which our *economic* base is infinitely the weaker?

If we take into consideration only the economic lever, it is clear that we in the USSR, and all the more so in China and India, have a far shorter arm of the lever than world capitalism. But the entire question is resolved by the *revolutionary struggle* of the two systems on a world scale. In the political struggle, the long arm of the lever is *on our side*, or, to put it more correctly, it can and must prove so in our hands, if our policy is correct.

Again, in the same article *On Our Revolution*, after stating that "a certain cultural level" is necessary for the creation of "socialism", Lenin adds: "although no one can tell what this certain cultural level is". Why can no one tell? Because the question is settled by the struggle, by the rivalry between the two social systems and the two cultures, *on an international scale*. Breaking completely with this idea of Lenin's, which flows from the very essence of the question, the draft program asserts that in 1917 Russia had precisely the "minimum technology" and consequently also the culture necessary for the building of socialism in one country. The authors of the draft attempt to tell in the program that which "no one can tell" *a priori*.

It is impermissible, impossible, and absurd to seek a criterion for the "sufficient minimum" within national states ("Russia prior to 1917") when the whole question is settled by international dynamics. In this false, arbitrary, isolated national criterion rests the theoretical basis of national narrowness in politics, the precondition for inevitable national-reformist and social patriotic blunders in the future.

7. On the Reactionary Idea of "Two-Class Workers' and Peasants' Parties" for the Orient

The lessons of the second Chinese Revolution are lessons for the entire Comintern, but primarily for all the countries of the Orient.

All the arguments presented in defense of the Menshevik line in the Chinese Revolution must, if we take them seriously, hold trebly good for India. The imperialist yoke assumes in India, the classic colony, infinitely more direct and palpable forms than in China. The survivals of feudal and serf relations in India are immeasurably deeper and greater. Nevertheless, or rather precisely for this reason, the methods which, applied in China, undermined the revolution, must result in India in even more fatal consequences. The overthrow of Hindu feudalism and of the Anglo-Hindu bureaucracy and British militarism can be accomplished only by a gigantic and an indomitable movement of the popular masses which precisely because of its powerful sweep and irresistibility, its international aims and ties, cannot tolerate any halfway and compromising opportunist measures on the part of the leadership.

The Comintern leadership has already committed not a few mistakes in India. The conditions have not yet allowed these errors to reveal themselves on such a scale as in China. One can, therefore, hope that the lessons of the Chinese events will permit of a more timely rectification of the line of the leading policy in India and in other countries of the Orient.

The cardinal question for us here, as everywhere and always, is the question of the communist party, its complete independence, its irreconcilable class character. The greatest danger on this path is the organization of so-called "workers' and peasants' parties" in the countries of the Orient.

Beginning with 1924, a year which will go down as the year of open revision of a number of fundamental theses of Marx and Lenin, Stalin advanced the formula of the "two-class workers' and peasants' parties for the Eastern countries". It was based on the self-same national oppression which served in the Orient to camouflage opportunism, as did "stabilization" in the Occident. Cables from India, as well as from Japan, where there is no national oppression, have of late frequently mentioned the activities of provincial "workers' and peasants' parties", referring to them as organizations which are close and friendly to the Comintern, as if they were almost our "own" organizations, without, however, giving any sort of concrete definition of their political physiognomy; in a word, writing and speaking about them in the same way as was done only a short while ago about the Kuomintang.

Back in 1924, *Pravda* reported that: "There are indications that the movement of national liberation in Korea is gradually taking shape in the form of the creation of a workers' and peasants' party."[10]

And in the meantime Stalin lectured to the communists of the Orient that

> The communists must pass from the policy of a united national front ... to the policy of a revolutionary bloc between the workers and petty-bourgeoisie, In such countries this bloc can assume the form of a single party, a workers' and peasants' party, akin to the Kuomintang ...[11]

The ensuing tiny "reservations" on the subject of the

independence of the communist parties (obviously, "independence" like that of the prophet Jonah inside the whale's belly) served only for the purpose of camouflage. We are profoundly convinced that the Sixth Congress must state that the slightest equivocation in this sphere is fatal and will be rejected.

It is a question here of an absolutely new, entirely false, and thoroughly anti-Marxian formulation of the fundamental question of the party and of its relation to its own class and other classes.

The necessity for the Communist Party of China to enter the Kuomintang was defended on the ground that in its social composition the Kuomintang is a party of workers and peasants, that nine-tenths of the Kuomintang—this proportion was repeated hundreds of times—belonged to the revolutionary tendency and were ready to march hand in hand with the communist party. However, during and since the *coups d' etat* in Shanghai and Wuhan, these revolutionary nine-tenths of the Kuomintang disappeared as if by magic. No one has found a trace of them. And the theoreticians of class collaboration in China, Stalin, Bukharin, and others, did not even take the trouble to explain what has become of the nine-tenths of the members of the Kuomintang, the nine-tenths workers and peasants, revolutionists, sympathizers, and entirely our "own". Yet, an answer to this question is of decisive importance if we are to understand the destiny of all these "two-class" parties preached by Stalin; and if we are to be clarified upon the very conception itself, which throws us far behind not only of the program of the CPSU of 1919, but also of the *Communist Manifesto* of 1847.

The question of where the celebrated nine-tenths vanished can become clear to us only if we understand, first, the impossibility of a bi-composite, that is a two-class party, expressing simultaneously two mutually exclusive historical lines—the proletarian and petty bourgeois lines; secondly, the impossibility of realizing in capitalist society an independent peasant party, that is, a party expressing the interests of the peasantry, which is at the same time independent of the proletariat and the bourgeoisie.

Marxism has always taught, and Bolshevism, too, accepted, and taught, that the peasantry and proletariat are two different classes, that it is false to identify their interests in capitalist society in any way, and that a peasant can join the communist party only if, from the property viewpoint, he adopts the views of the proletariat. The alliance of the workers and peasants under the dictatorship of the proletariat does not invalidate this thesis, but confirms it, in a different way, under different circumstances. If there were no *different* classes with *different* interests, there would be no talk even of an *alliance*. Such an alliance is compatible with the socialist revolution only to the extent that it enters into the iron framework of the dictatorship of the proletariat. In our country the dictatorship is incompatible with the existence of a so-called Peasants' League precisely because every "independent" peasant organization aspiring to solve all national political problems would inevitably turn out to be an instrument in the hands of the bourgeoisie.

Those organizations which in capitalist countries label themselves peasant parties are in reality one of the varieties of bourgeois parties. Every peasant who has not adopted the proletarian position, abandoning his proprietor psychology, will inevitably follow the bourgeoisie when it comes to fundamental political issues. Of course, every bourgeois party that relies or seeks to rely on the peasantry and, if possible, on the workers, is compelled to camouflage itself, that is, to assume two or three appropriate colorations. The celebrated idea of "workers' and peasants' parties" seems to have been specially created to camouflage bourgeois parties which are compelled to seek support from the peasantry but who are also ready to absorb workers into their ranks. The Kuomintang has entered the annals of history for all time as a classic type of such a party.

Bourgeois society, as is known, is so constructed that the propertyless, discontented, and deceived masses are at the bottom and the contented fakers remain on top. Every bourgeois party, if it is a real party, that is, if it embraces considerable masses, is built on the self-same principle. The exploiters, fakers, and despots compose the minority in class society. Every capitalist party is therefore compelled in its internal relations, in one way or another, to reproduce and reflect the relations in bourgeois society as a whole. In every mass bourgeois party the lower ranks are therefore more democratic and further to the "Left" than the tops. This holds true of the German Center, the French Radicals, and particularly the social democracy. That is why the constant complaints voiced by Stalin, Bukharin, and others that the tops do not reflect the sentiments of the "Left" Kuomintang rank and file, the "overwhelming majority", the "nine-tenths", etc., etc., are so naive, so unpardonable. That which they represented in their bizarre complaints to be a temporary, disagreeable misunderstanding which was to be eliminated by means of organizational measures, instructions, and circular letters, is in reality a cardinal and basic feature of a bourgeois party, particularly in a revolutionary epoch.

It is from this angle that the basic arguments of the authors of the draft program in defense of all kinds of opportunist blocs in general—both in England and China, must be judged. According to them, fraternization with the tops is done exclusively in the interests of the rank and file. The Opposition, as is known, insisted on the withdrawal of the party from the Kuomintang:

> The question arises," says Bukharin, "why? Is it because the leaders of the Kuomintang are vacillating? And what about the Kuomintang masses, are they mere 'cattle'? Since when is the attitude to a mass organization determined by what takes place at the 'high' summit![12]

The very possibility of such an argument seems impossible in a Revolutionary party. Bukharin asks, "And what about the Kuomintang masses, are they mere cattle?" Of course they are cattle. The masses of any bourgeois party are always cattle, although in different degrees. But for us, the masses are not cattle, are they? No, that is precisely why we are forbidden to drive them into the arms of the bourgeoisie, *camouflaging the latter under the label of a workers' and peasants' party*. That is precisely why we are forbidden to subordinate the proletarian party to a bourgeois party, but on the contrary, must at every step, oppose the former to the latter. The "high" summit of the Kuomintang of whom Bukharin speaks so ironically, as of something secondary, accidental, and temporary is in reality the soul of the Kuomintang, its social essence. Of course, the bourgeoisie constitutes only the "summit" in the party as well as in society. But this summit is powerful in its capital, knowledge, and connections: it can always fall back on the imperialists for support, and what is most important, it can always resort to the actual political and military power which is intimately fused with the leadership in the Kuomintang itself. It is precisely this summit that wrote laws against strikes, throttled the uprisings of the peasants, shoved the communists into a dark corner, and, at best, allowed them to be only one-third of the party, exacted an oath from them that petty-bourgeois Sun Yat-senism takes precedence over Marxism. The rank and file were picked and harnessed by this summit, serving it, like Moscow, as a "Left" support, just as the generals, compradores, and imperialists served it as a Right support. To consider the Kuomintang not as a *bourgeois party, but as a neutral arena of struggle for the masses*, to play with words about nine-tenths of the Left rank and file in order to mask the question as to who is the real master, meant to add to the strength and power of the summit, to assist the latter to convert ever broader masses into "cattle", and, under conditions most favorable to it to prepare the Shanghai *coup d'etat*. Basing themselves on the reactionary idea of the two-class party, Stalin and Bukharin imagined that the communists, together with the "Lefts", would secure a majority in the Kuomintang and thereby power in the country, for, in China, power is in the hands of the Kuomintang. In other words, they imagined that *by means of ordinary elections at Kuomintang Congresses power would pass from the hands of the bourgeoisie to the proletariat*. Can one conceive of a more touching and idealistic idolization of "party democracy" ... in a bourgeois part? For indeed, the army, the bureaucracy, the press, the capital are all in the hands of the bourgeoisie. Precisely because of this and this alone it stands at the helm of the ruling party. The bourgeois "summit" tolerates or tolerated "nine-tenths" of the Lefts (and Lefts of *this sort*), only in so far as they did not venture against the army, the bureaucracy, the press, and against capital. By these powerful means the bourgeois summit kept in subjection not only the so-called nine-tenths of the "Left" party members, but also the masses as a whole. In this the theory of the bloc of classes, the theory that the Kuomintang is a workers' and peasants' party, provides the best possible assistance for the bourgeoisie. When the bourgeoisie later comes into hostile conflict with the masses and shoots them down, in this clash between the two real forces, the bourgeoisie and the proletariat, not even the bleating of the celebrated nine-tenths is heard. The pitiful democratic fiction evaporates without a trace in face of the bloody reality of the class struggle.

Such is the genuine and only possible political mechanism of the "two-class workers' and peasants' parties for the Orient". There is no other and there will be none.

* * *

Although the idea of the two-class parties is motivated on national oppression, which allegedly abrogates Marx's class doctrine, we have already heard about "workers' and peasants' " mongrels in Japan, where there is no national oppression at all. But that isn't all, the matter is not limited merely to the Orient. The "two-class" idea seeks to attain universality. In this domain, the most grotesque features were assumed by the above-mentioned Communist Party of America in its effort to support the presidential candidacy of the bourgeois, "anti-trust" Senator LaFollette, so as to yoke the American farmers by this means to the chariot of the social revolution. Pepper, the theoretician of this manoeuver, one of those who ruined the Hungarian revolution because he overlooked the Hungarian peasantry, made a great effort (by way of compensation, no doubt) to ruin the Communist Party of America by dissolving it among the farmers. Pepper's theory was that the super-profit of American capitalism converts the American proletariat into a world labor aristocracy, while the agrarian crisis ruins the farmers and drives them onto the path of social revolution. According to Pepper's conception, a party of a few thousand members, consisting chiefly of immigrants, had to fuse with the farmers through the medium of a bourgeois party and by thus founding a "two-class" party, insure the socialist revolution in the face of the passivity or neutrality of the proletariat corrupted by super-profits. This insane idea found supporters and half-supporters among the upper leadership of the Comintern. For several weeks the issue swayed in the balance until finally a concession was made to the ABC of Marxism (the comment behind the scenes was: Trotskyist prejudices). It was necessary to lasso the American Communist Party in order to tear it away from the LaFollette party which died even before its founder.

Everything invented by modern revisionism for the Orient is carried over later to the West. If Pepper on one side of the Atlantic Ocean tried to spur history by means of a two-class party then the latest dispatches in the press inform us that the Kuomintang experience finds its imitators in Italy where, apparently, an attempt is being made to foist on our party the monstrous slogan of a "republican assembly on the basis [?!] of workers' and peasants' committees". In this slogan the spirit of Chiang Kai-shek embraces the spirit of Hilferding. Will we really come to that?

* * *

In conclusion there remains for us only to recall that the idea of a workers' and peasants' party sweeps from the history of Bolshevism the entire struggle against the Populists (Narodniks), without which there would have been no Bolshevik party. What was the significance of this historical struggle? In 1909, Lenin wrote the following about the Social-Revolutionists:

> The fundamental idea of their program was not at all that 'an alliance of the forces' of the proletariat and the peasantry is necessary, but that there is no *class abyss* between the former and the latter and that there is no need to draw a line of class demarcation between them, and that the social democratic idea of the petty bourgeois nature of the peasantry that distinguishes it from the proletariat is fundamentally false.[13]

In other words, the two-class workers' and peasants' party is the central idea of the Russian Narodniks. Only in the struggle against this idea could the party of the proletarian vanguard in peasant Russia develop.

Lenin persistently and untiringly repeated in the epoch of the 1905 revolution that

> Our attitude towards the peasantry must be distrustful, we must *organize separately from it*, be ready for a struggle against it, to the extent that the peasantry comes forward as a reactionary or anti-proletarian force.[14]

In 1906 Lenin wrote:

> Our last advice: proletarians and semi-proletarians of city and country, organize yourselves separately! Place no trust in any small proprietors, even the petty ones, even those who 'toil' ... We support the peasant movement to the end, but we must remember that it is a movement of another class, *not the one* that can or will accomplish the socialist revolution.[15]

This idea reappears in hundreds of Lenin's major and minor works. In 1908, he explained:

> The alliance between the proletariat and the peasantry must in no case be interpreted to mean a *fusion of the different classes or parties* of the proletariat and the peasantry. Not only fusion, but even *any sort of lasting concord* would be fatal for the socialist party of the working class and *weaken* the revolutionary democratic struggle.[16]

Could one condemn the very idea of a workers' and peasants' party more harshly, more ruthlessly, and more devastatingly? Stalin, on the other hand, teaches that

> The revolutionary anti-imperialist bloc ... must, though not always [!] necessarily [!], assume the form of a single workers' and peasants' party, bound formally [?] by a single platform.[17]

Lenin taught us that an alliance between workers and peasants must in no case and never lead to merger of the parties. But Stalin makes only one concession to Lenin: although, according to Stalin, the bloc of classes must assume "the form of a single party", a workers' and peasants' party like the Kuomintang—*is not always obligatory*. We should thank him for at least this concession.

Lenin put this question in the same irreconcilable spirit during the epoch of the October Revolution. In generalizing the experience of the three Russian revolutions, Lenin, beginning with 1918, did not miss a single opportunity to repeat that there are two decisive forces in a society where capitalist relations predominate—the bourgeoisie and the proletariat.

> If the peasant does not follow the workers, he marches behind the bourgeoisie. There is and there can be no middle course.[18]

Yet a "workers" and peasants' party" is precisely an attempt to create a middle course.

Had the vanguard of the Russian proletariat failed to oppose itself to the peasantry, had it failed to wage a ruthless struggle against the all-devouring petty-bourgeois amorphousness of the latter, it would inevitably have dissolved itself among the petty-bourgeois elements through the medium of the Social Revolutionary Party or some other "two-class party" which, in turn, would inevitably have subjected the vanguard to bourgeois leadership. In order to arrive at a revolutionary alliance with the peasantry—this does not come gratuitously— it is first of all necessary to separate the proletarian vanguard, and thereby the working class as a whole, from the petty bourgeois masses. This can be achieved only by training the proletarian party in the spirit of unshakable class irreconcilability.

The younger the proletariat, the fresher and more direct its "blood-ties" with the peasantry, the greater the proportion of the peasantry to the population as a whole, the greater becomes the importance of the struggle against any form of "two-class" political alchemy. In the West the idea of a workers' and peasants' party is simply ridiculous. In the East it is fatal. In China, India, and Japan this idea is mortally hostile not only to the hegemony of the proletariat in the revolution but also to the most elementary independence of the proletarian vanguard. The workers' and peasants' party can only serve as a base, a screen, and a springboard for the bourgeoisie.

It is fatal that in this question, fundamental for the entire East, modern revisionism only repeats the errors of old social democratic opportunism of pre-revolutionary days. Most of the leaders of European social democracy considered the struggle of our party against SRs to be mistaken and insistently advocated the fusion of the two parties, holding that for the Russian "East" a two-class workers' and peasants' party was exactly in order. Had we heeded their counsel, we should never have achieved either the alliance of the workers and the peasants or the dictatorship of the proletariat. The "two-class" workers' and peasants' party of the SRs became, and could not help becoming in our country, the agency of the imperialist bourgeoisie, i.e., it tried unsuccessfully to fulfil the same historic role which was successfully played in China by the Kuomintang in a different and "peculiar" Chinese way, thanks to the revisionists of Bolshevism. Without a relentless condemnation of the very idea of workers' and peasants' parties for the East, there is not and there cannot be a program of the Comintern.

8. The Advantages Secured from the Peasants' International Must be Probed

One of the principal, if not *the* principal, accusations hurled against the Opposition, was its "underestimation" of the peasantry. On this point, too, life has made its tests and rendered its verdict along national and international lines. In every case the official leaders proved guilty of *underestimating the rob and significance of the proletariat in relation to the peasantry*. In this the greatest shifts and errors took place, in the economic and political fields and internationally. At the root of the internal errors since 1923 lies an underestimation of the significance, for the whole of national economy and for the alliance with the peasantry, of state industry under the management of the proletariat. In China, the revolution was doomed by the inability to understand the leading and decisive role of the proletariat in the agrarian revolution.

From the same standpoint, it is necessary to examine and evaluate the entire work of the Krestintern, which from the beginning was merely an experiment—an experiment, moreover, which called for the utmost care and rigid adherence to principles. It is not difficult to understand the reason for this.

The peasantry, by virtue of its entire history and the

conditions of its existence, is the least international of all classes. What are commonly called national traits have their chief source precisely in the peasantry. From among the peasantry, it is only the semi-proletarian masses of the peasant poor who can be guided along the road of internationalism, and only the proletariat can guide them. Any attempt at a short-cut is merely playing with the classes, which always means playing to the detriment of the proletariat. The peasantry can be attracted to internationalist politics only if it is torn away from the influence of the bourgeoisie by the proletariat and if it recognizes in the proletariat not only its ally, but its leader. Conversely, attempts to organize the peasants of the various countries into an independent international organization, over the head of the proletariat and without regard to the national communist parties, are doomed in advance to failure. In the final analysis such attempts can only harm the struggle of the proletariat in each country for hegemony over the agricultural laborers and poor peasants.

In all bourgeois revolutions as well as counter-revolutions, beginning with the peasant wars of the sixteenth century and even before that time, the various strata of the peasantry played an enormous and at times even decisive role. But it never played an *independent* role. Directly or indirectly, the peasantry always supported one political force against another. By itself it never constituted an independent force capable of solving national political tasks. In the epoch of finance capital the process of the polarization of capitalist society has enormously accelerated in comparison to earlier phases of capitalist development. This means that the specific gravity of the peasantry has diminished and not increased. In any case, the peasant is less capable in the imperialist epoch of *independent* political action on a national, let alone international scale, than he was in the epoch of industrial capitalism. The farmers of the United States today are incomparably less able to play an independent political role than they were forty or fifty years ago when, as the experience of the Populist movement shows, they could not and did not organize an independent national political party.

The temporary but sharp filip to agriculture in Europe

resulting from the economic decline caused by the war gave rise to illusions concerning the possible role of the "peasant", i.e., of bourgeois pseudo-peasant parties demagogically counterposing themselves to the bourgeois parties. If in the period of stormy peasant unrest during the postwar years one could still risk the experiment of organizing a Peasants' International, in order to test the new relations between the proletariat and the peasantry and between the peasantry and the bourgeoisie, then it is high time now to draw the theoretical and political balance of the five years' experience with the Peasants' International, to lay bare its vicious shortcomings and make an effort to indicate its positive aspects.

One conclusion, at any rate, is indisputable. The experience of the "peasant" parties of Bulgaria, Poland, Rumania, and Yugoslavia (i.e., of all the backward countries); the old experience of our Social Revolutionists, and the fresh experience (the blood is still warm) of the Kuomintang; the episodic experiments in advanced capitalist countries, particularly the LaFollette-Pepper experiment in the United States, have all shown beyond question that in the epoch of capitalist decline there is even less reason than in the epoch of rising capitalism to look for *independent*, revolutionary, anti-bourgeois peasant parties.

> The city cannot be equated to the village, the village cannot be equated to the city in the historical conditions of the present epoch. The city inevitably *leads the village*, the village inevitably *follows the city*. The only question is *which* of the urban classes will lead the village.[19]

In the revolutions of the East the peasantry will still play a decisive role, but once again, this role will be neither leading nor independent. The poor peasants of Hupeh, Kwangtung, or Bengal can play a role not only on a national but on an international scale, but only if they support the workers of Shanghai, Canton, Hankow, and Calcutta. This is the only way out for the revolutionary peasant on an *international* road. It is hopeless to attempt to forge a direct link between the peasant of Hupeh and the peasant of Galicia or Dobrudja, the Egyptian fellah and the American farmer.

It is in the nature of politics that anything which does not serve a direct aim inevitably becomes the instrument of other aims, frequently the opposite of the one sought. Have we not had examples of a bourgeois party, relying on the peasantry or seeking to rely upon it, deeming it necessary to seek insurance for itself in the Peasants' International, for a longer or shorter period, if it could not do so in the Comintern, in order to secure protection from the blows of the communist party in its own country? Like Purcell, in the trade union field, protected himself through the Anglo-Russian Committee? If La Follette did not try to register in the Peasants' International, that was only because the American Communist Party was so extremely weak. He did not have to. Pepper, uninvited and unsolicited, embraced LaFollette without that. But Radic, the banker-leader of the Croatian rich peasants, found it necessary to leave his visiting card with the Peasants' International on his way to the cabinet. The Kuomintang went infinitely further and secured a place for itself not only in the Peasants' International and the League Against Imperialism, but even knocked at the doors of the Comintern and was welcomed there with the blessing of the Politbureau of the CPSU, marred by only one dissenting vote.

It is highly characteristic of the leading political currents of recent years that at a time when tendencies in favor of liquidating the Profintern [Red International of Labor Unions] were very strong (its very name was deleted from the statutes of the Soviet trade unions), nowhere, so far as we recall, has the question ever been raised in the official press as to the precise conquests of the Krestintern, the Peasants' International.

The Sixth Congress must seriously review the work of the Peasants' "International" from the standpoint of proletarian internationalism. It is high time to draw a Marxian balance to this long drawn-out experiment. In one form or another the balance must be included in the program of the Comintern. The present draft does not breathe a single syllable either about the "millions" in the Peasants' International, or for that matter, about its very existence.

Conclusion

We have presented a criticism of certain fundamental theses in the draft program; extreme pressure of time prevented us from dealing with all of them. There were only two weeks at our disposal for this work. We were therefore compelled to limit ourselves to the most pressing questions, those most closely bound up with the revolutionary and internal party struggles during the recent period.

Thanks to our previous experience with so-called "discussions", we are aware beforehand that phrases torn out of their context and slips of the pen can be turned into a seething source of new theories annihilating "Trotskyism". An entire period has been filled with triumphant crowing of this type. But we view with utmost calm the prospect of the cheap theoretical scorpions that this time, too, may descend upon us.

Incidentally, it is quite likely that the authors of the draft program, instead of putting into circulation new critical and expository articles, will prefer to resort to further elaboration of the old Article 58. Needless to say, this kind of argument is even less valid for us.

The Sixth World Congress is faced with the task of adopting a program. We have sought to prove throughout this entire work that there is not the slightest possibility of taking the draft elaborated by Bukharin and Stalin as the basis of the program.

The present moment is the turning point in the life of the CPSU and the entire Comintern. This is evidenced by all the recent decisions and measures of the CEC of our party and the February plenum of the ECCI. These measures are entirely inadequate, the resolutions are contradictory, and certain among them, like the February resolution of the ECCI on the Chinese Revolution, are false to the core. Nevertheless throughout all these resolutions there is a tendency to take a turn to the Left. We have no ground whatever for overestimating it, all the more so since it proceeds hand in hand with a campaign of extermination against the revolutionary wing, while the Right wing is being protected. Notwithstanding all this, we do not for a moment entertain the notion of ignoring this Leftward tendency, forced by the *impasse* created by the old course. Every genuine revolutionist at his post will do everything in his power to facilitate the development of these symptoms of a Left zigzag into a revolutionary Leninist course, with the least difficulties and convulsions in the party. But we are still far removed from this today. At present the Comintern is perhaps passing through its most acute period of development, a period in which the old course is far from having been liquidated, while the new course brings in eruptions of alien elements. The draft program reflects in whole and in part this transitional condition. Yet, such periods, by their very nature, are least favorable for the elaboration of documents that must determine the activity of our international party for a number of years ahead. Difficult as it may be, we must bide our time—after so much time has been lost already. We must permit the muddled waters to settle. The confusion must pass, the contradictions must be eliminated, and the new course take definite shape.

The Congress has not convened for four years. For nine years the Comintern has existed without a definitive program. The only way out at the present moment is this: that the Seventh World Congress be convened a year from today, putting an end once and for all to the attempts at usurping the supreme powers of the Comintern as a whole, a normal regime be re-established, such a regime as would allow of a genuine discussion of the draft program and permit us to oppose to the eclectic draft, another, a Marxist-Leninist draft. There must be no forbidden questions for the Comintern, for the meetings and conferences of its sections, and for its press. During this year the entire soil must be deeply plowed by the plow of Marxism. Only as a result of such labor can the international party of the proletariat secure a, program, a beacon which will illuminate with its penetrating rays, and throw reliable beams far into the future.

NOTES

1. *Minutes of the Seventh Plenum,* ECCI, Vol. I, p. 406.
2. Lenin, *Works,* Vol. XIV, part 1, p. 11.
3. *Minutes,* p. 205.
4. *Works,* Vol. XVIII, part 2, p. 119.
5. Ibid., p. 118.
6. *Works,* Vol. XIV, part 1, p. 29.

7. *Works*, Vol. VIII, p. 215.
8. *Works*, Vol. XVIII, Part 21, pp.118f.
9. Lenin, *Works*, "The Year 1919," Vol. XVI, p. 458.
10. *Pravda*, March 2, 1929.
11. Stalin, *Problems of Leninism*, p. 269.
12. *The Present Situation in the Chinese Revolution*.
13. *Works*, Vol. XI, Part 1, p. 198.
14. *Works*, Vol. VI, p. 113.
15. *Works*, Vol. IX, p. 410.
16. *Works*, Vol. XI, Part 1, p. 79.
17. *Problems of Leninism*, p. 265.
18. *Works*, Vol. XVI, *The Year 1919*, p. 219.
19. Lenin, *Works*, Vol. XVI, *The Year 1919*, p. 442.

31

Democratic Slogans in China

October 1928

The history of this work ("The Chinese Question After the Sixth Congress") is the following: When I wrote the criticism of the draft program, I wanted to include the call for a Constituent Assembly as one to be raised in China in the present period. Then I decided that it was better in a programmatic document for me to confine myself for the time being to a general description of the counter-revolutionary and non-revolutionary epoch that has come about in China, i.e., the epoch of a certain political and economic stabilization of the bourgeoisie (a "year of 1849 as Lenin put it 94). I thought that the only dispute over principles that could arise would be over whether the "year of 1849 has begun or not. If it has, the call for soviets as a practical slogan falls by the wayside as a matter of course. This is precisely why, in addition to demonstrating the reactionary nature of the call for a "democratic dictatorship", I also argued that a revolutionary situation did not exist in China and that there was a need for a policy that coincided with the inevitable intensification of the tendencies toward stabilization.

I admit that I was still apprehensive that if in passing I raised the call for a constituent assembly—especially important, in my opinion, for showing the character of the political change that had occurred—then Bukharin and Manuilsky would hasten to forbid a constituent assembly. So I decided to wait. But the discussion at the congress on the question of China showed that there could be no waiting. The fundamental features of my work had been written when I received the resolution of the ECCI declaring the call for a national assembly to be opportunistic. At that point I very much regretted that I had not included the call for a constituent assembly in my programmatic work. In the meantime I wrote a number of comrades very briefly about the need to advance in China the democratic demand for popular representation. It could be that excessive brevity gave rise to a misunderstanding. I have already received several telegrams raising objections to this demand. Some comrades inform me by telegram that they have sent detailed letters on this question. I am forwarding my work without waiting for these letters, which, very likely, will have to be answered individually. I must say, some of the objections in the telegrams did seem quite incredible to me. For example, two comrades say that the call for a constituent assembly is "not a class demand", and that, therefore, they reject it. Such an understanding of the class character of demands has an anarcho-syndicalist and not a Marxist character. To the extent that Chinese politics have switched from a revolutionary track to the track of bourgeois stabilization, with the question of a national assembly already having become the central question (tomorrow this will be conclusively revealed), to that extent the class interests of the proletariat, correctly understood, require that "democratic slogans be carried out to the fullest extent. Don't forget that in 1912 the Bolsheviks in the legal press called themselves "consistent democrats". This pseudonym to pass the censors expressed all the same a very important political tendency of the party's work at that time. Several telegrams advance the call for soviets instead of the call for a constituent assembly. This is not in the least a serious alternative. If it were, it would serve us well to re-examine either the entire question of the role of soviets or the question of the character of the period China is passing through. Otherwise we are only confusing the Chinese party and ourselves. But as I already said, I will have to speak about this a little more after receiving the letters, if the present work does not dispel some of the misunderstandings provoked, in part, by the brevity of my letter.

I believe that it is necessary to devote separate documents, like the one I was trying to do on China, to the most important countries ("The French Question After the Sixth Congress", "The English Question . . .", etc.). It would only be possible to carry out this work well by doing it collectively, for example, if Comrade Radek took responsibility for Germany, Holland, and Scandinavia, possibly England as well; Comrade Dingelsted-India; Comrade Rakovsky-France and possibly England, etc.

Other comrades could send me their observations on different questions or countries. It is necessary right now to pose all the questions raised in the Comintern fully in the concrete, but by separate countries—and in good time. From Comrades Smilga, Palatnikov, Livshits, and our economists in general we expect concrete theses on the internal working of the "present period", domestically. Of course it goes without saying, I am naming comrades here only by way of example. But time is precious.

Warm greetings.

Yours,
L. Trotsky

32

The Chinese Question after the Sixth Congress

October 4, 1928
Alma Ata

The lessons and the problems in the strategy and tactics of the Chinese Revolution constitute at the present time the greatest teaching for the international proletariat. The experience gained in 1917 has been altered, disfigured and falsified to the point of un-recognizability by the epigones brought to power on the waves of defeats of the world's working class. Henceforth, one is compelled to extract the 1917 revolution from beneath mountains of impurities under which it has been buried. The revolution has verified the policy of Bolshevism by resorting to the method of *reductio ad absurdum*. The strategy of the Communist International in China was a gigantic game of "losers win". The young generation of revolutionists must be taught the alphabet of Bolshevism by using the Chinese antithesis contrasted to the experience gained in October. China itself has a world importance. But what happens in this country decides not only its own fate, but the destiny of the Communist International in the full sense of the world. Not only has the Sixth Congress not drawn up the correct balance or introduced clarity, but on the contrary, it has consecrated the errors committed and has supplemented them by a new confusion which can create for the Chinese Communist Party a hopeless situation for a whole series of years. The bureaucratic thunderbolts of excommunication will manifestly fail to reduce us to silence when the fate of the international revolution is at stake. It is just those who excommunicate us who are the ones directly responsible for the defeats suffered; that is why they dread the shedding of light.

* * *

In the past five years, no party has suffered so cruelly from the opportunist leadership of the Communist International as the Chinese CP. We have had in China a perfect example (and that is just the reason why it led to a catastrophe) of the application of the Menshevik policy to a revolutionary epoch. What is more, Menshevism had a monopoly at its disposal, for it was protected against Bolshevik criticism by the authority of the Communist International and by the material apparatus of the soviet power. This combination of circumstances is unique in its kind. As a result, one of the greatest revolutions, according to its possibilities, was completely confiscated by the Chinese bourgeoisie; it served to strengthen the latter, something which, from all the data in our possession, the bourgeoisie had no reason to count on. The mistakes of opportunism have not yet been repaired. The whole course of the Congress discussion, the reports of Bukharin and Kuusinen, the speeches of the Chinese Communists—all these indicate that the line of conduct followed by the leadership in Chinese politics not only was false but remains false to this day. Passing over from the opportunism openly practised in the form of collaboration (1924–27), it made an abrupt zig-zag at the end of 1927 by resorting to adventures. After the Canton insurrection, it rejected putschism and passed into the third phase, the most sterile one, seeking to combine the old opportunistic premises with a purely formal, ineffectual radicalism, which at a certain period bore in Russia, the names of "ultimatism" and "Otzovism", and which constitutes the worst variety of ultra-leftism.

No Chinese Communist can any longer take a single step forward now without first having estimated at its right value the opportunist leadership which led to destruction in the three stages (Shanghai, Wuhan, Canton) and without having completely understood the immense break produced by these defeats in the social and political, the internal and international position of China.

The Congress discussion showed what gross and perilous illusions still subsist in the conceptions of Chinese Communist leaders. While defending the Canton insurrection, one of the Chinese delegates referred triumphantly to the fact that after the defeat suffered in this city, the membership of the Party did not decrease but grew. Even here, thousands of miles from the theatre of the revolutionary events, it seems incredible that such monstrous information could have been presented to a world Congress without immediately encountering an indignant refutation. However, thanks to observations made on another point by a speaker, we learn, that while the CPC has gained (for how long?) tens of thousands of new members among the peasants, it has on the other hand lost the majority of its workers. It is this menacing process, characterizing without the possibility of error a certain phase of *decline* of the Party, that the Chinese Communists describe at the Congress as a sign of growth and progress. While the revolution is beaten in the cities and in the most important centres of the workers' and the peasants' movement, there will always be, especially in a country as vast as China, fresh regions, fresh just because they are backward, containing not yet exhausted revolutionary forces. On the distant periphery, the beginnings of the revolutionary wave will yet swell for a long time. Without having direct data on the situation in the Chinese-Muslim regions of the south-west, it is difficult to speak with precision of the probability of a revolutionary ferment being produced there in the approaching period. But the whole past of China renders such an eventuality possible. It is quite evident that this movement would only be a belated echo of the battles of Shanghai, Hankow and Canton. After the decisive defeat suffered by the revolution in the cities, the Party, for a certain time, can still draw tens of thousands of new members from the awakening peasantry. This fact is important as a precursory sign of the great possibilities in the future. But in the period under consideration it is only one form of the dissolution and the liquidation of the CPC, for, by losing its proletarian nucleus, it ceases to be in conformity with its historical destiny.

An epoch of revolutionary decline is by its very essence pregnant with dangers for a revolutionary party. In 1852, Engels said that such a party, having let a revolutionary situation escape it, or having suffered a decisive defeat in it, inevitably disappears from the scene for a certain period of history. The counter-revolutionary epoch strikes a revolutionary party all the more cruelly if the crushing of the revolution is caused, not by an unfavorable relationship of forces, but by the patent and indisputable blunders of the leadership, as was exactly the case in China. Add to all this the brief existence of the Chinese party, the absence in it of firmly tempered cadres and solid traditions; add to it, finally, the alterations made so light-heartedly in the leadership which, there as everywhere else, was converted into the responsible manager expiating the mistakes of the Communist International. Taken together, all this creates veritably fatal conditions for the CPC during the counter-revolutionary epoch, the duration of which cannot be determined in advance.

It is only by clearly and courageously posing the fundamental questions of today and yesterday that one can avert for the CPC the fate which Engels spoke of, in other words, liquidation, from the political point of view, for a certain period.

We have examined—the class dynamics of the Chinese revolution in a special chapter of the criticism to which we submitted the fundamental theses of the draft program of the Communist International. Today, we see no need of adding anything to this chapter, or, for that matter, of introducing any modifications into it. We arrived there at the conclusion that the subsequent development of the Chinese Revolution can only take place in the form of the struggle of the Chinese proletariat, drawing hundreds of millions of poor peasants to the conquest of power. The solution of fundamental bourgeois-democratic problems in China depends entirely on the dictatorship of the proletariat. To oppose to this the democratic dictatorship of the proletariat and peasantry is to devote oneself to a reactionary attempt which seeks to drag the revolution back to stages already traversed by the coalition in the Guomindang. This general political diagnosis, containing the strategical line of conduct for the coming period of the Chinese revolution, or more exactly, of the third Chinese Revolution of the future, in no way annuls the question of the tactical problems of today and tomorrow.

1. The Permanent Revolution and the Canton Insurrection

In November 1927, the plenum of the Central Committee of the Chinese party decided that:

> The objective circumstances existing at the present time in China are such that the duration of a directly revolutionary situation will be measured not by weeks or by months, but by long years. The Chinese revolution has a lasting character, but on the other hand, it has no stops. By its character, it constitutes what Marx called a permanent revolution.

Is this right? Intelligently understood, it is right. But it must be understood according to Marx and not according to Lominadze. Bukharin, who showed up the latter precisely for having employed this formula, was no closer to Marx than the author of it. In capitalist society, every real revolution, above all if it takes place in a large country, and more particularly now, in the imperialist epoch, tends to transform itself into a permanent revolution; in other words, not to come to a halt at any of the stages it reaches, not to confine itself up to the complete transformation of society, up to the final abolition of class distinctions, consequently, up to the complete and final suppression of the very possibility of new revolutions. That is just what the Marxian conception of the proletarian revolution consists of, being distinguished by that from the bourgeois revolution, limited by its national scope as much as by its specific objectives. The Chinese Revolution contains within itself tendencies to become permanent in so far as it contains the possibility of the conquest of power by the proletariat. To speak of the permanent revolution without this and outside of it, is like trying to fill the cask of the Danaïds. Only the proletariat, after having seized the state power and having transformed it into an instrument of struggle against all the forms of oppression and exploitation, in the interior of the country as well as beyond its frontiers, gains therewith the possibility of assuring a continuous character to the revolution, in other words, of leading it to the construction of a complete socialist society. A necessary condition for this is to carry out consistently a policy which prepares the proletariat in good time for the conquest of power. Now, Lominadze has made of the possibility of a permanent development of the revolution (on the condition that the Communist policy be correct) a scholastic formula guaranteeing at one blow and for all time a revolutionary situation "for many years". The permanent character of the revolution thus becomes a law placing itself above history, independent of the policy of the leadership and of the material development of revolutionary events. As always in such cases, Lominadze and company resolved to announce their metaphysical formula regarding the permanent character of the revolution only after the political leadership of Stalin, Bukharin, Chen Tu Shiu and Tang Pingshan had thoroughly sabotaged the revolutionary struggle.

After having assured the continuity of the revolution for many years, the plenum of the Central Committee of the Chinese Communist Party, freed from any further doubts, deduces from this formula conditions favorable to the insurrection.

> Not only is the strength of the revolutionary movement of the toiling masses of China not yet exhausted, but it is precisely only now that it is beginning to manifest itself in a new advance of the revolutionary struggle. All this obliges the plenum of the Central Committee of the Chinese Communist Party to recognize that a directly revolutionary situation exists today (November 1927) throughout China.

The Canton insurrection was deduced from a similar evaluation of the situation with perfect inevitability. Had a revolutionary situation really existed, the mere fact of the defeat of Canton would have been a special episode, and in any case, would not have transformed the uprising of this city into an adventure. Even in face of unfavourable conditions for the insurrection of Canton itself or its environs, the leadership would have had as its duty to do all that was necessary to realize the revolt most rapidly in order thus to disperse and weaken the forces of the enemy and to facilitate the triumph of the uprising in the other parts of the country.

However, not after "many years" but after a few months, it had to be acknowledged that the political situation had declined abruptly, and that before the Canton insurrection. The campaign of Ho Lung and Ye Ting were already developing in an atmosphere of revolutionary decline, the workers were separating themselves from the revolution, the centrifugal tendencies were gaining in strength. This is in no way contradictory to the existence of peasant movements in various provinces. That is how it always is.

Let the Chinese Communist ask themselves now: Would they have dared to decide upon fixing the Canton insurrection for December had they understood that for the given period the fundamental forces of the revolution were exhausted and that the great decline had commenced? It is clear that if they had understood in good time this radical break in the situation, they would in no case have put on the order of the day the appeal for the armed uprising in Canton. The only way of explaining the policy of the leadership, in fixing and carrying out this revolt, is that it *did not understand the meaning* and the consequences of the defeats in Shanghai and Hupeh. There can be no other interpretation of it. But the lack of understanding can all the less excuse the leadership of the Communist International since the Opposition had warned in good time against the new situation and the new dangers. It found itself accused for this, by idiots and calumniators, of having the spirit of liquidators.

The resolution of the Sixth Congress confirms the fact that an inadequate resistance to "putschistic moods" produced the fruitless uprisings in Hunan, in Hupeh, etc. What is to be understood by "putschistic moods"? The Chinese Communists, in conformity with the directions of Stalin and Bukharin, judged that the situation in China was directly revolutionary and that the partial revolts had every chance of being extended successfully to the point of becoming a general insurrection. In this way, the launching of these surprise attacks resulted from an erroneous estimation of the circumstances in which China found itself towards the second half of 1927, as a result of the defeats suffered.

In Moscow, they could prattle about the "directly revolutionary situation", accuse the Oppositionists of being liquidators, while providing for themselves beforehand against the future (especially after Canton) by making reservations on the subject of "putschism". But on the theatre of events, in China itself, every honest revolutionist was duty bound to do everything he could in his corner to hasten the uprising, since the Communist International had declared that the general situation was propitious for an insurrection on a national scale. It is on this question that the régime of duplicity reveals its deliberately criminal character.

At the same time the resolution of the Congress says:

> The Congress deems it entirely inexact to attempt to consider the Canton insurrection as a putsch. It was a heroic rearguard [?] battle of the Chinese proletariat, fought in the course of the period which has just passed in the Chinese revolution; in spite of the crude mistakes committed by the leadership, this uprising will remain the standard of the new soviet phase of the revolution.

Here confusion reaches its zenith. The heroism of the Cantonese proletariat is brought in evidence as a screen to cover up the faulty leadership, not of Canton (which the resolution casts off completely) but of Moscow, which only yesterday spoke not of a "rearguard battle" but of the overthrow of the government of the Guomindang.

Why is the appeal to insurrection denounced as putschism *after* the experience of Canton? Because, thanks to this experience, the inopportuneness of the uprising was confirmed. The leadership of the Communist International had need of a new object lesson in order to discover what already appeared quite clear without it. But are not these supplementary lessons for backward people, given in life, too costly to the proletariat?

Lominadze, one of the infant prodigies of revolutionary strategy, swore at the Fifteenth Congress of the Communist Party of the Soviet Union that the Canton insurrection was necessary, right and salutary, precisely because it inaugurated an era of the direct struggle of the workers and peasants for the conquest of power. He met with agreement. At the Sixth Congress, Lominadze recognized that the insurrection did not inaugurate an era of triumph but concluded one of defeat. Nevertheless, just as before, the uprising is considered necessary, right and salutary. Its name has simply been changed: from a clash between the vanguard of the forces at hand, they made a "rearguard battle". Everything else remains as in the past. The attempt to escape the criticism of the Opposition by hiding behind the heroism of the Cantonese workers has as much weight as, let us say for example, the attempt of General Rennenkampf to take shelter behind the heroism of the Russian soldiers whom he drowned by his strategy in the Masurian swamps. The proletarians of Canton are guilty, without having committed mistakes, simply of an excess of confidence in their leadership. Their leadership was guilty of having had a blind confidence in the leadership of the Communist International which combined political blindness with the spirit of adventurism.

It is radically false to compare the Canton insurrection of 1927 with that of Moscow in 1905. During the whole of 1905, the Russian proletariat rose from one plane to the other, wresting concessions from the enemy, sowing disintegration in its ranks, concentrating around its vanguard ever greater popular masses. The October 1905 strike was an immense victory, having a world historical importance. The Russian proletariat had its own party, which was not subordinated to any bourgeois or petty-bourgeois discipline. The self-esteem, the intransigence, the spirit of offensive of the Party, rose from stage to stage. The Russian proletariat had created soviets in dozens of cities, not on the eve of the revolt but during the process of a strike struggle of the masses. Through these soviets, the Party established contact with the vast masses; it registered their revolutionary spirit; it mobilized them. The tsarist government, seeing that each day brought a change in the relationship of forces favorable to the revolution, passed over to the counter-offensive and thus prevented the revolutionary leadership from being able to gain the time needed for continuing to mobilize its forces. Under these conditions, the leadership could and should have staked everything so as to be able to test by deeds the state of mind of the last decisive factor: the army. This was the meaning of the insurrection of December 1905.

In China, events developed in a directly opposite way. The Stalinist policy of the Chinese Communist Party consisted of a series of capitulations before the bourgeoisie, accustoming the workers to support patiently the yoke of the Guomindang. In March 1926 the Party capitulated before Chiang Kai-shek; it consolidated his position while weakening its own; it discredited the banner of Marxism; it converted itself into an auxiliary instrument of the bourgeois leadership. The Party extinguished the agrarian movement and the workers' strikes by putting into practice the directions of the Executive Committee of the Communist International on the bloc of four classes. It renounced the organization of soviets so as not to disturb the situation at the rear of the Chinese generals. It thus delivered to Chiang Kai-shek the workers of Shanghai, bound hand to foot. After the crushing of Shanghai, the Party, in conformity with the directions of the Executive Committee of the Communist International, placed all its hopes in the Left Guomindang, the so-called "centre of the agrarian revolution". The Communists entered the Wuhan government, which repressed the strike struggle and the peasants' uprisings. They thus prepared a new and still crueller devastation of the revolutionary masses. After all this, an instruction entirely permeated with the spirit of adventurism was issued, ordering an immediate orientation towards the insurrection. It is from this that was first born the adventure of Ho Lung and Ye Ting, and the even more painful one of the Canton *coup d'état*.

No, all this does not resemble the insurrection of December 1905 at all.

If an opportunist calls the events of Canton an adventure it is because it was an *insurrection*. If a Bolshevik employs the same designation for these facts, it is because it was an *inopportune insurrection*. It is not for nothing that a German proverb says that when two men say the same thing it does not mean the same thing. The officials *à la* Thälmann can continue, on the subject of the Chinese revolt, to recount to the German Communists the "apostasy" of the Opposition. We will know how to teach the German Communists to turn their backs on the Thälmanns. In actuality, the question of evaluating the Canton insurrection is the question of the teachings drawn from the Third Congress, in other words, of a lesson where the life of the German proletariat was at stake.

In March 1921 the Communist Party of Germany sought to engage in an insurrection by basing itself upon an active minority of the proletariat in the face of the passive spirit of the majority, which was tired, distrustful, expectant, as a result of all the preceding defeats. Those who directed this attempt at the time also sought to take shelter behind the heroism of which the workers gave proof in the March battles. However, the Third Congress did not congratulate them for this attempt when it condemned the spirit of adventurism of the leadership. What was our judgement in those days of the March events?

> "Their essence," we wrote, "is summed up in the fact that the young Communist Party, alarmed by a manifest decline in the workers' movement, made a desperate attempt to profit by the intervention of one of the most active detachments of the proletariat in order to 'electrify' the working class and, if possible, to bring matters to a decisive battle."[1]

Thälmann has not understood a thing of all this.

From July 1923 on, we demanded, to the great astonishment of Clara Zetkin, Warski and other old, very venerable but incorrigible Social Democrats, that the date of the insurrection in Germany be fixed. Then, at the beginning of 1924, when Zetkin declared that at that moment she envisaged the eventuality of an uprising with much "more optimism" than during the preceding year, we could only shrug our shoulders.

> An *elementary truth* of Marxism says that the tactics of the socialist proletariat cannot be the same in face of a revolutionary situation as when this situation does not exist.[2]

Today, everybody acknowledges this ABC verbally, but how far they still are from applying it in reality!

It is not a question of knowing what the Communists must do when the masses are rebelling *of their own accord*. That is a special question. When the masses arise, the Communists must be with them, organizing and instructing them. But the question is posed differently: What did the leadership do and what should it have done during the weeks and months that immediately preceded the Canton insurrection? The leadership was duty bound to explain to the revolutionary workers that as a consequence of defeats, due to an erroneous policy, the relationship of forces had veered entirely in favor of the bourgeoisie. The great masses of workers who had fought tremendous battles, dispersed by the encounters, abandoned the field of battle. It is absurd to believe that one can march towards a peasant insurrection when the proletarian masses are departing. They must be grouped together again, fight defensive battles, avoiding a general battle, which obviously does not hold out any hope. If *in spite of* such a work of clarification and education, *contrary* to it, the masses of Canton had rebelled (which is very unlikely) the Communists would have had to put themselves at their head. But it is just the reverse that happened. The uprising had been commanded in advance, deliberately and with premeditation, based upon a false appreciation of the whole atmosphere. One of the detachments of the proletariat was drawn into a struggle which obviously held out no hope, and made easier for the enemy the annihilation of the vanguard of the working class. Not to say this openly, is to deceive the Chinese workers and to prepare new defeats. The Sixth Congress did not say it.

Does all this signify that the Canton insurrection *was only an adventure,* allowing of but one conclusion, that is, that the leadership was entirely incompetent? No, that is not the sense of our criticism. The Canton insurrection showed that even after enormous defeats, with the manifest decline of the revolution, even in non-industrialized Canton, with its petty-bourgeois traditions of Sun-Yat-Sen-ism, the proletariat was able to rise in revolt, to fight valiantly and to conquer power. We have here a fact of enormous importance. It shows anew how considerable is the weight of the proletariat in its own right, how great is the political role which it can eventually play, even if the working class is relatively weak in numbers, in a historically backward country, where the majority of the population is composed of peasants and scattered petty-bourgeois. This fact, once more after 1905 and 1917, completely demolishes the philistines *à la* Kuusinen, Martynov and consorts, who teach us that one cannot dream of speaking of the dictatorship of the proletariat in "agrarian" China. Yet the Martynovs and the Kuusinens are at the present time the daily inspirers of the Communist International.

The Canton insurrection showed at the same time that at the decisive moment the proletariat was unable to find, even in the petty-bourgeois capital of Sun-Yat-Sen-ism, a single *political ally* having a distinct form, not even among the debris of the Guomindang, of the left or the ultra-left. This means that the vital task of establishing the alliance between the workers and the poor peasants in China devolves exclusively and directly upon the Communist Party. The accomplishment of this task is one of the conditions for the triumph of the coming third Chinese Revolution. And the victory of the latter will restore the power to the vanguard of the proletariat, supported by the union of the workers and the poor peasants.

* * *

If "apostasy" must be spoken of, the traitors to the heroes and the victims of the Canton insurrection are those who seek to rid themselves of the teachings of this uprising in order to conceal the crimes of the leadership. The lesson to draw is the following:

1. The Canton insurrection showed that only the proletarian vanguard in China is capable of carrying out the uprising and of capturing power. The revolt showed, after the experience of collaboration between the Communist Party and the Guomindang, the complete lack of vitality and the reactionary character of the slogan of the democratic dictatorship of the proletariat and the peasantry, opposed to the slogan of the dictatorship of the proletariat drawing the poor peasants behind it.
2. The Canton insurrection, conceived and executed contrary to the course of development of the revolution, accelerates and deepens the decline of the latter, facilitating the annihilation of the proletarian forces by

> the bourgeois counter-revolution. This stamps the inter-revolutionary period with a painful, chronic and lasting character. The greatest problem now is the renascence of the Communist Party as the organization of the vanguard of the proletariat.

These two conclusions are equally important. It is only by considering them simultaneously that the situation can be judged and the perspectives fixed. The Sixth Congress did neither the one nor the other. By taking as its point of departure the resolutions of the Ninth Plenum of the Executive Committee of the Communist International (February 1928) which assured us that the Chinese revolution "is continuing", the Congress slipped up in its flight to the point of declaring that this revolution has now entered into a preparatory phase. But this flight will not help anything. We must speak clearly and sincerely, recognize firmly, openly, brutally the breach that has taken place, adapt the tactics to it and at the same time follow a line of conduct which leads the vanguard of the proletariat through the insurrection to its preponderant role in the soviet China of the future.

2. The Inter-Revolutionary Period and the Tasks that Present Themselves in the Course of it

Bolshevik policy is characterized not only by its revolutionary scope, but also by its political realism. These two aspects of Bolshevism are inseparable. The greatest task is to know how to recognize in time a revolutionary situation and to exploit it to the end. But it is no less important to understand when this situation is exhausted and is converted, from the political point of view, into its antithesis. Nothing is more fruitless and worthless than to show one's fist after the battle. That, however, is just where Bukharin's speciality lies. First, he proved that the Guomindang and the soviets are the same thing, and that the Communists can conquer power through the Guomindang, avoiding the fray. And when this same Guomindang, with the aid of Bukharin, crushed the workers, he began to show his fist. In so far as he did nothing but amend or "complete" Lenin, his caricatured aspect did not exceed certain modest limits. In so far as he pretends to give leadership himself, profiting by the total lack of knowledge in international questions on the part of Stalin, Rykov and Molotov, little Bukharin swells up until he becomes a gigantic caricature of Bolshevism. His strategy reduces itself to finishing off and mutilating, in the epoch of decline, that which escaped alive in the abortive and besmirched revolutionary period.

It must be distinctly understood that there is not, at the present time, a revolutionary situation in China. It is rather a counter-revolutionary situation that has been substituted there, transforming itself into an inter-revolutionary period of indefinite duration. Turn with contempt from those who would tell you that this is pessimism and lack of faith. To shut one's eyes to facts is the most infamous form of lack of faith.

There remains in China a revolutionary situation in all its profundity, in so far as all the internal and international contradictions of the country can find their solution only on the road of the revolution. But from this point of view, there is not a single country in the world where there does not exist a revolutionary situation which must inevitably manifest itself openly with the exception of the USSR, where, in spite of five years of opportunist back-sliding, the soviet form of the proletarian dictatorship still opens up the possibility of a renascence of the October Revolution by means of reformist methods.

In certain countries, the eventuality of the transformation of the potential revolution into an active revolution is closer; in others it is further off. It is all the more difficult to divine in advance what will be the rotation followed, since it is determined not only by the acuteness of the international contradictions, but also by the intersection of world factors. One may very reasonably assume that the revolution will be accomplished in Europe before taking place in North America. But the predictions which announce that the revolution will break out in Asia first and then in Europe already have a more conditional character. It is possible, even probable, but it is not at all inevitable. New difficulties and complications, like the occupation of the Ruhr in 1923, or else the accentuation of the commercial and industrial crisis, under the pressure of the United States, can in the nearest future confront the European states with a directly revolutionary situation, as was the case in Germany in 1923, in England in 1926 and in Austria in 1927.

The fact that only yesterday China was passing through a stirring revolutionary phase does not bring closer the revolution for today and tomorrow, but on the contrary, makes it more distant. In the course of the period which followed the revolution of 1905, it produced great revolutionary disturbances and *coups d'état* in the countries of the East (Persia, Turkey, China). But in Russia itself, the revolution revived only twelve years later, in connection with the imperialist war. Naturally, these intervals are not obligatory for China. The general speed of the evolution of world contradictions has now been accelerated. That is all that can be said. But one must take into account and bear in mind that in China itself the revolution is at the present time laid over into an indefinite future. And moreover: the consequences of the defeat of the revolution have not yet been completely exhausted. In Russia the wave of fall and decline went through the years 1907–08, 1909 and partly 1910, when, thanks in large measure to the revival of industry, the working class began to come to life. A no less abrupt descent confronts the Chinese Communist Party. The latter must know how to cling to every ledge, to hold tenaciously to every point of support so as not to tumble down and be smashed.

The Chinese proletariat, beginning with its vanguard, must assimilate the enormous experiences of the defeats and, by acting with new methods, recognize the new environment; it must redress its shattered ranks; it must renew its mass organizations; it must establish with greater clarity and distinctness than before what its attitude must be towards the problems which are arising before the country: national unity and liberation, revolutionary agrarian transformation.

On the other hand, the Chinese bourgeoisie must squander the capital accumulated by its victories. The contradictions which exist within itself, as well as between it and the outside world, must once more lay themselves bare and become sharpened. A new regrouping of forces must have its repercussions in the peasantry, reviving its activity. It is precisely all this that will signify that there is a renascence of the revolutionary situation on a higher historical basis.

"... Those who have had to live, said Lenin on February 23, 1918, through the long years of revolutionary battles at the time of the ascension of the revolution and at the time when it sank into the abyss, when the revolutionary appeals to the masses found no echo among them, know that in spite of everything the revolution always rose anew"[3]

The pace that the Chinese revolution will follow in "rising anew", will depend not only upon objective conditions but also upon the policy of the Communist International.

The resolution of the Congress wheels diplomatically around these essential questions, planting reservations to the right and the left which will permit it to save itself, that is, like the lawyers, it creates motives in advance which will permit it to squash the case or appeal it.

It is true that this resolution recognizes that "the slogan of mass uprising becomes a propaganda slogan and it is only to the extent ... that a new rise of the revolution matures that it will again become immediately applicable in practice". Let us point out in passing that as late as February of this year such an attitude was called Trotskyism. No doubt it must be understood that this term signifies the ability to take into account facts and their consequences more rapidly than is done by the leadership of the Communist International.

But the resolution of the Congress does not go beyond this transformation of the armed insurrection into a propaganda slogan. The reports say nothing more on this point. What is to be expected in the very next period? What must be prepared for? What line must be followed in the work to be effected? No perspective is established. To understand how much needs to be learned over again from the very bottom in this question, let us again cast a glance upon yesterday, upon the very same resolution of the Chinese Central Committee, which furnishes the most striking manifestation of "revolutionary" light-mindedness doubled by opportunism.[4]

The Plenum of the Central Committee of the Chinese Communist Party, directed by the infant prodigies of left centrism, decided in November 1927, on the eve of the insurrection at Canton:

> In evaluating the general political situation created in China after the counter-revolutionary *coup d'état* in Hunan, the Central Committee of the Chinese Communist Party, already in its theses of August, formulated the affirmation that stabilization of the bourgeois military reaction in China was *entirely impossible* on the basis of the present social, economic and political relationships.

In this remarkable thesis, dealing with *stabilization*, the same operation was carried through as was done with the *revolutionary situation*. These two conceptions have been transformed into certain substances, irremediably opposed to each other. If the revolutionary situation is assured for "many years" in the face of no matter what circumstances, it is clear that stabilization, no matter what happens, is "absolutely impossible". The one supplements the other in a system of metaphysical principles. Bukharin and his friendly enemy, Lominadze, do not understand in such a case that the *revolutionary situation*, as well as its opposite, *stabilization*, are not only the premises of the class struggle but also constitute its living content. Outside of this struggle, neither the one nor the other exists.

We once wrote that stabilization is an "object" of the class struggle and not an arena established for it in advance. The proletariat wants to develop and utilize a situation of crisis, the bourgeois wants to put an end to it and to overcome it by its stabilization. Stabilization is the "object" of the struggle of these fundamental class forces. Bukharin first sneered at this definition; then he introduced it textually, as contraband, into his printed report to one of the plenums of the Executive Committee of the Communist International. But in acknowledging our formula, directed especially against his scholasticism, Bukharin failed absolutely to understand the meaning of our definition. As to the capricious leaps that Lominadze executes towards the left, their radius is very restricted, for the valiant infant prodigy does not dare break Bukharin's thread. Naturally, absolute stabilization is absolutely opposed to an absolute revolutionary situation. The conversion of these absolutes into each other is "absolutely impossible". But if one descends from these ridiculous theoretical summits, it turns out that before the complete and final triumph of socialism, the relatively revolutionary situation will very likely be converted more than once into relative stabilization (and vice versa). All other conditions remaining equal, the danger of the conversion of a revolutionary situation into bourgeois stabilization is all the greater the less capable is the proletarian leadership of exploiting the situation.

The leadership of the Chiang Kai-shek clique was superior to that of Chen Duxiu and of Tang Pingshan. But it is not this leadership that decided: foreign imperialism guided Chiang Kai-shek by threats, by promises, by its direct assistance. The Communist International directed Chen Duxiu. Two leaderships of world dimensions crossed swords here. That of the Communist International, through all the stages of the struggle, appeared as absolutely worthless, and it thus facilitated to the highest degree the task of the imperialist leadership. In such conditions, the transformation of the revolutionary situation into bourgeois stabilization is not only not "impossible", but is absolutely inevitable. Even more: it is accomplished, and within certain limits it is completed.

Bukharin has announced a new period of "organic" stabilization for Europe. He gave assurances that one need not expect, in the course of the coming years in Europe, any renewal of the Vienna events or in general any revolutionary conclusions. Why? One does not know. The struggle for the conquest of power is entirely thrust aside by the struggle to be conducted against war. On the other hand, stabilization in China is denied, just as the Fifth Congress denied it in Germany after the defeat of the revolution of 1923. Everything passes and everything changes, except the mistakes of the leadership of the Communist International.

The defeat of the workers and the peasants in China corresponds inevitably to a political consolidation of the Chinese ruling classes; and that is precisely the point of departure for economic stabilization. A certain establishment of order in domestic circulation and in foreign commercial relations, following upon the pacification or the abatement of the civil war regions, automatically brings with it a restoration of economic activity. The vital needs of the completely devastated and exhausted country must make a path for themselves to some degree or other. Commerce and industry must begin to re-establish themselves. The number of employed workers must increase.

It would be blindness to close one's eyes to the existence of certain political premises for the subsequent development of the productive forces of the country which, of course, take on the forms of capitalist servitude. The political premises alone do not suffice. There is still needed an economic impulsion without which the disorganization could be overcome only with relative slowness. This external shock may be furnished by the influx of foreign capital. America has already cut across the field, outstripping Japan and Europe, by consenting, for the sake of form, to conclude an "equal treaty". The domestic depression, in the face of the available resources, makes more than likely an extensive economic intervention in China by the United States, before which the Guomindang will evidently hold the door wide "open". One cannot doubt the fact that the European countries, especially Germany, fighting against the rapidly aggravated crisis, will seek to debouch upon the Chinese market.

Given the vast area of China and its multitudinous population, even feeble success in the field of road construction, even a simple growth in transportation security, accompanied by a certain regulation of the exchange, must automatically produce a considerable increase of commercial circulation and by the same sign an enlivening of industry. At the present time, the most important capitalist countries, among them and far from occupying last place, the United States, preoccupied with an outlet for their automobiles, are interested in the establishment of all kinds of roads.

In order to stabilize the Chinese exchange and to mark out the roads, a large loan from abroad is required. The possibility of concluding it is discussed and recognized as quite real in the influential Anglo-Saxon financial press. They speak of an international banking consortium to amortize the old debts of China and to grant it new credits. The well-informed press is already calling the future affair "the most important in world history".

It is impossible to predict to what extent these grandiose projects will be put into effect without being better acquainted with all the documents, which relate in part to operations that take place behind the scenes. But there can be no doubt about the fact that for the near future the course of events will follow this direction. Right now, the press is bringing dozens of news items indicating that the extremely relative pacification of China and its still more relative unification have already given an impetus in the most diversified fields of economic life. A good harvest in almost the whole of China is acting in the same sense. The diagrams of domestic circulation, of imports and exports, show patent signs of progress.

Manifestly, one should not repeat the mistake committed yesterday, only the other way around. One should not attribute to semicolonial capitalist stabilization I do not know what rigid, unchangeable—in a word, metaphysical—traits. It will be a very lame stabilization, exposed to all the winds of world politics as well as to the still un-eliminated internal dangers. Nevertheless, this very relative bourgeois stabilization is radically distinguished from a revolutionary situation. To be sure, the fundamental material relations of the classes have remained the same. But the political relationships of their forces for the period in view have been rudely altered. This is expressed also by the fact that the Communist Party has been almost completely driven back to its starting point. It will have to regain its political influence by proceeding almost from the beginning.

What has been gained is experience. But this gain will be positive instead of negative on the single condition that the experience is judiciously assimilated. In the meantime, the bourgeoisie is acting with greater assurance, with greater cohesion. It has gone over to the offensive. It is setting itself great tasks for the morrow. The proletariat is falling back; it is far from always offering resistance to blows. The peasantry, deprived of any kind of centralized leadership, boils over here and there without having any real chances of success. Now, world capital is coming to the aid of the Chinese bourgeoisie with the clear intention of bowing down still lower to the ground, through the intermediary of the latter, the Chinese toiling masses. There is the mechanism of the process of stabilization. The day after tomorrow, when Bukharin runs his head into the facts, he will proclaim that heretofore the stabilization might have been considered as "incidental", but it is now clear that it is "organic".

The process of economic recovery will, in turn, correspond to the mobilization of new tens and hundreds of thousands of Chinese workers, to the tightening up of their ranks, to the increase of their specific gravity in the social life of the country and by that an increase in their revolutionary self-confidence. It is superfluous to explain that the re-animation of Chinese commerce and industry will soon give point to the problem of imperialism. However, were the Communist Party of China, influenced by the scholasticism of Bukharin and Lominadze, to turn its back to the process really taking place in the country, it would lose an economic point of support for the recovery of the workers' movement.

At the beginning, the augmentation of the specific gravity and the class self-confidence of the proletariat will make itself felt in a rebirth of the strike struggle, in the consolidation of the trade unions. It is needless to say that serious possibilities are thus opened up before the Chinese Communist Party. Nobody knows how long it will have to remain in a clandestine existence. In any case, it is necessary to reinforce and to perfect the illegal organizations in the course of the coming period. But this task cannot be accomplished outside of the life and the struggle of the masses. The illegal apparatus will have all the greater possibilities to develop itself if the legal and semi-legal organizations of the working class surround it closely and the more profoundly it will penetrate into them. The Chinese Communist Party must not have doctrinaire blinkers over its eyes, and it must keep its hands on the pulse of the economic life of the country. It must put itself at the head of strikes at the proper time, charge itself with the resurrection of the trade unions and the struggle for the eight-hour day. It is only under these conditions that its participation in the political life of the country can obtain a serious foundation.

* * *

"There cannot even be any question", said one of the Chinese delegates at the Congress, "of a consolidation of the power of the Guomindang."[5] This is false. There most assuredly can be a "question" of a certain consolidation, even fairly considerable, of the power of the Guomindang for a certain period of time, even for a fairly important period.

The Chinese bourgeoisie, with an ease which it never expected, has won decisive victories, for the period in view, against the workers and the peasants. The re-awakening of its class consciousness which followed made itself clearly felt at the economic conference which met at the end of June in Shanghai and which represented, so to speak, the economic pre-parliament of the Chinese bourgeoisie. It showed that it wanted to reap the fruits of its triumph. Across this road stand the militarists and the imperialists with whose aid it vanquished the masses. The bourgeoisie wants customs autonomy, that stumbling block to economic independence, to the completest possible unification of China; the abolition of internal customs which disorganize the market; suppression of the arbitrariness of the military authorities who confiscate the rolling stock of the railroads and encroach upon private property; finally, the reduction of armaments, which today constitute a too heavy burden upon the economy of the country. It is to this, also, that belongs the creation of a unified currency and the establishment of order in administration. The bourgeoisie has formulated all its demands in its economic pre-parliament. From the formal point of view, the Guomindang has taken note of it, but being entirely divided among the regional military cliques, it constitutes at the present time an obstacle to the realization of these measures.

The foreign imperialists represent an even stronger one. The bourgeoisie considers, and not without cause, that it will exploit the contradictions between the imperialists with all the greater success, and that it will obtain an all the more favorable compromise with them, should it be successful in compelling the military cliques of the Guomindang to submit to the centralized apparatus of the bourgeois state. It is in this sense that the aspirations of the most "progressive" elements of the bourgeoisie and of the democratic petty bourgeoisie are now being directed. It is out of this that is born the idea of the National Assembly to crown the victories won, a means of bridling the militarists, the authorized state representative of the Chinese bourgeoisie for doing business with foreign capital. The economic animation which is already visible cannot but give courage to the bourgeoisie, obliging it to regard with particular hostility anything that impairs the regularity of the circulation of merchandise and disorganizes the national market. The first stage of economic stabilization will certainly increase the chances of success of Chinese parliamentarism and will consequently require that the Chinese Communist Party give evidence, in this question too, of timely political initiative.

For the Chinese bourgeoisie, having vanquished the workers and the peasants, it can only be a question of an arch-censored assembly, perhaps by simply giving formal representation to the commercial and industrial associations on the basis of which the economic conference of Shanghai was convoked. The petty-bourgeois democracy, which will inevitably begin to stir, seeing that the revolution declines, will formulate more "democratic" slogans. In this manner, it will seek to establish contact with the higher strata of the popular masses of town and country.

The "constitutional" development of China, at least in its next stage, is intimately bound up with the internal evolution of the Guomindang, in whose hands the state power is at present concentrated in every respect. The last plenum of the Guomindang, in August, decided, so far as can be understood, to convene for the first of January 1929 the Party congress which was adjourned for so long a time owing to the centre's fear of losing power (as we see, the peculiarity of "China" is not very peculiar). The agenda of the congress includes the problem of the Chinese constitution. It is true that certain internal or external events may cause the collapse not only of the January congress of the Guomindang but also of the whole constitutional era of stabilization of the Chinese bourgeoisie. This eventuality always remains a possibility. But unless new factors intervene, the question of the state régime in China, the constitutional problems, will occupy the centre of public attention in the next period.

What attitude will the Communist Party take? What will it set up against the Guomindang's draft of a constitution? Can the Communist Party say that since it is preparing, as soon as a new rise takes place, to create soviets in the future, it makes no difference to it *up to then* whether there exists or does not exist in China a National Assembly, that it matters little if it is censored or embraces the whole people? Such an attitude would be superficial, empty and passive.

The Communist Party can and should formulate the slogan of a Constituent Assembly with full powers, elected by universal, equal, direct and secret suffrage. In the process of agitation for this slogan, it will obviously be necessary to explain to the masses that it is doubtful if such an assembly will be convened, and even if it were, it would be powerless so long as the material power remains in the hands of the Guomindang generals. From this flows the possibility of broaching in a new manner the slogan of the arming of the workers and the peasants. The revival of political activity, connected with that of economy, will once more bring the agrarian problem to the foreground. But for a certain period it may find itself posed on the parliamentary field, that is, on the field of the attempts by the bourgeoisie and primarily by the petty-bourgeois democracy to "solve" it by legislative means. Obviously, the Communist Party cannot adapt itself to bourgeois legality, that is, capitulate before bourgeois property. It can and should have its own finished and rounded-out project for the solution of the agrarian problem on the basis of the confiscation of landed property exceeding a certain area, varying in accordance with the different provinces. The Communist project of the agrarian law must be in essence the formula of the future agrarian revolution. But the Communist Party can and should introduce its own formula into the struggle for the National Assembly and into the Assembly itself, should this ever be convened.

The slogan of the National (or Constituent) Assembly is thus intimately linked up with those of the eight-hour day, the confiscation of the land and the complete national independence of China. It is precisely in these slogans that the democratic stage of the development of the Chinese Revolution will express itself. In the field of international policy, the Communist Party will demand an alliance with the USSR. By judiciously combining these slogans, by advancing each of them at the proper time, the Communist Party will be able to tear itself out of its clandestine existence, make a bloc with the masses, win their confidence, and thus speed the coming of the period of the creation of soviets and of the direct struggle for power.

Well-defined historical tasks are deduced from the democratic stage of the revolution. But by itself the democratic character of these tasks does not at all determine as yet what classes, and in which combination, will solve these problems. At bottom, all the great bourgeois revolutions solved problems of the same type, but they did it through a different class mechanism. By fighting for democratic tasks in China in the inter-revolutionary period, the Communist Party will re-assemble its forces, will check up on itself, upon its slogans and its methods of action. If it should succeed, in this connection, in passing over a period of parliamentarism (which is possible, even probable, but far from inevitable), this will permit the proletarian vanguard to scrutinize its enemies and adversaries by examining them through the prism of parliament. In the course of the pre-parliamentary and parliamentary period, this vanguard will have to conduct an intransigent struggle to win influence over the peasants, to guide the peasantry directly from the political point of view. Even if the National Assembly should be realized in an arch-democratic manner, the fundamental problems would nevertheless have to be solved by force. Through the parliamentary period, the Chinese Communist Party would arrive at a direct and immediate struggle for power, but by possessing a more mature historical basis, that is, surer premises for victory.

We have said that the existence of the parliamentary stage was probable, but not inevitable. A new disintegration of the country, as well as external causes, may prevent its realization; at all events, in the first case, a movement in favor of parliaments for various regions might come forward. But all this does not remove the importance of the struggle for a democratically convoked National Assembly which would by itself be an entering wedge between the groupings of the possessing classes and would broaden the framework of the proletariat's spirit of activity.

We know in advance that all the "leaders" who preached the bloc of the four classes, the arbitration commissions instead of strikes, who gave telegraphic orders that the agrarian movement should not be extended, who counselled that the bourgeoisie should not be terrorized, who prohibited the creation of soviets, who subordinated the Communist Party to the Guomindang, who acclaimed Wang Jingwei as the leader of the agrarian revolution—that all these opportunists, guilty of the defeat of the revolution, will now attempt to outbid the left wing and to charge our way of putting the question with containing "constitutional illusions" and a "Social-Democratic deviation". We deem it necessary to warn the Communists and the advanced Chinese workers in time against the hollow, false radicalism of yesterday's favourites of Chiang Kai-shek. One cannot rid oneself of a historical process by faked quotations, by confusion, by mile-long resolutions, in general, by every sort of apparatus and literary trick, which seeks to escape facts and classes. Events will come and furnish the test. Those for whom the tests of the past are not enough have only to wait for the future. Only, let them not forget that this verification nevertheless is effected on the bones of the proletarian vanguard.

3. The Soviets and the Constituent Assembly

We hope that it is not necessary to raise here the general question of formal, that is, of bourgeois democracy. Our attitude towards it has nothing in common with the sterile anarchist negation. The slogan and the norms of democracy, from the formal point of view, are deduced in a different way for the various countries of a well-defined stage in the evolution of bourgeois society. The democratic slogans contain for a certain period not only illusions, not only deception, but also an animating historical force.

> So long as the struggle of the working class for full power is not on the order of the day, it is our duty to utilize every form of bourgeois democracy.[6]

From the *political* point of view, the question of formal democracy is for us not only that of the attitude to be observed towards the petty-bourgeois masses, but also towards the worker masses, to the extent that the latter have not yet acquired a revolutionary class consciousness. Under the conditions of progress of the revolution, during the offensive of the proletariat, the eruption of the lower strata of the petty bourgeoisie in political life was manifested in China by agrarian revolts, by conflicts with the governmental troops, by strikes of all kinds, by the extermination of lower administrators. At the present moment, all the movements of this type are obviously diminishing. The triumphant soldiery of the Guomindang dominates society. Every day of stabilization will lead more and more to collisions between this militarism and the bureaucracy on the one hand, and on the other, not only the advanced workers but also the petty-bourgeois masses who predominate in the population of the country and towns, and even, within certain limits, the big bourgeoisie. Before these collisions develop to the point of becoming an open revolutionary struggle, they will pass, from all the available facts, through a "constitutional" stage. The conflicts between the bourgeoisie and its own military cliques will inevitably draw in the upper layer of the petty-bourgeois masses, through the medium of a "third party" or by other means. From the standpoint of economics and of culture, the former are extraordinarily feeble. Their political strength lies in their numbers. Therefore, the slogans of formal democracy win over, or are capable of winning over, not only the petty-bourgeois masses but also the broad working masses, precisely because they reveal to them the possibility, which is essentially illusory, of opposing their will to that of the generals, the country squires and the capitalists. The proletarian vanguard educates the masses by using this experience, and leads them forward.

The experience of Russia shows that during the progress of the revolution, the proletariat organized in soviets can, by a correct policy, directed towards the conquest of power, draw behind it the peasantry, fling it against the front of formal democracy embodied in the Constituent Assembly, and switch it on the rails of soviet democracy. In any case, these results were not attained by simply opposing the soviets to the Constituent Assembly, but by drawing the masses towards the soviets while maintaining the slogans of formal democracy up to the very moment of the conquest of power and even after it.

> That in the Russia of September–November 1917, the working class of the cities, the soldiers and the peasants, as a result of a number of special conditions, found themselves admirably prepared for the adoption of the soviet régime and the dissolution of the most democratic of the bourgeois parliaments—that is an undeniable and perfectly established historical fact. Yet the Bolsheviks did not boycott the Constituent Assembly; far from it, they participated in the elections not only before but even after the conquest of political power by the proletariat ...
>
> "Even a few weeks before the victory of the soviet republic, even *after* this victory, the participation in a parliament of bourgeois democracy, far from injuring the revolutionary proletariat, helps it to prove to the backward masses that these parliaments deserve to be dissolved, *facilitates* the success of their dissolution, *brings nearer* the moment when it could be said that bourgeois parliamentarism had 'had its day politically'.[7]

When we adopted direct practical measures to disperse the Constituent Assembly, I recall that Lenin insisted particularly on having sent to Petrograd one or two regiments of Lettish light infantry, composed largely of agricultural workers. "The Petrograd garrison is almost entirely peasants; may it not hesitate in face of the Constituent?" That is how Lenin formulated his preoccupations. It was not at all a question of political "traditions"; indeed, the Russian peasantry could have no serious traditions of parliamentary democracy. The essence of the question lies in the fact that the peasant mass, aroused to historical life, is not at all inclined to place confidence in advance in a leadership coming from the cities, even if it is proletarian, especially during a non-revolutionary period; this mass seeks a simple political formula which would express *directly* its own political strength, that is, the predominance of numbers. The political expression of the domination of the majority is formal democracy.

Naturally, to affirm that the popular masses can and should never and under no conditions "leap" over the "constitutional" step, would be to manifest a ridiculous pedantry in the spirit of Stalin. In certain countries, the epoch of parliamentarism lasts long decades and even centuries. In Russia, it was only prolonged for the few years of the pseudo-constitutional régime and the one day of existence of the Constituent. From the historical point of view, one can perfectly well conceive of situations where even these few years and this one day would not exist.

Also, if the revolutionary policy had been correct, if the Communist Party had been completely independent of the Guomindang, if the soviets had been established in 1925–27, the revolutionary development could already have led China today to the dictatorship of the proletariat by passing beyond the democratic phase. But even in that case, it is not impossible that the formula of the Constituent Assembly, not tried by the peasantry at the most critical moment, not tested, and consequently still containing illusions, could, at the first serious difference between the peasantry and the proletariat, on the very morrow of the victory, become the slogan of the peasants and the petty bourgeoisie of the cities against the proletariat. Important conflicts between the proletariat and the peasantry, even in face of favourable conditions for the alliance, are quite inevitable, as is witnessed by the experience of the October revolution. Our greatest advantage lay in the fact that the majority of the Constituent Assembly, which had grown in the struggle of the dominant parties for the continuation of the war and against the confiscation of the land by the peasants, had profoundly compromised itself, even in the eyes of the peasantry, already at the moment of the convocation of the Constituent Assembly.

* * *

How does the resolution of the Congress, adopted after a reading of Bukharin's report, characterize the present period of the development of China and the tasks to be deduced from this period? Paragraph 54 of this resolution says:

> At the present time, the principal task of the Party, in the period between two waves of revolutionary progress, is to fight to win the masses, that is, mass work among the workers and the peasants' the re-establishment of their organizations, the utilization of all discontentment against the landed proprietors, the bourgeoisie, the generals, the foreign imperialists ...

There is really a classic example of double meaning in the manner of the most renowned oracles of antiquity. The present period is characterized as being "between two waves of revolutionary progress". We know this formula. The Fifth Congress applied it to Germany. A revolutionary situation does not develop uniformly, but by successive waves of ebb and flow. This formula has been chosen with premeditation, so as to be able to interpret it as recognizing the existence of a revolutionary situation, in which there takes place simply a "calm" before the tempest. At all events, they will also be able to explain it by pretending to acknowledge a whole period between two revolutions. In both cases, they will be able to begin the new resolution with the words: "as we foresaw" or "as we predicted".

Every historical prognosis inevitably contains a conditional element. The shorter the period over which this prognosis extends, the greater is this element. In general, it is impossible to establish a prognosis with which the leaders of the proletariat would, in the future, no longer have need of analysing the situation. A prognosis has not the significance of command but rather of an orientation. One can and one must make reservations on the point up to which it is conditional. In certain situations, one can furnish a number of variants of the future, delimiting them with reflection. One can, finally, in a turbulent atmosphere, completely abandon prognosis for the time being and confine oneself to giving the advice: Wait and see! But all this must be done clearly, openly, honestly. However, in the course of the last five years, the prognoses of the Communist International have constituted not directives but rather traps for the leaderships of the parties of the various countries. The principal aim of the "prognoses" is: to inspire veneration towards the wisdom of the leadership, and in case of defeat, to save its "prestige", that supreme fetish of weak people. It is a method of oracular announcement and not of Marxian investigation. It presupposes the existence on the scene of action of "scapegoats". It is a demoralizing system. The ultra-leftist mistake committed by the German leadership in 1923 flowed precisely from this same perfidious, double-meaning manner of formulating the question on the subject of the "two waves of revolutionary progress". The resolution of the Sixth Congress can cause just as many misfortunes.

We have known the wave of the period before Shanghai, and then that of Wuhan. There have been many more partial and localized waves. They all rose in the general revolutionary progress of 1925–27. But this historical ascension is exhausted. This must be understood and said clearly. Important strategic consequences are to be deduced from it.

The resolution speaks of the necessity of utilizing "all discontentment against the landed proprietors, the bourgeoisie, the generals, the foreign imperialists". This is incontestable, but it is too indefinite. Utilize it how? If we find ourselves between two waves of continuous revolutionary progress, then every manifestation of discontentment, no matter how small its importance, can be considered as the famous (according to Zinoviev-Bukharin) "beginning of the second wave". Then the propaganda slogan of the armed insurrection will have to be transformed immediately into a slogan of action. From this can grow a "second wave" of putschism. The Party will utilize quite differently the discontentment of the masses, if it considers it by reckoning with a correct historical perspective. But the Sixth Congress does not possess this "bagatelle", a correct historical perspective, on any question. The Fifth Congress was a failure because of this deficiency. It is on this score that the whole Communist International can also break its neck.

After having once more condemned the putschistic tendencies for which it itself prepares the ground, the resolution of the Congress continues:

> On the other hand, certain comrades have fallen into an opportunist error: they put forward the slogan of the National Assembly.

The resolution does not explain what the opportunism of this slogan consists of. The scalded cat fears even cold water.

Only the Chinese delegate, Strakhov, in his closing speech on the lessons of the Chinese Revolution, tried to furnish an explanation. Here is what he says:

> From the experience of the Chinese revolution, we see that when the revolution in the colonies [?] draws close to the decisive moment, the question is clearly posed: Either the dictatorship of the landed proprietors and the bourgeoisie, or that of the proletariat and the peasantry.

Naturally, when the revolution (and certainly not only in the colonies) "draws close to the decisive moment", then every mode of action in the Guomindang style, that is to say, all collaborationism, is a crime involving fatal consequences: one can then conceive only of a dictatorship of the possessors or a dictatorship of the workers. But as we have already seen, even in such moments, in order to triumph over parliamentarism as revolutionists, one must have nothing in common with the sterile negation of it. Strakhov, however, goes even further:

> There [in the colonies], bourgeois democracy cannot exist; only the bourgeois dictatorship, operating openly, is possible. It cannot have there any constitutional path.

This is a doubly inexact extension of a correct thought. If, during "decisive moments" of the revolution, bourgeois democracy is inevitably torpedoed (and that not only in the colonies), this in no wise signifies that it is impossible during inter-revolutionary periods. But it is Strakhov and the whole Congress who do not want to recognize that the "decisive moment", during which it was precisely the Communists who occupied themselves with the worst democratic fictions within the Guomindang, has already passed. Now, before a new "decisive moment", a long period must be passed through, during which the *old* questions will have to be approached in a *new* manner.

To assert that in the colonies there can be no constitutional or parliamentary periods of evolution, is to renounce the utilization of methods of struggle which are essential to the highest degree, and is, above all, to make hard for oneself a correct political orientation, by driving the Party into a blind alley.

To say that for China, as, moreover, for all the other states of the world, there is no way out towards a free, in other words, a socialist development, by following the parliamentary path, is one thing, is right. But to claim that in the evolution of China, or of the colonies, there can be no constitutional period or stage, that is another thing, that is wrong. There was a parliament in Egypt, which is at the present time dissolved. It may come to life again. There is a parliament in Ireland, in spite of the semi-colonial situation of that country. The same holds true for all the states of South America, not to speak of the dominions of Great Britain. There exist semblances of "parliaments" in India. They can also develop later on: in such matters, the British bourgeoisie is pretty flexible. What reason is there for asserting that after the crushing of the revolution which has just taken place, China will not pass through a parliamentary or pseudo-parliamentary phase, or that it will not go through a serious political struggle to gain this stage of evolution? Such an assertion has no foundation at all.

The same Strakhov says that it is precisely the Chinese opportunists who aspire to substitute the slogan of the National Assembly for that of soviets. This is possible, probable, even inevitable. It was proved by all the experience of the world labor movement, of the Russian movement in particular, that the opportunists are the first to cling to parliamentary methods, in general to everything which resembles parliamentarism, or even approaches it. The Mensheviks clung to activity in the Duma *as against* revolutionary activity. The utilization of parliamentary methods inevitably brings up all the dangers connected with parliamentarism: constitutional illusions, legalism, a penchant for compromises, etc. These dangers and maladies can only be combated by a revolutionary course in policies. But the fact that the opportunists put forward the slogan of the struggle for the National Assembly in no way constitutes an argument in favor of a formal, negative attitude on our part towards parliamentarism. After the *coup d'état* of June 3, 1907 in Russia, the majority of the leading elements of the Bolshevik Party favoured boycotting the mutilated and tricked Duma. This did not prevent Lenin from coming forward resolutely in favour of the utilization of even the "parliamentarism" of June 3, at the Party conference which at that time still united the two factions.

Lenin was the only Bolshevik who voted with the Mensheviks in favour of participation in the elections. Obviously, Lenin's "participation" had nothing in common with that of the Mensheviks, as was shown by the whole subsequent march of events; it was not opposed to the revolutionary tasks, but served them for the epoch included between two revolutions. While utilizing the counter-revolutionary pseudo-parliament of June 3, our party, in spite of its great experience of the soviets of 1905, continued to conduct the struggle for the Constituent Assembly, that is, for the most democratic form of parliamentary representation. The right to renounce parliamentarism must be won by uniting the masses around the Party and by leading them to struggle openly for the conquest of power. It is naïve to think that one can simply substitute for this work the mere renunciation of the revolutionary utilization of the contradictory and oppressive methods and forms of parliamentarism. This is the crudest error of the resolution of the Congress, which makes here a flippant ultra-leftist leap.

Just see how everything is turned topsy-turvy. According to the logic of the present leadership, and in conformity with the sense of the resolutions of the Sixth Congress of the Communist International, China is not approaching its 1917, but rather its 1905. *That is why* the leaders conclude mentally: Down with the slogan of formal democracy! There really does not remain a single joint which the epigones have not taken care to dislocate. How can the slogan of democracy, and especially the most radical one, the democratic representation of the people, be rejected in the condition of a non-revolutionary period, if the revolution has not accomplished its most immediate tasks from the point of view of the unity of China and its purging of all its feudal and military-bureaucratic rubbish?

So far as I know, the Chinese party has not had a program of its own. The Bolshevik Party arrived at the October Revolution and accomplished it while armed with its old program, in the political part of which the slogans of democracy occupied an important place. In his time, Bukharin attempted to suppress this minimum program, just as he came forward later on against transitional demands in the program of the Communist International. But this attitude of Bukharin's remained recorded in the history of the Party only as an anecdote. As is known, it was the dictatorship of the proletariat which accomplished the democratic revolution in Russia. The present leadership of the Communist International absolutely does not want to understand this either. But our party led the proletariat to the dictatorship only because it defended with the greatest energy, doggedness and devotion all the slogans and demands of democracy, including popular representation based upon universal suffrage, responsibility of the government to the representatives of the people, etc. Only such an agitation permits the Party to preserve the proletariat from the influence of petty-bourgeois democracy, to undermine its influence among the peasantry, to prepare the alliance of the workers and the peasants, and to draw into its ranks the most resolute revolutionary elements. Was all this nothing but opportunism? *Spoitie, svietik, nie stydities!*

* * *

Strakhov says that we have the slogan of soviets and that only opportunists can substitute for it the slogan of the National Assembly. This argument unmasks in most exemplary manner the erroneous character of the Congress resolution. In the discussion, nobody confuted Strakhov. On the contrary, his position was approved; it was ratified in the principal tactical resolution. It is only now that one sees clearly how numerous are those in the present leadership who went through the experience of one, two, or even three revolutions, letting themselves be drawn in by the course of events and the leadership of Lenin, but without themselves reflecting upon the meaning of what was happening and without assimilating the greatest lessons of history. One is therefore obliged to repeat again certain elementary truths.

In my criticism of the program of the Communist International, I have shown how the epigones have monstrously disfigured and mutilated the thought of Lenin, which affirms that the soviets are organs of insurrection and organs of power. From it was drawn the conclusion that soviets can be created only on the "eve" of the insurrection. This grotesque idea found its most consummate expression in the same resolution, recently revealed by us, of the November Plenum of the Chinese Central Committee held last year. It says there:

> Soviets can and should be created as organs of revolutionary power only when we are in the midst of an important, incontestable progress of the revolutionary movement of the masses and when the solid victory of the uprising is *assured*.

The first condition: "important progress", is incontestable. The second condition: "guarantee of victory", and what is more, of a "solid" one, is simply pedantic stupidity. In the rest of the text of the resolution this stupidity, however, is developed at length:

> The creation of soviets obviously cannot be approached when victory is not yet absolutely guaranteed, for it might then happen that all attention is concentrated solely upon elections to the soviets and not upon the military struggle, as a consequence of which petty-bourgeois democratism might install itself, which would weaken the revolutionary dictatorship and would create a danger for the leadership of the Party.

The spirit of Stalin, refracted through the prism of the infant prodigy, Lominadze, hovers over these immortal lines. However, all this is simply absurd. During the Hong Kong strike, during the Shanghai strikes, during all the subsequent violent progress of the workers and the peasants, soviets should and could have created as organs of an open revolution mass struggle which, *sooner or later* and not at all at one blow, would lead to the insurrection and the conquest of power. If, in the phase under consideration, the struggle did not rise to the point of insurrection, obviously the soviets too would be reduced to nothing. They cannot become "normal" institutions of the bourgeois state. But in that case, too, that is, if the soviets are liquidated before the insurrection, the working masses make an enormous acquisition, familiarizing themselves with the soviets in practice, identifying themselves with their mechanism. During the following stage of the revolution, the more successful and more extensive creation of soviets will thus be guaranteed: although, even in the phase that follows it may be that they do not lead directly, not only to victory, but even not to the insurrection.

Let us recall this very distinctly: the slogan of soviets can and must be put forward from the first stages of the revolutionary progress of the masses. But it must be a real progress. The working masses must flock to the revolution, rally under its standard. The soviets furnish an expression, from the organizational point of view, to the centripetal force of revolutionary progress. But in this way, it holds true at the same time that during the period of revolutionary ebb-tide and of the development of centrifugal tendencies in the masses, the—slogan of soviets will be doctrinaire, lifeless, or what is just as bad, it will be the slogan of adventurists. The Canton experience showed this better than anything else, in a striking and tragic manner.

At the present time, the slogan of soviets in China has an importance only from the point of view of perspective, and in this sense it has a propaganda value. One would not be conforming to anything at all by opposing the soviets, the slogan of the third Chinese Revolution, to the National Assembly, that is, to the slogan that flows from the débâcle of the second Chinese Revolution. Abstentionism, in an inter-revolutionary period, especially after a cruel defeat, would be a suicidal policy.

One might say (for there are many sophists in the world) that the resolution of the Sixth Congress does not at all mean abstentionism: there is no National Assembly, nobody is as yet convoking it or promising to convoke it, consequently there is nothing to boycott. Such reasoning, however, would be too pitiable, purely formal, infantile, Bukharinistic. If the Guomindang were compelled to proclaim the convocation of a National Assembly, would we boycott it in the given situation? No. We would pitilessly unmask the lie and duplicity of the Guomindang's parliamentarism, the constitutional illusions of the petty bourgeoisie: we would demand the complete extension of electoral rights; at the same time we would throw ourselves into the political arena to oppose, in the struggle for the parliament, in the course of the elections and in the parliament itself, the workers and the poor peasants to the possessing class and their parties. Nobody would presume to foretell how great would be the results thus obtained for the present party, debilitated and reduced to a clandestine existence. If the policy were correct, the advantages could be very considerable. But in this case, is it not clear that the Party can and must not only participate in the elections if the Guomindang promulgates them, but also demand that they be held by mobilizing the masses around this slogan?

From the political point of view the question is already posed, every new day will confirm it. In our criticism of the program, we spoke of the probability of a certain economic stabilization in China. The newspapers have since then brought dozens of indications of the economic revival that is beginning (see the Bulletin of the Chinese University). Now it is no longer a supposition, but a fact, even though it is only in its very first phase. But it is just in the course of the first phase that the tendencies must be perceived, otherwise it will not be a revolutionary policy that is pursued, but a dragging at the tail of events.

The same holds true for the political struggle around the questions of the constitution. This is now no longer a theoretical forecast, that is, a simple possibility, but something more concrete. It is not for nothing that the Chinese delegate frequently recurs to the theme of the National Assembly; it is not by chance that the Congress thought it necessary to adopt a special (and a particularly false) resolution on the subject of this question. It is not the Opposition which has posed this question, but rather the evolution of Chinese political life. Here too one must know how to perceive a tendency at the very outset. The more audaciously and resolutely the Communist Party comes forward with the slogan of the democratic Constituent Assembly, the less place it will leave all sorts of intermediary parties, the more solid will be its own success.

If the Chinese proletariat is obliged to live a few more years (even if it were only another year) under the régime of the Guomindang, could the Chinese Communist Party abandon the struggle for the extension of legal possibilities of all sorts, for the freedom of press, of assembly, of organization, of strike, etc.? Were it to abandon this struggle, it would transform itself into a lifeless sect. But that is a struggle on the democratic plane. Soviet power signifies the monopoly of the press, of assembly, etc., in the hands of the proletariat. Perhaps the Chinese Communist Party will put forward these slogans precisely at this time? In the situation under consideration, it would be a mixture of childishness and madness. The Communist Party is fighting at present not for power, but to maintain, to consolidate and to develop its contact with the masses for the sake of the struggle for power in the future. The struggle to win the masses is inevitably bound up with the struggle conducted against the violence which the Guomindang bureaucracy practices towards the mass organizations, their meetings, their press, etc. During the period that is to follow immediately, will the Communist Party fight for freedom of the press or will it leave this to be done by a "third party"? Will the Communist Party confine itself to presenting democratic, isolated, partial demands (freedom of the press, of assembly, etc.), which would amount to liberal reformism, or will it put forward the most consistent slogans of democracy? In the political sphere, this signifies popular representation based upon universal suffrage.

* * *

One might ask if the Democratic Constituent Assembly is "realizable" after a defeated revolution in a semi-colonial China encircled by the imperialists. This question can only be answered by conjectures. But the simple criterion of the possibility of realizing some demand, in the face of conditions existing in bourgeois society or in a given state of this society, is not decisive for us. It is very probable, for example, that the monarchical power and the House of Lords will not be swept away before the establishment of the revolutionary dictatorship of the proletariat. Nevertheless, the British Communist Party must formulate among its partial demands this one as well.

It is not by devoting oneself to empirical conjectures as to the possibility of realizing some transitional demand or not, that the question relating to it is settled. It is its social and historical character that decides: is it progressive from the point of view of the subsequent development of society? Does it correspond to the historical interests of the proletariat? Does it strengthen the consciousness of the latter? Does it bring it closer to its dictatorship? Thus for example, the demand for the prohibition of trusts is petty-bourgeois and reactionary and, as the experiences of America have shown, it is completely utopian. Under certain conditions, on the contrary, it is entirely progressive and correct to demand workers' control over the trusts, even though it is more than doubtful that this will ever be realized within the framework of the bourgeois state. The fact that this demand is not satisfied so long as the bourgeoisie rules must push the workers to the revolutionary overthrow of the latter. Thus, the impossibility of realizing a slogan from the political point of view can be no less fruitful than the relative possibility of putting it into practice.

Will China come for a certain period to democratic parliamentarism? What will be the degree of its democratism? What strength and what duration will it have? All this is a matter of conjecture. But it would be radically wrong to base oneself on the supposition that parliamentarism is unrealizable in China in order to conclude that we cannot hale the cliques of the Guomindang before the tribunal of the Chinese people. The idea of the representation of the entire people, as has been shown by the experience of all the bourgeois revolutions and especially those which liberated nationalities, is the most elementary, the most simple and the one most apt to embrace really vast popular strata. The more the ruling bourgeoisie resists this demand of the "entire people", and the more the proletarian vanguard rallies around our banner, the riper the political conditions will become to win the real victory against the bourgeois state, little matter whether it be the military state of the Guomindang or the parliamentary.

It may be said: a real Constituent Assembly will not be convoked except through the soviets, that is through the insurrection. Would it not be simpler to begin with soviets and to confine oneself to them? No, it would not be simpler. It would be just like putting the cart before the horse. It is very likely that it will not be possible to convoke the Constituent Assembly except through the soviets and that in this way the Assembly might become superfluous even before its birth. This may happen, just as it may not happen. If the soviets, through whose medium a "real" Constituent Assembly might be called together, were already here, we would see if it was still necessary to proceed with its convocation. But there are no soviets at the present time. One cannot start to establish them except at the beginning of a new advance of the masses, which may take place in two or three years, in five years, or more. There are no soviet traditions at all in China. The Communist International conducted an agitation in that country against soviets and not in favour of them. In the meantime, however, constitutional questions are beginning to emerge from every cranny.

Can the Chinese Revolution, in the course of its new stage, leap over formal democracy? It follows from what has been said above that, from the historical point of view, such a possibility is not excluded. But it is entirely inadmissible to approach the question guided by this possibility, which is the most distant and the least likely. It is to manifest light-mindedness in the political domain. The Congress adopts its decisions for more than one month, and even, as we know, for more than a year. How then can the Chinese Communists be left bound hand and foot, by designating as opportunism the form of political struggle which, from the next stage onwards, may acquire the greatest importance?

* * *

It is incontestable that by entering the path of struggle for the Constituent Assembly, the Menshevik tendencies in the Chinese

Communist Party may be revived and strengthened. It is no less important to fight against opportunism when the policy is directed towards parliamentarism or towards the struggle for it, than when one is confronted with a direct revolutionary offensive. But, as has already been said, it does not follow from this that the democratic slogans should be called opportunistic, but that guarantees and Bolshevik methods of struggle for these slogans must be worked out. In broad outline, these methods and guarantees are the following:

1. The Party must have in mind and must explain that in comparison with its principal aim, the conquest of power with arms in hand, the democratic slogans have only an auxiliary, a provisional, an episodic character. Their fundamental importance consists of the fact that they permit us to debouch on the revolutionary road.
2. In the process of the struggle for these slogans of democracy, the Party must shatter the constitutional and democratic illusions of the petty bourgeoisie and of the reformists who express their opinions, by explaining that power in the state is not obtained by the democratic forms of the vote, but by property and by the monopoly of information and armaments.
3. While making full use of the differences of views existing within the petty and the big bourgeoisie on the subject of constitutional questions; while opening up every possible road towards an openly exercised field of activity; while fighting for the legal existence of the trade unions, the workers' clubs, the labour press; while creating, whenever and wherever possible, legal political organizations of the proletariat under the direct influence of the Party; while trying as soon as possible to legalize more or less the various fields of activity of the Party; the latter must above all assure the existence of its illegal, centralized, well-built apparatus, directing all the branches of the Party's activity, legal as well as illegal.
4. The Party must develop systematic revolutionary work among the troops of the bourgeoisie.

5. The leadership of the Party must implacably unmask all the opportunist hesitations seeking a reformist solution of the problems confronting the proletariat of China and must cut off all the elements who consciously pull towards the subordination of the Party to bourgeois legalism.

It is only by taking these conditions into account that the Party will preserve the necessary proportions in the various branches of its activity, will not let pass a new turn in the situation which leads towards a revolutionary advance, so that its first steps proceed along the road of the creation of soviets, of mobilizing the masses around them and of opposing them to the bourgeois state, with all its parliamentary and democratic camouflage, should this happen to be realized.

4. Once More on the Slogan of the Democratic Dictatorship

The slogan of the Constituent Assembly is just as little opposed to the formula of the democratic dictatorship as it is to that of the dictatorship of the proletariat. Theoretical analysis and the history of our three revolutions indicate that.

In Russia, the formula of the democratic dictatorship of the proletariat and the peasantry was the algebraic expression, in other words, the most general, the broadest expression of the collaboration of the proletariat and the lower strata of the peasantry in the democratic revolution. The logic of this formula was conditioned by the fact that its fundamental magnitude had not been checked up in action. In particular, it was not possible to predict quite categorically if, in the conditions of the new epoch, the peasantry would be capable of becoming a more or less *independent* political power, to what extent it would be such, and what would the reciprocal political relations of the allies in the dictatorship which would result from it.

The year 1905 did not bring the question to the point of a decisive verification. The year 1917 showed that when the peasantry bears on its back a party (the Socialist Revolutionaries) independent of the vanguard of the proletariat, this party proves to be in complete dependence upon the imperialist bourgeoisie. In the course of the period from 1905 to 1917, the growing imperialist transformation of the petty-bourgeois democracy as well as of international Social Democracy, made gigantic progress. It was because of this that in 1917 the slogan of the democratic dictatorship of the proletariat and the peasantry was really realized in the dictatorship of the proletariat, drawing with it the peasant masses. By this very token, the "transformation by growth" of the revolution, passing from the democratic phase to the socialist stage, took place with the dictatorship of the proletariat already established.

In China, the slogan of the democratic dictatorship of the proletariat and the peasantry might still have had a certain political logic, much more limited and episodic than in Russia, if it had been formulated at the right time in 1925–26, in order to test out the animating forces of the revolution, so as to be replaced, also at the right time, by the dictatorship of the proletariat, drawing behind it the poor peasants. All that is necessary has been said about this in 'The Criticism of the Draft Program'. Here, it still remains to ask: Does not the present inter-revolutionary period, bound up with a new regrouping of class forces, allow one to discern possibilities of the rebirth of the slogan of the democratic dictatorship? To this we reply: No, it makes this possibility disappear completely.

The period of inter-revolutionary stabilization corresponds to the development of the productive forces, to the growth of the national bourgeoisie, to the growth and the increase of the cohesion of the proletariat, to the accentuation of the differentiation in the villages and to the continuation of the capitalist degeneration of democracy *à la* Wang Jingwei or any other petty-bourgeois democrat, with their "third party", etc. In other words, China will pass through processes analogous in their broad outlines to those through which Russia passed under the régime of June 3. We were certain in our time that this régime would not be eternal, nor of long duration, and that it would terminate by a revolution. That is what happened (somewhat aided by the war). But the Russia which came out of the régime of Stolypin was no longer what it had been when it entered it.

The social changes which the inter-revolutionary régime will introduce in China depend especially upon the duration of this régime. But the general tendency of these modifications is henceforth indisputable: it is the sharpening of the class contradictions and the complete elimination of the petty-bourgeois democracy as an independent political power. But this signifies precisely that in the third Chinese Revolution, a "democratic" coalition of the political parties would acquire a still more reactionary and more anti-proletarian content than that of the Guomindang in 1925–27. There is therefore nothing left to do but to make a coalition of classes under the direct leadership of the proletarian vanguard. That is the road of October. It involves many difficulties, but there exists no other.

5. APPENDIX

A Remarkable Document on the Policy and the Régime of the Communist International

We referred above several times to the remarkable resolution of the Plenum of the Central Committee of the Chinese Communist Party (November 1927), precisely the one which the Ninth Plenum of the Executive Committee of the Communist International charged with "Trotskyism", and about which Lominadze justified himself in such a variegated manner while Stalin very monotonously slunk off in silence. In reality, this resolution is a combination of opportunism and adventurism, reflecting with perfect precision the policy of the Executive Committee of the Communist International before and after July 1927. In condemning this resolution *after the defeat of the Canton insurrection*, the leaders of the Communist International not only did not publish it but did not even quote from it. It was too embarrassing for them to show themselves in the Chinese mirror. This resolution was published in a special Documentation, accessible to very few, printed by the Chinese Sun Yat Sen University (no.10).

No. 14 of the same publication, which reached our hands when our work (The Chinese Question after the Sixth Congress) was already completed, contains a no less remarkable document, even though of a different, that is, of a critical character: it is a resolution adopted by the Kiangsu District Committee of the Chinese Communist Party on May 7, 1928, in connection with the decisions of the Ninth Plenum of the Executive Committee of the Comintern. Remember that Shanghai and Canton are part of the province of Kiangsu.

This resolution, as has already been said, constitutes a truly remarkable document, in spite of the errors in principle and the political misunderstandings it contains. The essence of the Resolution amounts to a deadly condemnation not only of the decisions of the Ninth Plenum of the Executive Committee of the Communist International, but in general, of the whole leadership of the Comintern in the questions of the Chinese revolution. Naturally, in conformity with the whole régime existing in the Comintern, the criticism directed against the Executive Committee of the CI bears a camouflaged and conventionally diplomatic character. The immediate point of the resolution is directed against the Central Committee itself as against a responsible ministry under an irresponsible monarch who, as is known, "can do no wrong". There are even polite eulogies for certain parts of the resolution of the ECCI. This whole way of approaching the question by "manoeuvring" is in itself a harsh criticism of the régime of the Communist International; hypocrisy is inseparable from bureaucratism. But what the resolution says in essence about the political leadership and its methods has a much more damning character.

> "After the August 7 (1927) conference," the Kiangsu Committee relates, "the Central Committee formulated a judgement on the situation which was tantamount to saying that even though the revolution had suffered a triple defeat, it is nevertheless going through a rising phase."

This appreciation is entirely in conformity with the caricature which Bukharin makes of the theory of the permanent revolution, a caricature which he applied first to Russia, then to Europe and finally to Asia. The actual events of the struggle, that is, the three defeats, are one thing and the permanent "rise" is another.

The Central Committee of the Chinese party draws the following conclusion from the resolution adopted by the Eighth

Plenum of the Executive Committee of the Communist International (in May):

> Wherever this is objectively possible, we must *immediately* prepare and organize armed insurrections.

What are the political premises for this? The Kiangsu Committee declares that in August 1927

> the political report of the Central Committee pointed out that the *workers* of Hunan, after the cruel *defeat, are abandoning the leadership of the Party,* that we are not confronted with an objectively revolutionary situation ... but in spite of this ... the Central Committee says plainly that the general situation, from the economic, political and social [precisely! – *L.T.*] point of view is favourable to the insurrection. Since *it is already no longer possible to launch revolts in the cities,* the armed struggle must be transferred to the villages. That is where the centres of the uprising must be, while the town must be an auxiliary force. (p. 4)

Let us recall that immediately after the May Plenum of the Executive Committee of the Communist International, which entrusted the leadership of the agrarian revolution to the Left Guomindang, the latter began to exterminate the workers and peasants. The position of the ECCI became completely untenable. At all costs, there had to be, and that without delay, "left" actions in China to refute the "calumny" of the Opposition, that is, its irreproachable prognosis. That is why the Chinese Central Committee, which found itself between the hammer and the anvil, was obliged, in August 1927, to turn the proletarian policy topsy-turvy all over again. Even though there was no revolutionary situation and the working masses were abandoning the Party, this Committee declared that the economic and social situation was, in its opinion, "favourable to the insurrection". In any case, a triumphant uprising would have been very "favourable" to the prestige of the Executive Committee of the Comintern. Given the fact that the workers were abandoning the revolution, it was therefore necessary to turn one's back to the towns and endeavour to launch isolated uprisings in the villages.

Already at the May Plenum (1927) of the ECCI, we pointed out that the adventurist uprisings of Ho Lung and Ye Ting were inevitably doomed to defeat because of insufficient political preparation and because they were bound up with no movement of the masses. That is just what happened. The resolution of the Kiangsu Committee says on this subject:

> In spite of the defeat of the armies of Ho Lung and Ye Ting in Guangdong, even after the November Plenum the Central Committee persists in clinging to the tactic of immediate uprisings and takes as its point of departure an estimation leading to the direct ascent of the revolution.

For understandable reasons, the Kiangsu Committee passes in silence over the fact that this appreciation was also that of the Executive Committee of the Comintern itself, which treated as "liquidators" those who correctly estimated the situation, and the fact that the Chinese Central Committee was forced, in November 1927, on pain of being immediately overthrown and expelled from the Party, to present the decline of the revolution as its rise.

The Canton insurrection sprang up by basing itself upon this tip-tilted manner of approaching the question; manifestly, this uprising was not regarded as a rearguard battle (only raging madmen could have urged passing over to the insurrection and to the conquest of power through a "rearguard battle"); no, this uprising was conceived as part of a general *coup d'état*. The Kiangsu resolution says on this point:

> During the Canton insurrection of December, the Central Committee decided once more to launch an immediate uprising in Hunan, Hupeh and Kiangsu in order to defend Guangdong, in order to extend the framework of the movement all over China (this can be verified from the information letters of the Central Committee, nos. 16 and 22). These measures flowed from a subjective estimation of the situation and did not correspond to the objective circumstances. Obviously, under such conditions defeats will be inevitable. (p.5)

The Canton experience frightened the leaders not only of China but also of Moscow. A warning was issued against putschism, but in essence the political line did not change. The orientation remained the same: towards insurrection. The Central Committee of the Chinese Communist Party transmitted this ambiguous instruction to the lower bodies; it also warned against the tactic of skirmishes, while setting down in its circulars academic definitions of adventurism.

"But being given the fact that the Central Committee based itself in its estimation of the revolutionary movement, upon an uninterrupted advance," as the Kiangsu resolution says correctly and pointedly,

> no modifications were brought into this question at the bottom. The forces of the enemy are far too greatly underrated and at the same time, no attention is paid to the fact that our organizations have lost contact with the masses. Therefore, in spite of the fact that the Central Committee had sent its information letter no.28 (on putschism) everywhere, it did not at the same time correct its mistakes. (p.5)

Once more, it is not a question of the Central Committee of the Chinese party. The February Plenum of the Executive Committee of the Communist International introduced no modifications into its policy either. While warning against the tactics of skirmishes in general (in order to insure itself against all eventualities), the resolution of this Plenum pounced furiously upon the Opposition which spoke of the necessity of a resolute change in the whole orientation. In February 1928, the course continued as before to lead towards insurrection. The Central Committee of the Chinese Communist Party only served as a mechanism to transmit this instruction. The Kiangsu Committee says:

> The Central Committee circular no.38, of March 6 [take careful note: March 6, 1928! – *L.T.*] shows very clearly that the Central Committee still finds itself under the influence of illusions about a favourable situation for general insurrection in Hunan, Hupeh and Kiangsu, and the possibility of conquering power throughout the province of Guangdong. The radical quarrel over the choice of Changsha or Hankow as the centre of insurrection still continued between—the Political Bureau of the Central Committee and the instructor of the Central Committee in Hunan and Hupeh. (p.5)

Such was the disastrous significance of the resolution of the February Plenum, not only false in principle, but deliberately ambiguous from the practical point of view. The thought concealed behind this resolution was always the same: if, contrary to expectations, the uprising extends itself, we shall refer to that part which speaks against the liquidators; if the insurrection goes no further than partisan affrays, we will point a finger at that part of the resolution which warns against putschism.

Even though the Kiangsu resolution nowhere dares to criticize the Executive Committee of the Communist International (everybody knows what this costs), nevertheless, in none of its documents has the Opposition dealt such deadly blows to the leadership of the Comintern as does the Kiangsu Committee in its arrangment, aimed formally at the Central Committee of the Chinese Communist Party. After listing chronologically the policies of adventurism month after month, the resolution turns to the general causes for the disastrous course.

> "How is one to explain," asks the resolution, "this erroneous estimation of the situation established by the Central Committee which influenced the practical struggle and contained serious errors? It is to be explained as follows:
>
> 1. The revolutionary movement was estimated as an uninterrupted ascent [the "permanent revolution" *à la* Bukharin-Lominadze! – *L.T.*].
>
> 2. No attention was paid to the loss of contact between our party and the masses, nor to the decomposition of the mass organizations at the turning point of the revolution.
>
> 3. No account was taken of the new regrouping of class forces inside the enemy camp during this turn.
>
> 4. No consideration was given to leading the movement in the cities.
>
> 5. No attention was paid to the importance of the anti-imperialist movement in a semicolonial country.
>
> 6. During the insurrection, no account was taken of the objective conditions, nor of the necessity of applying different methods of struggle in conformity with them.
>
> 7. A peasant deviation made itself felt.
>
> 8. The Central Committee, in its estimation of the situation, was guided by a subjective point of view."

It is doubtful if the Kiangsu Committee has read what the Opposition wrote and said on all these questions. One can even say with certainty that it did not read it. As a matter of fact, if it had, it would have feared to formulate with such precision its considerations, coinciding entirely in this part with ours. The Kiangsu Committee repeated our words without suspecting it.

The eight points enumerated above, characterizing the false line of the Central Committee (that is, the Executive Committee of the Communist International) are equally important. If we wish to say a few words on the fifth point, it is simply because we have here a particularly striking confirmation "by facts" of the justice of our criticism in its most essential features. The Kiangsu resolution charges the policy of the Central Committee with neglecting the problems of the anti-imperialist movement in a semicolonial country. How could this happen? By the force of the dialectic of the false political line; mistakes have their dialectic like everything else in the world. The point of departure of official opportunism was that the Chinese Revolution is essentially an anti-imperialist revolution, and that the yoke of imperialism welds together all the classes or at the very least "all the living forces of the country". We objected that a successful struggle against imperialism is only possible by means of an audacious extension of the class struggle, and consequently, of the agrarian revolution. We rose up intransigently against the attempt to subordinate the class struggle to the abstract criterion of the struggle against imperialism (substitution of arbitration commissions for the strike movement, telegraphic advice not to stir up the agrarian revolution, prohibiting the formation of soviets, etc.). This was the first stage of the question. After Chiang Kai-shek's *coup d'état*, and especially after the "treason" of the "friend" Wang Jingwei, there was a turn about face of 180 degrees. Now, it turns out to be that the question of customs independence, that is, of the economic "(and consequently, the political)" sovereignty of China is a secondary "bureaucratic" problem (Stalin).

The essence of the Chinese Revolution was supposed to consist of the agrarian upheaval. The concentration of power in the hands of the bourgeoisie, the abandonment of the revolution by the workers, the schism between the Party and the masses, were appraised as secondary phenomena in comparison with the peasant revolts. Instead of a genuine hegemony of the proletariat, in the anti-imperialist as well as in the agrarian struggle, that is, in the democratic revolution as a whole, there took place a wretched capitulation before the primitive peasant forces, with "secondary" adventures in the cities. However, such a capitulation is the fundamental premise of putschism. The whole history of the revolutionary movement in Russia, as well as in other countries, is witness to that. The events in China of the past year have confirmed it.

In its estimation and its warnings, the Opposition took as its point of departure general theoretical considerations, basing itself upon official information, very incomplete and sometimes deliberately distorted. The Kiangsu Committee has as its point of departure facts which it observed directly at the centre of the revolutionary movement; from the theoretical point of view this Committee still writhes in the toils of Bukharinist scholasticism. The fact that its empirical conclusions coincide completely with our own has, in politics, the same significance as, for example, the discovery in laboratories of a new element whose existence was predicted in advance on the basis of theoretical deductions has in chemistry. Unfortunately, the triumph from the theoretical point of view of our Marxian analysis, in the case before us, has as its political foundation mortal defeats for the revolution.

* * *

The abrupt and essentially adventurist turn in the policy of the Executive Committee of the Communist International in the middle of 1927 could not but provoke painful shocks in the Chinese Communist Party, which was taken off its guard by it. Here we pass from the political line of the Executive Committee of the Communist International to the régime of the Comintern and to the organizational methods of the leadership. Here is what the Kiangsu Committee resolution says on this point:

> After the conference of August 7 (1927), the Central Committee should have assumed the responsibility for the putschist tendencies, for it demanded rigorously of the local committees

> that the *new political line* be applied; if anybody was not in agreement with *the new line*, without further ceremony he was not permitted to renew his party card and even comrades who had already carried out this operation were expelled At this time, the putschist mood was making headway throughout the Party; if anybody expressed doubts about the policy of uprisings, he was immediately called an opportunist and pitilessly attacked. This circumstance provoked great friction within the Party organizations. (p.6)

All this took place with the accompaniment of pious academic warnings against the dangers of putschism "in general".

The policy of the sudden, hastily improvised armed insurrection demanded a speedy overhauling and a regrouping of the entire Party. The Central Committee tolerated in the Party only those who silently acknowledged the course of armed insurrection in the face of an obvious decline of the revolution. It would be well to publish the instructions furnished by the Executive Committee of the Communist International during this period. They could be reduced to one: an instruction for the organization of defeat. The Kiangsu resolution sets forth that

> The Central Committee continues not to take notice of the defeats and the depressed mood of the workers; it does not see that this situation is the result of the mistakes of its leadership. (p.6.)

But that is not all:

"The Central Committee accuses someone or other [just so! – *L.T.*] for the fact that:

> (a) *the local committees have not sufficiently well checked up on the reorganization;*
> (b) *the worker and peasant elements are not pushed ahead;*
> (c) *the local organizations are not purged of opportunist elements, etc."*

All this happens abruptly, by telegraph: somehow or other, the mouth of the Opposition must be closed. But nevertheless since matters are in a bad way, the Central Committee asserts that: "the disposition of the masses would be entirely different if the signal for revolt had been given at least in one single province. Does not this last indication bespeak a one hundred per cent putschism of the Central Committee itself?" (page 6) asks the

Kiangsu Committee with full justice, passing prudently over in silence that the Central Committee only executed the instructions of the Executive Committee of the Communist International.

For five years the Party was led and educated in an opportunist spirit. At the present moment, it is demanded of it that it be ultra-radical and "that it immediately put forward" worker-leaders. How? ... Very simply: by fixing a certain percentage of them. The Kiangsu Committee complains:

1. No account is taken of the fact that the ones who are to supplement the leading cadres should be advanced in the course of the struggle. Whereas the Central Committee confines itself to a formal establishment of a percentage fixed in advance of workers and peasants in the leading organs of the various organizations.
2. In spite of the numerous failures, they do not examine the point to which our party is already restored, but they simply say formally that it is necessary to reorganize:
3. The Central Committee simply says dictatorially that the local organizations do not put forward new elements, that they do not rid themselves of opportunism; at the same time, the Central Committee makes baseless attacks upon the militants of the cadres and replaces them light-mindedly.
4. Without paying attention to the mistakes of its own leadership, the Central Committee nevertheless demands the most severe party discipline from the rank-and-file militants.

Does it not seem as though all these paragraphs are copied from the Platform of the Opposition? No, they are copied from life. But since the *Platform* is also copied from life, there is no coincidence. Where then is the "peculiarity" of Chinese conditions? Bureaucratism levels down each and every peculiarity. The policy as well as the régime are determined by the Executive Committee of the Communist International, more exactly by the Central Committee of the Communist Party of the Soviet Union. The Central Committee of the Chinese Communist Party drives both of them down into the lower organs. Here is how this takes place according to the Kiangsu resolution:

The following declaration made by a comrade of a district

> committee is very characteristic: 'At present it is very difficult to work; but the Central Committee shows that it has a very subjective manner of regarding the problem. It pounces down with accusations and says that the Provincial Committee is no good; the latter in its turn accuses the rank-and-file organizations and asserts that the district committee is bad. The latter also begins to accuse and asserts that it is the comrades working on the spot who are no good. And the comrades declare that the masses are not revolutionary'. (p.8)

There you really have a striking picture. Only, there is nothing peculiarly Chinese about it.

Every resolution of the Executive Committee of the Communist International, in registering new defeats, declares that on the one hand all had been foreseen and that on the other it is the "executors" who are the cause of the defeats because they did not understand the line that had been pointed out to them from above. It remains unexplained how the perspicacious leadership was able to foresee everything save that the executors did not measure up to its instructions. The essential thing in the leadership does not consist of presenting an abstract line, of writing a letter without an address, but of selecting and educating the executors. The correctness of the leadership is tested precisely in execution. The reliability and perspicacity of the leadership are confirmed only when words and deeds harmonize. But if chronically, from one stage to the other, in the course of many years, the leadership is obliged *post factum* to complain at every turn that it has not been understood, that its ideas have been deformed, that the executors have ruined its plan, that is a sure sign that the fault devolves entirely upon the leadership. This "self-criticism" is all the more murderous by the fact that it is involuntary and unconscious. According to the Sixth Congress, the leadership of the Opposition must be held responsible for every group of turncoats; but *per contra* the leadership of the Communist International should in no wise have to answer for the Central Committee of all the national parties in the most decisive historical moments. But a leadership which is answerable for nothing is an irresponsible leadership. In that is to be found the root of all the evils.

In protecting itself against the criticism of the ranks, the Central Committee of the Chinese Communist Party bases itself on the Executive Committee of the Communist International, that is, it draws a chalk line on the floor which cannot be stepped over. Nor does the Kiangsu Committee overstep it. But within the confines of this chalk line, it tells some bitter truths to its Central Committee which automatically extend to the Executive Committee of the Communist International. We are once more forced to quote an extract from the remarkable document of Kiangsu:

> The Central Committee says that the whole past leadership was exercised in accordance with the instructions of the Communist International. As if all these hesitations and errors depended only upon the rank-and-file militants. If one adopts such a manner of regarding the question, the Central Committee will itself be unable either to repair the mistakes or to educate the comrades to study this experience. It will not be able to strengthen its ties with the lower Party apparatus. The Central Committee always says that its leadership was right; it charges the rank-and-file comrades with all the mistakes, always especially underscoring the hesitations of the rank-and-file Party committees.

A little further on:

> If the leadership only attacks light-mindedly the local leading comrades or organs by pointing out their errors, but without actually analysing the source of these mistakes, this only produces friction within the Party; such an attitude is disloyal ["rude and disloyal" – *L.T.*] and can do no good to the revolution and to the Party. If the leadership itself covers up its errors and throws the blame on others, such conduct will do no good to the Party or to the revolution. (p.10)

A simple but classic characterization of bureaucratic centrism's work of decaying and devastating the consciousness.

The Kiangsu resolution shows in an entirely exemplary manner how and by what methods the Chinese Revolution was led to numerous defeats, and the Chinese party to the brink of catastrophe. For the imaginary hundred thousand members who figure on paper in the Chinese Communist Party only represent a gross self-deception. They would then constitute one-sixth of the total membership of the Communist parties of all the capitalist countries. The payments which Chinese Communism must make for the crime of the leadership are still far from completed.

Further decline is ahead. There will be great difficulty in rising again. Every false step will fling the Party into a deeper ditch. The resolution of the Sixth Congress dooms the Chinese Communist Party to errors and false steps. With the present course of the Communist International, under its present régime, victory is impossible. The course must be changed. This is what the resolution of the Kiangsu Provincial Committee says once more.

NOTES

1. L. Trotsky, *Five Years of the Communist International*, p. 333.
2. Lenin, *The Proletarian Revolution and the Renegade Kautsky*, *Works*, Vol. XV, p. 499.
3. *Lenin,* Report at the Meeting of the All-Russia CEC, Works, Vol. XX, part 2, p. 217.
4. It goes without saying that *Pravda* has not published this resolution to which we have already referred above. It can only be found in the *Material on the Chinese Question* (no.10, 1928, issued by the Chinese Sun Yat-Sen University), and is very hard to procure. It is this same resolution that is officially charged with "Trotskyism", although it is, in reality, nothing but Stalinist-Bukharinist opportunism upside down. – *L.T.*
5. *Pravda,* August 28, 1928.
6. *Lenin,* Report at the 2nd All-Russia Trade Union congress, *Works, January 20, 1919,* Vol. XX, Part 2, p. 298.
7. Lenin, *Works,* Vol. XVII, 1920; *The Infantile Sickness of Communism,* p.149.

33

China and the Constituent Assembly

December 1928

Certain comrades, while completely agreeing with my point of view in estimating the forces behind the Chinese Revolution and in assessing the perspectives of this revolution, raise objections to the democratic slogan of the constituent assembly. Naturally this difference of opinion does not have the same importance from the standpoint of principles as the problem of evaluating the main tendencies and forces of the revolution. Nevertheless, at a certain point this question can acquire an enormous importance as was the case with the Bolsheviks in regard to the attitude to be taken toward the Third Duma. To my great surprise, one comrade, in criticizing the slogan for a constituent assembly, seriously claimed to see in this a manoeuver that I was supposedly carrying out with the aim of "deceiving" the Chinese bourgeoisie. It was for this reason that he cited against me a quotation drawn from my "Criticism of the Draft Program of the Communist International" that began with the following words: "Classes cannot be deceived...," etc.

There is an obvious misunderstanding here of the greatest importance. Everything of political significance on the slogan of the constituent assembly for China has been said in my essay, "The Chinese Question after the Sixth Congress". I will not repeat it here. If one looks in the "Criticism of the Draft Program" for the general theoretical basis given to the argumentation on this slogan, it will be found in the chapter on "The Fundamental Peculiarities Inherent in the Strategy of the Revolutionary Epoch," which says:

Without an extensive and generalized dialectical comprehension of the present epoch as an epoch of abrupt turns, a real education of the young parties, a correct strategical leadership of the class struggle, a correct combination of tactics, and, above all, a sharp and bold and decisive re-arming at each successive breaking point of the situation is impossible. [*The Third International AfterLenin* (New York: Pathfinder Press, 1970), p. 86.]

One of my critics declares: "It is the slogan of the abolition of the *tuchuns* and the unification of China under the power of the soviets that remains correct." As for the call for the constituent assembly, that would be "unacceptable." I ask why? If one regards as correct the resolution of the February plenum (1928) of the Executive Committee of the Communist International in declaring that "it is correct to continue to orient toward the insurrection," then, clearly, one must also grant the correctness of the slogan of soviets. This is only logical. But I considered, and I still consider, that proclaiming an insurrectional course in February 1928 was the most criminal stupidity that can be imagined.

Well before February, the counter-revolution in China overwhelmed the working class and the party. In "The Chinese Question after the Sixth Congress" I clearly established the main chronological milestones of the changes in the situation in China, basing my presentation on indisputable facts and documents. This country is at present going through not a revolution but rather a counter-revolution. In the course of such a period the slogan of soviets makes no sense *except for a limited number of cadres,* in preparing them for the third Chinese Revolution, in the future.

This preparation clearly has an enormous importance. To accomplish it, the slogan of soviets must be accompanied by the slogan of the struggle of the proletariat for its dictatorship at the head of all the impoverished masses of the population, and, above all, of the poor peasants. But side by side with theoretical and propagandistic preparation of the revolutionary cadres for the future revolution there still remains the question of *mobilizing the broadest possible layers of the workers to participate actively in the political life of the period we are in.*

The country is now being administered by a military dictatorship serving the top sectors of the bourgeoisie and the foreign imperialists This dictatorship, which was recently installed after the revolutionary struggle (which we shamefully and criminally lost), cannot yet be stable. It seeks only to become stable by establishing a "transitional regime" on the road to the creation of the Five Chambers of Sun Yat-sen. This absurd and reactionary invention (which one hears praised among ourselves without much critical sense, even at a time when these ideas above all retard the revolutionary development of China), this philistine fantasy now becomes an instrument serving as "national", "constitutional" camouflage for the fascist regime, that is to say, for the military domination by a centralized party, the Kuomintang, representing the interests of capital in their most concentrated form.

By the same token, questions of the political regime and of the state are on the agenda in China. These problems are inevitably of interest to large working class circles. In a situation that is not revolutionary it is impossible to give any other reply to these questions than the slogans and formulas of political democracy.

When the mass movement progresses, under the conditions of a general revolutionary crisis, the soviets, arising through this movement, serve its current needs, become a natural form of the unity of the masses, comprehensible, close to the "national" point of view, and aid the party to bring the masses to the insurrection. But what does the slogan of soviets signify now, under the present circumstances in China? Don't forget that there is no soviet tradition there. Such a tradition would have remained even in the event of a defeat, but it didn't exist. The cause of that is the reactionary leadership of Stalin-Bukharin. The slogan of soviets, which is not sustained by a mass movement and which is not even supported by the experience of the past, is only an empty phrase: *do as they did in Russia,* that is to say, it is the slogan of the socialist revolution in its purest, most abstract, and most absolute form.

Soviets have to be created to win power by the proletariat and the poor peasants through an insurrection. But *today* it is necessary to oppose to the fascist machine of the Kuomintang the slogans of democracy, that is, those which, under the domination of the bourgeoisie, open the widest avenue for popular political activity.

The stage of democracy has a great importance in the evolution of the masses. Under definite conditions, the revolution can allow the proletariat to pass beyond this stage. But it is precisely to facilitate this future development, which is not at all easy and not at all guaranteed to be successful in advance, that it is necessary to utilize to the fullest the inter-revolutionary period to exhaust the democratic resources of the bourgeoisie. This can be done by developing democratic slogans before the broad masses and by compelling the bourgeoisie to place itself in contradiction to them at each step.

The anarchists have never understood this Marxist policy. The opportunists conducting the Sixth Congress, mortally frightened by the fruits of their labor, do not understand it either. But we, thank heavens, are neither anarchists, nor opportunists covered with shame, but Bolshevik-Leninists, that is, revolutionary dialecticians who have understood the meaning of the imperialist epoch and the dynamic of its abrupt turns.

34

The Political Situation in China and the Tasks of the Bolshevik-Leninist Opposition

June 1929

At the February [1928] plenum of the ECCI and the Sixth Congress of the Comintern a basically false evaluation of the situation in China was made. So as to cover up for the terrible defeats, it was declared that the revolutionary situation is maintained ("between two waves"), and that as before the course is toward armed uprising and soviets.

In fact, the second Chinese Revolution of 1925–27 ended in a series of crushing defeats, without having completed its tasks. Now we have an inter-revolutionary period, under the complete sway of bourgeois counterrevolution and with a strengthening of the position of foreign imperialism.

It is impossible to predict how long the inter-revolutionary period will last, since it depends on many factors, internal and international. But the rise of a third revolution is inevitable; it is absolutely and completely grounded in the conditions of the defeat of the second revolution.

The tasks of the Chinese Communist Opposition, i.e., the Bolshevik-Leninists, are to understand the causes of the defeats clearly, to evaluate correctly the present situation, to regroup the staunchest, bravest, and most tested elements of the proletarian vanguard, to seek again the paths to the masses on the basis of transitional demands, and in all fields of social life to prepare the working class for the third Chinese Revolution.

The second Chinese Revolution was defeated in three stages in the course of 1927: in Shanghai, Wuhan, and Canton. All three defeats were the direct and immediate consequence of the basically false policy of the Communist International and the Central Committee of the Chinese Communist Party.

The completely opportunist line of the Comintern found its expression in the four questions which determined the fate of the Chinese revolution:

1. *The question of the party.* The Chinese Communist Party entered a bourgeois party, the Kuomintang, while the bourgeois character of this party was disguised by a charlatan philosophy about a "workers' and peasants' party" and even about a party of "four classes" (Stalin-Martynov). The proletariat was thus deprived of its own party at a most critical period. Worse yet: the pseudo-Communist Party was converted into an additional tool of the bourgeoisie in deceiving the workers. There is nothing to equal this crime in the whole history of the world revolutionary movement. The responsibility falls entirely on the ECCI and Stalin, its inspirers.

Since even now in India, Korea, and other countries "workers' and peasants'" parties, i.e., new Kuomintangs, are still being instituted, the Chinese Communist Opposition considers it necessary, on the basis of the experience of the second Chinese Revolution, to declare:

Never and under no circumstances may the party of the proletariat enter into a party of another class or merge with it organizationally. An absolutely independent party of the proletariat is a first and decisive condition for communist politics.

2. *The question of imperialism.* The false course of the Comintern was based on the statement that the yoke of international imperialism is compelling all "progressive" classes to go together. In other words, according to the Comintern's Stalinist theory, the yoke of imperialism would somehow change the laws of the class struggle. In fact, the economic, political, and military penetration of imperialism into China's life brought the internal class struggle to extreme sharpness.

While at the bottom, in the agrarian bases of the Chinese economy, the bourgeoisie is organically and unbreakably linked with feudal forms of exploitation, at the top it is just as organically and unbreakably linked with world finance capital. The Chinese bourgeoisie cannot on its own break free either from agrarian feudalism or from foreign imperialism.

Its conflicts with the most reactionary feudal militarists and its collisions with the international imperialists always take second place at the decisive moment to its irreconcilable antagonism to the poor workers and peasants.

Having always behind it the help of the world imperialists against the Chinese workers and peasants, the so-called national bourgeoisie raises the class struggle to civil war more rapidly and more mercilessly than any other bourgeoisie in the world, and drowns the workers and peasants in blood.

It is a gigantic and historical crime that the leadership of the Comintern helped the Chinese national bourgeoisie to mount the backs of the workers and peasants, while shielding it from the criticism and protests of revolutionary Bolsheviks. Never in the history of all revolutions has the bourgeoisie had such a cover-up and such a disguise as the Stalinist leadership created for the Chinese bourgeoisie.

The Opposition reminds the Chinese workers and the workers of the whole world that as little as a few days before the Shanghai coup of Chiang Kai-shek, Stalin not only suddenly called for trust and support for Chiang Kai-shek, but also subjected to fierce repressions the Bolshevik-Leninists ("Trotskyists") who had given warning in time of the defeat in store for the revolution.

The Chinese Opposition declares that all who support or spread or defend in relation to the past the legend that the "national" bourgeoisie is able to lead the masses to a revolutionary struggle are traitors. The tasks of the Chinese revolution can really be solved only on condition that the Chinese proletariat, at the head of the oppressed masses, throws off bourgeois political leadership and seizes power. There is no other way.

3. The question of the petty bourgeoisie and the peasantry. In this question too, which has decisive importance for China, just as for all countries of the East, the policy of the Comintern

constitutes a Menshevik falsification of Marxism. When we, the Opposition, spoke of the necessity for a revolutionary alliance of the proletariat and the petty bourgeoisie, we had in mind the oppressed masses, the tens and hundreds of millions of poor of town and countryside. The Comintern leadership understood and understands by the petty bourgeoisie those petty-bourgeois summits, overwhelmingly intellectuals, who, under the form of democratic parties and organizations, exploit the rural and urban poor, selling them out at the decisive moment to the big bourgeoisie. For us, it is not a matter of an alliance with Wang Ching-wei against Chiang Kai-shek, but of an alliance with the toiling masses against Wang Ching-wei and Chiang Kai-shek.

4. The question of soviets. The Bolshevik theory of soviets was replaced by an opportunist falsification, subsequently supplemented by adventurist practice.

For the countries of the East, just as for the countries of the West, soviets are the form of organization which can and must be created from the very first stage of a broad revolutionary upsurge. Soviets usually arise as revolutionary strike organizations, and then extend their functions and increase their authority in the eyes of the masses. At the next stage they become the organizations of a revolutionary uprising. Finally, after the victory of the uprising they are transformed into the organs of revolutionary power.

In hindering the Chinese workers and peasants from creating soviets, the Stalinist leadership of the Comintern artificially disarmed and weakened the toiling masses before the bourgeoisie and gave it the opportunity to crush the revolution. The subsequent attempt in December 1927 to set up a soviet in Canton in twenty-four hours was nothing but a criminal adventure, and it prepared only for the final defeat of the heroic workers of Canton by the unrestrained military.

These are the basic crimes of the Stalinist Comintern leadership in China. Taken together they indicate a substitution of Menshevism, perfected and taken to its limits, for Bolshevism. The crushing of the second Chinese Revolution is above all a defeat for the strategy of Menshevism, which this time appeared under a Bolshevik mask. It is not by chance that in this the whole of the international Social Democracy was in solidarity with Stalin and Bukharin.

Without understanding the great lessons for which the Chinese working class has paid so dearly there can be no movement forward. The Chinese Left Opposition bases itself on these lessons, wholly and completely. The Chinese bourgeoisie, after the defeat of the popular masses, was compelled to endure the dictatorship of the military. This is for the given period the only possible form of state power, flowing from the irreconcilable antagonisms of the bourgeoisie toward the popular masses on the one hand and the dependence of the bourgeoisie on foreign imperialism on the other. Individual layers and provincial groups of the bourgeoisie are not content with the rule of the sword, but the big bourgeoisie as a whole cannot keep itself in power otherwise than with the sword.

The inability of the "national" bourgeoisie to stand at the head of a revolutionary nation makes democratic parliamentarism unacceptable to it. Under the name of a temporary regime of "guardianship of the people", the "national" bourgeoisie is establishing the rule of military cliques.

These last, which reflect the special and local interests of various groups of the bourgeoisie, come one after the other into conflicts and open wars, which are the reward for a crushed revolution.

It would be pitiful and contemptible now to try to determine which of the generals is "progressive", so as to again bind up the fate of the revolutionary struggle to his sword.

The task of the Opposition is to counterpose the workers and the poor to the whole social mechanism of the counterrevolutionary bourgeoisie. It is not the Stalinist policy of collaboration and alliances with leaders, but the irreconcilable class policy of Bolshevism that will be the Opposition's line.

From the end of 1927 the Chinese Revolution gave way to counter-revolution which is still continuing to deepen. The clearest expression of this process is the fate of the Chinese party. At the Sixth Congress the number of members of the Chinese Communist Party was boastfully given as one hundred thousand. The Opposition said then that after 1927 the party would hardly be able to keep even ten thousand members. In fact, the party today musters not more than three to four thousand, and its decline is still going on. The false political orientation, which at every step comes into irreconcilable contradiction with the facts, is destroying the Chinese Communist Party and will inevitably lead it to its doom, if the Communist Opposition does not secure a basic change in its whole policy and in the whole party regime.

In continuing to cover up for its errors, the present leadership of the Comintern is clearing the way in the Chinese workers' movement for two enemies: *Social Democracy* and *anarchism.* The revolutionary movement can only be defended from these complementary dangers by the Communist Opposition, which wages an irreconcilable struggle against both the opportunism and the adventurism which inevitably flow from the Stalinist leadership of the Comintern.

There is at present no mass revolutionary movement in China. All that can be done is to prepare for it. The preparation must consist in attracting ever wider circles of workers into the political life of the country, on the basis that exists now in an epoch of triumphant counterrevolution.

The slogan of soviets, as a slogan for the present, is now adventurism or empty talk.

The struggle against the military dictatorship must inevitably assume the form of *transitional revolutionary democratic demands,* leading to the demand for a Chinese constituent assembly on the basis of universal direct, equal, and secret voting, for the solution of the most important problems facing the country: the introduction of the eight-hour day, the confiscation of the land, and the securing of national independence for China.

Having rejected transitional revolutionary democratic slogans the Sixth Congress left the Chinese Communist Party without any slogans and thereby denied it the possibility of approaching the task of mobilizing the masses under conditions of counterrevolution.

The Chinese Opposition condemns the lifeless irrelevance of such a policy. The Chinese Opposition predicts that as soon as the workers start to emerge from their paralysis they will inevitably put forward democratic slogans. If the communists stand back, the revival of political struggle will go to the benefit of petty-bourgeois democracy, and it is possible to predict in advance that the present Chinese Stalinists will follow in its wake, giving the democratic slogans not a revolutionary, but a conciliatory interpretation.

The Opposition therefore considers it necessary to make clear in advance that the real road to a solution of the problems of national independence and the raising of the standard of living of the mass of the people is a basic change in the whole social structure by means of a third Chinese Revolution.

At present, it is still difficult to predict when and in what ways the revolutionary revival in the country will start. There are, however, symptoms which allow the conclusion to be drawn that political revival will be preceded by a certain *economic revival* with a greater or lesser participation of foreign capital.

An economic upsurge, even a weak one of short duration, will again assemble the workers in the factories, raise their feeling of class self-confidence, and thereby create the conditions for the setting up of trade union organizations and for a new extension of the influence of the Communist Party. An industrial upsurge would in no case liquidate the revolution. On the contrary, in the last analysis it would revive and sharpen all the unsolved problems and all the now repressed class and subclass antagonisms (between the military, the bourgeoisie, and "democracy," between the "national" bourgeoisie and imperialism, and, finally between the proletariat and the bourgeoisie as a whole). The Upsurge would lead the Chinese popular masses out of oppression and passivity. The inevitable new crisis after this could serve as a new revolutionary impulse.

Of course, factors of an international character could hinder or possibly accelerate these processes.

The Opposition therefore does not bind itself to any ready-made scheme. Its duty is to follow the actual development of the internal life of the country and the whole world situation. All the tactical turns of our policy must be timed to the real situation of each new stage. And our general strategic line must lead to the conquest of power.

The dictatorship of the Chinese proletariat must include the Chinese Revolution in the international socialist revolution. The victory of socialism in China, just as in the USSR, is thinkable only in the conditions of a victorious international revolution. The Opposition categorically rejects the reactionary Stalinist theory of socialism in one country.

The immediate tasks of the Opposition are:

(a) to publish the most important documents of the Bolshevik-Leninists (Opposition);
(b) to commence as soon as possible publication of a weekly political and theoretical organ of the Opposition;
(c) to select, on the basis of a clear conception, the best, most reliable elements of communism, capable of withstanding the pressure of counterrevolution, creating a centralized faction of Bolshevik-Leninists (Opposition), and preparing themselves and others for a new upsurge;
(d) to maintain constant active contact with the Left Opposition in all other countries, so as to attain in the shortest possible time the construction of a strong, ideologically united international faction of Bolshevik-Leninists (Opposition).

Only such a faction, openly and boldly coming out under its own banner, both inside the Communist parties and outside them, is capable of saving the Communist International from decay and degeneration and returning it to the path of Marx and Lenin.

35

The Capitulation of Radek, Preobrazhensky, and Smilga*

July 27, 1929

As befits all self-respecting bankrupts, the trio certainly could not fail to cover themselves from *the permanent revolution* side. Of this powder, there is an inexhaustible supply in Yaroslavsky's snuffbox. What is most tragic in all the new historical experience of the defeats of opportunism—the Chinese Revolution—the three capitulators dismiss with a cheap oath in which they declare they have nothing in common with the theory of permanent revolution. It would be more correct to say that these gentlemen have nothing in common with Marxism on the fundamental questions of world revolution.

Radek and Smilga stubbornly supported the subordination of the Chinese Communist Party to the bourgeois Kuomintang, and this not only before Chiang Kai-shek's coup d'etat but also after. Preobrazhensky mumbled something vague, as he usually does on political questions. A remarkable fact: *all those in the Opposition who had supported the subordination of the Communist Party* to the Kuomintang have become capitulators. Not one of the Oppositionists who remained faithful to their banner carries this mark, a mark of notorious shame. Three-quarters of a century after the *Communist Manifesto* came into the world, a quarter of a century after the foundation of the Bolshevik party, these unfortunate "Marxists" thought it possible to defend the

---

* Excepted from the article *"A Wretched Document"*.

communists being in the Kuomintang cage! In reply to my accusation, Radek, as he now does in his letter of surrender, raised the fear of "the isolation" of the proletariat from the peasantry should the Communist Party leave the bourgeois Guomintang. Shortly before that, Radek described the Canton government as a *workers' and peasants'* government, helping Stalin to camouflage enslavement of the proletariat to the bourgeoisie. How cover oneself from these shameful acts consequences of this blindness and stupidity, this betrayal of Marxism? *How? With an indictment of the permanent revolution* Yaroslavsky's snuffbox is at your service.

As early as 1928, having begun to look for arguments in order to capitulate, Radek associated himself immediately with the *resolution of the February 1928 plenum* of the ECCI on the Chinese question. This resolution described the Trotskyists as liquidators because they called a defeat a defeat and did not agree to describe the victorious Chinese counter-revolution as the highest stage of the Chinese Revolution. In this February resolution the course toward armed insurrection and soviets was proclaimed. For anyone with the slightest political sense helped by revolutionary experience, this resolution offered itself as a sample of disgusting, irresponsible adventurism. Radek associated himself with it. Smilga was thoughtfully silent because what was the Chinese revolution to him when he had already begun to smell the "concrete" odor of the figures of the five-year plan?". Preobrazhensky involved himself in the matter in a no less subtle manner than Radek, but from the opposite end. The Chinese Revolution is defeated, he wrote, and will be for a long time. A new revolution won't come soon. In that case, is it worthwhile quarreling with the centrists over China? Preobrazhensky sent lengthy messages on the subject. Reading them at Alma-Ata, I had a feeling of shame. What had these people learned in the school of Lenin? I asked myself several times. Preobrazhensky's premises were completely the opposite of Radek's, yet their conclusions were identical: both would have liked very much for Yaroslavsky to embrace them fraternally, through the mediation of Menzhinsky. Oh, to be sure, it's for the good of the revolution. They aren't careerists;

no, they aren't careerists—they are simply people without hope, exhausted of ideas.

To the adventurist resolution of the plenum of the ECCI of February 1928, I had already counterposed at the time the course of mobilizing the Chinese masses around democratic slogans, including the slogan of *a Chinese constituent assembly.* But here the unfortunate trio rushed into ultra-leftism; that was cheap and committed them to nothing. Democratic slogans? Never. "It is a gross mistake by Trotsky." Only Chinese soviets, and not a penny less. It is difficult to invent anything more stupid than this apology for a position. To use the slogan of soviets in a period of bourgeois reaction is to trifle, i.e., to make a mockery of soviets. Even at the time of the revolution, i.e., in the period of directly-building soviets, we didn't withdraw democratic slogans. We withdrew them only when *the real soviets,* which had already captured power, clashed, before the eyes of the masses, with *the real institutions of democracy.* In the language of Lenin (and not in the mishmash of Stalin and his parrots) that meant: *not jumping over the democratic stage in the development of the country.*

Without a program for democracy—the constituent assembly, the eight-hour day, national independence for China, confiscation of the land, the right of nationalities to self-determination, etc.— without this program for democracy, the Chinese Communist Party would find itself bound hand and foot and would be obliged passively to clear the ground for the Chinese Social Democracy which, helped by Stalin, Radek, and Company, might supplant it.

So: when he followed in the wake of the Opposition, Radek missed what was most important in the Chinese Revolution, for he defended the subordination of the Communist Party to the bourgeois Kuomintang. Radek missed the Chinese counter-revolution, supporting the course to armed insurrection which followed the Canton adventure. Now, Radek jumps over the period of the counterrevolution and the struggle for democracy, keeping himself apart from the tasks of the transition period by the abstract idea of soviets outside of time and place. But in compensation, Radek swears he has nothing in common with permanent revolution. That is gratifying. That is comforting. It is true that Radek does not understand the motive forces of revolution; he does not understand its changing periods; he does not understand the role and meaning of the proletarian party; he does not understand the relation between democratic slogans and the struggle for power; but in compensation—oh, supreme compensation!—he takes no strong drink and if he comforts himself on difficult days, it is not with the alcohol of permanent revolution but with innocent pinches from Yaroslavsky's snuffbox.

But, no, these "pinches" are not so innocent. On the contrary, they are very dangerous. They bear in themselves a very great threat for the coming Chinese Revolution. The anti-Marxist theory of Stalin-Radek bears in itself a repetition, changed but not improved' of the Kuomintang experiment, for China, for India, and for all the other countries of the East.

On the basis of all the experiences of the Russian and Chinese revolutions, on the basis of the teachings of Marx and Lenin, having thought the matter out in the light of these experiences the Opposition affirms:

A new Chinese Revolution can overthrow the existing regime and hand power over to the mass of the people *only in the form of the dictatorship of the proletariat.*

"The democratic dictatorship of the proletariat and the peasantry"—substituting for *the dictatorship of the proletariat leading the peasantry and carrying out the democratic program*— is a fiction, a self-deception, or, worse still, Kerenskyism or Kuomintangism.

Between the regime of Kerensky or Chiang Kai-shek on the one hand and the dictatorship of the proletariat on the other, *there is not, nor can there be, any intermediate revolutionary regime,* and whoever puts forward such a naked formula shamefully deceives the workers of the East and prepares fresh catastrophes.

The Opposition says to the workers of the East: The machinations of the capitulators gnawing within the party help Stalin to sow the seeds of centrism, to throw sand in your eyes, to stop up your ears, to befog your minds. On the one hand, you are weakened in the face of the regime of an oppressive bourgeois dictatorship because you are forbidden to develop the struggle for democracy. On the other hand, there is drawn for you a perspective of some kind of dictatorship, cheap and non-proletarian, thus facilitating the future reshaping of the Kuomintang, i.e., the future defeat of the revolution of the workers and peasants.

Such forecasters utter treacheries. Workers of the East, learn to distrust them, learn to despise them, learn to drive them out of your ranks!

36

The Sino–Soviet Conflict and the Opposition

August 4, 1929

On July 22 I gave the following statement in answer to an American news agency questionnaire:

I can give my view on Sino–Soviet relations, of course, only as an individual. I have no information except what is in the newspapers. In cases of this kind, information in the newspapers is always insufficient.

There can be no doubt that aggressiveness has been manifested not by the Soviet, but by the Chinese government. The managing apparatus of the Chinese Eastern Railroad has existed for a number of years. The workers' organizations that the Chinese regime has attacked have also existed for some time. The existing administrative arrangement for the Chinese Eastern Railroad was carefully worked out this last time by a special commission under my chairmanship. The commission's decisions were approved in April 1926 and completely protect Chinese interests.

The conduct of the present Chinese government is explained by the fact that it was made stronger by the crushing defeat of the workers and peasants. I will not discuss here the reasons for the defeat of the revolutionary movement of the Chinese people because I have dealt sufficiently with this theme in my previously published works. The government, having risen out of a completely routed revolution, as always in such cases, feels weak in relation to those forces against which the revolution was directed, i.e., above all against British and Japanese imperialism. Therefore, it is compelled to try to enhance its power and influence by making adventuristic gestures toward its revolutionary neighbor.

Must this provocation that developed out of the defeat of the Chinese Revolution lead to war? I don't think so. Why? Because the *Soviet government does not want war,* and the Chinese government *is not capable of waging it.*

The army of Chiang Kai-shek was victorious in 1925–27 [against the warlords] thanks to the revolutionary upsurge of the masses. In turning against them, the army has forfeited its chief source of strength. As a purely military organization, Chiang Kai-shek's army is extremely weak. Chiang Kai-shek cannot help but realize that the Soviet government is well aware of the weakness of his army. It is unthinkable that Chiang Kai-shek could wage a war against the Red Army without the aid of other powers. It is more accurate to say that Chiang Kai-shek would wage war only if his army were merely the auxiliary detachment to the forces of another power. I do not believe that at this time such a combination is very likely, especially in light of the Soviet government's sincere desire, as indicated above, to settle problems by peaceful means....

It goes without saying that in the event that war is imposed on the Soviet people, the Opposition will devote itself fully to the cause of defending the October Revolution.

I thought that in this statement I had expressed the viewpoint of the Communist Left Opposition as a whole. I regret to say that this is not entirely true. Individuals and groups have come forward in the Opposition that, on the occasion of their first serious political test, have taken either an equivocal or a basically wrong position, a position outside their own revolutionary Opposition camp or one which brought them very close to the camp of the Social Democracy.

In *Die Fahne des Kommunismus,* no. 26, there was an article written by one H. P. According to this article, the conflict was caused by an encroachment on China's right of self-determination by the Soviet republic. In other words, it was in essence a defense of Chiang Kai-shek. I shall not deal with this article, since H. P. received a correct reply from Comrade Kurt Landau, who dealt with this question as behoves a Marxist.

The editor of *Fahne des Kommunismus* printed the article as a discussion article, with a note that he is not in solidarity with the author. It is incomprehensible that a discussion could be opened on a question that is so elementary for every revolutionary, particularly at a time political action is called for. The thing became even worse when the editor of the paper also published Landau's contribution as a "discussion article". H.P.'s article expresses the prejudices of vulgar democracy combined with those of anarchism. Landau's article formulates the Marxist position. And what about the position of the editor?

Something incomparably worse occurred in one of the numerous groups of the French Opposition. Number 35 of *Contre le Courant* (July 28, 1929) had an editorial on the Sino–Soviet conflict which is a sorry mess of errors from beginning to end partly of a Social Democratic and partly of an ultra-left character. The editorial begins with the statement that the adventuristic policy of the Soviet bureaucracy is responsible for the conflict; in other words, the paper assumes the role of Chiang Kai-shek's attorney. The editorial puts the policy of the Soviet government toward the Chinese Eastern Railroad in the category of a capitalist, imperialist policy, which resorts to the support of the imperialist powers.

"The Communist Opposition," the editorial states, "cannot support Stalin's war, which is not a defensive war of the proletariat but a semicolonial war." Elsewhere it says: "The Opposition must have the courage *to tell the working class that it is not falling into line with the Stalinist bureaucrats, that it is not for their adventuristic war."* This sentence is emphasized in the original, and not by accident. It expresses the whole point of the editorial and thereby puts the author into implacable opposition to the Communist Left.

In what sense is the Stalinist bureaucracy responsible for the present conflict? In this sense and no other: that it helped Chiang Kai-shek by its previous policy to destroy the revolution of the Chinese workers and peasants. I wrote about this in an article directed against Radek and Company: "Chiang

Kai-shek's provocation is the settlement of expenses incurred by Stalin in the defeat of the Chinese revolution. We gave warning hundreds of times: after Stalin has helped Chiang Kai-shek to settle in the saddle, Chiang Kai-shek would, at the first opportunity, draw his whip on him. That is what has happened."

Chiang Kai-shek's provocation was preceded by his crushing of the Chinese Revolution. What we have now is an adventure of the Bonapartist military power headed by Chiang Kai-shek. This provocation is at the root of the Sino–Soviet conflict.

According to the editorial, the principal cause of the conflict is the imperialist "claim" of the Soviet republic on the Chinese Eastern Railroad. Hands off China! shout the involuntary defenders of Chiang Kai-shek, repeating not only the slogans but also the basic arguments of the Social Democrats. Up until now we believed that only the capitalist bourgeoisie as a class could be the representatives of an imperialist policy. Is there anything to indicate the contrary? Or has such a class taken power in the USSR? Since when? We are fighting against the centrism of the Stalinist bureaucracy (remember: centrism is a tendency within the working class itself) because centrist policies may *help* the bourgeoisie to gain power, first the petty and middle bourgeoisie and, eventually, finance capital. This is the historical danger; but this is a process that is by no means at the point of completion.

In the same issue of *Contre le Courant*, there is a so-called draft of a platform. In it we read among other things: "We cannot say that Thermidor has already taken hold." This shows that continual repetition of the general formulas of the Opposition is far from equivalent to a political understanding of those formulas. If we cannot say that Thermidor is an accomplished fact, then we cannot say that Soviet policy has become a capitalist, or imperialist, policy. Centrism zigzags between the proletariat and the petty bourgeoisie. To identify centrism with big capital is to understand nothing, and thereby to support finance capital not only against the proletariat, but also against the petty bourgeoisie.

The theoretical wisdom of the ultra-lefts in Berlin and Paris boils down to a few democratic abstractions, which have a geographical, not a socialist basis. The Chinese Eastern Railroad runs through Mahchuria, which belongs to China. China has a right to self-determination; therefore, the claim of Soviet Russia to this railroad is imperialism. It should be turned over. To whom? To Chiang Kai-shek? Or to the son of Chang Tso-lin?

During the Brest-Litovsk peace negotiations, von Kublmann introduced the demand for an independent Latvia and Estonia, referring to the fact that the Landtags established there with the aid of Germany had instructed him to demand separation. We refused to sanction this, and we were denounced by the entire official German press as imperialists.

Let us assume that in the Caucasus there is an outbreak of counter-revolution which, with the help of, say, England, achieves victory. Let us also assume that the workers of Baku, with the help of the Soviet Union, succeed in keeping the whole area of Baku in their hands. It goes without saying that the Transcaucasian counter-revolution would lay claim to this district of Baku. It is perfectly clear that the Soviet republic would not consent to this. Is it not also clear that in such a case the enemy would accuse the Soviet government of imperialism?

Had the revolution of the Chinese workers and peasants been victorious, there wouldn't be any difficulty whatsoever about the Chinese Eastern Railroad. The lines would have been turned over to the victorious Chinese people. But the fact of the matter is that the Chinese people were defeated by the ruling Chinese bourgeoisie, with the aid of foreign imperialism. To turn over the railroad to Chiang Kai-shek under such conditions would mean to give aid and comfort to the Chinese Bonapartist counterrevolution against the Chinese people. This itself is decisive. But there is another consideration of equal weight. Chiang Kai-shek never could get those lines by virtue of his own financial-political means—let alone keep them. It is hardly an accident that he tolerates the actual independence of Manchuria existing under a Japanese protectorate. The railroad lines transferred to Chiang Kai-shek would only become security for the foreign loans he received. They would pass into the hands of the real imperialists and would become their most important economic and strategic outpost in the Far East—against a potential Chinese revolution and against the Soviet republic. We are well aware that the imperialists understand perfectly how to utilize the slogan of self-determination for their own dirty deals. But I don't believe that Marxists are under obligation to help them put it over.

The point of departure for the ultra-lefts is the fact that it was the greedy and thievish imperialism of the tsar that took the Chinese Eastern Railroad from the Chinese people. This is a fact that cannot be disputed. Yet they forget to point out this was the same imperialism that dominated the Russian people. Yes, this railroad was constructed for the purpose of robbing the Chinese workers and peasants. But it was constructed by the exploitation and the robbery of the Russian workers and peasants. Then the October Revolution took place. Did this alter the mutual relations of the Chinese and the Russians? On the foundation of the revolution, after a period of reaction, the state structure was rebuilt. Did Russia now return to the starting point? Can we now imagine, from a historical viewpoint—regardless of Stalin and Molotov, regardless of the exile of the Opposition, etc., etc.—can we imagine an ownership of the Chinese Eastern Railroad that would be more beneficial from the point of view of the international proletariat and the Chinese revolution than that of the Soviet Union? This is how we ought to put the question.

All the White Guard emigres look upon this question from a class viewpoint, not from a nationalist or a geographical one. In spite of internal dissension, the leading groups of the Russian emigres agree that the internationalization of the Chinese Eastern Railroad, that is, its transference to the control of world imperialism, would be more advantageous to the "coming", that is, bourgeois, Russia than leaving it in the possession of the Soviet state. By the same token, we can say that its remaining under the control of the Soviet government would be more advantageous to an independent China than turning it over to any of the present claimants.

Does this mean that the managing apparatus of the line is perfect? No! Indeed not. Tsarist imperialism has left its traces.

All the zigzags of Soviet internal policy are undoubtedly also reflected in the apparatus of the lines. The tasks of the Opposition extend to these questions as well.

I would like to refer to my personal experience in this matter. I had to fight more than once for an improvement in the administration of the Chinese railroad. The last time I worked on this question was in March 1926 on a special commission of which I was chairman. The members of the commission were Voroshilov, Dzerzhinsky, and Chicherin. In full agreement with the Chinese revolutionaries, not only the communists but also the representatives of the then functioning Kuomintang, the commission considered absolutely necessary: "strictly keeping the actual apparatus of the CER in the hands of the Soviet government—which in the next period is the only way to protect the railroad from imperialist seizure....

With regard to the administration in the interim, the resolution adopted on the question had this to say:

> It is necessary to immediately adopt broad measures of a cultural-political nature aimed at *Sinification* of the railroad.
>
> (a) The administration should be bilingual; station signs and instructions posted in the stations and in the cars, etc., should be bilingual. (b) Chinese schools for railroad workers should be established combining technical and political training. (c) At appropriate points along the railroad, cultural-educational institutions should be established for the Chinese workers and the Chinese settlements adjacent to the railroad. ["Problems of Our Policy with Respect to China and Japan" (March 25, 1926).]

With regard to the policy of the Russian representatives toward China, the resolution said:

> There is absolutely no doubt that in the actions of the various departmental representatives there were inadmissible great-power mannerisms compromising the Soviet administration and creating an impression of Soviet imperialism.

It is neccessary to impress upon the corresponding agencies and persons the vital importance for us of such a policy and of even such an external form of the policy in relation to China so that any trace of suspicion of great-power intentions will be eliminated. This policy—based on the closest attention to China's rights, on emphasizing its sovereignty, etc.—must be carried out on every level. In every individual instance of a violation of this policy, no matter how slight, the culprits should be punished and this fact brought to the attention of Chinese public opinion.

In addition to this I must point out that the Chinese owners of the railroad, including Chiang Kai-shek, put against the management of the railroad not a Chinese but mainly an apparatus on the payroll of the imperialists of the world. The White Guards employed in the police and military squads of the Chinese lines have frequently committed acts of violence against the railroad workers. Regarding this, the resolution passed by the commission said the following:

It is necessary right now to carefully compile (and subsequently examine) all cases of tyranny and violence on the part of Chinese militarists, police, and Russian White Guard elements against Russian workers and employees of the CER, and also all cases of conflict between Russians and Chinese on national-social grounds. It is also necessary to devise the course and means for defending the personal and national dignity of Russian workers so that conflicts on this basis rather than kindling chauvinist sentiments on both sides, on the contrary, will have a political and educational significance. It is necessary to set up special conciliation commissions or courts of honor attached to the trade unions, with both sides participating on an equal basis, under the actual guidance of serious communists who understand the full importance and acuteness of the national question.

I believe that this is a far cry from imperialism. I believe that the ultra-lefts have a good chance to learn something from this. I am also ready to admit that not all of our resolutions have been carried out. There were probably more unlawful acts on the railroad than in Moscow. That is precisely why the Opposition wages an implacable struggle. Yet it is a poor politician who throws out the baby with the bath water.

I have already shown the sense in which the Stalinist faction is responsible for Chiang Kai-shek's provocations. But even if we assume that Stalin's bureaucrats have acted foolishly again, and have thereby helped the enemy to strike a blow against the Soviet republic, what conclusions should we draw? The conclusion that we must not defend the Soviet republic? Or the conclusion that we must free the Soviet republic from the Stalinist leadership? The *Contre le Courant* editorial has outrageously come to the first conclusion. It states that we must not support Stalin's bureaucracy and its adventuristic war, as though in the event of war the Stalinist bureaucracy would be at stake and not the October Revolution and its potentialities. In order to display more of its wisdom, the editorial continues: "It is not up to the Opposition to find some special remedy in the present crisis." We cannot imagine a worse position. This is not the view of a revolutionary, but of a disinterested spectator. What shall the Russian revolutionary do? What shall the fighters of the Opposition do in case of war? Shall they perhaps take a neutral position? The author of the editorial does not seem to think of this. And that is because he is not guided by the viewpoint of a revolutionary who will unconditionally enlist in the war, but proceeds like a notary who records the actions of both parties without intervening.

The Stalinists have accused us more than once of being defeatists or conditional defencists. I spoke on this subject at a joint plenary session of the Central Committee and the Central Control Commission on August 1, 1927. I said: "The lie of conditional defencism . . . we fling back into the faces of the calumniators."

In this way I repudiated the idea of neutrality and of conditional defence, called it a slander, and hurled the slander back into the teeth of the Stalinists. Did the author of the editorial fail to notice this? And if he didn't—why did he not attack me? The speech to which I refer was printed in my recent book, published in French under the title *La Revolution defiguree.*

When I spoke, I did not deal with a specific war, but with any war that might be waged against the Soviet republic. Only an ignoramus could fail to see from the combination of the preceding events a basic antagonism between the imperialist powers and Soviet Russia. Yes, concerning my visa the imperialists are in cheerful accord with Stalin. But when it comes to the question of the Soviet republic, they all remain its mortal enemies, *irrespective of Stalin.* Every war would expose this antagonism and inevitably result in endangering the very existence of the Soviet Union. That is why I said in that speech:

Do we, the Opposition, cast any doubts on the defense of the socialist fatherland? Not in the slightest degree. It is our hope not only to participate in the defence, but to be able to teach others a few things. Do we cast doubts on Stalin's ability to sketch a correct line for the defense of the socialist fatherland? We do so and, indeed, to the highest possible degree....

The Opposition is for the victory of the USSR; it has proved and will continue to prove this in action, in a manner inferior to none. But Stalin is not concerned with that. Stalin has essentially a different question in mind, which he dares not express, namely, "Does the Opposition really think that the leadership of Stalin is incapable of assuring victory to the USSR?" Yes, we think so.

Zinoviev: Correct!

Not a single Oppositionist will renounce his right and his duty, on the eve of war, or during the war, to fight for the correction of the party's course—as has always been the case in our party—because therein lies the most important condition for victory. To sum up. For the socialist fatherland? Yes! For the Stalinist course? No!

I believe that this position retains its full force at the present moment as well.

37

What is Happening in China?

November 9, 1929
Prinkipo

A Question every Communist must ask Himself

Among the telegrams in *Pravda* there has been communicated several times during October, in the smallest type, that an armed Communist detachment under the command of comrade Zhu De is advancing successfully towards Chao-Cho (Guangdong), that this detachment has grown from 5,000 to 20,000, etc. Thus we learn, as if incidentally, from the laconic telegrams in *Pravda* that the Chinese Communists are conducting an armed struggle against Chiang Kai-shek. What is the meaning of this struggle? Its origins? Its perspectives? Not a word is breathed to us about it. If the new revolution in China has matured to the point that the Communists have taken to arms, then it would seem necessary to mobilize the whole International in the face of events of such gigantic historical importance. Why then do we hear nothing of the sort? And if the situation in China is not such as puts on the order of the day the armed struggle of the Communists for power, then how and why has a Communist detachment begun an armed struggle against Chiang Kai-shek, that is, against the bourgeois military dictatorship?

Yes, why have the Chinese Communists risen in rebellion? Perhaps because the Chinese proletariat has already found the time to heal its wounds? Because the demoralized and debilitated Communist Party has found the time to rise on the revolutionary wave? Have the city workers ensured their contact with the revolutionary masses of the country? Has the general strike pushed the proletariat to the insurrection? If such is the case, then everything is clear and in order. But then why does *Pravda* communicate these events in a few lines and in small type?

Or perhaps the Chinese Communists have risen in rebellion because they have received the latest comments of Molotov on the resolution on the "third period"? It is no accident that Zinoviev who, in distinction to the other capitulators, still pretends to be alive, has come out in *Pravda* with an article which shows that the domination of Chiang Kai-shek is entirely similar to the temporary domination of Kolchak, that is, is only a simple episode in the process of the revolutionary rise. This analogy is of course bracing to the spirit. Unfortunately, it is not only false, but simply stupid. Kolchak organized an insurrection in one province against the dictatorship of the proletariat already established in the greater part of the country. In China, bourgeois counter-revolution rules in the country and it is the Communists who have stirred up an insurrection of a few thousand people in one of the provinces. We think, therefore, we have the right to pose this question: Does this insurrection spring from the situation in China or rather from the instructions concerning the "third period"? We ask further, what is the political role of the Chinese Communist Party in all this? What are the slogans with which it mobilized the masses? What is the degree of its influence upon the workers? We hear nothing about all this. The rebellion of Zhu de appears to be a reproduction of the adventurist campaigns of Ho Lung and Ye Ting in 1927 and the Canton uprising timed for the moment of the expulsion of the Opposition from the Russian Communist Party.

Perhaps the rebellion broke out spontaneously? Well and good. But then what is the meaning of the Communist banner unfurled above it? What is the attitude of the official Chinese Communist Party towards the insurrection? What is the position of the Comintern in this question? And why, finally, in communicating this fact to us, does the Moscow *Pravda* abstain from any comment?

But there is still another explanation possible, which is perhaps the most alarming one: Have the Chinese Communists risen in rebellion because of Chiang Kai-shek's seizure of the Chinese Eastern Railway? Has this insurrection, wholly partisan in character, as its aim to cause Chiang Kai-shek uneasiness at his rear? If that is what it is, we ask who has given such counsel to the Chinese Communists? Who bears the political responsibility for their passing over to guerrilla warfare?

It was not long ago that we decisively condemned the ramblings on the necessity of handing over so important an instrument as the Chinese Eastern from the hands of the Russian Revolution to those of the Chinese counter-revolution. We called to mind the elementary duty of the international proletariat in this conflict to defend the Republic of the soviets against the Chinese bourgeoisie and all its possible instigators and allies. But on the other hand it is quite clear that the proletariat of the USSR, which has power and an army in its hands, cannot demand that the vanguard of the Chinese proletariat begin a war at once against Chiang Kai-shek, that is, that it apply the means which the Soviet government itself does not find possible, and correctly so, to apply.

Had a war begun between the USSR and China, or rather between the USSR and the imperialist patrons of China, the duty of the Chinese Communists would be to transform this war in the shortest time into a civil war. But even in that case the launching of the civil war would have to be subordinated to general revolutionary policy; and even then the Chinese Communists would be unable to pass over arbitrarily, and at any moment at all, to the road of open insurrection, but only after having assured themselves of the necessary support of the worker and peasants masses. The rebellion in Chiang Kai-shek's rear, in this situation, would be an extension of the front of the Soviet workers and peasants; the fate of the insurgent Chinese workers would be intimately bound up with the fate of the soviet republic; the tasks, the aims, the perspectives would be quite clear.

But what is the perspective opened up by this uprising of the today isolated Chinese Communists in the absence of war or revolution? The perspective of a terrific debacle and of an adventurist degeneration of the remnants of the Communist Party.

In the meantime, it must be said openly: calculations based upon guerrilla adventure correspond entirely to the general nature of Stalinist policy. Two years ago, Stalin expected gigantic gains for the security of the soviet state from the alliance with the imperialists of the General Council of the British trade unions. Today, he is quite capable of calculating that a rebellion of the Chinese Communists, even without any hope, would bring "a little profit" in a precarious situation. In the first case, the calculation was grossly opportunist, in the second, openly adventurist, but in both cases, the calculation is made independently of the general tasks of the world labour movement, against these tasks and to the detriment of the correctly understood interests of the Soviet Republic.

We have not at our disposal all the necessary data for a definite conclusion. That is why we ask:

What is happening in China? Let it be explained to us! The Communist who does not pose the question to himself and to the leadership of his party will be unworthy of the name of Communist. The leadership that would like to remain discreetly on the sidelines in order, in case of a defeat of the Chinese partisans, to wash its hands and transfer responsibility to the Central Committee of the Chinese Communist Party—such a leadership would dishonor itself—not for the first time. It is true—by the most abominable crime against the interests of the international revolution.

We ask: What is happening in China? We will continue to pose this question until we have forced a reply.

38

A Reply to the Chinese Oppositionists

December 22, 1929

In the bitter struggle that the Bolsheviks conducted against the Narodniks and the Mensheviks during the fifteen years that preceded the October Revolution, there was never a question of employing methods of physical violence. As for individual terror, we Marxists rejected it even with regard to the tsarist satraps. Nevertheless, in recent times the Communist parties, or rather their apparatus people, have resorted more and more frequently to the disruption of meetings and to other methods for the mechanical suppression of adversaries, notably the Left Opposition. Many bureaucrats are sincerely convinced that this is what real Bolshevism consists of. They avenge themselves on other proletarian groups for their impotence against the capitalist state, and thereby transform the bourgeois police into an arbiter between us.

It is difficult to imagine the depravity engendered by this combination of impotence and violence. The youth become more and more accustomed to thinking that the fist is a surer weapon than argument. In other words, political cynicism is cultivated, which more than anything else prepares individuals for passing over into the fascist camp. An implacable struggle must be waged against the brutal and disloyal methods of Stalinism, by denouncing them in the press and in meetings, by cultivating among the workers a hatred and contempt for all these pseudo-revolutionists who, instead of appealing to the brain, take a crack at the skull.

Concerning the Ch'en Tu-hsiu group, I am pretty well acquainted with the policy it followed in the years of the revolution: it was the Stalin-Bukharin-Martynov policy, that is, a policy in essence of right-wing Menshevism. Comrade N. wrote me, however, that Ch'en Tu-hsiu, basing himself on the experience of the revolution, has come considerably closer to our position. It goes without saying that this can only be welcomed. In your letter, however, you categorically dispute Comrade N.'s information. You even contend that Ch'en Tu-hsiu has not broken from Stalin's policy, which presents a mixture of opportunism and adventurism. But up to now I have read only one declaration of program by Chen Tu-hsiu and therefore am in no position to express myself on this question.

In other respects, I conceive a solidarity in principle on the Chinese question only on the basis of clear replies to the following questions:

As far as the first period of the revolution is concerned:

1. Did the anti-imperialist character of the Chinese revolution give the "national" Chinese bourgeoisie the leading role in the revolution (Stalin-Bukharin)?
2. Was the slogan of the "bloc of four classes"—the big bourgeoisie, the petty bourgeoisie, the peasantry, and the proletariat (Stalin-Bukharin)—correct, even for an instant?
3. Were the entry of the Chinese Communist Party into the Kuomintang and the admission of the latter into the Comintern (resolution of the Politburo of the Soviet Communist Party) permissible?
4. Was it permissible, in the interests of the Northern Expedition, to curb the agrarian revolution (telegraphic directives in the name of the Politburo of the Soviet Communist Party)?
5. Was it permissible to renounce the slogan of soviets at the time the broad movement of workers and peasants developed, that is, in 1925–27 (Stalin-Bukharin)?
6. Was the Stalinist slogan of a "workers' and peasants'" party, that is, the old slogan of the Russian Narodniks, acceptable for China, even for an instant?

As far as the second period is concerned:

7. Was the resolution of the Communist International which said that the crushing of the workers' and peasants' movement by the Kuomintang of the right and the left signified a "transition of the revolution to a higher stage" (Stalin-Bukharin) correct?
8. Under these conditions, was the slogan of insurrection, issued by the Communist International, correct?
9. Was the tactic of guerrilla warfare, reinstituted by Ho Lung and Yeh T'ing and approved by the Comintern at the moment of the political ebb tide of the workers and peasants, correct?
10. Was the organization of the Canton uprising by the agents of the Comintern correct?

As far as the past in general is concerned:

11. Was the 1924–27 struggle in the Communist International against the Opposition on the Chinese question a struggle of Leninism against Trotskyism or, on the contrary, a struggle of Menshevism against Bolshevism?
12. Was the 1927–28 struggle in the Communist International against the Opposition a struggle of Bolshevism against "liquidationism" or, on the contrary, a struggle of adventurism against Bolshevism?

As far as the future is concerned:

13. Under the present conditions of victorious counter-revolution, is the mobilization of the Chinese masses under democratic slogans, particularly that of the constituent assembly, necessary as the Opposition believes, or is there any ground for limitation to the abstract propaganda of the slogan of soviets, as the Comintern has decided?
14. Has the slogan of the "workers' and peasants' democratic dictatorship" still a revolutionary content, as the Comintern thinks, or is it necessary, on the contrary, to sweep away this masked formula of the Kuomintang and to explain that the victory of the

alliance of the workers and peasants in China can lead only to the dictatorship of the proletariat?

15. Is the theory of socialism in one country applicable to China or, on the contrary, can the Chinese Revolution triumph and accomplish its task to the very end only as a link in the chain of the world revolution?

These are, in my opinion, the principal questions that the platform of the Chinese Opposition must necessarily answer. These questions have great importance for the whole International. The epoch of reaction that China is now passing through must become, as has always happened in history, an epoch of theoretical preoccupation. What characterizes the young Chinese revolutionists at the present time is the passion to understand, to study, to embrace the question in its entirety. The bureaucracy lacking an ideological basis, stifles Marxist thinking. But I do not doubt that in the struggle with the bureaucracy the Chinese vanguard of the proletariat will produce from its ranks a nucleus of notable Marxists who will render service to the whole International.

With Opposition greetings,

L.D. Trotsky

39

Some Results of the Sino–Soviet Conflict

January 3, 1930

1. In its last stage the conflict revealed, as is known, the complete military impotence of the present Chinese government.

   This in itself clearly demonstrates that there has not been a victorious bourgeois revolution in China, as Louzon, Urbahns, and others think, for a victorious revolution would have consolidated the army and the state. In China there was a victorious counter-revolution, directed against the overwhelming majority of the nation and therefore incapable of creating an army.
2. At the same time it strikingly demonstrates the inconsistency of the Menshevik policy of Stalin-Martynov, based since the beginning of 1924 on the assumption that the "national" Chinese bourgeoisie is capable of leading the revolution. In reality the bourgeoisie, with political support from the Comintern and material aid from the imperialists, was capable only of smashing the revolution and thereby reducing the Chinese state to complete impotence.
3. The Sino–Soviet conflict, in its military stage, revealed the enormous superiority of the [Russian] proletarian revolution, although weakened by the erroneous policy of the leadership in the last years, over the [Chinese] bourgeois counterrevolution, which had at its disposal

substantial diplomatic and material support from imperialism.

4. The victory of the October Revolution over the April counter-revolution (the coup by Chiang Kai-shek in April 1927) can in no sense be considered a victory for Stalin's policy. On the Contrary, that policy has suffered a series of heavy defeats. The project of the railroad was Chiang Kai-shek's payment for the services rendered by Stalin. Stalin's subsequent wager on Feng Yu-hsiang was equally inconsistent. The Opposition warned against the adventurist anti-Chiang Kai-shek bloc with Feng Yuhsiang after April 1927 as energetically as it had protested against Stalin's bloc with Chiang Kai-shek.
5. The unprincipled wager on the Kellogg Pact also resulted in a heavy loss.125 The Soviet government's adherence to the pact of American imperialism was a capitulation of the Soviet government as shameful as it was useless. By signing the pact, the so-called instrument of peace, Stalin openly assisted the American government in deceiving the working masses of America and Europe. What was the purpose of adherence to the pact? Obviously to gain the goodwill of the United States and thereby hasten diplomatic recognition. As should have been expected this end was not achieved, for the American government had no reason to pay for what it got for nothing. New York, basing itself on the Kellogg Pact, took the first opportunity to play the role of China's protector against the Soviet republic. Moscow was obliged to reply with a sharp rebuke. That was correct and inevitable. But this necessary demonstration against the American government's attempt to intervene disclosed Stalin's criminal light-mindedness in joining the Kellogg Pact.
6. There still remains the question of the revolutionary communist detachment under the leadership of Chu Teh. *Pravda* wrote about this on the eve of the transition of the conflict into a military stage. After that, we heard no more about these Chinese workers and peasants

> whom someone sent into armed battle under the banner of communism. What were the aims of the struggle? What was the role of the party in it? What was the fate of this detachment? And, finally, in whose back room are all these questions decided?

On this last point, no less important than all the rest, a final balance sheet cannot yet be drawn. But everything points to the fact that bureaucratic adventurism in this instance as in the others bears the responsibility for the weakening and exhaustion of the reserves of the Chinese Revolution.

40

The Slogan of a National Assembly in China

April 2, 1930

It seems to me that our Chinese fiends deal with the question of political slogans of democracy too metaphysically, even scholastically.

The "intricacies" begin with the name: constituent assembly or national assembly. In Russia until the revolution we used the slogan of a constituent assembly because it most clearly emphasized a break with the past. But you write that it is difficult to formulate this slogan in Chinese. If so, the slogan of a national assembly can be adopted. In the consciousness of the masses, the slogan's content will depend, firstly, on the implication revolutionary agitation gives it and, secondly, on events. You ask, "Is it possible to carry on agitation for a constituent assembly while denying that it can be achieved?" But why should we decide in advance that it cannot be? Of course the masses will support the slogan only if they consider it feasible. Who will institute a constituent assembly and how will it function? Only suppositions are possible. In case of a further weakening of the military Kuomintang regime and increasing discontent among the masses, particularly in the cities, it is possible that an attempt will be made by a part of the Kuomintang together with the "Third Party" to convene something on the style of a national assembly. They will, of course, cut into the rights of the more oppressed classes and layers as much as they can.

Would we communists enter such a restricted and manipulated national assembly? If we are not strong enough to replace it, that is, to take power, we certainly would enter it. Such a stage would not at all weaken us. On the contrary, it would help us to gather together and develop the forces of the proletarian vanguard inside this spurious assembly, and particularly outside of it, we would carry on agitation for a new and more democratic assembly. If there were a revolutionary mass movement, we would simultaneously build soviets. It is very possible that in such a case the petty-bourgeois parties would convene a relatively more democratic national assembly, as a dam against the soviets. Would we participate in this kind of assembly? Of course we would participate; again, only if we were not strong enough to replace the assembly with a higher form of government, that is soviets. Such a possibility, however, reveals itself only at the apex of revolutionary ascent. But at the present time we are far from there.

Even if there were soviets in China—which is not the case—this in itself would not be a reason to abandon the slogan of a national assembly. The majority in the soviets might be—and in the beginning would certainly be—in the hands of the conciliatory and centrist parties and organizations. We would be interested in exposing them in the open forum of the national assembly. In this way, the majority would be won over to our side more quickly and more certainly. When we succeeded in winning a majority we would counterpose the program of the Soviets to the program of the national assembly, we would rally the majority of the country around the banner of the soviets, and this would enable us, in deed and not on paper, to replace the national assembly, this parliamentary-democratic institution, with soviets, the organ of the revolutionary class dictatorship.

In Russia the Constituent Assembly lasted only one day. Why? Because it made its appearance too late, the Soviet power was already in existence and came into conflict with it. In this conflict, the Constituent Assembly represented the revolution's yesterday. But let us suppose that the bourgeois Provisional Government had been sufficiently decisive to convene the

Constituent Assembly in March or April [1917]. Was that possible? Of course it was. The Cadets used every legal trick to drag out the convening of the Constituent Assembly in the hope that the revolutionary wave would subside. The Mensheviks and the Social Revolutionaries took their cue from the Cadets. If the Mensheviks and the Social Revolutionaries had had a little more revolutionary drive, they could have convened the Constituent Assembly in a few weeks. Would we Bolsheviks have participated in the elections and in the assembly itself? Undoubtedly, for it was *we who demanded all this time the speediest convening of the Constituent Assembly*. Would the course of the revolution have changed to the disadvantage of the proletariat by an early convening of the assembly? Not at all. Perhaps you remember that the representatives of the Russian propertied classes and, imitating them, also the conciliators, were for postponing all the important questions of the revolution "until the constituent assembly", meanwhile delaying its convening. This gave the landowners and capitalists a chance to mask to a certain degree their property interests in the agrarian question, industrial question, etc.

If the Constituent Assembly had been convened let us say in April 1917, then all the social questions would have confronted it. The propertied classes would have been compelled to show their cards; the treacherous role of the conciliators would have become apparent. The Bolshevik faction in the Constituent Assembly would have won the greatest popularity and this would have helped to elect a Bolshevik majority in the soviets. Under these circumstances the Constituent Assembly would have lasted not one day but possibly several months. This would have enriched the political experience of the working masses and, rather than retard the proletarian revolution, would have accelerated it. This in itself would have been of the greatest significance. If the second revolution had occurred in July or August instead of October, the army at the front would have been less exhausted and weakened and the peace with the Hohenzollerns might have been more favorable to us. Even if we assume that the proletarian revolution would not have come a single day sooner because of the Constituent Assembly, the school of revolutionary parliamentarism would have left its mark on the political level of the masses, making our tasks the day after the October Revolution much easier.

Is this type of variant possible in China? It is not excluded. To imagine and expect that the Chinese Communist Party can jump from the present conditions of the rule of the unbridled bourgeois-military cliques, the oppression and dismemberment of the working class, and the extraordinarily low ebb of the peasant movement to the seizure of power is to believe in miracles. In practice this leads to adventurist guerrilla activity, which the Comintern is now covertly supporting. We must condemn this Policy and guard the revolutionary workers from it.

The political mobilization of the proletariat in leadership of the peasant masses is the first task that must be solved under the present circumstances—the circumstances of the military-bourgeois counter-revolution. The power of the suppressed masses is in their numbers. When they awaken they will strive to express their strength of numbers politically by means of universal suffrage.

The handful of communists already knows that universal suffrage is an instrument of bourgeois rule and that this rule can be liquidated only by means of the proletarian dictatorship. You can educate the proletarian vanguard in this spirit beforehand. But the millions of the toiling masses can be drawn to the dictatorship of the proletariat only on the basis of their own political experience, and the national assembly would be a progressive step on this road. This is why we raise this slogan in conjunction with four other slogans of the democratic revolution: the transfer of the land to the peasant poor, the eight-hour working day, the independence of China, and the right of self determination of the nationalities included in the territory of China.

It is understood that we cannot rule out the perspective—it is theoretically admissible—that the Chinese proletariat, leading the peasant masses and basing itself on soviets, will come to power before the achievement of a national assembly in one or another form. But for the immediate period at any rate this is improbable, because it *presupposes the existence of a powerful and centralized revolutionary party of the proletariat.* In its absence, what other force will unite the revolutionary masses of your gigantic country? Meanwhile it is our misfortune that there is no strong centralized Communist Party in China; it has yet to be formed. The struggle for democracy is precisely the necessary condition for that. The slogan of the national assembly would bring together the scattered regional movements and uprisings, give them political unity, and create the basis for forging the Communist Party as the leader of the proletariat and all the toiling masses on a national scale.

That is why the slogan of the national assembly—on the basis of universal, direct, equal, secret ballot—must be raised as energetically as possible and a courageous, resolute struggle developed around it. Sooner or later the sterility of the purely negative position of the Comintern and the official leadership of the Chinese Communist Party will be mercilessly exposed. The more decisively the Communist Left Opposition initiates and develops its campaign for democratic slogans, the sooner this will happen. The inevitable collapse of the Comintern policy will greatly strengthen the Left Opposition and help it to become the decisive force in the Chinese proletariat.

41

Two Letters to China

August 22 and September 1, 1930

August 22, 1930

Dear Comrade "N."

1. Today I finally received a copy of Comrade Ch'en Tu-hsiu's letter of December 10, 1929. I feel that this letter is an extremely good document. Totally clear and correct attitudes are taken in answer to all the important questions; especially on the question of a democratic dictatorship, Comrade Tu-hsiu takes a completely correct stand. At the time you wrote to me explaining why you could not unite with Ch'en Tu-hsiu, your reason was that he still seemed to support the "democratic dictatorship" viewpoint. I feel this question to be a decisive one, because if you do not have a proletarian dictatorship leading the poor peasants, then it is the same as a democratic dictatorship, which in reality is only another name for a new Kuomintang policy, that's all! There can be no compromise on this question! But it is clear from the letter of December 10 that Comrade Ch'en's position is correct. Because of this, how can I explain and defend your position? What other differing opinions have you? None, I think, unless there are some unexpected difficulties. How can we get together on the question of a national assembly? What kind of role would the parliamentary system play in China? On fundamental questions we are in complete accord. As for the unexpected or more complicated questions, some are merely academic, while others are tactical questions. These questions will be decided as events

unfold. Here, I must honestly tell you that your opinions on the national assembly and the parliamentary system cannot stand, in my view. It is true that *Wo-men-tihua* says that this is Kautskyism, but there is no basis for this.

2. When we have such an outstanding revolutionary as Ch'en Tu-hsiu, who formally breaks with the party, is then thrown out of the party, and finally announces that his stand is 100 percent in accord with the International Opposition, how can we ignore him? Is it possible that you have many Communist Party members who are as experienced as Ch'en Tu-hsiu? He made many mistakes in the past, but he is already aware of them. To become aware of one's past mistakes is very valuable to revolutionists and leaders. We have many young people in the Opposition who can and should learn from Comrade Ch'en Tu-hsiu!

3. You attack the Wo-men-ti-hua group for incorrectly assessing the general political situation in China and denying the utility of slogans about striving for democracy. I have received a long letter from them, and it appears that the differences of principle about which you speak have all been eliminated. You wrote that they have revised the agenda of the conference. If this is so, they have revised it for the better and, moreover, are even closer to us. You attack them for their underhanded methods (such as bringing up old disputes and revising the agenda). Naturally, this problem carries its own meaning, but if they feel there are some mistakes, and everyone agrees to revise the agenda, that isn't such a terrible crime. Isn't it a fact that they are still doing all this revising in a Marxist spirit? The three other points that you raised (the most important being whether to work inside or outside the party) are really not questions of principle, for there has not been one Opposition section that has taken as its mission the creation of a second party. We must continue to look upon ourselves as factions within the party. Naturally, we must recruit new members into the Communist Party ranks, that is, into the Opposition. The correct mixture of work both inside and outside the party can only be attained through practical work. No matter what, our work outside the party must be of the

following nature: Comrades inside the party must look upon us as friends, not enemies. Let's look at the European experience. In that case, the opposition in France and Germany has recently grown closer to the party, and yet there has been absolutely no lessening in the struggle between the party and the Opposition. This strategy has already obtained the very best results in France and is fast doing so in Germany.

4. *Biulleten Oppozitsii,* in its current issue, is giving great space to the China question. It's too bad that, up to now, you have not sent any materials regarding China's peasant (Soviet) movement, in order that we might adopt a correct stand. It is very important that we collect all information and carefully research all facts; otherwise we just might kill our opportunity to affect the whole situation.

Isn't there still a chance that the peasant war will converge with the workers' movement? This is an extremely important question. Theoretically, it doesn't discard the possibility of making gains while underground. That is, under the influence of the peasant insurrection, the revolution in the cities can intensify and quickly move forward. If this comes about, then the peasant insurrection takes on a different objective meaning. Naturally, our fundamental mission is to improve upon the ordinary peasant insurrection and, at the same time, to fuse with it. In addition, we must explain to the workers the true nature of peasant insurrections and what might be obtained through them in the future. Furthermore, we must devise a means to raise the workers' spirits through these insurrections. At the same time, we must visibly support the insurrectionists in their demands and programs, while opposing the landlords, officials, and bourgeoisie in their rumors, slanders, and repression. It is upon this foundation, and only this foundation, that we can expose the tricks of the Comintern organizations. They say that "soviet regimes" have been established in China—without a proletarian dictatorship! It has even reached the point where the workers refuse to actively participate in the movement. I expect that the "International" [International Left Opposition] will soon issue a manifesto on this question to inform China's Communist Party members.

5. It seems to be a fine time for me to send you a copy of *The Permanent Revolution.* You should receive it soon.

6. I am afraid that the address I have for Chen Tu-hsiu is no good. Please send him my regards, and tell him that I was very happy to read his letter of last December 10. I firmly hope we can work together in the future.

A warm handshake,

Trotsky

September 1, 1930

Dear Comrades,

I have already received your letter of July 27 (from the Shihyueh she).

I will only answer very simply, because the International Left Opposition is at this time planning to discuss the problems of China's present situation in a special manifesto. So I will merely repeat what has been written to the other groups.

1. It is the policy of the International Opposition not to side with any particular group of the Chinese Left Opposition against any other group. The reason being: nothing in any of our materials suggests the existence of serious differences requiring continued disunity.
2. In light of this, no single group of the Chinese Left Opposition can consider itself the sole representative of the International Left Opposition and attack any other group.
3. The same goes for Comrade Chen Tuhsiu's group. Not long ago I received an English translation of Comrade Ch'en's open letter of December 10, 1929. Comrade Ch'en expressed views on fundamental issues which were in total agreement with our general stand. Realizing this, I fail to understand why some of our Chinese comrades still call Comrade Ch'en's group "rightist". At the same time, none of the other groups have furnished us with any documentary proof of this charge.
4. Because of this, we feel it is necessary that these four groups publicly unite in a sincere fashion, basing

themselves on commonly held principles. Recently, the International Opposition has advised these groups on the basic points that should be incorporated in the party platform to be drafted by the platform committee, and on the methods of organizing for unification.

5. As for the question of the national assembly, I have already discussed that in previous articles. It seems that some of our Chinese comrades seek to "split hairs" with us over this question. If we struggle amongst ourselves over this question and its concomitant problems (personally, I don't think this will happen), then this dispute will certainly manifest itself throughout the drafting of a party platform. Only after we have received alternate analyses can the International Opposition gauge the depth of this dispute. However, we sincerely hope that the analyses we do receive are not written in a contentious way; rather, they should be written in such a way as to enable the Chinese Left Opposition to unify on a firm foundation of commonly held principles.

Communist greetings,

Trotsky

P.S: I am sending you two copies of this letter; forward one to Comrade Ch'en Tu-hsiu, as I do not know his address.

42

Stalin and the Chinese Revolution

Facts and Documents

August 26, 1930
Prinkipo

Facts and Documents

The Chinese Revolution of 1925–27 remains the greatest event of modern history after the 1917 revolution in Russia. Over the problems of the Chinese Revolution the basic currents of Communism come to clash. The present official leader of the Comintern, Stalin, has revealed his true stature in the events of the Chinese Revolution. The basic documents pertaining to the Chinese Revolution are dispersed, scattered, forgotten. Some are carefully concealed.

On these pages we want to reproduce the basic stages of the Chinese Revolution in the light of articles and speeches by Stalin and his closest assistants, as well as decisions of the Comintern dictated by Stalin. For this purpose we use genuine texts from our archives. We especially present excerpts from the speech of Khitarov, a young Stalinist, at the 15th Congress of the Communist Party of the Soviet Union, which were concealed from the Party by Stalin. The readers will convince themselves of the tremendous significance of the testimony of Khitarov, a young Stalinist functionary—careerist, a participant in the Chinese events, and at the present time one of the leaders of the Young Communist International.

In order to make the facts and citations more comprehensible, we think it useful to remind the readers of the sequence of the most important events in the Chinese Revolution.

- March 20th, 1926—Chiang Kai-shek's first coup in Canton.
- Autumn 1926—the Seventh Plenum of the ECCI, with the participation of a Chiang Kai-shek delegate from the Guomindang.
- April 13, 1927—*coup d'état* by Chiang Kai-shek in Shanghai.
- The end of May 1927—the counter-revolutionary coup of the "Left" Guomindang in Wuhan.
- The end of May 1927—the Eighth Plenum of the ECCI proclaims it the duty of Communists to remain within the "Left" Guomindang.
- August 1927—the Chinese Communist Party proclaims a course toward an uprising.
- December 1927—the Canton insurrection.
- February 1928—the Ninth Plenum of the ECCI proclaims for China the course towards armed insurrection and soviets.

  July 1928—the Sixth Congress of the Comintern renounces the slogan of armed insurrection as a practical slogan.

1. The Bloc of Four Classes

Stalin's Chinese policy was based on a bloc of four classes. Here is how the Berlin organ of the Mensheviks appraised this policy:

> On April 10 [1927], Martynov, in *Pravda*, most effectively and in a quite Menshevik manner, showed the correctness of the official position which insists on the necessity of retaining the bloc of four classes, on not hastening to overthrow the coalition government, in which the workers sit side by side with the big bourgeoisie, not to impose 'socialist tasks' upon it prematurely.[1]

What did the policy of coalition with the bourgeoisie look like? Let us quote an excerpt from the official organ of the Executive Committee of the Comintern:

> On January 5, 1927, the Canton government made public a new

> strike law in which the workers are prohibited from carrying weapons at demonstrations, from arresting merchants and industrialists, from confiscating their goods, and which establishes compulsory arbitration for a series of conflicts. This law contains a number of paragraphs protecting the interests of the workers But along with these paragraphs there are others, which limit the freedom to strike more than is required by the interests of defence during a revolutionary war.[2]

In the rope placed around the workers by the bourgeoisie the threads ("paragraphs") favorable to the workers are traced. The shortcoming of the noose is that it is tightened more than is required "by the interests of defence" (of the Chinese bourgeoisie). This is written in the central organ of the Comintern. Who does the writing? Martynov. When does he write? On February 25, six weeks before the Shanghai bloodbath.

2. The Perspectives of the Revolution according to Stalin

How did Stalin evaluate the perspectives of the revolution led by his ally, Chiang Kai-shek? Here are the least scandalous parts of Stalin's declaration (the most scandalous parts of it were never made public):

> The revolutionary armies in China [that is, the armies of Chiang Kai-shek] are the most important factor in the struggle of the Chinese workers and peasants for their liberation. For the advance of the Cantonese means a blow at imperialism, a blow at its agents in China, and freedom of assembly, freedom of press, freedom of organization for all the revolutionary elements in China in general and for the workers in particular.[3]

The army of Chiang Kai-shek is the army of workers and peasants. It bears freedom for the whole population, "for the workers in particular".

What is needed for the success of the revolution? Very little:

> The student youth (the revolutionary youth), the working youth, the peasant youth—all these are a force that can advance the revolution with seven league boots, if it should be subordinated to the ideological and political influence of the Guomindang.[4]

In this manner, the task of the Comintern consisted not of

liberating the workers and peasants from the influence of the bourgeoisie but, on the contrary, of subordinating them to its influence. This was written in the days when Chiang Kai-shek, armed by Stalin, marched at the head of the workers and peasants subordinated to him, "with seven-league boots", towards the Shanghai *coup d'état*.

3. Stalin and Chiang Kai-shek

After the Canton *coup d'état*, engineered by Chiang Kai-shek in March 1926, and which our press passed over in silence, when the Communists were reduced to the role of miserable appendices of the Guomindang and even signed an obligation not to criticize Sun-Yat-Sen-ism, Chiang Kai-shek—a remarkable detail indeed!—came forward to insist on the acceptance of the Guomindang into the Comintern: in preparing himself for the role of an executioner, he wanted to have the cover of world Communism and—he got it. The Guomindang, led by Chiang Kai-shek and Hu Hanmin, was accepted into the Comintern (as a "sympathizing" party). While engaged in the preparation of a decisive counter-revolutionary action in April 1927, Chiang Kai-shek at the same time took care to exchange portraits with Stalin. This strengthening of the ties of friendship was prepared by the journey of Bubnov, a member of the Central Committee and one of Stalin's agents, to Chiang Kai-shek. Another "detail": Bubnov's journey to Canton coincided with the March *coup d'état* of Chiang Kai-shek. What about Bubnov? He made the Chinese Communists submit and keep quiet.

After the Shanghai overturn, the bureau of the Comintern, upon Stalin's order, attempted to deny that the executioner Chiang Kai-shek still remained a member of the Comintern. They had forgotten the vote at the Political Bureau, when everybody, against the vote of one (Trotsky), sanctioned the admission of the Guomindang into the Comintern with a consultative voice. They had forgotten that at the Seventh Plenum of the ECCI, which condemned the Left Opposition, "comrade Shao Li-tse", a delegate from the Guomindang, participated. Among other things he said:

> Comrade Chiang Kai-shek in his speech to the members of the Guomindang, declared that the Chinese revolution would be inconceivable if it could not correctly solve the agrarian, that is, the peasant question. What the Guomindang strives for is that there should not be created a bourgeois domination after the nationalist revolution in China, as happened in the West, as we see it now in all countries except the USSR, we are all convinced, that under the leadership of the Communist Party and the Comintern, the Guomindang will fulfil its historic task.[5]

This is how matters stood at the Seventh Plenum in the autumn of 1926. After the member of the Comintern, "comrade Chiang Kai-shek", who had promised to solve all the tasks under the leadership of the Comintern, solved only one: precisely the task of a bloody crushing of the revolution, the Eighth Plenum in May 1927 declared in the resolution on the Chinese question:

> The ECCI states that the events fully justified the prognosis of the Seventh Plenum.

Justified, and right to the very end! If this is humour, it is at any rate not arbitrary. However, let us not forget that this humour is thickly coloured with Shanghai blood.

4. The Strategy of Lenin and the Strategy of Stalin

What tasks did Lenin set before the Comintern with regard to the backward countries?

> It is necessary to carry on a determined struggle against the attempt to surround the bourgeois democratic liberation movements in the backward countries with a Communist cloak.

In carrying this out, the Guomindang, which had promised to establish in China "not a bourgeois régime", was admitted into the Comintern.

Lenin, it is understood, recognized the necessity of a temporary alliance with the bourgeois-democratic movement, but he understood by this, of course, not an alliance with the bourgeois parties, duping and betraying the petty-bourgeois revolutionary democracy (the peasants and the small city folk), but an alliance with the organizations and groupings of the masses themselves—against the national bourgeoisie. In what form, then, did Lenin visualize the alliance with the bourgeois democracy of the colonies? To these, too, he gives an answer in his thesis written for the Second Congress:

> The Communist International should enter into a temporary alliance with the democratic bourgeoisie of the colonies and backward countries, but should not fuse with it and must unconditionally maintain the independent character of the proletarian movement – even in its embryonic form.

It seems that in executing the decisions of the Second Congress, the Communist Party was made to join the Guomindang and the Guomindang was admitted into the Comintern. All this summed up is called Leninism.

5. The Government of Chiang Kai-shek as a Living Refutation of the State

How the leaders of the Communist Party of the Soviet Union appraised the government of Chiang Kai-shek one year after the first Canton *coup d'état* (March 20, 1926) may be seen clearly from the public speeches of the members of the Party Political Bureau.

Here is how Kalinin spoke in March 1927, at the Moscow factory *Goshnak*:

> All the classes of China, beginning with the proletariat and ending with the bourgeoisie, hate the militarists as the puppets of foreign capital; all the classes of China look upon the Canton government as the national government of the whole of China in the same way.[6]

Another member of the Political Bureau, Rudzutak, spoke a few days later at a gathering of the street car workers. The *Pravda* report states:

> Pausing further on the situation in China, comrade Rudzutak pointed out that the revolutionary government has behind it all the classes of China.[7]

Voroshilov spoke in the same spirit more than once.

Truly in vain did Lenin clear the Marxian theory of the state from the petty-bourgeois garbage. The epigones succeeded in a short time in covering it with twice as much refuse.

As late as April 5, Stalin spoke in the Hall of the Columns in defence of the Communists remaining inside the party of Chiang Kai-shek, and what is more, he denied the danger of a betrayal by his ally: "Borodin is on guard!" The coup occurred exactly one week later.

6. How the Shanghai Coup took Place

In this connection we have the exceptionally valuable testimony of a witness and participant, the Stalinist Khitarov, who arrived from China on the eve of the Fifteenth Congress and appeared there with his information. The most important points of his narrative have been deleted by Stalin from the Minutes with the consent of Khitarov himself: the truth cannot be made public if it so crushingly proves all the accusations the Opposition directed against Stalin. Let us give the floor to Khitarov[8]:

> The first bloody wound has been inflicted upon the Chinese revolution in Shanghai by the execution of the Shanghai workers on April 11–12.
>
> I would like to speak in greater detail about this coup because I know that in our party little is known about it. In Shanghai there existed for a period of 21 days the so-called People's Government in which the Communists had a majority. We can therefore say that for 21 days Shanghai had a Communist government. This Communist government, however, showed complete inactivity in spite of the fact that the coup by Chiang Kai-shek was expected any day.
>
> The Communist government, in the first place, did not begin to work for a long time under the excuse that, on the one hand, the bourgeois part of the government did not want to get to work, sabotaging it, and, on the other hand, because the Wuhan government did not approve of the composition of the Shanghai government. Of the activity of this government three decrees are known, and one of them, by the way, speaks of the preparation of a triumphal reception to Chiang Kai-shek who was expected to arrive in Shanghai.
>
> In Shanghai, at this time, the relations between the army and the workers became acute. It is known, for instance, that the army [that is, Chiang Kai-shek's officers – *L.T.*] deliberately drove the workers into slaughter. The army for a period of several days stood at the gates of Shanghai and did not want to enter the city because

> they knew that the workers were battling against the Shantungese, and they wanted the workers to be bled in this struggle. They expected to enter later. Afterwards the army did enter Shanghai. But among these troops there was one division that sympathized with the workers—the First Division of the Canton army. The commander, Say-O, was in disfavour with Chiang Kai-shek, who knew about his sympathies for the mass movement, because this Say-O himself came from the ranks. He was at first the commander of a company and later commanded a division.
>
> Say-O came to the comrades in Shanghai and told them that there was a military coup in preparation, that Chiang Kai-shek had summoned him to headquarters, had given him an unusually cold reception and that he, Say-O, would not go there any longer—because he feared a trap. Chiang Kai-shek proposed to Say-O that he get out of the city with his division and to go to the front; and he, Say-O, proposed to the Central Committee of the Communist Party that they agree that he should not submit to Chiang Kai-shek's order. He was ready to remain in Shanghai and fight together with the Shanghai workers against the military overthrow that was in preparation. To all this, our responsible leaders of the Chinese Communist Party, Chen Duxiu included, declared that they knew about the coup being prepared, but that they did not want a premature conflict with Chiang Kai-shek. The First Division was let out of Shanghai, the city was occupied by the Second Division of Bai-Sung Gee and, two days later, the Shanghai workers were massacred.

Why was this truly stirring narrative left out of the Minutes (p. 32)? Because it was not at all a question of the Chinese Communist Party but of the Political Bureau of the Soviet Union.

On May 24, 1927, Stalin spoke at the Plenum of the ECCI:

> The Opposition is dissatisfied because the Shanghai workers did not enter into a decisive battle against the imperialists and their myrmidons. But it does not understand that the revolution in China cannot develop at a fast tempo. It does not understand that one cannot take up a decisive struggle under unfavourable conditions. The Opposition does not understand that not to avoid a decisive struggle under unfavourable conditions (when it can be avoided), means to make easier the work of the enemies of the revolution ...

This section of Stalin's speech is entitled: *The Mistakes of the*

Opposition. In the Shanghai tragedy Stalin found mistakes ... by the Opposition. In reality the Opposition at that time did not yet know the concrete circumstances of the situation in Shanghai, that is, it did not know how much more favourable the situation still was for the workers in March and the beginning of April, in spite of all the mistakes and crimes of the leadership of the Comintern. Even from the deliberately concealed story of Khitarov it is clear that the situation could have been saved even at that time. The workers in Shanghai are in power. They are partly armed. There is all the possibility of arming them far more extensively. Chiang Kai-shek's army is unreliable. There are sections of it where even the commanding staff is on the side of the workers. But everything and everyone is paralysed at the top. We must not prepare for the decisive struggle against Chiang Kai-shek, but for a triumphal reception to him. Because Stalin gave his categorical instructions from Moscow: not only do not resist the ally, Chiang Kai-shek, but on the contrary, show your loyalty to him. How? Lie down on your back and play dead.

At the May Plenum of the ECCI, Stalin still defended on technical, tactical grounds this terrible surrender of positions without a struggle, which led to the crushing of the proletariat in the revolution. Half a year later, at the Fifteenth Congress of the CPSU, Stalin was already silent. The delegates at the Congress extended Khitarov's time so as to give him a chance to end his narrative which gripped even them. But Stalin found a simple way out of it by deleting Khitarov's narrative from the Minutes. We publish this truly historic document here for the first time.

Let us note in addition one interesting circumstance: While smearing up the course of events as much as possible and concealing the really guilty one, Khitarov singles out for responsibility Chen Duxiu whom the Stalinists had until then defended in every way against the Opposition, because he had merely carried out their instructions. But at that time it was already becoming clear that comrade Chen Duxiu would not agree to play the role of a silent scapegoat, that he wanted openly to analyse the reasons for this catastrophe. All the hounds of the Comintern were let loose upon him, not for mistakes fatal to the revolution but because he would not agree to deceive the workers and to be a cover for Stalin.

7. The Organizers of the "Infusion of Workers' and Peasants' Blood"

The leading organ of the Comintern wrote on March 18, 1927, about three weeks prior to the Shanghai overturn:

> The leadership of the Guomindang is at present ill with a lack of revolutionary workers' and peasants' blood. The Chinese Communist Party must aid in the infusion of this blood, and then the situation will radically change.

What an ominous play on words! The Guomindang is in "need of workers' and peasants' blood". The "aid" was rendered in the fullest measure: in April-May, Chiang Kai-shek and Wang Jingwei received a sufficient "infusion" of workers' and peasants' blood.

With regard to the Chiang Kai-shek chapter of Stalin's policy, the Eighth Plenum (May 1927) declared:

> The ECCI assumes that the tactic of the bloc with the national bourgeoisie in the already declining period of the revolution was absolutely correct. The Northern expedition alone [!] serves as historic justification for this tactic ...

And how it serves!

Here is Stalin all the way through. The Northern expedition, which incidentally proved to be an expedition against the proletariat, serves as a justification of his friendship with Chiang Kai-shek. The ECCI has done everything it could to make it impossible to draw the lessons of the bloodbath of the Chinese workers.

8. Stalin repeats his Experiment with the "Left" Guomindang

Further on, the following remarkable point is left out of Khitarov's speech:

> After the Shanghai *coup*, it has become clear to everyone that a new epoch is beginning in the Chinese revolution; that the bourgeoisie is retreating from the revolution. This was recognized

> and immediately so stated. But one thing was left out of sight in connection with this—that while the bourgeoisie was retreating from the revolution, the Wuhan government did not even think of leaving the bourgeoisie. Unfortunately, among the majority of our comrades, this was not understood; they had illusions with regard to the Wuhan government. They considered the Wuhan government almost an image, a prototype of the democratic dictatorship of the proletariat and peasantry. [The omission is on page 33.]
>
> After the Wuhan *coup*, it became clear that the bourgeoisie is retreating ...

This would be ridiculous if it were not so tragic. After Chiang Kai-shek slew the revolution in the face of the workers disarmed by Stalin, the penetrating strategists finally "understood" that the bourgeoisie is "retreating". But having recognized that his friend Chiang Kai-shek was retreating, Stalin ordered the Chinese Communists to subordinate themselves to that same Wuhan government which, according to Khitarov's information at the Fifteenth Congress, "did not even think of leaving the bourgeoisie". Unfortunately "our comrades did not understand this". What comrades? Borodin, who clung to Stalin's telegraph wires? Khitarov does not mention any names. The Chinese Revolution is dear to him, but his hide—is still dearer.

However, let us listen to Stalin:

> Chiang Kai-shek's *coup d'état* means that there will now be two camps, two armies, two centres in the South: a revolutionary centre in Wuhan and a counter-revolutionary centre in Nanking.

Is it clear where the centre of the revolution is located? In Wuhan!

> This means that the revolutionary Guomindang in Wuhan, leading a decisive struggle against militarism and imperialism, will in reality be transformed into an organ of the revolutionary democratic dictatorship of the proletariat and peasantry ...

Now we finally know what the democratic dictatorship of the proletariat and peasantry looks like!

> From this it follows further [Stalin continues], that the policy of close collaboration of the lefts and the Communists inside the

> Guomindang acquires a particular force and a particular significance at the present stage. That without such a collaboration the victory of the revolution is impossible.[9]

Without the collaboration of the counter-revolutionary bandits of the "Left" Guomindang, "the victory of the revolution is impossible"! That is how Stalin, step after step—in Canton, in Shanghai, in Hankow—assured the victory of the revolution.

9. Against the Opposition—for the Guomindang

How did the Comintern regard the "Left" Guomindang? The Eighth Plenum of the ECCI gave a clear answer to this question in its struggle against the Opposition.

"The ECCI rejects most determinedly the demand to leave the Guomindang ... The Guomindang in China is precisely that specific form of organization where the proletariat collaborates directly with the petty bourgeoisie and the peasantry."

In this manner the ECCI quite correctly saw in the Guomindang the realization of the Stalinist idea of the "two-class workers' and peasants' party".

The not unknown Rafes, who was at first a minister under Petlura and afterwards carried out Stalin's instructions in China, wrote in May 1927 in the theoretical organ of the Central Committee of the CPSU:

> Our Russian Opposition, as is known, also considers it necessary for the Communists to leave the Guomindang. A consistent defence of this viewpoint would lead the adherents of the policy to leave the Guomindang, to the famous formula proclaimed by comrade Trotsky in 1917: 'Without a tsar, but a labour government!', which, for China, might have been changed in form: 'Without the militarists, but a labour government!' We have no reason to listen to such consistent defenders of leaving the Guomindang.[10]

The slogan of Stalin-Rafes was: "Without the workers, but with Chiang Kai-shek!" "Without the peasants, but with Wang Jingwei!" "Against the Opposition, but for the Guomindang!"

10. Stalin again Disarms the Chinese Workers and Peasants

What was the policy of the leadership during the Wuhan period of the revolution? Let us listen to the Stalinist Khitarov on this question. Here is what we read in the Minutes of the Fifteenth Congress:

> What was the policy of the CC of the Communist Party at this time, during this whole [Wuhan] period? The policy of the CC of the Communist Party was carried on under the slogan of *retreat* ...
>
> Under the slogan of retreat—in the revolutionary period, at the moment of the highest tension of the revolutionary struggles—the Communist Party carries on its work, and under this slogan surrenders one position after another without a battle: To this surrender of positions belongs: the agreement to subordinate all the trade unions, all the peasant unions and other revolutionary organizations to the Guomindang; the rejection of independent action without the permission of the Central Committee of the Guomindang; the decision on the voluntary disarming of the workers' pickets in Hankow; the dissolution of the pioneer organizations in Wuhan; the actual crushing of all the peasant unions in the territory of the national government, etc.

Here is pictured quite frankly the policy of the Chinese Communist Party, the leadership of which actually helps the "national" bourgeoisie to crush the people's uprising and to annihilate the best fighters of the proletariat and the peasantry.

But the frankness here is treacherous: the above citation is printed in the Minutes after the omission cited above by the line of periods. Here is what the section concealed by Stalin says:

> At the same time, some responsible comrades, Chinese and *non-Chinese*, invented the so-called theory of retreat. They declared: the reaction is advancing upon us from all sides. We must therefore immediately retreat in order to save the possibility of legal work, and if we retreat, we will save this possibility, but if we defend ourselves or attempt to advance, we will lose everything.

Precisely in those days (end of May 1927), when the Wuhan counter-revolution began to crush the workers and peasants, in the face of the Left Guomindang, Stalin declared at the Plenum of the ECCI (May 24, 1927):

> The agrarian revolution is the basis and content of the bourgeois democratic revolution in China. *The Guomindang in Hankow and the Hankow government are the centre of the bourgeois-democratic revolutionary movement.*[11]

To a written question of a worker as to why no soviets were being formed in Wuhan, Stalin replied:

> It is clear that whoever calls at present for the immediate creation of soviets of workers' deputies in this [Wuhan] district, is attempting to jump [!] over the *Guomindang phase of the Chinese revolution*, and he risks putting the Chinese revolution in a most difficult position.

Precisely: In a "most difficult" position! On May 13, 1927, in a conversation with students, Stalin declared:

> Should soviets of workers' and peasants' deputies, in general, be created in China? Yes, they should, absolutely they should. They will have to be created *after the strengthening of the Wuhan revolutionary government*, after the unfolding of the agrarian revolution, in the transformation of the agrarian revolution, of the bourgeois-democratic revolution into the revolution of the proletariat.

In this manner, Stalin did not consider it permissible to strengthen the position of the workers and peasants through soviets, so long as the positions of the Wuhan government, of the counter-revolutionary bourgeoisie, were not strengthened.

Referring to the famous theses of Stalin which justified his Wuhan policy, the organ of the Russian Mensheviks wrote at that time:

> Very little can be said against the essence of the Ôline' traced there [in Stalin's theses]. As much as possible to remain in the Guomindang, and to cling to its left wing and to the Wuhan government to the last possible moment: 'to avoid a decisive struggle under unfavourable conditions'; not to issue the slogan 'All power to the soviets' so as not to give new weapons into the hands of the enemies of the Chinese people for the struggle against the revolution, for creating new legends that it is not a national revolution that is taking place in China, but an artificial transplanting of Moscow sovietization'—what can actually be more sensible ...?[12]

On its part, the Eighth Plenum of the ECCI, which was in session at the end of May 1927, that is, at a time when the crushing of the workers' and peasants' organizations in Wuhan had already begun, adopted the following decision:

> The ECCI insistently calls the attention of the Chinese Communist Party to the necessity of taking all possible measures for the strengthening and development of all mass organizations of workers and peasants ... within all these organizations it is necessary to carry on an agitation *to enter the Guomindang*, transforming the latter into a mighty mass organization of the revolutionary petty-bourgeois democracy and the working class.

"To enter the Guomindang" meant to bring one's head voluntarily to the slaughter. The bloody lesson of Shanghai passed without leaving a trace. The Communists, as before, were being transformed into cattle herders for the party of the bourgeois executioners (the Guomindang), into suppliers of "workers' and peasants' blood" for Wang Jingwei and company.

11. The Stalinist Experiment with Ministerialism

In spite of the experience of the Russian Kerenskiad and the protests of the Left Opposition, Stalin wound up his Guomindang policy with an experiment in ministerialism: two Communists entered the bourgeois government in the capacity of ministers of labour and agriculture—the classic posts of hostages!—under the direct instructions of the Comintern: to paralyse the class struggle with the aim of retaining the united front. Such directives were constantly given from Moscow by telegraph until August 1927.

Let us hear how Khitarov depicted Communist "ministerialism" in practice before the audience of delegates at the Fifteenth Congress of the CPSU. "You know that there were two Communist ministers in the government," says Khitarov. The rest of this passage is deleted from the Minutes:

> Afterwards, they [the Communist ministers] stopped coming around to the ministries altogether, failed to appear themselves and put in their places a hundred functionaries. During the activity of these ministers not a single law was promulgated which would ease the position of the workers and peasants. This reprehensible activity was wound up with a still more reprehensible, shameful end. These ministers declared that one of them was ill and the other wished to go abroad, etc., and therefore asked to be released. They did not resign with a political declaration in which they would have declared: You are counter-revolutionists, you are

> traitors, you are betrayers—we will no longer go along with you. No. They declared that one was allegedly ill. In addition, *Tang Pingshan* wrote that *he could not cope with the magnitude of the peasant movement*, therefore he asked that his release be granted. Can a greater disgrace be imagined? A Communist minister declares that he cannot cope with the peasant movement. Then who can? It is clear, the military, and nobody else. This was an open legalization of the rigorous suppression of the peasant movement, undertaken by the Wuhan government.

This is what the participation of the Communists in the "democratic dictatorship" of the workers and peasants looked like. In December 1927, when Stalin's speeches and articles were still fresh in the minds of all, Khitarov's narrative could not be printed, even though the latter—young but precocious! —in looking after his own welfare, did not say a word about the Moscow leaders of Chinese ministerialism and even referred to Borodin only as "a certain non-Chinese comrade".

Tang Pingshan complained—Khitarov raged hypocritically —that he could not cope with the peasant movement. But Khitarov could not help knowing that this was just the task that Stalin set before Tang Pingshan. Tang Pingshan came to Moscow at the end of 1926 for instructions and reported to the Plenum of the ECCI how well he coped with the "Trotskyists", that is, with those Communists who wanted to leave the Guomindang in order to organize the workers and peasants. Stalin was sending Tang Pingshan telegraphic instructions to curb the peasant movement in order not to antagonize Chiang Kai-shek and the bourgeois military staff. At the same time, Stalin accused the Opposition of underestimating the peasantry.

The Eighth Plenum even adopted a special *Resolution on the Speeches of comrades Trotsky and Vuyovitch at the Plenary Session of the ECCI*. It read:

> Comrade Trotsky ... demanded at the Plenary Session the immediate establishment of the dual power in the form of soviets and the immediate adoption of a course towards the overthrow of the Left Guomindang government. This apparently [!] ultra-left [!!] but in reality opportunist [!!!] demand is nothing but the repetition of the old Trotskyist position of jumping over the petty-bourgeois, peasant stage of the revolution.

We see here in all its nakedness the essence of the struggle against Trotskyism: the defence of the bourgeoisie against the revolution of the workers and peasants.

12. Leaders and Masses

All the organizations of the working class were utilized by the "leaders" in order to restrain, to curb, to paralyse the struggle of the revolutionary masses. Here is what Khitarov related:

> The congress of the trade unions [in Wuhan] was postponed from day to day and when it was finally convened no attempt whatsoever was made to utilize it for the organization of resistance. On the contrary, on the last day of the congress, it was decided to stage a demonstration before the building of the National government with the object of expressing their sentiment of loyalty to the government. (**Lozovsky:** I scared them there with my speech.)

Lozovsky was not ashamed at that moment to bring himself forward. "Scaring" the same Chinese trade unionists whom he had thrown into confusion, with bold phrases, Lozovsky succeeded on the spot, in China, in not seeing anything, not understanding anything, and not foreseeing anything. Returning from China, this "leader" wrote:

> The proletariat has become the dominant force in the struggle for the national emancipation of China.[13]

This was said about a proletariat whose head was being squeezed in the iron manacles of Chiang Kai-shek. This is how the general secretary of the Red International of Labour Unions deceived the workers of the whole world. And after the crushing of the Chinese workers (with the aid of all sorts of "general secretaries"), Lozovsky derides the Chinese trade unionists: those "cowards" got scared, you see, by the intrepid speeches of the most intrepid Lozovsky. In this little episode lies the art of the present "leaders", their whole mechanism, the whole of their morals!

The might of the revolutionary movement of the masses of the people was truly incomparable. We have seen that in spite of three years of mistakes the situation could still have been saved in Shanghai by receiving Chiang Kai-shek not as a liberator but as a mortal foe. Moreover, even after the Shanghai *coup d'état* the Communists could still have strengthened themselves in the provinces. But they were ordered to submit themselves to the "Left" Guomindang. Khitarov gives a description of one of the most illuminating episodes of the second counter-revolution carried out by the Left Guomindang:

> The *coup* in Wuhan occurred on May 21–22. The *coup* took place under simply unbelievable circumstances. In Changsha the army consisted of 1,700 soldiers, and the peasants made up a majority of the armed detachments gathered around Changsha to the number of 20,000. In spite of this, the military command succeeded in seizing power, in shooting all the active peasants, in dispersing all revolutionary organizations and in establishing its dictatorship only because of the cowardly, irresolute, conciliatory policy of the leaders in Changsha and Wuhan. When the peasants learned of the *coup* in Changsha they began to prepare themselves, to gather around Changsha in order to undertake a march on it. This march was set for May 21. The peasants started to draw up their detachments in increasing numbers towards Changsha. It was clear that they would seize the city without great effort. But at this point *a letter arrived from the Central Committee of the Chinese Communist Party in which Chen Duxiu wrote that they should presumably avoid an open conflict and transfer the question to Wuhan.* On the basis of this letter, the District Committee dispatched to the peasant detachments an order to retreat, not to advance any further; but this order failed to reach two detachments. Two peasant detachments advanced on Wuhan and were there annihilated by the soldiers.[14]

This is approximately how matters proceeded in the rest of the provinces. Under Borodin's guidance—"Borodin is on guard!" —the Chinese Communists carried out very punctiliously the instructions of Stalin: not to break with the Left Guomindang, the chosen leaders of the democratic revolution. The capitulation at Changsha took place on May 31, that is, a few days after the decisions of the Eighth Plenum of the ECCI and in full conformity with these decisions.

The leaders indeed did everything in order to destroy the cause of the masses!

In that same speech of his, Khitarov declares:

> I consider it my duty to declare that in spite of the fact that the Chinese Communist Party has for a long time committed unheard-of opportunist errors. We do not, however, need to blame the Party masses for them to my deep conviction (I have seen many sections of the Comintern), there isn't another such section so devoted to the cause of Communism, so courageous in its fight for our cause as are the Chinese Communists. There are no other Communists as courageous as the Chinese comrades.[15]

Undoubtedly, the revolutionary Chinese workers and peasants revealed exceptional self-sacrifice in the struggle. Together with the revolution, they were crushed by the opportunist leadership. Not the one that had its seat in Canton, Shanghai and Wuhan but the one that was commanding from Moscow. Such will be the verdict of history!

13. The Canton Uprising

On August 7, 1927, the special conference of the Chinese Communist Party condemned, according to previous instructions from Moscow, the opportunist policy of its leadership, that is, its whole past, and decided: to prepare for an armed insurrection. Stalin's special emissaries had the task of preparing an insurrection in Canton timed for the Fifteenth Congress of the Communist Party of the Soviet Union, in order to cover up the physical extermination of the Russian Opposition with the political triumph of the Stalinist tactic in China.

On the declining wave, while the depression still prevailed among the urban masses, the Canton "soviet" uprising was hurriedly organized, heroic in the conduct of the workers, criminal in the adventurism of the leadership. The news of the new crushing of the Canton proletariat arrived exactly at the moment of the Fifteenth Congress. In this manner, Stalin was smashing the Bolshevik-Leninists exactly at the moment when his ally of yesterday, Chiang Kai-shek, was crushing the Chinese Communists.

It was necessary to draw up new balance sheets, that is, once more to shift the responsibility on to the executors. On February 7, 1928, *Pravda* wrote:

> The provincial armies fought undividedly against Red Canton and this proved to be the greatest and *oldest shortcoming of the Chinese Communist Party, precisely insufficient political work for the decomposition of the reactionary armies*.

"The oldest shortcoming"! Does this mean that it was the task of the Chinese Communist Party to decompose the armies of the Guomindang? Since when?

On February 25, 1927, a month and a half prior to the crushing of Shanghai, the central organ of the Comintern wrote:

> The Chinese Communist Party and the conscious Chinese workers must not *under any circumstances* pursue a tactic which would disorganize the revolutionary armies just because the influence of the bourgeoisie is to a certain degree strong there.[16]

And here is what Stalin said – and repeated on every occasion— at the Plenum of the ECCI on May 24, 1927:

> Not unarmed people stand against the armies of the old régime in China, but an armed people in the form of the revolutionary army. In China, an armed revolution is fighting against armed counter-revolution.

In the summer and autumn of 1927, the armies of the Guomindang were depicted as an armed people. But when these armies crushed the Canton insurrection, *Pravda* declared the "oldest [!] shortcoming" of the Chinese Communists to be their inability to decompose the "reactionary armies", the very ones that were proclaimed "the revolutionary people" on the very eve of Canton.

Shameless mountebanks! Was anything like it ever seen among real revolutionists?

14. The Period of Putschism

The Ninth Plenum of the ECCI met in February 1928, less than two months after the Canton insurrection. How did it estimate the situation? Here are the exact words of its resolution:

> The ECCI makes it the duty of all its sections to fight against the slanders of the Social Democrats and the Trotskyists who assert that the Chinese revolution has been liquidated.

What a treacherous and at the same time miserable subterfuge! Social Democracy considers in reality that the victory of Chiang Kai-shek is the *victory* of the national revolution (the confused Urbahns went astray on this very same position). The Left Opposition considers that the victory of Chiang Kai-shek is the *defeat* of the national revolution.

The Opposition never said and never could have said that the Chinese Revolution *in general* is liquidated. What was liquidated, confused, deceived and crushed was "only" the second Chinese Revolution (1925–27). That alone would be enough of an accomplishment for the gentlemen of the leadership!

We maintained, beginning with the autumn of 1927, that a period of ebb is ahead in China, of the retreat of the proletariat, the triumph of the counter-revolution. What was Stalin's position?

On February 7, 1928, *Pravda* wrote:

> The Chinese Communist Party is heading towards an armed insurrection. The whole situation in China speaks for the fact that this is the correct course Experience proves that the Chinese Communist Party must concentrate all its efforts on the task of the day-to-day and widespread careful preparation of the armed insurrection.

The Ninth Plenum of the ECCI, with ambiguous bureaucratic reservations on putschism, approved this adventurist line. The object of these reservations is known: to create holes for the "leaders" to crawl into in the event of a new retreat.

The criminally light-minded resolution of the Ninth Plenum meant for China: new adventures, new skirmishes, breaking away from the masses, the loss of positions, the consuming of the best revolutionary elements in the fire of adventurism, the demoralization of the remnants of the Party. The whole period between the conference of the Chinese party on August 7, 1927, and the Sixth Congress of the Comintern on July 8, 1928, is permeated through and through with the theory and practice of putschism. This is how the Stalinist leadership was dealing with final blows to the Chinese Revolution and the Communist Party.

Only at the Sixth Congress did the leadership of the Comintern recognize that:

> The Canton uprising was objectively already a 'rearguard battle' of the receding revolution.[17]

"Objectively"! And subjectively? That is, in the consciousness of its initiators, the leaders? Such is the masked recognition of the adventurist character of the Canton insurrection. However that may be, one year after the Opposition, and what is more important, after a series of cruel defeats, the Comintern recognized that the second Chinese revolution had terminated together with the Wuhan period, and that it cannot be revived through adventurism. At the Sixth Congress the Chinese delegate, Chan Fi-Yun, reported:

> The defeat of the Canton insurrection has delivered a still heavier blow to the Chinese proletariat. The first stage of the revolution was in this manner ended with a series of defeats. In the industrial centres, a depression is being felt in the labour movement.[18]

Facts are stubborn things! This had to be recognized also by the Sixth Congress. The slogan of armed insurrection was eliminated. The only thing that remained was the name "second Chinese revolution" (1925–27), "the first stage" of which is separated from the future second stage by an undefined period. This was a terminological attempt to save at least a part of the prestige.

15. After the Sixth Congress

The delegate of the Chinese Communist Party, Duxiu, declared at the Sixteenth Congress of the CPSU:

> Only Trotskyist renegades and Chinese Chen Duxiuists say that the Chinese national bourgeoisie has a perspective of independent development [?] and stabilization [?].

Let us leave aside the abuse: these unfortunate people would never be in the Lux boarding house if they did not address their abuse to the Opposition. This is their only resource. Tang Pingshan thundered in exactly the same manner against the "Trotskyists" at the Seventh Plenum of the ECCI before he went over to the enemy. What is curious in its naked shamelessness is the attempt to father us, Left Oppositionists, with the idealization of the Chinese "national bourgeoisie" and its "independent development". Stalin's agents, as well as their leader, fulminate because the period after the Sixth Congress once more revealed their complete incapacity to understand the change in circumstances and the direction of its further development.

After the Canton defeat, at a time when the ECCI in February 1928—was steering the course towards an armed insurrection, we declared in opposition to this:

> The situation will now change in the exactly opposite direction; the working masses will temporarily retreat from politics; the Party will grow weak which does not exclude the continuation of peasant uprisings. The weakening of the war of the generals as well as the weakening of the strikes and uprisings of the proletariat will inevitably lead in the meantime to some sort of an establishment of elementary processes of economic life in the country and consequently to somewhat of an even, though very weak, commercial and industrial rise. The latter will revive the strike struggles of the workers and permit the Communist Party, under the condition of correct tactics, once more to establish its contact and its influence in order that later, already on a higher plane, the insurrection of the workers may be interlocked with the peasant war. That is what our so-called 'liquidationism' consisted of.

But, apart from abuse, what did Duxiu say about China in the last two years? First of all, he stated, after the fact:

> In Chinese industry and commerce a certain revival was to be marked in 1928.

And further:

> In 1928, 400,000 workers went on strike, in 1929, the number of strikers had already reached 750,000. In the first half of 1930, the labour movement was still further fortified in the tempo of development.

It is understood that we must be very cautious with the figures of the Comintern, including Duxiu's. But regardless of the possible exaggeration of the figures, Duxiu's exposition bears out entirely our prognosis at the end 1927 and the beginning of 1928.

Unfortunately, the leadership of the ECCI and the Chinese Communist Party took their point of departure from the directly opposite prognosis. The slogan of armed insurrection was dropped only at the Sixth Congress, that is, in the middle of 1928. But aside from this purely negative decision the Party did not receive any new orientation. The possibility of economic revival was not taken into consideration by it. The strike movement went on to a considerable extent apart from it. Can one doubt for an instant that if the leadership of the Comintern had not occupied itself with stupid accusations of liquidationism against the Opposition and had understood the situation in time, as we did, the Chinese Communist Party would have been considerably stronger, primarily in the trade-union movement? Let us recall that during the highest ascent of the second revolution, in the first half of 1927, there were 2,800,000 workers organized in trade unions under the influence of the Communist Party. At the present time, there are, according to Duxiu, around 60,000. This in the whole of China!

And these miserable "leaders", who have worked their way into a hopeless corner, who have done terrific damage, speak about the "Trotskyist renegades" and think that by this slander they can make good the damage. Such is the school of Stalin! Such are its fruits!

16. The Soviets and the Class Character of the Revolution

What, according to Stalin, is the role of the soviets in the Chinese Revolution? What place has been assigned to them in the alternation of its stages? With the rule of what class are they bound up?

During the Northern Expedition, as well as in the Wuhan period, we heard from Stalin that soviets can be created only *after* the completion of the bourgeois-democratic revolution, only on the *threshold* of the proletarian revolution. Precisely because of this the Political Bureau, following right behind Stalin, stubbornly rejected the slogan of soviets advanced by the Opposition:

> The slogan of soviets means nothing but an immediate skipping over the stage of the bourgeois-democratic revolution and the

> organization of the power of the proletariat.[19]

On May 24, after the Shanghai *coup d'état* and during the Wuhan *coup*, Stalin proved the incompatibility of soviets with bourgeois-democratic revolution in this manner:

> But the workers will not stop at this if they have soviets of workers' deputies. They will say to the Communists—and they will be right: If we are the soviets, and the soviets are the organs of power, then can we not squeeze the bourgeoisie a little, and expropriate 'a little'? The Communists will be empty windbags if they do not take the road of expropriation of the bourgeoisie with the existence of soviets of workers' and peasants' deputies. Is it possible to and should we take this road at present, at the present phase of the revolution? No, we should not.

And what will become of the Guomindang after passing over to the proletarian revolution? Stalin had it all figured out. In his discourse to the students on May 13, 1927 which we already quoted, Stalin replied:

> I think that in the period of the creation of soviets of workers' and peasants' deputies and the preparation for the Chinese October, the Chinese Communist Party will have to substitute for the present bloc inside the Guomindang the bloc outside the Guomindang.

Our great strategists foresaw everything—decidedly they foresaw everything, except the class struggle. Even in the matter of going over to the proletarian revolution Stalin solicitously supplied the Chinese Communist Party with an ally, with the same Guomindang. In order to carry out the socialist revolution, the Communists were only permitted to get out of the ranks of the Guomindang, but by no means to break the bloc with it. As is known, the alliance with the bourgeoisie was the best condition for the preparation of the "Chinese October". And all this was called Leninism.

Be that as it may, in 1925–27 Stalin posed the question of soviets very categorically, connecting the formation of soviets with the immediate socialist expropriation of the bourgeoisie. It is true he needed this "radicalism" at that time not in defence of the expropriation of the bourgeoisie but on the contrary in defence of the bourgeoisie from expropriation. But the principled posing of the question was at any rate clear: *the soviets can be only and exclusively organs of the socialist revolution*. Such was the position of the Political Bureau of the CPSU, such was the position of the ECCI.

But at the end of 1927 an insurrection was carried out in Canton to which a soviet character was given. The Communists had the power. They decreed measures of a purely socialist character (nationalization of the land, banks, dwellings, industrial enterprises, etc.) It would seem we were confronted with a proletarian revolution. But no. At the end of February 1928, the Ninth Plenum of the ECCI drew up the balance of the Canton insurrection. And what was the result?

"The current year in the Chinese revolution is a period of bourgeois-democratic revolution, which has not been completed. The tendency towards jumping over the bourgeois-democratic stage of the revolution with the simultaneous appraisal of the revolution as a 'permanent' revolution is a mistake similar to the one made by Trotsky in 1905."

But ten months before that (April 1927) the Political Bureau declared that the very slogan of soviets (not Trotskyism, but the slogan of soviets!) means the inadmissible skipping of the bourgeois-democratic stage. But now, after a complete exhaustion of all the variations of the Guomindang, when it was necessary to sanction the slogan of soviets, we were told that only Trotskyists can connect this slogan with the proletarian dictatorship. This is how it was revealed that Stalin, during 1925–27, was a "Trotskyist", even though the other way around.

It is true that the program of the Comintern also made a decisive turn in this question. Among the most important tasks of the colonial countries, the program mentioned: "The establishment of a democratic dictatorship of the proletariat and peasantry based on the soviets." Truly miraculous! What was yesterday incompatible with the democratic revolution was today proclaimed to be its foundation base. One would seek in vain for any theoretical explanation of this complete somersault. Everything was done in a strictly administrative manner.

In what instance was Stalin wrong? When he declared the

soviets incompatible with the democratic revolution or when he declared the soviets to be the basis of the democratic revolution? In both instances. Because Stalin does not understand the meaning of the democratic dictatorship, the meaning of the proletarian dictatorship, their mutual relationship, and what role the soviets play in connection with them.

He once more revealed it best, even though in a few words, at the Sixteenth Congress of the CPSU.

17. The Chinese Question at the Sixteenth Congress of the CPSU

In his ten-hour report Stalin, however anxious he was to do so, could not completely ignore the question of the Chinese revolution. He devoted to it exactly five phrases. And what phrases! Indeed, "a lot in a little", as the Latinists say (*multum in parvo*). Desiring to avoid all sharp corners, to refrain from risking generalizations and still more from concrete prognoses, Stalin in five phrases succeeded in making all the mistakes still left for him to make.

> It would be ridiculous to think, [Stalin said] that this misconduct of the imperialists will pass for them unpunished. The Chinese workers and peasants have already replied to this by the creation of soviets and a Red army. It is said that a soviet government has already been created there. I think that if this is true then there is nothing surprising in it. There is no doubt that only soviets can save China from complete dismemberment and impoverishment.[20]

"It would be ridiculous to think." Here is the basis for all the further conclusions. If the misconduct of the imperialists will inevitably provoke a reply in the form of soviets and a Red army, then how is it that imperialism still exists in the world?

"It is said that a soviet government has already been created there." What does it mean: "It is said"? Who says so? And what's most important, what does the Chinese Communist Party say about it? It is part of the Comintern and its representative spoke at the Congress. Does it mean that the "soviet government" was created in China without the Communist Party and without its knowledge? Then who is leading this government? Who are its members? What party holds power? Not only does Stalin fail to give a reply, but he does not even put the question.

> "I think that if [!] this is true then [!] there is nothing surprising in it." There is nothing surprising in the fact that in China a soviet government was created about which the Chinese Communist Party knows nothing and about whose political physiognomy the highest leader of the Chinese revolution can give us no information. Then what is there left in the world to be surprised at?

"There is no doubt that only soviets can save China from dismemberment and impoverishment." Which soviets? Up to now, we have seen all sorts of soviets: Tsereteli's soviets, Otto Bauer's and Scheidemann's, on the one hand, Bolshevik soviets on the other. Tsereteli's soviets could not save Russia from dismemberment and impoverishment. On the contrary, their whole policy went in the direction of transforming Russia into a colony of the Entente. Only the Bolsheviks transformed the soviets into a weapon for the liberation of the toiling masses. What kind of soviets are the Chinese? If the Chinese Communist Party can say nothing about them, then it means that it is not leading them. Then who is? Apart from the Communists, only accidental, intermediate elements, people of a "third party", in a word, fragments of the Guomindang of the second and third sort, can come to the head of the soviets and create a soviet government.

Only yesterday Stalin thought that "it would be ridiculous to think" of the creation of soviets in China prior to the completion of the democratic revolution. Now he seems to think —if his five phrases have any meaning at all—that in the democratic revolution the soviets can save the country even without the leadership of the Communists.

To speak of a soviet government without speaking of the dictatorship of the proletariat means to deceive the workers and to help the bourgeoisie deceive the peasants. But to speak of the dictatorship of the proletariat without speaking of the leading role of the Communist Party means once more to convert the dictatorship of the proletariat into a trap for the proletariat. The Chinese Communist Party, however, is now extremely weak. The number of its worker-members is limited to a few thousand. There are about fifty thousand workers in the Red trade unions. Under these conditions, to speak of the dictatorship of the proletariat as an *immediate* task is obviously unthinkable. On the other hand, in South China a broad peasant movement is unfolding itself in which partisan bands participate. The influence of the October Revolution, in spite of the years of epigone leadership, is still so great in China that the peasants call their movement "soviet" and their partisan bands—"Red armies". This shows once more the depths of Stalin's philistinism in the period when, coming out against soviets, he said that we must not scare off the masses of the Chinese people by "artificial sovietization". Only Chiang Kai-shek could have been scared off by it, but not the workers, not the peasants, to whom, after 1917, the soviets had become symbols of emancipation. The Chinese peasants, it is understood, inject no few illusions into the slogan of soviets. It is pardonable in them. But is it pardonable in the leading *chvostists* who confine themselves to a cowardly and ambiguous generalization of the illusions of the Chinese peasantry, without explaining to the proletariat the real meaning of events?

"There is nothing surprising in it," says Stalin, if the Chinese peasants, without the participation of the industrial centres and without the leadership of the Communist Party, created a soviet government. But we say that the appearance of the soviet government under these circumstances is absolutely impossible. Not only the Bolsheviks but even the Tsereteli government or half-government of the soviets could make its appearance only on the basis of the cities. To think that the peasantry is capable of creating its soviet government *independently*, means to believe in miracles. It would be the same miracle to create a peasant Red army. The peasant partisans played a great revolutionary role in the Russian Revolution, but under the existence of centres of proletarian dictatorship and a centralized proletarian Red army. With the weakness of the Chinese labour movement at the present moment, and with the still greater weakness of the Communist Party, it is difficult to speak of a dictatorship of the proletariat as the *task of the day* in China. This is why Stalin, swimming in the wake of the peasant uprising, is compelled, in spite of all his earlier declarations, to link the peasant soviets and the peasant Red army with the bourgeois-democratic dictatorship. The leadership of this dictatorship, which is too heavy a task for the Communist Party, is delivered to some other political party, to some sort of a revolutionary *x*. Being that Stalin hindered the Chinese workers and peasants from conducting their struggle for the dictatorship of the proletariat, then somebody must now help Stalin by taking in hand the soviet government as the organ of the bourgeois democratic dictatorship. As a motivation for this new perspective we are presented with five arguments in five phrases. Here they are:

1. "It would be ridiculous to think";
2. "it is said";
3. "if it is true";
4. "there is nothing surprising in it";
5. "there is no doubt".

Here it is, administrative argumentation in all its power and splendour!

We warn: the Chinese proletariat will again have to pay for this whole shameful concoction.

18. The Character of Stalin's "Mistakes"

There are mistakes and mistakes. In the various spheres of human thought, there can be very considerable mistakes which flow from the insufficient examination of the object, from insufficient factual data, from a too great complexity of the factors to be considered, etc. Among these we may consider, let us say, the mistakes of meteorologists in foretelling the weather, which are typical of a whole series of mistakes in the sphere of politics. However, the mistakes of a learned, quick-witted meteorologist are often more useful to science than the conjecture of an empiric, even though it is accidentally substantiated by facts. But what should we say of a learned geographer, of a leader of a polar expedition who would take as his point of departure that the earth rests on three whales? Yet the mistakes of Stalin are almost completely of this last category. Never rising to Marxism as a method, making use of one or the other "Marxian-like" formulas in a ritualistic manner, Stalin in his practical actions takes as his point of departure the crassest empirical prejudices. But such is the dialectic of the process: these prejudices became Stalin's main strength in the period of revolutionary decline. They were the ones that permitted him to play the role which subjectively he did not want. The cumbersome bureaucracy, separating itself from the revolutionary class that conquered power, seized upon Stalin's empiricism for his mercenariness, for his complete cynicism in the sphere of principles, in order to make him its leader and in order to create the legend of Stalin which is the holiday legend of the bureaucracy itself. This is the explanation of how and why the strong but absolutely mediocre person who occupied third and fourth roles in the years of the rise of the revolution proved called upon to play the leading role in the years of its ebb, in the years of the stabilization of the world bourgeoisie, the regeneration of Social Democracy, the weakening of the Comintern and the conservative degeneration of the broadest circles of the Soviet bureaucracy.

The French say about a man: His defects are his virtues. Of Stalin it can be said: his defects proved to be to his advantage. The gear teeth of the class struggle meshed into his theoretical limitedness, his political adaptability, his moral indiscriminateness, in a word, into his defects as a proletarian revolutionist, in order to make him a statesman of the period of the petty-bourgeois emancipation from October, from Marxism, from Bolshevism.

The Chinese Revolution was an examination of the new role of Stalin—by the inverse method. Having conquered power in the USSR with the aid of the strata who have been breaking away from the international revolution and with the indirect but very real aid of the hostile classes, Stalin automatically became the leader of the Comintern and by that alone the leader of the Chinese Revolution. The passive hero of the behind-the-scenes apparatus mechanism had to show his method and quality in the events of the great revolutionary flow. Within this lies the tragic paradox of Stalin's role in China. Having subordinated the Chinese workers to the bourgeoisie, put the brakes on the agrarian movement, supported the reactionary generals, disarmed the workers, prevented the appearance of soviets and liquidated those that did appear, Stalin carried out to the end that historic role which Tsereteli only attempted to carry out in Russia. The difference is that Tsereteli acted on the open arena, having arrayed against him the Bolsheviks—and he immediately and on the spot had to bear the responsibility for his attempt to betray to the bourgeoisie a fettered and duped working class. Stalin, however, acted in China primarily behind the scenes, defended by a powerful apparatus and draped in the banner of Bolshevism. Tsereteli supported himself on the repressions of the power of the Bolsheviks by the bourgeoisie. Stalin, however, himself applied these repressions against the Bolshevik-Leninists (Opposition). The repressions of the bourgeoisie were shattered by the rising wave. Stalin's repressions were fostered by the ebbing wave. This is why it was possible for Stalin to carry out the experiment with the purely Menshevik policy in the Chinese Revolution to the end, that is, to the most tragic catastrophe.

But what about the present left paroxysm of the Stalinist policy? To see in this episode—and the left zigzag with all its significance will nevertheless go down into history as an episode—a contradiction to what has been said, can be done only by very near-sighted people who are foreign to an understanding of the dialectic of human consciousness in connection with the dialectic of the historic process. The decline of the revolution as well as its rise does not move along a straight line. The empirical leader of the down-sliding of the revolution—"You think that you are moving but you are being moved" (Goethe)—could not help at a certain moment but take fright at that abyss of social betrayal to the very edge of which he was pushed in 1925–27 by his own qualities, utilized by forces half-hostile and hostile to the proletariat. And since the degeneration of the apparatus is not an even process, since the revolutionary tendencies within the masses are strong, then for the turn to the left from the edge of the Thermidorian abyss there were sufficient points of support and reserve forces already at hand. The turn assumed a character of panicky jumps, precisely because this empiric foresaw nothing until he had reached the very brink of the precipice. The ideology of the jump to the left was prepared by the Left Opposition—it only remained to utilize its work in bits and fragments, as befits an empiric. But the acute paroxysm of leftism does not change the basic processes of the evolution of the bureaucracy, nor the nature of Stalin himself.

The absence in Stalin of theoretical preparation, of a broad outlook and creative imagination—those features without which there can be no independent work on a large scale—fully explains why Lenin, who valued Stalin as a practical assistant, nevertheless recommended that the Party remove him from the post of general secretary when it became clear that this post might assume independent significance. Lenin never saw in Stalin a political leader.

Left to himself, Stalin always and invariably took up an opportunistic position on all big questions. If Stalin had no important theoretical or political conflicts with Lenin, like Bukharin, Kamenev, Zinoviev and even Rykov, it is because Stalin never held on to his principal views and in all cases of serious disagreement simply kept quiet, retreated to one side and waited. But for all that, Lenin very often had practical organizational-moral conflicts with Stalin, frequently very sharp ones, precisely for those Stalinist defects which Lenin, so carefully in form but so mercilessly in essence, characterized in his "testament".

To all that has been said we must add the fact that Lenin worked hand in hand with a group of collaborators, each of whom brought into the work knowledge, personal initiative, distinct talent. Stalin is surrounded, particularly after the liquidation of the right wing group, by accomplished mediocrities, devoid of any international outlook and incapable of producing an independent opinion on a single question of the world labour movement.

In the meantime, the significance of the apparatus has grown immeasurably since Lenin's time. Stalin's leadership in the Chinese Revolution is just the fruit of the combination of theoretical, political and national limitedness with huge apparatus power. Stalin has proved himself incapable of learning. His five phrases on China at the Sixteenth Congress are permeated through and through with that same organic opportunism which governed Stalin's policy at all the earlier stages of the struggle of the Chinese people. The undertaker of the second Chinese Revolution is preparing before our very eyes to strangle the third Chinese Revolution at its inception.

NOTES

1. *Sotsialisticheski Vestnik,* no. 8, April 23, 1927, p. 4.
2. *Die Kommunistische Internationale,* March 1, 1927, no. 9, p. 408.
3. *On the Perspectives of the Chinese Revolution*, p. 46.
4. *Ibid.*, p. 55.
5. *Minutes of the Enlarged Executive of the Communist International,* [German Edition], November 30, 1926, pp. 403-4.
6. *Izvestia,* March 6, 1927.
7. *Pravda,* March 9, 1927.
8. Sixteenth session of the XV Congress of the CPSU, December 11, 1927.
9. Problems of the Chinese Revolution, pp.125–7.
10. *Proletarskaya Revolyutsiya,* p. 54.
11. *Minutes* [German edition], p. 71.
12. *Sotsialisticheski Vestnik,* no.9 [151], p.1.
13. *Workers' China,* p. 6.
14. *Minutes,* p. 34.
15. *Minutes,* p. 36.
16. *Die Kommunistische Internationale,* February 25, 1927, p.19.
17. *Pravda,* July 27, 1928.
18. *Pravda,* July 17, 1928, No. 164.
19. From the written *Reply of the Political Bureau* to the Opposition theses, April 1927.
20. Political Report of the CC to the 16th Party Congress, *Pravda,* June 29, 1930.

43

A History of the Second Chinese Revolution is Needed

Published September 1930

A study of the Chinese Revolution is a most important and urgent matter for every communist and for every advanced worker. It is not possible to talk seriously in any country about the struggle of the proletariat for power without a study by the proletarian vanguard of the fundamental events, motive forces, and strategic methods of the Chinese Revolution. It is not possible to understand what day is without knowing what night is; it is not possible to understand what summer is without having experienced winter. In the same way, it is not possible to understand the meaning of the methods of the October uprising without a study of the methods of the Chinese catastrophe. In the meantime, the history of the Chinese Revolution has been a forbidden topic for the Comintern. There is not a single book which has summed up what the lessons are of the great experiences of the battles and defeats of 1925–27. This book has not been written, and it will not and cannot be written by the Comintern leadership for the same reason that the Roman conclave will not write a scientific history of the Holy Inquisition: it is not possible to demand or expect that any institution should write the history of its own crimes.

The working up of the history of the second Chinese Revolution (1925–27) can be done only by the Communist Left Opposition: First place here belongs, clearly, to our Chinese comrades. We think that this question must be included on the agenda of the international conference of the Left Opposition (Bolshevik-Leninists).

44

Manifesto on China of the International Left Opposition

September 1930

During the last few months a peasant movement of considerable scope has again appeared in certain provinces of southern China. Not only the world press of the proletariat, but the press of its enemies as well, is filled with the echoes of this struggle. The Chinese Revolution, betrayed, defeated, exhausted, shows that it is still alive. Let us hope that the time when it will again lift its proletarian head is not far off. And in order to be prepared for this, we must put the problems of the Chinese Revolution on the agenda of the working class of the world.

We, the International Communist Left Opposition (Bolshevik-Leninists), consider it our duty to raise our voices now in order to attract the attention of all communists, all advanced revolutionary workers, to the task of liberating this great country of East Asia and at the same time to warn them against the false policy of the dominant faction of the Communist International, which obviously threatens to undermine the coming Chinese Revolution as it ruined the 1925–27 revolution.

The signs of the rebirth of the Chinese Revolution in the countryside indicate its inner forces and immense potentialities. But the task is to transform these potentialities into reality. The first condition for success is to understand what is happening, that is, to make a Marxist analysis of the motive forces and to estimate correctly the current stage of the struggle. On both counts, the ruling circle of the Comintern is wrong.

The Stalinist press is filled with communications about a "soviet government" established in vast provinces of China under the protection of a Red army. Workers in many countries are greeting this news with excitement. Of course! The establishment of a soviet government in a substantial part of China and the creation of a Chinese Red army would be a gigantic success for the international revolution. But we must state openly and clearly: *this is not yet true.*

Despite the scanty information which reaches us from the vast areas of China, our Marxist understanding of the developing process enables us to reject with certainty the Stalinist view of the current events. It is false and extremely dangerous for the further development of the revolution.

For centuries the history of China has been one of formidable uprisings of a destitute and hungry peasantry. Not less than five times in the last two thousand years the Chinese peasants succeeded in effecting a complete re-division of landed property. Each time the process of concentration began anew and continued until the growth of the population again produced a partial or general explosion. This vicious cycle was an expression of economic and social stagnation.

Only the inclusion of China in the world economy opened up new possibilities. Capitalism invaded China from abroad. The backward Chinese bourgeoisie became the intermediary between foreign capital and the mercilessly exploited masses of their own country. The foreign imperialists and the Chinese bourgeoisie combine the methods of capitalist exploitation with the methods of feudal oppression and enslavement through usury.

The fundamental idea of the Stalinists was to transform the Chinese bourgeoisie into a leader of the national revolution against feudalism and imperialism. The results of this political strategy ruined the revolution. The Chinese proletariat paid a heavy price for knowledge of the truth that their bourgeoisie cannot, does not want to, and never will fight either against so-called feudalism, which constitutes the most important part of its own system of exploitation, or against imperialism, whose agent it is and under whose military protection it operates.

As soon as it was clear that the Chinese proletariat, in spite of all the obstacles put in its path by the Comintern, was ready to proceed on its own independent revolutionary road, the bourgeoisie, with the help of the foreign imperialists, beginning in Shanghai, crushed the workers' movement. As soon as it was clear that friendship with Moscow could not paralyze the uprising of the peasants, the bourgeoisie shattered the peasants' movement. The spring and summer of 1927 were the months of the greatest crimes of the Chinese bourgeoisie.

Frightened by the consequences of its mistakes, at the end of 1927 the Stalinist faction abruptly tried to compensate for its blunders of the past years. The Canton insurrection was organized. The Stalinist leaders assumed that the revolution was still on the rise; actually, it was already on the decline. The heroism of the vanguard workers could not prevent the disaster caused by the adventure of these leaders. The Canton insurrection was drowned in blood. The second Chinese Revolution was completely destroyed.

From the beginning, we, the representatives of the International Left Opposition, the Bolshevik-Leninists, were against entering the Kuomintang and for an independent proletarian policy. From the very beginning of the revolutionary upsurge, we urged that the organization of workers', soldiers', and peasants' soviets be initiated; we urged that the workers take their place at the head of the peasant insurrection and carry through the agrarian revolution to its conclusion. Our course was rejected. Our supporters were persecuted and expelled from the Comintern; those in the USSR were arrested and exiled. In the name of what? In the name of a bloc with Chiang Kai-shek.

After the counter-revolutionary coup d'etat in Shanghai and Wuhan we, the Communist Left Oppositionists, warned insistently that the second Chinese revolution was finished, that a temporary triumph of the counter-revolution had supervened, and that an attempt at insurrection by the advanced workers in the face of the general demoralization and fatigue of the masses would inevitably bring additional criminal blows against the revolutionary forces. We demanded a shift to the defensive, a strengthening of the underground organization of the party, the participation in the economic struggles of the proletariat, and the mobilization of the masses under democratic slogans: the independence of China, the right of self-determination for the different nationalities in the population, a constituent assembly, the confiscation of the land, the eight-hour workday. Such a policy would have allowed the communist vanguard to emerge gradually from its defeat, to re-establish connections with the trade unions and with the unorganized urban and rural masses, and to prepare to meet the new revolutionary upsurge fully armed.

The Stalinist faction denounced our policy as "liquidationist," while it, not for the first time, went from opportunism to adventurism. In February 1928, when the Chinese Revolution was at its lowest point, the Ninth Plenum of the Executive Committee of the Communist International announced a policy of armed insurrection in China. The results of this madness were the further defeat of the workers, the murder of the best revolutionaries, a split in the party, demoralization in the ranks of the workers.

The decline of the revolution and a temporary lessening of the struggle between the militarists permitted a limited economic revival in the country. Strikes occurred again. But these were conducted independently of the party, which, not understanding the situation, was absolutely unable to present a new perspective to the masses and to unite them under the democratic slogans of the transitional period. As a result of new errors, opportunism, and adventurism, the Communist Party now counts in its ranks only a few thousand workers. In the Red trade unions, according to the figures given by the party itself, there are about sixty thousand workers. In the months of the revolutionary upsurge there were about three million.

The counter-revolution left its mark more directly and much more ruthlessly on the workers than on the peasants. The workers in China are few in number and are concentrated in the industrial centers. The peasants are protected to a certain extent by their numbers and their diffusion over vast areas. The revolutionary years trained quite a few rural local leaders, and the counter-revolution did not succeed in eliminating them all. A considerable number of revolutionary workers hid from the militarists in the countryside. In the last decade a large amount of arms was widely dispersed. In conflicts with local administrators or military units, these arms were obtained by the peasants and Red guerrilla bands were organized. Agitation flared up in the armies of the bourgeois counter-revolution, at times leading to open revolts. Soldiers, with their guns, deserted to the side of the peasants, sometimes in groups, sometimes in whole companies.

It is quite natural, therefore, that even after the defeat of the revolution, waves of the peasant movement continued to roll through the various provinces of the country and have now forcefully rushed ahead. Armed peasant bands drive out and exterminate local landlords, as many as can be found in their regions, and especially the so-called gentry and *tuchuns,* the local representatives of the ruling class—the bureaucrat-proprietors, the usurers, the rich peasants.

When the Stalinists talk about a soviet government established by the peasants in a substantial part of China, they not only reveal their credulity and superficiality; they obscure and misrepresent the fundamental problem of the Chinese Revolution. The peasantry, even the most revolutionary, cannot create an independent government; it can only support the government of another class, the dominant urban class. The peasantry at all decisive moments follows either the bourgeoisie or the proletariat. So-called peasant parties may disguise this fact, but they cannot annul it. Soviets are the organs of power of a revolutionary class in opposition to the bourgeoisie. This means that the peasantry is unable to organize a soviet system on its own. The same holds true for an army. More than once in China, and in Russia and other countries too, the peasantry has organized guerrilla armies which fought with incomparable courage and stubbornness. But they remained guerrilla armies, connected to a local province and incapable of centralized strategic operations on a large scale. *Only the predominance of the proletariat in the decisive industrial and political centers of the country* creates the necessary basis for the organization of a Red army and for the extension of a soviet system into the coutryside. To those unable to grasp this, the revolution remains a book closed with seven seals.

The Chinese proletariat is just beginning to recover from the paralysis of the counter-revolution. The peasant movement at the present time is advancing, to a large degree, independently of the workers' movement, according to its own laws and at its own tempo. But the heart of the problem of the Chinese Revolution consists in the political coordination and organizational combination of the proletarian and peasant uprisings. Those who talk about the victory of the soviet revolution in China, although confined to separate provinces in the South and confronted with passivity in the industrial North, ignore the dual problem of the Chinese Revolution: the problem of an alliance between the workers and peasants and the problem of the leading role of the workers in this alliance.

The vast flood of peasant revolts can unquestionably provide the impulse for the revival of political struggle in the industrial centers. We firmly count on it. But this does not mean in any case that the revolutionary awakening of the proletariat would lead immediately to the conquest of power or even to the struggle for power. The resurgence of the proletariat might at first assume the character of partial economic and political defensive and offensive struggles. How much time would the proletariat, and particularly the communist vanguard, require to rise to its role as leader of a revolutionary nation? At any rate, more than weeks or months. Bureaucratic command is no substitute for the independent growth of the class and its party.

At this juncture the Chinese communists need a long-range policy. They must not scatter their forces among the isolated flames of the peasant revolt. Weak and small in number, the party will not be able to take hold of this movement. The communists must concentrate their forces in the factories and the shops and in the workers' districts in order to explain to the workers the meaning of what is happening in the provinces, to lift the spirits of the tired and discouraged, to organize groups of workers for a struggle to defend their economic interests, and to raise the slogans of the democratic-agrarian revolution. Only through the process of activating and uniting the workers will the

Communist Party be able to assume leadership of the peasant insurrection, that is, of the national revolution as a whole.

To support the illusions of adventurism and to conceal the weakness of the proletarian vanguard, the Stalinists say that a democratic dictatorship, not a proletarian, is the issue. On this central point their adventurism relies entirely on the premises of opportunism. Not satisfied with their Kuomintang experiment, the Stalinists are devising a new formula for the coming revolution with which to put to sleep and chain the working class, the "democratic dictatorship".

When the vanguard workers in China advanced the slogan of *soviets*, they were saying: we want to do what the Russian workers did. Only yesterday the Stalinists replied to this: no, you must not, you have the Kuomintang, and it will do what is necessary. Today the same leaders respond more cautiously: you will have to organize soviets, not for a proletarian but for a democratic dictatorship. They thereby tell the proletariat that the dictatorship will not be in their hands, that there is some other as-yet-undiscovered force which can introduce the revolutionary dictatorship in China. In this way the formula of the democratic dictatorship opens the gates to a new deception of the workers and peasants by the bourgeoisie.

To justify the slogan of the "democratic dictatorship", the Stalinists describe the Chinese counter-revolution as "feudal militarist and imperialist". Thus they exclude the bourgeoisie from the counter-revolution, that is, they again as before idealize the bourgeoisie. In reality the militarists express the interests of the Chinese bourgeoisie, which are inseparable from feudal interests and relations. The Chinese bourgeoisie is too hostile to the people, too closely tied up with the foreign imperialists, and too afraid of the revolution to be eager to rule in its own name by parliamentary methods. The militarist-fascist regime of China is an expression of the anti-national, anti-revolutionary character of the Chinese bourgeoisie. The Chinese counter-revolution is not a counter-revolution of feudal barons and slave-owners against bourgeois society. It is a counter-revolution of all property holders—and first of all bourgeois—against the workers and peasants.

The proletarian insurrection in China can and will develop only as a direct and immediate revolution against the bourgeois. The peasants' revolt in China, much more than it was in Russia, is a revolt against the bourgeoisie. A class of landlords as a separate class does not exist in China. The landowners and the bourgeoisie are one and the same. The gentry and *tuchuns*, against whom the peasant movement is immediately directed, represent the lowest link to the bourgeoisie and to the imperialist exploiters as well. In Russia the October Revolution, in its first stage, counterposed all the peasants as a class against all the landlords as a class, and only after several months began to introduce the civil war within the peasantry. In China every peasant uprising is, from the start, a civil war of the poor against the rich peasants, that is, against the village bourgeoisie.

The middle peasantry in China is insignificant. Almost 80 per cent of the peasants are poor. They and they alone play a revolutionary role. The problem is not to unite the workers with the peasants as a whole, but with the village poor. They have a common enemy: the bourgeoisie. No one but the workers can lead the poor peasants to victory. Their mutual victory can lead to no other regime but the dictatorship of the proletariat. Only such a regime can establish a soviet system and organize a Red army, which will be the military expression of the dictatorship of the proletariat supported by the poor peasants.

The Stalinists say that the democratic dictatorship, as the next stage of the revolution, will grow into a proletarian dictatorship at a later stage. This is the current doctrine of the Comintern, not only for China but for all the Eastern countries. It is a complete departure from the teachings of Marx on the state and the conclusions of Lenin on the function of the state in a revolution. The democratic dictatorship differs from the proletarian in that it is a *bourgeois democratic* dictatorship. The transition from a bourgeois to a proletarian dictatorship cannot occur as a peaceful process of "growing over" from one to the other. A dictatorship of the proletariat can replace a democratic, or a fascist, dictatorship of the bourgeoisie only through armed insurrection.

The peaceful "growing over" of a democratic revolution into a socialist revolution is possible only under the dictatorship of one class—the proletariat. The transition from democratic measures to socialist measures took place in the Soviet Union under the regime of the proletarian dictatorship. This transition will be accomplished much faster in China because its most elementary democratic problems have much more of an anti-capitalist and antibourgeois character than they had in Russia. The Stalinists apparently need one more defeat, paid for by the workers' blood, before they can bring themselves to say: "The revolution has reached the highest stage, whose slogan is the dictatorship of the proletariat."

At this moment nobody can tell the extent to which the present peasant insurrection combines the reflection of the second revolution with the summer lightning of the third. Nobody can foretell now whether the hearths of the peasant revolt can keep a fire burning through the whole long period of time which the proletarian vanguard will need to gather its own strength, bring the working class into the fight, and coordinate its struggle for power with the general offensive of the peasants against their most immediate enemies.

What distinguishes this movement in the countryside today is the desire of the peasants to give it the form of soviets, at least in name, and to fashion their own guerrilla armies as much as possible after the Red Army. This shows how intensely the peasants are seeking a political form that would enable them to overcome their dispersion and impotence. From this point of departure, the communists can proceed successfully.

But it must be understood in advance that in the consciousness of the Chinese peasant the general slogan of soviets does not by any means signify the dictatorship of the proletariat. The peasants cannot speak for the proletarian dictatorship a priori. They can be led to it only through the experience of a struggle that will prove to them in life that their *democratic* problems cannot be solved in any way except through the *dictatorship of the proletariat*. This is the fundamental reason why *the Communist Party cannot lead the proletariat to a struggle for power except under democratic slogans.*

The peasant movement, although adorned with the name of soviets, remains scattered, local, provincial. It can be elevated to a national movement only by connecting the struggle for land and against oppressive taxes and burdens of militarism with the ideals of the independence of China and the sovereignty of the people. A democratic expression of this connection is the sovereign constituent assembly. Under such a slogan the communist vanguard will be able to unite around itself the vast masses of workers, the oppressed small townspeople, and the hundreds of millions of poor peasants for an insurrection against foreign and native oppressors.

The organization of workers' soviets can be attempted only on a rising tide of revolution in the cities. In the meantime we can prepare for it. To prepare means to gather strength. At present we can do it only under consistent and courageous revolutionary democratic slogans.

And we must explain to the vanguard elements of the working class that a constituent assembly is only a step on the revolutionary road. We are setting our course toward the dictatorship of the proletariat in the form of a soviet regime.

We do not shut our eyes to the fact that such a dictatorship will place the most difficult economic and international problems before the Chinese people. The proletariat in China constitutes a smaller part of the population than the proletariat in Russia did on the eve of the October Revolution. Chinese capitalism is more backward than was Russia's. But difficulties are conquered not by illusions, not by an adventurist policy, not by hopes in a Chiang Kai-shek or in a "democratic dictatorship". Difficulties are conquered by clear thinking and revolutionary will.

The Chinese proletariat will take power not in order to resurrect the Chinese Wall and under its protection construct national socialism. By winning power the Chinese proletariat will win one of the most important strategic positions for the international revolution. The fate of China, like that of the USSR, is bound up with the fate of the revolutionary movement of the world proletariat. This is the source of greatest hope and the justification of highest revolutionary courage.

The cause of the international revolution is the cause of the Chinese Revolution. The cause of the Chinese Revolution is the cause of the international revolution.

45

A Retreat in Full Disorder

November 1930
Prinkipo

Manuilsky on the "Democratic Dictatorship"

In the anniversary number of *Pravda* (November 7), Manuilsky once more shows the value of the present leadership of the Comintern. We will analyse briefly that part of his anniversary reflections devoted to China, and which amounts in essence to a cowardly, deliberately confused, and therefore all the more dangerous, semi-capitulation to the theory of the permanent revolution.

1. "A revolutionary-democratic dictatorship of the peasantry and proletariat in China," writes Manuilsky, "will differ essentially from the democratic dictatorship outlined [!] by the Bolsheviks in the 1905–06 revolution."

The democratic dictatorship was "outlined" by the Bolsheviks not only in 1905, but also in 1917 and in all the years between the two revolutions. But only *outlined*. Events served as a test. Manuilsky, like his teacher Stalin, does not reflect upon the points of resemblance and the points of difference of the Chinese Revolution with the three Russian revolutions—no, with such comparison they would be unable to preserve the fiction of the democratic dictatorship, and along with it, the fiction of their theoretical reputations. Therefore these gentlemen do not compare the Chinese Revolution with the real Russian Revolution, but with the one that was "outlined". It is much easier in this way to confuse and to throw dust in the eyes.

2. In what respect then does the revolution taking place in China differ from the one "outlined" in Russia? In the fact, we are taught by Manuilsky, that the Chinese Revolution is directed against the "whole system of world imperialism"! It is true that this was the basis upon which Manuilsky yesterday depended for the revolutionary role of the Chinese bourgeoisie as against the Bolshevik position "outlined in 1905". Today, however, Manuilsky's conclusions are different: "The difficulties of the Chinese revolution are tremendous; and this is precisely why the victorious movement of the Chinese Red Army upon the industrial centres of China had to halt at Changsha." It would have been much more simple and honest to say that the partisan peasant detachments, *in the absence of revolutionary uprisings in the cities,* found themselves powerless to take possession of the industrial and political centres of the country. Wasn't this clear to Marxists beforehand?

But Manuilsky must needs save Stalin's speech at the Sixteenth Congress. Here is how he fulfils this task:

> The Chinese revolution has at its disposal a Red army, it is in possession of a considerable territory, at this very moment it is creating on this territory a soviet system of workers' and peasants' power in whose government the Communists are in the majority. And this condition permits the proletariat to realize not only an ideological but also a *state hegemony over the peasantry.* [Our emphasis.]

The fact that the Communists, as the revolutionary and most self-sacrificing elements, appear at the head of the peasant movement and the armed peasant detachments, is quite natural in itself and is also exceptionally important in the symptomatic sense. But this does not change the fact that the Chinese workers find themselves throughout their vast country under the heel of the Chinese bourgeoisie and foreign imperialism. In what way can the proletariat realize "state hegemony" over the peasantry, when the state power is not in its hands? It is absolutely impossible to understand this. The leading role of the isolated Communists and the isolated Communist groups in the peasant war does not decide the question of power. Classes decide and not parties. The peasant war may support the dictatorship of the proletariat, if they coincide in point of time, but under no circumstances can it be substituted for the dictatorship of the proletariat. Is it possible that the "leaders" of the Comintern have not learned even this from the experiences of the three Russian revolutions?

3. Let us listen further to Manuilsky: "All these [?] conditions lead to the fact that a revolutionary-democratic dictatorship in China will be confronted with the necessity of a *consistent confiscation of the enterprises belonging to foreign and Chinese capital*." (Our emphasis.)

"All these conditions" is a commonplace whose purpose is to cover up the gap created in the old position. But the centre of gravity in the phrase quoted above is not in "all these conditions" but in one single "condition": Manuilsky has been instructed to manoeuvre away from the democratic dictatorship and to cover up the traces. This is why Manuilsky so diligently, but not very skilfully, wags his tail.

The democratic dictatorship can be contrasted only to the proletarian socialist dictatorship. The one differs from the other by the character of the class holding power and by the social content of its historical work. If the democratic dictatorship is to occupy itself not with clearing the road for capitalist development, as stated in the Bolshevik schema "outlined in 1905", but on the contrary, with a "consistent confiscation of the enterprises belonging to foreign and Chinese capital", as "outlined" by Manuilsky, then we ask: wherein does this *democratic* dictatorship differ from the *socialist*? In no way. Then does it mean that Manuilsky, for the second time after a lapse of twelve years, has bitten into the apple of the "permanent" theory? He bit without really taking a bite: this will yet be seen.

4. We read one phrase after another. "The presence of socialist elements will be the specific [!] peculiarity of the revolutionary-democratic dictatorship of the proletariat and peasantry in China." Not a bad "specific" peculiarity!

The democratic dictatorship was always thought of by the Bolsheviks as a *bourgeois*-democratic dictatorship, and not as a supra-class one, and was contrasted to the socialist dictatorship only in this—the only possible—sense. Now it appears that in

China there will be a "democratic dictatorship with socialist elements". Between the bourgeois and socialist régimes, the class abyss thus disappears, everything is dissolved into pure democracy, and this pure democracy is supplemented gradually and planfully by "socialist elements".

Who did these people learn from? From Victor Chernov. It is precisely he who, in 1905–06, outlined such a Russian Revolution as would be neither bourgeois nor socialist, but democratic, and would gradually be supplemented by socialist elements. No, Manuilsky did not make much use of the apple of wisdom!

5. Further, the Chinese Revolution in its transition from capitalism to socialism will have more intermediate stages than our October Revolution: but the periods of its growing over into a socialist revolution will be considerably shorter than the periods outlined (!) by the Bolsheviks for the democratic dictatorship in 1905.

Our astrologer has drawn the balance to everything in advance: to the stages, the periods, and the length of the periods. He only forgot the ABC of Communism. It appears that under democracy, capitalism will *grow over* into socialism in a series of stages. And the power—will it remain the same in this process or will it change? What class will hold power under the democratic dictatorship and what class under the socialist? If different classes will hold power then they can supplant each other only by a new revolution, and not through the "growing over" of the power of one class into the power of another. On the other hand, if it is assumed that in both periods one and the same class will dominate, that is, the proletariat, then what is the meaning of the democratic dictatorship as against the proletarian? To this there can be no answer. And there will not be. Manuilsky is ordered not to clear up the question but to cover up the traces.

In the October Revolution, the democratic tasks grew over into socialist ones—under the unaltered domination of the proletariat. One can therefore draw a distinction (it is understood, only relatively) between the democratic period of the October Revolution and the socialist period; but one cannot distinguish between the democratic and the socialist dictatorships because the democratic was—non-existent.

In addition, we have heard from Manuilsky that in China the democratic dictatorship, from the very beginning, will be confronted with a consistent confiscation of the enterprises, which means the expropriation of the bourgeoisie. This means that there will not even be a democratic stage of the proletarian dictatorship. Under these conditions, where will the democratic dictatorship come from?

Manuilsky's injudicious construction would be entirely impossible were he to compare the Chinese Revolution with the Russian as it actually developed, and not with the one that was "outlined", and at that, to confuse and distort the outline. And all this to what end? In order to retreat without retreating, in order to give up the reactionary formula of the democratic dictatorship, or, as they say in China, to save face. But on the face of Stalin-Manuilsky have already written, first, Chiang Kai-shek and then Wang Jingwei! Enough! The face is already sufficiently descriptive. They cannot save it any more. Manuilsky's theoretical confusion is directed against the basic interests of the Chinese Revolution. The Chinese Bolshevik-Leninists will reveal this.

46

A Letter to Max Shachtman

December 10, 1930

You are quite right when you point out that the Russian Opposition, as late as the first half of 1927, did not demand openly the withdrawal from the Kuomintang. I believe, however, that I have already commented on this fact publicly somewhere. I personally was from the very beginning, that is, from 1923, resolutely opposed to the Communist Party joining the Kuomintang, as well as against the acceptance of the Kuomintang into the "Kuomintern". Radek was always with Zinoviev against me.

The younger members of the Opposition of 1923 were with me almost to a man. Rakovsky was in Paris and not sufficiently informed. Up to 1926, I always voted independently in the Political Bureau on this question, against all the others.

In 1925, simultaneously with the theses on the Chinese Eastern Railroad which I have quoted in the Opposition press, I once more presented the formal proposal that the Communist Party leave the Kuomintang instantly. 145 This was unanimously rejected and contributed a great deal to the baiting later on. In 1926 and 1927, I had uninterrupted conflicts with the Zinovievists on this question. Two or three times, the matter stood at the breaking point. Our center consisted of approximately equal numbers from both of the allied tendencies, for it was after all only a bloc. At the voting, the position of the 1923 Opposition was betrayed by Radek, out of principle, and by Pyatakov, out of unprincipledness. Our faction (1923) was furious about it, demanded that Radek and Pyatakov be recalled from the center.

But since it was a question of splitting with the Zinovievists, it was the general decision that I must submit publicly in this question and acquaint the Opposition in writing with my *standpoint.*

47

To the Chinese Left Opposition

January 8, 1931

Dear Comrades:

During the last few months I have received from you a great number of documents and letters in English, French, and well as a large number of Opposition publications in Chinese. Pressing work, followed by illness prevented me from answering you sooner. During the last days I have carefully studied all the documents received—except, alas, the Chinese—in order to be able to answer the questions you have raised.

To begin with, I will say that in studying the new documents I finally became convinced that there is no difference in principle at all among the various groups that have entered on the road to unification. There are nuances in tactics, which in the future depending on the course of events, *could* develop into differences. However, there are no grounds for assuming that these differences of opinion will necessarily coincide with the lines of the former groupings. Further on, I will attempt to analyze the controversial and semi controversial questions as I see them from here.

1. The entrance of the Communist Party into the Kuomintang was a mistake from the very beginning. I believe that this must be stated openly—in one or another document—especially since in this instance the Russian Opposition to a large extent shares the guilt. Our group (the 1923 Opposition) was from the first, with the exception of Radek and a few of his closest friends, *against* the entry of the Communist Party into the Kuomintang and against the admission of the Kuomintang into the

Comintern. The Zinovievists held the opposite position. With his vote, Radek put them in a majority in the Opposition center. Preobrazhensky and Pyatakov thought that we should not break our bloc with the Zinovievists because of this question. As a result, the United Opposition took an equivocal position on this question, which was reflected in a whole series of documents, even in the Opposition platform. It is worthy of note that all the Russian Oppositionists who adopted the Zinovievist or a conciliatory position on this question subsequently capitulated. On the other hand, all the comrades who are today in jails or in exile were from the very beginning opponents of the entry of the Communist Party into the Kuomintang. This shows the power of a principled position!

2. The slogan *dictatorship of the proletariat and the poor* does not contradict the slogan *dictatorship of the proletariat* but only supplements the latter, and makes it more understandable to the people. In China the proletariat is only a small minority. It can only become a force by uniting around it the majority, i.e., the city and village poor. This idea is in fact expressed by the slogan *dictatorship of the proletariat and the poor.* Naturally, we must point out in the platform and in programmatic articles clearly and distinctly that the role of leadership is concentrated in the hands of the proletariat, which acts as the guide, teacher, and defender of the poor. However, in agitation it is completely correct to employ the term *dictatorship of the proletariat and the poor* as a short slogan. In this form, it has nothing in common with "democratic dictatorship of the proletariat and the peasantry".

In a long document (December 15, 1929) signed by Ch'en Tuhsiu and others, the problem is formulated in the following manner: The tasks of the bourgeois-democratic revolution in China (national independence, state unity, and agrarian revolution) can be solved only on condition that the Chinese proletariat, in alliance with the city and village poor and *as their leader* seizes political power. In other words, the conclusion and the victory of the bourgeois democratic revolution in China can only be attained in the Russian way, i.e., by way of a Chinese October.

I believe that this formulation is completely correct and excludes the possibility of any misunderstandings whatever.

3. On the question of the character of the Chinese Revolution the Comintern leadership has reached an impasse. The experience of the events and the critiques of the Left Opposition have completely destroyed the conception of a "democratic dictatorship". However, if this formula is given up, then no other recourse is left except to turn to the theory of the permanent revolution. The pathetic "theoreticians" of the Comintern stand between these two theories in the unenviable position of Buridan's ass.

The anniversary article (*Pravda,* November 7, 1930) of Manuilsky is the very latest revelation on this subject. A baser mixture of ignorance, cretinism, and villainy cannot be imagined. The Buridanish theory of the Stalinist bureaucrats has been analyzed in the last number of the *Biulleten Oppozitsii* (nos. 17–18). On this fundamental question at any rate we do not have the least difference with you, as all your documents demonstrate.

4. In some letters, complaints have been made about some groups or individual comrades taking a wrong position with regard to the Chinese "Red Army" by likening its detachments to bandits. If that is true, then a stop must be put to it. Of course, lumpen proletarian elements and professional bandits are joining the revolutionary peasant detachments. Yet the movement as a whole arises from wellsprings deep in the conditions of the Chinese village, and these are the same sources from which the dictatorship of the proletariat will have to nourish itself later on. The policy of the Stalinists toward these detachments is a policy of criminal bureaucratic adventurism. This policy must be mercilessly exposed. We do not share or encourage the illusions of the leaders and the participants of the partisan detachments. We must explain to them that without a proletarian revolution and the seizure of power by the workers the partisan detachments of the peasantry cannot lead the way to victory. However, we must conduct this work of clarification as real friends, not detached onlookers and—especially—not as enemies. Without abandoning our own methods and tasks,

we must persistently and courageously defend these detachments against the Kuomintang repression and bourgeois slander and persecution. We must explain the enormous *symptomatic* significance of these detachments. Naturally, we cannot throw our own forces into the partisan struggle—at present we have another field of endeavor and other tasks. Nevertheless, it is very desirable to have our people, Oppositionists, at least in the larger divisions of the "Red Army", to share the fate of these detachments, to observe attentively the relations between these detachments and the peasantry, and to keep the Left Opposition informed.

In case of a postponement of the revolution, of a new economic revival in China, and of a development of parliamentary tendencies (all these are interconnected), the detachments will inevitably degenerate, antagonizing the poor peasantry. Therefore it is all the more necessary for us to keep an eye on these detachments, in order to be able to adjust our position as necessary.

5. In several letters, the question of a national assembly is brought up anew. The problem of our political tasks is lost beneath guesses as to whether a national assembly will be set up, in what form, the relationship that might develop between the national assembly and the soviets, etc. Running through such speculation is a strong thread of political scholasticism. Thus, for instance, one of the communications reads:

We believe that the national assembly will most likely not be realized. Even if it should be realized, it could not be transformed into a "provisional government", since all the material forces are in the hands of the Kuomintang militarists. Regarding the government that will be organized after the insurrection, that will undoubtedly be the government of the proletarian dictatorship, and in that case it will not convoke a national assembly.

This supposition is extremely incomplete and one-sided, and therefore, leaves considerable room for misunderstandings and mistakes.

(a) First of all, we must not exclude the possibility that the bourgeois classes themselves may be forced to convoke *something like* a national assembly. If the reports of the European papers are correct, Chiang Kai-shek is nursing the idea of substituting control over some kind of sham parliament for his control over the Kuomintang, which is now restricting him. Certain circles of the big and the middle bourgeoisie which have come into conflict with what they find to be an exasperating party dictatorship may look with favor upon such a project. At the same time, a "parliament" would serve better as a cover for the military dictatorship in face of American public opinion. As the papers report, Chiang Kai-shek has adopted Americanized Christianity in the not unfounded hope that this will facilitate his credit rating with the Jewish bankers in Wall Street; Americanized Christianity, American Jewish moneylenders, and a Chinese pseudo-parliament—all these harmonize splendidly with one another.

In case of a parliamentary variant, the urban petty bourgeoisie, the intellectuals, the students, the "Third Party"—all will be set into motion. The questions of a constitution, suffrage, and parliamentarism will come onto the agenda. It would be nonsense to contend that the masses of the Chinese people have already left all this behind them. Up to the present, they have only gone through the Stalin-Chiang Kai-shek school, i.e., the basest of all schools. The problems of democracy will inevitably, for a certain period, absorb the attention not only of the peasantry, but of the workers also. This must take place *under our leadership.*

Will Chiang Kai-shek convoke his own parliament? It is quite possible. But it is possible that the constitutional-democratic movement will go beyond the bounds planned by Chiang Kaishek, and this will force him to go further than he wants to at present. It is possible even that the movement will sweep away Chiang Kai-shek together with all his plans. No matter what the constitutional-parliamentary variants, we will not remain on the sidelines. We shall participate in the struggle under our slogans above all, under the slogans of revolutionary and consistent ("100 per cent") democracy. If the revolutionary wave does not immediately sweep away Chiang Kai-shek and his parliament, we will be forced to participate in this parliament, exposing the lies of comprador parliamentarism, and advancing our own tasks.

(b) Can we assume that the revolutionary democratic movement may take on such dimensions that Chiang Kai-shek will no longer be able to keep the military apparatus under control, while the communists are not yet in a position to seize power? Such a transitional period is very likely. It could advance some sort of Chinese variety of *dual power,* a new provisional government, a bloc of the Kuomintang with the Third Party, etc., etc. Such a regime would be very unstable. It could only be a step toward the dictatorship of the proletariat. But such a step is possible

(c) "After the victorious insurrection," says the document which we have quoted, "a proletarian dictatorship might be instituted and in that case a national assembly would not be convoked." Here, too, the question is oversimplified. At what moment will the insurrection take place and under what slogans? If the proletariat has assembled the poor peasantry under the slogans of democracy (land, national assembly, etc.) and in a united onslaught overthrows the military dictatorship of the bourgeoisie, then, when it comes into power, the proletariat will have to convoke a national assembly in order not to arouse the mistrust of the peasantry and in order not to provide an opening for bourgeois demagogy. Even after the October insurrection the Bolsheviks had to convoke the Constituent Assembly. Why should we conclude that this variant is impossible for China? The peasantry does not develop at the same rate as the proletariat. The proletariat can anticipate many things, but the peasantry will only learn from the facts. It may be that the Chinese peasantry will need to go through the living experience of a national assembly.

Since the bourgeoisie in Russia delayed convoking the Constituent Assembly for a long time, and the Bolsheviks exposed this, they were compelled, after they had come into power, to convoke the Constituent Assembly rapidly, on the basis of the old election results, which put them in a minority. The Constituent Assembly came into conflict with the soviets before the eyes of all the people and it was dissolved.

In China we can conceive of another variant. After it comes to power, the proletariat may, under certain conditions, postpone convoking a national assembly for several months, develop a broad agitation in the countryside, and assure a communist majority in the national assembly. The advantage would be that the soviet system would be formally sanctioned by the national assembly, immediately depriving the bourgeoisie of a popular slogan in the civil war.

6. Of course, the variations we have considered above are only *historical hypotheses.* There is no way of predicting what the actual course of developments will be. The general course, toward the dictatorship of the proletariat, is clear in advance. We should not engage in speculation over possible variations, stages, and combinations, but instead intervene as the revolutionary factor in what is happening and develop powerful agitation around democratic slogans. If we take the initiative in this field, the Stalinist bureaucracy will be brushed aside and the Bolshevik Leninists will become within a short time a powerful political force.

7. The question of determining what possibilities may open up in the near future for Chinese capitalism is not a matter of principle but of fact. To decide in advance that capitalist development in China can no longer take a step forward would be the purest doctrinairism. A significant inflow of foreign capital into China is not at all excluded. Because of the world crisis, idle capital is accumulating that needs a field of investment. It is true that at present even American capital, the most powerful of all, is paralyzed, perplexed, apprehensive, and deprived of initiative, since only recently it fell from the peaks of prosperity into the depths of the depression. But it has already begun to look for an international bridgehead as the springboard from which it could touch off a new economic upsurge. It is beyond doubt that under these conditions China offers serious possibilities. To what degree will these be realized? This is not easy to predict either. Here we must not guess a priori, but watch the actual economic and political processes. All the same, it is not at all excluded that while the bulk of the capitalist world is still struggling in the grip of the crisis, the inflow of foreign capital

will create an economic revival in China. We must be prepared for this variant, too, by focusing our attention in good time on organizing and strengthening the trade unions and assuring them a correct leadership.

Naturally, an economic upsurge in China would postpone immediate revolutionary perspectives for some time, but this revival will in turn open up new possibilities, new forces, and new sources of strength for victory. In any case, the future belongs to us.

8. Some of the letters from Shanghai pose the question: Should we carry out a complete unification in the individual localities, fuse the press of all the groups, and convoke a conference on the basis of the unification that has already been achieved, or should we permit separate groups to continue within the united Opposition until all the tactical problems have been solved? In such organizational matters, it is difficult to offer advice from afar. It is even possible that the advice would arrive too late. Still, I cannot refrain from saying this to you: *Dear friends, fuse your organizations and your press definitely this very day!* We must not drag out the preparations for the unification a long time, because in that way, without wanting to, we can create artificial differences.

By this I do not mean to say that all the questions have already been settled and that you (or more correctly, *we)* are assured that no differences will arise in the future. No, there is no doubt that the day after tomorrow and the day after that, new tasks will arise, and with them new differences. Without this the development of a revolutionary party is impossible. But the new differences will create new groupings in the framework of the united organization. We must not tarry too long over the past. We must not mark time. We must go onward toward the future.

9. That new differences are inevitable is proved by the experiences of all the sections of the Left Opposition. The French League, for example, was formed from various groups. Thanks to its weekly journal, the League has accomplished very serious and very valuable work, not only from the national, but from the international point of view as well. It has demonstrated

that the unification of the different groups was a progressive step. But in recent months some very serious differences have arisen in the League, particularly on the trade union question. A right wing has formed and taken a position that is false to the core. This question is so important and so profound that it can even lead to a new split. Naturally, absolutely everything will have to be done to avoid this. But if that does not succeed, it will not at all prove that the unification of yesterday was a mistake. We do not make a fetish of unity, nor of splits. It all depends upon the conditions of the moment, on the depth of the differences, on the character of the problems.

10. In Spain, conditions are apparently different from those in all the other countries. Spain is at present going through a period of clear and definite revolutionary upsurge. The heated political atmosphere should greatly facilitate the work of the Bolshevik-Leninists as the boldest and most consistent revolutionary wing. The Comintern has smashed the ranks of Spanish communism, it has weakened and rendered lifeless the official party. As in all other important cases, the Comintern leadership has let a revolutionary situation slip by. The Spanish workers have been left to their own devices at a most crucial moment. Left almost without leadership, they are developing a struggle through revolutionary strikes of notable scope. Under these conditions, the Spanish Bolshevik-Leninists are issuing the slogan of *soviets.* According to the theory of the Stalinists and the practice of the Canton insurrection, it appears that soviets must be created only on the eve of the insurrection. Disastrous theory and disastrous practice! Soviets must be created when the real and living movement of the masses manifests the need for that type of organization. Soviets are formed at first as broad strike committees. This is precisely the case in Spain. There is no doubt that under these conditions the initiative of the Bolshevik-Leninists (Opposition) will receive a sympathetic response from the proletarian vanguard. A broad perspective can open up in the near future for the Spanish Opposition. Let us wish our Spanish friends complete success.

11. In conclusion, I come once more to the question of unity, in order to point out the extremely pitiful experiences of Austria in this domain.

For a year and a half, three Austrian groups occupied themselves with "unification" and each thought up in turn such conditions as to make the unification impossible. This criminal game only reflected the generally sorry state of the Austrian Opposition which has been overcome by the decay of the official Communist Party. This year each of the Austrian groups has succeeded in more than amply demonstrating that it is ready to give up the ideas and principles of the International Opposition but in no case its own sectarian pretensions. The more barren the ideological base of these groups, the more venomous the nature of their internal struggles. They delight in dragging the banner of the International Opposition into the mud and demand that the International Opposition use its authority to cover up their unworthy work.

Obviously the International Opposition is not going to do this. To bring unprincipled groups into the International Opposition would mean poisoning one's own organism. In this respect, strict selection is demanded. I hope that at its conference the International Opposition will adopt the "twenty-one conditions" for the admission of organizations into its ranks and that these conditions will be sufficiently severe.

In contrast to the Austrian Opposition, the Chinese Opposition did not develop on the basis of petty backroom intrigues, but from the experiences of a great revolution that was lost by an opportunist leadership. Its great historic mission places exceptional responsibilities on the Chinese Opposition. All of us here hope that the Chinese Opposition will rid itself of the spirit of clannishness, and, rising to its full height, prove equal to the tasks it faces.

Yours,

L. Trotsky

48

The Strangled Revolution

February 9, 1931
Prinkipo

The book by André Malraux, *Les Conquérants*, was sent to me from various quarters and I think in four copies, but to my regret I read it after a delay of a year and a half or two. The book is devoted to the Chinese Revolution, that is, to the greatest subject of the last five years. A fine and well-knit style, the discriminating eye of an artist, original and daring observation —all confer upon the novel an exceptional importance. If we write about it here it is not because the book is a work of talent, although this is not a negligible fact, but because it offers a source of political lessons of the highest value. Do they come from Malraux? No, they flow from the recital itself, unknown to the author, and they go against him. This does honour to the author as an observer and an artist, but not as a revolutionist. However, we have the right to evaluate Malraux too from this point of view; in his own name and above all in the name of Garine, his other self, the author does not hesitate with his judgements on the revolution.

This book is called a novel. As a matter of fact, we have before us a romanticized chronicle of the Chinese Revolution, from its first period to the period of Canton. The chronicle is not complete. Social vigour is sometimes lacking from the picture. But for that there pass before the reader not only luminous episodes of the revolution but also clear-cut silhouettes which are graven in the memory like social symbols.

By little coloured touches, following the method of *pointillisme*, Malraux gives an unforgettable picture of the general strike, not, to be sure, as it is below, not as it is carried out, but as it is observed from above: the Europeans do not get their breakfast, they swelter in the heat, the Chinese have ceased to work in the kitchens and to operate the ventilators. This is not a reproach to the author: the foreign artist could undoubtedly not have dealt with his theme otherwise. But there is a reproach to be made, and not a small one: the book is lacking in a congenital affinity between the writer, in spite of all he knows, understands and can do, and his heroine, the revolution.

The active sympathies of the author for insurgent China are unmistakable. But chance bursts upon these sympathies. They are corroded by the excesses of individualism and by aesthetic caprice. In reading the book with sustained attention one sometimes experiences a feeling of vexation when in the tone of the persuasive recital one perceives a note of protective irony towards the barbarians capable of enthusiasm. That China is backward, that many of its political manifestations bear a primitive character—nobody asks that this be passed over in silence. But a correct perspective is needed which puts every object in its place. The Chinese events, on the basis of which Malraux's "novel" unfolds itself, are incomparably more important for the future destiny of human culture than the vain and pitiful clamour of Europe parliaments and the mountain of literary products of stagnant civilization. Malraux seems to feel a certain fear to take this into account.

In the novel, there are pages, splendid in their intensity, which show how revolutionary hatred is born of the yoke, of ignorance, of slavery, and is tempered like steel. These pages might have entered into the Anthology of the Revolution if Malraux had approached the masses with greater freedom and intrepidity, if he had not introduced into his observations a small note of *blasé* superiority, seeming to excuse himself for his transient contact with the insurrection of the Chinese people, as much perhaps before himself as before the academic mandarins in France and the traffickers in spiritual opium.

* * *

Borodin represents the Comintern in the post of "high counsellor" in the Canton government. Garine, the favourite of the author, is in charge of propaganda. All the work is done within the framework of the Guomindang. Borodin, Garine, the Russian "General" Galen, the Frenchman Gérard, the German Klein and others, constitute an original bureaucracy of the revolution raising itself above the insurgent people and conducting its own "revolutionary" policy instead of the policy of the revolution.

The local organizations of the Guomindang are defined as follows: "groups of fanatics—brave of a few plutocrats out for notoriety or for security—and crowds of students and coolies". (p. 24) Not only do bourgeois enter into every organization but they completely lead the Party. The Communists are subordinate to the Guomindang. The workers and the peasants are persuaded to take no action that might rebuff the devoted friends of the bourgeoisie. "Such are the societies that we control (more or less, do not fool yourself on this score)." An edifying avowal! The bureaucracy of the Comintern tried to "control" the class struggle in China, like the international bankocracy controls the economic life of the backward countries. But a revolution cannot be controlled. One can only give a political expression to its internal forces. One must know to which of these forces to link one's destiny.

"Today coolies are beginning to discover that they exist, simply that they exist." (p. 26) That's well aimed. But to feel that they exist, the coolies, the industrial workers and the peasants must overthrow those who prevent them from existing. Foreign domination is indissolubly bound up with the domestic yoke. The coolies must not only drive out Baldwin or MacDonald but also overthrow the ruling classes. One cannot be accomplished without the other. Thus, the awakening of the human personality in the masses of China, who exceed ten times the population of France, is immediately transformed into the lava of the social revolution. A magnificent spectacle!

But here Borodin appears on the scene and declares: "In the revolution the workers must do the coolie work for the bourgeoisie," wrote Chen Duxiu in an open letter to the Chinese

Communists. The social enslavement from which they want to liberate themselves, the workers find transposed into the sphere of politics. To whom do they owe this perfidious operation? To the bureaucracy of the Comintern. In trying to "control" the Guomindang, it actually aids the bourgeoisie which seeks "notoriety and security" in enslaving the coolies who want to exist.

Borodin, who remains in the background all the time, is characterized in the novel as a "man of action", as a "professional revolutionist", as a living incarnation of Bolshevism on the soil of China. Nothing is further from the truth! Here is the political biography of Borodin: in 1903, at the age of 19, he emigrated to America; in 1918, he returned to Moscow where, thanks to his knowledge of English, he "ensured contact with the foreign parties"; he was arrested in Glasgow in 1922; then he was delegated to China as representative of the Comintern. Having quit Russia *before* the first revolution and having returned *after* the third, Borodin appeared as the consummate representative of that state and Party bureaucracy which recognized the revolution only after its victory. When it is a question of young people, it is sometimes nothing more than a matter of chronology. With people of 40 or 50, it is already a political characterization. If Borodin rallied successfully to the victorious revolution in Russia, it does not in the least signify that he was called upon to assure the victory of the revolution in China. People of this type assimilate without difficulty the gestures and intonations of "professional revolutionists". Many of them, by their protective colouration, not only deceive others but also themselves. The audacious inflexibility of the Bolshevik is most usually metamorphosed with them into that cynicism of the functionary ready for anything. Ah! to have a mandate from the Central Committee! This sacrosanct safeguard Borodin always had in his pocket.

Garine is not a functionary, he is more original than Borodin and perhaps even closer to the revolutionary type. But he is devoid of the indispensable formation; dilettante and theatrical, he gets hopelessly entangled in the great events and he reveals it at every step. With regard to the slogans of the Chinese revolution, he expresses himself thus: "democratic chatter—'the rights of the proletariat', etc." (p.32.) This has a radical ring but it is a false radicalism. The slogans of democracy are execrable chatter in the mouth of Poincaré, Herriot, Léon Blum, sleight-of-hand artists of France and jailers of Indochina, Algeria and Morocco. But when the Chinese rebel in the name of the "rights of the proletariat", this has as little to do with chatter as the slogans of the French Revolution in the eighteenth century. At Hong Kong, the British birds of prey threatened, during the strike, to re-establish corporal punishment. "The rights of man and of the citizen" meant at Hong Kong the right of the Chinese not to be flogged by the British whip. To unmask the democratic rottenness of the imperialists is to serve the revolution: to call the slogans of the insurrection of the oppressed "chatter", is involuntarily to aid the imperialists.

A good inoculation of Marxism would have preserved the author from fatal contempt of this sort. But Garine in general considers that revolutionary doctrine is "doctrinaire rubbish" (*le fatras doctrinal*). He is, you see, one of those to whom the revolution is only a definite "state of affairs". Isn't this astonishing? But it is just because the revolution is a "state of affairs", that is, a stage in the development of society conditioned by objective causes and subjected to definite laws, that a scientific mind can foresee the general direction of processes. Only the study of the anatomy of society and of its physiology permits one to react to the course of events by basing oneself upon scientific foresight and not upon a dilettante's conjectures. The revolutionist who "despises" revolutionary doctrine is not a bit better than the healer who despises medical doctrine which he does not know, or than the engineer who rejects technology. People who without the aid of science, try to rectify the "state of affairs" which is called a disease, are called sorcerers or charlatans and are prosecuted by law. Had there existed a tribunal to judge the sorcerers of the revolution, it is probable that Borodin, like his Muscovite inspirers, would have been severely condemned. I am afraid Garine himself would not have come out of it unscathed.

Two figures are contrasted to each other in the novel, like

the two poles of the national revolution; old Chen Dai, the spiritual authority of the right wing of the Guomindang, the prophet and saint of the bourgeoisie, and Hong, the young leader of the terrorists. Both are depicted with great force. Chen Dai embodies the old Chinese culture translated into the language of European breeding; with this exquisite garment, he "ennobles" the interests of all the ruling classes of China. To be sure, Chen Dai wants national liberation, but he dreads the masses more than the imperialists; he hates the revolution more than the yoke placed upon the nation. If he marches towards it, it is only to pacify it, to subdue it, to exhaust it. He conducts a policy of passive resistance on two fronts, against imperialism and against the revolution, the policy of Gandhi in India, the policy which, in definite periods and in one form or another, the bourgeoisie has conducted at every longitude and latitude. Passive resistance flows from the tendency of the bourgeoisie to canalize the movement of the masses and to make off with it.

When Garine says that Chen Dai's influence rises above politics, one can only shrug his shoulders. The masked policy of the "upright man", in China as in India, expresses in the most sublime and abstractly moralizing form the conservative interests of the possessors. The personal disinterestedness of Chen Dai is in no sense in opposition to his political function: the exploiters need "upright men" as the corrupted ecclesiastical hierarchy needs saints.

Who gravitate around Chen Dai? The novel replies with meritorious precision: a world of "aged mandarins, smugglers of opium and of obscene photographs, of scholars turned bicycle dealers, of Parisian barristers, of intellectuals of every kind". (p.124) Behind them stands a more solid bourgeoisie bound up with England, which arms General Tang against the revolution. In the expectation of victory, Tang prepares to make Chen Dai the head of the government. Both of them, Chen Dai and Tang, nevertheless continue to be members of the Guomindang which Borodin and Garine serve.

When Tang has a village attacked by his armies, and when he prepares to butcher the revolutionists, beginning with Borodin and Garine, his party comrades, the latter with the aid of Hong, mobilize and arm the unemployed. But after the victory won over Tang, the leaders do not seek to change a thing that existed before. They cannot break the ambiguous bloc with Chen Dai because they have no confidence in the workers, the coolies, the revolutionary masses, they are themselves contaminated with the prejudices of Chen Dai whose qualified arm they are.

In order "not to rebuff" the bourgeoisie they are forced to enter into struggle with Hong. Who is he and where does he come from? "The lowest dregs." (p. 36) He is one of those who are making the revolution and not those who rally to it when it is victorious. Having come to the idea of killing the British governor of Hong Kong, Hong is concerned with only one thing: "When I have been sentenced to capital punishment, you must tell the young to follow my example." (p. 36) To Hong a clear program must be given: to arouse the workers, to assemble them, to arm them and to oppose them to Chen Dai as to an enemy. But the bureaucracy of the Comintern seeks Chen Dai's friendship, repulses Hong and exasperates him. Hong exterminates bankers and merchants one after another, the very ones who "support" the Guomindang, Hong kills missionaries: "those who teach people to support misery must be punished, Christian priests or others". (p. 274) If Hong does not find the right road, it is the fault of Borodin and Garine who have placed the revolution in the hands of the bankers and the merchants. Hong reflects the mass which is already rising but which has not yet rubbed its eyes or softened its hands. He tries by the revolver and the knife to act *for* the masses whom the agents of the Comintern are paralysing. Such is the unvarnished truth about the Chinese Revolution.

* * *

Meanwhile, the Canton government is "oscillating, in its attempt to stay straight, between Garine and Borodin, who control the police and the trade unions, on the one hand, and Chen Dai, who controls nothing, but who exists all the same, on the other." (p. 68) We have an almost perfect picture of the duality of power. The representatives of the Comintern have in their hands the trade unions of Canton, the police, the cadet school of Whampoa, the sympathy of the masses the aid of the Soviet Union. Chen Dai has a "moral authority", that is, the prestige of the mortally distracted possessors. The friends of Chen Dai sit in a powerless government willingly supported by the conciliators. But isn't this the régime of the February revolution, the Kerenskyist system, with the sole difference that the role of the Mensheviks is played by the pseudo-Bolsheviks? Borodin has no doubt of it even though he is made up as a Bolshevik and takes his make-up seriously.

The central idea of Garine and Borodin is to prohibit Chinese and foreign boats, cruising towards the port of Canton, from putting in at Hong Kong. By the commercial boycott these people, who consider themselves revolutionary realists, hope to shatter British domination in southern China. They never deem it necessary first of all to overthrow the government of the Canton bourgeoisie which only waits for the moment to surrender the revolution to England. No, Borodin and Garine knock every day at the door of the "government", and hat in hand, beg that the saving decree be promulgated. One of them reminds Garine that at bottom the government is a phantom. Garine is not disconcerted. Phantom or not, he replies, let it go ahead while we need it. That is the way the priest needs relics which he himself fabricates with wax and cotton. What is concealed behind this policy which weakens and debases the revolution? The respect of a petty-bourgeois revolutionist for a solid conservative bourgeois. It is thus that the reddest of the French radicals is always ready to fall on his knees before Poincaré.

But perhaps the masses of Canton are not yet mature enough to overthrow the power of the bourgeoisie? From this whole atmosphere, the conviction arises that without the opposition of the Comintern the phantom government would long before have been overthrown under the pressure of the masses. But let us admit that the Cantonese workers were still too weak to establish their own power. What, generally speaking, is the weak spot of the masses? Their inclination to follow the exploiters. In this case, the first duty of revolutionists is to help the workers liberate themselves from servile confidence. Nevertheless, the work done by the bureaucracy of the Comintern was diametrically opposed to his. It inculcated in the masses the notion of the necessity to submit to the bourgeoisie and it declared that the enemies of the bourgeoisie were their own enemies.

Do not rebuff Chen Dai! But if Chen Dai withdraws in spite of this, which is inevitable, it would not mean that Garine and Borodin will be delivered of their voluntary vassaldom towards the bourgeoisie. They will only choose as the new focus of their activity, Chiang Kai-shek, son of the same class and younger brother of Chen Dai. Head of the military school of Whampoa, founded by the Bolsheviks, Chiang Kai-shek does not confine himself to passive resistance; he is ready to resort to bloody force, not in the plebeian form, the form of the masses, but in the military form and only within limits that will permit the bourgeoisie to retain an unlimited power over the army. Borodin and Garine, by arming their enemies, disarm and repulse their friends. This is the way they prepare the catastrophe.

But are we not overestimating the influence of the revolutionary bureaucracy upon the events? No, it showed itself stronger than it might have thought, if not for good then at least for evil. The coolies who are only beginning to exist politically require a courageous leadership. Hong requires a bold program. The revolution requires the energies of millions of rising men. But Borodin and his bureaucrats require Chen Dai and Chiang Kai-shek. They strangle Hong and prevent the worker from raising his head. In a few months, they will stifle the agrarian insurrection of the peasantry so as not to repulse the bourgeois army command. Their strength is that they represent the Russian October, Bolshevism, the Communist International. Having usurped authority, the banner and the material resources of the greatest of revolutions, the bureaucracy bars the road to another revolution which also had all chances of being great.

The dialogue between Borodin and Hong (pp.182–84) is the most terrific indictment of Borodin and his Moscow inspirers. Hong, as always, is after decisive action. He demands the punishment of the most prominent bourgeois. Borodin finds this sole objection: Those who are "paying" must not be touched. "Revolution is not so simple," says Garine for his part. "Revolution involves paying an army," adds Borodin. These aphorisms contain all the elements of the noose in which the Chinese Revolution was strangled. Borodin protected the bourgeoisie which, in recompense, made contributions to the "revolution", the money going to the army of Chiang Kai-shek. The army of Chiang Kai-shek exterminated the proletariat and liquidated the revolution. Was it really impossible to foresee this? And wasn't it really foreseen? The bourgeoisie pays willingly only for the army which serves it against the people. The army of the revolution does not wait for donations: it makes them pay. This is called the revolutionary dictatorship. Hong comes forward successfully at workers' meetings and thunders against the "Russians", the bearers of ruin for the revolution. The way of Hong himself does not lead to the goal but he is right as against Borodin. "Had the Tai Ping leaders Russian advisers? Had the Boxers?" (p.190) Had the Chinese revolution of 1924–27 been left to itself it would perhaps not have come to victory immediately but it would not have resorted to the methods of hara-kiri, it would not have known shameful capitulations and it would have trained revolutionary cadres. Between the dual power of Canton and that of Petrograd there is the tragic difference that in China there was no Bolshevism in evidence; under the name of Trotskyism, it was declared a counter-revolutionary doctrine and was persecuted by every method of calumny and repression. Where Kerensky did not succeed during the July Days, Stalin succeeded ten years later in China.

Borodin and "all the Bolsheviks of his generation", Garine assures us, were distinguished by their struggle against the anarchists. This remark was needed by the author so as to prepare the reader for the struggle of Borodin against Hong's group. Historically it is false. Anarchism was unable to raise its head in Russia not because the Bolsheviks fought successfully against it but because they had first dug up the ground under its feet. Anarchism, if it does not live within the four walls of intellectuals' cafés and editorial offices, but has penetrated more deeply, translates the psychology of despair in the masses and signifies the political punishment for the deceptions of democracy and the treachery of opportunism. The boldness of Bolshevism in posing the revolutionary problems and in teaching their solution left no room for the development of anarchism in Russia. But if the historical investigation of Malraux is not exact, his recital shows admirably how the opportunist policy of Stalin-Borodin prepared the ground for anarchist terrorism in China.

Driven by the logic of this policy, Borodin consents to adopt a decree against the terrorists. The firm revolutionists, driven on to the road of adventurism by the crimes of the Moscow leaders, the bourgeoisie of Canton, with the benediction of the Comintern, declares them outlaws. They reply with acts of terrorism against the pseudo-revolutionary bureaucrats who protect the moneyed bourgeoisie. Borodin and Garine seize the terrorists and destroy them, no longer defending the bourgeois alone but also their own heads. It is thus that the policy of conciliation inexorably slips down to the lowest degree of treachery.

The book is called *Les Conquérants*. With this title, which has a double meaning when the revolution paints itself with imperialism, the author refers to the Russian Bolsheviks, or more exactly, to a certain part of them. The conquerors? The Chinese masses rose for a revolutionary insurrection, with the influence of the October upheaval as their example and with Bolshevism as their banner. But the "conquerors" conquered nothing. On the contrary, they surrendered everything to the enemy. If the Russian Revolution called forth the Chinese Revolution, the Russian epigones strangled it. Malraux does not make these deductions. He does not even suspect their existence. All the more clearly do they emerge upon the background of his remarkable book.

49

What is Happening in the Chinese Communist Party?*

Published March 1931

Pravda of December 25, 1930, tells us:

In the fall of 1930, the Chinese Communist Party numbered 200,000 members. The party has uprooted the remnants of the ideas of Ch'en Tu-hsiu and has destroyed Trotskyism ideologically. [!]

However, the complicated circumstances of struggle have recently given rise to certain reservations of a "leftist" semi-Trotskyist character inside the party. A whole number of leading comrades, who believe that a revolutionary situation has matured on an international scale, have posed the question of beginning an immediate struggle for power on a full national plane, ignoring the necessity of consolidating the soviet power in the regions already occupied by the Red Army. Proceeding from such an estimate, they consider it possible to cease the economic struggle of the proletariat and to liquidate the revolutionary unions.

This quotation gives one an idea of the chaos that reigns in the minds of the leading functionaries of the Chinese party. They have destroyed Trotskyism "ideologically"—that goes without saying—but immediately following this destruction, reservations of a "semi-Trotskyist character" rise anew. Such things have happened time and again. These reservations have

* Excerpted from the article *"Notes of a Journalist"*.

arisen even among a "number of leading comrades." That also has happened before.

What are these new semi-Trotskyist reservations? They manifest themselves, first of all, in the demand to begin an "immediate struggle for power on a full national plane". But the Left Opposition since the fall of 1927 has advanced the exact opposite demand: to withdraw the slogan of armed insurrection as an immediate slogan. Even today our Chinese comrades put on the agenda not the armed uprising, but the mobilization of the masses around the social demands of the proletariat and the peasantry and the slogans of revolutionary democracy; not adventurist experiments in the countryside, but the building up of the trade unions and the party! If *Pravda is* not indulging in slander (which is very likely), if the new opposition really voices demands "to cease the economic struggle of the proletariat and to liquidate the unions", then this is directly contrary to the proposals of the Left Opposition (Bolshevik-Leninists).

We read further on that the new opposition ignores "the necessity of consolidating the soviet power in the regions already occupied by the Red Army". Instead of such consolidation, it is as though the opposition were calling for a general national uprising. This too has nothing in common with the position of Bolshevik-Leninists. If the Chinese "Red Army" is regarded as the weapon of a proletarian uprising, then the Chinese communists must be guided by the laws of every revolutionary uprising. They must take the offensive, extend their territory, conquer the strategic centers of the country. Without this, every revolutionary uprising is hopeless. To delay, to remain on the defensive instead of taking the offensive, spells defeat for the uprising. In this sense, the new opposition, if its point of view has been correctly stated, is far more consistent than the Stalinists, who believe that "soviet power" in the countryside can be maintained for years or that soviet power can be transported from one end of the country to another in the baggage car of the partisan detachments labeled the "Red Army". But neither position resembles our own; both flow from a wrong point of departure. They renounce the class theory of soviet power. They dissolve the revolution into provincial peasant revolts, linking up the entire fate of the Chinese Communist Party with them in an adventurist manner.

What does the Communist Party represent? Quite unexpectedly we learn from this article that the Communist Party in the fall of 1930 numbered about "200,000 members." The figure is given without explanation. Last year, however, the Chinese party numbered only about six to seven thousand members. If this tremendous growth of the party during the last year is a fact, then this should be a symptom of a radical change in the situation in favor of the revolution. Two hundred thousand members! If in reality the party were to number fifty, forty, or even twenty thousand workers, after it had experienced the second Chinese Revolution and had absorbed its lessons, we would say that this is a powerful force, and invincible; with such cadres, we can transform all of China. But we would also have to ask: Are these twenty thousand workers members of the unions? What kind of work are they carrying on within them? Is their influence growing? Are they linking up their organizations with the masses of the unorganized and of the rural periphery? And under what slogans?

The fact is that the leadership of the Comintern is concealing something from the proletarian vanguard. We can be certain that the lion's share of these 200,000—let us say from 90 to 95 per cent—come from regions where the detachments of the "Red Army" are active. One has only to imagine the political psychology of the peasant detachments and the conditions under which they carry on their activity to get a clear political picture: the partisans, most probably, are almost all enrolled in the party, and after them the peasants in the occupied regions. The Chinese party, as well as the "Red Army" and the "soviet power," has abandoned the proletarian rails and is heading toward the rural districts and the countryside.

In seeking a way out of the impasse, the new Chinese opposition advances, as we have read, the slogan of a proletarian uprising on a national plane. Obviously this would be the best outcome, if the prerequisites for it were to exist. But they do not exist today. What, then, can be done? We must develop slogans for the interval between revolutions, the length of which no one can tell in advance. These are the slogans of the democratic revolution: land to the peasants, the eight-hour workday, national independence, the right of national self-determination for all people, and, finally, the constituent assembly. Under these slogans the provincial peasant uprisings of the partisan detachments will break out of their provincial isolation and fuse with the general national movement, linking their own fate with it. The Communist Party will emerge, not as the technical guide of the Chinese peasantry, but as the political leader of the working class of the entire country. There is no other road!

50

A Strangled Revolution and its Stranglers

June 13, 1931
Kadikoy

Urgent work prevented me from reading sooner the article by Malraux in which he defends, against my criticism, the Communist International, Borodin, Garine, and himself. As a political publicist, Malraux is at a still greater distance from the proletariat and from the revolution than as an artist. By itself, this fact would not justify these lines, for it is nowhere said that a talented writer must necessarily be a proletarian revolutionist. If I nevertheless return to the same question again, it is for the sake of the subject, and not of Malraux.

The best figures of the novel, I said, attained the stature of social symbols. I must add: Borodin, Garine and all their "collaborators" constitute symbols of the quasi-revolutionary bureaucracy, of that new "social type" which was born thanks to the existence of the soviet state on the one hand, and on the other to a definite régime in the Comintern.

I declined to classify Borodin among the "professional revolutionists", as he is characterized in the novel. Malraux endeavours to show me that Garine has enough mandarin's buttons to give him the right to this title. Here, Malraux finds it in place to add that Trotsky has a greater quantity of buttons. Isn't it ridiculous? The type of the professional revolutionist is not at all some sort of an ideal type. But in all events, it is a *definite* type, with a definite political biography and with salient traits. Only Russia created this type during the last decades; in Russia, the most perfect of this type was created by the Bolshevik Party. The professional revolutionists of the generation to which Borodin belonged began to take shape on the eve of the first revolution, they were put to the test in 1905, they tempered and educated (or decomposed) themselves during the years of the counter-revolution; they stood the supreme test in 1917. From 1903 up to 1918, that is, during the whole period when, in Russia, was being formed the type of professional revolutionist, Borodin, and hundreds, thousands of Borodins, remained outside of the struggle. In 1918, after the victory, Borodin arrived to offer his services. This does him honour: it is worthier to serve the proletarian state than the bourgeois state. Borodin charged himself with perilous missions. But the agents of bourgeois states in foreign countries, especially in colonial countries, also and that quite frequently, accomplish perilous tasks. Yet they do not become revolutionists because of that. The type of the functionary-adventurer and the type of the professional revolutionist, at certain moments and by certain qualities, can find points of similarity. But by their psychological formation as much as by their historical function, they are two opposite types.

The revolution pursues its course together with its class. If the proletariat is weak, if it is backward, the revolution confines itself to the modest, patient and persevering work of the creation of propaganda circles, of the preparation of cadres; supporting itself upon the first cadres, it passes over to mass agitation, legal or illegal, according to the circumstances. It always distinguishes its class from the enemy class, and conducts only such a policy as corresponds to the strength of its class and consolidates this strength. The French, the Russian or the Chinese proletarian revolutionist, will look upon the Chinese workers as his own army, of today or of tomorrow. The functionary-adventurer raises himself above all the classes of the Chinese nation. He considers himself predestined to dominate, to give orders, to command, independently of the internal relationship of forces in China. Since the Chinese proletariat is weak today and cannot assure the commanding positions, the functionary conciliates and joins together the different classes. He acts as the inspector of the nation, as the viceroy for the affairs of the colonial revolution. He arranges combinations between the conservative bourgeois and the anarchist, he improvises a program ad hoc, he erects policies upon ambiguities, he creates a bloc of four classes, he swallows swords and scoffs at principles. With what result? The bourgeoisie is richer, more influential, more experienced. The functionary-adventurer does not succeed in deceiving it. But for all that, he deceives the workers, filled with the spirit of abnegation, but not experienced, by turning them over to the hands of the bourgeoisie. Such was the role of the bureaucracy of the Comintern in the Chinese Revolution.

Considering as natural the right of the "revolutionary" bureaucracy to command independently of the forces of the proletariat, Malraux informs us that one could not participate in the Chinese Revolution without participating in the war, and one could not participate in the war without participating in the Guomindang, etc. To this, he adds: the break with the Guomindang would have meant, for the Communist Party, the necessity of passing into illegality. When one thinks that these arguments sum up the philosophy of the representatives of the Comintern in China, he cannot refrain from saying: Indeed, the dialectic of the historical process sometimes plays bad jokes upon organizations, upon men and upon ideas! How easy it is to solve the problem: in order to participate successfully in the events directed by the enemy class, one must submit to this class; in order to avoid repressions on the part of the Guomindang, one must paint oneself up in its colours! There you have the secret of Borodin-Garine.

Malraux's political estimate of the situation, of the possibilities and the tasks in China in 1925, is entirely false; it hardly reaches the border line where the real problems of the revolution begin. I have said elsewhere all that had to be said on this subject, and Malraux's article gives no ground for a re-examination of what has been said. But even by standing on the ground of the false estimate Malraux gives of the situation, one can in no case justify the policy of Stalin-Borodin-Garine.

In order to protest in 1925 against this policy, certain things had to be foreseen. In order to defend it in 1931, one must be incurably blind.

Did the strategy of the functionaries of the Comintern bring the Chinese proletariat anything but humiliations, the extermination of its cadres and above all, a terrific confusion in the mind? Did the shameful capitulation before the Guomindang avert repression for the Party? On the contrary, it only accumulated and concentrated the repressions. Was not the Communist Party compelled to pass into illegality? And when? In the period of the crushing of the revolution! If the Communists had begun by illegal work, at the beginning of the revolutionary tide, they would have emerged upon the open arena at the head of the masses. By effacing and demoralizing the Party with the aid of the Borodins and Garines, Chiang Kai-shek compelled it later, with all the greater success to take refuge in illegality during the years of the counter-revolution. The policy of Borodin-Garine entirely served the Chinese bourgeoisie. The Chinese Communist Party must begin all over again at the beginning, and that on an arena encumbered with debris, with prejudices, with uncomprehended mistakes and with the distrusts of the advanced workers. Those are the results.

The criminal character of this whole policy reveals itself with particular acuteness in isolated questions. Malraux presents as a merit of Borodin and Company the fact that in turning over the terrorists to the hands of the bourgeoisie, he deliberately pushed under the knife of the terror the leader of the bourgeoisie, Chen Dai. This machination is worthy of a bureaucratic Borgia or of the "revolutionary" Polish *szlachta* (gentry and nobility) who always preferred to fire with the hands of others behind the backs of the people. No, the task was not to kill Chen Dai in ambush, but to prepare the overthrow of the bourgeoisie. When the party of the revolution is obliged to kill, it does it on its open responsibility, in the name of tasks and immediate aims understood by the masses.

Revolutionary morals are not abstract Kantian norms, but rules of conduct which place the revolutionist under the control of the tasks and aims of his class. Borodin and Garine were not bound up with the masses, they did not absorb the spirit of responsibility before the class. They are bureaucratic supermen who consider that "everything is permitted" within the limits of the mandate received from above. The activity of such men, effective as it may be at certain moments, can only be directed, in the last instance, against the interests of the revolution.

After having killed Chen Dai with the hands of Hong, Borodin and Garine then turn over Hong and his group to the hands of the executioners. This stamps their whole policy with the brand of Cain. Here too Malraux poses as a defender. What is his argument? Lenin and Trotsky also punished the anarchists. It is hard to believe that this is said by a man who came near the revolution, even if but for a moment. Malraux forgets or does not understand that the revolution takes place in the name of the domination of one class over another, that it is only from this task that revolutionists draw their right to violence. The bourgeoisie exterminates the revolutionists, sometimes also the anarchists (more and more infrequently, because they become ever more obedient) in the name of safeguarding the régime of exploitation and baseness. Under the domination of the bourgeoisie, the Bolsheviks always defend the anarchists against the Chiappes. After having conquered power, the Bolsheviks did everything to draw the anarchists over to the side of the dictatorship of the proletariat. They succeeded in actuality in drawing the majority of the anarchists behind them. Yes, the Bolsheviks severely punished those anarchists who undermined the dictatorship of the proletariat. Were we right or weren't we? That depends upon the manner in which one evaluates our revolution and the régime instituted by it. But can one imagine for a single instant that the Bolsheviks—under Prince Lvov or under Kerensky, under the bourgeois régime—would act as its agents in the extermination of anarchists? It is enough to formulate the question clearly, to turn aside in disgust. Just as Bridoison interests himself only in the form and ignores the essence, so the quasi-revolutionary bureaucracy and its literary attorney interest themselves only in the mechanics of the revolution, ignoring the question of what class and what régime they should serve. Here lies the abyss between the revolutionist and the functionary of the revolution.

What Malraux says about Marxism is a joke. The Marxian policy was not applicable in China because, you see, the proletariat was not class-conscious. It would seem then that from this flows the task of awakening this class-consciousness. But Malraux deduces a justification of the policy directed against the interests of the proletariat. The other argument is no more convincing and still less amusing: Trotsky speaks of the need of Marxism for revolutionary politics; but isn't Borodin a Marxist? And Stalin, isn't he a Marxist? Then it is not a question of Marxism. I defend, against Garine, the revolutionary doctrine, just as I would defend, against a sorcerer, the medical sciences. The sorcerer will say to me in his defence that diplomaed doctors also very often kill their patients. It is an argument unworthy of a moderately educated burgher, and not only of a revolutionist. The fact that medicine is not omnipotent, that the doctors do not always effect cures, that one finds among them ignoramuses, blockheads and even poisoners—can this fact serve as an argument for giving the right to practise medicine to sorcerers, who have never studied medicine and who deny its significance?

I must make one correction, after having read Malraux's article. In my article I expressed the idea that an inoculation of Marxism would do Garine good. I don't think so any more.

51

The Soviet Union and Japan's Manchurian Adventure*

November 26, 1931

1, 2, 3, 4, ...

5. The tsarist adventure in Manchuria led to the Russo Japanese War; the war—to the 1905 revolution. The present Japanese adventure in Manchuria can lead to revolution in *Japan.*

At the beginning of the century, the feudal-military regime of that country could still successfully serve the interests of the young Japanese capitalism. But in the last quarter of a century, capitalist development has brought extraordinary decomposition in the old social and political forms. Since that time, Japan has more than once been on the brink of revolution. But she lacked a strong revolutionary class to accomplish the tasks imposed on it by the developments. The Manchurian adventure may accelerate the revolutionary catastrophe for the Japanese regime.

Present-day China, no matter how enfeebled it may be by the dictatorship of the Kuomintang clique, differs greatly from the China which Japan, following the European powers, despoiled in the past. China has not the strength to drive out the Japanese expeditionary forces immediately, but the national consciousness and activity of the Chinese people have grown enormously; hundreds of thousands, millions of Chinese have

---

* Excerpted from the article *"Germany, the Key to the International Situation"* in 'The Struggle Against Fascism in Germany'.

gone through military training. The Chinese will rig up newer and yet newer armies. The Japanese will feel themselves besieged. The railroads will be of far greater service for war than for economic purposes. More and more new troops will have to be sent out. The Manchurian expedition spreading out will begin to exhaust Japan's economic organism, increase the discontent inside the country, sharpen the contradictions, and thereby accelerate the revolutionary crisis.

6. In *China,* the necessity for a determined defense against the imperialist invasion will also provoke serious internal political consequences. The Kuomintang regime arose out of the national revolutionary mass movement which was exploited and strangled by the bourgeois militarists (with the aid of the Stalinist bureaucracy). Precisely for this reason, the present regime, shaky and full of contradictions, is incapable of initiating a revolutionary war. The necessity for a defense against the Japanese tyrants will turn more and more against the Kuomintang regime, nourishing the revolutionary sentiments of the masses. With a correct policy, the proletarian vanguard can, under these conditions, make up for all that was so tragically lost in the course of the years 1924–27.

7. The present events in *Manchuria* prove particularly how naive those gentlemen were who demanded of the Soviet Union the simple return of the Chinese Eastern Railroad to China. That would have meant surrendering it voluntarily to Japan, in whose hands the railroad would have become a weapon against China as well as against the USSR. If anything at all had hitherto prevented the Japanese military cliques from intervention in Manchuria, and if anything may still hold them within the bounds of caution today, it is the fact that the Chinese Eastern Railroad is the property of the Soviets.

8. Cannot the Manchurian adventure of the Japanese nevertheless lead to war with the USSR? It goes without saying that this is not excluded even with the wisest and most cautious policy on the part of the Soviet government. The internal contradictions of feudal-capitalistic Japan have obviously unbalanced her government. There is no lack of instigators (France). And from the historical experiences of tsarism in the

Far East, we know what an unbalanced military-bureaucratic monarchy is capable of.

The struggle unfolding in the Far East is, of course, carried on not for the sake of the railroads, but over the fate of all of China. In this gigantic historical struggle, the Soviet government cannot be neutral, cannot take the same position with regard to China and Japan. It is duty bound to stand completely and fully on the side of the Chinese people. Only the unflinching loyalty of the Soviet government to the struggle for the liberation of the oppressed peoples can really protect the Soviet Union on the eastern frontier against Japan, Britain, France, the United States.

The ways in which the Soviet government will support the struggle of the Chinese people in the coming period depend upon the concrete historical circumstances. If it would have been absurd to surrender the Chinese Eastern Railroad voluntarily to Japan earlier, then it would be just as absurd to subordinate the entire policy in the Far East to the question of the Chinese Eastern Railroad. There is much to suggest that the behavior of the Japanese military clique on this question has a consciously provocatory character. The direct instigators of this provocation are the French rulers. The aim of the provocation is to tie the Soviet Union down in the East. All the more firmness and farsightedness is required on the part of the Soviet government.

The fundamental conditions of the East—its immense expanse, its countless human masses, its economic backwardness—give all processes a slow, drawn out, and crawling character. In any case, there is no immediate or acute threat to the existence of the Soviet Union from the Far East. During the coming period, the main events will unfold in Europe. Here great opportunities may arise, but from the same source also, great dangers threaten. For the present, only Japan has tied its hands in the Far East. The Soviet Union must, for the present, keep its hands free.

52

Peasant War in China and the Proletariat

September 22, 1932

Dear Comrades:

After a long delay, we received your letter of June 15. Needless to say we were overjoyed by the revival and the renascence of the Chinese Left Opposition, despite the most ferocious police persecutions it had endured.

Our irreconciliable attitude toward the vulgar democratic Stalinist position on the peasant movement has, of course, nothing in common with a careless or passive attitude toward the peasant movement itself. The manifesto of the International Left Opposition that was issued two years ago and that evaluated the peasant movement in the southern provinces of China declared: "The Chinese revolution, betrayed, defeated, exhausted, shows that it is still alive. Let us hope that the time when it will again lift its proletarian head is not far off." Further on it says: "The vast flood of peasant revolts can unquestionably provide the impulse for the revival of political struggle in the industrial centres. We firmly count on it."

Your letter testifies that under the influence of the crisis and the Japanese intervention, against the background of the peasant war, the struggle of the city workers is burgeoning once again. In the manifesto we wrote about this possibility with necessary caution: "Nobody can foretell now whether the hearths of the peasant revolt can keep a fire burning through the whole long period of time which the proletarian vanguard will need to gather its own strength, bring the working class into the fight, and co-ordinate its struggle for power with the general offensive of the peasants against their most immediate enemies."

At the present time it is evident that there are substantial grounds for expressing the hope that, through a correct policy, it will be possible to unite the workers' movement, and the urban movement in general, with the peasant war; and this would constitute the beginning of the third Chinese Revolution. But in the meantime this still remains only a hope, not a certainty. The most important work lies ahead.

In this letter I want to pose only one question which seems to me, at least from afar, to be the most important and acute. Once again I must remind you that the information at my disposal is altogether insufficient, accidental, and disjointed. I would indeed welcome any amplification and correction.

The peasant movement has created its own armies, has seized great territories, and has installed its own institutions. In the event of further successes—and all of us, of course, passionately desire such successes—the movement will become linked up with the urban and industrial centres and, through that very fact it will come face to face with the working class. What will be the nature of this encounter? Is it certain that its character will be peaceful and friendly?

At first glance the question might appear to be superfluous. The peasant movement is headed by Communists or sympathizers. Isn't it self-evident that in the event of their coming together the workers and the peasants must unanimously unite under the Communist banner?

Unfortunately the question is not at all so simple. Let me refer to the experience of Russia. During the years of the civil war the peasantry in various parts of the country created its own guerrilla detachments, which sometimes grew into full-fledged armies. Some of these detachments considered themselves Bolshevik, and were often led by workers. Others remained non-party and most often were led by former non-commissioned officers from among the peasantry. There was also an "anarchist" army under the command of Makhno.

So long as the guerrilla armies operated in the rear of the

White Guards, they served the cause of the revolution. Some of them were distinguished by exceptional heroism and fortitude. But within the cities these armies often came into conflict with the workers and with the local party organizations. Conflicts also arose during encounters of the partisans with the regular Red Army, and in some instances they took an extremely painful and sharp character.

The grim experience of the civil war demonstrated to us the necessity of disarming peasant detachments immediately after the Red Army occupied provinces which had been cleared of the White Guards. In these cases the best, the most class-conscious and disciplined elements were absorbed into the ranks of the Red Army. But a considerable portion of the partisans strived to maintain an independent existence and often came into direct armed conflict with the Soviet power. Such was the case with the anarchist army of Makhno, entirely kulak in spirit. But that was not the sole instance; many peasant detachments, which fought splendidly enough against the restoration of the landlords, became transformed after victory into instruments of counter-revolution.

Regardless of their origin in each isolated instance—whether caused by conscious provocation of the White Guards, or by tactlessness of the Communists, or by an unfavourable combination of circumstances—the conflicts between armed peasants and workers were rooted in one and the same social soil: the difference between the class position and training of the workers and of the peasants. The worker approaches questions from the socialist standpoint; the peasant's viewpoint is petty bourgeois. The worker strives to socialize the property that is taken away from the exploiters; the peasant seeks to divide it up. The worker desires to put palaces and parks to common use; the peasant, insofar as he cannot divide them, inclines to burning the palaces and cutting down the parks. The worker strives to solve problems on a national scale and in accordance with a plan; the peasant, on the other hand, approaches all problems on a local scale and takes a hostile attitude to centralized planning, etc.

It is understood that a peasant also is capable of raising

himself to the socialist viewpoint. Under a proletarian regime more and more masses of peasants become re-educated in the socialist spirit. But this requires time, years, even decades. It should be borne in mind that in the initial stages of revolution, contradictions between proletarian socialism and peasant individualism often take on an extremely acute character.

But after all aren't there Communists at the head of the Chinese Red armies? Doesn't this by itself exclude the possibility of conflicts between the peasant detachments and the workers' organizations? No, that does not exclude it. The fact that individual Communists are in the leadership of the present armies does not at all transform the social character of these armies, even if their Communist leaders bear a definite proletarian stamp. And how do matters stand in China?

Among the Communist leaders of Red detachments there indubitably are many declassed intellectuals and semi-intellectuals who have not gone through the school of proletarian struggle. For two or three years they live the lives of partisan commanders and commissars; they wage battles, seize territories, etc. They absorb the spirit of their environment. Meanwhile the majority of the rank-and-file Communists in the Red detachments unquestionably consists of peasants, who assume the name Communist in all honesty and sincerity but who in actuality remain revolutionary paupers or revolutionary petty proprietors. In politics he who judges by denominations and labels and not by social facts is lost. All the more so when the politics concerned is carried out arms in hand.

The true Communist party is the organization of the proletarian vanguard. But we must not forget that the working class of China has been kept in an oppressed and amorphous condition during the last four years, and only recently has it evinced signs of revival. It is one thing when a Communist party, firmly resting on the flower of the urban proletariat, strives through the workers to lead a peasant war. It is an altogether different thing when a few thousand or even tens of thousands of revolutionists, who are truly Communists or only take the name, assume the leadership of a peasant war without having serious support from the proletariat. This is precisely the situation in China. This acts to augment to an extreme the danger of conflicts between the workers and the armed peasants. In any event, one may rest assured there will be no dearth of bourgeois provocateurs.

In Russia, in the period of civil war, the proletariat was already in power in the greater part of the country, the leadership of the struggle was in the hands of a strong and tempered party, the entire commanding apparatus of the centralized Red Army was in the hands of the workers. Notwithstanding all this, the peasant detachments, incomparably weaker than the Red Army, often came into conflict with it after it victoriously moved into peasant guerrilla sectors.

In China the situation is radically different and moreover completely to the disadvantage of the workers. In the most important regions of China the power is in the hands of bourgeois militarists; in other regions, in the hands of leaders of armed peasants. Nowhere is there any proletarian power as yet. The trade unions are weak. The influence of the party among the workers is insignificant. The peasant detachments, flushed with victories they have achieved, stand under the wing of the Comintern. They call themselves "the Red Army", i.e., they identify themselves with the armed forces of the Soviets. What results consequently is that the revolutionary peasantry of China, in the person of its ruling stratum, seems to have appropriated to itself beforehand the political and moral capital which should by the nature of things belong to the Chinese workers. Isn't it possible that things may turn out so that all this capital will be directed at a certain moment *against* the workers?

Naturally the peasant poor, and in China they constitute the overwhelming majority, to the extent they think politically, and these comprise a small minority, sincerely and passionately desire alliance and friendship with the workers. But the peasantry, even when armed, is incapable of conducting an independent policy.

Occupying in daily life an intermediate, indeterminate, and vacillating position, the peasantry at decisive moments can follow either the proletariat or the bourgeoisie. The peasantry does not find the road to the proletariat easily but only after a series of mistakes and defeats. The bridge between the peasantry and the bourgeoisie is provided by the urban petty bourgeoisie, chiefly by the intellectuals, who commonly come forward under the banner of socialism and even communism.

The commanding stratum of the Chinese "Red Army" has no doubt succeeded in inculcating itself with the habit of issuing commands. The absence of a strong revolutionary party and of mass organizations of the proletariat renders control over the commanding stratum virtually impossible. The commanders and commissars appear in the guise of absolute masters of the situation and upon occupying cities will be rather apt to look down from above upon the workers. The demands of the workers might often appear to them either inopportune or ill-advised.

Nor should one forget such "trifles" as the fact that within cities the staffs and offices of the victorious armies are established not in the proletarian huts but in the finest city buildings, in the houses and apartments of the bourgeoisie; and all this facilitates the inclination of the upper stratum of the peasant armies to feel itself part of the "cultured" and "educated" classes, in no way part of the proletariat.

Thus in China the causes and grounds for conflicts between the army, which is peasant in composition and petty bourgeois in leadership, and the workers not only are not eliminated but on the contrary, all the circumstances are such as to greatly increase the possibility and even the inevitability of such conflicts; and in addition the chances of the proletariat are far less favorable to begin with than was the case in Russia.

From the theoretical and political side the danger is increased many times because the Stalinist bureaucracy covers up the contradictory situation by its slogan of "democratic dictatorship" of workers and peasants. Is it possible to conceive of a snare more attractive in appearance and more perfidious in essence? The epigones do their thinking not by means of social concepts, but by means of stereotyped phrases; formalism is the basic trait of bureaucracy.

The Russian Narodniks used to accuse the Russian Marxists of "ignoring" the peasantry, of not carrying on work in the villages, etc. To this the Marxists replied: "We will arouse and organize the advanced workers and through the workers we shall arouse the peasants." Such in general is the only conceivable road for the proletarian party.

The Chinese Stalinists have acted otherwise. During the revolution of 1925–27 they subordinated directly and immediately the interests of the workers and the peasants to the interests of the national bourgeoisie. In the years of the counter-revolution they passed over from the proletariat to the peasantry, i.e., they undertook that role which was fulfilled in our country by the SRs when they were still a revolutionary party. Had the Chinese Communist Party concentrated its efforts for the last few years in the cities, in industry, on the railroads; had it sustained the trade unions, the educational clubs and circles; had it, without breaking off from the workers, taught them to understand what was occurring in the villages—the share of the proletariat in the general correlation of forces would have been incomparably more favourable today.

The party actually tore itself away from its class. Thereby in the last analysis it can cause injury to the peasantry as well. For should the proletariat continue to remain on the sidelines, without organization, without leadership, then the peasant war even if fully victorious will inevitably arrive in a blind alley.

In old China every victorious peasant revolution was concluded by the creation of a new dynasty, and subsequently also by a new group of large proprietors; the movement was caught in a vicious circle. Under present conditions the peasant war by itself, without the direct leadership of the proletarian vanguard, can only pass on the power to a new bourgeois clique, some "left" Kuomintang or other, a "third party", etc., etc., which in practice will differ very little from the Kuomintang of Chiang Kai-shek. And this would signify in turn a new massacre of the workers with the weapons of "democratic dictatorship".

What then are the conclusions that follow from all this? The first conclusion is that one must boldly and openly face the facts as they are. The peasant movement is a mighty revolutionary factor insofar as it is directed against the large landowners, militarists, feudalists, and usurers. But in the peasant movement itself are very powerful proprietary and reactionary tendencies, and at a certain stage it can become hostile to the workers and sustain that hostility already equipped with arms. He who forgets about the dual nature of the peasantry is not a Marxist. The advanced workers must be taught to distinguish from among "communist" labels and banners the actual social processes.

The activities of the "Red armies" must be attentively followed, and the workers must be given a detailed explanation of the course, significance, and perspectives of the peasant war; and the immediate demands and the tasks of the proletariat must be tied up with the slogans for the liberation of the peasantry.

On the bases of our own observations, reports, and other documents we must painstakingly study the life processes of the peasant armies and the regime established in the regions occupied by them; we must discover in living facts the contradictory class tendencies and clearly point out to the workers the tendencies we support and those we oppose.

We must follow the inter-relations between the Red armies and the local workers with special care, without overlooking even the minor misunderstandings between them. Within the framework of isolated cities and regions, conflicts, even if acute, might appear to be insignificant local episodes. But with the development of events, class conflicts may take on a national scope and lead the revolution to a catastrophe, i.e., to a new massacre of the workers by the peasants, hoodwinked by the bourgeoisie. The history of revolutions is full of such examples.

The more clearly the advanced workers understand the living dialectic of the class interrelations of the proletariat, the peasantry, and the bourgeoisie, the more confidently will they seek unity with the peasant strata closest to them, and the more successfully will they counteract the counter-revolutionary provocateurs within the peasant armies themselves as well as within the cities.

The trade-union and the party units must be built up; the

advanced workers must be educated, the proletarian vanguard must be brought together and drawn into the battle.

We must turn to all the members of the official Communist Party with words of explanation and challenge. It is quite probable that the rank-and-file Communists who have been led astray by the Stalinist faction will not understand us at once. The bureaucrats will set up a howl about our "underestimation" of the peasantry, perhaps even about our "hostility" to the peasantry. (Chernov always accused Lenin of being hostile to the peasantry.) Naturally such howling will not confuse the Bolshevik-Leninists. When prior to April 1927 we warned against the inevitable coup d'tat of Chiang Kai-shek, the Stalinists accused us of hostility to the Chinese national revolution. Events have demonstrated who was right. Events will provide a confirmation this time as well.

The Left Opposition may turn out to be too weak to direct events in the interests of the proletariat at the present stage. But we are sufficiently strong right now to point out to the workers the correct road and, in the development of the class struggle, to demonstrate to the workers our correctness and political insight. Only in this way can a revolutionary party gain the confidence of the workers, only in this way will it grow, become strong, and take its place at the head of the popular masses.

Postscript, September 26, 1932

In order to express my ideas as clearly as possible, let me sketch the following variant which is theoretically quite possible.

Let us assume that the Chinese Left Opposition carries on in the near future widespread and successful work among the industrial proletariat and attains the preponderant influence over it. The official party, in the meantime, continues to concentrate all its forces on the "Red armies" and in the peasant regions. The moment arrives when the peasant troops occupy the industrial centres and are brought face to face with the workers. In such a situation, in what manner will the Chinese Stalinists act?

It is not difficult to foresee that they will counterpose the peasant army to the "counter-revolutionary Trotskyists" in a hostile manner. In other words, they will incite the armed peasants against the advanced workers. This is what the Russian SRs and the Mensheviks did in 1917; having lost the workers, they fought might and main for support among the soldiers, inciting the barracks against the factory, the armed peasant against the worker Bolshevik. Kerensky, Tsereteli, and Dan, if they did not label the Bolsheviks outright as counter-revolutionists, called them either "unconscious aides" or "involuntary agents" of counter-revolution. The Stalinists are less choice in their application of political terminology. But the tendency is the same: malicious incitement of the peasant, and generally petty-bourgeois, elements against the vanguard of the working class.

Bureaucratic centrism, as centrism, cannot have an independent class support. But in its struggle against the Bolshevik-Leninists it is compelled to seek support from the right, i.e., from the peasantry and the petty bourgeoisie, counterposing them to the proletariat. The struggle between the two Communist factions, the Stalinists and the Bolshevik-Leninists, thus bears in itself an inner *tendency* toward transformation into a class struggle. The revolutionary development of events in China may draw this tendency to its conclusion, i.e., to a civil war between the peasant army led by the Stalinists and the proletarian vanguard led by the Leninists.

Were such a tragic conflict to arise, due entirely to the Chinese Stalinists, it would signify that the Left Opposition and the Stalinists ceased to be Communist factions and had become hostile political parties, each having a different class base.

However is such a perspective inevitable? No, I don't think so at all. Within the Stalinist faction (the official Chinese Communist Party) there are not only peasant, i.e., petty-bourgeois tendencies but also proletarian tendencies. It is extremely important for the Left Opposition to seek to establish connections with the proletarian wing of the Stalinists by presenting to them the Marxist evaluation of "Red armies" and the interrelations between the proletariat and the peasantry in general.

While maintaining its political independence, the

proletarian vanguard must be ready always to assure united action with revolutionary democracy. While we refuse to identify the armed peasant detachment with the Red Army as the armed power of the proletariat and have no inclination to shut our eyes to the fact that the Communist banner hides the petty-bourgeois content of the peasant movement, we, on the other hand, take an absolutely clear view of the tremendous revolutionary-democratic significance of the peasant war. We teach the workers to appreciate its significance and we are ready to do all in our power in order to achieve the necessary military alliance with the peasant organizations.

Consequently our task consists not only in preventing the political-military command over the proletariat by the petty-bourgeois democracy that leans upon the armed peasant, but in preparing and ensuring the proletarian leadership of the peasant movement, its "Red armies" in particular.

The more clearly the Chinese Bolshevik-Leninists comprehend the political events and the tasks that spring from them, the more successfully will they extend their base within the proletariat. The more persistently they carry out the policy of the united front in relation to the official party and the peasant movement led by it, the more surely will they succeed not only in shielding the revolution from a terribly dangerous conflict between the proletariat and the peasantry and in ensuring the necessary united action between the two revolutionary classes, but also in transforming their united front into the historical step toward the dictatorship of the proletariat.

53

For A Strategy of Action and Not of Speculation

Letter to Peking Friends

What are, at Present, the Chief Elements of the Political Situation in China?

October 3, 1932

The two most important revolutionary problems, the national problem and the agrarian problem have again become aggravated. The pace of the peasant war, slow and crawling but generally victorious, is evidence that the dictatorship of the Kuomintang has proved incapable of satisfying the countryside or of intimidating it further. The Japanese intervention in Shanghai and the effective annexation of Manchuria have placed partly revealed the military bankruptcy of Kuomintang dictatorship. The crisis of power which at bottom, has not stopped for a single moment during these last years had to grow fatally worse. The struggle between the militarist cliques is destroying what remains of the unity of the country.

If the peasant war has radicalized the intellectuals who have connections in the countryside, the Japanese intervention, on the contrary, gave a political stimulation to the petty-bourgeoisie of the cities. This has only again aggravated the crises of power. There is not a single section of the bourgeoisie called "Nationalists" which does not tend to arrive at the conclusion that the Kuomintang regime devours much and gives little. To demand an end of the period of "education" of the Kuomintang is to demand that the military dictatorship give way to parlimentarism.

The Left Opposition press has sometimes labeled as fascist the regime of Chiang Kai Shek. This definition was formed from the fact that in China as in Italy, the military-police power is concentrated in the hands of one bourgeois party alone to the exclusion of all other parties and notably, of the workers organizations. But after the experience of the last years, an experience complicated by the confusion the Stalinists brought to the question of fascism, it would not be very correct, nevertheless, to identify the dictatorship of the Cementing with fascism. Hitler, as in his time Mussolini, supports himself, before all, on the counter-revolutionary petty bourgeoisie; there is the essence of fascism. The Cementing has not this point of support. Thus in Germany the peasants march behind Hitler and by this fact indirectly support Von Papen; in China the peasants carry on the raging struggle against Chiang Kai Shek.

The regime of the Kuomintang contains more of Bonapartist traits than of fascism: Not possessing a social base, no matter how small, the Kuomintang, is half between the pressure of the imperialists and compradores on the one hand, and the revolutionary movement on the other. But Bonapartism can pretend to stability only when the land hunger of the peasants is satisfied. This is not true in the case of China. Hence the impotence of the military dictatorship which maintains itself only thanks to the dispersion of its enemies. But under their growing attack even this begins to be unhinged.

It is the proletariat which in the revolution of 1925–1927 morally and physically suffered the most. That is why at the present time it is the workers who are in the rear of the other classes and in fact not only of the petty bourgeoisie, beginning with the students, but also in a certain sense, of the peasants. On the other hand it is just this which proves that the third Chinese Revolution not only will win but will not even be produced as long as the working class has not again entered into the lists.

The Slogans of the revolutionary democracy correspond in the best possible way to the political pre-revolutionary situation in China.

That the peasants, whatever their banner, fight for the aims or agrarian petty bourgeois democracy is what, for a Marxist, does not have to be demonstrated. The slogan of independence of China, raised to a white heat by the Japanese intervention, is a slogan of the national democracy. The powerlessness of the military dictatorship and the partition of the country among the militarist dictatorship and the partition of the country among the militarist cliques put on the end of the day the slogan of political democracy.

The students cry: "Down with the Kuomintang government". The groups of workers' vanguard support this slogan. The "National" bourgeoisie demands they go on to a constitutional regime. The peasant revolt against the dearth of land, the yoke of the militarists, government officials and of usurious loans. Under there circumstances the party of the proletariat cannot favor any other political central slogan than that of the NATIONAL ASSEMBLY (Constitutional).

Does this mean, it will be asked, that we demand from the present government the convocation of the National Assembly or that we should strive to convoke it ourselves? This way of posing the question, at least on the present stage, it too formalistic. During a certain number of years, the Russian Revolution coordinated two slogans: "Down with Absolutism****" and "Long Live the Constituent Assembly". To the question who will convoke the Constituent Assembly for a long time we answered: the future will show, that is to say, the relation of forces, as they are established in the process of the revolution itself. This manner of approaching the question remains equally correct for China. Will the government of the Kuomintang try, at the moment of its disappearance, to convoke such or such representative assembly, what will be the attitude that we shall adopt in regard to this, that is to say how shall we utilize it in the interests of the revolution, whether we should boycott the elections or whether we should participate in them; will the revolutionary masses succeed in giving rise to an independent government organism which will take upon itself the convocation of the National Assembly; will the proletariat succeed, in the course of the struggle for the slogans of democracy, in creating the soviets; will the latter not render superfluous the convocation of the National Assembly? This is what is actually impossible to foretell. After all the tasks consists not in making prognostications from the calendar but in mobilizing the workers around the slogans flowing from the political situation. Our strategy is a strategy of revolutionary action and not of abstract speculations.

Today, by the force of events, the revolutionary agitation is directed above all against the government of the Kuomintang. We explain to the masses that the dictatorship of Chiang Kai Shek is the main obstacle which stands in the way of the National Assembly and that we can clean China from the militarist cliques only by means of an armed insurrection. Agitation, spoken and written, strikes, meetings, demonstrations, boycotts whatever may be the concrete questions to which they are consecrated, must have a corollary the slogans: "Down with the Kuomintang, Long live the Constituent Assembly!"

In order to arrive at a real national liberation it is necessary to overthrow the Kuomintang. But this does not mean that we postpone the struggle until the time when the Kuomintang is overthrown. The more the struggle against foreign oppression spreads the more difficulties the Kuomintang will have. The more we line up the masses against the Kuomintang the more the struggle against imperialism will develop.

At the acute moment of Japanese intervention the workers and the students called for arms. From whom? Again from the Kuomintang. It would be a sectarian absurdity to abandon this demand under the pretext that we wish to overthrow the Kuomintang. We wish to overthrow it but we have not yet reached that point. The more energetically we demand the arming of the workers the sooner we shall reach it.

The official Communist Party, in spite of its ultra-leftism. favors "the resumption of the Russian-Chinese diplomatic relations". Now this slogan is addressed directly against the Kuomintang. To formulate it does not at all mean that one has "confidence" in the Kuomintang. On the contrary, this slogan has to render more difficult the situation of the latter before the masses. Certain Kuomintang loaders have had already to take up on their own account the slogan of the re-establishment of relations with the USSR. We know that with these gentlemen it is a long way between works and acts. But here, as in all the other questions, everything depends on the force that the pressure of the masses will attain.

If under the whip of the revolution, the Kuomintang government begins to make petty concessions of the agrarian question, tries to call a semblance of a National Assembly, sees itself obliged to give arms to the workers or to take up relations with the USSR it goes without saying that we will at once exploit these concessions, that we will cling to them firmly at the same time that we show with perfect correctness their insufficiency so as to make of the concessions by the Kuomintang a weapon to overthrow it. Such is in general the reciprocal relation of reforms and of revolution in Marxist politics.

Does not the scope the peasant war is reaching mean that there is no longer time nor place for the slogans and problems of parliamentary democracy in China? Let us go back to that question.

If the revolutionary Chinese peasants today call their fighting organizations "soviets" we have no reason to give up the name. We must simply not get intoxicated with words. To believe that the soviet power in essentially rural regions can be an important, stable revolutionary power is to give proof of great frivolity. It is not possible to be ignorant of the experience offered by the only country where the soviet power has effectively won. Although in the Petrograd, Moscow and other industrial centers and basins of Russia, the soviet power has held firmly and constantly since November 1917, in all the immense periphery (Ukrain, Northern Caucasus, Transcaucasia, Urals, Siberia, Central Asia, Archangel Murmansk) this power has appeared and disappeared several times not only because of foreign interventions, but also as a consequence of internal revolts. The Chinese soviet power has an essential rural, peripheral character, and still entirely lacks a point of support in the industrial proletariat. The less stable and sure this power is, the less of a soviet power it is.

Ko-Lin's article which appeared in the German paper *Der*

Rote Aufbau, claims that in the red armies the workers represent 36 per cent, the peasants 57 per cent, the intellectuals 7 per cent. I confess that these figures arouse in me serious doubts. If the percentages apply to all the armed forces of the insurrection, forces which according to the author reach 350,000 men, the result is that the army includes about 125,000 workers. If the 36 per cent only applies to the red armies, it appears that of 150,000 soldiers, there are more than 50,000 workers. Is this really so? Did they belong to the unions before, to the party, and did they take part in the revolutionary struggle? But even that does not clinch the question. On account of the absence of strong, independent proletarian organizations in the industrial centers, the revolutionary workers, inexperienced or too little experienced, become fatally lost in the peasant, petty-bourgeois environment.

Van-Ming's article, which appeared at the beginning of the year in the CI press, singularly exaggerates, as far as I can judge, the scope of the movement in the cities, the degree of independence of the workers in the movement and the importance of the influence of the Communist Party. The misfortune of the present official press is that its mercilessly deforms facts in the name of its factional interest. Hence it is not hard to realize, even by Van-Ming's article, that the leading place in the movement which began in the autumn of last year (1931) belonged to the students or in general to the school youth. The university strikes had an appreciable importance, greater than the factory strikes.

To arouse the workers, to group them, to give them the possibility of leaning on the national and agrarian movements in order to take the head of both: such is the task that falls to us. The immediate demands of the proletariat as such (length of work day, wages, right to organize, etc.) must form the basis of our agitation. But that alone is not sufficient. Only three slogans can raise the proletariat to the role of head of the nation: the independence of China, land to the poor peasants, the National Assembly.

The Stalinists imagine that the minute the insurgent peasants call their organizations soviets, the stage of revolutionary parliamentarism has already passed. This is a serious mistake. The rebels peasants can serve as a point of support to the soviets if the proletariat only if the latter shows practically its ability to lead. Hence, without the leadership of the proletariat, the peasant movement can only assure the advantage of one bourgeois clique over another in order to break up finally into provincial fractions. The National Assembly, thanks to its centralizing importance, would constitute a serious stage in the development of the agrarian revolution. The existence of rural "soviets", and "red armies" would help the peasants elect revolutionary representatives. This is the only way at the present stage to link up the peasant movement politically with the national and proletarian movements.

The official Chinese Communist Party declares that its "principal slogan" is at present that of the national revolutionary war against Japanese imperialism (see Van-Ming's article in the *Communist International #1,* 1932). That is a one-sided and even an adventurist way to pose the question. It is certain that the struggle against imperialism, which is the essential task of the Chinese proletariat, cannot be carried through to the end except by insurrection and revolutionary war. But it does not in the least follow that the struggle against Japanese imperialism constitutes the central slogan of the present moment. The question must be solved from the international angle.

At the beginning of this year, they thought in CI circles that Japan had entered upon its military action against China in order to push things immediately to war against the Soviet Union. I wrote then that the Tokyo government would have to be completely out of its head to run the risk of a war with the Soviet Union without having beforehand at least somewhat consolidated the military base which Manchuria constitutes for it. In reply to this estimation of the situation, the American Stalinists, the most vulgar and stupid of all, declared that I worked in the interest of the Japanese general-staff. —And yet, what have the events of these last months shown? The fear of Japan's leading circles for the consequences of a military adventure was so great that the military clique had to send from life to death a certain number of Japanese statesmen in order to arouse the Mikado's government to follow up the annexation of Manchuria to the end. That even today the war against the Soviet Union remains a very real perspective, there is no doubt, but in politics time has a great value.

If the soviet government considered war with Japan to be inevitable right now, it would have neither the right nor the possibility of carrying out a peace policy that is, an ostrich policy. In reality, in the course of the year, the Soviet government has concluded an arrangement with Japan to furnish Soviet naphtha to the Japanese war fleet. If war is right now inevitable, to furnish naphtha to Japan is equivalent to committing a real treason towards the proletarian revolution. We will not discuss here the question of knowing to what extent this or that declaration or step of the Soviet government is correct. One thing is clear: contrary to the American Stalinists whose zeal is beyond measure the Moscow Stalinists have been oriented towards peace with Japan and not towards war.

Pravda of Sept. 24th writes: "With vast impatience the world bourgeoisie was expecting a Nippo-Soviet war. But the fact that the USSR has rigorously abstained from mixing in the Sino-Japanese conflict and the firm peace policy she is following, has forestalled war"—admitting that the attitude of the American and other windbags has any political meaning at all, it had only one meaning: they pushed the Soviet power on the same road where the world bourgeoisie pushed it. We do mean that they consciously served the Japanese general staff. Suffice it to state they are incapable of consciously serving the proletarian revolution.

The Chinese proletariat inscribes on its banner not only resumption of diplomatic relations with the Soviet Union but the conclusion of a close offensive and defensive alliance with it. This implies that the policy of the Chinese proletariat must be in conformity with the whole of the international situation and above all with the policy of the Soviet Union. If Japan were today to thrust war upon the Soviet Union, the fact of drawing China into that war would be a question of life or death for the Chinese proletariat and its party. The war would open up boundless horizons before the Chinese Revolution. But to the extent that the international situation and internal conditions oblige the Soviet Union to make serious concessions in the Far-East in order to avoid war, that is, to defer it as far as possible, and to the extent that Japan does not find itself strong enough to begin hostilities, the war against Japanese imperialism cannot constitute, in any case at the present time, the central fighting slogan of the Chinese Communist Party.

Van-Ming quotes the following slogans of the Left Opposition in China: "Reconstitution of the mass movement". "Convocation of the National Assembly" and "Resumption of diplomatic relations between China and the Soviet Union". Under the simple pretext that these slogans are it seems poorly motivated, in an article appearing in the legal organ of the opposition, Van Ming calls the Left Opposition in China a "counter-revolutionary Trotskyist-Chen Du Hsiu group".

Now, even if we admit that the motivation of the revolutionary slogans was not fortunate, this does not give them, nor the organization which formulated them, a counter-revolutionary character. But Van Ming and his like are obliged to speak of the counter-revolutionary spirit of the "trotskyists" if they do not wish their posts and emoluments withdrawn.

At the same time that they declare themselves so severe against the Bolshevik Leninists who have proved they have been right in the course of the events which have taken place in China from 1932, the Stalinists show themselves as indulgent as possible towards themselves that is towards the uninterrupted chain of their errors.

In the days when Japan was attacking Shanghai, the Kuomintang supported "the united front of the workers, peasants, soldiers, merchants and students to combat imperialism". But this is the famous "bloc of four classes" of Stalin-Martinov! Since the second revolution, foreign oppression in China has not weakened, but on the contrary has grown. The antagonism between the needs of the country's evolution and the regime or imperialism has likewise become sharpened. Since then, all the old Stalinist arguments in favor of the bloc of four classes have acquired double strength. Now this time, the Stalinists have interpreted the Kuomintang's proposal as a new attempt to deceive the masses. Very well! But they have forgotten to explain why from 1924 to 1927 the CI leadership helped the Chinese bourgeoisie deceive to the end, and why the philosophy which consisted in being at the Kuomintang's beck and call has found expression in the program of the CI.

It is evident that we can and must support the slogan of democratic self-government of the election of functionaries by the people, etc. The program of democracy constitutes a great step forward in relation to the regime of military dictatorship. We must just bring together each time the isolated, partial democratic slogans with the essential slogans and attach them to the problems of revolutionary grouping and the arming of the workers.

The question of "patriotism" and "nationalism" like certain other questions contained in your letter, deal with terminology rather than with the essence of things. The Bolsheviks, favoring the national liberation of oppressed peoples by revolutionary means support by all means the movement of the masses of the people for national liberation not only against the foreign imperialists, but also against the bourgeois exploiters inside the national movement, in the nature of the Kuomintang.

Must we still introduce the term "patriotism" discredited and soiled enough? I doubt it. Must we not see in this attempt a tendency to want to adapt oneself to the petty-bourgeois ideology and terminology? If this tendency were to really appear in our ranks, we would have to fight it mercilessly.

Many questions of tactical and strategical character will appear insoluble if approached in a formalistic way. But they will fall into their right place if we pose them dialectically, that is, in the perspective of the living struggle of classes and parties. It is in real action that revolutionary dialectic is best assimilated. I do not doubt that our comrades in ideas and our Chinese friends the Bolshevik Leninists not only discuss passionately the complex problems of the Chinese Revolution, but also participate not less passionately in the developing struggle. We are for a strategy of action—not for speculation.

L.Trotsky *Prinkipo, Oct. 3, 1932*

54

On the War in China

1933

Japan's military procedure in China is developing in spiral fashion: its scope is increasing from month to month. Such a system offers political and diplomatic advantages: by degrees first their own people and then the opponents are drawn in, while the world is confronted by a series of accomplished facts. But at the same time it also knows that the military clique at present has to overcome not only external but international difficulties. From the purely military point of view such action "*par petits paquets*" (in sections) carries a disadvantage with it. Evidently the powerful circles in Japan are of the opinion that China's military weakness and the insoluble contradictions in the enemy's camp permit them a certain loss of time, which is connected with a spiral advance.

In the meantime, with or without delay, the second phase (the phase of a real war) must inevitably follow the first. What is Japan's political object? The leading Paris papers, which carefully render in the French tongue the views and remarks of the Japanese general staff, have continually emphasized that there cannot be talk of war but only of police measures. This information belongs as a necessary constituent to the "section method" of the spiral system. It will fall apart of itself as soon as the military action has come to a full development and as the defensive forces stand before the sought-for aims.

Japan's aim is the colonization of China, a really grandiose plan. But we can also say that it surpasses Japan's strength. Japan has arrived too late upon the scene. At a time when Great

Britain must contemplate the loss of India, Japan will not succeed in making a new India out of China.

Is it however not possible that the rulers in Tokyo are pursuing a different aim, namely a drive against the Soviet Republic? It would be hasty to declare such a plan as completely excluded. It can however surely not be placed in the front ranks. Only when Manchuria has been occupied and its position there consolidated can it be thought of, to make a drive in a northwestern direction. But while the Soviet government neither will nor can lead a war, evidently Japan will not decide to undertake an immediate aggressive path against Soviet Russia, before it has assured and strengthened its position in China and Manchuria.

A war against the Soviet Union would have to be carried on with quite other methods. Without strong allies in a position to finance the war extensively, it must be considered doubtful whether Japan will decide to overstep the boundaries of Manchuria. How far Tokyo today or tomorrow can count on million-dollar loans for military purposes, can be established better in Paris, London, or New York than here in Prinkipo.

Every attempt to repeat the Soviet Government's aggressive plans in the Far East comes up against a lack of support. A war would mean a severe blow to the industrial plan with which Russia's whole future is closely bound up. A factory which is 99 per cent finished is yet no factory, and in Soviet Russia there are hundreds and thousands of factories which are still in the building. Through a war they would be for a long time turned into dead capital. All this is really so clear, that it does not need to be brought out further.

If we admit then a military conflict in the far East is nevertheless inevitable—and of this not only many politicians in Japan, but also elsewhere are convinced—in this case there is no ground for the Soviet Union to hasten this event. Japan has forced its way into China in consequence of a high-flown enterprise, which will have unexpected consequences. It can and will have military and diplomatic partial results, but these will be of a negligible nature, while the difficulties will be not only enduring, but will also increase. In Korea Japan already posses her Ireland. In China she is trying to get her India. One must be a completely dumb general of the feudal type to look down with contempt upon the national movement in China. A powerful nation of 450 millions of people which has awakened to self-consciousness by a display of arms. Japan will sink to her knees, if not to her waist, in the fat Manchurian soil, and will stick fast there. And since in Japan itself the industrial development has prospered in complete contradiction with the feudal structure of society, we must regard an inner crisis as quite inevitable. First the Selyakai Party must clear the field for the Minsei Party, which will develop further to the Left. Then the revolutionary party will lift its head. France has lost not a little through the financing of Tzarism. She is making a mistake if she believes that she has assured herself against losses by the financing of Mishado. It is quite plain in the Far East the Soviet Regime has no occasion to make haste or to sacrifice.

Consequently a war between Soviet Russia and Japan could only arise if the conflict were provoked by Japan designedly and knowingly with the consent of strong allies. The object of such a war could be incomparably greater than the question of the Chinese Eastern railway and the whole Manchurian problem together. Certain French papers have been rather hasty with the prediction that Bolshevism will go to ruin in the Siberian steppes. The steppes and the forests of Siberia have room enough to make way for the fall of many things, but is it so sure that it must be Bolshevism which is to go down there?

The idea of a war between Soviet Russia and Japan like the parallel thought of a war between Japan and the United States brings the problem of distances before us: a land ocean or a water ocean as probable scenes of military operation. At the very first glance the strategic problem goes straight to the question of distances. Which brings up the point, many people come quickly to conclusions which are disagreeable for Russia; the weak protection of the Asiatic districts of the Soviet Union, the industrial backwardness and the lack of railroad connections must be seen as so many factors which are unfavorable to the Soviet Union. This is correct to a certain point. If however one approaches the question first from a purely military-technical standpoint, it must not be overlooked that these same powerful distances will likewise be allies for the Soviets. When we also admit the possibility of military success of the Japanese in the advance to the West, it can be easily seen that its difficulties in the section which lies behind the Japanese troops would increase with the distances. Its successes would be thereby complicated, and in the bargain Japan would leave behind its back its Ireland and its India.

Meanwhile we cannot contemplate the problem within such narrow limits. The war would not be carried out entirely by military means ... Soviet Russia would not stand alone. China is awakened. It will fight for its existence, and is in a position to do this. Whoever overlooks this factor, risks to lose his head.

The transportation of millions of soldiers on the Siberian railroad and their provisioning with all that belongs to the conduct of a war is certainly no light problem. But since now Russia's industrial facilities are greatly improved, transportation by rail in case of necessity could be considerably increased. This will certainly take time. But a war over great distances would also be a war of long duration. One could perhaps propose a 5-year war plan or alter the industrial 5-year plan to correspond with the requirements of the war. Naturally the industry and culture of the countries affected by the war would be dealt a terrible blow. I proceed from the proposition that there is no other way. Once a war is inevitable it must be conducted thoroughly, and no help and means must be spared. The participation of Soviet Russia in the war through which the Chinese people would gain new prospects, would have to open up a patriotic movement of powerful scope in China. Of this there can be no doubt for anyone who understands anything of the logic of events and of mass psychology. In China there is no lack of human material. Millions of Chinese have learned to go around with a gun. They do not lack the will to struggle, but only an ordered military preparation, an organization, a system and a trained leadership. Here the Red Army could render the Chinese very efficacious help. The qualified units in Chang Kai-Shek's army as is known, have been built up under the leadership of Russian instructors. The experiment of the military school at Whampoa could, if it were put on a different political foundation (this question I will not broach here) be built up to powerful proportions. Then the Transiberian Railway, as the necessary military instrument, would have to advance not an army but only the quintessence of an army.

How troops can be improvised out of awakened and aroused human material the Bolsheviks have thoroughly learned, and should not have forgotten. I do not doubt that it would be possible in 12 or 18 months to mobilize a million fighters, to clothe, arm and train them and place them on the battle line, and that these troops would not fall behind the Japanese in anything which concerns training. With regard to preparation for fight they would be even superior to the Japanese. For the second million, six months would not be needed. I speak of China, and beside China stand the Soviet Republic, the Red Army, their powerful reserves ... The leading French papers, which hold the world's regard for reaction, have really been too hasty to bury the Soviet in Siberia's cities. Hatred is generally a bad counsellor and it is particularly so in making prophecies.

But if, you will ask me, the prophets are so hopeful, why does the Soviet Government try with all means to avoid war? To this question I have already answered; the time factor in the Far East worked against Japanese imperialism which has already passed its peak and is moving to ruin. But setting this aside, it must not be forgotten, and this side of the problem is not to be underestimated, that the world does not consist of the Far East alone. The key to the world situation lies for the moment not in Mukden, but in Berlin. If Hitler attains power, it would be a far greater danger to Soviet Russia than all the plans of the Tokyo military clique.

55

Discussions with Harold R. Isaac

August 1935

August 8, 1935 ... On the problem of the united front with the bourgeoisie: Trotsky did not believe Liu Jen-ching's conclusion that Chen Tuhsiu has become an opportunist. He thinks that Liu's argument was un-dialectical and that it tended to throw around ambiguous terminology. For instance, Trotsky thinks there should be a distinction between "united fronts" and "common action" . . . and he was rather amused by Liu's arrogant attitude of being a self-appointed representative of the Bolshevik tendency in the Chinese revolutionary movement.

AUGUST 9, 1935

To resume yesterday's discussion, Trotsky read my draft and pointed out a few weaknesses on the first page. He felt that my analysis of the different layers of the bourgeoisie and their subjective and objective viewpoints was insufficient and un-dialectical. He said that if we used such a pat formula, we would tend to be dogmatic and opportunist. He emphasized:

"Common action, especially a short-term common action, is one thing, but capitulation to the bourgeoisie in the form of a permanent 'united front' such as the French Popular Front is another. They are entirely different. It is good to keep our organization completely independent; but the heart of the matter is how to use this independence. We should continually carry out 'common action' with the students' and peasants' organizations."

I said that the question is not one of our relationship to the petty bourgeoisie and the peasantry. On this point, Ch'en Tu-hsiu had adopted an emptier and more abstract formula than Liu Jen ching. At any rate, I had to send Sneevliet a telegram to ask him to send me Liu's document, "Five Years of the Chinese Left Opposition." (I had not brought it with me because I had thought Trotsky already had this document. We will discuss it more fully later on.)

AUGUST 9 (AFTERNOON)

My oral report on the Chinese Red Army took up almost the whole meeting. In this report I also touched on the general political situation in China. Dr. F. and N. Sedova were also present. I drew a map and talked for an hour and a half. I talked about the origins, initial development, internal evolution, and eventual fate of the Chinese Red Army. I dealt with it as completely as possible so that at the conclusion there were almost no questions to be answered.

Trotsky only said that its general development verified the Opposition's prediction that without the leadership of the working class movement, the fate of the Red Army would either depend on the upper strata (merchants and middle and rich peasants) within its jurisdiction, or it would be suppressed by the superior military forces of the Kuomintang and the imperialists. Our viewpoint was that at present the Red Army wanted to go to Sinkiang province because only there could they answer the Soviet Union's diplomatic needs by establishing a buffer zone between the Soviet Union and the Japanese forces from Mongolia. Trotsky considered this viewpoint correct, logical, and most likely. Near the end of the meeting, I raised the problem of the political perspective in China. I described Liu's ideological evolution on the problem of economic reconstruction, and also mentioned his search for a new solution and his attention to the Red Army and the possibility of its expansion into Szechwan province. At the end, I mentioned that the political perspective had to be clarified because this will be the foundation of the program of the Chinese Bolshevik-Leninist faction. This problem will be discussed in the later meetings.

AUGUST 13 (MORNING)

We discussed Liu's document. I could only cite major arguments and read the important quotations to him, and let him read it. We only had time to discuss the introduction and the chapters on the national assembly and the bourgeoisie. When I read the part (page 14) where Liu said the masses considered the national assembly and the dictatorship of the proletariat to be "the same thing" (i.e., the national assembly is the popular formula for the dictatorship of the proletariat), Trotsky interrupted me and said: "It would be more exact to say that Liu considers what is in his mind and what is in the minds of the masses to be 'the same thing.'" He continued:

"One might say, looking at the historical development of countries such as England and France, that a long period of democracy is required before reaching socialism, and that this period could last several centuries. But in Russia, semi-democracy of the parliamentary period lasted only several years. Democracy during the February revolution lasted only eight months. In China, this period may not even last eight months. At any rate, the masses always want democracy in the beginning. Only when they follow this road will they be able to accept the soviet system and to seize power. For this matter we cannot form a detailed plan in advance; we have to rely on the thinking and actions of the masses to determine our action. In China the period of democracy may be very short, or even nonexistent. But this does not mean that the masses will think of the national assembly, or any democratic concept, and the dictatorship of the proletariat as 'the same thing.'"

I continued to read. He shook his head and said: "It is ridiculous to hinder our first steps with worrying about future problems. The first step should be to conduct propaganda and agitation for the national assembly. When the Kuomintang capitulates to the Japanese imperialists, the people should do something themselves. How? Call a national assembly! As simple as that! We should spread this idea among all strata of the people. The students, as before, could play a very big role in the initial stage. We have two tasks: (*i*) to arouse and to participate in the democratic mass movement; (*ii*) to draw the proletariat into this movement so as to prepare them for the proletarian revolution. If we can recruit ten or a hundred cadres, they will be the future leaders of the proletariat.

"The problems of the future perspective are part of cadre education, but these problems should not be allowed to paralyze and interfere with our propaganda work for a national assembly. The most important task at the moment is to do everything possible to promote the idea of a national assembly. Then we will watch the result of this agitation closely. For instance, if Chiang Kai-shek attempts to call his own national assembly—which will eventually cause a split among the bourgeoisie—the right wing will oppose this idea and the left wing will try to utilize the movement. Then we will attack it and expose it. If the radical wing of the bourgeoisie attempted to carry out the national assembly, we should on the one hand push them to act, for instance to overthrow Chiang Kai-shek and form their own government; and on the other hand we have to expose their deception to the masses. We should start now to agitate for the national assembly. We will discuss the second step later."

"But," I interrupted, "you said we should participate in this democratic mass movement. This is a problem, because at the moment we do not have such a movement. Our task is to create one in order to resurrect mass activity." I then briefly described the present situation of pessimism, discontent, and lack of organization of the workers and of the petty-bourgeois intellectuals. Trotsky said:

"It frequently happens that we cannot push the masses forward. We cannot create a miracle. The defeat of the revolution was deeply felt by the masses. It is a fact that we recognized the defeat in 1928. On the one hand, there was a certain impulse imparted by this defeat (the Red Army, etc.), and on the other hand there were the deepening psychological effects among the masses. If simultaneously the economic crisis deepens, the number of workers declines, production shrinks, and the peasant movement is suppressed, this will mean that the counter-revolution has deepened. But its basis is still undetermined. We will then have to carry out the task of education through our cadres. We will use all means to spread the idea of a national assembly, and we will watch the effect of our propaganda. If there is not yet a response, we will try again, again, and again, until we get a response.

"In the past, we made a theoretical assumption that if the Red Army were to occupy large cities, it would awaken the workers' movement. We also said that this was probable but not inevitable, and that if an economic boom should coincide with advances by the Red Army, it could accelerate the rise of the mass movement. But these lucky coincidences did not occur. Therefore we have to start over again, go back to 1922–23. But if and when the movement rises for the second time, its tempo will be much quicker. The entire contents of the second revolution will be run through again as a brief overture to the third revolution. We will start with our democratic slogan. The slogan of the national assembly can play a big role among the masses. We will talk to the workers through literature and conversations. We should get some response from the workers. This is the only way to advance our work."

Trotsky then described the circumstances of the revival of mass political activity in Russia in 1893, after ten years of reaction following the suppression of the "People's Will". Plekhanov and his group published a document that year evaluating the progress of the Marxist movement in which they expressed their disappointment at the small results. But it was to be in that very year that Marxism was to grow into a big movement that swept the whole country.

"But I have to explain that the revival was the result of ten years of growth and development of Russian capitalism, which had completely changed the face of the nation. If the deepening of the counter-revolution in China is paralleled by an economic crisis, then our agitation will have no results. Then we will have to prepare our cadres and wage our propaganda. Although our results seem small, we are preparing our future leaders and we do not expect any miracles. What then can bring about the revival of the revolutionary mass movement? Various factors can have this effect: war or revolution in other countries—a new war will bring a new revolution—such was the effect of the Russo-Japanese War in 1905. Don't forget that without our 1905 revolution, there would have been no Prussian revolution, and there would have been no 1911 revolution in China. Our 1905 made a big impact on the Far East.

"As for who will convoke the national assembly, at the moment that is still a hypothetical question. Our agitation should concentrate on the need for a national assembly. First the masses must become convinced of the need for a national assembly. As our agitation progresses, we will proceed further on the basis of the results of the last step. In all events, we must start to agitate around the demand for a national assembly to oppose Kuomintang rule. Comrades participating in this struggle must have an adequate slogan, a slogan that covers various possible circumstances.

"I do not yet thoroughly understand these controversies [between Chen and Liu] so I cannot express my opinion. I shall study them more carefully. But I can say one thing: even if Ch'en Tu-hsiu holds some opportunist ideas, he is, after all, older and has a lifetime of experience. It is possible that he can contribute many good ideas. I have the impression—with some reservations—that Liu Jen-ching has exaggerated this disagreement. Maybe Ch'en posed his opinion as a tactical formula, and Liu considered it a strategic one. If this is Ch'en's strategic line then many of Liu's criticisms may be right. But I think these differences have been greatly exaggerated. I think it is impermissible to conduct a split with Ch'en Tu-hsiu. We need his cooperation in the Fourth International. The unfortunate thing is not that a serious dispute has arisen over a small difference, but that this small difference has blocked our action."

56

On the Sino–Japanese War

September 23, 1937

Dear Comrade Diego Rivera:

During the past few days I have been reading some of the lucubrations of the Oehlerites and the Eiffelites (yes, there is a tendency of that sort!) on the civil war in Spain and on the Sino–Japanese War. Lenin called the ideas of these people "infantile disorders". A sick child arouses sympathy. But twenty years have passed since then. The children have become bearded and even bald. But they have not ceased their childish babblings. On the contrary, they have increased all their faults and all their foolishness tenfold and have added ignominies to them. They follow us step by step. They borrow some of the elements of our analysis. They distort these elements without limit and counterpose them to the rest. They correct us. When we draw a human figure, they add a deformity. When it is a woman, they decorate her with a heavy moustache. When we draw a rooster, they put an egg under it. And they call all this burlesque Marxism and Leninism.

I want to stop to discuss in this letter only the Sino–Japanese War. In my declaration to the bourgeois press, I said that the duty of all the workers' organizations of China was to participate actively and in the front lines of the present war against Japan, without abandoning, for a single moment, their own program and independent activity. But that is "social patriotism"! the Eiffelites cry. It is capitulation to Chiang Kai-shek! It is the abandonment of the principle of the class struggle! Bolshevism preached revolutionary defeatism in the imperialist war. Now, the war in Spain and the Sino–Japanese War are both imperialist wars. "Our position on the war in China is the same. The only salvation of the workers and peasants of China is to struggle independently against the two armies, against the Chinese army in the same manner as against the Japanese army." These four lines, taken from an Eiffelite document of September 10, 1937, suffice entirely for us to say: we are concerned here with either real traitors or complete imbeciles. But imbecility, raised to this degree, is equal to treason.

We do not and never have put all wars on the same plane. Marx and Engels supported the revolutionary struggle of the Irish against Great Britain, of the Poles against the tsar, even though in these two nationalist wars the leaders were, for the most part, members of the bourgeoisie and even at times of the feudal aristocracy . . . at all events, Catholic reactionaries. When Abdel-Karim rose up against France, the democrats and Social Democrats spoke with hate of the struggle of a "savage tyrant" against the "democracy". The party of Leon Blum supported this point of view. But we, Marxists and Bolsheviks, considered the struggle of the Riffians against imperialist domination as a progressive war. Lenin wrote hundreds of pages demonstrating the primary necessity of distinguishing between imperialist nations and the colonial and semicolonial nations which comprise the great majority of humanity. To speak of "revolutionary defeatism" in general, without distinguishing between exploiter and exploited countries, is to make a miserable caricature of Bolshevism and to put that caricature at the service of the imperialists.

In the Far East we have a classic example. China is a semicolonial country which Japan is transforming, under our very eyes, into a colonial country. Japan's struggle is imperialist and reactionary. China's struggle is emancipatory and progressive.

But Chiang Kai-shek? We need have no illusions about Chiang Kai-shek, his party, or the whole ruling class of China, just as Marx and Engels had no illusions about the ruling classes of Ireland and Poland. Chiang Kai-shek is the executioner of the Chinese workers and peasants. But today he is forced, despite himself, to struggle against Japan for the remainder of the independence of China. Tomorrow he may again betray. It is possible. It is probable. It is even inevitable. But today he is struggling. Only cowards, scoundrels, or complete imbeciles can refuse to participate in that struggle.

Let us use the example of a strike to clarify the question. We do not support all strikes. If, for example, a strike is called for the exclusion of Negro, Chinese, or Japanese workers from a factory, we are opposed to that strike. But if a strike aims at bettering— insofar as it can—the conditions of the workers, we are the first to participate in it, whatever the leadership. In the vast majority of strikes, the leaders are reformists, traitors by profession, agents of capital. They oppose every strike. But from time to time the pressure of the masses or of the objective situation forces them into the path of struggle.

Let us imagine, for an instant, a worker saying to himself: "I do not want to participate in the strike because the leaders are agents of capital". This doctrine of this ultra-left imbecile would serve to brand him by his real name: *a strikebreaker.* The case of the Sino–Japanese War, is from this point of view, entirely analogous. If Japan is an imperialist country and if China is the victim of imperialism, we favor China. Japanese patriotism is the hideous mask of worldwide robbery. Chinese patriotism is legitimate and progressive. To place the two on the same plane and to speak of "social patriotism" can be done only by those who have read nothing of Lenin, who have understood nothing of the attitude of the Bolsheviks during the imperialist war, and who can but compromise and prostitute the teachings of Marxism. The Eiffelites have heard that the social patriots accuse the internationalists of being the agents of the enemy and they tell us: "You are doing the same thing." In a war between two *imperialist* countries, it is a question neither of democracy nor of national independence, but of the oppression of backward non-imperialist peoples. In such a war the two countries find themselves on the same historical plane. The revolutionaries in both armies are defeatists. But Japan and China are not on the same historical plane. The victory of Japan will signify the enslavement of China, the end of her economic and social development, and the terrible strengthening of Japanese imperialism. The victory of China will signify, on the contrary, the social revolution in Japan and the free development, that is to say unhindered by external oppression, of the class struggle in China.

But can Chiang Kai-shek assure the victory? I do not believe so. It is he, however, who began the war and who today directs it. To be able to replace him it is necessary to gain decisive influence among the proletariat and in the army, and to do this it is necessary not to remain suspended in the air but to place oneself in the midst of the struggle. We must win influence and prestige in the *military* struggle against the foreign invasion and in the *political* struggle against the weaknesses, the deficiencies, and the internal betrayal. At a certain point, which we cannot fix in advance, this political opposition can and must be transformed into armed conflict, since the civil war, like war generally, is nothing more than the continuation of the political struggle. It is necessary, however, to know when and how to transform political opposition into armed insurrection.

During the Chinese Revolution of 1925–27 we attacked the policies of the Comintern. Why? It is necessary to understand well the reasons. The Eiffelites claim that we have changed our attitude on the Chinese question. That is because the poor fellows have understood nothing of our attitude in 1925–27. We never denied that it was the duty of the Communist Party to participate in the war of the bourgeoisie and petty bourgeoisie of the South against the generals of the North, agents of foreign imperialism. We never denied the necessity of a military bloc between the CP and the Kuomintang. On the contrary, we were the first to propose it. We demanded, however, that the CP maintain its entire political and organizational independence, that is, that during the civil war against the internal agents of imperialism, as in the national war against foreign imperialism, the working class, while remaining in the front lines of the *military* struggle, prepare the *political* overthrow of the bourgeoisie. We hold the same policies in the present war. We have not changed our attitude one iota. The Oehlerites and the Eiffelites, on the other hand, have not understood a single bit of our policies, neither those of 1925–27, nor those of today.

In my declaration to the bourgeois press at the beginning of the recent conflict between Tokyo and Nanking, I stressed above all the necessity of the active participation of revolutionary workers in the war against the imperialist oppressors. Why did I do it? Because first of all it is correct from the Marxist point of view; because, secondly, it was necessary from the point of view of the welfare of our friends in China. Tomorrow the GPU, which is in alliance with the Kuomintang (as with Negrin in Spain), will represent our Chinese friends as being "defeatists" and agents of Japan. The best of them, with Chen Tu-hsiu at the head, can be nationally and internationally compromised and killed. It was necessary to stress, energetically, that the Fourth International was on the side of China as against Japan. And I added at the same time: *without abandoning either their program or their independence.*

The Eiffelite imbeciles try to jest about this "reservation." "The Trotskyists," they say, "want to serve Chiang Kai-shek in action and the proletariat in words." To participate actively and consciously in the war does not mean "to serve Chiang Kai-shek" but to serve the independence of a colonial country *in spite of* Chiang Kai-shek. And the words directed against the Kuomintang are the means of educating the masses for the overthrow of Chiang Kai-shek. In participating in the *military* struggle under the orders of Chiang Kai-shek, since unfortunately it is he who has the command in the war for independence—to prepare *politically* the overthrow of Chiang Kai-shek . . . that is the only revolutionary policy. The Eiffelites counterpose the policy of "class struggle" to this "nationalist and social patriotic" policy. Lenin fought this abstract and sterile opposition all his life. To him, the interests of the world proletariat dictated the duty of aiding oppressed peoples in their national and patriotic struggle against imperialism. Those who have not yet understood that, almost a quarter of a century after the World War and twenty years after the October Revolution, must be pitilessly rejected as the worst enemies on the inside by the revolutionary vanguard. This is exactly the case with Eiffel and his kind!

L. Trotsky

57

Pacifism in China

September 25, 1937

The so-called peace organizations, including the working class organizations, do not in the least constitute an obstacle to the war. The numerous peace conferences, organized mainly by the Comintern, are purely theatrical enterprises without the least effectiveness; in time of war all these peace leaders, all these pious and humanitarian ladies and gentlemen, will return to their governments to support them in the war as they did in 1914–18.

The only political factor which today hinders the outbreak of war is the fear, on the part of the governments, of the social revolution. Hitler himself has said it many times. We must draw the logical conclusions from this: the more revolutionary the working class, the more it opposes the ruling imperialist class, the more are these latter prevented from carrying out their designs to make a new division of the world by armed force.

At the same time we must carefully distinguish between the imperialist countries and the backward countries, colonial and semicolonial. The attitude of the working class organiza-tions in and toward these two groupings cannot be the same. The present war between China and Japan is a classic example. It is absolutely indisputable that, on the part of Japan, it is a war of rapine and that, on the part of China, it is a war of national defence. Only conscious or unconscious agents of Japanese imperialism can put the two countries on the same plane.

That is why we can only feel pity or hatred for those who in the face of the Sino–Japanese War declare that they are opposed to all wars, to wars altogether. The war is already a fact. The working class movement cannot remain neutral in a struggle between those who wish to enslave and those who are enslaved. The working class movement in China, Japan, and in the entire world must oppose with all its strength the Japanese imperialist bandits and support the people of China and their army.

This does not at all suppose a blind confidence in the Chinese government and in Chiang Kai-shek. In the past, above all in 1925–27, the general was already dependent upon working class organizations in his military struggle against the Chinese generals of the North, agents of foreign imperialism. In the end, he crushed the working class organizations by armed force in 1927–28. We must learn the lessons from this experience which resulted from the fatal policies of the Comintern. In participating in the legitimate and progressive national war against Japanese invasion, the working class organizations must preserve their entire *political independence* of the Chiang Kai-shek government. The Communist Party of China again, as in 1924–25, is making violent efforts to turn over the Chinese working class movement politically to Chiang Kai-shek and the Kuomintang. It is a crime all the more horrible because it is being committed for the second time.

At the same time, the remedy does not lie in the working class organizations declaring themselves "against all wars" and folding their arms in an attitude of passive treason, but rather in participating in the war, aiding the Chinese people materially and morally, and simultaneously educating the masses of peasants and workers in a spirit of total independence of the Kuomintang and its government. We do not attack Chiang Kai-shek for conducting the war. Oh, no. We attack him for doing it badly, without sufficient energy, without confidence in the people and especially in the workers.

A pacifist who has the same attitude toward China as toward Japan in this terrible conflict is like one who would identify a lockout with a strike. The working class movement is against a lockout by the exploiters and for a strike of the exploited. At the same time, strikes are often led by misleaders who are capable of betraying the working class movement during the strike. This is no reason for workers to refuse to participate in the strike but it is reason for mobilizing the working masses against the defections and the treason of the leadership. It often happens that during or after a strike the organized masses change their leadership. This can very well happen in China. But this change can be favorable for the people only if the Chinese and international working class organizations support China against Japan.

58

The Chinese Revolution

London 1938

Introduction to Harold R. Isaac's—'The Tragedy of the Chinese Revolution'

First of all, the mere fact that the author of this book belongs to the school of historical materialism would be entirely insufficient in our eyes to win approval for his work. In present-day conditions the Marxist label would predispose us to mistrust rather than to acceptance. In close connection with the degeneration of the Soviet State, Marxism has in the past fifteen years passed through an unprecedented period of decline and debasement. From an instrument of analysis and criticism, it has been turned into an instrument of cheap apologetics. Instead of analyzing facts, it occupies itself with selecting sophisms in the interests of exalted clients.

In the Chinese Revolution of 1925–27 the Communist International played a very great role, depicted in this book quite comprehensively. We would, however, seek in vain in the library of the Communist International for a single book which attempts in any way to give a rounded picture of the Chinese Revolution. Instead, we find scores of "conjunctural" works' which docilely reflect each zigzag in the politics of the Communist International, or, more correctly, of Soviet diplomacy in China, and subordinating to each zigzag facts as well as general treatment. In contrast to this literature, which cannot arouse anything but mental revulsion, Isaacs' book represents a scientific work from beginning to end. It is based on a conscientious study of a vast number of original sources and supplementary material. Isaacs spent more than three years on this work. It should be added that he had previously passed about five years in China as a journalist and observer of Chinese life.

The author of this book approaches the revolution as a revolutionist, and he sees no reason for concealing it. In the eyes of a philistine a revolutionary point of view is virtually equivalent to an absence of scientific objectivity. We think just the opposite: only a revolutionist—provided, of course, that he is equipped with the scientific method—is capable of laying bare the objective dynamics of the revolution. Apprehending thought in general is not contemplative, but active. The element of will is indispensable for penetrating the secrets of nature and society. Just as a surgeon, on whose scalpel a human life depends, distinguishes with extreme care between the various tissues of an organism, so a revolutionist, if he has a serious attitude toward his task, is obliged with strict conscientiousness to analyse the structure of society, its functions and reflexes.

To understand the present war between Japan and China one must take the Second Chinese Revolution as a point of departure. In both cases we meet not only identical social forces, but frequently the same personalities. Suffice it to say that the person of Chiang Kai-shek occupies the central place in this book. As these lines are being written it is still difficult to forecast when and in what manner the Sino–Japanese war will end. But the outcome of the present conflict in the Far East will in any case have a provisional character. The world war which is approaching with irresistible force will review the Chinese problem together with all other problems of colonial domination. For it is in this that the real task of the second world war will consist: to divide the planet anew in accord with the new relationship of imperialist forces. The principal arena of struggle will, of course, not be that Lilliputian bath-tub, the Mediterranean, nor even the Atlantic Ocean, but the basin of the Pacific. The most important object of struggle will be China, embracing about one-fourth of the human race. The fate of the Soviet Union—the other big stake in the coming war—will also to a certain degree be decided in the Far East. Preparing for this clash of Titans, Tokyo is attempting today to assure itself of the broadest possible drill-ground on the continent of Asia. Great Britain and the United States are likewise losing no time. It can, however, be predicted with certainty—and this is in essence acknowledged by the present makers of destiny—that the world war will not produce the final decision: it will be followed by a new series of revolutions which will review not only the decisions of the war but all those property conditions which give rise to war.

History is no Pacifist

This prospect, it must be confessed, is very far from being an idyll, but Clio, the muse of history, was never a member of a Ladies' Peace Society. The older generation which passed through the war of 1914–18 did not discharge a single one of its tasks. It leaves to the new generation as heritage the burden of wars and revolutions. These most important and tragic events in human history have often marched side by side. They will definitely form the background of the coming decades. It remains only to hope that the new generation, which cannot arbitrarily cut loose from the conditions it has inherited, has learned at least to understand better the laws of its epoch. For acquainting itself with the Chinese Revolution of 1925–27 it will not find today a better guide than this book.

Despite the unquestionable greatness of the Anglo-Saxon genius, it is impossible not to see that the laws of revolutions are least understood precisely in the Anglo-Saxon countries. The explanation for this lies, on the one hand, in the fact that the very appearance of revolution in these countries relates to a long-distant past, and evokes in official "sociologists" a condescending smile, as would childish pranks. On the other hand, pragmatism, so characteristic of Anglo-Saxon thinking, is least of all useful for understanding revolutionary crises.

The English Revolution of the seventeenth century, like the French Revolution of the eighteenth, had the task of "rationalizing" the structure of society, i.e., cleansing it of feudal stalactites and stalagmites, and subjecting it to the laws of free competition, which in that epoch seemed to be the laws of "common sense". In doing this, the Puritan revolution draped itself in Biblical dress, thereby revealing a purely infantile incapacity to understand its own significance. The French Revolution, which had considerable influence on progressive thought in the United States, was guided by formulas of pure rationalism. Common sense, which is still afraid of itself and resorts to the mask of Biblical prophets, or secularized common sense, which looks upon society as the product of a rational "contract", remain to this day the fundamental forms of Anglo-Saxon thinking in the domains of philosophy and sociology.

Yet the real society of history has not been constructed, following Rousseau, upon a rational "contract", nor, as according to Bentham, upon the principle of the "greatest good", but has unfolded "irrationally", on the basis of contradictions and antagonisms. For revolution to become inevitable class contradictions have to be strained to the breaking point. It is precisely this historically inescapable necessity for conflict, which depends neither on good nor ill will but on the objective inter-relationship of classes, that makes revolution, together with war, the most dramatic expression of the "irrational" foundation of the historic process.

"Irrational" does not, however, mean arbitrary. On the contrary, in the molecular preparation of revolution, in its explosion, in its ascent and decline, there is lodged a profound inner lawfulness which can be apprehended and, in the main, foreseen. Revolutions, as has been said more than once, have a logic of their own. But this is not the logic of Aristotle, and even less the pragmatic demi-logic of "common sense". It is the higher function of thought: the logic of development and its contradictions, i.e., the dialectic.

The obstinacy of Anglo-Saxon pragmatism and its hostility to dialectical thinking thus have their material causes. Just as a poet cannot attain to the dialectic through books without his own personal experiences, so a well-to-do society, unused to convulsions and habituated to uninterrupted "progress", is incapable of understanding the dialectic of its own development. However, it is only too obvious that this privilege of the Anglo-Saxon world has receded into the past. History is preparing to give Great Britain as well as the United States serious lessons in the dialectic.

Character of the Chinese Revolution

The author of this book tries to deduce the character of the Chinese Revolution not from *a priori* definitions and not from historical analogies, but from the living structure of Chinese society and from the dynamics of its inner forces. In this lies the chief methodological value of the book. The reader will carry away not only a better-knit picture of the march of events but—what is more important—will learn to understand their social mainsprings. Only on this basis is it possible correctly to appraise political programs and the slogans of struggling parties—which, even if neither independent nor in the final analysis the decisive factors in the process, are nevertheless its most manifest signs.

In its immediate aims the uncompleted Chinese Revolution is "bourgeois". This term, however, which is used as a mere echo of the bourgeois revolutions of the past, actually helps us very little. Lest the historical analogy turn into a trap for the mind, it is necessary to check it in the light of a concrete sociological analysis. What are the classes which are struggling in China? What are the inter-relationships of these classes? How, and in what direction, are these relations being transformed? What are the objective tasks of the Chinese Revolution, i.e., those tasks dictated by the course of development? On the shoulders of which classes rests the solution of these tasks? With what methods can they he solved? Isaacs' book gives the answers to precisely these questions.

Colonial and semicolonial—and therefore backward—countries, which embrace by far the greater part of mankind, differ extraordinarily from one another in their degree of backwardness, representing an historical ladder reaching from nomadry, and even cannibalism, up to the most modern industrial culture. The combination of extremes in one degree or another characterizes all of the backward countries. However, the hierarchy of backwardness, if one may employ such an expression, is determined by the specific weight of the elements of barbarism and culture in the life of each colonial country. Equatorial Africa lags far behind Algeria, Paraguay behind Mexico, Abyssinia behind India or China. With their common economic dependence upon the imperialist metropolis, their political dependence bears in some instances the character of open colonial slavery (India, Equatorial Africa), while in others it is concealed by the fiction of State independence (China, Latin America).

In agrarian relations backwardness finds its most organic and cruel expression. Not one of these countries has carried its democratic revolution through to any real extent. Half-way agrarian reforms are absorbed by semi-serf relations, and these are inescapably reproduced in the soil of poverty and oppression. Agrarian barbarism always goes hand-in-hand with the absence of roads, with the isolation of provinces, with "medieval" particularism, and absence of national consciousness. The purging of social relations of the remnants of ancient and the encrustations of modern feudalism is the most important task in all these countries.

The achievement of the agrarian revolution is unthinkable, however, with the preservation of dependence upon foreign imperialism, which with one hand implants capitalist relations while supporting and re-creating with the other all the forms of slavery and serfdom. The struggle for the democratization of social relations and the creation of a national state thus uninterruptedly passes into an open uprising against foreign domination.

Historical backwardness does not imply a simple reproduction of the development of advanced countries, England or France, with a delay of one, two, or three centuries. It engenders an entirely new "combined" social formation in which the latest conquests of capitalist technique and structure root themselves into relations of feudal or pre-feudal barbarism, transforming and subjecting them and creating peculiar relations of classes.

Bourgeoisie Hostile to People

Not a single one of the tasks of the "bourgeois" revolution can be solved in these backward countries under the leadership of the "national" bourgeoisie, because the latter emerges at once with foreign support as a class alien or hostile to the people.

Every stage in its development binds it only the more closely to the foreign finance capital of which it is essentially the agency. The petty bourgeoisie of the colonies, that of handicrafts and trade, is the first to fall victim in the unequal struggle with foreign capital, declining into economic insignificance, becoming declassed and pauperized. It cannot even conceive of playing an independent political role. The peasantry, the largest numerically and the most atomized, backward, and oppressed class, is capable of local uprisings and partisan warfare, but requires the leadership of a more advanced and centralized class in order for this struggle to be elevated to an all-national level. The task of such leadership falls in the nature of things upon the colonial proletariat, which, from its very first steps, stands opposed not only to the foreign but also to its own national bourgeoisie.

Out of the conglomeration of provinces and tribes, bound together by geographical proximity and the bureaucratic apparatus, capitalist development has transformed China into the semblance of an economic entity. The revolutionary movement of the masses translated this growing unity for the first time into the language of national consciousness. In the strikes, agrarian uprisings, and military expeditions of 1925–1927 a new China was born. While the generals, tied to their own and the foreign bourgeoisie, could only tear the country to pieces, the Chinese workers became the standard-bearers of an irresistible urge to national unity. This movement provides an incontestable analogy with the struggle of the French Third Estate against particularism, or with the later struggle of the Germans and Italians for national unification. But in contrast to the first-born countries of capitalism, where the problem of achieving national unity fell to the petty bourgeoisie, in part under the leadership of the bourgeoisie and even of the landlords (Prussia!), in China it was the proletariat that emerged as the primary motive force and potential leader of this movement. But precisely thereby, the proletariat confronted the bourgeoisie with the danger that the leadership of the unified fatherland would not remain in the latter's hands. Patriotism has been throughout all history inseparably bound up with power and property. In the face of danger the ruling classes have never stopped short of dismembering their own country so long as they were able in this way to preserve power over one part of it. It is not at all surprising, therefore, if the Chinese bourgeoisie, represented by Chiang Kai-shek, turned its weapons in 1927 against the proletariat, the standard-bearer of national unity. The exposition and explanation of this turn, which occupies the central place in Isaacs' book, provides the key to the understanding of the fundamental problems of the Chinese Revolution as well as of the present Sino–Japanese war.

The so-called "national" bourgeoisie tolerates all forms of national degradation so long as it can hope to maintain its own privileged existence. But at the moment when foreign capital sets out to assume undivided domination of the entire wealth of the country, the colonial bourgeoisie is forced to remind itself of its "national" obligations. Under pressure of the masses it may even find itself plunged into a war. But this will be a war waged against one of the imperialist powers, the one least amenable to negotiations, with the hope of passing into the service of some other, more magnanimous power. Chiang Kai-shek struggles against the Japanese violators only within the limits indicated to him by his British or American patrons. Only that class which has nothing to lose but its chains can conduct to the very end the war against imperialism for national emancipation.

Grandiose Historical Test

The above developed views regarding the special character of the "bourgeois" revolutions in historically belated countries are by no means the product of theoretical analysis alone. Before the second Chinese Revolution (1925–1927) they had already been submitted to a grandiose historical test. The experience of the three Russian Revolutions (1905, February and October 1917) bears no less significance for the twentieth century than the French Revolution bore for the nineteenth. To understand the destinies of modern China the reader must have before his eyes the struggle of conceptions in the Russian revolutionary movement, because these conceptions exerted, and still exert, a direct and, moreover, powerful influence upon the politics of the Chinese proletariat and an indirect influence upon the politics of the Chinese bourgeoisie.

It was precisely because of its historical backwardness that Czarist Russia turned out to be the only European country where Marxism as a doctrine and the Social Democracy as a party attained powerful development before the bourgeois revolution. It was in Russia, quite naturally, that the problem of the correlation between the struggle for democracy and the struggle for socialism, or between the bourgeois revolution and the socialist, was submitted to theoretical analysis. The first to pose this problem in the early eighties of the last century was the founder of the Russian Social Democracy, Plekhanov. In the struggle against so-called Populism (Narodnikism), a variety of socialist Utopianism, Plekhanov established that Russia had no reason whatever to expect a privileged path of development, that like the "profane" nations, it would have to pass through the stage of capitalism and that along this path it would acquire the regime of bourgeois democracy indispensable for the further struggle of the proletariat for socialism. Plekhanov not only separated the bourgeois revolution as a task distinct from the socialist revolution—which he postponed to the indefinite future—but he depicted entirely different combinations of forces. The bourgeois revolution was to be achieved by the proletariat in alliance with the liberal bourgeoisie, and thus clear the path for capitalist progress; after a number of decades and on a higher level of capitalist development, the proletariat would carry out the socialist revolution in direct struggle against the bourgeoisie.

Lenin—not immediately, to be sure—reviewed this doctrine. At the beginning of the present century, with much greater force and consistency than Plekhanov, he posed the agrarian problem as the central problem of the bourgeois revolution in Russia. With this he came to the conclusion that the liberal bourgeoisie was hostile to the expropriation of the landlords' estates, and precisely for this reason would seek a compromise with the monarchy on the basis of a constitution on the Prussian pattern. To Plekhanov's idea of an alliance between the proletariat and the liberal bourgeoisie, Lenin opposed the idea of an alliance between the proletariat and the peasantry. The aim of the revolutionary collaboration of these two classes he proclaimed to be the establishment of the "bourgeois-democratic dictatorship of the proletariat and the peasantry" as the only means of cleansing the Czarist empire of its feudal-police refuse, of creating a free farmers' system, and of clearing the road for the development of capitalism along American lines. Lenin's formula represented a gigantic step forward in that, in contrast to Plekhanov's it correctly indicated the central task of the revolution, namely, the democratic overturn of agrarian relations, and equally correctly sketched out the only realistic combination of class forces capable of solving this task. But up to 1917 the thought of Lenin himself remained bound to the traditional concept of the "bourgeois" revolution. Like Plekhanov, Lenin proceeded from the premise that only after the "completion of the bourgeois democratic revolution" would the tasks of the socialist revolution come on the order of the day. Lenin, however, contrary to the legend later manufactured by the epigones, considered that after the completion of the democratic overturn, the peasantry, as peasantry, could not remain the ally of the proletariat. Lenin based his socialist hopes on the agricultural laborers and the semi-proletarianized peasants who sell their labor power.

An Internal Contradiction

The weak point in Lenin's conception was the internally contradictory idea of the "bourgeois-democratic dictatorship of the proletariat and the peasantry". A political bloc of two classes whose interests only partially coincide excludes a dictatorship. Lenin himself emphasized the fundamental limitation of the "dictatorship of the proletariat and the peasantry" when he openly called it bourgeois. By this he meant to say that for the sake of maintaining the alliance with the peasantry the proletariat would, in the coming revolution, have to forego the direct posing of the socialist tasks. But this would signify, to be precise, that the proletariat would have to give up the dictatorship. In that event, in whose hands would the revolutionary power be concentrated? In the hands of the peasantry? But it is least capable of such a role.

Lenin left these questions unanswered up to his famous Theses of April 4, 1917. Only here did he break for the first time with the traditional understanding of the "bourgeois" revolution and with the formula of the "bourgeois-democratic dictatorship of the proletariat and the peasantry". He declared the struggle for the dictatorship of the proletariat to be the sole means of carrying out the agrarian revolution to the end and of securing the freedom of the oppressed nationalities. The regime of the proletarian dictatorship, by its very nature, however, could not limit itself to the framework of bourgeois property. The rule of the proletariat automatically placed on the agenda the socialist revolution, which in this case was not separated from the democratic revolution by any historical period, but was uninterruptedly connected with it, or, to put it more accurately, was an organic outgrowth of it. At what tempo the socialist transformation of society would occur and what limits it would attain in the nearest future would depend not only upon internal but upon external conditions as well. The Russian Revolution was only a link in the international revolution. Such was, in broad outline, the essence of the conception of the permanent (uninterrupted) revolution. It was precisely this conception that guaranteed the victory of the proletariat in October.

But such is the bitter irony of history: the experience of the Russian Revolution not only did not help the Chinese proletariat but, on the contrary, it became in its reactionary, distorted form, one of the chief obstacles in its path. The Comintern of the epigones began by canonizing for all countries of the Orient the formula of the "democratic dictatorship of the proletariat and peasantry" which Lenin, influenced by historical experience, had acknowledged to be without value. As always in history, a formula that had outlived itself served to cover a political content which was the direct opposite of that which the formula had served in its day. The mass plebeian, revolutionary alliance of the workers and peasants, sealed through the freely elected Soviets as the direct organs of action, the Comintern replaced by a bureaucratic bloc of party centres. The right to represent the peasantry in this bloc was unexpectedly given to the Kuomintang, i.e., a thoroughly bourgeois party vitally interested in the preservation of capitalist property, not only in the means of production but in land. The alliance of the proletariat and the peasantry was broadened into a "bloc of four classes"; workers, peasants, urban petty bourgeoisie, and the so-called "national" bourgeoisie. In other words, the Comintern picked up a formula discarded by Lenin only in order to open the road to the politics of Plekhanov and, moreover, in a masked and therefore more harmful form.

To justify the political subordination of the proletariat to the bourgeoisie, the theoreticians of the Comintern (Stalin, Bukharin) adduced the fact of imperialist oppression which supposedly impelled "all the progressive forces in the country" to an alliance. But this was precisely in its day the argument of the Russian Mensheviks, with the difference that in their case the place of imperialism was occupied by Czarism. In reality, the subjection of the Chinese Communist Party to the Kuomintang signified its break with the mass movement and a direct betrayal of its historical interests. In this way the catastrophe of the second Chinese Revolution was prepared under the direct leadership of Moscow.

Significance of Russian Marxism

To many political philistines who in politics are inclined to substitute "common sense" guesses for scientific analysis, the controversy among the Russian Marxists over the nature of the revolution and the dynamics of its class forces seemed to be sheer scholasticism. Historical experience revealed, however, the profoundly vital significance of the "doctrinaire formulas" of Russian Marxism. Those who have not understood this up to today can learn a great deal from Isaacs' book. The politics of the Communist International in China showed convincingly what the Russian Revolution would have been converted into if the Mensheviks and the Social Revolutionaries had not been thrust aside in time by the Bolsheviks. In China the conception of the permanent revolution was confirmed once more, this time not in the form of a victory, but of a catastrophe.

It would, of course, be impermissible to identify Russia and China. With all their important common traits, the differences are all too obvious. But it is not hard to convince oneself that these differences do not weaken but, on the contrary, strengthen the fundamental conclusions of Bolshevism. In one sense Czarist Russia was also a colonial country, and this found its expression in the predominant role of foreign capital. But the Russian bourgeoisie enjoyed the benefits of an immeasurably greater independence from foreign imperialism than the Chinese bourgeoisie. Russia itself was an imperialist country. With all its meagreness, Russian liberalism had far more serious traditions and more of a basis of support than the Chinese. To the left of the liberals stood powerful petty bourgeois parties, revolutionary or semi-revolutionary in relation to Czarism. The party of the Social Revolutionaries managed to find considerable support among the peasantry, chiefly from its upper layers. The Social Democratic (Menshevik) Party led behind it broad circles of the urban petty bourgeoisie and labour aristocracy. It was precisely these three parties—the Liberals, the Social Revolutionaries, and the Mensheviks—who for a long time prepared, and in 1917 definitely formed, a coalition which was not yet then called the People's Front but which had all of its traits. In contrast to this the Bolsheviks, from the eve of the revolution in 1905, took up an irreconcilable position in relation to the liberal bourgeoisie. Only this policy, which achieved its highest expression in the "defeatism" of 1914–1917, enabled the Bolshevik Party to conquer power.

The differences between China and Russia, the incomparably greater dependence of the Chinese bourgeoisie on foreign capital, the absence of independent revolutionary traditions among the petty bourgeoisie, the mass gravitation of the workers and peasants to the banner of the Comintern—demanded a still more irreconciliable policy—if such were possible, than that pursued in Russia. Yet the Chinese section of the Comintern, at Moscow's command, renounced Marxism, accepted the reactionary scholastic "principles of Sun Yat-Sen", and entered the ranks of the Kuomintang, submitting to its discipline. In other words, it went much further along the road of submission to the bourgeoisie than the Russian Mensheviks or Social Revolutionaries ever did. The same fatal policy is now being repeated in the conditions of the war with Japan.

New Methods of Bureaucracy

How could the bureaucracy emerging from the Bolshevik Revolution apply in China, as throughout the world, methods fundamentally opposed to those of Bolshevism? It would be far too superficial to answer this question with a reference to the incapacity or ignorance of this or that individual. The gist of the matter lies in this: together with the new conditions of existence the bureaucracy acquired new methods of thinking. The Bolshevik Party led the masses. The bureaucracy began to order them about. The Bolsheviks won the possibility of leadership by correctly expressing the interests of the masses. The bureaucracy was compelled to resort to command in order to secure its own interests against those of the masses. The method of command was naturally extended to the Communist International as well. The Moscow leaders began quite seriously to imagine that they could compel the Chinese bourgeoisie to move to the left of its interests and the Chinese workers and peasants to the right of theirs, along the diagonals drawn in the Kremlin. Yet it is the very essence of revolution that the exploited as well as the exploiters invest their interests with the most extreme expression. If hostile classes would move along diagonals, there would be no need for a civil war. Armed by the authority of the October Revolution and the Communist International, not to mention inexhaustible financial resources, the bureaucracy transformed the young Chinese Communist Party from a motive force into a brake at the most important moment of the revolution. In contrast to Germany and Austria, where the bureaucracy could shift part of the responsibility for defeat to the Social Democracy, there was no Social Democracy in China. The Comintern had the monopoly in ruining the Chinese Revolution.

The present domination of the Kuomintang over a

considerable section of Chinese territory would have been impossible without the powerful national revolutionary movement of the masses in 1925–1927. The massacre of this movement on the one hand concentrated power in the hands of Chiang Kai-shek, and on the other doomed Chiang Kai-shek to half-measures in the struggle against imperialism. The understanding of the course of the Chinese Revolution has in this way the most direct significance for an understanding of the course of the Sino–Japanese war. This historical work acquires thereby the most actual political significance.

War and revolution will be interlaced in the nearest future history of China. Japan's aim, to enslave forever, or at least for a long time to come, a gigantic country by dominating its strategic centres, is characterized not only by greediness but by wooden-headedness. Japan has arrived much too late. Torn by internal contradictions, the empire of the Mikado cannot reproduce the history of Britain's ascent. On the other hand, China has advanced far beyond the India of the seventeenth and eighteenth centuries. Old colonial countries are nowadays waging with ever greater success a struggle for their national independence. In these historic conditions, even if the present war in the Far East were to end with Japan's victory, and even if the victor himself could escape an internal catastrophe during the next few years—and neither the former nor the latter is in the least assured—Japan's domination over China would be measured by a very brief period, perhaps only the few years required to give a new impulse to the economic life of China and to mobilize its laboring masses once more.

The big Japanese trusts and concerns are already following in the wake of the army to divide the still unsecured booty. The Tokyo Government is seeking to regulate the appetites of the financial cliques that would tear North China to pieces. If Japan were to succeed in maintaining its conquered positions for an interval of some ten years, this would mean, above all, the intensive industrialization of North China in the military interests of Japanese imperialism. New railways, mines, power stations, mining and metallurgical enterprises, and cotton plantations would rapidly spring up. The polarization of the

Chinese nation would receive a feverish impulse. New hundreds of thousands and millions of Chinese proletarians would be mobilized in the briefest possible space of time. On the other hand, the Chinese bourgeoisie would fall into an ever greater dependence on Japanese capital. Even less than in the past would it be capable of standing at the head of a national war, no less a national revolution. Face to face with the foreign violator would stand the numerically larger, socially strengthened, politically matured Chinese proletariat, called to lead the Chinese village. Hatred of the foreign enslaver is a mighty revolutionary cement. The new national revolution will, one must think, be placed on the agenda still in the lifetime of the present generation. To solve the tasks imposed upon it, the vanguard of the Chinese proletariat must thoroughly assimilate the lessons of the Chinese Revolution. Isaacs' book can serve it in this sense as an irreplaceable aid. It remains to be hoped that the book will be translated into Chinese as well as other foreign languages.

Coyoacan, D.F., 1938

59

The Great Lesson of China*

May 1940

The tragic experience of China is a great lesson for the oppressed peoples. The Chinese Revolution of 1925–27 had every chance for victory. A unified and transformed China would constitute at this time a powerful fortress of freedom in the Far East. The entire fate of Asia and to a degree the whole world might have been different. But the Kremlin, lacking confidence in the Chinese masses and seeking the friendship of the generals, utilized its whole weight to subordinate the Chinese proletariat to the bourgeoisie and so helped Chiang Kai-shek to crush the Chinese Revolution. Disillusioned, disunited, and weakened, China was laid open to Japanese invasion.

Like every doomed regime, the Stalinist oligarchy is already incapable of learning from the lessons of history. At the beginning of the Sino–Japanese War, the Kremlin again placed the Communist Party in bondage to Chiang Kai-shek, crushing in the bud the revolutionary initiative of the Chinese proletariat. This war, now nearing its third anniversary, might long since have been finished by a real catastrophe for Japan, if China had conducted it as a genuine people's war based on an agrarian revolution and setting the Japanese soldiery aflame with its blaze. But the Chinese bourgeoisie fears its own armed masses more than it does the Japanese ravishers. If Chiang Kai-shek,

---

* Excerpted from *"Manifesto of the Fourth International on the Imperialist War and the Proletarian World Revolution,"* in Writings of Leon Trotsky (1939–40).

the sinister hangman of the Chinese revolution, is compelled by circumstances to wage a war, his program is still based, as before, on the oppression of his own workers and compromise with the imperialists.

The war in eastern Asia will become more and more interlocked with the imperialist world war. The Chinese people will be able to reach independence only under the leadership of the youthful and self-sacrificing proletariat, in whom the indispensable self-confidence will be rekindled by the rebirth of the world revolution. They will indicate a firm line of march. The course of events places on the order of the day the development of our Chinese section into a powerful revolutionary party.

60

China and the Russian Revolution

July 1940

The day I learned that my *History of the Russian Revolution* was to be published in the Chinese language was a holiday for me. Now I have received word that the work of the translation has been speeded up and that the first volume will be issued next year.

Let me express the firm hope that the book will prove profitable to Chinese readers. Whatever may be the shortcomings of my work, one thing I can say with assurance: Facts are there presented with complete conscientiousness, that is, on the basis of verification with original sources; and in any case, not a single fact is altered or distorted in the interests of this or that preconceived theory or, what is worse yet, in the interests of this or that personal reputation.

The misfortune of the present young generation in all countries, among them China, consists in this: that there has been created under the label of Marxism a gigantic factory of historical, theoretical, and all other kinds of falsifications. This factory bears the name "Communist International". The totalitarian regime, i.e., the regime of bureaucratic command in all spheres of life, inescapably seeks to extend its rule also over the past. History becomes transformed into raw material for whatever constructions are required by the ruling totalitarian clique. This fate was suffered by the October Revolution and by the history of the Bolshevik party. The latest and to date most finished document of falsification and frame-up is the *History of the Communist Party of the Soviet Union*, issued some time ago under the personal direction of Stalin. In the entire library of mankind I do not know, and hardly anyone else knows, of a book in which facts, documents—and furthermore facts known to everyone—are so dishonestly altered, mangled, or simply deleted from the march of events in the interests of glorifying a single human being, namely Stalin.

Thanks to the unlimited material resources at the disposal of the falsifiers, the rude and untalented falsification has been translated into all the languages of civilized mankind and circulated by compulsion in millions and tens of millions of copies.

We have at our disposal neither such financial resources nor such a colossal apparatus. But we do dispose of something greater: concern for historical truth and a correct scientific method. A falsification, even one compiled by a mighty state apparatus, cannot withstand the test of time and in the long run is blown up because of its internal contradictions. On the contrary, historical truth, established through a scientific method, has its own internal persuasiveness and in the long run gains mastery over minds. The very necessity of reviewing, i.e., recasting and altering—still more precisely, falsifying—the history of the revolution, arose from this: that the bureaucracy found itself compelled to sever the umbilical cord binding it to the Bolshevik party. To recast, i.e., to falsify the history of the revolution, became an urgent necessity for the bureaucracy which usurped the revolution and found itself compelled to cut short the tradition of Bolshevism.

The essence of Bolshevism was the class policy of the proletariat, which alone would bring about the conquest of power in October. In the course of its entire history, Bolshevism came out irreconcilably against the policy of collaboration with the bourgeoisie. Precisely in this consisted the fundamental contradiction between Bolshevism and Menshevism. Still more, the struggle within the labor movement, which preceded the rise of Bolshevism and Menshevism, always in the last analysis revolved around the central question, the central alternative: either collaboration with the bourgeoisie or irreconcilable class struggle. The policy of "People's Fronts" does not include an iota of novelty, if we discount the solemn and essentially charlatan name. The matter at issue in all cases concerns the political subordination of the proletariat to the left wing of the exploiters, regardless of whether this practice bears the name of coalition or Left Bloc (as in France) or "People's Front" in the language of the Comintern.

The policy of the "People's Front" bore especially malignant fruit because it was applied in the epoch of the imperialist decay of the bourgeoisie. Stalin succeeded in conducting to the end, in the Chinese Revolution, the policy which the Mensheviks tried to realize in the revolution of 1917. The same thing was repeated in Spain. Two grandiose revolutions suffered catastrophe owing to this: that the methods of the leadership were the methods of Stalinism, i.e., the most malignant form of Menshevism.

In the course of five years, the policy of the "People's Front", by subjecting the proletariat to the bourgeoisie, made impossible the class struggle against war. If the defeat of the Chinese Revolution, conditioned by the leadership of the Comintern, prepared the conditions for Japanese occupation, then the defeat of the Spanish revolution and the ignominious capitulation of the "People's Front" in France prepared the conditions for the aggression and unprecedented military successes of Hitler.

The victories of Japan, like the victories of Hitler, are not the last word of history. War this time, too, will turn out to be the mother of revolution. Revolution will once again pose and review all the questions of the history of mankind in advanced as well as in backward countries, and make a beginning for overcoming the very distinction between advanced and backward countries.

Reformists, opportunists, routinists will be flung aside by the course of events. Only revolutionists, tempered revolutionists enriched by the experience of the past, will be able to rise to the level of great events. The Chinese people are destined to occupy the first place in the future destinies of mankind. I shall be happy if the advanced Chinese revolutionists will assimilate from this history certain fundamental rules of class politics which will help them to avoid fatal mistakes in the future, mistakes that led to the shipwreck of the revolution of 1925–27.

APPENDIX

Appeal to all Comrades of the Chinese Communist Party

December 10, 1929
Chen Tu Shiu

Dear Comrades,
Since 1920 (the ninth year of the republic) I have worked with the comrades, in founding the party, in sincerely carrying out the opportunist policy of the International's leaders, Stalin, Zinoviev, Bukharin, and others bringing the Chinese Revolution to a shameful and sad defeat. Though I have worked night and day, yet my demerits exceed my merits.

Of course, I should not imitate the hypocritical confessions of some of the ancient Chinese emperors: "I, one person, am responsible for all the sins of the people"; take upon my own shoulders all the mistakes that caused the failure. Nevertheless I feel ashamed to adopt the attitude of some responsible comrades at times—only criticizing the past mistakes of opportunism and excluding oneself. Whenever my comrades have pointed out my past opportunist errors, I earnestly acknowledged them. I am absolutely unwilling to ignore the experiences of the Chinese revolution obtained at the highest price paid by proletarians in the past. (From the August 7 Conference [1927] to the present time, I not only did not reject proper criticism against me, but I even kept silent about the exaggerated accusations against me.)

Not only am I willing to acknowledge my past errors, but now or in the future, if I should make any opportunist errors in thought or action, I likewise expect comrades to criticize me mercilessly with theoretical argument and fact. I humbly accept or shall accept all criticism, but not rumors and false accusations. I cannot have such self-confidence as Ch'u Ch'iu-pai and Li Li-san. I clearly recognize that it is never an easy thing for anybody or any party to avoid the errors of opportunism. Even such veteran Marxists as Kautsky and Plekhanov were guilty of unpardonable opportunism when they were old; those who followed Lenin for a long time like Stalin and Bukharin are now also acting like shameful opportunists. How can superficial Marxists like us be self-satisfied? Whenever a man is self-satisfied, he prevents himself from making progress.

Even the banner of the Opposition is not the incantation of the "Heavenly Teacher" Chang [the Taoist pope]. If those who have not fundamentally cleared out the ideology of the petty bourgeoisie, and have not plainly understood the system of past opportunism, and decisively participated in struggles, merely stand under the banner of the Opposition to revile the opportunism of Stalin and Li Li-san, and then think that the opportunist devils will never approach, they are suffering from an illusion. The only way of avoiding the errors of opportunism is continually and humbly to learn from the teachings of Marx and Lenin in the struggles of the proletarian masses and in the mutual criticism of comrades.

I decisively recognize that the objective conditions were second in importance as the cause of the failure of the last Chinese Revolution. The main cause was the error of opportunism, the error of our policy in dealing with the bourgeois Kuomintang. All the responsible comrades of the Central Committee at that time, especially myself, should openly and courageously recognize that this policy was undoubtedly wrong. But it is not enough merely to recognize the error. We must sincerely and thoroughly acknowledge that the past error was the internal content of the policy of opportunism examine the causes and results of that policy, and reveal them clearly. Then we can hope to stop repeating the errors of the past, and the repetition of former opportunism in the next revolution. When our party was first founded, though it was quite young, yet, under the guidance of the Leninist International, we did not commit any great mistakes. For instance, we decisively led the struggle of the workers and recognized the class nature of the Kuomintang. In 1921, our party induced the delegates of the Kuomintang and other social organizations to participate in the conference of the Toilers of the Far East, which was called by the Comintern. The conference resolved that in the colonial countries of the East the struggle for the democratic revolution must be carried out, and that in this revolution peasant soviets should be organized.

In 1922, at the Second Congress of the Chinese party, the policy of the united front in the democratic revolution was adopted, and based upon this we expressed our attitude toward the political situation. At the same time, the representative of the Communist Youth International, Dalin, came to China and suggested to the Kuomintang the policy of a united front of the revolutionary groups. The head of the Kuomintang, Sun Yat-sen, stubbornly rejected this, agreeing only to allow the members of the Chinese Communist Party and the Youth League to join the Kuomintang as individuals and obey it, denying any unity outside of the party.

Soon after the adjournment of our party congress the Communist International sent its delegate Maring to China. He invited all the members of the Central Committee of the Chinese Communist Party to hold a meeting at the West Lake in Hangchow, in Chekiang province, at which he suggested to the Chinese party that it join the Kuomintang organization. He strongly contended that the Kuomintang was not a party of the bourgeoisie but the joint party of various classes and that the proletarian party should join it in order to improve this party and advance the revolution.

At that time, the five members of the Central Committee of the CCP-Li Shou-ch'ang, Chang T'e-li, Ts'ai Ho-sen, Kao Chu-n-yu, and I—unanimously opposed the proposal. The chief reason was: To join the Kuomintang was to confuse the class organizations and curb our independent policy. Finally, the delegate of the Third International asked if the Chinese party would obey the decision of the International.

Thereupon, for the sake of respecting international discipline the Central Committee of the CCP could not but accept the proposal of the Communist International and agree to join the Kuomintang. After this, the international delegate and the representatives of the Chinese party spent nearly a year in carrying out the reorganization of the Kuomintang. But from the very outset the Kuomintang entirely neglected and resisted it. Many times Sun Yat-sen said to the delegates of the International: "Since the Chinese CP has joined the Kuomintang, it should obey the discipline of the KMT and should not openly criticize it. If the communists do not obey the Kuomintang I shall expel them from it; if Soviet Russia stands on the side of the CCP I shall immediately oppose Soviet Russia." As a result, a dejected Maring returned to Moscow. Borodin, who took over Maring's post in China, brought with him a large sum of material aid for the Kuomintang. It was then, in 1924, that the KMT began the policy of reorganization and alliance with Soviet Russia.

At this time the Chinese communists were not very much tainted with opportunism. We were able to lead the railroad workers' strike on February 7, 1923, and the May Thirtieth Movement of 1925, since we were not restrained by the KMT and at times severely criticized its compromising policy. But as soon as the proletariat raised its head in the May Thirtieth Movement, the bourgeoisie was immediately aroused. In response, Tai Chi-t'ao's anti-Communist pamphlet appeared in July.

At the enlarged plenum of the Central Committee of the CCP held in Peking in October of 1925, I submitted the following proposal to the Political Resolution Committee: Tai Chi-t'ao's pamphlet was not accidental but the indication that the bourgeoisie was attempting to strengthen its own power for the purpose of checking the proletariat and going over to the counterrevolution. We should be ready immediately to withdraw from the Kuomintang. We should maintain our [public] political face, lead the masses, and not be held in check by the policy of the Kuomintang.

At that time both the delegate of the Comintern and the responsible comrades of the Central Committee unanimously opposed my suggestion, saying that it was to propose to the comrades and the masses to take the path of opposing the Kuomintang. I, who had no decisiveness of character, could not insistently maintain my proposal. I respected international discipline and the opinion of the majority of the Central Committee.

Chiang Kai-shek's coup d'etat on March 20, 1926, was made to carry out Tai Chi-t'ao's principles. Having arrested the communists in large numbers, disarmed the Canton-Hong Kong Strike Committee's guards for the visiting Soviet group (most of whom were members of the Central Committee of the AUCP) and for the Soviet advisers, the Central Committee of the Kuomintang decided that all communist elements should be removed from the supreme party headquarters of the KMT, that criticism of Sun-Yat-senism by communists be prohibited, and that a list of the names of the members of the Communist Party and of the [Youth] League who had joined the KMT should be handed over to the latter. All these conditions were accepted.

At the same time we resolved to prepare our independent military forces in order to be equal to the forces of Chiang Kai-shek. Comrade P'eng Shu-chih was sent to Canton as representative of the Central Committee of the Chinese party to consult the international delegate about our plan. But the latter did not agree with us, and tried his best to continually strengthen Chiang Kai- shek. He insistently advocated that we use all our strength to support the military dictatorship of Chiang Kai-shek, to build up (the Canton government, and to carry on the Northern Expedition. We demanded that he take 5,000 rifles out of those given to Chiang Kai-shek and Li Chi-shen, so that we might arm the peasants of Kwangtung province. He refused, saying:

"The armed peasants cannot fight against the forces of Ch'en Chiung-ming nor take part in the Northern Expedition, but they can incur the suspicion of the Kuomintang and make the peasants oppose it."

This was the most critical period. Concretely speaking it was the period when the bourgeois KMT openly compelled the proletariat to follow its guidance and direction, when we formally called on the proletariat to surrender to the bourgeoisie, to follow it, and be willing to be subordinates of the bourgeoisie. (The international delegates said openly: "The present period is a period in which the communists should do the coolie service for the Kuomintang.") By this time the party was already not the party of the proletariat, having become completely the extreme left wing of the bourgeoisie, and beginning to fall into the deep pit of opportunism.

After the coup of March 20, I stated in a report to the Comintern my personal opinion that cooperation with the Kuomintang by means of joint work within it should be changed to cooperation outside the KMT. Otherwise, we would be unable to carry out our own independent policy or win the confidence of the masses. After having read my report, the International published an article by Bukharin in *Pravda* severely criticizing the Chinese party on [the question of] withdrawing from the Kuomintang, saying:

"There have been two mistakes: the advocacy of withdrawal from the yellow trade unions and from the Anglo-Russian Trade Union Unity Committee; now the third mistake has been produced: the Chinese party advocates withdrawal from the Kuomintang." At the same time, the head of the Far Eastern Bureau, Voitinsky, was sent to China to correct our tendency to withdraw from the KMT. At that time, I again failed to maintain my proposal strongly, for the sake of honoring the discipline of the International and the opinion of the majority of the members of the Central Committee.

Later on, the Northern Expedition army set out. We were very much persecuted by the KMT because in Hsiang-tao we criticized the curbing of the labor movement in the rear, and the compulsory collection of the military fund from the peasants for the use of the Northern Expedition. In the meantime the workers in Shanghai were about to rise up to oust the Chihli-Shantung troops. If the uprisings were successful, the problem of the ruling power would be posed. At that time, in the minutes of the [discussion of the] political resolution of the enlarged plenum of the Central Committee I suggested:

The Chinese Revolution has two roads: One is that it be led by the proletariat, then we can reach the goal of the revolution; the other is that it be led by the bourgeoisie, and in that case the latter must betray in the course of the revolution. And though we may cooperate with the bourgeoisie at the present, we must nevertheless seize the leading power. However, all the members of the Far Eastern Bureau of the Comintern residing in Shanghai unanimously opposed my opinion, saying that such an opinion would influence our comrades to oppose the bourgeoisie too early. Further, they declared, if the Shanghai uprising succeeds, the ruling power should belong to the bourgeoisie and that it was unnecessary to have any participation by workers' delegates. At that time, I again could not maintain my opinion because of their criticism.

About the time the Northern Expedition army took Shanghai in 1927, [Ch'u] Ch'iu-pai paid great attention to the selection of the Shanghai municipal government and how to unite the petty bourgeoisie (the middle and small traders) in opposition to the big bourgeoisie. P'eng Shu-chih and Lo-nung were in agreement with my opinion, that the immediate problem was not the municipal elections. The central problem was that if the proletariat was not strong enough to win a victory over Chiang Kai-shek's military forces the petty bourgeoisie would not support us. Chiang Kai-shek, at the instigation of the imperialists, would be certain to carry out a massacre of the masses. Then not only would the municipal elections be reduced to empty talk, but we would face the beginning of a defeat throughout China. When Chiang Kai-shek openly betrayed the revolution it could not be just an individual action but would be the signal for the bourgeoisie in the whole country to go over to the reactionary camp.

At that time [P'eng] Shu-chih went to Hankow to state our opinion before the international delegate and the majority of the members of the Central Committee of the Chinese Communist Party and to consult with them on how to attack Chiang Kai- shek's forces. But they did not care very much about the impending coup in Shanghai. They telegraphed to me several times urging me to go to Wuhan. They thought that since the Nationalist government was then at Wuhan, all important problems should be solved there. At the same time, the International telegraphed to us instructing us to hide or bury all the workers' weapons to avoid a military conflict between the workers and Chiang Kai-shek, in order not to disturb the occupation of Shanghai by the armed forces. Having read this telegram, Lo-nung became very angry, and threw it on the floor. At that time I again obeyed the order of the International and could not maintain my own opinion. Based upon the policy of the International toward the Kuomintang and the imperialists, I issued a shameful manifesto with Wang Ching-wei.

At the beginning of April I went to Wuhan. When I first

met Wang Ching-wei, I heard some reactionary things from him, far different from what he had said while in Shanghai. I told this to Borodin; he said that my observations were right and that as soon as Wang Ching-wei reached Wuhan he was surrounded by Hsu Ch'ien, Ku Meng-yti, Ch'en Kung-po, T'an Yen-k'ai, and others, and became gradually colder. After Chiang Kai-shek and Li Chi-shen began their massacre of the workers and peasants, the [Wuhan] Kuomintang came to hate the power of the proletariat more every day, and the reactionary attitude of Wang Ching-wei and of the Central Committee of the Kuomintang rapidly hardened. At the meeting of our Political Bureau, I made a report on the status of the joint meeting of our party and of the Kuomintang:

"The danger involved in cooperation between our party and the Kuomintang is more and more serious. What they tried to seize on seemed to be this or that small problem; what they really wanted was the whole of the central power. Now there are only two roads before us: either to give up the authority of leadership or to break with them."

Those attending the meeting answered my report with silence. After the coup [May 21 at Changsha] in Hunan province, I twice suggested withdrawal from the Kuomintang. Finally, I said: "The Wuhan Kuomintang has followed in the footsteps of Chiang Kai-shek! If we do not change our policy, we too will end up on the same road."

At that time only Jen Pi-shih said, "That is so!" Chou EnLai said, "After we withdraw from the Kuomintang the labor and peasant movement will be freer but the military movement will suffer too much." All the rest still answered my suggestion with silence. At the same time I discussed this with [Ch'u] Ch'iu.pai. He said: "We should let the Kuomintang expel us; we cannot withdraw by ourselves." I consulted Borodin. He said: "I quite agree with your idea but I know that Moscow will never permit it."

At that time I once more observed the discipline of the International and the opinion of the majority of the Central Committee and was unable to maintain my own opinion. From the beginning I could not persistently maintain my opinion; but this time I could no longer bear it. I then tendered my resignation to the Central Committee. My chief reason for this was:

"The International wishes us to carry out our own policy, on the one hand, and does not allow us to withdraw from the Kuomintang on the other. There is really no way out and I cannot continue with my work."

From the beginning to the end, the International recognized the Kuomintang as the main body of the Chinese national democratic revolution. In Stalin's mouth, the words "leadership of the Kuomintang" were shouted very loudly (see "The Errors of the Opposition" in "Questions of the Chinese Revolution"). So it wished us throughout to surrender in the organization of the Kuomintang and to lead the masses under the name and the banner of the Kuomintang. This was continued up to the time when the whole Kuomintang of Feng Yu-hsiang, Wang Ching-wei, T'ang Sheng-chih, Ho Chien, etc., became openly reactionary and abolished the so-called three-point policy: to unite with the Soviet Union. to allow the CP to join the Kuomintang, and to help the labor and peasant movement. The International instructed us by telegram: "Only withdraw from the Kuomintang government, not from the Kuomintang."

So, after the August 7 Conference, from the Nanchang uprising to the capture of Swatow, the Communist Party still hid behind the blue-white banner of the left clique of the Kuomintang. To the masses it seemed that there was trouble within the Kuomintang, but nothing more. The young Chinese Communist Party, produced by the young Chinese proletariat, had not had a proper period of training in Marxism and class struggles. Shortly after the founding of the party, it was confronted by a great revolutionary struggle. The only hope of avoiding a very grave error was correct guidance by the proletarian policy of the International. But under the guidance of such a consistently opportunist policy how could the Chinese proletariat and the Communist Party clearly see their own future? And how could they have their own independent policy? They only surrendered to the bourgeoisie step by step and subordinated themselves to the bourgeoisie. So when the latter suddenly massacred us we did not know what to do about it. After the coup in Changsha, the policy given to us by the International was:

1. Confiscate the land of the landowners from the lower strata, but not in the name of the Nationalist government, and

do not touch the land of military officers. (There was not a single one of the bourgeoisie, landlords, tuchtins, and gentry of Hunan and Hupeh provinces who was not the kinsman, relative, or old friend of the officers of that time. All the landowners were directly or indirectly protected by the officers. To confiscate the land is only empty words if it is conditioned by "do not touch the land of the military officers.")

2. Restrain the peasants' "over-zealous" actions with the power of the party headquarters. (We did execute this shameful policy of checking the peasants' over-zealous actions; afterward the International criticized the Chinese party for having "often become an obstacle to the masses" and considered it as one of the greatest opportunist errors.)

3. Destroy the present unreliable generals, arm twenty thousand communists, and select fifty thousand worker and peasant elements from Hunan and Hupeh provinces for organizing a new army. (If we could get so many rifles, why should we not directly arm the workers and peasants and why should we still recruit new troops for the Kuomintang? Why couldn't we establish soviets of workers, peasants, and soldiers? If there were neither armed workers and peasants nor soviets, how and with whom could we destroy the said unreliable generals? I suppose that we could have continued to pitifully beg the Central Committee of the Kuomintang to discharge them. When the Comintern representative Roy showed Wang Ching-wei these instructions from the International it was, of course, for this purpose.'

4. Put new worker elements into the Central Committee of the Kuomintang to take the place of old members. (If we had the power to deal freely with the old committee and reorganize the Kuomintang, why could we not organize soviets? Why must we send our worker and peasant leaders to the bourgeois Kuomintang, which has already been massacring the workers and peasants? And why should we decorate such a Kuomintang with our leaders?)

5. Organize a revolutionary court with a well-known member of the Kuomintang (one who is not a member of the CCP) as its chairman, in order to judge the reactionary officers. (How can an already reactionary leader of the Kuomintang judge the reactionary officers in the revolutionary court?)

Those who attempted to implement such a policy within the Kuomintang were still opportunists, of a left stripe. There was no change at all in the fundamental policy; it was like taking a bath in a urinal vessel! At that time, if we wanted to carry out a genuinely left, that is, a revolutionary, policy, the fundamental line had to be changed. The Communist Party had to withdraw from the Kuomintang and be really independent. It had to arm the workers and peasants, as many as possible, establish soviets of workers, peasants, and soldiers, and seize the leading power from the Kuomintang. Otherwise, no matter what kind of left policy was adopted, there was no way to realize it.

At that time the Central Political Bureau wired to the Communist International in answer to its instructions: We accept the instructions and will work according to their directions, but they cannot be realized immediately. All the members of the Central Committee recognized that the International's instructions were impractical. Even Fan K'e, a participant in the Central Committee meeting (it was said that he was Stalin's private deputy), also thought that there was no possibility of carrying them out. He agreed with the telegraphic answer of the Central Committee, saying: "This is the best reply we can give".

After the August 7 Conference, the Central Committee tried to propagate the idea that the Chinese Revolution had failed because the opportunists did not accept the Communist International's instructions to immediately change tactics. (Of course, the instructions were the above mentioned ones; besides these, there were no instructions!) We did not know: How could the policy be changed from inside the Kuomintang? And who were the so-called opportunists?

Once the party had committed such a fundamental error, a continual series of other smaller or larger subordinate errors were naturally inevitable. I, whose perception was not clear, whose opinion was not decisive, became immersed in the atmosphere of opportunism and sincerely carried out the opportunist policy of the Third International. I unconsciously became the tool of the narrow faction of Stalin. I could not save the party and the revolution. All this, both I and other comrades should be held responsible for. The present Central Committee says: "You attempt to place the failure of the Chinese revolution on the shoulders of the Comintern in order that you might throw off your own responsibility!" This statement is ridiculous. One does not permanently lose his right to criticize the opportunism of the party leadership, or to return to Marxism and Leninism because he has himself committed opportunist errors.

At the same time, nobody can take the liberty of avoiding his responsibility for executing an opportunist policy because the opportunism originated in high places. The source of the opportunist policy is the Comintern; but why did not the leaders of the Chinese party protest against the Comintern, and instead loyally carry out its policies? Who can absolve us of this responsibility? We should very frankly and objectively recognize that all the past and present opportunist policies originated in the Communist International. The International should bear the responsibility. The young Chinese party has not yet the ability of itself to invent any theories and settle any policy; but the leading organ of the Chinese party ought to bear the responsibility for blindly implementing the opportunist policy of the Comintern without a little bit of judgment and protest.

If we mutually excuse each other and all of us think that we have committed no mistakes, was it then the error of the masses? This is not only too ridiculous but also does not assume any responsibility toward the revolution! I strongly believe that if I, or other responsible comrades, could at that time have clearly recognized the falsity of the opportunist policy and made a strong argument against it, even to the point of mobilizing the entire party for a passionate discussion and debate, as Comrade Trotsky has been doing, the result would inevitably have been a great help to the revolution. It would not have made the revolution such a shameful failure, though I might have been expelled from the Communist International and a split in the party might have taken place. I, whose perception was not clear and whose opinion was not resolute, did not do so after all! If the party were to base itself on such past mistakes of mine or on the fact that I strongly maintained the former erroneous line, as grounds for giving me some severe punishment, I would earnestly accept it without uttering a word.

But these are the reasons given by the present Central Committee for expelling me from the party:

1. They said: "Fundamentally, he is not sincere in recognizing his own error of opportunist leadership in the period of the great revolution, and has not decided to recognize where his real past error lies, so it is inevitable that he will continue his past erroneous line." In reality, I was expelled because I sincerely recognized where the error of the former opportunist leadership lay, and decided to oppose the present and future continuation of wrong lines.

2. They said: "He is not satisfied with the decisions of the Communist International. He is obdurately unwilling to go to Moscow to be trained by the International." I have been trained enough by the Communist International. Formerly, I made many mistakes because I accepted the opinions of the Third International. Now I have been expelled because I am not satisfied with those opinions.

3. Last August 5, I wrote a letter to the Central Committee in which there were the following sentences: "Besides, what is the continuing fundamental contradiction of 'economic class interests' between these two classes [the bourgeoisie and the landlords]?!" "Before and after the Canton uprising. . . .I wrote several letters to the Central Committee pointing out that the ruling power of the Kuomintang would not collapse as quickly as you estimated." "At present, though there are some mass struggles it is not enough to take them as the symptoms of the coming revolutionary wave." "The wholly legal movement, of course, is an abandonment of the attempt at revolution. But under certain circumstances, when it is necessary to build up our strength, as Lenin said, 'except in eruptions of a white-hot intensity, we should also make use of all possible legal measures in this (transitional) period.'"

The Central Committee changed these sentences to read ambiguously:

"There is no contradiction between the bourgeoisie and the feudal forces." "The present ruling class is not going to be overthrown and the revolutionary struggle is not beginning to revive but is declining more and more." He advocates "the adoption of legal forms".

Furthermore, they put quotation marks around each

sentence so as to make them seem like my original statements. This is another reason for my expulsion.

4. I wrote another letter to the Central Committee on October 10 saying: "The present period is not a period of the revolutionary wave, but a period of counter-revolution. We should elaborate democratic slogans as our general demands. For instance, besides the eight-hour-day demand and the confiscation of land, we should issue the slogans 'Nullify the unequal treaties,' 'Against the military dictatorship of the Kuomintang,' 'Convoke the national assembly,' etc., etc. It is necessary to bring the broad masses into activity under these democratic slogans; then we can shake the counterrevolutionary regime, go forward to the revolutionary wave, and make our fundamental slogans—'Down with the Kuomintang government,' 'Establish the soviet regime,' etc.—the slogans of action in the mass movement."

On October 26, Comrade P'eng Shu-chih and I wrote a letter to the CC saying: "This is not the transitional period to direct revolution, and we must have general political slogans adapted to this period; then we can win the masses. The workers' and peasants' soviets is merely a propaganda slogan at present. If we take the struggle to organize soviets as a slogan of action, we will certainly get no response from the proletariat." But the CC claimed that in place of the slogans "Down with the Kuomintang government" and "Establish the soviet regime" we wish to substitute as the present general political slogan the demand "Convoke the national assembly". This is also one of the reasons for my expulsion.

5. I said in a letter that we should point out "the policy of treason or spoliation of the country by the Kuomintang in the handling of the Chinese Eastern Railroad", making the "broad masses still imbued with nationalist spirit able to sympathize with us and oppose the maneuver of the imperialists to attack the Soviet Union by utilizing the Kuomintang and making the Chinese Eastern Railroad problem an excuse". This was to help the slogan of defense of the USSR penetrate the masses. But the CC said I wanted to issue the slogan of opposing the spoliation of the country by the Kuomintang in place of the slogan of supporting the USSR. This is another reason why I was expelled.

6. I wrote the CC several letters dealing with the serious

political problems within the party. The CC kept them from the party for a long time. Further, the delegates of the Comintern and the CC told me plainly that the principle is that different political opinions cannot be expressed in the party. Because there is no hope of correcting the mistakes of the Central Committee by means of a legal comradely discussion, I hold that I should not be bound by the routine discipline of the organization, and still less should comrades be prevented from passing my letters to others to be read. This is also one of the reasons why I am expelled.

7. Since the August 7 Conference, the CC has not allowed me to participate in any meetings, nor has it given me any work to do. Then, on October 6 (only forty days before my expulsion), they suddenly wrote me a letter saying: "The CC has decided to ask you to undertake the work of editing in the CC under the political line of the party, and to write an article, 'Against the Opposition,' within a week." As I had criticized the Central Committee more than once for continuing the line of opportunism and putschism, they tried to create some excuse for my expulsion. Now I have recognized fundamentally that Comrade Trotsky's views are identical with Marxism and Leninism. How would I be able to write false words, contrary to my opinions?

8. We know that Comrade Trotsky has decisively opposed the opportunist policy of Stalin and Bukharin. We cannot listen to the rumors of the Stalin clique and believe that Comrade Trotsky, who led the October Revolution hand in hand with Lenin, really is a counter-revolutionist. (It may be "proved" by rumors created about us by the Chinese Stalinist clique, Li Li-san, etc.) Because we spoke of Trotsky as a comrade, the Central Committee accused us of "having already left the revolution, left the proletariat, and gone over to the counter-revolution", and expelled us from the party.

Comrades! The Central Committee has now invented these false reasons in order to expel me from the party and brand me as a "counter-revolutionist" without any proof. I believe that most of the comrades are not clear about this case. Even the CC itself has said: "There may be some who do not understand it!" But they expelled me and said I went over to the counter-revolution even though some comrades do not understand it.

Nevertheless, I understand quite well why they falsely accuse us as "counter-revolutionists". This is a weapon created by up-to-date Chinese for attacking those who differ from them. For instance, the Kuomintang accuses the communists of being "counter-revolutionists" in order to cover its own sins. Chiang Kai-shek tries to deceive the masses with the signboard of revolution, portraying himself as the personification of revolution. Those who oppose him are "counter-revolutionists" and "reactionary elements".

Many comrades know that the false reasons I have cited, given by the CC for expelling me, are only the formal and official excuse. In reality, they have become tired of hearing my opinions expressed in the party and of my criticism of their continued opportunism and putschism and their execution of a bankrupt policy.

In any number of the bourgeois countries of the world, there are feudal survivals and methods of semi-feudal exploitation (Blacks, and slaves of the South Sea archipelago, are like those of the pre-feudal slave system), and there exist remnants of feudal LA forces. China is even more like this. In the revolution, of course, we cannot neglect this; but the Comintern and the CC unanimously hold that in China the feudal remnants still occupy the dominant position in the economy and politics and are the ruling power. As a result, they consider these survivals as the object of the revolution and disregard the enemy, the suppressor of the revolution—the forces of the bourgeoisie. They pass off all reactionary actions of the bourgeoisie as those of the feudal forces.

They say that the Chinese bourgeoisie is still revolutionary that it can never be reactionary, and that all those who are reactionary cannot be the bourgeoisie. Thus, they do not recognize that the Kuomintang represents the interests of the bourgeoisie or that the Nationalist government is the regime representing the interests of the bourgeoisie. The conclusion must be that besides the Kuomintang, or the Nanking section of it, there is or will be, now or in the future, a non-reactionary, revolutionary bourgeois party Therefore, in tactics and in practical actions they now simply follow the Re-organization-ists and do the military work of overthrowing Chiang Kai-shek.' In the platform they say that the character of the third revolution in the future must still be that of a bourgeois-democratic revolution, opposing anything that would antagonize the economic forces of the bourgeoisie and opposing issuing the slogan for the dictatorship of the proletariat. Such illusions in the bourgeoisie and such continual attraction to it are calculated not only to perpetuate the opportunism of the past but to deepen it. It must lead to a more shameful and miserable failure in the future revolution.

If we consider the slogan "Establish the soviet regime" as a slogan of action, we can issue it only when the objective conditions have ripened into a revolutionary wave. It cannot be issued at any time at will. In the past, during the revolutionary wave, we did not adopt the slogans "Organize soviets" and "Establish the soviet regime". Naturally, this was a grave error. In the future, when the revolution takes place, we shall immediately have to organize the workers', peasants', and soldiers' soviets. Then we shall mobilize the masses to struggle for the slogan "Establish the soviet regime". Furthermore, it would be the soviet of the dictatorship of the proletariat, and not the soviet of the workers' and peasants' democratic dictatorship.

In the present period when the counter-revolutionary forces are entirely victorious and when there is no wave of mass revolutionary action, the objective conditions for "armed uprising" and the establishment of soviets have not matured. At the present time, "Organize soviets" is only a propaganda and educational slogan. If we use it as a slogan of action, and mobilize the working class at once to struggle in practice to "Organize soviets" we will be completely unable to generate a response from the masses.

In the present situation, we should adopt the democratic slogan, "Struggle for the convocation of the national assembly". The objective conditions for this movement have matured and at present only this slogan can take large masses through the legal political struggle and toward the revolutionary rise and the struggle for the "armed uprising" and the "Establishment of the soviet regime".

The present CC, continuing its putschism, does not do this. They consider that the rebirth of the revolution has matured, and reproach us for regarding the slogan of the "Establishment of workers' and peasants' soviets" as only a propaganda slogan; thus, they logically consider it a slogan of action. In consequence, they are continually ordering party members into the streets for demonstrations in workers' quarters, and ordering employed comrades to strike. Every small daily struggle is artificially blown up into a big political battle, leading to more and more defections from the party by the working masses and employed comrades.

More than that, at the Kiangsu representative conference recently, it was resolved "to organize the great strike movement," and "local uprisings". Since last summer there have been signs of small struggles among the Shanghai workers, but as they appear they have been defeated through the party's putschist policy. Henceforth, of course, they will all be crushed; if the resolutions of the Kiangsu representative conference are carried out, these workers' struggles will be destroyed. Our party is no longer the guide, helping the coming wave of workers' revolutionary struggles; it is becoming the executioner destroying the workers' struggles at their roots.

The present Central Committee, sincerely basing itself upon the bankrupt line of the Sixth Congress, and under the direct guidance of the Comintern, is executing the above bankrupt policy and capping the opportunism and putschism of the past by liquidating the party and the revolution. No matter whether it was the Comintern or the Chinese Communist Party that committed the opportunist errors in the past and made the revolution fail, it was a crime. Now these errors have been pointed out plainly by the comrades of the Opposition, but they still do not acknowledge their past mistakes and consciously continue their past erroneous line. Moreover, for the sake of covering up the errors of a few individuals, they deliberately violate the organizational norms of Bolshevism, abuse the authority of the supreme party organs, and prevent self-criticism within the party, expelling numerous comrades from the party for expressing different political opinions and deliberately splitting the party. This is the crime of crimes, the most stupid and the most shameful.

No Bolshevik should be afraid of open self-criticism before the masses. The only way for the party to win the masses is to carry out self-criticism courageously, never losing the masses for fear of self-criticism. To cover up one's own mistakes, like the present Central Committee, is certainly to lose the masses.

The majority of comrades have felt these mistakes and the party crisis to varying degrees. As long we do not simply expect to make our living through the party, as long as we have some feeling of responsibility for the party and the revolution, any comrade should stand up and resolutely make a self-criticism of the party in order to rescue it from this crisis. To silently watch, arms folded, while our party comes close to destruction would surely be criminal!

Comrades! We all know that whoever opens his mouth to express some criticism of the errors of the party is himself expelled, while the mistake remains uncorrected. But we should draw a balance. Which is more important: to save the party from danger or save ourselves from having our names dropped from the party list?

Since the August 7 Conference, which adopted the "general line of armed uprising", and the uprisings that followed in several places, I have written many letters to the Central Committee, pointing out that the revolutionary sentiment of the masses was not then at a high point, that the Kuomintang regime could not be quickly exploded, that uprisings that lacked objective conditions only weaken the power of the party and isolate it further from the masses. I proposed that we change from the policy of uprisings to a policy of winning and uniting the masses in their daily struggles. The Central Committee thought that widespread uprisings were an absolutely valid new line for correcting opportunism, and that to take account of the objective conditions for the uprisings and to consider how to insure the success of the uprisings, is opportunism. Of course, they never took my opinion into consideration and regarded my words as a joke. They propagated them everywhere, saying that it was proof that I had not corrected my opportunist mistakes. At that time, I was bound by the discipline of the party organization, and took a negative attitude, being unable to go over the head of the organization to wage a determined struggle against the policy of the Central Committee which was destroying the party.

I accept responsibility for this. After the Sixth Congress, I still and a false comprehension and still entertained the illusion that the new Central Committee had received so many lessons from events that they themselves would awaken to the fact that it was not necessary after all to follow blindly the erroneous line of the Comintern. I still continued my negative attitude and did not hold any different theories that would have involved a dispute within the party, though I was fundamentally dissatisfied with the line of the Sixth Congress. After the war between Chiang Kai- shek and the Kwangsi cliques, and the "May 30 anniversary movement", I felt deeply that the Central Committee would obstinately continue its opportunism and putschism, and manifestly could not change by itself: that except through an open discussion and criticism by the party members, from the lowest to the highest ranks, the seriously false line of the leading organ could not be corrected. But all the party members are under the domination and restriction of party discipline, in a state of "daring to be angry but not daring to speak".

At that time, I could not bear to see the party (created by the warm blood of innumerable comrades) destroyed and ruined by the enduring and essentially false line. Thus I could not do otherwise than to begin to express my opinion, from August onward, in order to fulfil my responsibility. Some comrades sought to dissuade me, saying that the people in the Central Committee regard the interests of a few leaders as more important than the interests of the party and the revolution, that they have attempted everywhere to cover up their mistakes and could never accept the criticism of comrades, and that since I was criticizing them so frankly, they would use it as an excuse for expelling me from the party. But my regard for the party compelled me to resolutely follow the path of not caring for my own interests.

The Communist International and the Central Committee have for a long time opposed any review of the record of failure of the Chinese Revolution. And now, because I have continued to criticize them, they have suddenly invented the following declaration: "He [i.e., I] is not sincere in recognizing his own error of opportunist leadership in the period of the great revolution and has not decided to recognize where his real past error lies, so it is inevitable that he will continue his past erroneous line."